WRITERS INC

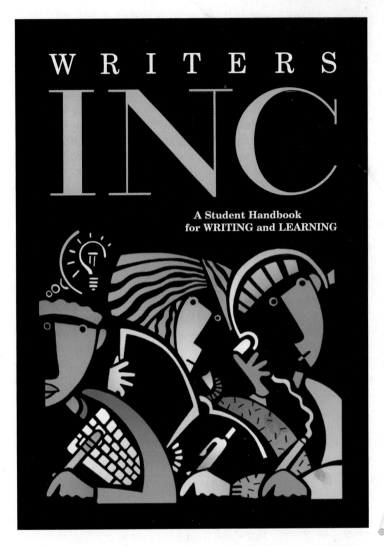

A Student Handbook for WRITING and LEARNING

Written and Compiled by
Patrick Sebranek, Dave Kemper, and Verne Meyer

Illustrated by **Chris Krenzke**

WRITE SOURCE®

GREAT SOURCE EDUCATION GROUP
a Houghton Mifflin Company
Wilmington, Massachusetts

Acknowledgements

Writers INC is a reality because of the help and advice of our team of educators, editors, and designers: Laura Bachman, Colleen Belmont, Carol Elsholz, Sherry Gordon, Mariellen Hanrahan, Mary Anne Hoff, Stuart Hoffman, Pat Kornelis, Lois Krenzke, Ellen Leitheusser, Barb Lund, Candyce Norvell, Randy Rehberg, Kelly Brecher Saaf, Linda Sivy, Lester Smith, Vicki Spandel, Connie Stephens, Ken Taylor, Travis Taylor, John Van Rys, Jean Varley, Sandy Wagner, and Claire Ziffer.

A special thanks also goes to all the teachers and students who sent us the writings used as samples throughout the handbook. (Visit our Web site for additional student models, as well as the latest information on evaluating and documenting Internet sources.)

Printed in the United States of America

International Standard Book Number: 0-669-47164-X (hardcover)
5 6 7 8 9 10 -RRDC- 05 04 03 02 01

International Standard Book Number: 0-669-47186-0 (softcover)
4 5 6 7 8 9 10 -RRDC- 05 04 03 02 01

Using the Handbook

Your *Writers INC* handbook provides concise, easy-to-use guidelines, samples, and strategies to help you with all of your writing. If that's not enough, you can also refer to our Web site <**thewritesource.com**> for more information. Here are some of the writing aids you will find on the Web site:

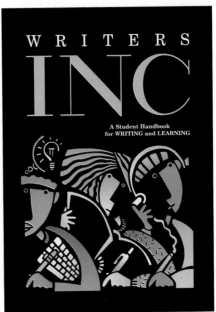

○ links to publishing sites,

○ additional writing samples, including an APA research paper,

○ MLA and APA documentation updates, and

○ a sample multimedia report.

W R I T E R S

INC

A Student Handbook
for WRITING and LEARNING

Writers INC will also help you with your other learning skills, including study-reading, test taking, note taking, and Internet searches. In addition, the "Student Almanac" in the back of the handbook contains tables, lists, maps, terms, and charts covering everything from science to history.

Your handbook guide . . .

The **Table of Contents** (starting on the next page) lists the five major sections of the handbook and the chapters found in each. Use the table of contents when you're looking for a *general* topic.

The **Index** (starting on page 589) provides a thorough listing of the information covered in *Writers INC*. Use the index when you're looking for a *specific* topic.

The **Color Coding** used for the "Proofreader's Guide" (the yellow pages) makes this important section easy to find. The guide covers punctuation, capitalization, spelling, usage, grammar, and more.

The **Cross-References** throughout the handbook tell you where to turn for more information about a topic. Some of these references are within the text. *Example:* (See page 5). Other cross-references are set off from the text because of their importance. (See *example* below.)

[**HOT LINK**] See "Assessment Rubric," page 154, for a helpful revising and editing guide.

Table of **Contents**

The **Process** of Writing

The **Forms** of Writing

The **Forms** of Writing

WRITING ABOUT LITERATURE

RESEARCH WRITING

WORKPLACE WRITING

The **Tools** of Learning

Proofreader's Guide

Student Almanac

LANGUAGE

SCIENCE

MATHEMATICS

GEOGRAPHY

GOVERNMENT

HISTORY

Understanding the
WRITING
PROCESS

> "Writing is the most powerful means of discovery available to all of us throughout life."
> —Peter Stillman

WHY Write?

You write essays, compile reports, and answer essay-test questions. These are important *practical* types of writing that you complete in school. Be prepared. You'll continue to do a lot of practical writing in your chosen profession. As writer Patricia T. O'Conner states, "Because of computers, we're suddenly a nation of writers." Doctors, mechanics, lawyers, florists, fitness trainers—everyone is "wired in" and writing reports, requests, proposals, briefs, and whatnot.

You may also keep a daily journal, write about your course work in a learning log, e-mail your friends and family members, and send letters. These are important *personal* types of writing that help you figure things out and determine where you fit in. According to writer Natalie Goldberg, personal writing "allows you to penetrate your life and learn to trust your own mind." If you don't already do any personal writing, get started as soon as possible.

Preview

○ **Reasons to Write**

○ *Writers INC* **and You**

Reasons to Write

Why should you make writing an important part of your life? Here are a few good reasons.

To become a better thinker and learner

Writing about new ideas and recent happenings helps you to better understand them and make them part of your own thinking. As writer Ray Bradbury once said, writing "lets the world burn through you."

To share your experiences

Writing satisfies your need to connect with other people, to let them know what's going on in your life. The more you write, the better you will be able to share these experiences with different audiences. So get into a regular writing routine—and stick to it.

To improve your performance in school

Writing about the subjects you are studying can help you do better in just about any class. It will help you master challenging concepts and remember information longer.

To get you ready for the next step

How far you go in school—whether it's high school, tech school, or college—actually depends on your ability to take charge of your own learning. The extra effort you put into your writing and learning now will make you a better student next month, next semester, next year, forever.

To shape a meaningful life

A lot of what is important to you right now is surface stuff—wearing the right clothes, hanging out with certain people, and fitting in. When you start writing and learning for yourself, you'll begin to appreciate life on a whole different level.

Writers INC and You

Writers INC is a portable resource containing all sorts of valuable information, from writing guidelines to test-taking strategies. What you won't find are exercises or assignments—not one. Note the subtitle on the cover: *A Student Handbook for Writing and Learning.* *Writers INC* is a guide for your *own* writing and learning. Now and for years to come, it will help you complete your practical writing tasks and make personal writing and learning an important part of your life.

"When I write, I am always struck at how magical and unexpected the process turns out to be." —Ralph Fletcher

Writing as a
PROCESS

At the start of her career, author Annie Dillard thought that all you really needed was "paper, pen, and a lap" to write something. But before too long, she discovered that "in order to write so much as a sonnet [a 14-line poem], I needed a warehouse." Of course, the author is exaggerating, but only to make a point. Dillard soon learned that she had to spend a lot of time—and write numerous drafts—to produce effective finished products.

You may know from experience what Dillard is talking about. Think of your best essays, reports, and stories. You probably put forth a great deal of effort (enough to fill a warehouse?) to produce each one, changing some parts many times from draft to draft. You may also know that writing really becomes satisfying when it reflects your best efforts. If you work hard at your writing, you—and your readers—will almost always be pleased with the results.

Preview

- Writing Is Discovering
- The Writing Process in Action
- A Closer Look at the Process
- Advice from the Pros

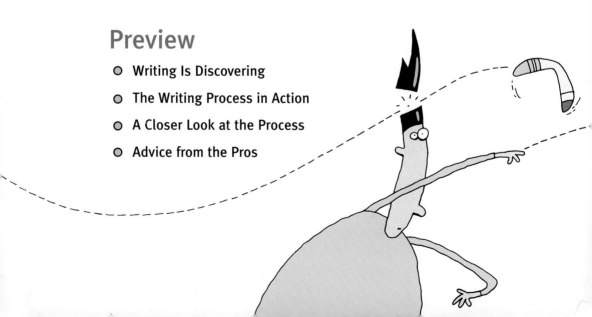

Writing Is **Discovering**

Writing is not trying to figure out everything you want to say *before* you put pen to paper or fingers to the keyboard. Working in this way will result in having very little to say, or worse yet, having nothing to say at all. (Ever hear of writer's block?) Writing almost always works best when it springs from the discoveries you make *during* the writing process.

Take NOTE   The five steps in the writing process discussed in your handbook are **prewriting, writing the first draft, revising, editing and proofreading,** and **publishing.**

Setting the Stage

Before you use the writing process, it's important that you understand the following points about writing:

- **Experience shapes writing.** Each of your experiences becomes part of what you know, what you think, and what you have to say in your writing. Writing is the process of capturing those thoughts and experiences on paper.

- **Writing never follows a straight path.** Writing is a backward as well as a forward activity, so don't expect to move neatly through the steps in the writing process. Writing by its very nature includes detours, wrong turns, and repeat visits.

- **Each assignment presents special challenges.** For one assignment, you might search high and low for a subject. For another one, you might do a lot of prewriting and planning. For still another, you might be ready to write your first draft almost immediately.

- **Each writer works differently.** Some writers work more in their heads, while others work more on paper. Some writers need to talk about their writing early on, while others would rather keep their ideas to themselves. As you continue to work with the writing process, your own writing personality will develop.

How can I become a better writer?

If you do the following four things, you are sure to improve your writing ability: become a regular reader, write every day, write about subjects that truly interest you, and experiment with different forms of writing. *Remember:* Writing is like any other skill. It takes a lot of practice and patience to become good at it.

The **Writing Process** in Action

The next two pages provide a basic look at the writing process in action. Use this information as a general guide whenever you write.

■ PREWRITING

Choosing a Subject and Gathering Details

1. Search for a meaningful writing idea—one that truly interests you and meets the requirements of the assignment.

2. Use a selecting strategy (listing, clustering, freewriting, and so on) to identify possible subjects. (See pages 43-45.)

3. Learn as much as you can about the subject you choose. (See pages 46-49.)

4. Decide on an interesting or important part of the subject—your focus—to develop. Express your focus in a thesis statement, a statement that helps map out your writing. (See page 51.)

5. Think about an overall plan or design for organizing your writing. This plan can be anything from a brief list to a detailed outline. (See page 52.)

■ WRITING THE FIRST DRAFT

Connecting Your Ideas

1. Write the first draft while your prewriting is still fresh in your mind.

2. Set the right tone by giving your opening paragraph special attention. (See page 55.)

3. Refer to your plan for the main part of your writing, but be flexible. A more interesting route may unfold as you write.

4. Don't worry about getting everything right at this point; just concentrate on developing your ideas. (If you're working on a computer, save a paper copy of each draft.)

HELP FILE

Experienced writers often view the drafting process as a stimulating release, especially if they have spent a lot of time researching a subject and have a lot of ideas percolating in their minds. Approach your own drafting with the same kind of energy and enthusiasm, and you'll do your best work.

■ REVISING

Improving Your Writing

1. Review your first draft, checking the ideas, organization, and voice of your writing. (See pages 63-67.)

2. Ask at least one classmate to react to your work.

3. Add, cut, reword, or rearrange ideas as necessary. (You may have to change some parts several times before they say what you want them to say.)

4. Carefully assess the effectiveness of your opening and closing paragraphs.

5. Look for special opportunities to make your writing as meaningful and interesting as possible. (See page 62.)

■ EDITING AND PROOFREADING

Checking for Style and Accuracy

1. Edit your revised writing for sentence smoothness and word choice. (See pages 77-78.)

2. Then check for errors in usage, punctuation, capitalization, spelling, and grammar.

3. Have a dictionary, thesaurus, and your *Writers INC* handbook close at hand as you work.

4. Ask a reliable editor—a friend, a classmate, a parent, or a teacher—to check your writing for errors you may have missed.

5. Prepare a neat final copy of your writing.

6. Proofread the final draft for errors before submitting it.

■ PUBLISHING

Sharing Your Work

1. Share the finished product with your teacher, writing peers, friends, and family members.

2. Decide if you are going to include the writing in your portfolio. (See page 35.)

3. Post it on your personal or class Web site or publish it on-line. (See pages 38-39.)

4. Consider submitting your work to a school, a local, or a national publication. (Ask your teacher for recommendations for places to publish.) Make sure to follow the requirements for submitting manuscripts. (See pages 36-37.)

A **Closer Look** at the Process

Keep the following tips in mind whenever you write. They will help make each of your writing projects satisfying and meaningful.

Keep time on your side. Effective writing requires a lot of searching, planning, writing, reflecting, and revising. In order to do all of these things, you must give yourself plenty of time. If your teacher provides you with a timetable for your writing, make sure to follow it. Otherwise, create your own. (Always reserve plenty of time for revising.) As you probably know, waiting until the last minute takes all of the fun out of writing.

Remember: Good writing takes time.

Work from a position of authority. The more you know about your subject, the easier it is to write about it. So collect as much information as you can during prewriting—tapping into your own thoughts, asking other people for their ideas, consulting print material, surfing the Net, and so on.

Remember: Good writing requires good information.

Limit your subject. It would be almost impossible to write an effective essay or report about a general subject such as photography. You wouldn't know where to begin or end. But if you limited this subject to a specific aspect of photography—let's say, the use of photography by investigative reporters—then you would find it much easier to manage your writing.

Remember: Good writing has a focus, meaning that it stems from and is built around a limited subject.

Take some risks. Don't be afraid to experiment in your writing. For example, you might share a personal story in an essay or develop an interview report in a question-and-answer format, much like you would find in many magazine articles. Then again, you might change the sequence of events in a narrative to add suspense. If one experiment doesn't work out, you can always try something else.

Remember: Good writing is a process of discovery.

Pace yourself when you revise. Many of the pros believe that the real writing takes place when they add, cut, rearrange, and rewrite different parts of their first drafts. They do not rush these changes or make them all at once. Instead, they pace themselves, working very patiently and methodically at times, making revisions until all of the parts seem clear and complete.

Remember: Good writing usually requires a series of changes before it says exactly what you want it to say.

Advice from the Pros

Keep the following thoughts in mind as you develop your writing. They come from experienced authors who appreciate writing as a process of discovery.

"I don't pick subjects so much as they pick me."

—Andy Rooney

**"When I speak to students about writing,
I hold myself up as an example of that ancient
axiom—write about what you know."**

—Robert Cormier

"The inspiration comes while you write."

—Madeleine L'Engle

**"I think one is constantly startled by the
things that appear before you on the page while
you write."**

—Shirley Hazzard

**"The faster I write, the better my output.
If I'm going slow, I'm in trouble. It means I'm pushing
the words, instead of being pulled by them."**

—Raymond Chandler

**"No tears in the writer, no tears in the reader.
No surprise for the writer, no surprise for the reader."**

—Robert Frost

"Half of my life is an act of revision."

—John Irving

**"There is no such thing as good writing,
only good rewriting."**

—Louis D. Brandeis

**"I believe in impulse and naturalness, but followed
by discipline in the cutting."**

—Anaïs Nin

**"Write visually, write clearly, and
make every word count."**

—Gloria D. Miklowitz

> "Writing is really rewriting—making the story better, clearer, truer."
>
> —Robert Lipsyte

ONE WRITER'S Process

When you install new computer software, the instructions guide you through the set-up process one step at a time. In a similar way, the writing process helps you produce effective essays, narratives, and reports—one step at a time. To become a skilled and confident writer, you must gain a working knowledge of these steps: prewriting, writing, revising, editing and proofreading, and publishing. *Remember:* Developing a piece of writing can be a complex undertaking; breaking it down into steps keeps you on track and helps you do your best work.

This chapter shows how student writer Todd Michaels developed an expository essay using the steps in the writing process. As you follow his work, you'll see how he shaped his initial idea into an effective finished piece of writing.

Preview

- Prewriting: Selecting and Gathering
- Writing the First Draft: Connecting the Ideas
- Revising: Improving the Writing
- Editing: Checking for Style
- Editing: Checking for Accuracy
- Publishing: Sharing the Final Copy

■ **PREWRITING**

Selecting and Gathering

In an environmental science class, Todd Michaels' teacher gave the following assignment:

> **In an expository essay, examine one example of the reduce-reuse-recycle principle in action.**

On the next two pages, you'll see how Todd selected a subject, gathered information about it, and focused his thoughts for writing.

1. **Choosing a Subject . . .** Todd freely listed possible subjects—glass recycling, secondhand stores, paper recycling, e-mail versus paper mail, new automotive technology, and so on. After discussing his list with a classmate, he selected "paper recycling" as his subject.

2. **Exploring First Thoughts . . .** To collect his initial thoughts about his subject, Todd wrote freely for 10 minutes about paper recycling. Here is one passage from this writing.

> *I must have delivered thousands of newspapers when I had a paper route. I wonder how many pounds I carried? A lot of that paper came from recycled stuff, and lots of people recycled their newspapers and other paper scraps. Today, we're still recycling, but how's it going? Is America still dumping a lot of paper in landfills? Are we wasting less paper because of e-mail and recycling . . . ?*

3. **Gathering Details . . .** To explore his subject further, Todd completed a "paper-recycling" cluster. (See page 43.)

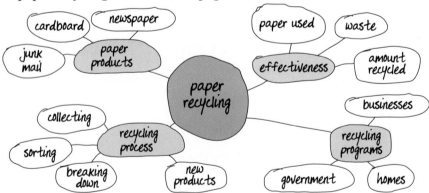

4. **Generating Questions . . .** After reviewing his cluster, Todd decided to explore the following questions: *How does paper recycling work? What paper gets recycled? Who uses recycling programs?*

5. Carrying Out Research . . . With these questions in mind, Todd read articles, searched Web sites, and visited a recycling plant. Here are some of his notes:

Paper Recycling

Stover, Dawn. "Do-It-Yourself Paper Recycling." Popular Science (March 99: vol. 254, 3: 32)
- not all paper can be recycled
- work is being done to recycle glossy paper

Statistical Abstract of the United States (1998, pp. 243-244).
- 80 million tons of paper waste generated per year; 32.6 million tons recovered (41%)
- paper accounts for 38% of total waste generated in U.S.
- total waste is 209.7 million tons

"U.S. Postal Service Named Environmental Mailer of the Year at Ceremony in Washington, D.C."
- USPS program: recycles more than a million tons; buys $160 million in recycled paper

6. Forming a Thesis . . . To guide his writing, Todd needed a thesis statement. (See page 51.) Based on his thinking and research, he came up with the following statement:

Paper recycling has become part of the daily lives of many Americans.

(As Todd's essay evolves, he may revise this statement once or twice.)

7. Planning the First Draft . . . After forming his thesis, Todd created a basic writing plan by listing the main ideas he wanted to cover in his writing.

Writing Plan
1. Extent of paper recycling
2. Businesses that recycle paper
3. How paper recycling works
4. Problems with paper recycling

■ **WRITING THE FIRST DRAFT**

Connecting the Ideas

Todd wrote his first draft freely, using his writing plan and notes as a general guide. His goal was to get his ideas on paper, without worrying about every word and comma being right.

Paper Recycling

The opening paragraph leads up to the thesis statement.

From the home to large paper chutes at the office, paper recycling has become an everyday occurrence. Americans have stopped there throwaway attitudes with a committment to recycle. Last year 32 million tons of paper like newspapers were recycled. Paper recycling is very important to America and the enviroment. Because it makes sense and it works, paper recycling has truly become a big part of the daily lives of many Americans

Paper recycling has indeed become a big deal, and a big business. Businesses and other organizations recycle paper because it is a good thing to do. Americans they through away more paper (38 percent of the total waste) than anything else so recycling means big gains. Businesses save lots of paper just by using e-mail to communicate with each other and the Internet to advertise. For example, Fort Howard Corp. at Green Bay uses recycled paper for all its bathroom tissue, it recycles enough paper to cover 100 acres 18 ft deep. The U.S. Postal Service recycles more than a million tons of material and buys $160 million worth of recycled paper each year. Foreign countries are buying our paper waste. If you see a MADE IN TAIWAN tag, it probably was a newspaper in America.

The writer develops each main point with details.

The recycling process is explained.

Paper recycling works by first getting paper collected and sorted. Recyclable paper includes computer printouts, newspaper, scrap paper, and cardboard boxes. The paper is turned into pulp which is dried and the new paper is formed on cylinders. A large spinning blade mixes the paper to a pulp. This new paper is used to make newspapers, cereal and shoe boxes, toilet tissue, egg cartons, and even in building insulation and cow bedding!

Each paragraph covers a different aspect of recycling.

But not all types of paper can be recycled. Carbon paper, glossy paper, photographs, or paper with tape, glue or staples. The recycling equipment can't take that stuff out. Changes are being made that might make it possible to work with these items. Equipment is currently under development to remove ink from glossy magazines and catalogs.

Although landfills are still filling up with more than 2/3 of our recyclable waste, paper recycling has become a success story. While only 18 percent of metal cans and 2 percent of plastics are recycled, 40 percent of white paper is too. 5,000 community programs exist nationwide for the recycling. Big business is very involved. Recycling fever hasn't been this high in the U.S. since World War II when

The writer concludes by restating his main point.

people felt it was there duty to recycle. Americans are recycling paper on a daily basis so they can save the environment and there future.

■ REVISING

Improving the Writing

Todd took a break after finishing his first draft. When he was ready to review his work, he looked carefully at the developing ideas. He wrote brief notes in the margin, identifying parts that needed to be changed. Below, you can see the changes he made.

Todd's comments

Paper Recycling

From the home *curbside collection* to large paper chutes at the office, paper recycling has become an everyday occurrence. Americans have stopped *replaced* there throwaway attitudes with a committment to recycle *and they are recycling in record numbers* Last year 32 million tons of paper like newspapers were recycled. ~~Paper recycling is very important to America~~

Cut sentence— doesn't add anything new.

~~and the enviroment.~~ Because it makes sense and it works, paper recycling has truly become a big part of the daily lives of many Americans

Paper recycling has indeed become a big deal, and a big business. Businesses and other organizations recycle paper, *not just* because it is a good thing to do, *but because it makes good sense.* Americans they through away more paper (38 percent of the total waste) than *there is much to be gained by recycling paper.*

Cut unnecessary idea.

anything else so recycling means big gains. ~~Businesses save lots of paper just by using e-mail to communicate with each other and the Internet to advertise.~~ For example, Fort Howard Corp. at Green Bay uses recycled paper for all its

Tell how often.

bathroom tissue, it recycles enough paper *each year* to cover 100 acres 18 ft deep. The U.S. Postal Service recycles more than a

Add information about the award.

million tons of material and buys $160 million worth of *and it won the 1999 Environmental Mailer of the Year Award.* recycled paper each year. Foreign countries are buying our *on a manufactured paper product* paper waste. If you see a MADE IN TAIWAN tag, it probably was a newspaper in America.

Include a topic sentence.

¶ The process of paper recycling is simple. First paper is ~~Paper recycling works by first getting paper~~ collected and sorted. Recyclable paper includes computer printouts, newspapers ~~newspaper,~~ scrap paper, and cardboard boxes. ~~The paper is turned into~~ pulp ~~which~~ is dried and the new paper is formed on cylinders. A large spinning blade mixes the paper to a pulp. This new paper is used to make newspapers, cereal and shoe boxes, toilet tissue, egg cartons, and even in building insulation and cow bedding!

Reorder these items.

Clarify this idea.

But not all types of paper can be recycled. Recycling equipment cannot handle Carbon paper, glossy paper, photographs, or paper with tape, glue or staples. These types of paper must be sorted out. ~~The recycling equipment can't take that stuff out.~~ Advancements ~~Changes~~ are being made that might make it possible to work with these items. Equipment is currently under development to remove ink from glossy magazines and catalogs.

Although landfills are still filling up with more than 2/3 of our recyclable waste, paper recycling has become a success story. While only 18 percent of metal cans and 2 percent of plastics are recycled, 40 percent of white paper is in fact, recycled. ~~too.~~ 5,000 community programs exist nationwide for the of paper products recycling. Big business ~~is very involved.~~ has discovered the advantages of paper recycling. Recycling fever hasn't been this high in the U.S. since World War II when people felt it was there duty to recycle. ~~Americans are recycling paper on a daily basis so they can save the environment and there future.~~ Perhaps people today feel that the world is in a different kind of emergency situation and that, again, it is there duty to recycle.

Be more specific here.

Rework the closing sentence so it has more impact.

■ **EDITING**

Checking for Style

After revising his draft, Todd was ready to edit for style. He read his work aloud, checking for sentence smoothness and strong nouns, verbs, and modifiers. He made his changes on a printout of his revised paper.

Paper Recycling

> Phrasing clarified.

From the ~~home~~ curbside collection *at* to large *scrap* paper chutes at the office, paper recycling has become an everyday occurrence. Americans have replaced there throwaway attitudes with a committment to recycle and they are recycling in record numbers. Last year 32 million tons of

> Extra words cut; important idea added.

paper ~~like newspapers~~ were recycled *—a substantial increase from the previous year*. Because it makes sense and it works, paper recycling has truly become a big part of the daily lives of many Americans

Paper recycling has indeed become a big deal, and a big business. Businesses and other organizations recycle paper not just because it is a good thing to do, but because it makes good sense. Americans they through away more paper (38 percent of the total waste) than anything else so there is much to be gained by recycling paper. For example, Fort Howard Corp. at Green Bay uses recycled paper for all its bathroom tissue, it recycles enough paper each year to cover 100 acres 18 ft deep. The U.S. Postal Service recycles

> Specific noun used.

more than a million tons of *scrap paper* ~~material~~ and buys $160 million worth of recycled paper each year ~~and~~ it won the 1999

> Rambling sentence fixed.

Environmental Mailer of the Year Award. Foreign countries are *even* buying our paper waste. If you see a MADE IN

> Modifying phrase added.

TAIWAN tag on a manufactured paper product, *in another life* it probably was a newspaper in America.

The process of paper recycling is simple. First paper is collected and sorted. Recyclable paper includes computer printouts, newspapers, scrap paper, and cardboard boxes. A large spinning blade mixes the paper to a pulp. The pulp is dried *on screens* and the new paper is formed on cylinders. This new paper is used to make newspapers, cereal and shoe boxes, toilet tissue, egg cartons, ~~and even in~~ building insulation, *livestock* and ~~cow~~ bedding!

But not all types of paper can be recycled. Recycling equipment cannot handle carbon paper, glossy paper, photographs, or paper with tape, glue or staples. These types of papers must be sorted out. ~~Advancements are being made that might~~ *However, new technologies may* make it possible to work with these items. *For example* Equipment is currently under development to remove ink from glossy magazines and catalogs.

Although landfills are still filling up with more than 2/3 of our recyclable waste, paper recycling has become a success story. While only 18 percent of metal cans and 2 percent of plastics are recycled, 40 percent of white paper is in fact, recycled. 5,000 community programs exist, nationwide for the recycling of paper products, *and* Big business has discovered the advantages of paper recycling. Recycling fever hasn't been this high in the U.S. since World War II when people felt it was there duty to recycle. Perhaps people today *realize* ~~feel~~ that the world is in a different kind of emergency situation, and that, again, it is there duty to recycle.

Modifying phrase added.

Ideas made parallel.

Specific subject used; passive verb "are being made" cut.

Transitional words used.

Two sentences combined.

Stronger verb used.

■ **EDITING**

Checking for Accuracy

Having edited his essay for style, Todd turned his attention to the accuracy of his writing. He checked for spelling, grammar, usage, and punctuation errors. He also added the sources he used for outside information. (Some sources are in parentheses.)

Hyphen added to compound adjective.	**Paper Recycling** From curbside collection at home to large scrap-paper chutes at the office, paper recycling has become an everyday
Usage and spelling error corrected.	occurrence. Americans have replaced ~~there~~ *their* throwaway attitudes with a ~~committment~~ *commitment* to recycle, and they are recycling
Sources and page numbers added.	in record numbers. ~~Last year,~~ *According to the 1999 Statistical Abstract,* 32 million tons of paper were *last year* recycled—a substantial increase from the previous year *(235)*. Because it makes sense and it works, paper recycling has truly become a big part of the daily lives of many Americans.
	Paper recycling has indeed become a big deal, and a big business. Businesses and other organizations recycle paper not just because it is a good thing to do, but because it
Double subject "they" deleted; usage error corrected.	makes good sense. Americans ~~they through~~ *throw* away more paper (38 percent of the total waste) than anything else, so there is much to be gained by recycling paper. For example, Fort Howard ~~Corp.~~ *Corporation* at Green Bay uses recycled paper for all
Comma splice corrected; an abbreviation spelled out.	its bathroom tissue; it recycles enough paper each year to cover 100 acres 18 ~~ft~~ *feet (Howard, 230)* deep. The U.S. Postal Service recycles more than a million tons of scrap paper and buys $160 million worth of recycled paper each year. It won the 1999 Environmental Mailer of the Year Award. Foreign countries are even buying our paper waste. If you see a MADE IN TAIWAN tag on a manufactured paper product, in another life it probably was a newspaper in America.

The process of paper recycling is simple. First paper is collected and sorted. Recyclable paper includes computer printouts, newspapers, scrap paper, and cardboard boxes. A large spinning blade mixes the paper to a pulp. The pulp is dried on screens and the new paper is formed on cylinders. This new paper is used to make newspapers, cereal and shoe boxes, toilet tissue, egg cartons, building insulation, and livestock bedding!

Commas added to compound sentence; end punctuation changed.

Not all types of paper can be recycled. Recycling equipment cannot handle carbon paper, glossy paper, photographs, or paper with tape, glue, or staples. These types of papers must be sorted out. However, new technologies may make it possible to work with these items. For example, equipment is currently under development to remove ink from glossy magazines and catalogs.

Comma added to a series.

Although landfills are still filling up with more than two-thirds ~~2/3~~ of our recyclable waste, paper recycling has become a success story. While only 18 percent of metal cans and 2 percent of plastics are recycled, 40 percent of white paper is, in fact, recycled. Five thousand ~~5,000~~ community programs exist nationwide for the recycling of paper products, and big business has discovered the advantages of paper recycling (Howard, 232). Recycling fever hasn't been this high in the United States ~~U.S.~~ since World War II when people felt it was their ~~there~~ duty to recycle. Perhaps people today realize that the world is in a different kind of emergency situation and that, again, it is their ~~there~~ duty to recycle.

Fraction spelled out.

Comma added; number spelled out at a sentence beginning.

Usage errors corrected; unnecessary comma deleted.

■ **PUBLISHING**

Sharing the Final Copy

Todd produced a neat final copy of his essay. He proofread this copy for errors before sharing it with his classmates. Here is a portion of Todd's first page.

Follow your teacher's directions for placement of name, class, etc.

Todd Michaels

Ms. Herman

Environmental Science

January 20, 2000

Paper Recycling

From curbside collection at home to large scrap-paper chutes at the office, paper recycling has become an everyday occurrence. Americans have replaced their throwaway attitudes with a commitment to recycle, and they are recycling in record numbers. According to the 1999 *Statistical Abstract,* 32 million tons of paper were recycled last year—a substantial increase from the previous year (235). Because it makes sense and it works, paper recycling has truly

Points to Remember

Do the necessary prewriting. Todd gathered a great deal of information about his subject before he started writing. Thorough prewriting makes the rest of the writing process go more smoothly.

Write with confidence. Because of his thorough preparation, Todd was able to get all of his thoughts on paper freely and smoothly.

Expect to make many changes. Todd wasn't satisfied with just making a few changes. He wanted to make all of his ideas as clear and complete as possible. *Remember:* No writer, not even the most accomplished author, ever gets it right the first or the second time.

"Good writing excites me and makes
life worth living."   —Harold Pinter

Traits of
EFFECTIVE Writing

When you think of creative writing, you probably think of stories, poems, and plays—forms of writing that require a lot of imagination. This is creative writing in the traditional sense: an inventive, somewhat playful form of writing. And when you think of academic writing, you probably think of essays, reports, and research papers—forms of writing that require a lot of factual information, but not a lot of imagination.

However, it shouldn't be that way. In their own way, essays and reports can be just as creative as stories and poems. Simply put, a creative essay or report exhibits the basic traits found in all good writing: stimulating ideas, clear organization, engaging voice, and so on.

Learning about these traits of good writing—and putting them into practice—will help you write better in all of your classes.

Preview

- Quick Guide
- The Traits in Action
- Checklist for Effective Writing

"The greatest courtesy of all is to
make [your writing] interesting."

—Scott Rice

Quick Guide

The six traits listed below identify the main features found in effective essays, reports, stories, and articles. If you write with these traits in mind, you will most likely be pleased with the results.

STIMULATING IDEAS: Effective writing presents interesting and vital information about a specific subject. It has a clear purpose or focus, or as writer Donald Murray states, "It has a controlling vision which orders what is being said." The ideas are thoroughly explored and hold the reader's attention from start to finish.

LOGICAL ORGANIZATION: In terms of basic structure, good writing has a clearly developed beginning, middle, and ending. Within the text, each main point is supported with examples, explanations, definitions, and specific details. The overall arrangement of ideas unifies the writing and makes clear the writer's purpose.

ENGAGING VOICE: In the best writing, you can hear the writer's voice—her or his special way of expressing ideas and emotions. Voice gives writing personality: it shows that the writer sincerely cares about her or his subject and audience. Writer Donald Graves calls voice the "imprint of the writer in the writing."

ORIGINAL WORD CHOICE: In good writing, the nouns and verbs are specific. The modifiers are colorful (and used somewhat sparingly). The overall level of language helps to communicate the message and set an appropriate tone. In short, all the right words are in all the right places.

EFFECTIVE SENTENCE STYLE: Effective writing flows from sentence to sentence. But it isn't, by any means, predictable. Sentences vary in length, and they don't all begin in the same way. Sentence fluency gives rhythm to writing, which helps make it enjoyable to read.

CORRECT, ACCURATE COPY: Good writing follows the accepted standards of punctuation, mechanics, usage, and spelling. It is edited with care to ensure that the work is accurate and easy to follow.

The Traits in Action

On the next three pages, writing samples exhibit each of the traits of effective writing. These samples show quality writing in action.

Stimulating Ideas

The following passage comes from *Sacred Hoops* by Phil Jackson. In this one short paragraph, Jackson, the former coach of the Chicago Bulls, presents an interesting Native American perspective on teamwork.

> **The Lakota's concept of teamwork was deeply rooted in their view of the universe. A warrior didn't try to stand out from his fellow band members; he strove to act bravely and honorably, to help the group in whatever way he could to accomplish its mission. If glory befell him, he was obligated to give away his most prized possessions to relatives, friends, the poor, and the aged. As a result, the leaders of the tribe were often its poorest members. A few years ago I received a beautiful hand-woven blanket from a Sioux woman in North Dakota who said her brother had broken the state championship scoring record I had set in the 1960s. His achievement had brought so much honor to her family, she thought it only fitting to send me a gift.**

○ Phil Jackson first describes the Lakota's notion of teamwork. He then explains how a successful warrior is expected to act in this culture. Finally, he shares an engaging personal story to illustrate his point.

Logical Organization

In this passage from *For the Time Being,* writer Annie Dillard develops an odd but interesting topic. She presents the main point, or topic, in the first sentence, and then adds supporting information in an orderly fashion.

> **It is interesting, the debris in the air. A surprising portion of it is spider legs, and bits thereof. Spider legs are flimsy, Oxford writer David Bodanis says, because they are hollow. They lack muscles; compressed air moves them. Consequently, they snap off easily and go blowing about. Another unexpected source of aerial detritus [debris] is tires. Eroding tires shed latex shreds at a brisk clip, say the folks who train their microscopes on air. Farm dust joins sulfuric acid drops (from burned fossil fuels) and sand from the Sahara Desert to produce the summer haze that blurs and dims valleys and coasts.**

○ The topic of this passage is the types of debris floating in the air. Dillard provides three detailed examples to support her topic and enhance the reader's understanding of the floating debris.

Engaging Voice

In *Neither Here nor There,* writer Bill Bryson shares his wacky thoughts and experiences related to his travels across Europe. In the paragraph below, he discusses his special relationship with dogs.

> I don't know why it is, but something about me incites dogs to a frenzy. I would be a rich man if I had a nickel for every time a dog tried to get at the marrow in my ankle bone while the owner just stood there and said, "Well, I don't understand it; he's never done anything like this before. You must have said something to him." That always knocks me out. What would I say to the dog? "Hello, boy, like to open a vein in my leg?"

○ Note how Bryson establishes an entertaining, personal voice in the first line ("I don't know why it is . . . ") and maintains this voice throughout the passage. Expressions such as "tried to get at the marrow in my ankle bone" and "that always knocks me out" add to the conversational tone and overall appeal of the passage.

Original Word Choice

In this passage from *A Crossing,* writer Brian Newhouse describes a personal camping experience in the state of Washington. As you will see, he pays careful attention to word choice throughout the text.

> Why at that moment, I have no idea, but as if by signal Washington's mosquito population swarmed us. Lars dove to his tent. I swatted myself and stamped around the campsite. But Duncan walked placidly into the pines and returned with dried branches and long wet grasses. He laid boughs on the fire. Sparks geysered into the blue-black sky, and the heat pulled the skin tight across my cheekbones. Next came several handfuls of grass. The heavy white smoke smelled like Christmas and summer at the same time.

○ Notice the vivid verbs Newhouse uses—"swarmed," "dove," "swatted," "stamped," and "geysered." Also note the modifiers that help you to visualize the scene—"walked *placidly,*" "*dried* branches," "*long wet* grasses," "*blue-black* sky," and "*heavy white* smoke."

 How can I focus on word choice in longer pieces of writing?

According to writer Barry Lane, writers often think of their writing as a series of "snapshots." Snapshots are specific images that writers attempt to capture using the best words. Try this in your own writing. Focus on one "snapshot" at a time.

"The bottom line for me is the sentence in front of my face. If nine out of ten of them hit the mark, then I'm satisfied." —Gloria Naylor

Effective Sentence Style

In the following passage from *Good Old Boy,* writer Willie Morris gives some of the geological background of Yazoo City, a small delta city in Mississippi. Note how he pays careful attention to the sound and flow of each sentence.

> The town sits there crazily, half on the green hills and half on the delta. Once, many thousands of years ago, this flat delta land was the very floor of the sea. Later it was covered with great swampy forests, and any person who wandered into them by himself would get very lonely and afraid. He would have to be wary of the quicksand, not to mention the giant lizards, snakes, alligators, spiders, and Indians. Now it is the richest land in the world. Some say if you plant a cotton seed in it, you have to jump away quickly to avoid being hit by the growing stalk.

○ Note how Morris varies the sentence beginnings in this passage. No two sentences start in the same way. Also note the varying lengths—the longest sentence contains 24 words; the shortest one contains 9. The style of his sentences helps make this passage interesting for readers.

Correct, Accurate Copy

In the following passage from *West with the Night,* writer Beryl Markham shares a childhood memory, the time she encountered a dangerous lion roaming around the neighboring (Elkington's) farm in East Africa. Note how precise punctuation helps control the flow of her ideas.

> I was within 20 yards of the Elkington lion before I saw him. He lay sprawled in the morning sun, huge, black-maned, and gleaming with life. His tail moved slowly, stroking the rough grass like a knotted rope end. His body was sleek and easy, making a mould where he lay, a cool mould, that would be there when he had gone. He was not asleep; he was only idle. He was rusty-red, and soft, like a strokable cat.

○ See how the commas draw attention to each detail about the lion. Overall, the carefully selected punctuation establishes an effective, smooth-reading rhythm in the passage.

Checklist for Effective Writing

If a piece of writing meets the following standards, it exhibits the traits of effective writing. Check your work using these standards.

Stimulating Ideas

The writing . . .

_____ presents interesting and valuable information.

_____ maintains a clear, specific focus or purpose.

_____ holds the reader's attention (and answers his or her questions about the subject).

Logical Organization

_____ includes a clear beginning, middle, and ending.

_____ contains specific details—arranged in the best order—to support the main ideas.

Engaging Voice

_____ speaks in a sincere, natural way.

_____ shows that the writer really cares about the subject.

Original Word Choice

_____ contains specific, clear words.

_____ presents an appropriate level of language.

Effective Sentence Style

_____ flows smoothly from sentence to sentence.

_____ displays varied sentence beginnings and lengths.

Correct, Accurate Copy

_____ adheres to the rules of grammar, spelling, and punctuation.

_____ follows established formatting guidelines.

"For me, it [the computer] was obviously the perfect new toy. I began playing on page 1 . . . and have been on a rewriting high ever since."   —William Zinsser

Writing with a
COMPUTER

Pens, pencils, notebooks, and folders—all of these might prove useful during a writing project. However, no writing tool is more valuable than the personal computer. When you write with a computer, you stay at a piece of writing longer, take more risks, and get more feedback from your writing peers.

Writing with a computer may be most helpful when you revise. First drafts that are written longhand often contain crossed-out lines, squeezed-in words, and arrows connecting different parts. They're usually a mess, and hard to work with. By contrast, revising on the computer is a much easier process. You can add, delete, and rearrange copy right on the screen—or on a clean printed copy. And you can continue to make changes until your writing says exactly what you want it to say.

Preview

- O **A Guide to the Process**
- o **Designing Your Writing**
- o **Effective Design in Action**

A **Guide** to the Process

■ PREWRITING

THE UPSIDE

- Using a computer allows you to gather your thoughts and feelings without worrying about sloppy handwriting.
- Using a computer allows you to get more ideas on paper—in less time.
- Using a computer can bring out your inventiveness and creativity.
- Using a computer can be especially helpful during freewriting. You can fill the screen and keep going, without so much as having to flip over a sheet of paper.

THE DOWNSIDE

- You may do less prewriting and planning with a computer, partly because you can't use certain prewriting techniques like clustering.
- You may constantly stop to read or rewrite what you have written, disrupting the free flow of your thoughts. *Solution:* Turn down the resolution of the monitor to discourage yourself from stopping to revise or edit.

Best Advice: **Try both methods. Find out whether prewriting on a screen or prewriting on paper is better for you. It's your choice.**

■ WRITING THE FIRST DRAFT

THE UPSIDE

- Using a computer may help you stay with a piece of writing longer and develop it more thoroughly.
- Computers allow you to concentrate on ideas rather than on the appearance of your writing.
- Writing on a computer makes it easier for you to share early drafts. You can simply print out a copy for others to read. By sharing, you also become more aware of a real audience.

THE DOWNSIDE

- Deleting whole sections of copy on a computer is very tempting. But most experts agree that it is important to save all of your ideas in early drafts. *Solution:* Don't push that "delete" key.

Best Advice: **Do your drafting on a computer; then save, print out, share, and keep paper copies of what you've written.**

■ REVISING

THE UPSIDE

- Using a computer saves you time and toil during each step in the revising process, especially for longer writing assignments.
- Using a computer allows you to move, delete, and add large chunks of information by using a few simple commands. As a result, you have more time to improve the quality of your writing.
- Using a computer makes group advising sessions easier because everyone gets a quick, clean printout to read and react to.

THE DOWNSIDE

- Some people find it difficult to reread and evaluate writing on a screen. *Solution:* Simply print out the document, make the changes on paper, and then input them.

Best Advice: Use your computer for revising. Take advantage of the speed and ease a computer offers, but slow down long enough to reflect on your writing. (If you print out a copy of your work first, and then revise on screen, you can easily undo any hasty revising later.)

■ EDITING AND PROOFREADING

THE UPSIDE

- Use the spell and grammar checkers and the search-and-replace capabilities (available in most word-processing programs) to help you prepare your writing for publication.
- Use the formatting features (if provided) to create the table of contents, outline, and graphics for a research paper.

THE DOWNSIDE

- You may not see errors such as missing words, misplaced commas, or misspelled words as easily on a screen as on paper.
- You may also come to rely too much on your spell and grammar checkers. These checkers aren't foolproof. For example, a spell checker won't be able to distinguish between words that sound the same (*hole* and *whole*) but are spelled differently. *Solution:* Use these programs; then do a careful final read yourself.

Best Advice: Do your editing and proofreading on a computer. Clearly, the computer is valuable in this final step of preparing a paper for publication. But also carefully check for errors yourself.

Designing Your Writing

The test of good page design is that your writing is clear and easy to follow. Consider these tips for creating clean, attractive essays, reports, and research papers. (Also see pages 31-32.)

TYPOGRAPHY

- **Use an easy-to-read serif font for the main text.**
  (*Serif* type, like this type, has "tails" at the tops and bottoms of the letters.) For most types of writing, use a 10- or 12-point type size.

- **Make titles and headings short and to the point.**
  Headings of equal importance should be stated in the same way. Follow the basic rules for capitalizing titles and headings. (See page 476.6.)

- **Consider using a sans serif font for the title and headings.**
  (*Sans serif* type, like this type, does not have "tails.") Use larger type, perhaps 18-point, for your title and 14-point type for any headings. (Use **boldface** for headings if they seem to get lost on the page.)

Take NOTE On screen, most people find a sans serif font easier to read. So for writing that you publish on-line, consider a **sans serif font** for the body and a **serif font** for the title and any headings.

SPACING AND MARGINS

- **Maintain a one-inch margin around each page** (top, bottom, left, and right).

- **Hit the tab key to indent the first line of each paragraph.** This key should be set at five spaces.

- **Leave only one space after each sentence** to make your writing easier to read.

- **Avoid placing headings, hyphenated words, and starts of new paragraphs at the bottom of a page.** Also avoid single words at the bottom of a page or carried over to the top of a page.

GRAPHIC DEVICES

- **Create bulleted lists to highlight important points.** Most programs allow you to do this. (See page 32.) Be selective; you don't want too many lists in your writing.

- **Include charts or other graphics.** Graphics should not be so small that they get lost on the page, nor so large that they overpower the page. You can also put graphics on separate pages. (See page 32.)

Effective Design in Action

The following two pages (page 1 and page 5) from a student report show effective design features.

Kendall McGinn
Mr. Gilding
Social Studies
Feb. 25, 2000

The title is 18-point sans serif type.

The Return of the Buffalo

At one point in the early twentieth century, it seemed that the American buffalo would continue to exist only in pictures or on the buffalo nickel. Its population of 100 million in 1700 had been reduced to 1,000 by 1889. In recent years, that number has increased to nearly 400,000 (Hodgson 71). The buffalo, once endangered, has returned.

The main text is 10-point serif type.

Before the Europeans came to North America, the native people of the North American plains and the buffalo were one *Pte Oyate,* or Buffalo Nation. The big bull *tantanka* was life itself. These Native Americans followed the herds and used the buffalo for food, clothing, shelter, religious ceremonies, and medicine. A Lakota leader summed up this unity between human and animal: "When the Creator made the buffalo, he put power in them. When you eat the meat, that power goes into you, heals the body and spirit" (qtd. in Hodgson 69).

The heading is 14-point sans serif.

Open Season on Buffalo

During the expansion of the United States, a cultural clash occurred, and the Europeans practically destroyed the buffalo. By the year 1800, it was reported that there were only about 30 million buffalo left in the United States.

McGinn 5

A graphic adds visual appeal.

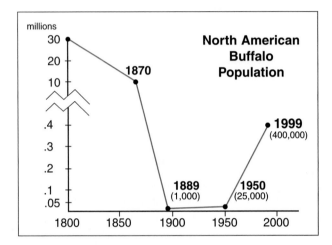

The buffalo is "returning" to North America in ever-increasing numbers. Cable Network News owner Ted Turner and actress Jane Fonda raise almost 10,000 buffalo on their Montana and New Mexico ranches. "I guess I've gone buffalo batty," Turner says. Both he and Fonda support the raising of buffalo as an excellent source of low-fat meat and as a way to help save this once endangered species (Hodgson 75).

Buffalo ranchers are, in fact, learning that raising buffalo has many benefits. Raising buffalo is more cost-effective and more environmentally safe than raising cattle. Here are four main benefits:

A bulleted list is easy to read.

- Buffalo don't overeat.
- Their sharp hooves loosen hard soil.
- Buffalo improve grass crops.
- They adapt to any climate.

Buffalo living in Florida seem just as happy as those living in Alaska. In Hawaii, they even survived a hurricane. Hawaiian rancher Bill Mowry recalls how the buffalo "loved every minute of it."

"Writing becomes real when it has an audience." —Tom Liner

PUBLISHING
Your Writing

Publishing is the driving force behind writing. It makes all of your prewriting, drafting, and revising worth the effort. Publishing is to a writer what a live performance is to a musician or an exhibit is to an artist. It is why you have worked so hard in the first place—to share a finished piece of writing that effectively expresses your thoughts and feelings.

The easiest and by far the most helpful form of publishing is sharing a finished project with your classmates. As writer Tom Liner states, "You learn ways to improve your writing by seeing its effect on others."

You can also select a piece of writing for your classroom portfolio or submit something to your school newspaper or literary magazine. If you're really adventurous, you may even want to submit your writing outside of school, perhaps to a national literary magazine. This chapter will help you with all your publishing needs.

Preview

- ○ Publishing Ideas
- ○ Preparing a Portfolio
- ○ Sending Your Writing Out
- ○ Places to Publish
- ○ Publishing On-Line
- ○ Creating Your Own Web Page

Publishing Ideas

As you will see in the ideas listed below, publishing covers a great deal of territory. Some of these ideas are easy to carry out, like sharing your writing with your classmates. Others are more challenging and take more time and effort, such as entering a favorite piece in a writing contest.

PERFORMING

Sharing with Classmates
Reading to Other Audiences
Producing a Video
Performing on Stage

DISPLAYING

Bulletin Boards / Display Cases
Libraries
Business Windows
Clinic Waiting Rooms
Literary/Art Fairs

SELF-PUBLISHING

Family Newsletter
Greeting/Special-Occasion Cards
Booklets
Personal Web Sites (See page 39.)

SUBMITTING (In School)

School Newspaper
Literary Magazine
Classroom Collection
Class-Project Display
Writing Portfolio (See page 35.)

SUBMITTING (Outside of School)

City Newspaper
Area Historical Society
Local Arts Council
Church Publications
Young Writers' Conferences
Magazines/Contests (See page 37.)
On-Line Publications (See page 38.)

Publishing TIPS

These tips will help you prepare your writing for publication.

- Work with your writing until you feel good about it from start to finish.
- Ask for input and advice throughout the writing process.
- Save all drafts of your writing for reference.
- Carefully edit your work for style and correctness.
- Present your final copy clearly and neatly. (See pages 30-32 and 75-79.)
- Know your publishing options.
- Follow the necessary publication guidelines. (See pages 36 and 38.)

Preparing a Portfolio

A **writing portfolio** is a collection of your work that shows your skill as a writer. It is different from a writing folder that contains writing in various stages of completion. In most cases, you will be asked to compile a *show-case portfolio*—a collection of your best writing for a quarter or a semester. Compiling a showcase portfolio allows you to participate in the assessment process. You decide which writing and samples to include; you reflect upon your writing progress; you make sure that all the right pieces are in all the right places. You are in control.

What You Should Include

Most showcase portfolios contain the following basic components. (Check with your teacher for the specific requirements.)

- **A table of contents** listing the pieces included in your portfolio
- **An opening essay or letter** detailing the story behind your portfolio (how you compiled it, how you feel about it, what it means to you, etc.)
- **A specified number of finished pieces** representing your best writing in the class (Your teacher may require you to include all of your prewriting, drafting, and revising work for one or more of these pieces.)
- **A best "other" piece** related to your work in another content area
- **A cover sheet** attached to each piece of writing, discussing the reason for its selection, the amount of work that went into it, and so on
- **Evaluation sheets or checklists** charting the basic skills you have mastered as well as the skills you still need to work on (Your teacher will supply these sheets. You may also be asked to include samples that demonstrate specific skills.)

How You Should Work

1. Keep track of all of your writing (including planning notes and drafts). This way, when it comes to compiling your portfolio, you will have all the pieces to work with.
2. Make sure that you understand all of the specific requirements for your portfolio.
3. Use an expandable folder for your portfolio to avoid dog-eared or ripped pages. Keep your papers in a "safe environment."
4. Maintain a regular writing/compiling schedule. It will be impossible to produce an effective portfolio if you approach it as a last-minute project.
5. Develop a feeling of pride in your portfolio. Make sure that it reflects a positive image of yourself. Look your best!

Sending Your Writing Out

Q. *What types of writing can I submit?*

A. There are markets for all types of writing—essays, articles, stories, plays, poems, and children's books. Newspapers are most interested in essays and articles. With magazines, it depends. Some magazines publish essays, reports, stories, and poetry; others accept only essays.

HELP FILE

Check the *Writer's Market* (Writer's Digest Books) or the *Writer's Market: The Electronic Edition* (CD-ROM) to find out who publishes what. If your school library doesn't have either of these resources, your public library will.

Q. *Where should I submit my writing?*

A. You will probably have better success if you try to publish your work locally. Consider area newspapers and publications put out by local organizations. If you're interested in submitting something to a national publication, turn again to the *Writer's Market*. It includes a special section devoted to teen and young-adult publications. (Also see page 37 in this handbook for additional ideas.)

Q. *How should I submit my work?*

A. Check the publication's masthead for submission guidelines. (The *masthead* is the small print on one of the opening pages identifying the publishers and editors of the publication, subscription rates, the mailing address, and so on.) You can also call the publication or go to its Web site. Most publications expect you to include . . .

- **a brief cover letter** (addressed to a specific editor) identifying the title and form of your writing, and the word count;
- **a neatly printed copy of your work** with your name on each page—double-spaced and paper-clipped; and
- **a SASE** (self-addressed stamped envelope) large enough to hold your manuscript so that it can be returned after it has been read.

Q. *What should I expect?*

A. First, you should expect to wait a long time for a reply. (It may take up to two months in some cases.) Second, you should not be surprised or disappointed if your writing is not accepted for publication at the first place you send it. Consider it a learning experience and keep submitting.

Places to Publish

Listed below are five well-respected publications that accept student submissions and three writing contests to enter. (Refer to the *Writer's Market*—found in most libraries—for more places to publish.)

PUBLICATIONS

Kids Byline: A Magazine for Kids by Kids (Grades 2-12)
FORMS: Fiction, nonfiction, poetry
SEND TO: P.O. Box 1838
              Frederick, MD 21702

Merlyn's Pen (Grades 6-12)
FORMS: Fiction, poetry, essays, reviews
SEND TO: P.O. Box 910
              E. Greenwich, RI 02818

Writing! (Grades 6-12)
FORMS: Fiction, essays, book reviews, poetry
SEND TO: 900 Skokie Boulevard
              Suite 200
              Northbrook, IL 60062

The 21st Century (Grades 9-12)
FORMS: Fiction, poetry, nonfiction
SEND TO: Box 30
              Newton, MA 02461

The High School Writer
(Grades 9-12)
FORMS: Fiction, poetry, nonfiction
SEND TO: Senior High Edition
              P.O. Box 718
              Grand Rapids, MN 55744

WRITING CONTESTS

Read Writing Contests
(Grades 9-12)
FORMS: Short stories, personal essays
SEND TO:
    Read Writing and Art Awards
    Weekly Reader Corporation
    200 First Stamford Place
    P.O. Box 120023
    Stamford, CT 06912-0023

National Council of Teachers of English (NCTE) Achievement Awards in Writing (Grade 11)
FORMS: Sampler of best writing plus one impromptu theme on a topic selected by NCTE
SEND TO: NCTE, Achievement
              Awards in Writing
              1111 Kenyon Road
              Urbana, IL 61901-1096

Scholastic Writing Awards
(Grades 9-12)
FORMS: Short story, essay, dramatic script, poetry, humor, science fiction, fantasy, writing portfolio
SEND TO: The Scholastic Art and
              Writing Awards
              555 Broadway
              New York, NY 10012

Take NOTE Always check with the contest or publication and with your teacher about guidelines for submitting your writing. Include a self-addressed stamped envelope (SASE) with any inquiry.

Publishing On-Line

The Internet offers many publishing opportunities. There are on-line magazines, writing contests, and other sites that accept submissions. The questions and answers below will help you prepare to publish your writing on the Net.

Q. *What should I do first?*

A. Begin by checking with your teachers to see if your school has its own Internet site where students can post their work. If not, suggest that one be started. Also ask your teachers about Web sites they know of that accept student submissions.

Q. *How should I begin my Web search?*

A. Use a search engine to find places to publish. (See pages 332-334.) Here's one starting point: Refer to the search engine's index of topics, and look for an "Education" topic; then click on the "K-12" subheading to see what develops. You can also enter "student and publish" as a search phrase, and go from there.

Q. *Does the Write Source have a Web site?*

A. Yes, you can visit our Web site at <thewritesource.com>. Follow the "Publish It" link for a list of Web sites that accept student submissions.

Q. *How should I submit my work?*

A. Before you do anything, make sure that you understand the publishing conditions related to a particular site and share this information with your parents. Then follow these guidelines:

- Include a message explaining why you are contacting the site. Most publishers receive many messages each day, so keep your message brief and make your purpose clear.
- Send your work in an appropriate format. Some sites have on-line forms into which you can paste a text. Others list the electronic file formats they prefer to receive.
- Provide the publisher with correct information for contacting you. E-mail addresses sometimes change, so a site may ask for other information. (However, don't give your home address or other personal information unless your parents approve.)

Q. *What should I expect?*

A. Within a week or so of your submission, you should receive a note from the publisher verifying that your work has been received. However, it may take many weeks for the publisher to make a decision about publishing your work. If one site doesn't publish your work, you can always submit it to another one.

Creating Your Own Web Page

To create a Web site on your home computer, check with your Internet service provider to find out how to get started. If you are using a school computer, ask your teacher for help. Then start designing your site. Use the questions and answers below as a starting point.

Q. *How do I plan my site?*

A. Think about the number of pages you want on your Web site. Should you put everything on one page, or would you like to have a number of pages (perhaps a home page, a page of poetry, a page of short stories, a page of favorite links, and so forth)? Check out other student sites for ideas. Then plan your pages by sketching them out. Note how the pages will be linked by marking the hot spots on your sketches.

Q. *How do I make the pages?*

A. Start each page as a separate file. Many word-processing programs let you save a file as a Web page. If yours doesn't, you will have to add HTML (hypertext markup language) codes to format the text and make links to graphics and other pages. Your teacher may be able to explain how to do this. Otherwise, you can find instructions about HTML on the Net. (See our Web site at <thewritesource.com> for help.)

Q. *How do I know whether my pages work?*

A. You should always test your pages. Using your browser, open your first page. Then follow the links to make sure they work correctly and that all the pages look right.

Q. *How do I get my pages on the Net?*

A. You must upload your finished pages to your Internet provider's computer. Ask your provider how to do this. (If you're working on your home computer, make sure to get your parents' approval first. If you're using the school's equipment, work with your teacher.) Your provider will also tell you how you can access the pages later, in case you want to make changes. After you upload a page, visit your site to make sure it still works.

HELP FILE

Once your site is up and working, e-mail your friends and tell them to visit it. Ask visitors to your site to spread the word to other people they know. In addition, mention your page in chat rooms and post announcements on electronic bulletin boards. Ask your provider for tips on how to "advertise" your page to the rest of the Net.

Using the

WRITING PROCESS

"As soon as you connect with your true subject, you will write."

—Joyce Carol Oates

A Guide to
PREWRITING

Author Barry Lane says writers "continually move back and forth between the sea and the mountain" during a writing project. As Lane explains it, writing begins in the "sea of experience," which contains the memories, experiences, and information that writers work with. When they actually write, writers begin to climb the "mountain of perception," forming new understandings, linking ideas, and drawing conclusions. If they need more details, they head back to the sea.

Prewriting refers to the beginning of a writing project—when you're still at sea—selecting a subject, gathering information about it, and so on. Prewriting also refers to trips back to the sea—when you need to carry out additional research and planning in the middle of a writing project. If you give prewriting the proper attention, you've laid a solid foundation for all of the other steps in the writing process.

Preview

- Quick Guide
- Using Selecting Strategies
- Freewriting Tips
- Using Collecting Strategies
- Using Graphic Organizers
- A Closer Look at Prewriting

Quick Guide

PURPOSE: The main purpose of prewriting is to select and develop specific subjects for writing. It deals with all of the brainstorming, talking, collecting, and planning you do before you write.

✱ You may also do some prewriting activities later in the writing process. For example, once you review your first draft, you may decide to gather some additional information about your subject. (Writing is a recursive process, meaning that a writer may repeat or revisit steps during the writing process.)

STARTING POINT: During prewriting, you do the following:
- select a specific subject,
- collect information about it,
- focus on a specific part of the subject for writing, and
- plan how to use the supporting information.

Remember: Always select a subject that interests you and meets the requirements of the assignment.

FOCUS: Prewriting can be carried out in a variety of ways. You may start by making a list or a cluster of possible subjects. This activity may prompt you to write freely about some item from that list or cluster. Then you may do some research before focusing on a specific way to write about the subject. Once you've established a focus, or thesis, you may arrange your supporting information with an outline or some other graphic organizer.

THE BIG PICTURE: When prewriting, pay special attention to three traits of good writing: ideas, organization, and voice.

Ideas: Collect as much information as you can. The more you know about your subject, the easier it will be to write about it.

Organization: Decide on the best arrangement of the facts and details you have collected. There has to be a master plan that holds all of the information together. (See page 52.)

Voice: Make sure that your subject still interests you after you've done some collecting and planning. In order to write with voice and personality, you must have a sincere interest in your topic.

Using **Selecting** Strategies

The following strategies will help you select a specific subject for your writing. Read through the entire list before you choose a strategy to begin your subject search.

1. **Journal Writing . . .** Write in a journal on a regular basis. Explore your personal feelings, develop your thoughts, and record events and happenings of each day. Underline ideas in your journal writing that you would like to explore further. (See pages 144-146.)

2. **Freewriting . . .** Write nonstop for 5-10 minutes to discover possible writing ideas. Begin writing with a particular focus in mind that is somehow related to your assignment. (See page 45 for tips.)

3. **Clustering . . .** Begin a cluster with a nucleus word related to your writing topic or assignment. Then cluster ideas around the nucleus word. Circle each idea you write and draw a line connecting it to the closest related idea. (See the sample below.)

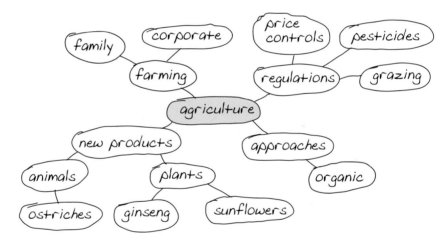

★ After 3 or 4 minutes of clustering, scan your cluster for an idea to explore in a freewriting. (A specific writing subject should begin to emerge during this freewriting.)

4. **Listing . . .** Begin with a thought or a key word related to your assignment and simply start listing words and ideas. Listing ideas with a group of friends or classmates (brainstorming) is also an effective way to search for writing ideas.

5. **Reflecting, Participating, and Listening . . .** Think about possible writing ideas as you read, as you ride (or drive) to school, and as you wait in the cafeteria line. Be alert for potential subjects as you visit with friends, or as you shop, work, or travel. Participate in activities related to your writing assignment. Also, talk to other people who are knowledgeable about your possible writing idea.

6. **Using the "Essentials of Life Checklist" . . .** Below you will find a checklist of the essential elements in our lives. The checklist provides an endless variety of subject possibilities. Consider the third category, *food*. It could lead to the following writing ideas:

- sensible eating habits
- fast-food overload
- a favorite type of food
- truth in labeling on food packages

ESSENTIALS OF LIFE CHECKLIST

clothing	communication	exercise/training
housing	purpose/goals	community
food	measurement	arts/music
education	machines	faith/religion
family	intelligence	trade/money
friends	agriculture	heat/fuel
love	environment	rules/laws
senses	plant life	science/technology
energy	land/property	work/occupation
entertainment	health/medicine	private/public life
recreation	literature/books	natural resources
personality	tools/utensils	freedom/rights

HELP FILE

Many writing assignments are related to a general subject area you are studying. Let's say, for example, you were asked to write a report about exercise and training, or about opportunities in education. Your writing task would be to focus on a specific aspect of that subject:

General Subject Area: Exercise and Training
Specific Writing Subject: Aerobic Spinning

General Subject Area: Opportunities in Education
Specific Writing Subject: Internships for High School Students

Freewriting **TIPS**

The Process . . .

- Write nonstop and record whatever comes into your head. Write for at least 10 minutes if possible.

- Begin writing about a particular subject if you have one in mind. Otherwise, pick anything that comes to mind and begin writing.

- Don't stop to judge, edit, or correct your writing. Freewriting is exploratory writing, nothing more.

- Keep writing even when you seem to be drawing a blank. If necessary, switch to another subject, or write "I'm drawing a blank" until a new idea comes to mind.

- When a certain subject seems to be working, stick with it as long as you can. Record as many specific details about it as possible.

  * Keep a small notebook close at hand, and write freely in it whenever you have an idea you don't want to forget, or write in it just for something to do. These freewritings will help you become a better writer.

The Result . . .

- Review your writing and underline ideas you like. These ideas may serve as starting points for writing assignments.

- Share your writing with your peers. You can learn a great deal by reading and reacting to the freewriting of your fellow writers.

- Continue freewriting about ideas you want to explore further. (You could approach this focused freewriting as a first draft for an assignment.)

Some Reminders . . .

- Thoughts are constantly passing through your head; you always have something on your mind.

- Freewriting helps you get these thoughts on paper.

- Freewriting helps you develop your thoughts by exploring, connecting, and making meaning out of them.

- Many things seem awkward or difficult when you first try them; freewriting will probably be no different.

- Just stick with it and don't become discouraged.

Using Collecting Strategies

Once you've selected a subject, you need to gather details for writing. The activities and strategies that follow should help you do this. If you need to explore your writing ideas in great detail, and if time permits, use two or more of these strategies.

Gathering Your Thoughts

Freewriting @ At this point, you can approach freewriting in two ways. (1) You can do a focused freewriting, exploring your subject from a number of different angles. (2) You can approach your freewriting as if it were a quick version of the actual paper. A quick version will give you a good feel for your subject and will also tell you how much you know about it or need to find out.

Clustering @ Try clustering again, this time with your subject as the nucleus word. This clustering will naturally be more focused or structured than an initial clustering since you now have a specific subject in mind.

5 W's of Writing @ Answer the 5 W's—*Who? What? When? Where?* and *Why?*—to identify basic information about your subject. (Add *How?* to the list for even better coverage.)

Directed Writing @ Write whatever comes to mind about your subject, using one of the modes listed below. (Repeat the process as often as you need to, selecting a different mode each time.)

Describe it.	What do you see, hear, feel, smell, taste . . . ?
Compare it.	What is it similar to? What is it different from?
Apply it.	What can you do with it? How can you use it?
Associate it.	What connections between this and something else come to mind?
Analyze it.	What parts does it have? How do they work together?
Argue for or against it.	What do you like about it? Not like about it? What are its strengths and its weaknesses?

Directed Dialoguing @ Create a dialogue between two people in which your specific subject is the topic of the conversation. The two speakers should build on each other's comments about the subject.

Audience Appeal @ Select a specific audience to address in an exploratory writing. Consider a group of preschoolers, a live television audience, the readers of a popular teen magazine, the local school board. This writing will help you see your subject in new ways.

Questioning ℮ Ask questions to gather information about your subject. You can use the questions in the chart below if your subject falls into any of these three different categories: **problems** (student apathy), **policies** (grading), or **concepts** (student internships).

	Description	Function	History	Value
PROBLEMS	What is the problem? What are the signs of the problem?	Who or what is affected by it? What new problems may it cause in the future?	What is the current status of the problem? What or who caused it?	What is the significance? Why is it more (or less) important than other problems?
POLICIES	What type of policy is it? What are its most important features?	What is the policy designed to do? What is needed to make it work?	What brought this policy about? What are the alternatives to this policy?	Is the policy working? What are its advantages and disadvantages?
CONCEPTS	What type of concept is it? Who or what is related to it?	Who has been influenced by this concept? Why is it important?	When did it originate? How has it changed over the years?	What practical value does it hold? What is its social worth?

Researching Your Topic

Reading ℮ Refer to nonfiction books, magazines, pamphlets, and newspapers for information about your subject. Take notes as you read.

Surfing ℮ Explore the Internet for information about your writing idea. (See pages 332-335 for help.) Jot down Web addresses as you go.

Viewing and Listening ℮ Watch relevant television programs and videos or listen to tapes about your subject.

Talking to Others

Interviewing ℮ Interview an expert about your subject. Meet the expert in person, communicate by phone, or send questions to be answered. (See page 330 for more information on interviewing.)

Discussing ℮ Talk with your classmates, teachers, or other people to find out what they know about your subject. Take notes to help you remember the important things they say.

Using Graphic **Organizers**

Graphic organizers can help you gather and organize your details for writing. Clustering is one method (see page 43); these next two pages list other useful organizers.

Cause/Effect Organizer

Use to collect and organize details for cause/effect essays.

Subject: _____

Causes (Because of . . .)	Effects / . . . these \ (conditions) \ resulted. /
.	.
.	.
.	.
.	.

Problem/Solution Web

Use to map out problem/solution essays.

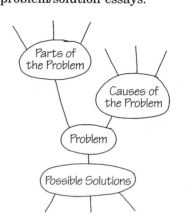

Time Line

Use to collect details for personal narratives and for reports recalling important events.

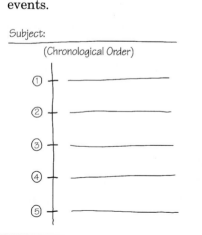

Evaluation Collection Grid

Use to collect supporting details for essays of evaluation.

Subject: _____

Points to Evaluate	Supporting Details
1.	
2.	
3.	
4.	

Venn Diagram

Use to collect details to compare and contrast two subjects.

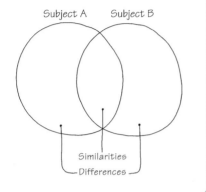

Subject A   Subject B

Similarities
Differences

5 W's Chart

Use to collect the *Who? What? When? Where?* and *Why?* details for personal narratives and news stories.

Subject: _____

Who?	What?	When?	Where?	Why?

Line Diagram

Use to collect and organize details for expository essays.

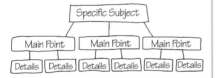

Specific Subject

Main Point | Main Point | Main Point

Details | Details | Details | Details | Details | Details

Definition Diagram

Use to gather information for extended definition essays.

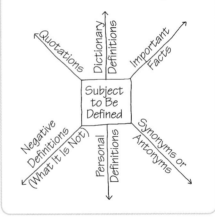

Quotations | Dictionary Definitions | Important Facts

Subject to Be Defined

Negative Definitions (What It Is Not) | Personal Definitions | Synonyms or Antonyms

Process (Cycle) Diagram

Use to collect details for science-related writing, such as how a process or cycle works.

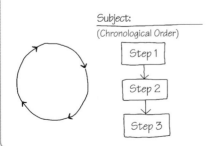

Subject: _____
(Chronological Order)

Step 1
Step 2
Step 3

Sensory Chart

Use to collect details for descriptive essays and observation reports.

Subject: _____

Sights	Sounds	Smells	Tastes	Textures

"Good writing is formed partly through plan and partly through accident."

—Ken Macrorie

A **Closer Look** at Prewriting

What should you do after you've gathered information about your writing idea? Well, you can either plan and write your first draft, or you can stop and consider how well you match up with your subject before you go any further.

Taking Inventory of Your Thoughts

After carefully considering the questions that follow, you will be ready to (1) move ahead with your writing or (2) change your subject.

Purpose: Does my subject meet the assignment requirements? Am I writing to explain, describe, persuade, entertain, or retell?

Self: How do I feel about the subject? Do I have enough time to develop this subject?

Subject: How much do I know about this subject? Can I think of an interesting way to write about it? Is additional information available?

Audience: Who are my readers? How much do they already know about this subject? How can I get them interested in my ideas?

Form and Style: How should I present my ideas—in a narrative, an essay, a report, or an article? Can I think of an interesting way to begin or lead into my paper?

 How much information do I have to collect before I write my first draft?

That depends on the type of writing you are doing. If you are developing a personal narrative, collecting information may not be a big issue. But suppose you are developing a persuasive essay about the misuse of megavitamins. You would have to do some research to collect enough information to develop a convincing argument. In short, the closer you are to your subject, the less collecting you will have to do.

Forming Your Thesis Statement

After you have completed enough exploring and collecting, you should begin to develop a more focused interest in your subject. If all goes well, this interest will become the thesis of your writing. **A thesis statement identifies the focus for your writing.** It usually highlights a special condition or feature of the subject, expresses a specific feeling, or takes a stand.

State your thesis in a sentence that effectively expresses what you want to explore in your essay. Write as many versions as it takes to come up with a sentence that sets the right tone and direction for your writing. Use the following formula to write a thesis statement.

FORMULA

> **A specific subject**
> **+ a specific condition, feeling, or stand**
> **= an effective thesis statement.**

Thesis Statement: **Young children exposed to low levels of lead** (*specific subject*) **may face health problems later in life.** (*specific condition*)

SAMPLE THESIS STATEMENTS

Writing Assignment: Essay about opportunities in education
Specific Subject: High school internships
Thesis Statement: **High school internship programs** (*specific subject*) **benefit students in three ways** (*specific features*).

Writing Assignment: Essay on the Civil War
Specific Subject: General George McClellan
Thesis Statement: **General George McClellan's overcautious tactics** (*specific subject*) **prolonged the war** (*specific feeling*).

Writing Assignment: Essay about an outdoor activity
Specific Subject: Use of barbed hooks for fishing
Thesis Statement: **Barbed hooks** (*specific subject*) **should be banned from fishing** (*specific stand*).

HELP FILE

If you try to cover too much ground, your essays, reports, and research papers will go on and on and be hard to follow. That is why it is so important to establish a specific thesis for your writing assignments.

Organizing Your Details

With a clear thesis in mind, you may need to design a writing plan before you start your first draft. Your plan can be anything from a brief list of ideas to a detailed sentence outline. (See page 108.) Use the guidelines that follow to help organize your details for writing.

1. **Study your thesis statement.** It may suggest a logical method of organization.

2. **Review the details that support your thesis.** See if an overall plan of organization begins to emerge.

3. **Consider the methods of organization listed below.**

Methods of Organization

Listed below are some useful ways to organize details in your writing. (See pages 100-103 for writing samples and pages 48-49 for organizers.)

- **Chronological order** (*time*) is effective for sharing personal narratives, summarizing steps, and explaining events.

- **Order of location** (*spatial*) is useful for many types of descriptions. Details can be described from left to right, from right to left, from top to bottom, from edge to center, and so on.

- **Illustration** (*deductive*) is a method of arrangement in which you first state a general idea (thesis statement) and follow with specific reasons, examples, and facts.

- **Climax** (*inductive*) is a method of arrangement in which you present specific details followed by a general statement or a conclusion.

- **Compare/contrast** is a method of arrangement in which you compare one subject to another subject. In the process of your writing, you show how the subjects are alike and how they are different.

- **Cause/effect** is a type of arrangement that helps you make connections between a result and the events that came before it. Usually, you begin with a general statement giving the cause of something, and then you discuss a number of specific effects.

- **Problem/solution** is a type of arrangement in which you state a problem and explore possible solutions.

- **Definition** or **classification** is a type of arrangement that can be used to explain a term or a concept (a machine, a theory, a game, and so on). Begin by placing the subject in the appropriate *class,* and then provide details that show how your subject is different from and similar to others in the same class. (See pages 208-209.)

"All writing begins life as a first draft, and first drafts
are never any good.   They're not supposed to be."

—Patricia T. O'Conner

A Guide to
DRAFTING

This is it—your first draft, your first complete look at a writing idea.
All of your searching and planning have led up to this point. Write as
much of your first draft as possible in the first sitting while all of your
prewriting is still fresh in your mind. Think of drafting as the process of
connecting all of the ideas that you have collected about your subject. Refer
to your planning notes as you write, but be open to new ideas as they
emerge. Keep these additional points in mind as you write:

- Concentrate on developing your ideas, not on producing a final copy.
- Include as much detail as possible.
- Continue writing until you make all of your main points, or until
  you come to a logical stopping point.

Preview

- Quick Guide
- Writing an Opening Paragraph
- Developing the Middle
- Bringing Your Writing to a Close

"The only true creative aspect of writing is the first draft. That's when it's coming straight from your head and your heart."   —Evan Hunter

Quick Guide

PURPOSE: Drafting shows you how well you match up with your subject and sets into motion the actual development of your writing.

STARTING POINT: You're ready to write a first draft once you . . .
- know enough about your subject,
- establish a thesis (focus) for your writing, and
- organize your supporting ideas.

Some writers pay special attention to the specific wording in their opening paragraph before they dive headfirst into their first draft. Once the beginning part is set, they find it much easier to carry out the rest of their writing. Other writers are more interested in getting all of their thoughts on paper right away. Author John Steinbeck supports the second approach. As he advises: "Write freely and as rapidly as possible and throw the whole thing on paper."

FORM: When drafting with pen and paper, write on every other line, and use only one side of the paper. Double-space when using a computer. This will make revising by hand much easier.

Remember to write your first draft freely, without being too concerned about neatness and correctness. This is why a first draft is often called a *rough draft*. Just make sure that your writing is legible.

THE BIG PICTURE: When writing a first draft, give special attention to these traits of effective writing: ideas, organization, and voice.

Ideas: Develop all the worthwhile thoughts and ideas you have collected, and consider new ideas or directions as they come to mind. (A first draft is your first look at a developing writing idea.)

Organization: Use your prewriting and planning as a general guide when you write. Try to work logically through your draft from the opening to the closing paragraph.

Voice: Speak honestly and naturally so the real you comes through in your writing.

Writing an **Opening** Paragraph

For almost all of your writing—narratives, essays, reviews, and reports—you need to plan an opening or lead paragraph. Your opening should help clarify your thinking about your subject and accomplish three things: It should introduce your subject, gain your reader's attention, and identify your thesis, or focus. The opening paragraph is one of the most important elements in any composition because it sets the tone and establishes the basic organization for your writing.

There are many ways to begin an opening paragraph. Several possible starting points are listed below:

- Share some thought-provoking details about the subject.
- Ask your reader a challenging question.
- Begin with an informative quotation.
- Provide a dramatic, eye-opening statement.
- Open with some thoughtful dialogue or an engaging story.
- Identify the main points you plan to cover.

HELP FILE

Your opening affects the direction and style of your entire piece of writing. If you don't like how the first or second draft of your opening sounds, keep trying. You'll know when you hit the right version because it will help you visualize the rest of your draft.

Sample **Opening Paragraph**

The following opening paragraph comes from student writer Steve Crandall's essay about driver education. Note how effectively he gains the reader's attention by offering thought-provoking ideas about his subject. He also establishes a serious tone and sets down a basic organization for the rest of the writing in his thesis statement. (From *The 21st Century.* Copyright by the Young Authors Foundation, Inc. All rights reserved.)

The results of today's driver education programs are visible every day, on every road. You can see them in the guy who squeals dangerously into traffic on a busy street or in the girl who nearly blows through a stop sign while talking on a cell phone. Many people say younger drivers are to blame for the problems on our roads; but, if they are to be blamed, it is only because they were poorly prepared. Young drivers are products of driver education programs that are outdated, ineffective, and in need of improvement.

Developing the Middle

The middle paragraphs in your draft should support your thesis. Make sure to use your planning notes (outline, list, cluster) as a general guide for your writing. Here are some ways to support your thesis:

Explain: Provide important facts, details, and examples.

Narrate: Share a brief story (anecdote) or re-create an experience to illustrate or clarify an idea.

Describe: Tell in detail how someone appears or how something works.

Define: Identify or clarify the meaning of a specific term or idea.

Argue: Use logic and evidence to prove something is true.

Compare: Provide examples to show how two things are alike or different.

Analyze: Examine the parts of something to better understand the whole.

Reflect: Express your thoughts or feelings about something.

How many different methods of support should I use?

For most essays and other longer compositions, you should use at least two or three of these methods to develop your thesis. For example, in an essay of definition, you might provide one or two dictionary definitions, compare your subject to something similar, and share a brief story about it.

Supporting Your Thesis

The paragraphs in the middle part of an essay contain the main points and supporting details that develop your thesis. In most cases, you should develop each main point in a separate paragraph. Remember that specific details add meaning to your writing and make it worth reading. Writing that lacks effective detail gives an incomplete picture.

A well-written supporting paragraph often contains three levels of detail:

Level 1: Controlling sentences name the topic:
Some states have adopted graduated licensing programs to produce better drivers.

Level 2: Clarifying sentences support the main point:
Such programs require that beginning drivers receive three different types of licenses.

Level 3: Completing sentences add details to complete the point:
First, they must obtain a learner's permit, then, after six months, a Junior Operator's License. . . .

Sample **Middle Paragraphs**

Provided below are three sample paragraphs from Steve Crandall's essay on driver education. In the first paragraph, he *describes* and *reflects* upon a special type of licensing program.

> Some states have adopted graduated licensing programs to produce better drivers. Such programs require that beginning drivers receive three different types of licenses. First, they must obtain a learner's permit, then, after six months, a Junior Operator's License. After another six months, they are eligible for a full license. Before getting this license, a new driver cannot have anyone under 18 in the car unless an over-21 adult is in the front passenger seat. A new driver is also not allowed to drive between midnight and 5 a.m. This approach seems good in theory, but is it really effective? For example, do the drivers in these programs receive enough behind-the-wheel experience during their training period? In addition, can any over-21 adult accompany a junior operator? What if this adult has a poor driving record?

In this paragraph, the writer *analyzes* the existing driver education program in his state and *compares* it to those in other countries.

> A few simple changes in the existing driver ed program would do a great deal to improve the quality of new drivers. On the written test in our state, a score of 14 on a 20-question test is a passing grade. It would not be unreasonable to require at least a score of 18 on this test. Currently, only 54 total hours of training are deemed necessary, with 30 of these hours completed in the classroom. Some countries, including Canada, require many more hours of training (triple or quadruple the time), with a higher percentage of in-car training. Those same countries also require beginning drivers to spend a significant amount of money (up to $2,000) to receive their training. This is not necessarily what should be done here, but certainly many more hours of behind-the-wheel training are necessary.

Later in the essay, the writer *reflects* on the cause and possible prevention of most traffic accidents.

> Human error accounts for most traffic accidents. Weather would not have to be a major factor if drivers were taught how to drive on wet or icy roads. Road rage may cause some accidents, but many could also be avoided if drivers were properly trained. Unfortunately, no training can help drivers in certain situations, such as confronting drunk drivers. Still, new drivers ought to receive training in night driving, driving in rainy and foggy conditions, and in defensive driving.

Bringing Your Writing to a **Close**

Closing paragraphs are important when you need to tie up any loose ends or clarify certain points in your essay. They help readers see the importance of your thesis or message. Experiment with possible closings before you settle on one. Closing paragraphs should do one or more of the following things:

- Restate the thesis.
- Answer any questions left unanswered in the middle paragraphs.
- Review the main points.
- Emphasize the special importance of one of the main points.
- Connect with the reader's experience or with life in general.

> **HELP FILE**
>
> An effective closing is an ending—plus more to think about. In the first part of your closing, review specific points you covered in your writing. In the second part, broaden your scope by saying something more general about the subject, something that will keep the subject alive in the reader's mind.

Sample **Closing Paragraph**

In this sample closing, the writer restates the thesis of his essay and reviews some of his main points. In addition, the final point emphasizes the importance of the subject.

> The current driver education programs don't meet the needs of today's young drivers. What's needed are new, more extensive programs, producing young drivers who are much better prepared for the road and much less likely to have careless accidents. Human error, which causes most accidents, will never be totally eliminated; but it can be reduced if young drivers are prepared in the proper way. In the end, this training may mean fewer traffic injuries and deaths on the road, something that would benefit everyone.

 How can I make my drafts sound natural and sincere?

Your writing will be natural and honest if you remember one thing: The writer is never alone. Think of your writing as one-half of a conversation with a reader you invent. Talk to your silent partner. In addition, relax when you write rather than nervously bouncing around. Think about what you've already said, and let that help you decide what you should say next.

"I tend to do as much revising
as editors will let me do."

—Tom Wolfe

A Guide to
REVISING

In most cases, experienced writers have one important advantage over you when it comes to developing a piece of writing. They have time—time to step away from a completed first draft before they do any revising, and time to shape and reshape their writing into an effective finished product. They also have another advantage—an extensive working knowledge of the revising process. More specifically, with a first draft in hand, they know just how much work is ahead of them.

In basic terms, revising deals with making changes in your writing until it says what you want it to say. Author Ernest Hemingway rewrote one of his endings 27 times before he felt satisfied with it. Now, you may have neither the time nor the desire to rework any part of your writing 27 times, but you should always make as many improvements as possible before turning in your paper. You owe it to yourself and to your readers.

Preview

- Quick Guide
- Using Basic Revising Guidelines
- A Closer Look at Revising
- Revising for Ideas, Organization, and Voice
- Revising Checklist

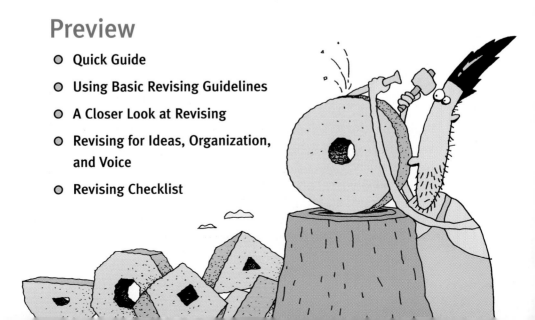

Quick Guide

PURPOSE: Revising is the process of improving the thoughts and details that carry the message in your writing. It consists of adding new information, rewriting or rearranging parts, cutting unnecessary ideas, and so on.

✱ Don't pay undue attention to surface issues (spelling, usage, grammar, and so on) too early in the process; otherwise, you may overlook ways to improve the *content* of your writing.

STARTING POINT: You're ready to revise once you . . .
- complete a first draft,
- set it aside for a day or two (if possible), and
- closely review your writing.

Focus first on the big picture—the thesis and overall organization of your writing. Then carefully examine the specific parts, which should support or develop the thesis. (See pages 56-57 for more information.)

FORM: If you're writing with pen and paper, make your changes on your first draft. Then recopy your work, incorporating your changes. If you're using a computer, you may make your changes by hand on a printed copy of your draft or enter your changes on the computer.

✱ No matter how you revise, always save your original copy for future reference. You may want to add something back in later.

THE BIG PICTURE: When revising, pay special attention to the following traits of good writing: ideas, organization, and voice.

Ideas: Make sure that you have included sufficient information to support or develop your thesis. Always keep your readers in mind when you evaluate the effectiveness of your ideas. Have you answered their most pressing questions about your subject?

Organization: Check the overall design of your writing, making sure that it moves smoothly and logically from one main point to the next. Also check the effectiveness of each main part—the beginning, the middle, and the ending—in your writing.

Voice: Does your writing sound like you are genuinely interested in your subject? Does the tone of your writing match your purpose (polite, serious, lighthearted)?

"In the writing process, the more a thing
cooks, the better."   —Doris Lessing

Using Basic Revising Guidelines

No writer gets it right the first time. Few writers even get it right the second time. In fact, professional writers almost always carry out many revisions before they are satisfied with their work. Don't be surprised if you have to do the same. To help you make the best revising moves, follow the guidelines listed below:

- **Set your writing aside.** Get it out of your mind for awhile. This will help you see your first draft more clearly when you're ready to revise.

- **Carefully review your draft when you're ready.** It also helps to have at least one other person react to your writing—someone whose opinion you trust.

- **Look at the big picture.** Take in the entire piece, deciding if you've effectively stated and developed a thesis. If your thinking about your subject has changed, write a new thesis statement.

- **Look at specific chunks of information.** Rewrite any parts that aren't as clear as you would like them to be. Also cut information that doesn't support your thesis, and add ideas if you feel your readers will need more information.

- **Evaluate your opening and closing paragraphs.** Make sure that they effectively introduce and wrap up your writing.

Revising on the Run

Writer Peter Elbow recommends "cut-and-paste revising" when you have little time to make changes in your writing. For example, let's say you are working on an in-class, timed writing assignment, and you have only 15 minutes to revise your writing. The five steps that follow describe this quick revising technique:

1. Don't add any new information to your writing.

2. Remove unnecessary facts and details.

3. Find the best possible information and go with it.

4. Put the pieces in the best possible order.

5. Do what rewriting is necessary.

A **Closer Look** at Revising

Knowing Your **Purpose and Audience**

Always know why you are writing—your purpose. Are you sharing information, arguing for or against something, explaining a process? When you have a clear purpose, it is much easier to know what to change in your writing. Also consider your readers—your audience. How much do they know about your subject? How much do they need to know? How can you gain and hold their attention?

Escaping the "Badlands"

The later stage of revising is one of the most important in the whole composing process. Why? Because here you can escape the "badlands" of writing—those stretches of uninspired ideas that can make a composition seem boring. Use these questions as a guide to check for these "badlands."

- **Is your topic worn-out?** An essay entitled "Lead Poisoning" sounds like a real yawner. With a new twist, you can revive it: "Get the Lead Out!"

- **Is your approach stale?** If you have been writing primarily to please a teacher or to get a good grade, start again. Try writing to learn something or to trigger a particular emotion in your readers.

- **Is your voice predictable or fake?** If it is ("A good time was had by all"), start again. This time, be honest. Be real.

- **Does your draft sound boring?** Maybe it's boring because it pays an equal amount of attention to everything. Try skimming through the less significant parts by "telling" what happened; then focus on the more important parts by "showing" what happened. (See page 127.)

- **Does your essay follow the "formula" too closely?** For example, the "five-paragraph essay" provides you with an organizing frame to build on. However, if a frame is followed too closely, it may get in the way. Read your draft again, and if your inner voice says "formula," try something new.

Take NOTE   Think of revising as an opportunity to try a number of new and different ways to energize your writing. If you need to refuel your thinking at any point during the revising process, consider using one of the prewriting activities in the handbook. (See pages 43-49.)

Revising for Ideas

Use these next two pages as a guide to revising the information or ideas in your writing.

Check for Depth (Level of Detail)

Let's say you are writing a technical essay explaining how the healing process works, and you realize that a certain passage needs more support. To improve the passage, you add more details.

Original Passage (Too general)

As soon as you receive a minor cut, the body's healing process begins to work. Blood from tiny vessels fills the wound and begins to clot. In less than 24 hours, a scab forms.

Revised Version (More specific)

As soon as you receive a minor cut, the body's healing process begins to work. In a simple wound, the first and second layers of skin are severed along with tiny blood vessels called capillaries. As these vessels bleed into the wound, disklike structures called platelets help stop the bleeding by sticking to the edges of the cut and to one another, forming a plug. The platelets then release chemicals that react with certain proteins in the blood to form a clot. The blood clot, with its fiber network, begins to join the edges of the wound together. As the clot dries out, a scab forms, usually in less than 24 hours.

Check the Overall Focus

After reviewing your essay about teen magazines, you notice that your opening paragraph lacks a specific focus. You revise the opening so that it builds to a specific thesis statement.

Opening Paragraph (Lacks focus or direction)

Teen magazines are popular with young girls. These magazines contain a lot of how-to articles about self-image, fashion, and boy-girl relationships. Girls read these magazines for advice on how to act and how to look. There are many popular magazines to choose from, and girls who don't really know what they want are the most eager readers.

Revised Version (Builds to a specific thesis statement)

Adolescent girls often see teen magazines as handbooks on how to be teenagers. These magazines influence the way they act and the way they look. For girls who are unsure of themselves, these magazines can exert an enormous amount of influence. Unfortunately, the advice these magazines give about self-image, fashion, and boys may do more harm than good.

Check the Focus of Each Supporting Paragraph

Suppose you are developing an expository essay about paper recycling, and you discover that one of the paragraphs lacks focus. You change it and narrow the discussion to just one aspect of paper recycling (the fact that it has become a big business).

Original Paragraph (Not focused on one main point)

Paper recycling has indeed become big business. Since Americans throw away more paper than anything else, there is much to be gained by recycling paper. For example, Fort Howard Corporation of Green Bay, Wisconsin, uses recycled paper to produce bathroom tissue. Recycling equipment at this time cannot handle certain types of paper, including paper with staples, glossy paper, envelopes, and so on. Five thousand community programs exist nationwide for the recycling of paper products.

Revised Version (One main point developed in detail)

Paper recycling has indeed become big business. Manufacturers use recycled paper to make cardboard, paper napkins, printing paper, and toweling, as well as insulation and animal bedding. The demand for recycled products of all kinds is increasing daily. To help meet the demand, U.S. papermakers have invested $10 billion in new recycling capacity in the past 10 years. As a result, the use of recycled paper has grown more than four times faster than the overall growth in paper consumption. Recycled paper now provides more than 37 percent of the raw material fiber used at U.S. mills. This percentage should continue to grow well into the 21st century.

Check for Clarity and Completeness

Let's say a classmate has a few questions about a paragraph in your narrative. She doesn't know who Mary is or what blue and pink dresses you are talking about. In your revision, you answer these questions.

Original Paragraph (Confusing ideas)

Mary and I played make-believe a lot. She was my constant companion in our long dresses or in our ballerina dresses. They were blue and pink and also itchy. We wore them when we played house and a lot of other things, including riding our tricycles.

Revised Version (A clear, more unified paragraph)

My days of make-believe sometimes included my sister Mary, who was my constant companion. We played in long dresses or dressed up in our ballerina dresses. Her ballerina dress was blue and mine was pink. They itched worse than poison ivy, but we'd wear them for hours. We wore them when we played house and store and restaurant . . . and even when we rode our tricycles down the driveway.

Revising for **Organization**

Good writing has structure. It leads readers logically and clearly from one point to the next. You can have great ideas in your writing; but if they are not organized effectively, readers won't be able to follow them. There are four general areas to consider when revising: the overall plan, the opening, the flow of ideas, and the closing.

Check the Overall Plan of Your Writing

Let's say that after reviewing your biographical essay, you realize that one section is vague or goes nowhere. The best way to correct this is to revisit your writing plan and the prewriting notes you gathered. Check your plan to see if there is something missing. Then check your notes to see if there is some information you could use to clarify or replace the vague writing. You should also see if there might be a better place to add this information. Of course, if the vague information is not necessary, you may want to delete it altogether. Here's a quick checklist to follow:

1. Recheck your plan for missing information.

2. Check your notes for additional details.

3. Consider moving information to another place in your writing.

4. Think about deleting unnecessary details.

Check Your Opening

Suppose the opening paragraph in your persuasive essay isn't very well developed and doesn't tell readers the specific focus of your writing. In the revised version, you add a series of questions and a thought-provoking thesis to lead the readers into the rest of the essay.

Original Opening (Lacks interest and purpose)

The lack of student motivation is a common subject in the news. Educators want to know how to get students to learn. Today's higher standards mean that students will be expected to learn even more. Another problem in urban areas is that large numbers of students are dropping out. How to interest students is a challenge.

Revised Version (Effectively leads readers into the essay)

How can we motivate students to learn? How can we get them to meet today's rising standards of excellence? How can we, in fact, keep students in school long enough to learn? The answer to these problems is quite simple. Give them money. Pay students to study and learn and stay in school.

Check for Flow of Ideas

Let's say a classmate cannot follow your descriptive essay about a home in the country because you haven't connected your thoughts well enough. In the revision, you add words and phrases to make it easier for your reader to follow the sense and flow of your ideas. (See page 104 for a list of "connecting words.")

Original First Words in the Four Middle Paragraphs

> There was a huge, steep hill . . .
> Buffalo Creek ran . . .
> A dense "jungle" covered . . .
> Within walking distance from my house . . .

Revised Version (Words and phrases connect ideas)

> <u>Behind the house,</u> there was a huge, steep hill . . .
> <u>Across the road from the house,</u> Buffalo Creek ran . . .
> <u>On the far side of the creek bank</u> was a dense "jungle" covered . . .
> <u>Up the road,</u> within walking distance from my house . . .

How do I know how to organize my essay?

There is a specific method of organization that is best suited for each type of writing you do. For example, narratives are usually organized by time; descriptive essays are often organized by location; persuasive essays, by order of importance. Of course, you may also customize or combine these methods to suit your particular essay. (See pages 52 and 100-103 for more information.)

Check Your Closing

Suppose that the closing for your book review is too general and flat. It doesn't effectively summarize the main points in the review, nor does it provide any final thought-provoking ideas. In your revision, you help readers understand the importance of the book by summarizing your main points or adding a strong recommendation.

Original Closing (Sketchy and uninteresting)

Native Son deals with a young man's struggle against racism. It shows the effects of prejudice. Everyone should read this book.

Revised Version (More specific and relevant)

Native Son deals with a young man's struggle in a racist society, but it deals with so much more. It shows how prejudice affects people, how it closes in on them, and what some people will do to find a way out. Anyone who wants to better understand racism in America should read this book.

"Once you begin to hear your own voice, it's easier to find it again and to sustain it longer."   —Vicki Spandel

Revising for **Voice**

Author William Zinsser advises young writers to "be yourself" in your writing. Let your voice come through in your essays and reports. Writing that has voice sounds genuine, and it holds your reader's attention.

Check Your Purpose

After reviewing the first draft of your feature article, you realize that it lacks personality. This is a definite problem since the purpose of your writing is to share a personal experience. To make a personal connection with your readers, you rewrite your draft in the first-person point of view. (See page 239.)

Original Passage (Lacks personality)

Cemeteries can teach us a lot about history. They make history seem more real. There is an old grave of a Revolutionary War veteran in the Union Grove Cemetery. . . .

Revised Version (Connects with the readers)

I've always had a special feeling for cemeteries. It's hard to explain any further than that, except to say history never seems quite as real as it does when I walk between rows of old gravestones. One day I discovered the grave of a Revolutionary War veteran. . . .

Check Your Enthusiasm

While reviewing your biographical essay, a classmate notes that the writing doesn't express any strong feelings. To take care of this problem, you inject more energy and genuine feelings into your writing.

Original Version (Lacks feeling and energy)

She turned to me. My grandmother was 86 years old. Her skin was wrinkled, but she had youthful blue eyes. She placed her gnarled hand upon mine and squeezed it.

Revised Version (Expresses real feelings)

She turned to me. My grandmother was 86 years old, and she was beautiful. Her wrinkled skin was an intricate map of wisdom and hard times, but the spark in her blue eyes hinted at eternal youth and vibrancy. In a soothing expression of tenderness, she placed her gnarled hand upon mine and squeezed it gently.

Revising Checklist

Use this checklist as a guide when you revise your writing. *Remember:* When you revise, you improve the thoughts and details that carry your message.

✔ **Does my writing have a clear focus?**

_____ Do I focus on an interesting part of my subject?

_____ Do I express my feelings about the subject in a thesis statement? (See page 51.)

✔ **Does my writing follow a clear method of organization?**

_____ Do I use a method of organizing my ideas? (See page 52.)

✔ **Do I need to add any information?**

_____ Do I need to make my opening clearer and more interesting?

_____ Do I need to add details to support my thesis?

_____ Do I need to make my closing more effective?

✔ **Do I need to cut any information?**

_____ Do any of my details not belong?

_____ Do I repeat myself in parts?

_____ Do I say too much about a certain idea?

✔ **Do I need to rewrite any parts?**

_____ Do some of my ideas sound unclear?

_____ Do I need to reword any explanations?

✔ **Do I need to reorder any parts?**

_____ Do any ideas or details seem out of place?

_____ Does the most important point come either near the beginning or near the end?

"The hardest part of writing is letting other writers read it. Sometimes I feel that they won't understand my ideas."

—Abby Sime, student writer

A Guide to
GROUP Advising

All writers can benefit from an interested audience, especially one that offers helpful advice. And who could make a better audience than your fellow writers? Those of you who work in writing groups already know the value of writers sharing their work. The rest of you should try it as soon as possible—no matter how nerve-racking it may seem to let your peers read your writing. You can handle it.

Exactly how can a writing group help you? Well, your fellow writers can tell you what does and doesn't work for them in your writing. This feedback is valuable throughout the writing process, but it is especially helpful during the early stages of revising when you are evaluating your first draft. Some experts go so far as to say that talking about your work will help you more than anything else you do during the writing process.

Preview

- ○ **Using Writing-Group Guidelines**
- ○ **A Closer Look at Responding**
- ○ **Group-Advising Strategies**
- ○ **Peer Response Sheet**

Using Writing-Group Guidelines

The guidelines below will help you conduct effective group-advising sessions. (If you're just starting out, work in small groups of two or three classmates.)

Role of the Writer-Reader

- **Come prepared with a meaningful piece of writing.** Make a copy for each group member (if this is what the group usually does).

- **Introduce your writing.** However, don't say too much; let your writing do the talking.

- **Read your copy out loud.** Speak confidently and clearly.

- **Listen and take notes as the group reacts to your writing.** Don't be defensive about your writing since this will stop some members from commenting honestly about your work. Answer all of their questions.

- **Share your concerns with your fellow writers.** If, for example, you're not sure about your ending, ask your listeners to pay special attention to it.

Role of the Listener-Responders

- **Listen carefully and take notes as the writer reads.** Keep your notes brief so you don't miss any part of the reading. (Afterward, read the text silently if the writer has supplied individual copies.)

- **Imagine yourself as the intended audience.** If, for example, the writing was meant for younger readers, a business, or the writer's peers, react to it with that audience in mind.

- **Keep your comments positive and constructive.** Instead of saying, "Great job," make more meaningful comments: "Sharing the personal story in the opening really grabbed my attention."

- **Focus your comments on specific things you observe.** An observation such as "I notice that many of your sentences start in the same way" is much more helpful than "Add some style to your writing."

- **Ask questions of the author.** "What do you mean when you say . . . ?" "Where did you get your facts about . . . ?"

- **Listen to other comments and add to them.** In this way, you help one another become better writers and better group advisors.

A **Closer Look** at Responding

Remember that the goal of group-advising sessions is to help each writer develop her or his writing into an effective finished product. The information on this page will help group members achieve this goal.

Making Your **Responses Count**

As a listener-responder, you will make two general types of responses: descriptions and assessments.

1. **Describing What You've Heard or Read** A writer may simply want responders to say what they think the writing is about. (*Can you follow my main points?*) As a responder, you listen attentively and describe what you've heard without making any comments about the effectiveness of the writing. A writer may, however, ask you to identify parts that are not clearly stated.

2. **Assessing the Writing** At other times, a writer may want responders to evaluate a piece of writing. (*What are the strengths and weaknesses in my writing? Does the opening work for you? What changes should I make?*) As a responder, you should note specific things you like or have questions about, and you should be prepared to make specific suggestions for revisions. (See pages 26 and 74.)

Asking the Writer Questions

Writer and teacher Nancie Atwell suggests that listener-responders ask the following types of questions while reviewing a piece of writing.

To help writers reflect on their purpose and audience . . .
Why are you writing this?
Who will read this, and what do they need to know?

To help writers focus their thoughts . . .
What message are you trying to get across?
Do you have more than one main point?
What are the most important examples?

To help writers think about their information . . .
What do you know about the subject?
Does this part say enough?
Does your writing cover all of the basics (*Who? What? Where? When? Why? and How?*)?

To help writers with their opening and closing . . .
What are you trying to say in the opening?
How else could you start your writing?
How do you want your readers to feel at the end?

Group-Advising Strategies

These next two pages provide four different strategies that you can use in group-advising sessions.

1 Critiquing a Paper

Use the checklist that follows as a basic guide when you assess a piece of writing in progress.

___ **Purpose:** Is it clear what the writer is trying to do—entertain, inform, persuade, describe?

___ **Audience:** Does the writing address a specific audience? Will the readers understand and appreciate this subject?

___ **Ideas:** Does the writer develop the subject with enough information?

___ **Organization:** Are the ideas arranged in the best way, making the main points clear to the readers?

___ **Voice:** Does the writing sound sincere and honest? That is, do you "hear" the writer when you read his or her paper?

___ **Readability:** Do the ideas read smoothly from start to finish? Are there parts that cause you to stumble or backtrack?

___ **Personal Thoughts:** Does the writer include any personal thoughts or comments? Are they needed or desirable?

___ **Purpose Again:** Does the writing succeed in making you smile, nod, or react in some other way? What is especially good about the writing?

2 Reacting to Writing

Peter Elbow, in *Writing Without Teachers,* offers four types of reactions group members might have to a piece of writing:

○ **Pointing** refers to a reaction in which a group member "points out" words, phrases, or ideas in the writing that make a positive or a negative impression on her or him.

○ **Summarizing** refers to a reader's general reaction to the writing. It may be a list of main ideas, or a single sentence that summarizes the writing.

○ **Telling** refers to readers describing what happens in a piece of writing: first this happens, then this happens, later this happens, and so on.

○ **Showing** refers to feelings expressed about the piece. Elbow suggests that readers express these feelings metaphorically. A reader might, for example, refer to something in the writing as if it were a voice quality, a color, a shape, a piece of clothing, and so on. ("Your writing has a neat, tailored quality.")

3 Appreciating Good Writing

What makes for good writing? The "Checklist for Effective Writing" on page 26 in this handbook lists the traits that show up in effective essays, stories, and reports. The list below approaches the qualities of good writing in a somewhat different way. Use either list as a guide during group-advising sessions. Good writing is . . .

- **original** (the subject or the way the subject is covered is lively and energized),
- **organized** (the ideas are presented in a sensible or effective order),
- **detailed** (the details are specific and colorful),
- **clear** (the sentences clearly and smoothly move the writing forward),
- **correct** (the final product is clean and correct), and
- **effective** (the writing is engaging and informative).

4 Feeling Your OAQS

Here's a simple and effective four-step scheme that can be used when discussing early drafts during group-advising sessions.

Observe
Appreciate
Question
Suggest

Observe means to notice what another person's essay is designed to do, and to say something about the design or purpose. For example, you might say, "Even though you are writing about your boyfriend, it appears that you are trying to get a message across to your parents."

Appreciate means to praise something in the writing that impresses or pleases you. You can find something to appreciate in any piece of writing. For example, you might say, "You make a very convincing point" or "With your description, I can actually see his broken tooth."

Question means to ask whatever you want to know after you've read the essay. You might ask for background information, a definition, an interpretation, or an explanation. For example, you might say, "Why didn't you tell us what happened when you got to the emergency room?"

Suggest means to give helpful advice about possible changes. Offer this advice honestly and courteously. Be specific, and be positive. For example, you might say, "With a little more physical detail—especially more sounds and smells—your third paragraph could be the highlight of the whole essay. What do you think?"

Peer Response Sheet

Use a response sheet, such as the one below, to make comments about another person's writing in progress. (You may not always make responses under each category.)

Response Sheet

Name:

Title:

I noticed . . .

I liked (enjoyed, appreciated) . . .

I wondered . . .

I would suggest . . .

Strong words, phrases, and images in the writing:

"In writing, punctuation plays the role of body language. It helps readers hear you the way you want to be heard."

—Russell Baker

A Guide to EDITING and PROOFREADING

There comes a point in any writing project (like a fast-approaching due date) when you must prepare your work for publication. At this point you must edit and proofread your writing so that it speaks clearly, smoothly, and accurately. Your first concern when editing is to check the style and clarity of your revised writing, paying special attention to any sentences and words that sound awkward or confusing. Then you should check your writing for spelling, punctuation, mechanics, usage, and grammar errors.

Student writer Katie Pingle knows about the importance of this step in the writing process. In fact, one of the essential things she has learned about writing is the need to edit again and again. As she states, "There is nothing worse than reading a final piece of work with a lot of errors. It's so frustrating."

Preview

- ○ **Quick Guide**
- ○ **Checking for Effective Sentence Style**
- ○ **Checking for Word Choice**
- ○ **Editing and Proofreading Checklist**

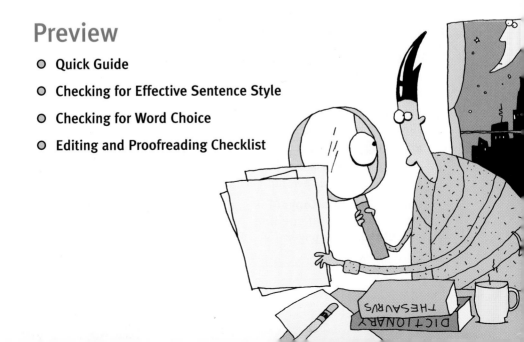

"I can't find five words but that I change seven."

—Dorothy Parker

Quick Guide

PURPOSE: Editing and proofreading deal with the line-by-line changes you make to improve the readability and accuracy of your writing. More specifically, when you edit, you make sure that the words and sentences in your revised writing are clear and correct. When you proofread, you need to make sure that the final copy of your writing is free of errors.

STARTING POINT: You're ready to edit, once you . . .

- complete your major revisions—adding, cutting, rewriting, or rearranging the ideas in your writing;
- make a clean copy of your revised writing; and
- set your writing aside for a day or two (if time permits).

First, check for the style of your writing, and then check its accuracy, focusing on one type of error at a time. (See page 79 for a checklist.)

Remember: Have a reliable editor check your work as well. You're too close to your writing to spot everything that needs to be changed.

FORM: If you're working on a computer, do your editing on a printed copy. Then enter the changes on the computer, and save the edited copy so you have a record of the changes you've made.

If you're working with pen and paper, do your editing on a neat copy of your revised writing. Then recopy your work and save the edited copy for your records. Proofread your final copy for errors.

THE BIG PICTURE: When you edit and proofread, pay extra-special attention to the following three traits of effective writing: sentence style or smoothness; word choice; and correct, accurate copy.

Sentence Style: Rewrite any sentences that disrupt the fluency or flow of your writing. Vary sentence beginnings and lengths.

Word Choice: Replace any words or phrases that get in the way of your message or set the wrong tone. Also replace any overused words, words that are not specific enough, and so on.

Correct, Accurate Copy: Make sure that your writing follows the basic standards of spelling, punctuation, mechanics, grammar, and usage. (See pages 455-531.)

Checking for **Effective Sentence Style**

Writer E. B. White advises young writers to "approach sentence style by way of simplicity, plainness, orderliness, and sincerity." That's good advice from a writer steeped in style. It's also important to know what to look for when reviewing your sentences. The following information will help you edit your sentences for style and smoothness.

Avoiding Sentence Problems

Always check for and correct the following types of sentence problems.

- **Short, Choppy Sentences** Combine any short, choppy sentences, following the examples and guidelines in the handbook. (See page 91.)

- **Incorrect Sentences** Check carefully for fragments, run-ons, and rambling sentences and correct them accordingly. (See pages 83-84.)

- **Unclear Sentences** Rewrite any sentences that contain unclear wording, misplaced modifiers, dangling modifiers, or incomplete comparisons. (See pages 85-86.)

- **Unacceptable Sentences** Change any sentences that include nonstandard language, double negatives, or unparallel construction. (See pages 89-90.)

- **Unnatural, Flowery Sentences** Simplify any sentences that contain flowery language, deadwood, or cliches. (See pages 87-88.)

 How can I tell if my sentences read smoothly?

Read your writing out loud, paying special attention to the flow of your ideas. Then have someone else read it aloud as you listen carefully for anything that causes the reader to stumble. Edit your writing until all of your sentences read smoothly.

HELP FILE

Use the following strategy to add variety to your sentences:

- In one column on a piece of paper, list the opening words in each of your sentences. Then decide if you need to vary some of your sentence beginnings.

- In another column, list the verbs in each sentence. Then decide if you need to replace any overused "be" verbs (*is, are, was, were*) with more vivid ones (*snap, stare, stir*).

- In a third column, identify the number of words in each sentence. Then decide if you need to change the length of some of your sentences.

Checking for **Word Choice**

The best words are the ones that add to the meaning, tone, and sound of your writing. Here are some things you should look for when editing for word choice.

Locating Problems with Word Choice

○ **Redundancy** Avoid any words or phrases that are used together but mean the same thing, or close to the same thing.

    repeat again   red in color   refer back

○ **Repetition** Watch for words that are unnecessarily repeated in a series of sentences.

    The man looked as if he was in his late seventies. The man was dressed in an old, blue suit. I soon realized that the man was homeless. . . .

○ **Usage Errors** Check for words used incorrectly. (See pages 491-500.)

    you're, your   there, their   effect, affect

○ **General Nouns and Verbs** Note instances where general nouns and verbs are used instead of specific ones.

    General noun and verb: The girl moved to the end of the bench.
    Specific noun and verb: Rosie slid to the end of the bench.

○ **Vague Modifiers** Watch for the overuse of vague words.

    Vague modifiers: nice, neat, good, great, funny, big
    Colorful modifiers: sympathetic, intricate, sleek

○ **Technical Terms** Check for technical words that are not explained.

    As the capillaries bleed, platelets work with fibrinogens to form a clot.

Using the Right Level of Language

Make sure that the words in your writing match your purpose and audience. Informal English is appropriate for most personal writing, while formal English is best suited for most persuasive and academic writing.

Informal English is characterized by a personal tone, the occasional use of popular expressions (*you know, forget it*), contractions, shorter sentences, and so on. Informal English sounds like one person talking to another in a somewhat relaxed setting.

Formal English is characterized by a serious tone, a careful attention to appropriate word choice, longer sentences, and so on. Formal English, such as you are reading in this sentence, is carefully worded so that it can withstand repeated readings without sounding trite or stale.

Editing and Proofreading Checklist

Use this checklist as a guide when you edit and proofread your writing. *Remember:* Edit your writing only after you have revised it.

✔ **Sentence Structure** (See pages 81-94.)

_____ Did I write clear and complete sentences?

_____ Do my sentences flow smoothly?

_____ Did I use sentences of different lengths and with a variety of beginnings?

✔ **Word Choice and Usage** (See pages 130-131 and 491-500.)

_____ Did I avoid redundancy and unnecessary repetition?

_____ Did I use the correct word (*their, there,* or *they're*)?

_____ Did I use specific nouns, vivid verbs, and colorful modifiers?

✔ **Punctuation** (See pages 455-474.)

_____ Does each sentence have the correct end punctuation?

_____ Did I use commas and apostrophes correctly?

_____ Did I punctuate dialogue correctly?

✔ **Capitalization** (See pages 475-477.)

_____ Did I start all of my sentences with capital letters?

_____ Did I capitalize the proper names of people, places, things, and ideas?

✔ **Grammar** (See pages 518-531.)

_____ Do the subjects and verbs agree in all my sentences?

_____ Do the pronouns agree with their antecedents?

_____ Did I use the correct verb tenses?

✔ **Spelling** (See pages 484-490.)

_____ Did I check for spelling errors (including those the spell checker may have missed)?

BASIC
ELEMENTS
of Writing

"A writer is not someone who expresses
his thoughts, his passion, or his
imagination in sentences but someone
who thinks sentences." —Roland Barthes

Writing
SENTENCES

Sentences are basic to written communication. A well-chosen word or phrase can do the job of expressing a complete thought, but a solid sentence is still your best bet for getting a point across. This is true in e-mail messages, writing assignments, business letters, notes to friends, applications, and so on.

You can learn the most about writing effective sentences by reading lots of them—in books, magazines, and newspapers, and on the Internet. Then you have to practice by writing regularly in a variety of forms (not all of them formal). This chapter provides guidelines for writing effective sentences that say what you mean to say. (See pages 518-528 for more on sentences.)

Preview

- ○ Understanding the Basics
- ○ Writing Complete and Clear Sentences
- ○ Writing Natural and Acceptable Sentences
- ○ Combining Sentences
- ○ Modeling Sentences
- ○ Expanding Sentences
- ○ Sentence-Writing Tips

Understanding the **Basics**

Simple sentences in the English language follow five basic patterns. (See pages 524-525 for more information.)

Subject + Verb

┌─S─┐ ┌─V─┐
Naomie winked.
Some verbs like *winked* are intransitive. Intransitive verbs *do not* need a direct object to express a complete thought. (See 507.2.)

Subject + Verb + Direct Object

┌─S─┐ ┌─V─┐ ┌─DO─┐
Harris grinds his teeth.
Some verbs like *grinds* are transitive. Transitive verbs *do* need a direct object to express a complete thought. (See 508.1.)

Subject + Verb + Indirect Object + Direct Object

┌─S─┐ ┌─V─┐ ┌─IO─┐ ┌─DO─┐
Elena offered her friend an anchovy.
The direct object names who or what receives the action; the indirect object names to whom or for whom the action was done.

Subject + Verb + Direct Object + Object Complement

┌───S───┐ ┌─V─┐ DO ┌──────OC──────┐
Room 222 named Ravi the class Web master.
The object complement renames or describes the direct object.

Subject + Linking Verb + Predicate Noun (or Predicate Adjective)

┌─S─┐LV┌──PN──┐   ┌─S─┐LV┌───PA───┐
Paula is a math whiz.   **Paula is very intelligent.**
A linking verb connects the subject to the predicate noun or predicate adjective. The predicate noun renames the subject; the predicate adjective describes the subject.

Inverted Order

In the sentence patterns above, the subject comes before the verb. In a few types of sentences, such as those below, the subject comes *after* the verb.

LV┌─S─┐ ┌─PN─┐
Is Larisa a poet? (A question)

LV ┌──S──┐
There was a meeting. (A sentence beginning with "there")

"To err is human, but when the eraser wears out ahead of the pencil, you're overdoing it."

—J. Jenkins

Writing **Complete** Sentences

By definition, a complete sentence expresses a complete thought and contains both a subject and a predicate. Several ideas, not just one, may make up this complete thought. The trick is getting those ideas to work together in a clear, interesting sentence that expresses your exact meaning.

The most common sentence errors are **fragments, comma splices, rambling sentences,** and **run-ons.**

Fragment A fragment is a group of words used as a sentence. It is not a sentence, though, because it lacks a subject, a verb, or some other essential part. Because of the missing part, the thought is incomplete.

Fragment: Lettuce all over the table. (This fragment lacks a verb.)
Sentence: Lettuce flew all over the table.

Fragment: When Herbie tossed the salad. (This fragment has a subject and verb, but it does not convey a complete thought. We need to know what happened "when Herbie tossed the salad.")
Sentence: When Herbie tossed the salad, lettuce flew all over the table.

Fragment: Laughing and scooping up a pile of lettuce. Kate remarked, "Now, that's what I call a tossed salad!" (The fragment is followed by a complete sentence. This fragment, a participial phrase, can be combined with the sentence to form a complete thought.)
Sentence: Laughing and scooping up a pile of lettuce, Kate remarked, "Now, that's what I call a tossed salad!"

FAQ *Is it ever acceptable to use fragments?*

Yes, when you have good reason. For example, single words or phrases set off as sentences can have a dramatic effect. In one of her articles, writer Anna Quindlan uses the following three fragments to dramatize the problems facing urban youths:

"**Teenage mothers. Child abuse. Crowded schools.**"

✱ You can also use fragments when you write dialogue because people often use incomplete thoughts when they talk.

"**Hey, Rico. My house?**"
"**Yeah, right. On Tuesday afternoon.**"
"**Whatever.**"

Comma Splice

A comma splice results when two independent clauses are connected ("spliced") with only a comma. The comma is not enough: a period, a semicolon, or a conjunction is needed. (*Note:* An independent clause presents a complete thought and can stand alone as a sentence.)

Splice: The concertgoers had been waiting in the hot sun for two hours, many were beginning to show their impatience by chanting and clapping.

Corrected: The concertgoers had been waiting in the hot sun for two hours, **and** many were beginning to show their impatience by chanting and clapping. (A coordinating conjunction has been added.)

Corrected: The concertgoers had been waiting in the hot sun for two hours; many were beginning to show their impatience by chanting and clapping. (A comma has been changed to a semicolon.)

Rambling Sentence

A rambling sentence seems to go on and on in a monotonous fashion (often because of too many *and*'s.) To correct this error, remove some of the *and*'s, fix the punctuation, and reword different parts if it results in a better passage.

Rambling: The intruder entered through the window and tiptoed down the hall and stood under the stairwell and waited in the shadows.

Corrected: The intruder entered through the window. He tiptoed down the hall and stood under the stairwell, waiting in the shadows.

Corrected: The intruder, who had entered through the window, tiptoed down the hall. He stood under the stairwell and waited in the shadows.

Run-On Sentence

A run-on is two (or more) sentences joined without adequate punctuation or a connecting word.

Run-on: I thought the ride would never end my eyes were crossed, and my fingers were numb.

Corrected: I thought the ride would never end. My eyes were crossed, and my fingers were numb.

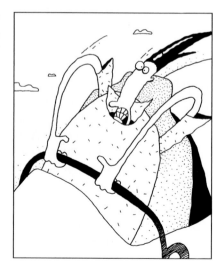

"If any man wishes to write in a clear style,
let him first be clear in his thoughts."

—Johann Wolfgang von Goethe

Writing **Clear** Sentences

Nothing is more frustrating for readers than writing that has to be reread just to understand its basic meaning. Look carefully at the common errors that follow. Do you recognize any of them as errors you sometimes make in your own writing? If so, use this section as a checklist when you revise. Conquering these errors will help to make your writing clear and readable.

Incomplete Comparison ◎ An incomplete comparison is the result of leaving out a word or words that are necessary to show exactly what is being compared to what.

Incomplete: I get along with Rosa better than my sister.
(Do you mean that you get along with Rosa better than you get along with your sister . . . or that you get along with Rosa better than your sister does?)

Clear: I get along with Rosa better than my sister does.

Ambiguous Wording ◎ Ambiguous wording is wording that is unclear because it has two or more possible meanings.

Ambiguous: Mike decided to take his new convertible to the drive-in movie, which turned out to be a real horror story.
(What turned out to be a real horror story—Mike's taking his new convertible to the drive-in, or the movie?)

Clear: Mike decided to take his new convertible to the drive-in movie, a decision that turned out to be a real horror story.

Indefinite Reference ◎ An indefinite reference is a problem caused by careless use of pronouns. As a result, readers are not sure who or what the pronoun(s) is referring to.

Indefinite: In *To Kill a Mockingbird*, **she** describes the problems faced by Atticus Finch and his family. (Who is *she*?)

Clear: In *To Kill a Mockingbird*, the author, Harper Lee, describes the problems faced by Atticus Finch and his family.

Indefinite: As he pulled his car up to the service window, **it** made a strange rattling sound. (Which rattled, the car or the window?)

Clear: His car made a strange rattling sound as he pulled up to the service window.

Misplaced Modifiers @ Misplaced modifiers are modifiers that have been placed incorrectly; therefore, the meaning of the sentence is not clear. (Modifiers should be placed as close as possible to the word they modify.)

Misplaced: We have an assortment of combs for physically active people with unbreakable teeth. (People with unbreakable teeth?)

Corrected: For physically active people, we have an assortment of combs with unbreakable teeth. (Corrected by rearranging the sentence.)

We have an assortment of combs for physically active people with unbreakable teeth.

Dangling Modifiers @ Dangling modifiers are modifiers that appear to modify the wrong word or a word that isn't in the sentence.

Dangling: Trying desperately to get under the fence, Paul's mother called him.
(The phrase *trying desperately to get under the fence* appears to modify *Paul's mother.*)

Corrected: Trying desperately to get under the fence, Paul heard his mother call him.
(Corrected by rewording and adding *Paul,* the person being referred to by the modifier.)

Dangling: After standing in line for five hours, the manager announced that all the tickets had been sold.
(In this sentence, it appears as if the manager had been *standing in line for five hours.*)

Corrected: After I stood in line for five hours, the manager announced that all the tickets had been sold.
(Corrected by rewording the sentence.)

"Read over your compositions and, when you meet a passage which you think is particularly fine, strike it out."

—Samuel Johnson

Writing **Natural** Sentences

Samuel Johnson was undoubtedly talking about one of the greatest temptations facing writers—to use lots of words (big words, clever words, fancy words). For some reason, we get the idea into our heads that writing *simply* is not writing effectively. Nothing could be further from the truth.

The best writing is honest and natural, not fancy or artificial. That's why it is so important to master the art of freewriting. It is your best chance at developing a sincere, simple style. The samples that follow demonstrate wordy and artificial writing; rewrite any passages in your own work that sound like these sentences.

Deadwood @ Deadwood is wording that fills up lots of space but does not add anything important or new to the overall meaning.

> **Wordy:** At this point in time, I feel the study needs additional work before the subcommittee can recommend it be resubmitted for further consideration.
>
> **Concise:** The study needs more work.

Flowery Language @ Flowery language is writing that uses more or bigger words than needed. It is writing that often contains too many adjectives or adverbs.

> **Flowery:** The cool, fresh breeze, which came like a storm in the night, lifted me to the exhilarating heights from which I had been previously suppressed by the incandescent cloud in the learning center.
>
> **Concise:** The cool breeze was a refreshing change from the muggy classroom air.

Trite Expression @ A trite expression is one that is overused and stale; as a result, it sounds neither sincere nor natural.

> **Trite:** It gives all of us a great deal of pleasure to present to you this plaque as a token of our appreciation.
>
> **Natural:** Please accept this plaque with our heartfelt thanks.

Jargon @ Jargon is language used in a certain profession or by a certain group of people. It is usually very technical and not at all natural.

> **Jargon:** I'm having conceptual difficulty with these employee mandates.
>
> **Natural:** I don't understand these work rules.

Euphemism @ A euphemism is a word or a phrase that is substituted for another because it is considered a less offensive way of saying something.

Euphemism: I am so exasperated that I could expectorate.

   Natural: I am so mad I could spit.

Wordiness @ Wordiness occurs when extra words are used in a sentence, such as when a word, phrase, or synonym is repeated unnecessarily.

   Redundant: He had a way of keeping my attention by raising and lowering his voice all the time throughout his whole speech.

   Concise: He kept my attention by raising and lowering his voice when he spoke.

   Double Subject: Some people they don't use their voices as well as they could. (Drop *they; people* is the only subject needed.)

   Concise: Some people don't use their voices as well as they could.

   Tautology: repeat again, descend down, audible to the ear, refer back, unite together (Each word group says the same thing twice.)

Cliche @ A cliche is an overused word or phrase that springs quickly to mind but just as quickly bores the user and the audience. A cliche gives the reader nothing new or original to think about.

   Cliche: Her face was as red as a beet.

   Natural: Her face turned a deep shade of red.

CLICHES TO AVOID

after all is said and done	food for thought
beat around the bush	grin and bear it
believe it or not	in a nutshell
best foot forward	in one ear and out the other
better late than never	in the nick of time
calm before the storm	last but not least
cart before the horse	lesser of two evils
chalk up a victory	more than meets the eye
come through with flying colors	no time like the present
crying shame	put your foot in your mouth
don't rock the boat	quiet enough to hear a pin drop
drop in the bucket	raining cats and dogs
easier said than done	see eye to eye
face the music	shot in the arm
fish out of water	sink or swim
flat as a pancake	so far, so good

"You can be a little ungrammatical if you come from the right part of the country."   —Robert Frost

Writing **Acceptable** Sentences

What Robert Frost says is certainly true. Much of the color and charm of literature comes from the everyday habits and customs—and especially the speech—of its characters. Keep that in mind when you write fiction of any kind. However, when you write essays, reports, and most other assignments, keep in mind that it's just as important to use language that is correct, appropriate, and therefore acceptable.

Nonstandard Language @ Nonstandard language is often acceptable in everyday conversation, but seldom in formal writing.

Colloquial: Avoid the use of colloquial language such as *go with, wait up.*

Mr. Park went with to the meeting. (Nonstandard)

Mr. Park went with them to the meeting. (Acceptable)

Double Preposition: Avoid the use of certain double prepositions: *off of, off to, in on.*

Reggie went off to the movies. (Nonstandard)

Reggie went to the movies. (Acceptable)

Substitution: Avoid substituting *and* for *to* in formal writing.

Try and get here on time. (Nonstandard)

Try to get here on time. (Acceptable)

Avoid substituting *of* for *have* when combining with *could, would, should,* or *might.*

I should of studied for that test. (Nonstandard)

I should have studied for that test. (Acceptable)

Slang: Avoid the use of slang or any other "in" words.

The museum trip was way cool. (Nonstandard)

The museum trip was wonderful. (Acceptable)

Double Negative @ A double negative is the improper use of two negative words to perform the same function in a sentence. In standard English, use only one negative word in a sentence.

Awkward: I haven't got no money.

(This actually says—with the two negatives—*I have money.*)

Corrected: I haven't got any money. / I have no money.

✱ Using the words *hardly, barely,* or *scarcely* with the words *no* or *not* also results in a double negative.

Shifts in Construction @ A shift in construction is a change in the structure or style midway through a sentence. (See pages 526-527.)

Shift in Number: When a person has the flu, they ought to stay at home.

Corrected: When people have the flu, they ought to stay at home.

Shift in Person: When you are well again, you can do all the things a person loves to do.

Corrected: When you are well again, you can do all the things you love to do.

Shift in Voice: Marcia is playing soccer again and many new skills are being learned by her. (The shift is from *active* to *passive voice.* See page 510.3.)

Corrected: Marcia is playing soccer again and learning many new skills. (Both verbs are in the *active voice.*)

Shift in Tense: Marcia drinks lots of juice and got plenty of rest.

Corrected: Marcia drinks lots of juice and gets plenty of rest.

✻ A tense shift is acceptable in a sentence that states one action as happening before another action.

I think (present tense) he completed (past tense) his assignment last night.

Unparallel Construction @ Unparallel construction occurs when the kind of words or phrases being used changes in the middle of a sentence. (See page 129.)

Unparallel: In my hometown, folks pass the time shooting pool, pitching horseshoes, and at softball games.
(The sentence switches from the *-ing* words, *shooting* and *pitching,* to the prepositional phrase *at softball games.*)

Parallel: In my hometown, folks pass the time shooting pool, pitching horseshoes, and playing softball.
(Now all three activities are *-ing* words—they are consistent, or parallel.)

Unparallel: For the open house, teachers prepare handouts for parents and are organizing the students' work for display.
(In this sentence, the verbs *prepare* and *organizing* are unparallel—not stated in the same way.)

Parallel: For the open house, teachers prepare handouts for parents and organize the students' work for display.
(Now both verbs are stated in the same way.)

Combining Sentences

If you were to write a sentence about a tornado that struck a small town without warning, causing a great deal of damage, a number of serious injuries, and several deaths, you would really be working with six different ideas:

1. There was a tornado.
2. The tornado struck a small town.
3. The tornado struck without warning.
4. The tornado caused a great deal of damage.
5. The tornado caused a number of serious injuries.
6. The tornado caused several deaths.

Of course, you wouldn't express each idea separately like this. Instead, you would combine the ideas into longer, more detailed sentences. **Sentence combining,** which can be done in a variety of ways (see below), is one of the most effective writing techniques you can practice.

1. Use a **series** to combine three or more similar ideas.
   The tornado struck the small town without warning, causing extensive damage, numerous injuries, and several deaths.

2. Use a **relative pronoun** *(who, whose, that, which)* to introduce the subordinate (less important) ideas.
   The tornado, which was completely unexpected, swept through the small town causing extensive damage, numerous injuries, and several deaths.

3. Use an **introductory phrase** or **clause** for the less important ideas.
   Because the tornado was completely unexpected, it caused **extensive damage, numerous injuries, and several deaths.**

4. Use a **participial phrase** *(-ing, -ed)* to begin or end a sentence.
   The tornado swept through the small town without warning, leaving a trail of death and destruction.

5. Use a **semicolon.** (Also use a **conjunctive adverb** if appropriate.)
   The tornado struck the town without warning; therefore, it caused extensive damage, numerous injuries, and several deaths.

6. Repeat a **key word** or phrase to emphasize an idea.
   The unexpected tornado left a permanent scar on the small town, a scar of destruction, injury, and death.

7. Use **correlative conjunctions** *(not only, but also; either, or)* to compare or contrast two ideas in a sentence.
   The unexpected tornado inflicted not only immense property damage, but also immeasurable human suffering.

8. Use an **appositive** (or an appositive phrase) for emphasis.
   A single incident, a tornado that came without warning, changed the face of the small town forever.

Modeling Sentences

Study the writing of your favorite authors, and you may find sentences that seem to flow on forever, sentences that are direct and to the point, and "sentences" that aren't by definition complete thoughts. (Writers do occasionally break the rules.)

Take NOTE Generally speaking, most popular authors write in a relaxed, informal style. This style is characterized by sentences with a lot of personality, rhythm, balance, and variety.

The Modeling Process

Imitating certain sentences because you like the way they sound, or the way they make a point, is sometimes called **modeling.** Here's how you can get started:

- **Reserve** a special section in your notebook to list effective sentences you come across—those that flow smoothly, use effective descriptive words, and contain original figures of speech such as metaphors, similes, and personifications. (See pages 136-138.)
- **Copy** the well-made sentences (or short passages) into your notebook.
- **Study** each sentence so you know how it is put together. Read it out loud. Look for phrases and clauses set off by commas. Also focus on word endings (*-ing, -ed*) and on the location of articles (*a, an, the*) and prepositions (*to, by, of*).
- **Write** your own version of the sentence, imitating it part by part. Try to use the same word endings, articles, and prepositions, but work in your own nouns, verbs, and modifiers.
- **Continue** imitating a number of different sentences in order to fine-tune your sense of sentence style.

THE PROCESS IN ACTION

Study the following sentence:

> **He has a thin face with sharp features and a couple of eyes burning with truth oil.** —Tom Wolfe

Now look carefully at the sentence below. Compare it part by part to the original sentence. Can you see how the modeling was done?

> **He has an athletic body with a sinewy contour and a couple of arms bulging with weight-room dedication.**

Expanding Sentences

Details seem to spill out of accomplished writers' minds naturally. Readers marvel at how effectively these authors can expand a basic idea with engaging details. Maybe you envy good writers because of this special ability, and wish you could write in the same way. The truth is you can. All it takes is a little practice.

Cumulative Sentences

Above all other types of sentences, the *cumulative sentence* marks an accomplished writer. What you normally find in a cumulative sentence is a main idea that is expanded by modifying words, phrases, or clauses. (See page 522.1 for more information.) Here's a sample cumulative sentence with the expanding modifiers coming *after* the main clause (in red).

> **Sam was studying at the kitchen table,** memorizing a list of vocabulary words, completely focused, intent on acing tomorrow's Spanish quiz.

Discussion: Notice how each new modifier adds another level of meaning to the sentence. Three modifying phrases have been added. Here's another cumulative sentence with expanding modifiers coming *before* and *after* the main clause (in red).

> Before every practice, **Kesha Sims and Tonya Harper work on free throws,** taking 50 shots each.

Discussion: In this case, a prepositional phrase (**Before every practice**) and a participial phrase (**taking 50 shots each**) add important details to the main clause.

Expanding with Details

When you practice expanding sentences on your own, remember that there are five basic ways to expand upon an idea:

- **Individual words:** José prepared his breakfast *quickly.*
- **Prepositional phrases:** José ate *with his cat on his lap.*
- **Participial (*-ing* or *-ed*) phrases:** *Looking at the clock,* José gobbled his first piece of toast.
- **Subordinate clauses:** José was still eating *when his mother left for work.*
- **Relative clauses:** The cat, *who loves leftovers,* purred for a treat.

HELP FILE

To write stylistic sentences, you need to practice sentence modeling and sentence expanding. You also need to become a regular and attentive reader who notices the style as well as the content of what you read.

Sentence-Writing **TIPS**

How can you make sure that your sentences are effective? Keep these important points in mind:

Vary the pattern of your sentences.

Your writing will be interesting if you use a variety of sentence patterns. (See page 82.)

Express complete thoughts.

Your writing will be easy to follow if it has no sentence errors such as fragments and comma splices. (See pages 83-84.)

Be clear in your thinking.

Your writing will be clear if it is free of ambiguous wording and incomplete comparisons. (See pages 85-86.)

Speak honestly and naturally.

Your writing will sound natural if you avoid flowery language, jargon or technical language, deadwood, wordiness, euphemisms, and cliches. (See pages 87-88.)

Follow the rules of standard English.

Your writing may cause readers to stumble if it contains substandard language, double negatives, or shifts in construction. (See pages 89-90.)

Combine short, choppy sentences.

Your writing will lack smoothness, or fluency, if it contains too many short sentences. (See page 91.)

Imitate stylistic sentences.

Your writing will have style if you pay special attention to the sound and rhythm of your sentences. (See page 92.)

Practice expanding basic ideas.

Your writing will lack specific details unless you learn how to expand basic sentences. (See page 93.)

"The paragraph [is] a mini-essay; it
is also a maxi-sentence." —Donald Hall

Writing
PARAGRAPHS

   In the real world of literature, the paragraph is not considered a form
of writing. You wouldn't, for example, head to the local bookstore to buy a
book of paragraphs. Nor would you pursue a writing career because you
want to write award-winning paragraphs.

   But paragraphs are very important as building blocks for other kinds
of writing. When you write an essay, for instance, you develop paragraphs
to organize your thoughts into manageable units. The paragraphs work
together to build a clear, interesting essay. Learning how to write effective
paragraphs will give you control of all of your academic writing—from
essays to reports to research papers.

Preview

- ○ **The Parts of a Paragraph**
- ○ **Types of Paragraphs**
- ○ **A Closer Look at Paragraphing**
- ○ **Arranging Your Details**
- ○ **Connecting Your Details**

"Constructing a paragraph requires a simple, clear, logical manner of thinking." —Jonathan Snyder

The Parts of a Paragraph

Most paragraphs begin with a topic sentence, identifying the subject of the writing. The sentences in the body of the paragraph support or explain the subject, while the closing sentence brings the paragraph to a logical stopping point. (See the expository paragraph on page 97.)

The Topic Sentence @ The topic sentence tells your readers what your paragraph is about. Here is a formula for writing good topic sentences:

> Formula   **An interesting subject**
> **+   a specific feeling or feature about the subject**
> **=   an effective topic sentence.**

Topic Sentence   **The average cost of a Hollywood film** *(interesting subject)* **runs between $30 and $50 million** *(specific feature).*

Is a topic sentence always the first sentence in a paragraph?

No, you can position a topic sentence anywhere in a paragraph, just as long as it works there. For example, you can present details that build up to an important summary statement (topic sentence). This strategy is especially effective in persuasive writing. (See page 115.)

The Body @ The body is the main part of the paragraph. This is where you place all of the information readers need to understand the subject. The sentences in the body should contain details that clearly support the topic sentence. Arrange these details in the best possible order.

Body Sentence   **The salary of a top star such as Bruce Willis or Harrison Ford can add $20 million to the cost of a major film.**

[HOT LINK] Turn to "Arranging Your Details," pages 100-103, when you have questions about how to organize the details in a paragraph.

The Closing @ The closing (clincher) sentence comes after all the details have been included in the body of the paragraph. This sentence may (1) remind readers of the subject, (2) keep them thinking about it, or (3) link the paragraph to the next one if this is part of a longer composition.

Closing Sentence   **Anyone who has bought a movie ticket recently knows that the consumer pays for these extravagant productions.**

Types of Paragraphs

There are four types of paragraphs: expository, descriptive, narrative, and persuasive. (Notice how the details support each topic sentence.)

EXPOSITORY

An **expository paragraph** presents facts, gives directions, defines terms, and so on. It should clearly inform readers about a specific subject.

> The average cost of a Hollywood film runs between $30 and $50 million. There are many reasons for this outlandish expense. The currently popular action-adventure productions are filled with special effects that cost huge amounts of money. In addition, most producers think in terms of blockbuster films. Instead of making a number of smaller, less-expensive films, they focus on big, elaborate films that could be smash hits. Of course, blockbuster films require big stars, which adds significantly to the production costs. The salary of a top star such as Bruce Willis or Harrison Ford can add $20 million to the cost of a major film. Then, the nonstop, full-throttle promotion of a film adds another enormous expense. All of these factors have contributed to the inflated costs of making and watching movies. Anyone who has bought a movie ticket recently knows that the consumer pays for these extravagant productions.

DESCRIPTIVE

A **descriptive paragraph** presents a single clear picture of a person, a place, a thing, or an idea. It should contain plenty of sensory details—specific sights, sounds, and smells.

> My Uncle John is normally a likable and friendly man, but when there is a group of people and one of those instant cameras around, he becomes a real pest. No matter what the occasion, even something as uneventful as a few of our relatives getting together for a visit after work, Uncle John appoints himself official photographer. He spends the whole time with one eye looking through the lens and the other scoping out the potential subjects for his pictures. In most situations, taking pictures is a great way to spend some time and have a little fun, but when Uncle John is pushing the button, it's quite another story. He doesn't believe in candids. Instead, Uncle John insists upon interrupting all activity to persuade his prey to pose for his pictures. In return, he gets photographs of people arranged in neat rows smiling through clenched teeth. Although we have tried again and again to convince Uncle John that his old, traditional methods of photography aren't necessarily the best, he continues to insist that we "Come over here, so I can take your picture." About the only solution is to convince Uncle John that he should be in some of these pictures and that you'd be happy to snap a few. Then, once you get the camera in your hands, don't stop shooting until all the film is gone.

NARRATIVE

A **narrative paragraph** tells a story. It should include details that answer the 5 W's (*Who? What? When? Where?* and *Why?*) about the experience or event.

> In first grade, I learned some of the harsh realities of life. I found out that circuses aren't all they're supposed to be. We were going to the circus for our class trip, and I was really excited about it because I had never been to one before. Our class worked for weeks on a circus train made of shoe boxes, and Carrie Kaske told me her mom had fainted once when she saw the lion trainer. The day of the trip finally came, and my wonderful circus turned out to be nothing but one disappointment after another. First, I couldn't see much of anything. I could just barely make out some tiny figures scurrying around in the three rings that seemed to be a hundred miles away from my seat. After the first half hour, all I wanted to do was buy a soda and a monkey-on-a-stick and get out of there. Of course, nothing in life is that easy. We weren't allowed to buy anything, so I couldn't have my souvenir; and instead of a cold soda to quench my thirst, I had warm, curdled milk that the room mothers had so thoughtfully brought along. I returned to school tired and a little wiser. I remember looking at our little circus train on the window ledge and thinking that I'd rather sit and watch it do nothing than go to another circus.

PERSUASIVE

A **persuasive paragraph** expresses an opinion and tries to convince the reader that the opinion is valid. It should contain supporting points that help solidify your argument.

> Capital punishment should be abolished for three major reasons. First, common sense tells me that two wrongs don't make a right. To kill someone convicted of murder contradicts the reasoning behind the law that taking another's life is wrong. The state is committing the same violent, dehumanizing act it is condemning. Second, the death penalty is not an effective deterrent. Numerous studies show that murder is usually the result of a complex psychological and sociological problem and that most murderers do not contemplate the consequences of their acts; or, if they do, any penalty is seen as a far-off possibility. The offense, on the other hand, brings immediate gratification. The third and most serious objection is that death is final and cannot be altered. Errors in deciding guilt or innocence will always be present in our system of trial by jury. There is too great a risk that innocent people will be put to death. Official records show that it has happened in the past. For these reasons, I feel capital punishment should be replaced with a system that puts all doubt on the side of life—not death.

A Closer Look at Paragraphing

Paragraph Unity

Every sentence in a paragraph should support the topic sentence and fit in well with the other sentences. This relationship creates a sense of unity in a paragraph. Notice how the **boldfaced sentences** disrupt the flow in the following paragraph. With these sentences removed, the paragraph is unified.

> Before the car accident paralyzed his left side, Randy thought about life in terms of jump shots, fast breaks, and high-flying layups. But when the passenger door banged open, and no seat belt held him down, he bounced out of the car into a paralytic's world that had completely different challenges. **Things might have been different if Randy had been wearing a seat belt.** How do you wash both hands when only one hand can hold the soap? How do you cut your right-hand fingernails when your left-hand fingers can't squeeze the clipper? How do you look cool while walking with friends and the clop-clop noise of your left-footed limp sounds louder than a bleacher full of fans? **The limp was really bad.** Eventually, Randy found joy in his new world, but first he had to learn to accept new challenges and to find fulfillment in different victories.

Paragraph Details

Your paragraphs need interesting, specific details to make them worth reading. Broadly speaking, you can gather details in the following four ways. (See pages 46-49 for more information.)

- **Reflect.** By brainstorming, mapping, and freewriting, you can unlock memories, explanations, and descriptions.
- **Observe.** By looking and listening attentively, you can discover important details and facts.
- **Talk.** By talking with knowledgeable people, you can gather material from their firsthand experiences and research.
- **Read.** By reading newspapers, journals, books, or periodicals (in print or on the Internet), you can find facts and quotations.

HELP FILE

There are many types of details you can gather, including . . .

facts	anecdotes	reasons	paraphrases
statistics	quotations	explanations	comparisons
examples	definitions	summaries	analyses

"I want to get the structural problems out of the way first, so I can get to what matters more."   —John McPhee

Arranging Your **Details**

On the next four pages, you will find sample paragraphs following seven basic methods of organization. Review these samples when you have questions about arranging the details in your own writing.

Classification

Classification is an effective method of organization for explaining a complex term or concept. To classify, you break a subject down into categories and subcategories to help readers better understand it. The following paragraph classifies the main groups of people that make up the population of Canada.

> Canada's 29-30 million people can be divided into three main groups: founding people, descendants of Europeans, and more recent immigrants. Founding people, about 2 percent of the population, are those who came across the Bering Strait from Asia thousands of years ago. This group includes Inuit (northern aboriginal people) and Métis (people of mixed heritage). The second group, those with European heritage, make up about 85 percent of the population. Most of this group are descended from British and French colonists, although almost all the other European countries are represented. The third group, recent immigrants, makes up the rest of the population and adds more diversity to the mix. These immigrants come from all over the world, including Vietnam, China, Haiti, and Jamaica. All three groups help give Canada a rich and interesting culture.

Order of Location

Order of location is a useful method for describing a person, a place, or a thing. It provides unity by arranging details in a logical way—left to right, right to left, top to bottom, and so on. In the sample paragraph that follows, Tony Rogers describes the condition of his bike after a serious crash. The description moves from the handlebars to the seat to the frame.

> As the dust and debris settled, I slowly got to my feet and examined my raw flesh and bleeding scrapes. Nothing broken. But my heart sank when I went to retrieve my bike. Lying on its side, the bike was breathing its last. The once proud handlebars were twisted into an agonizing position. The leather seat showed seams ripped open, and the frame that once had been so shiny and pure now lay bent and twisted into the rear wheel. It had been such an exquisite performer, but now it was destined for the junk heap.

"First, work hard to master the tools.
Simplify, prune, and strive for order."
—William Zinsser

Chronological Order

SHARING A STORY

Chronological (time) **order** is effective for sharing a story or explaining a process. Information is organized according to what happens first, second, third, and so on. The paragraph below uses chronological order to tell about a morning in the life of Michael Dayne.

When Michael heard the alarm at 5:30 a.m., his legs automatically swung to the floor. Groggy but awake, he pulled on his work clothes, stumbled downstairs, laced up his boots, and hurried across the farmyard. His first stop was the chicken house where he scooped the metal feeders full of ground oats and cleaned the water trays. Then it was off to the barn to pump water for the horses and fill their feedboxes with hay. From there, he hurried to the hog house, poked down ground corn into the self-feeders, and checked the automatic floats in the water troughs. His chores finished, Michael jogged back to the house, washed up, changed clothes, and ate his own breakfast. He then grabbed his book bag, trotted out to the road, and hopped on the school bus. Settling into the back seat, Michael checked his watch. "It's 6:45," he thought, "and the 'townies' are just waking up."

EXPLAINING A PROCESS

The paragraph below explains a process—how hair grows. The writer first introduces the topic, and then he describes the process chronologically.

Did you ever wonder what makes your hair grow? To understand the process, you first have to look at your scalp—just common skin. About 100,000 tiny holes, called follicles, poke through the top layer of skin (epidermis) and into the bottom layer (dermis). At the bottom of each follicle lies a seed-like pocket called a papilla. A small blood vessel carries food into the papilla, which works like a little factory, using the food to build hair cells. The cells form a strand that grows up through the dermis and past an oil gland that provides a coating to keep the hair soft and moist. The strand continues to grow through the epidermis and into the air above. Now and then, each papilla pauses, rests awhile, and then goes back to work again. However, if all your papillae stop working for good, you've reached that stage in your life called *baldness*.

Illustration

Illustration (general to specific) is a method of organization in which a general idea (the topic sentence) is stated and followed with specific details, facts, and examples. The paragraph below opens with a main point about humpback whales and follows with an explanation of the current research on the subject.

It's hard to say how humpback whales find their way. They may rely on their excellent sense of hearing to pick up low-frequency sound waves that bounce off common ocean features such as rock and coral. Scientists also believe that they may look for familiar landforms. Two researchers recently detected a small amount of magnetic material in humpbacks, which may allow them to migrate by sensing the earth's magnetic field. This may explain why whales get stranded. Some researchers think it's because they are drawn to coasts with low magnetic forces, thinking they are clear waterways. This would also explain how they could follow such precise migration paths.

Climax

Climax (specific to general) is a method of organization in which the specific details lead up to an important summary statement. (If a topic sentence is used, it is placed at the end.) The following paragraph shows the excitement building as the writer waits for a concert to begin.

As the lights dimmed in the amphitheater, multicolored spotlights began to circle overhead, bouncing off the ceiling and swirling over the heads of the crowd. The sound began to build. At first, it sounded like thunder rumbling in the distance, but soon it grew to a deafening roar. People all around were stamping their feet, clapping their hands, and whistling through their fingers to show that they were ready for the show to begin. The crowd noise was soon drowned out by a blast of bass guitar and drums that seemed to come out of nowhere. Behind a blinding flash of light and a shower of glittering sparks, the band appeared on stage and began to play. At last, the concert had begun.

HELP FILE

When you organize a paragraph from general to specific, you are working deductively. Most scientific and informative writing requires deductive reasoning because it helps make complicated material easy to understand. When you organize from specific to general, you are working inductively. Inductive reasoning is often used in personal essays and short stories.

Cause and Effect

Cause-and-effect organization helps show the relationship between events and their results. A piece organized this way can begin with a general statement about the *effect* and follow with specific *causes,* or it can begin with a general statement about the cause and follow with specific effects. In the paragraph below, Laura Black defines hypothermia, briefly explains its cause, and then discusses its effects on the human body.

Hypothermia means that a person's body temperature has dropped below the normal 98.6° F. This condition usually results from prolonged exposure to cold. As hypothermia sets in, it causes all bodily functions to slow down. At first, the dropping temperature affects blood flow and breathing. Heart rate and blood pressure decrease, and breathing becomes slower and shallower. As body temperature drops further, these effects become even more dramatic until somewhere between 86° and 82° F, the person lapses into unconsciousness. When body temperature reaches between 65° and 59° F, heart action, blood flow, and electrical brain activity stop. You would think that at this point the body would give out, but that does not necessarily happen. As the body cools down, the need for oxygen also slows. A person can be in a deep hypothermic state for an hour or longer and still be revived without serious long-term effects or complications.

Comparison

Organizing by comparison helps show the similarities or differences between two subjects. Often, you will end up showing both the similarities and differences. (See pages 202-203 for more information.) In the paragraph that follows, the writer compares the dedicated, humanitarian work of two contemporary First Ladies.

Former First Ladies Eleanor Roosevelt and Barbara Bush shared a concern for social change. Even though they supported different causes, both women worked to improve the lives of the young. Eleanor, wife of Democratic President Franklin D. Roosevelt, lectured about youth unemployment and supported the National Youth Administration, a program that found jobs for young people. Barbara, wife of Republican President George Bush, helped young people by starting reading programs for children throughout the United States and establishing the Barbara Bush Foundation for Family Literacy. However, both First Ladies also championed their own special concerns. Eleanor promoted racial equality, argued for desegregation, and chaired the commission that drafted the Universal Declaration of Human Rights. For her part, Barbara promoted better health care, raised money for cancer research, and assisted social agencies such as soup kitchens and shelters for the homeless. In the end, both women used their positions to improve our society.

Connecting Your Details

Once you've arranged all the details in your writing, you need to tie them together so they read smoothly. The words below can help.

Words used to **SHOW LOCATION**:

above	away from	beyond	into	over
across	behind	by	near	throughout
against	below	down	off	to the right
along	beneath	in back of	on top of	under
among	beside	in front of	onto	
around	between	inside	outside	

Words used to **SHOW TIME**:

about	before	later	second	today
after	during	meanwhile	soon	tomorrow
afterward	finally	next	then	until
as soon as	first	next week	third	when
at	immediately	now	till	yesterday

Words used to **COMPARE THINGS** (show similarities):

also	likewise	in the same way
as	similarly	like

Words used to **CONTRAST THINGS** (show differences):

although	even though	still	on the other hand
but	however	yet	otherwise

Words used to **EMPHASIZE A POINT**:

this reason	truly	to emphasize
especially	to repeat	in fact

Words used to **CONCLUDE** or **SUMMARIZE**:

all in all	finally	therefore	in summary
as a result	last	to sum up	in conclusion

Words used to **ADD INFORMATION**:

additionally	for example	also	as well	likewise
again	for instance	and	besides	moreover
along with	in addition	another	finally	next

Words used to **CLARIFY**:

for instance	in other words	that is	put another way

"Essays are experiments in making sense of things."
—Scott Russell Sanders

Writing
EXPOSITORY Essays

The expository essay is the basic form of writing assigned in most of your classes. You write expository essays about important concepts covered in your reading and in class discussions. You explore topics related to your course work. You compose procedure (how-to) papers. You take essay tests. Anytime you are asked to inform, explain, examine, discuss, or illustrate in writing, you are developing an expository essay.

Expository essays follow the thesis-statement-plus-support structure. That is, a successful expository essay includes a clear thesis statement (identifying an important or interesting aspect of a subject) with effective supporting ideas (facts, details, examples, and so on). The best essays begin and end with good information, so the key is to work with solid information right from the start.

Preview

- The Importance of Structure, Support, and Organization
- Writing Guidelines
- Tips for Writing Expository Essays
- Expository Essay
- Assessment Rubric

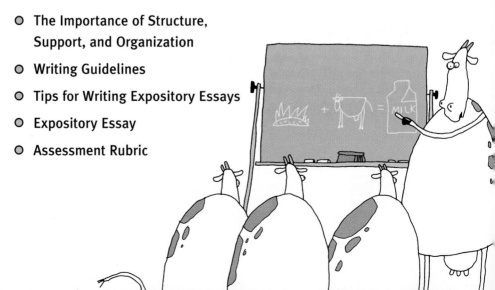

The Importance of **Structure**

An expository essay is usually tightly structured, like the graphic below. It contains an opening paragraph, several supporting paragraphs, and a closing paragraph.

Beginning **Your opening paragraph should gain your reader's interest and identify the thesis you plan to develop.** To get your reader's interest, you can use one or more of the following methods. You can . . .

  1. ask one or more questions about the topic,
  2. provide an interesting story about the subject,
  3. present a significant fact or statistic,
  4. quote an expert on the subject, or
  5. define an important term.

Middle **The supporting paragraphs present the main points or reasons supporting your thesis.** They are the heart of your essay. If, for instance, you plan to present information about the devastating effects of childhood malnutrition, each supporting paragraph in your essay should be about those effects.

In addition, knowing when to start a new paragraph is a key to writing a good essay. You should start a new paragraph whenever there is a shift or change in the essay. Such changes are called *paragraph shifts* and can take place for any of the following reasons: to introduce a new main point, to shift emphasis, or to indicate a change in time or place.

It's also important that the middle paragraphs are arranged in the best possible way—by order of importance, by classification, by time, and so on. And these paragraphs should flow clearly and smoothly from one to the next. To achieve this flow, the first sentence in each new paragraph should somehow be linked to the preceding one. Transitions or linking words are often used for this purpose.

Ending **Your closing paragraph should tie the main points in the essay together and draw a final conclusion.** It should also leave readers with a clear understanding of the importance of your subject. (See page 58.)

The Importance of Support

Without adequate support or evidence, you cannot effectively develop an expository essay. Here are three ways to support your thesis.

Include Facts

Facts are statements and statistics that add support and validity to your essays; they help you prove your main points. In the sample expository essay (see pages 112-113), the writer claims that childhood malnutrition is a tremendous problem. Here are two facts she presents to support this claim:

1. About 18 million people, mostly children, die each year from starvation, malnutrition, and related causes.
2. Nearly 200 million children under the age of five—40 percent of all of the children this age—lack sufficient nutrition to develop properly.

Give Examples

Examples are a way of "showing" your ideas to readers. In the sample expository essay, the writer discusses the general problems resulting from malnutrition. She then gives two examples of malnutrition and the specific problems of each:

1. Marasmus is a form of malnutrition occurring when children are weaned too soon and receive very few nutrients.
2. Kwashiorkor is another form of malnutrition occurring when children are weaned later than normal and do not receive the necessary protein and nutrients.

Add Quotations

Quotations from experts add authority to your writing. In the sample essay, the writer quotes an authority on malnutrition:

According to Dr. Hiroshi Nakajima, Director-General of the World Health Organization, "Much of the sickness and death attributed to major communicable diseases is, in fact, caused by malnutrition."

HELP FILE

In some cases, supporting your main point with facts, examples, and quotations may not be enough. You may also need to comment on or analyze the subject to complete the picture. For example, in the closing paragraph of the sample essay on page 113, the writer comments on the future outlook for overcoming malnutrition.

The Importance of **Organization**

Always organize the information you plan to use in your essay. One way to do this is to use an outline, either a **topic outline** or a **sentence outline**.

**Sample
Topic
Outline**

I. Effects of malnutrition on the body
   A. Extreme weight loss and stunted growth
   B. Frequent infections
   C. Lower resistance to life-threatening diseases
II. Marasmus—a form of malnutrition
   A. Extremely underweight
   B. Lack of body fat or defined muscles
   C. Puppet-like appearance
   D. Increased internal problems
III. Kwashiorkor—another form of malnutrition
   A. Badly swollen bellies
   B. Pale or red skin
   C. Thinning hair
IV. Effects of malnutrition on development
   A. Limited ability to walk and to talk
   B. Stunted intellectual development
   C. Effects continuing into adulthood

Sample Sentence Outline

I. Malnutrition limits the physical development of children.
   A. Malnutrition causes extreme weight loss and stunted growth.
   B. Malnutrition can result in children getting frequent infections.
   C. Malnutrition can lower children's resistance to diseases.
II. Marasmus is one form of malnutrition.
   A. Children with this condition lack body fat and muscle.
   B. They appear puppet-like.
   C. This condition causes the skin to sag and wrinkle.
   D. It also decreases the size of internal organs.
III. Kwashiorkor is another form of malnutrition.
   A. Children with this condition have swollen bellies.
   B. Kwashiorkor causes pale or red skin and thinning hair.
   C. This condition causes growth to stop.
IV. Malnutrition limits the mental development of children.
   A. It hinders toddlers' ability to walk and to talk.
   B. Iron and iodine deficiencies stunt intellectual development.
   C. Malnutrition in early childhood affects ongoing learning.

WRITING GUIDELINES
Expository Essay

In an expository essay, you inform readers about a meaningful and interesting subject. You are not arguing for or against the subject or reflecting upon its value or worth. Your main purpose is to convey a certain amount of information clearly and completely.

✱ Before you get started, make sure that you clearly understand the assignment, including the standards that will be used to assess your work.

■ PREWRITING

1. **Choosing a Subject . . .** In most cases, your teacher will give you a general subject or a writing prompt to get you started on your subject search. Carry out your search until you discover a specific subject that interests you and meets the requirements of the assignment. Then determine a focus (a specific angle or direction) for your writing.

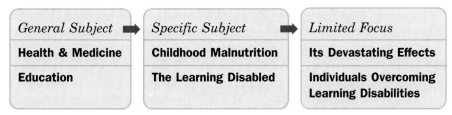

General Subject ➡	*Specific Subject* ➡	*Limited Focus*
Health & Medicine	**Childhood Malnutrition**	**Its Devastating Effects**
Education	**The Learning Disabled**	**Individuals Overcoming Learning Disabilities**

2. **Gathering Details . . .** Carry out as much research (interviewing, reading, observing) as necessary to collect a variety of information. (See pages 46-49 for collecting strategies and graphic organizers.)

3. **Forming a Thesis Statement . . .** A thesis statement identifies the focus for your writing. It usually highlights a special condition or feature of the subject, expresses a specific feeling, or takes a stand. You can use the formula below to help you form this statement. You need to know, too, that you may revise your thesis statement a few times during the writing process as you find new information. (See page 51 for more information.)

> **A specific subject** *(Children suffering from malnutrition)*
>
> **+ a limited focus** *(have little chance of living long, productive lives)*.
> _____
> **= an effective thesis statement.**

4. **Planning and Organizing Your Essay . . .** Review your research, highlighting the facts and details that support your thesis. (Do more research if necessary.) Then decide on the best way to organize this information. You may find it helpful to outline your ideas (see page 108) or to arrange them using a graphic organizer (see pages 48-49).

■ WRITING AND REVISING

5. **Connecting Your Ideas . . .** Write as freely as you can, using your prewriting and planning as a general guide. Your goal is to get all of your ideas on paper. You may have to write one or two more early drafts before your essay really begins to take shape.

HELP FILE

Devote extra time to your opening paragraph, which should catch your reader's attention and identify the thesis of your writing. Once you are satisfied with this paragraph, you'll find it much easier to develop the rest of your essay.

---

6. **Improving Your Writing . . .** Carefully review your draft for completeness, organization, and writing voice: *Do you sound interested in and knowledgeable about your subject?* Also have a classmate read and react to your draft. Be prepared to do some adding, cutting, and rearranging to make your essay say what you want it to say.

■ EDITING AND PROOFREADING

7. **Checking for Style and Accuracy . . .** Review your revised writing for style. Make sure that your sentences read smoothly and clearly, and that you have used the best words to express your ideas. Then check your writing for spelling, grammar, punctuation, and sentence errors.

   [HOT LINK] See "Assessment Rubric," page 114, for a helpful revising and editing guide.

8. **Sharing Your Work . . .** Prepare a neat final copy of your work, following your teacher's directions or the guidelines in your handbook. (See pages 30-32.) Proofread the final copy before sharing it with others.

"Bring ideas in and entertain them royally,
for one of them may be the king."
—Mark Van Doren

TIPS for Writing Expository Essays

If your essay needs a shot of energy, try one or more of the following activities. Each one is guaranteed to refuel your thinking.

- **Pretend** that you are the first person to know about and understand your subject in the way that you do; write freely about your ideas and discoveries. Some fresh ideas are bound to develop.

- **Write** a negative definition of your subject (what it is *not*). Then expand upon this definition in a freewriting, working in new thoughts and ideas as they come to mind.

- **Ask yourself,** "What am I trying to say here?" And then answer the question in your mind or out loud. Pick up on anything that sounds better than the way you initially expressed yourself.

- **Re-examine** your subject from a number of different angles. (See pages 46-47 for ideas.)

- **Get into** your writing. Grumble and mumble when the words aren't coming the way you want them to, and whoop it up or clap your hands when you hit on the right way to say something.

- **Bend** the rules (if you have your teacher's okay). If you don't feel like starting with a typical opening paragraph, open in a way that feels right to you—perhaps with a personal story about how you got interested in your subject in the first place.

- **Step back** and reassess your feelings about your subject. Do you still feel that your thesis is effective? Can you effectively support it?

- **Talk** about your subject with someone new. How about your younger brother, your grandmother, or your guidance counselor? What are their feelings about your subject, and why do they feel the way they do?

- **Find** new sources of information, new points of view. Decide if this information changes your thinking on the subject.

Sample **Expository Essay**

In this essay, student writer Dawn Wielenga informs readers about a world health problem: childhood malnutrition. The writer provides enough facts and details to help readers appreciate the seriousness of the situation.

No Escape for Malnourished Children

Hunger and malnutrition are tremendous problems in our world today. According to the magazine *Population Reports,* about 18 million people, mostly children, die each year from starvation, malnutrition, and related causes. This magazine also states that nearly 200 million children under age five—40 percent of all children this age—lack sufficient nutrition to develop fully (79-80). **Tragically, children suffering from malnutrition have little chance of living long, productive lives.**

Malnutrition can lead to death, but long before that happens, poorly nourished children suffer from a number of physical problems. Extreme weight loss, stunted growth, and frequent infections are just a few of the physical problems resulting from poor nutrition. Because the immune system often begins to shut down in malnourished children, they are also very susceptible to life-threatening diseases such as tuberculosis, measles, and diarrhea. According to Dr. Hiroshi Nakajima, Director-General of the World Health Organization, "Much of the sickness and death attributed to major communicable diseases is, in fact, caused by malnutrition" (81).

One form of malnutrition is called *marasmus* and occurs when children are weaned too soon and receive very few nutrients. Children with marasmus are extremely underweight, lack any body fat or defined muscles, and appear almost puppet-like—with large heads, small bodies, and thin arms and legs. Eventually their skin sags, and their faces wrinkle. To compound the problem, their body organs decrease in size, their intestines begin to fail, and their pulse rate slows down. Simply put, marasmus causes the child's body to waste away.

Another form of malnutrition is called *kwashiorkor* and occurs when children are weaned later than normal and do not receive the necessary protein and nutrients. Children

The opening paragraph leads up to the thesis statement (boldfaced).

An authority on the subject is quoted.

Specific details are added.

with this disease have badly swollen bellies that actually make them look somewhat healthy. However, their stomachs appear large because their abdominal muscles are loose and weak. Their skin is often pale or red, and their hair becomes very thin. Eventually, children who suffer from this form of malnutrition simply stop growing.

The writer demonstrates a clear understanding of the subject.

In terms of their mental development, children lacking proper food become sleepy, dull, and withdrawn. As a result, their ability to learn decreases. Because these children have no energy, it's difficult for them to even learn how to walk and talk. According to *The Public Health News and Notes,* iron and iodine deficiencies in children often impair their intellectual development. Even a small deficiency in iodine can reduce a child's development by as much as 10 percent. Studies have shown that poor nutrition in early childhood can continue to hinder development well into adulthood (15).

The closing paragraph summarizes the essay and comments on the future.

Malnutrition is a serious problem for people of all ages, but it takes its greatest toll on innocent children. And the problem is not likely to go away soon. New methods of farming, food distribution, and health care will be needed before a significant number of children can be helped. Those changes are just now beginning to take place. ∎

For more information on giving credit to the sources you use in your writing, turn to pages 260-264.

Assessment Rubric

Use this rubric as a checklist to assess the effectiveness of your expository essays. The rubric is arranged according to the traits of effective writing. (See pages 21-26.)

Stimulating Ideas

The writing . . .

_____ focuses on a specific informational subject clearly expressed in a thesis statement.

_____ contains specific facts, examples, or quotations to support the thesis.

_____ thoroughly informs readers.

Logical Organization

_____ includes a clear beginning, a strong middle, and an effective ending.

_____ presents ideas in an organized manner.

_____ uses transitions to link sentences and paragraphs.

Engaging Voice

_____ speaks clearly and knowledgeably.

_____ shows that the writer is truly interested in the subject.

Original Word Choice

_____ explains or defines any unfamiliar terms.

_____ contains specific nouns and active verbs.

Effective Sentence Style

_____ flows smoothly from one idea to the next.

_____ shows a variety of sentence lengths and structures.

Correct, Accurate Copy

_____ exhibits the basic rules of writing.

_____ follows the format required by the teacher or follows some other effective design. (See pages 30-32.)

"The best advice on writing I've ever received is 'Write with authority.' "

—Cynthia Ozick

Writing
PERSUASIVE Essays

Writing is a lot of things, all of which are good for you. Writing is a way to better understand your personal world. It is a way to think more logically and more creatively about your course work, and it is a way to gain insights into important news events of the day. Not bad for something that you can do whenever you want—free of charge.

Persuasive writing requires all of the understanding, creativity, and logic that you can muster. First you must learn as much as you can about your subject. In the process, you form an opinion about it that you can effectively support. Then you must connect all of your thoughts in an essay that sounds convincing to your readers. Persuasive writing succeeds when it presents a solid argument from start to finish.

Preview

- Writing Guidelines
- Thinking Through an Argument
- Using a Graphic Organizer
- Sample Persuasive Essay
- Assessment Rubric

WRITING GUIDELINES

Persuasive Essay

The primary purpose of a persuasive essay is to convince readers to think the way that you do about a subject. To accomplish this goal, you will have to establish a reasonable and thoughtful argument supporting a subject or a position you have strong feelings about.

■ PREWRITING

1. **Choosing a Subject . . .** For most persuasive writing assignments, you will search for a subject related to your course work. You will also need to make sure that the subject you choose is controversial (has at least two sides) and that it is specific enough to be handled in a multi-paragraph essay. The following chart shows the difference between expository and persuasive subjects.

Subjects for an Expository Essay	Subjects for a Persuasive Essay
How creatine works as a diet supplement	High school athletes should avoid creatine.
How barbless fishing hooks work	Only barbless fishing hooks should be used for recreational fishing.

2. **Gathering Details . . .** Gather your own thoughts about your subject (freewriting, listing, clustering). Then collect information from as many other sources as necessary. Consider newspapers, news magazines, books, and the Internet. (See page 47 for help.)

3. **Forming an Opinion Statement . . .** After reviewing your notes, express in a sentence your opinion about the subject. (This statement will be the thesis of your essay.) You may need to write several versions of this statement before it says what you want it to say.

4. **Planning and Organizing Your Thoughts . . .** Once you have your opinion statement, list the main points that support your opinion. (See the list below.) Or, you can organize your thoughts using a graphic organizer like the one shown in this chapter. (See page 120.)

> **Opinion Statement:** High school athletes should not use creatine.
>
> **Main Supporting Points:**
> 1. "Loading up" on creatine is unnatural.
> 2. Harmful side effects are possible.
> 3. It isn't used wisely.

HELP FILE

In a persuasive essay, you may want to lead off with your most significant argument to get your reader's attention. Or you may want to save your best argument for last to solidify your opinion. Then again, your supporting points may fall into a logical order in which one main point naturally leads to the next and so on. (If you plan to concede or counter any opposing opinions, it's best to do so early in your essay. See "Making concessions" on page 119.)

■ WRITING AND REVISING

5. **Connecting Your Ideas . . .** Write your first draft according to your planning and organizing, but feel free to add any new ideas as they come to mind. *Remember:* You may need to write more than one early draft before your essay really begins to take shape.

   [HOT LINK] See "The Importance of Structure," page 106, for help with the beginning, middle, and ending parts in your essay.

6. **Improving Your Writing . . .** Carefully review your first draft for completeness, organization, and voice: *Do you sound knowledgeable about your subject and confident in the position you've taken?* Have at least one classmate react to your first draft as well. Then add, cut, and rearrange information as necessary to make your essay as persuasive as possible.

■ EDITING AND PROOFREADING

7. **Checking for Style and Accuracy . . .** Review your revised essay for style, making sure that all of your sentences read smoothly and clearly. Also make sure that you have used the best words to express your ideas. Then check for spelling, grammar, punctuation, and sentence errors.

   ✱ If you have cited sources in your essay, make sure that you have documented them correctly. (See pages 259-274 for MLA documentation and pages 285-295 for APA documentation.)

   [HOT LINK] See "Assessment Rubric," page 123, for a helpful revising and editing guide.

8. **Preparing a Final Copy . . .** Write or keyboard a neat final copy of your essay according to your teacher's requirements or the guidelines in your handbook. (See pages 30-32.) Proofread the final copy before sharing it with others.

Thinking Through an Argument

The next two pages will help you state and support opinions as well as help you make concessions for any arguments opposing your line of thinking.

Stating an opinion. A reasonable and logical opinion statement is at the core of an effective persuasive essay. Opinion statements fall into three main categories: statements of fact, statements of value, and statements of policy.

- **Statements of fact** claim that something is true or not true.

  > Athletes who take supplemental creatine can weight-train longer and harder than athletes who rely on natural sources of the nutrient.

- **Statements of value** claim that something does or does not have worth.

  > In the long run, creatine really isn't worth the risk to athletes' health.

- **Statements of policy** claim that something should or should not be done.

  > Adults responsible for young athletes should forbid the use of creatine.

Using qualifiers. Qualifiers are terms that make an opinion easier to support. Note the difference between the two opinions below:

> Creatine makes athletes stronger, but it won't make them better.

> Creatine may make athletes stronger, but it won't necessarily make them better.

"May" and "necessarily" qualify the above opinion statement, changing it from an all-or-nothing claim to one that can more effectively be defended. Here are some other useful qualifiers:

almost	usually	maybe	probably
often	some	most	in most cases
if . . . then . . .	likely	many	frequently

Take NOTE

Opinions that include words that are strongly positive or negative—such as *all, best, every, never, none,* or *worst*—may be difficult to support. For example, an exaggerated opinion statement like "Creatine is the worst supplement on the market today" would certainly be impossible to support.

Adding support. Support your opinion with effective evidence. The more types of convincing evidence you offer, the stronger your argument will be. Here are different types of evidence you might use:

> **Statistics:** This magazine also states that nearly 200 million children under age five—40 percent of all children this age—lack sufficient nutrition.
>
> **Predictions:** This condition will surely affect the intellectual development of a particular country.
>
> **Observation:** Samantha appears quiet and withdrawn when math class starts.
>
> **Expert testimony:** Dr. Michael Colgan, a clinical nutritionist, states, "Taken in doses of more than 25 grams per day, creatine can crucify your kidneys. . . . "
>
> **Comparison:** To understand cerebral thrombosis (a type of stroke), one must imagine a highway, not a large highway, but a busy one.
>
> **Experience:** Although these cases are rare, a local high school football player was taken to the hospital for dehydration due to the use of the "power powder."
>
> **Analysis:** Realizing their own potential and building on their strong points have helped them overcome their disabilities, even enabling them to be examples for the rest of us.

Making concessions. When you make a concession, you identify other valid opinions about your subject. Making a concession often makes your overall argument more convincing. Note the following concession made by a student writer:

> I realize that you are worried about our safety, but there are dangers in nearly all things, including driving cars and playing sports.

The phrase "I realize that" introduces this concession in a way that shows respect for the other side of the argument. Here are some other useful expressions for making concessions:

even though	I agree that	I cannot argue with
while it is true that	admittedly	granted
I will admit	you're right	I accept the fact

Using a **Graphic Organizer**

Using an outline is a precise, tightly structured way to organize your writing. (See page 108.) Using a graphic organizer like the one below is a free-flowing, looser way. It's as though you were laying your main ideas and details on a table and moving them all around.

The organizer on this page represents a plan for the model persuasive essay on the next two pages. The thesis of this essay appears in the oval; each main supporting point (numbers 1-3) completes a "because" statement. For example, **High school athletes should not use creatine** *because* it is unnatural to "load up" on a supplement. The outlined boxes contain details supporting the main points.

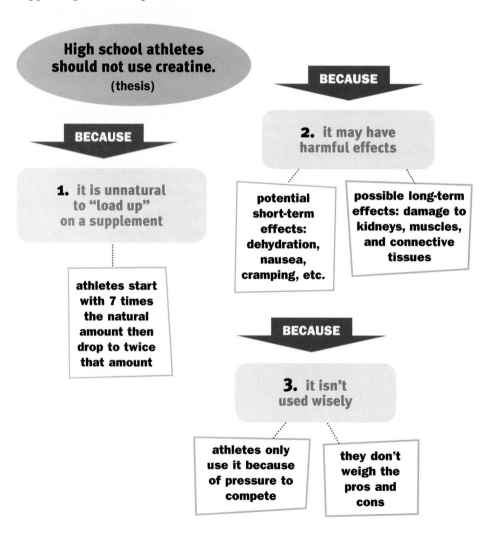

High school athletes should not use creatine. (thesis)

BECAUSE

1. it is unnatural to "load up" on a supplement

athletes start with 7 times the natural amount then drop to twice that amount

BECAUSE

2. it may have harmful effects

potential short-term effects: dehydration, nausea, cramping, etc.

possible long-term effects: damage to kidneys, muscles, and connective tissues

BECAUSE

3. it isn't used wisely

athletes only use it because of pressure to compete

they don't weigh the pros and cons

Sample **Persuasive Essay**

In this persuasive essay, student writer Brian Sonke speaks out against the use of creatine by high school athletes. Notice that the writer covers all the points listed in the graphic organizer on the previous page.

Creatine Crazy

The opening paragraph introduces the subject and identifies the thesis of the essay (boldfaced).

Walk into almost any fitness club today, and you will find someone who is taking creatine, a training supplement that has become popular with athletes from high school on up. For the last decade, athletes around the world have been taking it to gain muscle mass. If athletes work out regularly, follow a good diet, and take creatine, they'll get results. But are bigger muscles worth it? **For high school athletes, the answer is *no* because creatine presents too many risks.**

The supporting points are explained clearly.

One of the concerns with high school athletes is the overload creatine use creates. To help build muscles, the body actually produces creatine naturally—at the rate of 2 to 3 grams a day. The problem is that athletes who take supplemental creatine start with a loading-up phase, taking 20 to 25 grams a day for a week. They then follow with an eight-week cycle of 5 grams a day. In other words, athletes on the supplement start by taking more than seven times the natural daily amount before dropping down to twice the daily amount.

In the short term, creatine use may be more harmful than people believe. The side effects may include diarrhea, dehydration, nausea, cramping, bloating, muscle strains, and increased blood pressure. While these effects are rare, at least one local high school football player was taken to the hospital for dehydration from using creatine, or "power powder" as it is often called.

A quotation from an expert adds a level of authority to the argument.

Doctors are even more concerned about possible long-term problems. As Dr. Michael Colgan, a clinical nutritionist, states in *Today's Health* magazine, "Taken in doses of more than 25 grams per day, creatine can crucify [torture] your kidneys, and there's also evidence that it can contribute to muscle cramping and the tearing of connective tissues" (67). Experts worry about the kidneys having to filter all that extra creatine, and some believe that the body might actually stop producing creatine naturally. ▶

Creatine Crazy
(continued)

A transitional paragraph introduces the final argument.

Even with these possible harmful effects, more and more high school athletes are using creatine. Why? They feel pressure to become bigger, stronger, and faster. George Hurley, a football coach from Newbury Park High in California, said in a recent interview in *Sportz* magazine, "Kids come to the conclusion that if the guy next to me in the weight room is doing creatine and I'm not doing it, he is ahead of me" (117). The result is that teen athletes believe they must take creatine to compete in high school sports, and to have any chance of competing at the next level.

Given the pressure, few young athletes (or parents) take time to weigh the pros and cons of their decision about creatine. They fail to consider that very few high school athletes go on to play in college, and only a tiny minority of those will play professionally. They don't understand that they are risking a lifetime of health problems for a short-term gamble at the big leagues. They don't listen to the cautions that come their way. For example, the National Federation of High School Sports Medicine has stated in its *NFSM Journal* that "school personnel and coaches should not dispense any drug, medication, or food supplement except with extreme caution" (42). Adults responsible for young athletes should not promote the use of creatine in their schools.

Each quotation in the paper is identified by title and page number.

In the closing paragraph, the writer speaks directly and confidently in support of his thesis.

Today, teenage athletes are under a lot of stress. There is way too much emphasis placed on performing well in a society that seems to eat, sleep, and breathe sports. Coaches, administrators, and parents should de-emphasize winning at all costs and keep teens away from supplements like creatine, at least until more is known about them. Young athletes should be encouraged to rely on their natural talents and strength so that sports are fair and safe for everybody. Creatine may make athletes stronger, but it won't necessarily make them better, and in the long run, it really isn't worth the risk. ■

For more information on giving credit to the sources you use in your writing, turn to pages 260-264.

Assessment Rubric

Use this rubric as a checklist to assess the effectiveness of your persuasive essays. The rubric is arranged according to the traits of effective writing described in the handbook. (See pages 21-26.)

Stimulating Ideas

The writing . . .

_____ focuses on a statement of opinion about a timely subject.

_____ contains specific facts and details to support the opinion.

_____ maintains a clear, consistent stand from start to finish.

Logical Organization

_____ includes a clear beginning, strong support, and a convincing conclusion.

_____ arranges ideas in an organized manner (perhaps offering the strongest point first or last).

_____ presents logical arguments. (See pages 118-119.)

Engaging Voice

_____ speaks in a convincing way, using an appropriate tone.

_____ shows that the writer feels strongly about his or her position.

Original Word Choice

_____ explains or defines any unfamiliar terms.

_____ uses language that shows an understanding of the subject.

Effective Sentence Style

_____ flows smoothly from one idea to the next.

_____ displays varied sentence beginnings and lengths.

Correct, Accurate Copy

_____ adheres to the basic rules of writing.

_____ follows the appropriate format for citing sources.

The ART of
WRITING

"When I write, I read everything
out loud to get the right rhythm."

—Fran Lebowitz

Writing with
STYLE

Think about your hair. This morning when you first yawned into the mirror, you had to make some choices: Should I wash my hair? Should I blow it dry or just comb it? Should I use mousse, gel, or spritz? Should I try something new—braid it, rubber-band it, slick it, tease it—or just leave it? Do I want my jersey number shaved in back or should I get a Mohawk? Whatever you do—or don't do—that is your style.

Your writing style, similarly, comes from the choices you make. It is *your* words, *your* sentences, *your* paragraphs—nobody else's. Fortunately, you don't have to change your style every month to be in fashion. Your writing will always be in style if you make sure that it sounds like you, an honest and interested writer.

Preview

- ○ **Key Stylistic Reminders**
- ○ **Using Anecdotes**
- ○ **Writing with Metaphors**
- ○ **Using Repetition**
- ○ **Using Strong, Colorful Words**
- ○ **Avoiding the Ailments of Style**

"Have something to say and say it as clearly as you can. That is the only secret of style."

—Matthew Arnold

Key **Stylistic** Reminders

What really makes a good writing style? Not much. As odd as it may sound, the less you try to add style to your writing, the more stylistic it will probably be. Style is not using flowery language, nor is it trying to sound as if you are the supreme authority on your subject.

Your writing will always be in style if you follow three simple rules: (1) Be purposeful. (2) Be clear. (3) Be sincere. (See page 26 for another guide to good writing.)

1. **Be purposeful.** Writer Kurt Vonnegut states, "It is the genuine caring [about a subject], and not your games with language, which will be the most compelling and seductive element in your style." The bottom line is this: If you expect to produce effective writing, select subjects that interest you.

2. **Be clear.** Keep things simple, orderly, and direct in your writing. Many of our best writers such as Mark Twain and Rachel Carson have been plain talkers, speaking directly and clearly to their readers. Stylistic writing doesn't play games with readers, making them try to figure things out. Instead, it is easy to understand and follow from start to finish.

3. **Be sincere.** Writing works best when it sounds like one person (you) sincerely communicating with another person. It doesn't sound uncertain, phony, or pushy. Nor does it try to impress readers with a lot of ten-dollar words. It's honest and heartfelt and rings true for the reader.

 Why is it important to write with style?

"Do so, if for no other reason, out of respect for your readers," says Kurt Vonnegut. If your writing is dull, your readers will think that you don't care about your subject, or about them. They, in turn, will show little interest in your writing. On the other hand, if you speak honestly in your writing and engage your readers' interest, they will appreciate what you have to say.

Using Anecdotes

Writer Donald Murray suggests that you put people in your writing whose actions communicate important ideas. Brief "slices of life" add a spark to your writing. They allow you to **show** your readers something in a lively and interesting manner rather than just to **tell** them matter-of-factly.

Take NOTE

"Anecdote" is the more technical term for brief "slices of life." The *American Heritage College Dictionary* (3rd edition) defines an anecdote as "a short account of an interesting or humorous incident."

Showing ✎ In the following anecdote, student writer Sheila Maldonado shares a slice of life about her Coney Island (New York) neighborhood.

> **Under the boardwalk, a few homeless people find shelter; they hang up sheets, lay out their old clothes, and stack up plastic bags full of empty cans and other things they've collected on the streets. Even though the boardwalk doesn't provide them with walls, it does give them a roof over their heads. In the winter, they make fires on the beach and keep warm in tents. Some of them even have dogs, strays that probably approached them for food one day and stayed.**

Telling: This brief story brings part of Coney Island alive by *showing* it to readers. It is much more revealing than simply *telling* readers, "Some homeless people live around Coney Island."

Showing ✎ In this anecdote, professional writer Mary Anne Hoff shares the story of a visitor to her childhood home, North Dakota.

> **His "bee-yoo-tee-ful" stopped me short. This lanky Mr. Sophisticate from outside Paris was describing the North Dakota prairie. The wild grasses and big sky, the black-eyed Susan and sagebrush, the hum of dog days were new to him. Now all he could say as he lay exhausted in Mother's recliner was "bee-yoo-tee-ful."**
>
> **Two days later we all huddled around a book about Paris, every picture in full color. Suddenly our guest pointed to a photo and repeated "bee-yoo-tee-ful." It was the Champs Elysees at night. The Champs Elysees and the North Dakota prairie described with the same word? My prairie and a Parisian street linked? That was when I knew I would like him.**

Telling: Note how much more effective this *showing* story is than a *telling* statement such as "A visitor helped me see my North Dakota home in a new way."

"Metaphors create tension and excitement by producing new connections, and in doing so reveal a truth about the world we had not previously recognized." —Gabriele Rico

Using **Metaphors**

A metaphor compares an idea or an image in your writing to something new and brings your basic ideas to life for your readers.

To Create a Picture @ In the examples that follow, note how the basic ideas become a powerful picture when they are stated metaphorically.

> **Basic idea:** My performance was a real disappointment.
>
> **Metaphor:** My performance was a real choke sandwich, all peanut butter and no jelly.
>
> **Basic idea:** The sunset changed the color of our rivers.
>
> **Metaphor:** Our rivers were red and purple streaks of sunset.

To Expand an Idea @ Because a metaphor can unify ideas in a series of sentences, extending a metaphor can help you to expand and clarify your ideas. Note how the metaphor (comparing family relationships to fabric) is extended in the following passage.

> **Metaphor:** My family is a rich tapestry of personalities bound together by affection and respect.
>
> **Extended:** My family is a rich **tapestry** of personalities bound together by affection and respect. But my family was at **loose ends** last summer, at least until the reunion in August. Whatever feelings had been **torn** over my brother's divorce, whatever emotions had **frayed** over my grandmother's lingering illness, they were **mended** at the county park under a grove of red oak trees.

✱ Be careful with this technique. Your writing will sound unnatural or forced if you use too many extended metaphors.

HELP FILE

Make sure your metaphors are original and clear. Be especially careful not to *mix* your metaphors. For example, the reporter who wrote "In the final debate, Senator Jones fielded each of his opponent's accusations and eventually scored the winning shot" has created a mixed metaphor. He carelessly shifts from one comparison (*fielded* in baseball) to another (*the winning shot* in basketball).

Using **Repetition**

There's a good chance that your writing will be in style if you use repetition for the purpose of rhythm, emphasis, or unity. Just remember to keep the repeated words or ideas *parallel,* or stated in the same way. (The examples below show you parallelism in action. Also see page 432.) As with any stylistic technique, repetition is effective only when used selectively.

For Rhythm and Balance ℰ Notice how the patterns of words or phrases flow smoothly from one to the next in the following sentences:

> At one time or another, **the Austrians, the Russians,** and **the British** fought against Napoleon's army.

> That scrumptious sandwich contains **tender ham, crisp lettuce,** and **juicy tomatoes.**

> Jumal wants to **graduate from college, become a volunteer medic,** and **work in the African sub-Sahara.**

For Emphasis and Effect ℰ Notice the intensity created by repetition of a basic sentence structure in the following passages:

> Dad and Mr. Harmel danced in the rain. **They waltzed cheek to cheek; they schottisched side by side; they do-si-doed arm in arm.** Because the drought had broken, the wheat would grow. —Mary Anne Hoff

> **We shall fight on the beaches, we shall fight on the landing grounds, we shall fight in the fields and in the streets, we shall fight in the hills; we shall never surrender.** —Winston Churchill

For Unity and Organization ℰ Note in the passage below how the use of repetition in the beginning sentences unifies and helps organize all of the ideas:

> **Let the smell of mint touch me.** I am kneeling along a little stream, the water numbing my hands as I reach for a trout.
> **Let me see a certain color** and I am standing beside the threshing machine, grain cascading through my hands. The seeds we planted when snow was spitting down have multiplied a hundred times, returning in a stream of bright gold, still warm with the sunlight of the fields.
> **Let me hear an odd whirring.** I am deep in the woods, following an elusive sound, looking in vain for a last passenger pigeon, a feathered lightning I have never seen, unwilling to believe no person will ever see one again. —Ben Logan

Using **Strong, Colorful** Words

Suppose, at a basketball game, you see a soaring power-forward slam home a dunk shot. Then, suppose you write "The player scored a basket." How effectively do you think you have communicated your thought? Obviously, not very well. By using specific, colorful words, you can create clear and colorful word pictures for your reader.

Specific Nouns @ Some nouns are **general** (*vegetable, pants, computer*) and give the reader a vague, uninteresting picture. Other nouns are more **specific** (*okra, corduroys, laptop*) and give the reader a much clearer, more detailed picture. In the chart that follows, the italicized word at the top of each column is a general noun. The second word in each column is more specific. The third term is more specific yet. Finally, the word at the bottom of each column is a very specific noun. These last nouns are the type that can make a big difference in your writing.

person	*place*	*thing*	*idea*
woman	landmark	drink	belief
scientist	national landmark	coffee	strong belief
Marie Curie	Mount Rushmore	cappuccino	conviction

Vivid Verbs @ Like nouns, verbs can be too general to create a vivid word picture. For example, the verb *looked* does not say the same thing as *stared, glared, glanced, peeked,* or *inspected*. The statement "Ms. Shaw *glared* at the two goof-offs" is much more vivid and interesting than "Ms. Shaw *looked* at the two goof-offs."

- Whenever possible, use a verb that is strong enough to stand alone without the help of an adverb.

  A verb and an adverb: Hashim sat down on the couch.
  A vivid verb: Hashim plopped on the couch.

- Avoid overusing the "be" verbs (*is, are, was, were . . .*). Often a better verb can be made from another word in the same sentence.

  A "be" verb: Yolanda is someone who plans for the future.
  A stronger verb: Yolanda plans for the future.

- Use active rather than passive verbs.

  A passive verb: Another deep pass was launched by Gerald.
  An active verb: Gerald launched another deep pass.

- Use verbs that show rather than tell.

  A verb that tells: Greta is very tall.
  A verb that shows: Greta towers over her teammates.

Specific Adjectives ℮ Use precise adjectives to describe the nouns in your writing. Strong adjectives can help make the nouns you choose even more interesting and clearer to the reader. For example, describing your uncle's new car as a "*sleek, red* convertible" offers your reader a definite mental image of the car.

○ Avoid using adjectives that carry little meaning: *neat, big, pretty, small, cute, fun, bad, nice, good, great, funny,* and so on.

> **Overused adjective:** The big house on the square belongs to an architect.
>
> **Specific adjective:** The Victorian house on the square belongs to an architect.

○ Use adjectives selectively. If your writing contains too many adjectives, they will simply get in the way and lose their effectiveness.

> **Too many adjectives:** A tall, shocking column of thick, yellow smoke marked the exact spot where the unexpected explosion had occurred.
>
> **Selective use:** A column of thick, yellow smoke marked the spot where the explosion had occurred.

Specific Adverbs ℮ Use adverbs when you think they can add detail or color to a sentence. For example, the statement "Mayor Meyer *reluctantly* agreed to meet the protesters" presents a clearer picture than "Mayor Meyer agreed to meet the protesters." Don't, however, use a verb and an adverb when a single vivid verb would be better. (See page 130.)

The "Right" Words ℮ The words in your writing should not only be specific and colorful, they should also have the right *connotation,* or feeling. The connotation of a word is the meaning or feeling it suggests beyond its dictionary meaning. Note how the underlined words in the passage below suggest negative, almost frightening feelings about the subject, the writer's new teacher.

> A small woman stood at the front of the class fixing me with a look of hostile disapproval. She was as colorless as the classroom. Dressed in a black skirt and drab cardigan, she wore no makeup and even her short straight hair seemed to have no particular color. She leveled her pointer directly at me and unleashed a stream of angry words. Janine said something, clearly in my defense, and the pointer went down. The hostile stare did not.
>
> —Ruth Reichl

Avoiding the **Ailments of Style**

Primer Style ℮ If your writing contains many short sentences, one right after another, it may sound like a grade school textbook:

> Our policy for makeup assignments is unfair. The teachers go strictly by the rules. They don't care about the amount of work we have. They don't care about our other activities.

The Cure: The main cure is to combine some of your ideas into longer, smoother-reading sentences. (See page 91.) Here's the revised passage:

> When it comes to makeup assignments, our teachers go strictly by the rules. They don't care about the amount of work we have or about our other activities.

Passive Style ℮ If your writing seems slow-moving and impersonal, you may have used too many passive verbs. With passive verbs, the subject of the sentence receives the action. Here's an example written in the passive voice:

> Our biology teacher was loved by us. He was often asked for extra help, which was always given. He was visited by his students before and after school and often was at the center of some lively discussions.

The Cure: Flip the sentence. Make the subject give or do the action, not receive it. Here's the same passage written in the active voice:

> We loved our biology teacher. We were always asking for extra help, and he was always willing to give it. Students often dropped in before and after school to visit and share in some lively discussions.

Insecurity ℮ Does your writing contain many qualifiers (*to be perfectly honest, it seems to me, maybe*) or intensifiers (*really, truly, totally*)? These words and phrases suggest that you lack confidence in your ideas:

> I totally and completely agree with Mr. Grim about changing the school's dress code, but that's only my opinion.

The Cure: Visualize yourself standing before an audience and say exactly what you mean. Here is the revised version:

> I agree with Mr. Grim about changing our school's dress code.

[HOT LINK] For other ailments of style, see "Flowery Language," "Jargon," "Wordiness," and "Cliche." (See pages 87-88.)

"You always feel that you could
have put more into [your writing]."

—Emily Carr

Writer's
RESOURCE

Are you a free spirit, ready to write on just about any topic, at any time? Or are you more systematic, a clock puncher, interested in keeping track of each writing move as you go along? Then again, are you a detail person, always asking yourself, "What is my *purpose*? Who is my *audience*? Should I add a *modifier*?" Or are you a visionary, a dreamer, always looking for different forms of writing to experiment with?

In all probability, you don't fit just one of these writing personalities. Maybe you're a free-spirited visionary, or a free-spirited detail person. (Is that possible?) No matter how you approach writing, you'll find valuable information in this chapter.

Preview

- Thinking and Writing Moves
- Writing Topics
- Writing Techniques
- Writing Terms
- A Survey of Writing Forms

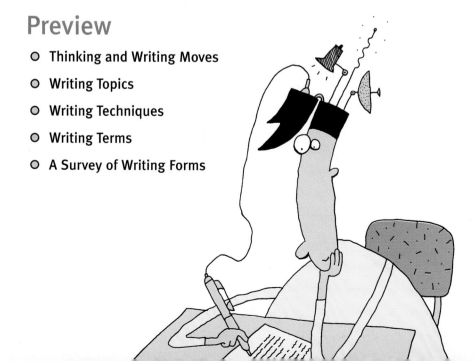

Thinking and Writing Moves

Writing is really thinking on paper. For example, you start a writing project by *gathering* information. Soon after, you *focus* and *organize* your thoughts, and so on. Use this chart as a basic thinking guide whenever you write essays, reports, and research papers.

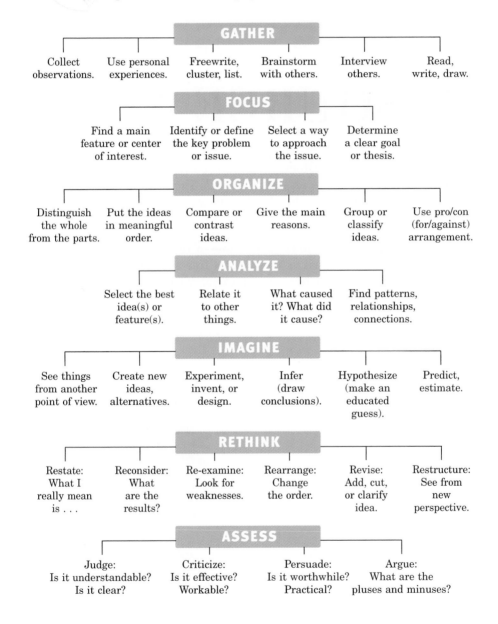

GATHER

| Collect observations. | Use personal experiences. | Freewrite, cluster, list. | Brainstorm with others. | Interview others. | Read, write, draw. |

FOCUS

| Find a main feature or center of interest. | Identify or define the key problem or issue. | Select a way to approach the issue. | Determine a clear goal or thesis. |

ORGANIZE

| Distinguish the whole from the parts. | Put the ideas in meaningful order. | Compare or contrast ideas. | Give the main reasons. | Group or classify ideas. | Use pro/con (for/against) arrangement. |

ANALYZE

| Select the best idea(s) or feature(s). | Relate it to other things. | What caused it? What did it cause? | Find patterns, relationships, connections. |

IMAGINE

| See things from another point of view. | Create new ideas, alternatives. | Experiment, invent, or design. | Infer (draw conclusions). | Hypothesize (make an educated guess). | Predict, estimate. |

RETHINK

| Restate: What I really mean is . . . | Reconsider: What are the results? | Re-examine: Look for weaknesses. | Rearrange: Change the order. | Revise: Add, cut, or clarify idea. | Restructure: See from new perspective. |

ASSESS

| Judge: Is it understandable? Is it clear? | Criticize: Is it effective? Workable? | Persuade: Is it worthwhile? Practical? | Argue: What are the pluses and minuses? |

Writing Topics

Whenever you need a writing topic for a narrative or an essay, review these lists for ideas. *Tip:* Compile your own list of possible writing ideas in a notebook. (See pages 43-45.)

Descriptive

Person: friend, teacher, relative, classmate, minister (priest, rabbi), coworker, neighbor, teammate, coach, entertainer, politician, sister, brother, bus driver, an older person, a younger person, someone who spends time with you, someone you wish you were like

Place: school, neighborhood, the beach, the park, the hangout, the bus stop, your room, the locker room, a restaurant, the library, a church, a stadium, the cafeteria, the hallway

Thing: a billboard, a photograph, a poster, a computer, a video game, a musical instrument, a tool, a pet, a bus, a boat, a book, a car, a cat, a dog, a drawing, a collection, a junk drawer

Narrative

During school: first memories, lunch hour, stage fright, learning to drive, odd field trips, asking for help, the big game, the school play, a school project

After school: just last week, on the bus, learning a lesson, a kind act, homesick, a big mistake, a reunion, getting lost, being late, Friday night, an embarrassing moment, staying overnight, getting hurt, success, a practical joke, being a friend, a family visit, on your own, moving, building a _____, the first day of _____, the last day of _____, a miserable time, cleaning up

Expository

How to . . . surf the Net, make spaghetti sauce, get a job, entertain a child, get in shape, study for a test, conserve energy, take a good picture

How to operate . . . control . . . run . . .
How to choose . . . select . . . pick . . .
How to build . . . grow . . . create . . .
How to fix . . . clean . . . wash . . .
How to protect . . . warn . . . save . . .

The causes of . . . global warming, snoring, inflation, shinsplints, tornadoes, urban sprawl, poor grades, overpopulation

Kinds of . . . music, crowds, friends, teachers, love, rules, compliments, commercials, dreams, happiness, neighbors, pollution, taxes, heroes, vacations, pain, communication

Definition of . . . best friend, poverty, generation gap, greed, the metric system, loyalty, a newsgroup, bioengineering, a team, literature, humor, courage, pressure, faith, personality, entertainment

Persuasive

For / Against . . . study halls, donating organs, capital punishment, the current speed limit, gun control, courtroom television, current graduation requirements, final exams, a career in the armed forces, teen centers, open lunch hours, girls on the football team, limited work hours for teens during the school year

Writing Techniques

Review the following writing techniques and then experiment with some of them in your own stories and essays.

Allusion @ A reference to a familiar person, place, thing, or event.

> I have feet that put Steven Spielberg's ET to shame. They are a tangle of toes held together by bunions.

Analogy @ A comparison of ideas or objects that are completely different but that are alike in one important way.

> Benjamin Franklin witnessed the first successful balloon flight. When asked what good such an invention was, Franklin answered, "What good is a newborn baby?" (Both are valuable simply for being, and no one knows what the future holds for either one.)

Anecdote @ A brief story used to illustrate or make a point. (See page 127.)

> In a passenger train compartment, a lady lit a cigarette, saying to Sir Thomas Beecham, a famous orchestra conductor, "I'm sure you don't object."
> "Not at all," replied Beecham, "provided you don't mind if I'm sick."
> "I don't think you know who I am," the lady pointed out. "I'm one of the railroad director's wives."
> "Madam," said the conductor, "if you were the director's *only* wife, I should still be sick." (The story makes a point about the unpleasantness of secondhand smoke.)

Antithesis @ Using opposite ideas in the same thought or sentence to emphasize a point. (See page 431.)

> There was no possibility of being hired at the town's cotton gin or lumber mill, but maybe there was a way to make the two factories work for her.
> —Maya Angelou, *Wouldn't Take Nothing for My Journey Now*

Colloquialism @ A common word or phrase suitable for ordinary, everyday conversation but not for formal speech or writing.

> you-all listen up   run this by her . . .   no way

Exaggeration @ An overstatement or stretching of the truth to emphasize a point. (See *hyperbole* and *overstatement*.)

> The Danes are so full of *joie de vivre* [joy of life] that they practically sweat it.   —Bill Bryson, *Neither Here nor There*

Flashback @ A technique in which a writer interrupts a story to go back and explain an earlier time or event for the purpose of making something in the present more clear.

> In *The Outsiders*, readers first meet Ponyboy as he leaves a movie theater and is jumped by gang members. Later, the author goes back and explains Ponyboy's background.

Foreshadowing @ Hints or clues that suggest what will happen next or later in a story.

> Now that she was out of the sun, Caro's eyes adjusted to the dimness. Someone had been there after all. There were markings on the walls, random doodlings as if someone had occupied him- or herself by drawing circles and jagged lines of lightning and stick figures. . . . There had been a terrible rain—the slanting dashes couldn't be anything else.   —Ardath Mayhar

Note: Later in the story, this bit of foreshadowing is borne out when Caro finds the skeletal remains of a Native American girl inside the cave.

Hyperbole @ (hi-pur´-ba-lē) Exaggeration used to emphasize a point.

> We didn't need to [read] because my father has read everything . . . and people in town have said that talking to him about anything is better than reading three books.   —Cynthia Marshall Rich, "My Sister's Marriage"

Irony @ An expression in which the author says one thing but means just the opposite. (See page 237.)

> But then I was lucky enough to come down with the disease of the moment in the Hamptons, which was Lyme disease.
>   —Kurt Vonnegut, *Fates Worse Than Death*

Juxtaposition @ Putting two words or ideas close together to create a contrasting of ideas or an ironic meaning.

> Just remember, we're all in this alone.   —Lily Tomlin

Local color @ The use of details that are common in a certain place. (The following passage lists foods common to small-town Southern life.)

> Folks had already brought over more cakes and pies, and platters of fried chicken and ham, and their good china bowls full of string beans, butterbeans, okra, and tomatoes.   —Olive Ann Burns, *Cold Sassy Tree*

Metaphor @ A figure of speech that compares two things without using the words *like* or *as*.

> Perfectionism is the voice of the oppressor, the enemy of the people.
>   —Anne Lamott, *Bird by Bird*

Overstatement @ An exaggeration or a stretching of the truth. (See *exaggeration* and *hyperbole*.)

> I bet you could set off dynamite in an A & P and the people would by and large keep reaching and checking oatmeal off their lists and muttering "Let me see, there was a third thing, began with an A, asparagus, no, ah, yes, applesauce!"   —John Updike, "A & P"

Oxymoron @ A technique in which two words with opposite meanings are put together for a special effect.

> war for peace   black light   controlled chaos

Paradox @ A statement that is true even though it seems to be saying two opposite things.

> **I shall always bear the deformities with which I have been blessed.**

Parallelism @ Repeating similar grammatical structures (words, phrases, or sentences) to give writing rhythm.

> **All this waste happens before any lid is popped, any can is opened, or any seal is broken.** —Allison Rozendaal, student writer

Personification @ A figure of speech in which a nonhuman thing is given human characteristics.

> **And what I remember next is how the moon, the pale moon with its one yellow eye . . . stared through the pink plastic curtains.**
> —Sandra Cisneros, "One Holy Night"

Pun @ A phrase that uses words that sound the same in a way that gives them a funny effect.

> **I have come to believe that opposing gravity is something not be taken—uh, lightly.** —Daniel Pinkwater, "Why I Don't Fly"

Sensory details @ Details that are experienced through the senses. They help readers to see, feel, smell, taste, and hear what is being described.

> **A tall, hawk-faced woman, her hair cropped off just below the ears, peered suspiciously at us. The sour smell of disinfectant came rushing toward me; behind the woman I could see a line of girls in blue filing silently up a staircase. . . . I shivered.** —Ruth Reichl, *Tender at the Bone*

Simile @ A figure of speech that compares two things using *like* or *as*.

> **They [the old men] had hands like claws, and their knees were twisted like the old thorn trees.** —William Butler Yeats

Slang @ Informal words or phrases used by a particular group of people among themselves.

> **dis   ain't   chill out**

Symbol @ A concrete object used to represent an idea. (See page 241.)

> **hourglass = time passing   dove = peace**

Synecdoche @ Using part of something to represent the whole.

> **Idle hands are the devil's playground.** (*Hands* represent the whole person.)

Understatement @ The opposite of exaggeration. By using very calm language, an author can bring special attention to an object or an idea.

> **He [our new dog] turned out to be a good traveler, and except for an interruption caused by my wife's falling out of the car, the journey went very well.** —E. B. White, "A Report in Spring"

Writing Terms

On the next two pages you will find a glossary of terms used to describe different aspects of the writing process.

Argumentation: Writing or speaking in which a point of view is debated.

Arrangement: The order in which details are placed in a piece of writing.

Audience: Those people who read or hear what you have written.

Balance: The arranging of words or phrases so they are parallel—given equal emphasis in a passage.

Body: The main part of a piece of writing, supporting or developing the thesis statement.

Brainstorming: Collecting ideas by thinking freely about all the possibilities; used most often with groups.

Case study: The in-depth story of one individual whose experiences speak for the experiences of a larger group.

Central idea: The main point of a piece of writing, often stated in a thesis statement or a topic sentence.

Closing sentence: The sentence that summarizes the point being made in a paragraph.

Coherence: The logical arrangement of ideas in writing.

Deductive reasoning: A logical presentation of information in which a main idea is stated early in a piece of writing and supporting details follow.

Description: Writing that paints a colorful picture of a person, a place, or a thing.

Details: Words used to describe a person, convince an audience, explain a process, and so on; to be effective, details should appeal to the senses.

Editing: (See pages 75-79.)

Emphasis: Placing greater stress on the most important idea in a piece of writing by giving it special treatment.

Essay: A multiparagraph composition in which ideas on a special topic are presented, explained, argued for, or described in an interesting way.

Exposition: Writing that explains. (See page 235.)

Extended definition: Writing that offers an in-depth examination of a concept including personal definitions, negative definitions (what it is not), uses of the concept, and so on.

Figurative language: Language that goes beyond the normal meaning of the words used.

Focus: Concentrating on a specific aspect of a subject in writing. (Often called the *thesis*.)

Freewriting: Writing openly, without strict structure; focused freewriting is writing openly on a specific topic or angle.

Generalization: An idea emphasizing the general characteristics rather than the specific details of a subject.

Grammar: Rules that govern the standard structure and features of a language.

Idiom: A phrase or an expression that means something different from what the words actually say (using *over his head* for *didn't understand*).

Illustration: Using an experience to make a point or clarify an idea.

Inductive reasoning: A logical presentation of information in which specific examples and details lead up to the main concluding idea.

Inverted sentence: A sentence in which the normal word order is reversed or switched; usually the verb comes before the subject.

Journal: Personal exploratory writing that often contains impressions and reflections; a journal is often a source of ideas for writing.

Limiting the subject: Narrowing a general subject to a specific topic that is suitable for a writing assignment.

Literal: The actual, dictionary meaning of a word; language that means what it appears to mean.

Loaded words: Words that are slanted for or against the subject.

Logic: Correct reasoning; correctly using facts, examples, and reasons to support your point.

Modifier: A word, a phrase, or a clause that limits or describes another word or group of words.

Narration: Writing that tells a story or recounts an event.

Objective: Relating information in an impersonal manner without feelings or opinions.

Observation: Paying close attention to people, places, things, and events to collect details for later use.

Overview: A general idea of what is or will be covered in a piece of writing.

Personal narrative: Writing that covers an event in the writer's life.

Persuasion: Writing that is meant to change a reader's thinking or action.

Poetic license: The freedom a writer has to bend the rules of writing to achieve a certain effect.

Point of view: The position or angle from which a story is told. (See page 239.)

Premise: A statement or central idea that serves as the basis of a discussion or a debate.

Process: A method of doing something that involves several steps or stages.

Profile: Writing that reveals an individual or re-creates a time period, using interviews and research.

Proofreading: (See pages 75-79.)

Prose: Writing in the usual sentence form. Prose becomes poetry when it takes on rhyme and rhythm.

Purpose: The specific reason a person has for writing; the goal of writing.

Reminiscence: Writing that focuses on a memorable past experience.

Report: A multiparagraph form of writing that results from gathering and organizing facts on a topic.

Revision: Changing a piece of writing to improve the content (ideas).

Subjective: Thinking or writing that includes personal feelings, attitudes, and opinions.

Syntax: The order and relationship of words in a sentence.

Theme: The message in a piece of writing (lengthy writings may have several themes). (See page 241.)

Thesis statement: A statement of the purpose, intent, or main idea of an essay.

Tone: The writer's attitude toward her or his subject; a writer's tone can be serious, sarcastic, solemn, and so on.

Topic: The specific subject for a writing assignment.

Transitions: Words or phrases that connect or tie ideas together. (See page 104.)

Unity: A sense of oneness in writing in which each sentence helps to develop the main idea.

Universal: A topic or an idea that applies to everyone.

Usage: The way in which individuals use language; language is generally considered to be standard (formal and informal) or nonstandard.

Vivid details: Details that appeal to the senses and help the reader see, feel, smell, taste, or hear the subject being written about.

A Survey of **Writing Forms**

The chart that follows classifies the forms of writing covered in this handbook. You can learn a great deal about writing by experimenting with a variety of forms.

PERSONAL WRITING	(See pages 143-154.)
Remembering & Sharing *(Exploring Experiences)* Promotes writing fluency.	Journals • Reminiscences • Logs • Diaries • Personal Essays and Narratives • Listing • Freewriting • Clustering • Brainstorming
SUBJECT WRITING	(See pages 155-166.)
Searching & Reporting *(Investigating)* Broadens writing experiences.	Descriptions • Profiles • Case Studies • Firsthand Experiences • Summary Reports • Eyewitness Accounts • Observation Reports • Personal Research Reports • Interviews
CREATIVE WRITING	(See pages 167-184.)
Inventing & Imitating *(Reshaping Ideas)* Encourages creativity.	Poems • Plays • Stories • Fictionalized Journal Entries • Monologues
PERSUASIVE WRITING	(See pages 115-123 and 185-198.)
Arguing & Evaluating *(Judging the Worth of Something)* Reinforces complex thinking.	Persuasive Essays • Pet Peeves • Personal Commentaries • Editorials • Essays of Argumentation • Essays of Opposing Ideas
ACADEMIC WRITING	(See pages 199-213 and 245-295.)
Informing & Analyzing *(Shaping Information into Clear Essays)* Develops organizing skills.	Expository Essays • Process Essays • Essays of Definition • Cause/Effect Essays • Problem/Solution Essays • Summaries • Comparison/Contrast Essays • Research Papers
WRITING ABOUT LITERATURE	(See pages 215-243.)
Understanding & Interpreting *(Reacting to Texts)* Fosters critical reading.	Journal Entries • Letters to the Author • Character Sketches • Book Reviews • Literary Analyses • Dialogues
WORKPLACE WRITING	(See pages 297-321.)
Questioning & Answering *(Writing to Get a Job Done)* Builds real-world writing skills.	Letters of Inquiry • Résumés • Memos • Letters of Application • Messages • Follow-up Letters • Writing Instructions

The FORMS of WRITING

> "Writing is not apart from living.
> Writing is a kind of double living."
>
> —Catherine Drinker Bowen

PERSONAL Writing

Suppose you've been given the following assignment: Write about an important experience in your life. If you're like most students, you may think, "Write about my life? What's there to write about? I wake up, go to school, come home, do homework, watch TV, and go to bed. Not much to write about." But believe it or not, your life *is* worth writing about, no matter how ordinary it may seem at times.

Once you get into personal writing, you'll realize that your thoughts and experiences are as interesting as anyone else's. And you'll also realize that this is just a starting point. You'll learn to turn these thoughts and experiences inside out and see them in new ways. You'll dig deeper to discover something more meaningful and exciting. This may sound like complicated stuff, but it really isn't. Personal writing is simply an effective way to examine your world. This chapter includes guidelines and samples that will help you get the most out of your personal writing.

Preview

- Journal Writing
- Personal Narrative
- Extended Personal Narrative
- Personal Essay
- Assessment Rubric

Journal Writing

It doesn't take much to keep a journal: a notebook, a handy supply of your favorite pens or pencils (or a computer), and a promise on your part to write regularly. The last point is the key. Journal writing works best when it is done on a regular basis.

If you get into a writing routine, you will begin to discover meaning in your writing. You'll begin to enter the world of your inner thoughts; and in time, you'll feel a little sharper, as if your senses have been fine-tuned. A squeaky car door will no longer go unnoticed. You'll begin to wonder, "How long has it been squeaky, why hasn't anyone fixed it, and what else is 'squeaky' in my life?"

Diary **and** Journal

You may have kept a diary at some time. Journals and diaries have similar purposes. Read the samples that follow. The first entry comes from Kate Kullberg's **diary** when she was a middle-school student.

> Well, I had a great birthday! At school on Monday, Mom brought caramel brownies. That was cool. That night, Ron, Barb, and Allison came over for dinner. I opened presents after dinner. I got lots of great stuff.

The second entry comes from Kate's **journal** when she was a sophomore in high school.

> Do you ever feel as though your life is right on the verge of drastically changing? I feel like that at this very moment as I sit here in my room—my last few hours of being 15. I feel like I'm about to cross a bridge, not a huge bridge like the kind that makes you feel freaked out, but a medium one that makes your stomach drop a little. I really feel like I'm ready to take the first step across, to be given some of my first chances at freedom and independence. And it all starts with the number SIXTEEN. A driver's license helps, too.

Both entries focus on a birthday, but unlike the diary entry, the journal entry reveals more of the student's inner thoughts and feelings and shows her growth as a writer. She has found her own writing voice and uses effective details to describe her feelings about becoming 16.

HELP FILE

In the best of all worlds, journal writing will become a very important part of your life, right up there with good friends and good food. But we'll settle for something more down to earth: that through journal writing you will begin to feel more comfortable with the act of writing and more confident in your ability to express yourself.

Journal-Writing TIPS

There's an old joke about a tourist in New York who asks a cab driver, "How do I get to the Metropolitan Opera House?" And the cabbie replies, "Practice, practice, practice." Old joke . . . great advice. Whether you're involved in music, sports, or writing, you have to practice the necessary skills over and over again.

Journal writing is a great way to practice writing because it is free from the gravitational pull of grades and expectations. You can work on your writing fluency, experiment with different forms, or try out new styles. Listed below are a few tips to get you started.

- **Write nonstop.** Your goal should be to write for at least 10-15 minutes at a time. If you get stuck, write "I'm drawing a blank" until something comes to mind.

- **Focus on ideas.** The real satisfaction in keeping a journal is making new discoveries. Make that your goal.

- **Always date your entries.** And make sure to read them from time to time to see how far you've come.

- **Push an idea as far as you can.** You'll discover new thoughts and feelings when you write about an idea from many different angles. (Keep asking yourself *why* as you write.)

- **Experiment in your writing.** Write like your favorite author or like someone you know. Write in a foreign language or in jazzy street language. Write to make yourself laugh or to give yourself a pep talk. Write using your own rules.

Other Types of Journals

Learning Log @ Writing in a learning log or class journal gets you more actively involved in your course work. It helps you make important facts and ideas part of your own thinking. (See pages 398-399 for more.)

Response Journal @ Writing in a reader-response journal enriches each of your reading experiences—whether you are reading the newest title by your favorite author, an article in a magazine, or a chapter in a class text.

Dialogue Journal @ In a dialogue journal, you and a partner carry on a conversation (first one person writes, then the other) about experiences you have had, books you have read, and issues that concern you.

Journal-Writing Ideas

Most of the ideas for your journal writing will come from your personal experiences. However, when nothing personal moves you to write, use the experiences of a friend or a family member, or page through a newspaper or a magazine for ideas. On those occasions when you still draw a blank, consider the following starting points.

Open-Ended Sentences @ Complete one of the following open-ended sentences and then continue to write about whatever topic pops up. Write about it from as many angles as possible.

> I wonder . . .
> I question whether . . .
> I hope . . .
> I was surprised to find that . . .
> I wish . . .
> I decided to . . . instead of . . .
> If only . . .
> I need help with . . .
> I have learned that . . .
> I should make a contract with myself to . . .
> They say . . . but my experience tells me . . .
> I never thought I would see the day . . .
> I was once . . . but now I am . . .

Unsent Letters @ Write a letter to anyone (a friend, an ancestor, a famous person) to see what develops. Share recent experiences, ask questions, reflect upon a newsworthy event, and so on.

Story Starters @ Write a quick rough draft of a story based directly or indirectly on something you see, hear, feel, or happen to be thinking about. Perhaps your growling stomach gets you thinking about lunch, so write a story that starts in a kitchen, a cafeteria, or a fast-food restaurant.

Essentials-of-Life Checklist @ Review the "Essentials" checklist in the handbook (see page 44) for possible writing ideas. Consider the first category, *clothing*. It could lead to a journal entry about . . .

> the clothes you are wearing,
> the wardrobe of a friend,
> present fashion trends, or
> what you will be wearing 10 years from now.

WRITING GUIDELINES
Personal Narrative

In a personal narrative, you re-create an incident that happened to you over a short period of time. This incident could be an emotional experience, a silly or serious event, or a frightening encounter. Be sure to include enough specific details to make the incident come alive for your readers. If you can't remember everything, fill in the gaps with details that seem right. (The pros do this all the time.)

◼ PREWRITING

1. **Choosing a Subject . . .** Think of a specific incident from your life that you think will appeal to your readers. (See page 135 for ideas.)

2. **Gathering Details . . .** Jot down all of the ideas and details that come to mind when you think of the experience. If necessary, collect more information from other people involved in the event.

3. **Focusing Your Efforts . . .** Decide on a particular feeling or mood that you want to convey in your story. For example, do you want to surprise your readers, make them laugh, have them share in your sorrow or fear?

◼ WRITING AND REVISING

4. **Hooking Your Reader . . .** First, try to start right in the middle of the action or introduce the people in your story and get them talking. Build the action by adding specific details, feelings, suspense—whatever it takes to pull in the reader.

5. **Improving Your Writing . . .** Read over your first draft (silently and aloud) for overall effectiveness: *Have you said everything you intended to say? Will your reader be able to follow your story, including any changes in time, place, or speaker? Does your story entertain, surprise, or make a point?* Revise your writing as necessary.
   [HOT LINK] See "Assessment Rubric," page 154, for a helpful revising and editing guide.

◼ EDITING AND PROOFREADING

6. **Checking for Style and Accuracy . . .** Review your revised writing for style, making sure that all of your sentences read smoothly and clearly and that you have used the best words to express your ideas. Then check your work for spelling, grammar, and punctuation errors.

7. **Preparing a Final Copy . . .** Write or keyboard a neat final copy of your narrative; proofread your copy before sharing it.

Sample **Personal Narrative**

In this personal narrative, student writer Matt Vice focuses on a recent event in his life, a memorable football game. The strong sensory details make this event come alive for readers.

The Game

The narrative starts right in the middle of the action.

The rain hit my helmet lightly, like a soft tapping on a door. I pulled my chin strap tightly around my face and snapped it on the other side. Forty-three teammates standing beside me started to jog, workhorses on the move, the clip-clop of our spikes the only sound.

As we approached the field, the rain picked up. I looked at my teammates after hearing the cheers from our fans. I said to myself, "This is why I play football; this is what it's all about." As we burst through the gate, the roar of the crowd engulfed us. Our coach gathered us together on the sidelines and barked the game plan to us. Forty-four sets of eyes locked on him as if we were hypnotized. We broke the huddle, and the receiving team trotted out onto the field.

> "I said to myself, 'This is why I play football; this is what it's all about.'"

The ball was kicked. It soared high above our heads as the two teams ran full charge at each other. I found my man and fixed on him like a missile locking on to its target. The return man was hit hard and brought down around the 50-yard line.

This paragraph serves as a transition between two parts of the game.

The crowd was yelling; the cheerleaders were pumped. I heard the chanting fade into the background as the game progressed. Two quarters passed, then three. Hard-hitting crunches and cracks could be heard play after play. Each team traded scores.

With less than a minute left in the game, we had a 24-to-17 lead. The rain was running down my helmet like an overflowing gutter. With time running out, the opposing quarterback dropped back. The crowd went silent as he passed to an open receiver in the end zone. Everything seemed to go into slow motion as the ball dropped securely into his hands. I stood openmouthed, dumbfounded, and barely breathing. They made the extra point, so the score was tied, which meant overtime.

The opposing team won the coin toss and went first. The official put the ball on the 10-yard line. In three short plays, they scored again, putting them ahead by six. I felt like I was in a bad dream. After the extra point, it was our turn. Our first two plays were stopped cold by their tenacious defense. On third down, our quarterback dropped back and connected with the tailback a yard short of the end zone. I snapped my helmet, anticipating heading out onto the field for the extra point.

> "Fourth down in overtime . . . this is the stuff dreams are made of."

Fourth down in overtime . . . this is the stuff dreams are made of. A quarterback sneak was our money play, a play we had executed to perfection at least 30 times throughout the season. How could it go wrong?

Specific details re-create the final play for readers.

Eleven men broke the huddle and slowly walked to the line. The center placed his hands on the ball, keeping the laces up for luck. The quarterback barked his cadence like a general shouting orders. Eyes were locked; the crowd was silent. At the snap of the ball, their linemen charged us, trying to crack the wall. Our quarterback took a hit and fumbled before he could cross the line. The game was over. We lost by inches.

I went still and fell to my knees. Our quarterback sat in the end zone, alone. I could hear sobs from the crowd. Tears ran down my face, or maybe it was just the rain. I couldn't tell. Some teammates were consoled by their families or hugged by their friends. Our last game was not supposed to end in this way.

The closing is neatly tied to the opening.

Heads down, our team walked slowly back to the locker room, the once thunderous footsteps now silent. For the first time that night, I felt the cold. ∎

Sample **Extended Personal Narrative**

An extended narrative, or phase autobiography, covers an important period in your life. In this sample, student writer Natalie Garcia shares the story of her search for her father, a search that spanned a number of years. Note the "I remember" details she includes.

Finding My Family

The opening provides important background information.

When I was four years old, I saw my dad all of the time. Although my parents were divorced, he used to drive all the way from Michigan just to see me. Sometimes he'd pick me up in his old blue pickup truck, and I'd travel back to his house, bumping along the potholed streets, listening to the radio.

I remember always waking up early in the morning, running into his room, and jumping on his bed to wake him. Soon after, I would smell homemade tortillas and eggs. Sometimes he even made breakfast burritos for a special treat. On other days, I just ate cereal.

I remember the sound of music from the ice-cream truck that would cruise through his neighborhood. We would run out of the house, and my dad would pick me up and hold me while I chose what I wanted. Sometimes I'd choose an orange push-up, but most of the time, I picked the green ice-cream frog on a stick with gum-ball eyes. It was my favorite.

"All of a sudden, my dad stopped visiting, and I was devastated."

My dad worked as a truck driver, and he'd often bring crates of produce home—bushels of bumpy brown potatoes, bright green peppers, and juicy orange-red tomatoes. I loved to eat the tomatoes whole, sprinkled with salt. I still do that now.

The writer shares deep feelings and concerns.

All of a sudden, my dad stopped visiting, and I was devastated. I wrote to him as many times as I could, but he never answered my letters. I thought that he didn't love me anymore. I asked my mom over and over why he didn't write to me. She said he probably didn't have the time. But how could someone not have enough time for his own child?

About a year ago, I finally received a return letter from my dad. There was a phone number on the letter, so I called. I asked about all of the letters he never answered, and he said, "I never got them." I didn't believe that, but I didn't care. I now had him back in my life, and that's all I wanted.

Then last year I came home from school and found an unexpected letter. When I read it, I found out that I had an older half-sister, which really shocked me. (My family was suddenly growing.) She told me the real reason that my dad had never answered my letters: His English skills weren't very good. That, I understood, and I cried with joy after reading the letter.

In the final paragraph, the writer shares the resolution to the problem.

I called my dad. During our conversation, for the first time since I was four years old, I heard him say, "I love you." I now know that I have family—here with Mom, of course, but now there's also Dad and a half-sister. My family may be scattered over three states, but knowing that everyone is out there is the best feeling in the world. It makes me feel like a hole in my heart has been filled. ■

Narrative-Writing TIPS

The following activities will help you find additional subject ideas for personal narratives:

- **Page through** family photo albums.
- **Talk** to your grandparents.
- **Complete** a series of "I remember . . . " statements.
- **Draw** a winding highway on your paper, representing a map of your life. Note memorable experiences on the map.
- **Collect** possible writing ideas related to different categories: early childhood, elementary school, holidays, and so on.

WRITING GUIDELINES
Personal Essay

A personal essay shares the details of a specific event or time in your life, emphasizing what you have learned from the experience. In this way, a personal essay is part recollection and part reflection. It entertains or informs, plus it gets your readers thinking. An effective personal essay leaves readers with something to talk about.

■ PREWRITING

1. **Choosing a Subject . . .** Review your journal entries for subjects, or list ideas that come to mind as you read the sample essay on the next page. Any important part of your life has personal-essay potential.

2. **Gathering Details . . .** Write freely about your subject for 10 minutes or more, letting your ideas take you where they will. One of the following open-ended sentences could serve as a starting point for your writing:

   ○ (*The subject*) makes me remember . . .
   ○ (*The subject*) causes me to . . .
   ○ (*The subject*) concerns me because . . .

3. **Focusing Your Efforts . . .** Study your freewriting to help you get a feel for your subject. Look for parts that you want to explore further. Also look for a main idea or feeling that could serve as the focus for your essay. Continue gathering details and focusing your thinking until you are ready to write your first draft.

■ WRITING AND REVISING

4. **Connecting Your Ideas . . .** Write your first draft freely, letting your true personality come through in your writing. (Write what you are thinking and feeling.) Your opening should pull readers into your essay, the middle should discuss the experience, and the closing should reflect upon its significance.

5. **Improving Your Writing . . .** Carefully review your first draft; then make the necessary revisions.

   [HOT LINK] See "Assessment Rubric," page 154, for a helpful revising and editing guide.

■ EDITING AND PROOFREADING

6. **Checking for Style and Accuracy . . .** Edit your revised writing for style; then check it for spelling, grammar, and punctuation errors.

7. **Preparing a Final Copy . . .** Write or keyboard a neat final copy of your essay; then proofread your copy carefully before sharing it.

Sample **Personal Essay**

In this personal essay, the student writer reflects upon an important aspect of her life—dealing with orthopedic deformities. As you will see, she approaches her subject with maturity and courage.

Stronger at the Broken Places

The opening details lead up to the focus, or thesis, of the essay.

Although I have no memory of the ordeals I faced during my first years of life, I shall always bear the orthopedic deformities that I was handed at birth. I have feet that put Steven Spielberg's E.T. to shame. They are a tangle of toes held together by bunions. In addition, my right knee, with its underdeveloped muscle and bone, is chronically dislocated. These deformities have been difficult to accept, but they have provided me with a unique life. My physical challenges have greatly influenced the development of my character.

Throughout my early years, I quickly learned that children can be cruel. It was difficult to explain my physical oddities to my elementary school peers; I hardly understood them myself. All my friends knew was that I couldn't play soccer or walk without pain. But it wasn't until I started wearing a knee brace and orthopedic shoes that the situation became almost unbearable. Being called *crippled,* getting kicked in the knee, and being tripped pricked my soul; but it also strengthened it in the process.

The writer expresses herself honestly and openly.

I have the athletic ability of a snail, so I decided to be the manager of the middle-school track team. Every other activity, including art, drama, and music, I have embraced with a passion. I am a firm believer that with determination, the individual can accomplish anything. Extraordinary people have lived as examples of this philosophy. I have used their triumphs as guides toward my own achievements.

I have now grown to realize the importance of self-worth, and I wish to share this lesson with others. For the past three years, I have spoken to the school's child-development class. I share my struggles in order to make others more sensitive to those who are different.

In the final paragraph, the writer reflects upon her circumstances.

My disabilities only "disable" me in the physical sense. They have strengthened my mind and my spirit. I will never be ashamed of my feet or my knee, for they have guided me in the past and will lead me into the future. ■

Assessment Rubric

Use this rubric as a checklist to assess your personal narratives and personal essays. This rubric is arranged according to the traits of effective writing described in your handbook. (See pages 21-26.)

Stimulating Ideas

The writing . . .

_____ focuses on a specific experience or event.

_____ presents an engaging picture of the action and people involved.

_____ contains specific details and dialogue.

_____ makes readers want to know what happens next.

Logical Organization

_____ includes a clear beginning that pulls readers into the essay.

_____ presents ideas in an organized manner.

_____ uses transitions to link sentences and paragraphs.

Engaging Voice

_____ speaks knowledgeably and/or enthusiastically.

_____ shows that the writer is truly interested in the subject.

Original Word Choice

_____ contains specific nouns, vivid verbs, and colorful modifiers.

Effective Sentence Style

_____ flows smoothly from one idea to the next.

_____ shows variation in sentence structure and length.

Correct, Accurate Copy

_____ adheres to the basic rules of writing.

_____ follows the form suggested by the teacher, or another effective design. (See pages 30-32.)

"To write about people, you have to know people; to write about bloodhounds, you have to know bloodhounds; to write about the Loch Ness monster, you have to find out about it."

—James Thurber

SUBJECT Writing

Look through a current issue of nearly any magazine, and you'll find the following types of stories:

- A description of a new product
- An eyewitness account of an important event
- An interview with an important public figure
- A profile of an influential personality
- A report about an innovative business

These stories are all examples of subject writing, writing carried out to share information about newsworthy people, places, and events. The best subject writing contains important information plus personality—it educates and entertains. Writers of these stories rely almost exclusively on primary sources (visits, observations, interviews, and so on) for the facts and details they need. This chapter includes guidelines and samples to help you with many forms of subject writing.

Preview

- Descriptive Writing
- Eyewitness Account
- Interview Report
- Profile of a Person
- Assessment Rubric

WRITING GUIDELINES
Descriptive Writing

In a good description, you write from a position of authority. Either you must know your subject well, or you must closely observe the person, place, or thing you are describing. Use vivid sensory and memory details to bring your subject to life, and make it clear why the subject is important to you.

■ PREWRITING

1. **Choosing a Subject . . .** Select a subject that is worthy of description. Consider people (individuals you admire), places (favorite gathering spots), or things (special gifts).

   ✱ If you choose a person, get his or her permission before you start, and by all means, use good judgment in your description.

2. **Gathering Details . . .** Imagine that you are planning a painting of your subject; jot down every shape, color, texture, or feature that comes to mind. Also record details firsthand as you observe your subject. (Include sensory details—sights, sounds, smells, and so on.)

3. **Focusing Your Efforts . . .** Review your collecting and decide which idea or feeling would work best as the focus of your writing. Plan your description to support this focus.

■ WRITING AND REVISING

4. **Connecting Your Ideas . . .** Write your first draft freely, working in the memory and sensory details according to your prewriting and planning. (Show, don't tell.)

5. **Improving Your Writing . . .** Read your first draft silently, and then read it out loud. Close your eyes and take a mental tour of your description: *Have you included all of the important details? Have you organized these details so they are easy to follow? Will readers understand why the subject is important to you?*

■ EDITING AND PROOFREADING

6. **Checking for Style and Accuracy . . .** Edit your revised writing for smoothness and word choice (especially precise, colorful modifiers). Then check your work for spelling, grammar, and punctuation errors.

   [HOT LINK] See "Assessment Rubric," page 166, for a helpful revising and editing guide.

7. **Preparing a Final Copy . . .** Write or keyboard a neat final copy of your description; proofread your copy before sharing it.

Sample **Descriptive Writing**

In this essay, student writer Roel Zinkstok describes one of his favorite settings, the garden behind his house. The garden serves as a pleasurable meeting place for his family.

Leaving the Garden

The opening shows readers the garden during the day.

Usually, our back garden is not very special. Most of it is laid with terra-cotta orange and dark gray stones. Our house rises three stories on the west side of it; the garage borders on the south end and is thickly covered with dark green ivy. Along the north side grows a hedge with tiny leaves that turn rusty red in the fall. A row of low yew trees runs parallel to the house, and towering over them are two tall birches and a huge conifer, some 45 feet tall. A few flower beds strive to brighten the garden's edges.

This garden changes magically on a warm summer's evening. As the sun sets, the garden seems to slowly shrink in the darkness. When it gets too dark to see, my mother puts a table lamp or candles on an old, paint-chipped table. This lamp creates a small bubble of golden light in the center of the

The details in the body focus on the garden's nighttime mystique.

garden, and casts grotesque shadows along the borders, making our seats around the table feel even more cozy. Over our heads, the starry dome of night makes it seem as though we are sitting on the brink of the universe.

Throughout the years, we have all sat there together—my father, my mother, my twin brother, and my two older sisters— talking, reading, or just sharing the silence. Here my father and I have discussed religion and faith, literature and science, or simply the day just passed. Here I have read great books, following their stories in my imagination from my garden chair. At times, soft music wafts toward us from the nearby house of a concert pianist, forming wonderful melodies that dance through the trees. Here my family has sat till far past midnight in the halo of light—with the bugs and the music.

In closing, the writer discusses the garden's importance in his life.

In recent years, my sisters have left home to study in Amsterdam. Now it is my turn to leave, my turn to become independent. That means letting go of the guiding hand of my parents. But I know that they will always be sitting there in the garden, leaving a chair vacant for me and my siblings, like the Jews at Pesach leave a chair for Elijah. When I return next summer, I will find my father and mother waiting in the garden with the lamp on the old table . . . and we will talk together for the rest of the night—and, in a way, forever. ■

WRITING GUIDELINES

Eyewitness Account

In an eyewitness account, you share the details of an event that you recently witnessed. You may develop your account in a number of ways—as a news story, as a traditional report, as an account of an event answering the 5 W's and H (*Who? What? When? Where? Why?* and *How?*), or as a flow of sensory impressions. The best eyewitness accounts contain a wide range of sights, sounds, and smells.

■ PREWRITING

1. **Choosing a Subject . . .** If no event from your recent past comes to mind, keep your eyes open for possible subjects during a typical day. You might, for example, focus on an action that regularly takes place in the school cafeteria. Or you could plan to attend a specific event—a game, a meeting, a concert, whatever you think would work as a subject.

2. **Gathering Details . . .** List the sights, sounds, and smells as you remember them from a recent event. Or record sensory observations (including bits of dialogue) as an event unfolds. (See page 49 for a graphic organizer to use for your collecting.)

3. **Focusing Your Efforts . . .** As you review your notes, identify (1) a main idea or feeling that can serve as the focus of your writing and (2) the best way to present your ideas—as a news story, as a sensory report, or so on.

■ WRITING AND REVISING

4. **Connecting Your Ideas . . .** Write your first draft according to your prewriting and planning. Work in a wide range of sensory details.

5. **Improving Your Writing . . .** As you review your first draft, ask yourself if you have included all of the important details and arranged them in the best order (according to your focus). Revise your writing accordingly.

■ EDITING AND PROOFREADING

6. **Checking for Style and Accuracy . . .** Review your revised writing for style, making sure that your sentences read smoothly and clearly and that you have used the best words and images to capture the event. Then check your work for spelling, grammar, and punctuation errors.

   [HOT LINK] See "Assessment Rubric," page 166, for a helpful revising and editing guide.

7. **Preparing a Final Copy . . .** Write or keyboard a neat final copy of your eyewitness account; proofread your copy before sharing it.

Sample Eyewitness Account

In the following sample, student writer Ron St. Germain describes a fire at his neighbor's house. His observations highlight the destruction caused by the fire.

One Hot Night

The opening grabs the reader's attention.

It was three o'clock when my mother came screaming down the hall waking us up. She told us to grab the dog and to get out of the house. The temperature began to rise as I ran down the stairs, and I was hit with a blast of hot air and the sound of exploding glass when I opened the side door. The first thing I saw was my neighbor's sleek red motorcycle explode with shrapnel shooting in all directions, and I saw a bright blaze engulf the once shiny, beautiful Honda.

My family gathered in the front yard and watched with our neighbors as the house across the street went up in flames. No one spoke as the fire trucks came up the hill with lights flashing, but with no sirens blaring. The firefighters got the hoses attached together faster than lightning, but couldn't get any water pressure. As a result, the fire spread through the old house and flames leaped to a black Toyota. The car's brakes

The event is recalled in great detail.

must have melted because the Toyota started rolling toward our house with flames billowing from the windows, hood, and muffler. Luckily, it stopped as the rear wheel hit a fire hose.

Minutes later the water pressure from another hydrant was strong enough so the firefighters were able to extinguish part of the fire. More people gathered in horror as the smoke seemed to cover the sky and made our eyes tear. It was getting hard to breathe, and I was getting burned by the ashes as they flew by. Two other cars parked in the charred garage slowly began to melt. As dawn approached, no one could see the rising sun because of the thick smoke.

My friends and I were still on our front lawn as the last of the flames were extinguished. The firefighters then grabbed axes and charged into the house, cutting holes in the roof. They threw out mattresses and clothing that were smoldering. They also brought down a guitar case. We all gathered around as the

The closing adds a personal touch to the report.

firefighter opened it. There lay a metallic blue guitar with only slight water damage. They also found a jar of jewelry cleaner with a diamond ring at the bottom of the pink liquid.

I got mad at the people who walked or drove slowly by and stared at the house as the owners sat crying, wearing their only possessions. After a few hours of sleep my friends and I took up a collection for our three homeless neighbors. That night, I wrapped $233 to present to them the next day. ■

WRITING GUIDELINES
Interview Report

In an interview report, your writing is based on the facts and details you gather while interviewing a person. The success of your writing depends upon your ability to conduct an interview, as well as your ability to shape the information you have collected into a meaningful report.

■ PREWRITING

1. **Choosing a Subject . . .** Interview someone you know well who has an interesting story to tell, or someone you would like to know better. Consider relatives, neighbors, family friends, community leaders, skilled workers, students, and so on.

2. **Preparing for the Interview . . .** Gather background information about your subject (if necessary). Then write questions you would like to ask this person. Shape your questions so that the interviewee cannot answer them with a simple "yes" or "no." Also set a time and a place to meet or call your subject. (See page 330 for more information.)

3. **Gathering Details . . .** Take brief notes during the interview; fill in any gaps soon after the interview. (Consider recording the session, if the person agrees to this.)

4. **Focusing Your Efforts . . .** Determine how you want to shape your writing. One way is to present your findings in a report by introducing your subject and highlighting important details in a question-and-answer script. Or you can present your findings in a story about the interviewing experience (*I asked her about . . . The real surprise was . . .*).

■ WRITING AND REVISING

5. **Connecting Your Ideas . . .** Develop your interview according to your planning. Refer to your notes whenever necessary.

6. **Improving Your Writing . . .** Read your first draft silently, then out loud. Make sure that you have captured the essence of your subject's story and that readers will be able to follow it. Revise accordingly.

■ EDITING AND PROOFREADING

7. **Checking for Style and Accuracy . . .** Review your revised writing for sentence style and word choice. Then check your work for spelling, grammar, and punctuation errors.

   [HOT LINK] See "Assessment Rubric," page 166, for a helpful revising and editing guide.

8. **Preparing a Final Copy . . .** Write or keyboard a neat final copy of your report; then proofread your copy before sharing it.

Sample **Interview Report**

In this report, student writer Kristine Vallila shares the story of an enterprising businesswoman with an unusual job. Note how the writing flows from one main point to the next.

Lunchtime with Miss Carol

The opening introduces us to the subject in an interesting way.

She is a hot-dog vendor, and she always wears a hat. Her hats are sleek and simple straw models, in tan or hot pink, with no bows or flowers. They always coordinate with what she is wearing.

When I asked her if she would agree to be interviewed for an article on offbeat jobs, she seemed offended.

"I don't have an offbeat job—I have a real job," she said, before pausing to greet a customer. "May I help you, Sweetie?"

"It's my livelihood," she continued. "What kinds of questions are you going to ask? I stopped doing interviews years ago."

She helped another customer to a sausage dog with chili. A cab driver honked as he drove past.

After this pause, I tried to explain to her that I had chosen to interview her because of her hats. Today's hat was tan, with yellow and green stripes woven through the brim.

"Ah," she replied, "I think you just came up with that, but you redeemed yourself. Let me hear some of your offbeat questions."

So I began. Her name is Miss Carol. That is all she would say, and after my first blunder, I was not going to press her for a last name. She sells hot dogs from her own grill, and greets everyone with "Darlin'," "Sugar," or "Sweetie." She knows her customers, and they know her.

The report highlights important points shared by the subject.

"I don't have my own children. I have a lot of customers and some are like my kids. But the majority are like nieces and aunts. On holidays, they remember me. And that's why I think I've been out here a long time."

She owns the stand and has been running it on the Fayetteville Street Mall for almost 10 years. She does not employ anyone besides herself and keeps supplies in five blue coolers behind the stand. She said that she knows how many supplies she will need each day: "I've been in the business for 10 years. If I don't know by now, I'll never know."

Her spot on the mall is permanent, but the stand is movable. She unloads the equipment, including the metal stand, each day from a truck. "I try to make my hours between 10 and 5," she said. She sells hot dogs year-round. ▶

Lunchtime with Miss Carol
(continued)

She started vending after working behind a desk. "The corporate world is a jungle, and I got tired. I wanted something new, and this is different. Sometimes in the corporate world, you have to make difficult choices. I think I made a good one."

Before working as a vendor, she had a job with a parcel-post company in customer service, then with a bank. Now she sells hot dogs from a stand across the street from that bank.

Miss Carol has two rules: "Always be able to do more than one thing, and enjoy what you do. I wouldn't give this up for nothing, but it's good to have experience on both sides of the fence. If my business goes bad, I can go back into the office."

> The subject's actual words give insights into her personality.

> "Miss Carol has two rules: 'Always be able to do more than one thing, and enjoy what you do.' "

A man came up to her while she ladled sauerkraut onto a hot dog and said, "My buddy says, 'Hey!' He had Bible study, but he told me to say, 'Hey.' " She nodded in return.

Another customer handed her a dollar for his hot dog. "You know a hot dog don't cost a dollar," she said. "You been buyin' from me long enough to know." (They cost $1.50.)

He replied that the sun was making him lose his memory. "I'm gonna refresh your memory right quick," she said. He grinned widely. I had a feeling they had had this talk before.

The wind picked up and blew the edges of the parasol shading her stand. She noticed another customer.

"You smellin' mighty good today," she told him.

"I just got a haircut," he replied.

"Ah . . . Sookie, Sookie." Her earrings jingled as she moved her head from side to side.

As I finished my interview, I told her that I hoped I had not offended her by calling her job offbeat.

> In closing, the writer reflects upon her experience.

"No, if you're where I'm at, you don't offend easily. Now, if you'd come up and messed with me, then I'd be offended. I've got a good job here and plan on doing it for a long time."

As I thanked her for the interview, said good-bye, and then walked away, I knew that the way sales had been going during the last half hour, she would indeed be in business for a long time. ∎

WRITING GUIDELINES
Profile of a Person

In a profile of a person or biographical story, you discuss a special part of the subject's life. To develop an effective profile, you must gather a great deal of information about the person through interviewing, corresponding, reading, observing, and reflecting.

■ PREWRITING

1. **Choosing a Subject . . .** Write your profile about someone who interests you and will also interest your readers. (Just make sure that you can gather plenty of information about this person.)

2. **Collecting Your Thoughts . . .** Write nonstop about your subject for at least 10 minutes. Consider what you already know about your subject, what puzzles or interests you about this person, what you hope to find out, and so on. Review this writing, looking for angles to explore, questions to answer, or special features to highlight in your profile.

3. **Gathering Details . . .** Collect information about your subject through interviews, phone conversations, letters, readings, and so on. (See page 330 for interviewing tips.)

4. **Focusing Your Efforts . . .** Decide what it is you want to focus on or emphasize about your subject. Plan and organize your writing to support this focus.

■ WRITING AND REVISING

5. **Connecting Your Ideas . . .** Write your first draft using your planning and prewriting as a general guide. Speak sincerely and honestly; keep your readers interested and entertained.

6. **Improving Your Writing . . .** As you review your first draft, pay close attention to the completeness of your profile: *Did you say enough about your subject? Do all of the ideas support your focus? Are your ideas easy to follow?* Revise your writing accordingly.

■ EDITING AND PROOFREADING

7. **Checking for Style and Accuracy . . .** Edit your revised writing for style, making sure that your sentences read smoothly and clearly and that you have used the best words to express your ideas. Then check your work for spelling, grammar, and punctuation errors.

    [HOT LINK] See "Assessment Rubric," page 166, for a helpful revising and editing guide.

8. **Preparing a Final Copy . . .** Write or keyboard a neat final copy of your profile; proofread your copy before sharing it.

Sample Profile of a Person

The following profile reflects student writer Karina Sang's effort to learn about her Chinese grandfather. She relies on her father's stories for most of her information. (This article first appeared in *New Youth Connections: The Magazine Written By and For New York Youth.*)

Grandfather's Journey from China to Santo Domingo

I have often wondered about my Chinese grandfather. He died before I was born, and my family has never really said much about him. Someday I would like to go to China and find what is left of my Chinese family. But for now, I must be satisfied with the few stories my father has told me.

The writer highlights important events in her grandfather's life.

My grandfather left China for Santo Domingo in 1916 with his brother. Their father had been a wealthy merchant, and his two sons decided to search for new horizons. They settled in the Dominican town of Bonao and opened a restaurant they called "Sang Lee Long." Even though it had a Chinese name, the restaurant served Dominican food and was very popular.

My grandfather's name was Luis Sang. He never told anyone in our family his Chinese name. He had gone through an arranged marriage in China and left his wife

> "My grandfather's name was Luis Sang. He never told anyone in our family his Chinese name."

and two sons behind when he moved to the Dominican Republic. In his new country he married again and had 10 children: 7 daughters and 3 sons. My father was one of them.

Grandfather's restaurant got most of its business from travelers. But when the old highway that had united the south of the Dominican Republic with the capital closed in late 1959, Bonao was isolated. As a result, my grandfather's restaurant went bankrupt. He stayed home after that and never opened another restaurant.

Details include the grandfather's interests and personality.

Over the years, my grandfather had acquired Dominican customs. He liked to hunt, play dominoes and poker, and drink Dominican rum.

In 1961, when people protested the actions of the country's dictator, Rafael Trujillo, he did, too. He believed so much in the opposition that he wanted to participate in politics, but he couldn't because he wasn't a citizen.

The ending mirrors the beginning, further explaining the author's interest.

He suffered a heart attack in 1968. His doctor told him he didn't have much time left, three months at the most. He lived another year doing everything the doctor had forbidden. He ate pork, drank, played poker, and smoked. "He died January 26, 1969," says my father in a proud voice, "but the fruits he left behind are still here, and I'm part of them."

—— My father does not feel a connection to his Chinese heritage. It may be because he was never taught anything about that culture. Unlike my father, I do feel a connection to my Chinese heritage. I keep asking questions about my grandfather's life and wait for the day I can visit Canton, China, to learn more about him. ■

Additional Types of Subject Writing

To sharpen your reporting skills, experiment with the following types of subject writing.

Historical Profile ◎ Present an accurate report about an interesting place, time, or event from the past. Your writing must somehow bring the subject to life for the reader.

Venture Report ◎ Provide an in-depth report on a specific occupation or business. Base your report on information from interviews, job-site visits, and other types of firsthand research.

Case Study ◎ Tell the story of one individual whose experiences speak for a larger group (disaster victims, recent immigrants, groupies, etc.). The effectiveness of a case study depends on your ability to gather information over an extended period of time.

Personal Research Report ◎ Present the detailed story of your investigation of a subject of personal interest (a new form of technology, a current fad, an unusual hobby or pastime, etc.).

Assessment Rubric

Use this rubric as a checklist to evaluate your subject writing. This rubric is arranged according to the traits of effective writing described in your handbook. (See pages 21-26.)

Stimulating Ideas

The writing . . .

_____   focuses on an inviting subject.

_____   contains a variety of supporting information (sensory details, memory details, and so on).

_____   informs and entertains the reader.

Logical Organization

_____   includes an engaging beginning, strong development, and an effective ending.

_____   forms a meaningful whole, moving smoothly from one main point to the next.

Engaging Voice

_____   displays a thorough knowledge of the subject.

_____   speaks with an appropriate voice.

Original Word Choice

_____   contains specific nouns, vivid verbs, and colorful modifiers.

_____   captures the subject's ideas and feelings in dialogue.

Effective Sentence Style

_____   flows smoothly from one idea to the next.

_____   shows variation in sentence structure.

Correct, Accurate Copy

_____   adheres to the basic rules of grammar, spelling, and punctuation.

_____   follows the appropriate formatting guidelines.

"Fact and fiction, fiction and fact.
Shapeshifting into one another . . . "

—Gail Godwin

CREATIVE Writing

Imagine writing a story about a high school student who has to move (this is *fact*). Also imagine including two main characters in your story—the girl who is moving and her boyfriend (this, too, may be *true*). The plot of your story revolves around how these friends spend their remaining time together (this is the *fiction* part).

This example illustrates how creative writing works—"fact and fiction, fiction and fact," blending together to form imaginative pieces of writing. A memory may develop into a poem, an image (like a special gift) may inspire a story, a recent experience may be portrayed in a play.

Remember: Creative writing is the process of inventing, the process of making something new and different, something made-up. But it also has solid roots in the real-world experiences and memories of the writer—fact and fiction, blending together. This chapter includes guidelines and samples for several types of creative writing.

Preview

- Story Writing
- Playwriting
- Assessment Rubric
- Poetry Writing
- Assessment Rubric

WRITING GUIDELINES
Story Writing

Story writing often begins with a question: "What can I create out of this image, memory, or feeling?" The image of a rickety, old tree house can grow into a story about the builders. The memory of a former classmate can evolve into a story about losing a friend. Build your story with several interesting characters, realistic dialogue, and believable action.

■ PREWRITING

1. **Getting Started . . .** All you're looking for is a seed, a starting point for your story. Let's say that you had spent a lot of time by a river when you were young. That river could be the setting for a story. And let's also say you recall that both good and bad things had happened there. Those happenings could spark ideas for the story line or plot.

   ✱ If no ideas come to mind, review your journal entries, freewrite about your experiences, or refer to the information on the next page.

2. **Focusing Your Efforts . . .** With a starting point in mind (a strong memory, image, or feeling), organize your thoughts for writing. Use this basic formula for your planning: In most stories, there are people (characters) in a place (setting) dealing with a problem (plot) that leads to a new understanding about life (theme).

■ WRITING AND REVISING

3. **Connecting Your Ideas . . .** Write your first draft freely, using your planning and prewriting as a guide. Start right in the middle of the action, and let your characters tell the story by what they say and do. (See the sample story beginning on page 170.)

4. **Improving Your Writing . . .** Carefully review your first draft to be sure your story develops in an interesting way: life for your main character (or characters) should become increasingly difficult because of the problem. Near the end of the story, the main character should come face-to-face with the problem and resolve it.

■ EDITING AND PROOFREADING

5. **Checking for Style and Accuracy . . .** Edit your revised writing for sentence style and word choice; then check your writing for spelling, grammar, and punctuation errors.
   [HOT LINK] Use "Assessment Rubric," page 178, as a helpful revising and editing guide.

6. **Preparing a Final Copy . . .** Write or keyboard a neat final copy of your writing; proofread your copy before sharing it.

Patterns of Fiction

The following patterns of fiction are not based on any hard-and-fast rules that must be followed during the story-writing process. Think of them more as general approaches to story writing. After reviewing these patterns, you may think of many good ideas for stories.

The Quest (Return) ℮ In a quest, the main character sets out in search of something, experiences various adventures, and finally returns—either triumphant or wiser. (A freshman sets out to make the basketball team and succeeds against significant odds.)

Sample Stories

"A Worn Path" by Eudora Welty

"My Kinsman, Major Molineaux" by Nathaniel Hawthorne
(Any of the heroic myths)

The Initiation ℮ A main character (usually a young person) is faced with a new situation that tests his or her abilities or beliefs. How the character deals with the situation determines the direction of his or her life. (A young boy loses a dog that he worships, and learns something about life in the process.)

Sample Stories

"The Haunted Boy" by Carson McCullers

"Marigolds" by Eugenia Collier
"a list of ten things" by Loubel Cruz (See page 170.)

The Union ℮ In this pattern, a boy and girl grow fond of each other, but their parents or some other authority figure or circumstance comes between them. The couple usually gets together in the end after overcoming various obstacles. (A teenage boy and the teenage daughter of a migrant worker meet secretly in spite of their parents' objections.)

Sample Stories

"Hoods I Have Known" by Sondra Spatt

"Horsetrader's Daughter" by D. H. Lawrence
(Any romantic stories)

The Choice ℮ The main character is faced with a difficult decision near the end of this type of story. Making this decision is the high point of the plot. (An out-of-work laborer must decide if he should work for someone he dislikes.)

Sample Stories

"A & P" by John Updike

"The Bass, The River, and Sheila Mant" by W.D. Wetherell
"When the Bough Breaks" by Elizabeth Enright

Sample **Short Story**

A boy-girl breakup (because of a move) serves as the starting point for this story by student writer Loubel Cruz. (From *Merlyn's Pen: Fiction, Essays, and Poems by America's Teens.* Copyright by Merlyn's Pen, Inc. All rights reserved.)

a list of ten things

The story starts right in the middle of the action.

—— The day had been terrible. I spent most of it trying to avoid my friends and trying not to cry. Davis knew something was wrong, but he was smart enough not to ask what it was. I knew I had to tell him, though.

"I'm moving."

"Yeah, right," Davis said.

"Davis," I said angrily, slamming his geometry book closed, "I'm serious."

Davis looked straight in my eyes. He knew the truth.

"Where?"

"Boston."

"Why?"

I started to feel my heart knot. "It's not my decision."

Davis looked down and pretended to be engrossed in the design of my sofa. He said nothing, but I knew exactly how he felt. Finally, without looking up, he spoke.

"Boston's pretty cool, I guess. The Red Sox and all. There'll be a lot of snow. You can ice-skate." He picked up the geometry book and continued to study.

"Geez, Davis, you sound like my mother." I was getting angry now. He acted like he didn't care.

"Well, Colleen, what do you want me to say? That I'm really glad you're moving so I can hang out with Herman Wallflower? I can't say what I want. I can't say, 'Don't go' because I know you have to." There was anger and confusion in his eyes. I had never seen him this way. It scared me. He had called me Colleen, and he always called me Marshall, my last name.

"It's not my fault," I said, tears starting to flow.

"Look, I gotta go now." Davis got up, gathered his things, and without another word, he left.

The main character's thoughts add an important level of detail.

—— I didn't cry anymore that night. I was too mad—at everybody: at my dad for accepting a job thousands of miles away, at my mom for agreeing to go along with it, at Davis for being such a lousy friend when I needed him most, and at myself for being mad.

The next day I tried to find Davis, but at the same time, I tried to avoid him. The first time I saw him was in Mrs. Drew's English class. He didn't look my way, so I tried not to look his. We were busy studying poetry, and our assignment was to write a list of ten things. God only knows how that is poetry, but I was too preoccupied to think about it. I looked over at Davis to see if he would give me one of his this-is-such-a-stupid-class looks, but he didn't. He just stared straight ahead, very intent on what Mrs. Drew was saying. He didn't talk to me for the rest of the school day.

That evening the doorbell rang. Davis gave me a shy grin and invited himself inside. "Could you help me with geometry? I have no idea what's going on."

"Davis, I'm sorry. I really shouldn't have . . . "

"Hey, Marshall, forget about it. It's not your fault. I should be the one who's sorry. Boston, huh? No offense, but you're going to freeze your rear up there."

I laughed. This was the way it was supposed to be.

"Let's not talk about you moving anymore, OK?" Davis said. "Promise?"

"Promise."

Davis smiled, satisfied. "So what did you think about the poem thing today? I wrote ten reasons why the Astros never made it to the World Series."

And that was that.

A transitional paragraph moves the story ahead.

Two months passed. As promised, Davis and I didn't mention moving. We went on with our daily routine as if I weren't leaving: him copying my geometry, me watching his football games, him proofreading my newspaper articles.

Then the day came: moving day. Davis and I were in my room. We laughed and talked, but we knew the time to say good-bye was coming nearer.

"Uh, well, Merry Christmas," he said, giving me a small wrapped box.

"Thanks," I said, opening the gift. Inside the box was a beautiful golden locket.

"Uh, my mom picked it out because you know how I am with girl presents," he said. "I thought you would like it, though. I didn't put my picture in it 'cause you might find a really cute guy up there in Massachusetts. But there's something engraved in it so you won't forget me."

"Thanks." I immediately put it on.

"Oh, here's another thing." He gave me a small envelope. "This is really from me. Don't open it yet, though." I nodded obediently. "Well, I gotta go now. It's getting late." He got up and headed for the door. "Boston will be great, I promise. You'll be fine." He smiled at me as he headed for the door. "Later, Marshall."

A final interchange adds intensity to the story.

I felt tears running down my face. "I love you, Davis."

He turned around and smiled. His eyes sparkled with little teardrops. "I know, Marshall." And with that, he walked away. ▶

a list of ten things
(continued)

I sat down on the floor, and through my tears I opened the envelope to read what Davis had written.

TEN THINGS COLLEEN K. MARSHALL SHOULD
ALWAYS REMEMBER IN BOSTON:

1) **Don't get one of those gross New England accents.**
2) **In association with #1, say "Ya'll" as much as possible.**
3) **She's beautiful.**
4) **Even if she's in Boston, she will always be a Texan at heart.**
5) **Her name is Marshall.**
6) **No matter what anyone tells her, she's going to be a writer. She will only write the truth.**
7) **It's not her fault if a certain person flunks geometry. Ha, ha.**
8) **She's not fat, she's not fat, she's not fat.**
9) **Astros rule!**
10) **And the last thing Colleen K. Marshall should always remember in Boston is that even though he never says it, Davis R. Vaughn loves her, too.**

Despite my tears, I found myself laughing. Davis knew me so well, and I was leaving him. But as the gold locket said, "We'll always be together."

> **Another transitional paragraph moves the story ahead.**

—— So here I was in Boston, going to a Catholic private school, wearing a red plaid uniform that I wouldn't be caught dead wearing in Houston.

The bell rang. I slowly gathered my things from Sister Mary Catherine's literature class and walked out the door. I hadn't made many friends—well, I really hadn't tried that hard, so it surprised me when I heard someone call my name. I turned and saw a guy running toward me, panting.

"Hi, I'm Richard Luis. I'm the editor of the newspaper here. Call me Rick, though . . . "

"Oh, hi. I'm Colleen Marshall. Call me . . . " I thought about it . . . "Colleen."

"I know." I felt surprised and kind of flattered that he did. "Sister Agnes says you're a very talented writer. We heard you were on the news staff at your old school . . . in Texas?"

"Yes, I was, in Houston."

"Houston, huh? The Astros are pretty good."

I smiled.

"Well, anyway," he continued, "we really need good writers, so I was wondering if you'd like to be on the staff."

> **The ending neatly links the old with the new.**

"Yeah, that would be great." I couldn't believe my luck.

"Great. What do you write?"

—— I thought of Davis's list and said, "Only the truth." ∎

Sample **Fictionalized Journal Entry**

For a history assignment, Heather Bachman writes a fictional journal entry about planning for a camel-caravan trip to Baghdad. Obviously, she has spent time researching her subject.

Journal Entry . . .

Today I went to the market to buy supplies for my trip to Baghdad.

Authentic names and unusual details immediately draw the reader into this journal entry.

Sheira, the butcher, sold me the pot of grease my servants and I will need to protect our lips from chapping. The hot desert winds are particularly bad this year.

There was a good crop of dates this year, so I bought thirty pounds of them very cheaply. Dates are very good and very filling, a good thing to have on a trip. Olpim had many bags of dried rice that were full of plump, bright grains, well worth the price for fifty bags.

I was surprised to find that Bahir, the camel man, did not have the long, tender strips of dried camel meat. Even though camel meat is tough, it is a good thing to have for food, so I had to slaughter one of my own yearling calves. Not only will I use the meat, but the fat in the hump can be used for butter. The hide will be tanned and can be used for clothing, tents, shoes, water bags, and pack saddles. The hair will be woven by my wife into fine cloth for warm blankets and garments.

I was happy to discover that all five of my female camels are nursing babies. My wife will care for the babies while I am gone, and I will milk the camels every night for myself and the six servants in my caravan.

The writer smoothly works interesting facts into her writing.

My wife spent all day filling the huge goatskin water bags. Although I have mapped out water holes where we can stop, the desert is too untrustworthy not to take water along. The five bags hold enough water for us to survive quite a long time.

My wife also has spent the last two days collecting the camels' dung and letting it dry into "chips." These chips are a reliable fuel; and if we run out, it will be easy enough to get more from the camels in the caravan.

It has been very rainy this year, so I will have two servants walk ahead to look for the deadly mud traps. They are formed by heavy rains when the deceivingly dry crust hides deadly "snares." Knowing where the traps are will help keep us from harm in the days to come. ■

WRITING GUIDELINES

Playwriting

A play script explores a conflict in the lives of two or more characters. In a play, the characters do almost all of the work—from revealing their personalities to advancing the plot, from identifying the setting to dealing with the theme. So as your script develops, so should your characters, to a point where you know them well. (See pages 176-177 for a sample script.)

■ PREWRITING

1. **Getting Started . . .** To start out, think of an actual situation or conflict to build a script around: You and a family member may argue about your future. Someone you know may be headed for big trouble. If you can't "find" an idea, invent one: A girl tries out for the varsity football team. An elderly gentleman can't remember where he lives.

2. **Focusing Your Efforts . . .** Once you have a situation in mind, identify your main characters and consider how this situation complicates their lives. Then decide how your play will start (who will be doing what and where).

■ WRITING AND REVISING

3. **Connecting Your Ideas . . .** Write your first draft freely, using your planning and prewriting as a general guide. After introducing the main characters and their problem, let the rest of the play "write itself" as you listen to and imagine your characters' interactions. Include stage directions as necessary. (See page 175 for additional tips.)

4. **Improving Your Writing . . .** Read your first draft silently, and then read it out loud, paying special attention to the plot and character development. *Does your script develop a complete, but brief storyline? Does the problem complicate the characters' lives? Do the characters' words and actions reveal enough about their personalities?* Revise your script accordingly.

■ EDITING AND PROOFREADING

5. **Checking for Style and Accuracy . . .** Edit your revised writing for style. Make sure that each character's lines sound natural and are in keeping with her or his personality. Then check your work for spelling, grammar, and punctuation errors.

   [HOT LINK] See "Assessment Rubric," page 178, for a helpful revising and editing guide.

6. **Preparing a Final Copy . . .** Prepare your final copy in appropriate script form. Proofread your copy before submitting it.

Playwriting TIPS

Pay special attention to each of the following elements as you write your play scripts.

Dialogue ⊘ How the characters speak should reveal something about their identity. (Clues to voice or delivery can be included in stage directions as well as in word choice.) Write the dialogue as speakers actually speak. People often interrupt each other and, at times, talk past or ignore one another.

Conflict ⊘ Build your play around a believable situation or problem, one that makes sense in the lives of the characters. (The conflict should make life increasingly difficult for the main characters until the play reaches a breaking point.)

Stage Directions ⊘ In the stage directions, indicate the time and place of the action, entrances and exits, and so on. Your directions may also indicate what each of the characters is doing on stage. However, don't complicate your play with too many directions.

Form ⊘ Follow the accepted format for a script, beginning with the title and following with a list of characters and an explanation of the setting *before* the first words are spoken.

Related Forms

If you enjoy writing scripts, here are two more forms to try:

Monologue ⊘ Have a character carry on a one-way conversation. The main challenge of this type of writing is to have your character reveal something important about his or her personality during the monologue. You often find monologues in longer pieces of writing—plays, novels, or short stories. A monologue within a play is called a *soliloquy*.

Ad Script ⊘ Create a television (or radio) ad script for a real or imagined product. To get started, determine what your product can do, how it can do it better than related products, and what kind of story would best sell this idea to your audience. Tell a very brief story, one that covers either 30 or 60 seconds.

✻ There are special stage directions to consider for ad scripts: *Add graphic, Add music, Cut to, Fade in, Insert,* and so on.

Sample **Play**

This brief one-act play by student writer Travis Taylor focuses on two friends dealing with different problems.

Small Tragedies

Characters: **Mike,** a high school student
Craig, Mike's high school friend
Kate, Mike's former girlfriend
Jake, Kate's present boyfriend

Scene I

The scene opens with Mike standing in the doorway of a nicely furnished study. His friend Craig is sitting at a computer playing a video game.

Mike: I need a ride, Craig.
Craig: No.
Mike: Please?
Craig: Silence. I am about to beat this.

Craig stops, stands up, and starts jumping around.

Craig: I can't believe I lost again!
Mike: Can I please get a ride downtown? There's somewhere I've got to be.
Craig: Ever feel like cosmic forces are aligning against you? All you want to do is play one stinking game, but you can't even do that because there's some secret weapon that . . .
Mike: Calm down.
Craig: *(sighing)* It's frustrating. That's all. I finally get to use my dad's computer, but the game just keeps . . . keeps . . . It's just frustrating. No matter what I do, I'll still wind up losing.
Mike: Looks like it. How about that ride downtown?
Craig: Hang on. Let me try this one more time.

More sounds emanate from the computer, then a gory "splat."

Craig: What? I can't believe it got me again! It . . .

Craig stands up and waves his arms in frustration, knocking over a huge crystal vase on the desk. The vase breaks.

Mike: Now can I get a ride to town? It's urgent.
Craig: Uh . . . that was a really expensive vase. My dad's gonna . . .
Mike: Come on, you can think about it on the way. Let's go.
Craig: *(excited)* Yeah, let's get out of here! *(The two exit.)*

The opening scene establishes differences between the two characters.

Scene II

Craig and Mike are sitting on a curb facing a line of stores.

Craig: I can't believe I broke that vase.

Mike: Quiet down, will you?

Craig: Why should I quiet down? I'm dead. That's it. *(pause)* Why are we here, anyway?

Mike: Would you rather be at home?

Craig: No, but why here?

Mike: I don't know. I feel like sitting here.

Craig: I hate this curb. It's hot. My father is going to disown me. The least you could do is tell me why we're here.

Mike: *(mutters something)*

Craig: What?

Mike: I said Kate came back yesterday.

Craig: Oh. *(a brief pause)* So?

Mike: So she always comes here. We're sitting in front of her favorite store. *(Mike sighs. Craig groans.)*

Craig: I can't believe that happened.

Mike: He can get another vase. I wonder when she'll pop up.

Craig: Will you get over her? She ripped your heart out.

Mike: Yeah, but that was before she left for France. You see, she wanted to cut off her attachments before leaving.

Craig: That's why she started seeing Jake.

Mike: She wasn't attached to him. But us . . . it's like . . . fate.

Craig: Great. I smashed my father's priceless vase, and I have to listen to you find yourself on the karmic circle.

Mike: Will you stop whining about the vase? This is serious.

Craig: You're still trapped in the sixth grade.

Mike: It was the fifth grade when I first laid eyes on her. I knew when I first saw her—

Craig: *(interrupting)* That you would become obsessed by her?

Mike: She's the one, that's all. That's what I mean by fate.

Craig: Right. *(Craig is looking more and more miserable.)* Wait a minute. . . .

Just then, Kate walks by, holding hands with Jake.

Craig: Ah . . . fate. Beautiful, isn't it?

Mike: Shut up!

The two sit on the curb in defeated silence.

Mike: Now what?

Craig: We could get something to eat.

Mike: I don't think I'm in the mood to eat.

Craig: Me neither. Any other suggestions?

Mike: I suppose I could wander around being depressed about Kate, and you could go home and get in trouble. . . .

Craig: Hmmm . . . I think I'm in the mood for a burrito.

Mike: Yeah, me too. Let's go. *(The two exit.)* ■

The brief give and take between the characters reflects real conversation.

Stage directions explain critical actions.

Assessment Rubric

Use this checklist to evaluate your fiction and script writing. This rubric is arranged according to the traits of good writing described in your handbook. (See pages 21-26.)

Stimulating Ideas

The writing . . .

_____ contains an engaging setting, story line, and theme.

_____ brings the action alive with dialogue and details.

_____ develops interesting characters.

Logical Organization

_____ follows a basic plot line, building effectively to a climax, or high point of interest. (See page 239.)

_____ progresses in a storylike way with the characters' words and actions moving things along. (Explanations or stage directions are kept to a minimum.)

Engaging Voice

_____ sounds realistic, in terms of the characters' dialogue.

_____ maintains a consistent voice for each character.

Original Word Choice

_____ contains specific nouns, vivid verbs, and colorful modifiers.

_____ employs a level of language appropriate to each character.

Effective Sentence Style

_____ flows smoothly from one idea (or line) to the next.

Correct, Accurate Copy

_____ follows the basic rules of spelling, grammar, and punctuation.

_____ uses appropriate formatting guidelines for final copies.

WRITING GUIDELINES
Poetry Writing

In a poem, you try to capture the essence (most important element) of a person, a memory, a belief, a feeling, or a dream. Since a poem is usually brief or compact, you must choose your words carefully. Each image (word picture) should hold meaning for your readers. (See page 180 for additional ideas.)

■ PREWRITING

1. **Choosing a Writing Idea . . .** To generate ideas for your poem, write freely in 5-minute bursts. Also look through your journal entries and current newspapers for ideas, and be on the lookout for intriguing sights and sounds around you. All you're looking for is an initial thought burst—a memory, a feeling, or an idea to get you started.

2. **Gathering Details . . .** List words and phrases that come to mind as you think about your writing idea. (Push yourself.) As your list grows, look for words or phrases that stand out. (They will give you a focus.) Continue listing until you feel a poem taking shape.

3. **Considering the Form . . .** Think about the form of your poem. Some poems are written in basic list form. Others follow specific guidelines (ballads, haiku, and so on). And some take on a form of their own. (See the sample poems, pages 181-183.)

■ WRITING AND REVISING

4. **Shaping Your Poem . . .** Present your idea in an interesting way. Then explore (compare, describe, clarify) the idea until you find a key insight or a surprise (like the climax in fiction). You might end with a final twist or a deepening of the meaning.

5. **Revising Your Writing . . .** Keep working with your poem until every word, phrase, and line says exactly what you want it to say.

■ EDITING AND PROOFREADING

6. **Checking for Style and Accuracy . . .** Make sure that each word, phrase, and line adds to the overall sound and meaning of your poem. Then check your spelling and grammar. (In a traditional poem like a ballad, the first word of each line is usually capitalized.)

   [HOT LINK] Use "Assessment Rubric," page 184, as a helpful revising and editing guide.

7. **Preparing a Final Copy . . .** Write or keyboard a neat final copy of your poem; proofread your copy before sharing it.

A **Closer Look** at Poetry Writing

Poets Some people think that poets are way out there . . . strange beings from a strange land. But in truth, poets are very much of this world; each poem they write is an attempt to interpret some part of life—an everyday occurrence (tending a garden), a difficult aspect of life (isolation in modern society), or something in between.

And Their Poems Since poems are almost always brief expressions of experience, every word and phrase is important. Prose writers think in terms of sentences, but poets think in terms of images (word pictures). Poets pay close attention to the sound and flow of their words—not to draw undue attention to them, but to help express a precise meaning. How poets arrange the images on a page depends on two things: (1) the type of poem they are writing and (2) the message they want to communicate.

FAQ *How can I become a good poet?*

No one really knows the answer to this question, not even our most celebrated poets. Without a doubt, however, reading good poetry is the best preparation. (Ask your teacher for suggested titles.) Then experiment with the different approaches to poetry, including some of the suggestions listed below. Above all else, keep writing. You may discover your best poems while writing your worst.

Starting Points for Poems

- **Share a memory** by writing freely about a vivid experience from your past; review this writing for a strong image that can serve as a starting point for a poem. (See page 181 for a sample.)
- **Create a springboard poem** by completing a starter line such as "I am the person who . . . ," "The time is right for . . . ," or "When I . . . , I feel . . . ." Then list thoughts and images that "spring" to mind as you think about this statement. When you run out of ideas, repeat the starter line. (See page 182 for a sample.)
- **Piece together a "found" poem** by searching newspapers, magazine ads, and pamphlets for snatches of prose that, when cut and pasted into poetic lines, make a new kind of sense. (See page 182 for a sample.)
- **Capture a person in a poem** by focusing on a family member, a friend, or an intriguing acquaintance. Share something unique or special about your subject. (See page 183 for a sample.)

Sample **Memory Poem**

   In this poem, student writer Lisa Prusinski investigates her feelings about a childhood friend. Note how the writer takes you from spring through summer, when the friend leaves. (From *Merlyn's Pen: Fiction, Essays, and Poems by America's Teens.* Copyright by Merlyn's Pen Inc. All rights reserved.)

To Steven, My Childhood Friend

The poem has a personal tone as if written directly to Steven.

In June we went crayfishing;
You broke my pail.
You made me red-faced and angry
Cheating in board games,
Scribbling in my coloring book.
I tried to be your friend,
But you wrecked my block house in one blow.

For your birthday, a mud-puddle day in July,
We gave you a T-shirt that read
"Joe Cool";
You lived up to it well
Standing on a swing like a mighty warrior.
Never were you content with peace—

The writer includes visual details, making it easy to see the subject.

Blocking the sidewalk with your bike
Creating havoc.
I wished and wished that you would go away,
and late one afternoon
I heard the rumor goin' round the block
That your dad was transferred
To Indiana.
I rejoiced:
No more broken dolls or fixed games of tag.

For the remaining part of that dusty August
The neighborhood was quiet and still;
We were restless and antsy,
Only hushed board games

The writer comes full circle, picking up details from the beginning.

And calm-weathered days with our blocks.
No more art contests or anticipated warfare.
No one knocking on our doors
With invitations
To crayfish anymore. ∎

Sample **Springboard Poem**

This poem by student writer Shannon Spencer begins and ends with the same "I am . . . " statement. In between, she lists thoughts that this statement "springs" to mind.

> ### I Am
>
> I am a romantic girl who loves to dream.
> I see exotic lands on the other side of the world.
> I hear waves crashing on a distant shore.
> I see a setting sun and a rising moon.
>
> I pretend to be someone else.
> I feel the wind on my face; I stand in a golden meadow.
> I touch the infinite sky as I soar with silver wings.
> I worry that I will be trapped in this town forever.
>
> I understand that I am a dreamer.
> I dream of magical, fantasy worlds.
> I try to hold on to this wild imagination.
> I am a romantic girl who loves to dream. ■

The poem consists of "romantic" images.

Sample **Found Poem**

Common street signs are the source of this sample poem by teacher and writer Ken Taylor. The choice of signs and the position of the words say something about the pace and quality of modern life.

> ### Life Signs
>
> GO! GO!   STOP!
> ENTER   DO NOT ENTER   EXIT   WAIT!
> WAIT WAIT WAIT WAIT WAIT WAIT WAIT WAIT
> WALK   WALK DO NOT RUN
> WRONG WAY   ONE WAY   NO THRU PASSAGE   NO
> WAY?
> NO   NO   NO   NO   NO
> STOPPINGSTANDINGPARKINGSMOKINGLOITERING
> EXIT
> ENTRANCE?   NOT AN ENTRANCE
> SLIPPERY
> WHEN
> WET PAINT
> SILENCE ■

The signs are repeated, run together, and broken apart.

Sample **Poem About a Person**

In this poem, student writer Jessica Feeney presents a dreamlike picture of her mother.

Transplanting Life

I reach out my hand and wipe away a small circle
    of condensation from my bedroom window.
How long has she been down there at the bottom of the hill?
In that other world.

The writer captures her mother at work in her own special world.

There stands my mother, her back to me,
    hair flying with the breeze,
    hands in the dark, cool soil,
Bending over what the earth has given her to work with.
She stays right there, filling the world with rich colors,
    deep green foliage, and lush petals.
I watch her move under the thin, transparent ray of sunlight
    that seems to illuminate only her.
It seems so lonely down there.
I will never comprehend what it is that attracts her to nature,
    never understand the peace and calmness it provides her.
But she comes into the house
    bringing a rush of clean, healthy air,
Runs her rough hands and long fingers
    with black soil under the nails
    under a stream of warm water.

A sense of calm is created through a series of images.

I close my eyes and visualize
    the beauty and happiness in her face
    when the smooth round tomatoes she has given birth to
    lie on our plates,
    when the crimson petals unfold and look toward the sun. ■

Assessment Rubric

Use this checklist to evaluate your poetry writing. This rubric is arranged according to the traits of good writing described in your handbook. (See pages 21-26.)

Stimulating Ideas

The writing . . .

_____ focuses on a specific memory, feeling, belief, or person.

_____ brings the subject to life.

_____ contains strong images (word pictures).

Logical Organization

_____ forms a meaningful whole—an idea is creatively presented and developed.

_____ ends with a final twist or deepening of meaning.

Engaging Voice

_____ speaks in a voice that reflects the poem's intent.

_____ maintains a consistent voice throughout.

Original Word Choice

_____ contains specific sensory details.

_____ employs poetic devices (metaphors, repetition, and so on).

Effective Sentence Style

_____ moves smoothly from one image to the next.

_____ sounds effective when read out loud.

Correct, Accurate Copy

_____ adheres to the basic rules of spelling and grammar.

_____ follows the appropriate formatting guidelines (if it is a traditional poem).

_____ looks interesting on the page (if it is a free-verse poem).

"It is not best that we should all think alike; it is the difference of opinion which makes horse races." —Mark Twain

PERSUASIVE Writing

Talk. Talk. Talk. In truth, talk takes up a lot of your time—be it mindless chatter, playful kidding, heartfelt exchanges, or serious discussions. Even when you're alone, you talk (in your mind, of course) to work things out in your life: *Should I or shouldn't I? What if I . . . ?*

In a sense, your writing is a form of talking, too, since every piece of writing that you develop is part of a dialogue with an intended audience. In persuasive writing, the subject of this chapter, your goal is to get your audience to think the way that you do about a timely and controversial issue, so you need to make your "talk" especially convincing. This chapter includes guidelines and samples to help you do just that.

Preview

- Pet Peeve Essay
- Editorial
- Personal Commentary
- Essay of Opposing Ideas
- Essay of Argumentation
- Assessment Rubric

WRITING GUIDELINES

Pet Peeve Essay

In a pet peeve essay, you react to a common, everyday annoyance. Maybe a button on a shirt or blouse always seems to fall off when you are in a hurry, your deodorant never works when you really need it, or people always seem to push or cut ahead of you when you are waiting in line. Remember to share specific details that show why the behavior or situation affects you as it does.

■ PREWRITING

1. **Choosing a Subject . . .** For your subject, you may choose something that really "grinds your beans" or something that is just irritating enough to be memorable. Review your personal journal or think about a typical day in your life for ideas.

2. **Gathering Details . . .** Once you have a subject in mind, collect your thoughts about it: *How do you feel about this subject? What exactly causes your negative reactions? Why do you react the way you do?*

3. **Focusing Your Efforts . . .** Determine how you want to write about your pet peeve: *Are you going to focus on one specific experience or discuss the subject in more general terms?* Also consider the voice or tone of your writing: *Are you going to be serious, playful, or sarcastic?*

■ WRITING AND REVISING

4. **Connecting Your Ideas . . .** Freely develop your first draft, working in the thoughts and details you've collected as well as anything new that occurs to you. Let the real "you" shine through in your writing.

5. **Improving Your Writing . . .** Read over your first draft (silently and aloud), making sure it forms a meaningful and engaging whole. Also have a classmate react to your work. Then revise your essay until it says exactly what you want it to say from start to finish.

■ EDITING AND PROOFREADING

6. **Checking for Style and Accuracy . . .** Review your revised writing for style, making sure that all of your sentences read smoothly and clearly and that you have used the best words to express your ideas. Then correct any grammar, spelling, and punctuation errors.

   [HOT LINK] See "Assessment Rubric," page 198, for a helpful revising and editing guide.

7. **Preparing a Final Copy . . .** Write or keyboard a neat final copy of your pet peeve essay, and proofread it before sharing it with others.

Sample **Pet Peeve Essay**

This pet peeve summarizes writer Ken Taylor's ongoing (and losing) battle with telephones of assorted sizes and shapes, a war being waged on a variety of fronts.

Telephone Tyranny

The opening lines describe a series of frustrating incidents involving the telephone.

I get into the shower. The phone rings. I drip my way to the phone. The caller has hung up. I have an urgent call to make and hurry to a pay phone on the corner. The phone is out of order. I try a half dozen phones. They are all inoperable. After I find a phone with a dial tone, it eats my only quarter, and I dial the wrong number. The phone rings on my nightstand at 4:00 a.m. I jump a good three feet and knock the lamp off the stand on my way back to earth. A voice I never heard before wants to know if Harry is there. I don't know any Harrys.

The listing of incidents implies an ongoing war with telephones.

I'm on the parkway going 65 miles an hour. I look in the rearview mirror. There's a car about to drive right through me. The driver is talking on his cell phone. I just sit down to dinner, and the phone rings. There's a recorded voice wanting to know if I'm happy with my present insurance coverage. I return to my food. The phone rings again. This time someone wants to sell me "call-waiting."

I can hear the phone ringing as I get off the elevator for my apartment. The phone keeps on ringing. I fumble for my keys, open the door, rush to the phone, and the caller has hung up. (Probably the same person who calls when I'm in the shower.)

I call a friend at his office. A secretary tells me I can call him direct on a different extension. Would I like to hang up and make the call again? No, I wouldn't. Okay, she will "try" to transfer my call. She tries. The next thing I hear is a dial tone.

The final suggestion indicates that a real solution to the writer's problem doesn't exist.

I dial a friend at home. She has "call-waiting," and asks if I'd mind calling her back. She's right in the middle of an important conversation. I call another friend at his office. He sounds as if he were talking from the moon. He says he's using his "speaker phone" and isn't it great?

I'm seriously thinking of taking up letter writing. The convenience of technology has me at my wit's end. ∎

WRITING GUIDELINES

Editorial

In an editorial, you present a brief essay of opinion about a timely and important topic. An effective editorial presents an informed argument that suggests a new course of action or a possible solution to a problem. When developing an editorial, make sure to state your position and provide solid evidence to support your point of view.

■ PREWRITING

1. **Choosing a Subject . . .** If you don't already have a subject in mind, review stories in a current edition of a local newspaper. Or you can write general categories such as "school," "sports," "entertainment," and "environment" across the top of a piece of paper. Then, under each of the headings, list current topics that come to mind. Choose one that you feel strongly about.

2. **Gathering Details . . .** Jot down everything you know and feel about your subject. Then refer to other sources of information if necessary.

3. **Focusing Your Efforts . . .** Review what you have gathered to see if you have sufficient evidence to support your opinion. (To help clarify your thinking, put your opinion in writing.) Also consider the opposing arguments that you may need to counter.

■ WRITING AND REVISING

4. **Connecting Your Ideas . . .** Build your argument in the most logical way. (You may want to save your best point for last.) Remember that editorials are usually published in the newspaper, so use a strong, to-the-point style and write brief paragraphs.

5. **Improving Your Writing . . .** Review your first draft carefully, paying special attention to any "loose ends" in your argument. If you have time, test your editorial on someone. Ask for suggestions. Then make the necessary changes to improve your editorial.

■ EDITING AND PROOFREADING

6. **Checking for Style and Accuracy . . .** Review your revised writing for style, making sure that all of your sentences read smoothly and clearly, and that you have used the best words to express your ideas. Then check for grammar, spelling, and punctuation errors.

   [HOT LINK] See "Assessment Rubric," page 198, for a helpful revising and editing guide.

7. **Preparing a Final Copy . . .** Write or keyboard a neat final copy of your editorial, and proofread your copy carefully before submitting it.

Sample **Editorial**

In this editorial, student writer Jeff Bulthuis promotes work-study programs as valuable learning experiences. He supports his claim very effectively by sharing his own experiences as a volunteer in a local hospital.

Education Through Application

The opening paragraph establishes an engaging personal tone.

Rather than spend my senior year taking a lot of elective courses, I wanted to get involved in a special work-study program where I could volunteer my services at the local hospital. My proposal was accepted without complaint by the high school principal, the dean of students, and the superintendent. It's the best decision I ever made.

As students, we aren't always able to retain information in our classes because we hardly ever see it applied in everyday life. We are taught a new concept one day, and the next day we have no recollection of what the teacher was even talking about. Studies have shown that students become more knowledgeable through visual aids. If the learning process can be greatly improved by seeing concepts in the classroom, imagine the possibilities of retaining new information by experiencing it in real-life situations. I know firsthand how valuable such experience can be.

Specific examples support the writer's claim.

I learned a lesson in faithfulness when I met Tommy, a father who has visited his comatose daughter in the hospital three times a week for the past 14 years. I came to appreciate my Spanish classes when I invited Antonio, a Hispanic American struggling through rehab, to the chapel service in the hospital. I came to value the strength of human contact when I held another patient's hand while a doctor made his examination. I also learned about the importance of choosing a career that I really like, because on many occasions, doctors told me, "Don't ever become a doctor; it's not worth all of the stress."

In closing, the writer recommends a specific course of action.

I have seen time and time again the beneficial results of learning through experience. My high school gave me a firm foundation in education, but it was only through application that I truly learned. All students should have the opportunity to volunteer at places that interest them. I was given the chance, and every day I reap the rewards of that experience. ■

WRITING GUIDELINES

Personal Commentary

In a personal commentary, you react thoughtfully to some aspect of your life. Think of a commentary as one step removed from an editorial. An editorial expresses a specific opinion about a newsworthy event, often calling for a particular course of action. A commentary makes a more even-handed and reflective statement about life and may be either serious or playful in tone.

■ PREWRITING

1. **Choosing a Subject . . .** Think about some recent experiences or conversations for possible ideas. Also review your journal entries. A commentary could focus on some aspect of school life (*athletes*), popular culture (*tattoos*), or life in general (*growing up*).

2. **Gathering Details . . .** Write freely about your subject to determine what you already know about it and what you need to find out. Continue by gathering information from other sources as needed.

3. **Focusing Your Efforts . . .** Review your freewriting and other notes; ask at least one of your classmates to react to your ideas. Then state a possible focus for your work—a sentence (or two) expressing the main point you want to convey in your commentary.

■ WRITING AND REVISING

4. **Connecting Your Ideas . . .** Think of an engaging way to start your commentary. Then write your first draft, working in those observations and details that support your focus.

5. **Improving Your Writing . . .** Carefully review your first draft, paying special attention to its completeness and consistency in tone. *Did you say everything you wanted to say? Do you sound sincere and interested in your subject?* Then add, cut, and rearrange ideas as necessary.

■ EDITING AND PROOFREADING

6. **Checking for Style and Accuracy . . .** Review your revised writing for style. Make sure that all of your sentences read smoothly and clearly, and that you have used the best words to express your ideas. Then check for grammar, spelling, and punctuation errors.

   [HOT LINK] See "Assessment Rubric," page 198, for a helpful revising and editing guide.

7. **Preparing a Final Copy . . .** Write or keyboard a neat final copy of your commentary; proofread your copy before sharing it.

Sample **Personal Commentary**

In this personal commentary, student writer Matt Ostwalt focuses on the pressures of high school athletics. It is his contention that the emphasis on winning takes most of the fun out of participating in sports. See if you agree.

The Demands of Winning

The writer presents his thesis in the opening paragraph.

As a wrestler, I know how much fun it is to win. In fact, there are few things that I enjoy more. However, I think it is important that we teach athletes how to love a sport and enjoy it for all it has to offer. Competitiveness is great, but sometimes the pressures of being the best can overload teenagers.

Personal reflections enhance the commentary.

I see and hear wrestlers day in and day out talk about how hard it is to love the sport because of the demands it takes to be the best. Pressure to win is laid upon wrestlers in many different ways. For example, our coach is a great coach, and I know that he cares about every one of his wrestlers, but every time that I walk out on that mat, I hear his words echoing in my mind: "You are a West Lincoln wrestler, and you will win." How can I not feel pressure to win, and anguish after losing, with that in mind? So if I do lose, I go home and mope around because I feel that I have let my coach and myself down. However, this doesn't last long because homework has to be done, and I have to sleep sometime, too. Then there is the never-ending concern with making weight for the next match.

I often wonder what I am doing to myself. I wonder if it would be any different if I still loved what I did, or if I were not as good as I am. If I had a penny for every time I have these thoughts, I could balance the budget.

In closing, the writer remembers an earlier time.

I remember how much fun wrestling was in eighth grade, even though I did not win a single match. I always loved practices, and I always thought they ended too quickly. I know I would miss wrestling if I decided to quit. I just wish I could return to the time when making weight was not a problem and when losing did not matter as long as I gave 100 percent. Now when I walk off that mat, I know I have given 100 percent, but it never seems to be enough. ■

WRITING GUIDELINES
Essay of Opposing Ideas

In an essay of opposing ideas, you present two (or more) points of view related to an important issue. Think of issues that are important to you as well as issues that concern young people in general. If you're speaking from personal experience, the opposing ideas will naturally unfold as you tell your story. If you are sharing facts and details from other sources, you will have to think about the best way to shape your essay.

■ PREWRITING

1. **Choosing a Subject . . .** In a small group, or on your own, produce a list of some of the hottest topics in your world (grades, college, teenage drinking, driving, boy-girl relationships, generation gap, culture clash, and so forth). Review your list for potential subjects.

2. **Gathering Details . . .** After you choose a subject, collect information using the following strategy: Fold a piece of paper two or three times—lengthwise—depending upon the number of opposing viewpoints (two or three) related to your subject. Use each folded column to list the facts and details related to a specific viewpoint.

3. **Focusing Your Efforts . . .** Review your collecting, and think about the focus, shape, and voice of your essay: *What message do you want to get across? What will you say first, second, and third? Will you speak in a formal or informal voice?*

■ WRITING AND REVISING

4. **Connecting Your Ideas . . .** Write your first draft freely, using your prewriting and planning, but work in other details that occur to you as you write.

5. **Improving Your Writing . . .** Carefully review your first draft, paying special attention to the development of the opposing points of view: *Have you addressed all the ideas fairly and completely?* Revise your writing as necessary.

■ EDITING AND PROOFREADING

6. **Checking for Style and Accuracy . . .** Review your revised writing for style; then check for mechanical errors.

   [HOT LINK] See "Assessment Rubric," page 198, for a helpful revising and editing guide.

7. **Preparing a Final Copy . . .** Write or keyboard a neat final copy of your essay; proofread your copy before sharing it.

Sample **Essay of Opposing Ideas**

In the following essay, student writer Sue Chong speaks from personal experience about the challenges of being a young Korean woman growing up in America. (This essay first appeared in *New Youth Connections: The Magazine Written By and For New York Youth*.)

He Said I Was Too American

The opening introduces the players in the conflict and the source of their opposing ideas.

My friend Kevin and I dated for a year, and during that time, we argued until we got sick of it. We argued about the stupid things all couples fight about, but the main thing that came between us was something that other couples probably don't have to deal with. We constantly argued about whether I was too Americanized.

Kevin and I both came to the United States from Korea five years ago. Although we had this in common, we had different points of view on everything. He would ask me why I couldn't be like other Korean girls. If I were a "real" Korean girl, I would listen to him when he told me to do something, depend on him for most things, and think his way instead of my way. When I didn't agree with him, we would have another fight. To me, he was too narrow-minded. He refused to accept any culture except his own, and he always thought his way was the only way.

> "He would ask me why I couldn't be like other Korean girls."

I eat Korean food, speak Korean, respect my parents, and celebrate Korean holidays and traditional days. I even joined the Korean Club in school so that I can observe my customs with Korean friends.

The author provides specific examples of the conflict.

During the past five years, however, I have come to like certain customs from other cultures. For example, I see the way my Hispanic friends greet people with affection. They kiss and hug when they say "hello," and I love this. (In Korea, people are much more formal; they just shake hands and bow to each other out of respect.) So I started kissing my friends on the cheek, too.

Kevin didn't like this, and he told me so. He even asked me to stop it. I asked him why, and he told me that he didn't like it and that other Koreans didn't act that way. I didn't want to stop, so I did it anyway—but not as much. ▶

He Said I Was Too American
(continued)

Korean men like to tell their wives and girlfriends what to do. He would always tell me how to dress and how to act in front of others. He wanted me to stay next to him all the time. I would complain that I was not his little toy and that he couldn't just order me around.

When I would go against his wishes, Kevin would say, "Why are you so Americanized?" I didn't know how to respond to his question. He said I must be ashamed of my country and my culture to act the way I did. I was shocked, and it hurt me deeply. I was not ashamed of my country or culture. I am proud of being a Korean. I just want to accept other cultures, too.

I can't deny that I sometimes act like an American, trying to be more independent and outgoing than other Korean girls. But I still act like a Korean. I want to go with the flow, and that doesn't mean that I don't like my own culture. I am trying to balance two cultures. Through my boyfriend, I got a chance to think about who I am. I realized that I am a Korean and an American, too. ■

> The closing provides a thoughtful analysis of the conflict.

Writing **Two-Part Essays**

The guidelines on page 192 show one way to write an essay of opposing ideas. The two-part strategy that follows offers another:

- **Begin** with a starter sentence about your subject after you have done some thinking about it. Consider these two examples:

    I think . . .   *but*   he or she thinks or says . . .
      Part 1   Part 2

    You can . . .   *but*   you can also . . .
      Part 1   Part 2

- **Write freely** about each part of your starter statement. Keep the ideas flowing for 10 minutes or more.

- **Review** your writing for ideas that you would like to explore further or use in your essay.

- **Develop** your essay by connecting the thoughts and ideas you have gathered.

WRITING GUIDELINES
Essay of Argumentation

The purpose of an essay of argumentation is to convince readers to accept your position on an important subject that you have strong, genuine feelings about. The quality of your argument depends upon your ability to support your position with solid facts and details and to counter significant opposing points of view. (See pages 115-123 and 445-446 for help.)

▪ PREWRITING

1. **Choosing a Subject . . .** Review your texts or class notes for possible subjects. Also think about issues or problems you hear debated locally or nationally.

   ✸ Test a possible subject in this way: (a) identify a reasonable claim to argue for, and (b) list at least two points that support the claim.

2. **Gathering Details . . .** Collect your own thoughts about the subject; then refer to books, magazines, newspapers, and the Internet for additional information. While you take notes, label points in support of your position "pro" and those against "con."

3. **Focusing Your Efforts . . .** Review all of the information you have gathered to determine whether or not you have enough good evidence to support your position or claim.

4. **Planning and Organizing . . .** Decide on the best arrangement of your ideas. If possible, deal with any opposing arguments early in your essay and save your best supporting argument for last.

▪ WRITING AND REVISING

5. **Connecting Your Ideas . . .** Write the first draft of your argument, using your prewriting and planning as a guide. If you get stuck, talk through your argument with a classmate.

6. **Improving Your Writing . . .** Review your essay from start to finish, paying special attention to the overall logic and completeness of your argument. Revise your essay as necessary.

▪ EDITING AND PROOFREADING

7. **Checking for Style and Accuracy . . .** Review your revised writing for style; then check for mechanical errors.

   [HOT LINK] See "Assessment Rubric," page 198, for a helpful revising and editing guide.

8. **Preparing a Final Copy . . .** Write or keyboard a neat final copy of your essay, and proofread it before sharing it with others.

Sample Essay of Argumentation

In this essay, scientist William C. Stevens argues that it is becoming more and more difficult in this country to find employment in the sciences. He cites a number of sources in support of his position.

Who Will Hire Our Scientists?

In the opening paragraph, the writer effectively leads up to his position.

I used to preach that the world was an oyster for anyone achieving a science degree. The Department of Labor had been forecasting a dramatic shortage of scientists, and immigration policies were designed to recruit as many scientists as possible from foreign countries. But those forecasts turned out to be wrong, and today we have a country that doesn't want many scientists.

I recently attended a meeting in Grand Rapids of the Analytical Laboratory Managers Association, and I took part in a roundtable discussion called "The Talent Pool." One member from the Philadelphia area said there were over 1,500 applicants for each entry-level chemist position. Another from a smaller city said there were "only" 150 applicants per position there.

My friends at the meeting from a major petrochemical company were depressed from watching the decline of the research and development (R & D) effort they spent 25 years building. "It used to be you couldn't get a spot in a 150-space parking lot if you got to work after 8 a.m.," one said. "Now there are never more than 25 or 30 cars in the lot." Pharmaceutical firms are scaling back R & D, too, closing American laboratories while continuing work in European labs. For computer scientists, the assurance that they would always have work ended when the computer programming work started to be shipped to countries such as India.

The engaging personal voice holds the readers' interest.

I subscribed to the *Young Scientists Network* on the Internet back in the early '90s when there were only a few hundred members. I saw that number swell to over 3,000 practically overnight. This is a group dedicated to fighting "the myth" of a scientists shortage and was started by unemployed physics Ph.D.'s. There is almost no hope at all of a Ph.D. physicist working in his or her chosen field these days, and this is growing increasingly true for other science Ph.D.'s as well. This has not been helped by the government's egregious [terrible] immigration policy to import foreign scientists and mathematicians.

— Is this all because our education system is producing inferior scientists? I don't think so. I think it is simply the economics of corporate greed. If scientists elsewhere work cheaper, then elsewhere is where the science will be done. I will admit that I have noticed a steady decline in the science and math training of incoming college students and, subsequently, beginning graduate students, but the science departments of our good universities are among the best in the world . . . for now.

The writer's analysis makes a convincing point for his position.

It is clear to me that we scientists need to tell the public that what we do is important—but not always easy to justify in concrete terms. My own field began as an idle physicist's curiosity a little over 50 years ago. It was never imagined that nuclear magnetic resonance (my field) would spawn powerful techniques for determining molecular structure in the laboratory or diagnosing illness and injury in the hospital MRI unit.

I was born a couple of years before *Sputnik,* and I've always known an American society that gives at least casual approval to the advancement of science. Now that the Cold War is over, it seems that we no longer have a sense of urgency

"Can we afford to have other countries do our scientific thinking for us?"

Two questions keep the argument alive in the readers' minds.

that scientific excellence is necessary to the nation's safety, its economic security, and the public good. These are the big questions I wish to raise: Can we, as a nation, afford to be less and less involved in the practice of science? Can we afford to have other countries do our scientific thinking for us? ■

Assessment Rubric

Use this rubric as a checklist to assess the effectiveness of your persuasive essays. The rubric is arranged according to the traits of effective writing as described in this handbook. (See pages 21-26.)

Stimulating Ideas

The writing . . .

_____ establishes an opinion or a position about a timely subject.

_____ contains specific facts, details, and examples to support the opinion or position.

_____ maintains a clear, consistent stand from start to finish.

Logical Organization

_____ includes a clear beginning, strong support, and a convincing conclusion.

_____ arranges ideas in an organized manner (point by point; opposing arguments first, then supporting arguments; etc.).

_____ presents reasonable, logical arguments. (See pages 445-446.)

Engaging Voice

_____ speaks in a convincing and knowledgeable way.

_____ shows that the writer feels strongly about his or her position.

Original Word Choice

_____ explains or defines any unfamiliar terms.

_____ uses specific nouns, vivid verbs, and convincing language.

Effective Sentence Style

_____ flows smoothly from one idea to the next.

_____ displays varied sentence beginnings and lengths.

Correct, Accurate Copy

_____ adheres to the basic rules of writing.

_____ follows the appropriate form and design for final copies.

"I hear and I forget;
   I see and I remember;
   I write and I understand."
                —Chinese Proverb

ACADEMIC Writing

Define the universe and give three examples. This assignment almost looks and sounds real, doesn't it? But . . . define the universe? I don't think so. This message was scrawled on a wall by a clever student, or former student, who was poking fun at school-related writing.

Of course, your academic writing is serious business, assigned to help you form your thoughts about the different subjects you are studying. For example, in a science class you may be asked to explain how a complex process works, or in a history class you may be asked to analyze the causes and effects of an important event.

The best academic writing sounds like the writer knows what he or she is talking about. It flows logically from one point to the next. It is the end product of careful planning, writing, and revising. This chapter includes guidelines and samples for the many types of academic writing.

Preview

- ○ Process Essay
- ○ Essay of Comparison
- ○ Cause/Effect Essay
- ○ Essay of Definition
- ○ Problem/Solution Essay
- ○ Assessment Rubric

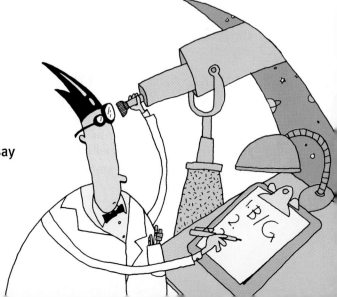

WRITING GUIDELINES

Process Essay

In a process essay, you explain how something works or how to do or make something. Your challenge is to write clearly and completely so that readers can easily follow the explanation. To do that, you must have a thorough understanding of your subject.

■ PREWRITING

1. **Choosing a Subject . . .** If your assignment is to explain how something works, review your class notes or text for ideas. For example, in a science class you might explain how a cut heals or a seed germinates. In a more general assignment, you might explain a certain job or chore, a hobby, or a special talent—like changing a flat tire or designing a Web site.

2. **Gathering Details . . .** List facts and details about your subject as they come to mind, or freewrite an instant version of your essay to see how much you already know about your subject—and how much you need to find out. Collect additional information as necessary.

3. **Planning and Organizing . . .** Arrange the information you have collected according to the steps in the process. Also write down the main point you want your audience to understand or appreciate.

■ WRITING AND REVISING

4. **Connecting Your Ideas . . .** Write your first draft freely, working in details according to your prewriting and planning. As you develop your writing, be sure you cover all the steps—including those steps that you may take for granted, but your reader will need to know.

5. **Improving Your Writing . . .** As you review your first draft, make sure you have included all the necessary information and that it is arranged chronologically. Ask yourself what added steps or details could make the process even clearer. Also ask at least one classmate to check your paper for clarity and completeness. Revise your work as needed.

■ EDITING AND PROOFREADING

6. **Checking for Style and Accuracy . . .** Review your revised writing for style and accuracy. Make sure that your sentences read smoothly and clearly, and that you have used the best words to express your ideas. Then check for spelling, grammar, and punctuation errors.

   [HOT LINK] See "Assessment Rubric," page 213, for a helpful revising and editing guide.

7. **Preparing a Final Copy . . .** Write or keyboard a neat final copy of your essay. (See pages 30-32 for formatting ideas.) Proofread your final copy.

Sample **Process Essay**

In this paper, student writer Julisa Rios leads the reader step-by-step through both the donor and recipient process of a bone marrow transplant.

The Gift of Life

The writer states her thesis in the opening sentence.

The procedure for donating bone marrow is fairly simple and very interesting. To start, a small amount of blood is taken from the volunteer at an approved donor center. The sample is then typed for antigens (immunity factors), and the results are entered on a computer registry. If all six of the donor's antigens match the patient's, the donor is counseled about the donation process and given a physical examination.

After the exam, potential donors go through a thorough information session during which they are advised about the risks of the procedure. If all goes well, the donor makes the decision to donate and signs an "intent to donate" form.

The writer provides step-by-step details.

Marrow is extracted from the donor in a simple surgical procedure under general or spinal anesthesia. Two to five percent of the donor's marrow is extracted from the back of the pelvis through a special needle and syringe. The extraction is fairly simple—only a few tiny incisions are made. They are so small, in fact, they require no stitches. The whole procedure takes only about an hour to complete. The donor is usually kept in the hospital overnight for observation.

As to the transplantation process, the donated marrow is transfused directly into the bloodstream, much like a blood transfusion. Healthy marrow cells travel to bone cavities, where they begin to grow and replace the old marrow. The patient must be isolated in a protected environment until the new marrow produces enough white blood cells to fight off the disease.

An increased white blood count, a sign that the new marrow is beginning to function, generally appears about three to four weeks after the procedure. The patient may be removed from protective isolation three to six weeks after the transplant, as long as the new marrow continues to produce white blood cells and there are no serious complications.

The closing answers the question "Who can donate?"

Any person between the ages of 18 and 60 who is in generally good health may become a bone marrow donor. All that person has to do is go to a National Marrow Donor Program center, get a blood test, and enter the tissue type in the National Registry. Then it's time to wait until a match is found. It's a life-saving process that more and more people are choosing to do. ■

WRITING GUIDELINES

Essay of Comparison

In an essay of comparison, you examine the similarities and differences between two or more subjects. Your subjects can come from any number of categories, including people, books, movies, events, experiments, feelings, and products. Just make sure that they come from the same category and that they would be interesting to compare.

■ PREWRITING

1. **Choosing a Subject . . .** Unless you already have two subjects in mind, review your class notes or text for ideas. You may also want to brainstorm for ideas with classmates, or write freely about your course work, noting potential subjects as they come to mind.

2. **Gathering Details . . .** Collect facts and details related to your subjects; consider taking notes on a graphic organizer. (See page 49.)

3. **Reviewing Your Work . . .** Study your notes to determine if you have enough information or need to find out more about your two subjects. Continue collecting as necessary.

4. **Focusing Your Efforts . . .** Write a possible thesis for your essay. Then plan your writing accordingly. (You can do a point-by-point comparison of the subjects, or you can address each subject separately, whichever seems more natural to you.)

■ WRITING AND REVISING

5. **Connecting Your Ideas . . .** Write your first draft, working in details according to your prewriting and planning. Pay special attention to the opening paragraph. It should gain your reader's attention and state the thesis of your essay.

6. **Improving Your Writing . . .** Carefully review your first draft, making sure that it is clear and logical from start to finish. (*Remember:* Your purpose is to help readers better understand the similarities and differences between the subjects.)

■ EDITING AND PROOFREADING

7. **Checking for Style and Accuracy . . .** Review your revised writing for style, making sure that your sentences read smoothly and clearly. Then check your work for spelling, grammar, and punctuation errors.

   [HOT LINK] See "Assessment Rubric," page 213, for a helpful revising and editing guide.

8. **Preparing a Final Copy . . .** Write or keyboard a neat final copy of your essay; then proofread your copy before submitting it.

Sample **Essay of Comparison**

In the following essay, the student writer talks about the effects of a personal struggle as she compares her relationship with friends at two different schools.

If Only They Knew

The writer's personal story leads readers into the essay.

Anorexia nervosa is an eating disorder that I struggled with for the majority of my middle school years and a portion of my high school years. My classmates at Riverview High School were aware of my disorder, and it greatly affected the way they treated me. At the start of my junior year, I transferred to Madison High School. I decided not to tell anyone at that school about my eating disorder since I was mostly recovered by that time. Even though my friends at Riverview and Madison all showed concern for my well-being, their approaches differed greatly, especially in lunchroom behavior, conversation, and individual opinions about my personality and character.

At Riverview, lunchtime was usually a nightmare for me. I would enter the cafeteria, and in my mind, all eyes would fix themselves upon my gangly figure. I would take my place at a table full of friends and try to enjoy a "normal" lunch. The problem was that I would not always eat lunch, and that greatly concerned my friends. They would watch to make sure that I was eating properly, almost forcing food into my mouth. Sometimes I would pretend to eat and then drop pieces of food into a napkin and throw it out with the trash. When some of my friends found out, they were furious, which seemed to cause even more trouble. Lunch was obviously not my favorite time of the day, and it involved a lot of stress.

A topic-by-topic comparison is made throughout the essay. (The first topic is lunchtime.)

Strangely, I stopped dreading lunch when I started at Madison. No one knew that I had an eating disorder, so they did not care what I ate. This lifted an enormous amount of stress from my life. I finally had the freedom to eat what I wanted without being harassed. It was still hard for me to eat in front of other people, which is common for anorexics, but I was able to put some of my fears aside. I began to enjoy lunch instead of disposing of it.

With my Riverview friends, instead of chatting about boys and other "girl things," we would discuss my disorder. Girls would follow me into the bathroom, and instead of styling their hair, they would check to see if I was throwing up. We never got to gossip together like normal middle-school girls because we had to focus on anorexia instead. All I really wanted to talk about was how cute Mike Reynolds looked that day. ▶

If Only They Knew
(continued)

I was totally shocked to find that all the life-and-death conversations disappeared when I went to Madison. It was so much fun to talk about the little things that occurred in everyday life. The subject of eating disorders rarely came up, and when it did, I was not the focus. I loved having the freedom to go into the bathroom without being followed. High school is meant to be filled with frivolous chatter, and at Madison I participated in more than my fair share.

I found that the students at Riverview had made many generalizations about my character, and their behavior was guided by those generalizations. Their natural instincts told them to help me. I appreciated their concern, but they never took the time to find out who I was as a person. They knew me only as an anorexic. My friends cared about my health, but they failed to care about me. Truthfully, all I wanted was for them to love me for me and not to obsess over my shortcomings.

The people at Madison took the time to know who I really was. They had no idea that I had been an anorexic, so that particular stereotype did not color their opinions of me. I was finally recognized for my talents and achievements, not my failures. I was honored as a good student. I was also honored as a cheerleader, and no one cared how I looked in my skirt. I could finally be viewed as a real person. I liked the way that people saw me at Madison, and I was no longer afraid to show my true character and personality.

> "The people at Madison took the time to know who I really was."

My days as an anorexic taught me many lessons that I would not trade for the world. They taught me about life and how to be a better friend. I learned about the joys of routine tasks such as eating lunch. I learned to appreciate the simple things in life like the gossip shared by a group of teenage girls. I gained an understanding of what true character is. I hold no grudges against those who so desperately tried to help me. In fact, I owe them a great debt. And I appreciate the people who helped me to see that there is more to life than having an eating disorder. ∎

WRITING GUIDELINES
Cause/Effect Essay

In a cause/effect essay, you present a thoughtful analysis of a timely subject. When you develop this type of essay, your first task is to identify the most important points related to your subject. Your second task is to make clear cause/effect connections between these points.

■ PREWRITING

1. **Choosing a Subject . . .** Consider recent experiences, conversations, and headlines for possible ideas. A cause/effect essay could focus on an improved situation in your school or community. It could focus on a recent development in medicine, on an exciting discovery, or on a milestone in history. Also consider personal events that have changed your life: gaining or losing a friend, learning about your family tree, and so on.

2. **Gathering Details . . .** Once you have a subject in mind, determine what you already know about it and what you need to find out. Refer to a variety of sources (books, magazines, the Internet, class notes, etc.) to gather details.

3. **Focusing Your Efforts . . .** Plan your essay by establishing a thesis as well as an effective order for presenting your ideas. (As always, your thesis statement may change as your writing and thinking develop.)

■ WRITING AND REVISING

4. **Connecting Your Ideas . . .** Develop your first draft, using your prewriting and planning as a general guide. Don't, however, be afraid to follow a new line of thinking if one begins to emerge. (Remember to identify your thesis in the opening paragraph.)

5. **Improving Your Writing . . .** Carefully examine your first draft to make sure that you have clearly established the cause/effect aspects of your subject. Ask at least one other person to react to your work as well. Add, cut, rearrange, or rewrite parts as necessary.

■ EDITING AND PROOFREADING

6. **Checking for Style and Accuracy . . .** Review your revised writing for style. Make sure that your sentences read smoothly and clearly, and that you have used the best words to express your ideas. Then check for spelling, punctuation, and grammar errors.

   [HOT LINK] See "Assessment Rubric," page 213, for a helpful revising and editing guide.

7. **Preparing a Final Copy . . .** Write or keyboard a neat final copy of your essay, and proofread your copy before submitting it.

Sample **Cause/Effect Essay**

In this essay, student writer Nathan Borgen explores the renewed interest in major league baseball. He cites the historic performances of two players as the major cause of this renaissance.

Saving Baseball

The opening gains the readers' interest with some baseball history.

—— Back in 1994, professional baseball players went on strike because they felt that they were underpaid for their services—underpaid to the tune of an average annual salary of just over $1 million. The strike cost baseball the World Series that year, which at the time was one of the holiest of all major sports championships. During the year and a half that baseball was on strike, I, along with most of the free world, had a hard time sympathizing with players who made so much money. Even when the strike ended, baseball had a hard time attracting fans, and some that did show up wore bags over their heads so as not to be noticed and disowned by friends and family.

It wasn't until 1998 that baseball became popular again. A gentle giant named Mark McGwire and a 37-year-old record for home runs in a season (61) played a major role in baseball's renaissance. Factor in someone named Ken Griffey, Jr., and another player named Sammy Sosa, and the executives in charge of baseball's public relations were happier than kids on Christmas morning.

> "People started coming out to ballparks in huge numbers, and the ball clubs had trouble keeping their concession stands stocked . . . "

Specific statistics add authority to the essay.

—— McGwire and Griffey drew crowds wherever they went because both of them were hitting home runs at a record pace. Then June rolled around, and Sammy Sosa got hot— so hot that he ended up breaking the record for most home runs in one month (20) while keeping his perennial cellar-dwelling team at least 10 games above .500 throughout most of the early season. People started coming out to ballparks in huge numbers, and the ball clubs had trouble keeping their concession stands stocked because of the large crowds.

Sosa's team, referred to as the "lovable losers" for nearly half a century, started playing before standing-room-only crowds because of their success and because of Sosa's power hitting. Things were going so well that sports fans in Chicago all but forgot about the retirement of a certain basketball star (Michael Jordan).

Everyone wanted to interview McGwire, the player most people thought would break the season home-run record. He was asked time and time again whether he thought he could do it. He almost always gave the same answer: "Once someone hits 50 by September 1, then he has a chance. But until then, I really don't want to talk about it."

Fast-forward again to September 1. McGwire had 55 home runs and Sosa had 52. That's when things got really exciting. Every game that these two played in was sold out. When McGwire reached 60 home runs, McGwire's team and Sosa's team met in a weekend series. In the first game of the series, McGwire hit a towering drive to tie the record at 61 home runs. The next night McGwire hit a screaming line drive over the left-field wall for number 62, ensuring his place in baseball's storied history.

The sum-up of the season ties everything together. —— The home-run race continued right to the end of the season. McGwire ended up with 70 home runs and Sosa ended up with 66. The entire country was mesmerized by these two men. Sosa's team also earned a position in the play-offs, which thrilled all of their fans across the country. Add in events such as pitcher David Wells's perfect game and pitcher Roger Clemens's incredible winning streak, and baseball again became America's game. All it took was the impressive performances of a few very impressive players. ■

WRITING GUIDELINES

Essay of Definition

In this type of essay, you explain a commonly used term or concept that is not easy to define. It may be that the term is complicated (*inflation, cancer,* or *democracy*) or that it means different things to different people (*love, courage,* or *fairness*). Consider including the following elements in your essay: dictionary definitions, personal definitions, negative definitions (telling what it is not), comparisons, quotations, and anecdotes (stories).

■ PREWRITING

1. **Choosing a Subject . . .** Select a term or concept that is complex enough to require some real thought on your part. If no subject comes to mind, write freely about your course work, about current events, or about your personal life. Also consider terms people either misuse or use too often.

2. **Gathering Details . . .** Collect information about your subject by referring to dictionaries, interviews, song lyrics, personal anecdotes, newspapers, the Internet, and so on.

3. **Focusing Your Efforts . . .** Plan how you want to arrange the details. You may want to begin with a dictionary definition, then include a quotation or two, follow with an important comparison, and so on. Experiment with a number of combinations.

■ WRITING AND REVISING

4. **Connecting Your Ideas . . .** Use your prewriting and planning as a guide when you write your first draft. In the opening, tell your readers what you are defining and why it's important to know more about it.

5. **Improving Your Writing . . .** Review your first draft and decide if it offers your readers a thorough and engaging examination of the subject. Add, cut, rearrange, and rewrite parts as necessary.

■ EDITING AND PROOFREADING

6. **Checking for Style and Accuracy . . .** Review your revised writing for style. Make sure that all of your sentences read smoothly and clearly and that you have used the best words to express your ideas. Then check for grammar, spelling, and punctuation errors.

   [HOT LINK] See "Assessment Rubric," page 213, for a helpful revising and editing guide.

7. **Preparing a Final Copy . . .** Write or keyboard a neat final copy of your essay. (See pages 30-32 for formatting ideas.) Proofread your copy before submitting it.

Sample **Essay of Definition**

In the following essay, student writer Martina Lowry defines, explains, and clarifies the meaning of the word "tact." Note how she summarizes the definition in her concluding paragraph.

Break It to 'Em Gently

The first paragraph ends with a basic definition of "tact."

There is a boy in my gym class (I'll call him Bill) who has unbearably yellow teeth that gross everyone out. Recently, another boy told Bill that he should "go Ajax" his teeth. Bill was crushed. Had the other boy been thinking, he would have realized that there is a better way to handle such a situation. He could have handled it with tact. He could have conveyed this hurtful truth in a more careful, sensitive way—that's "tact."

If a person isn't sensitive to another's feelings, there is no way he or she can be tactful. Yesterday, my 5-year-old brother proudly announced that he had cleaned the screen on our television set. Unfortunately, he used furniture polish, which produced a smeared, oily film on the television screen. My mother smiled and thanked him for his efforts—and then showed him how to clean the screen properly. Her sensitivity enabled my brother to keep his self-respect. Yet, sensitivity alone does not make tact.

Each new aspect of tact is followed by an example.

"Tactfulness" also requires "truthfulness." Doctors, for example, must be truthful. If a patient has just been paralyzed in an accident, a tactful doctor will tell the truth—but express it with sensitivity. The doctor may try to give the patient hope by telling of new healing techniques under study or about advanced equipment now available. Doctors must use tact with patients' relatives as well. Instead of bluntly saying, "Your husband is paralyzed," a doctor might say, "I'm sorry, but your husband has lost feeling in his legs and . . . "

Tact should not be confused with trickery. Trickery occurs when a nurse is about to give a patient an injection and says, "This won't hurt a bit." Instead of trickery, the nurse can use careful thought. For example, the nurse might assure the patient that the discomfort of the sting of a needle is a small thing compared to the benefits of the shot. It would also be thoughtful for the nurse to tell the patient about some of these benefits.

The closing lines stress the importance of tact in society.

Sensitivity, truthfulness, and careful thought—all are necessary components of tact. No one component will do. They must all be used in situations where people's feelings are at stake. Tact is a wonderful skill to have, and tactful people are usually admired and respected. Without tact our society would become an intolerable place to live. ■

WRITING GUIDELINES
Problem/Solution Essay

In a problem/solution essay, you provide readers with a detailed analysis of a subject—from a clear statement of the problem to a full discussion of possible solutions. It is important to examine your subject from a number of different angles before proposing any solutions.

■ PREWRITING

1. **Choosing a Subject . . .** If your assignment is related to a specific course, review your text and class notes for possible topics. Otherwise, think about the things students complain about most: homework, school spirit, jobs, grades, and so on. Or consider problems that have come up recently in your neighborhood or in your personal life.

2. **Gathering Details . . .** Write out your problem in a clear statement. Then research it thoroughly, collecting information about its history and causes. List possible solutions. Consider why different solutions may or may not work well.

3. **Focusing Your Work . . .** Review your collecting to decide if you are dealing with a manageable problem and if you have enough background information to write intelligently about it. (You may need to gather more facts and statistics to discuss the problem or propose solutions.)

■ WRITING AND REVISING

4. **Connecting Your Ideas . . .** Develop your first draft, discussing the problem and possible solutions as clearly and completely as you can. In the opening part of your essay, give enough background information so your readers fully understand the subject.

5. **Improving Your Writing . . .** Carefully review your first draft for logic and clarity: *Have you answered the questions readers would likely have? Do you sound knowledgeable about and interested in your subject?* Revise your writing accordingly.

■ EDITING AND PROOFREADING

6. **Checking for Style and Accuracy . . .** Review your revised writing for style. Make sure that all of your sentences read smoothly and clearly, and that you have used the best words to express your ideas. Then check your work for spelling, grammar, and punctuation errors.

   [HOT LINK] See "Assessment Rubric," page 213, for a helpful revising and editing guide.

7. **Preparing a Final Copy . . .** Write or keyboard a neat final copy of your essay; proofread your copy before submitting it.

Sample Problem/Solution Essay

In this essay, student writer Darin Fey examines a problem developing in his hometown—the lack of volunteers for the ambulance service. The "real-world" treatment of this subject makes the problem come alive for the readers.

Emergency Volunteers: Where Are They?

A personal story leads readers into the essay.

With a fever soaring well above 104°, a toddler goes into convulsions and needs immediate medical attention. Luckily for the parents, help is only a few minutes away. With a quick call to 911, an ambulance soon arrives. Because of the fast response of the ambulance personnel, the child is promptly and properly cared for.

This child was me, and I am very thankful for the volunteers who looked after me many years ago. But I am also afraid because my hometown of Edgerton, Minnesota, is facing a serious problem. Over the past year, a shortage of emergency volunteer technicians has developed. Without the help of these fine people, stories like mine might not end quite so happily.

The writer includes many specific details.

The ambulance association reports that over the last couple of years, the number of volunteers has significantly dropped, from 35 to 26. At least three, possibly up to six, additional people plan to quit at the end of the year. At this rate there won't even be an ambulance service in a few years.

> "At this rate there won't even be an ambulance service in a few years."

Nothing the ambulance association has done to encourage more people to join has worked. There have been numerous ads in the paper, people have written many letters to the editor, and there have been informational meetings. Nothing has come of these efforts. What are the reasons for this lack of support, and what can be done to turn things around?

One of the biggest problems that people see is the number of training hours needed to become a volunteer. To get started, each person must receive 140 hours of training and take a six-hour defensive-driving course. Then once a month there are more training sessions, plus a ▶

Emergency Volunteers: Where Are They?
(continued)

mandatory refresher course every two years. These strict regulations seem excessive for volunteers in a small community. The state of Minnesota must realize that these regulations negatively affect the number of volunteers across the state. A less extensive training schedule needs to be established.

Another problem is that many people are reluctant to get involved because they don't get anything in return for their services. To address this, the city established a retirement fund a few years ago for the volunteers. But in order to receive any payment, a person has to stay in the association for at least 10 years. The Edgerton City Council has also come up with a proposal to pay volunteers a small yearly fee for being on call. But where all of this money will come from is still to be determined. A plan is currently being developed that would charge each township in the ambulance-service area according to the number of people living there.

The insights of the community members help readers appreciate the problem.

But is this the best solution? A representative from the ambulance service said he liked it because it might entice people to take the training. But others, including Mel DeBoer, the editor of the local newspaper, is disheartened that the city has to offer monetary rewards in order to encourage people to serve the community. There are many others who also feel this plan might not solve the problem. Irene Reitsma, a volunteer member for over 20 years, feels that a plan has to come from the townspeople themselves. She states, "Volunteers have to make a clear commitment, and you just don't find that in people today. The pay isn't going to keep the volunteers; they have to be committed."

In closing, the writer proposes his own solution.

Perhaps the solution to this problem has nothing to do with training hours or payments received. Maybe what needs to happen is a change in the attitude and values of the people of Edgerton. The citizens must realize that service to the community is an honor and a duty—something that should be valued by everyone, young and old. The state of Minnesota and the city of Edgerton can try all they want, but until a change comes about in the people themselves, nothing will work. Let's hope that this attitude adjustment will happen before it's too late. ■

Assessment Rubric

Use this rubric as a checklist to evaluate your academic writing. It is arranged according to the traits of effective writing described in your handbook. (See pages 21-26.)

Stimulating Ideas

The writing . . .

_____ focuses on an important subject (a process, a problem, a term to define) that meets the requirements of the assignment.

_____ presents a clearly expressed thesis statement.

_____ thoroughly informs readers.

Logical Organization

_____ includes an interesting beginning, strong development, and an effective ending.

_____ arranges details in a logical way. (See page 52.)

_____ uses transitions to link sentences and paragraphs.

Engaging Voice

_____ speaks knowledgeably.

_____ shows that the writer is truly interested in the subject.

Original Word Choice

_____ explains or defines any unfamiliar terms.

_____ contains specific nouns and vivid verbs.

Effective Sentence Style

_____ flows smoothly from one idea to the next.

_____ shows variation in sentence structure.

Correct, Accurate Copy

_____ sticks to the basic rules of writing.

_____ follows the formatting requirements for the assignment.

Writing About
LITERATURE

"I am part of what I have read."   —John Kieran

Personal
RESPONSES TO LITERATURE

How do you react after attending an incredible concert or seeing a great movie? If you're like most people, you can't wait to talk about it. Movies and music can do that to you. Are you just as quick to talk about a good book? Probably not. Books are usually complex, containing many levels of meaning, and your feelings about your reading may develop slowly from chapter to chapter. Instead of going crazy over a good book, you may need time to think and reflect before reacting.

Writing about your reading helps you explore your thoughts about a book (or any other form of literature). It allows you to respond to a text on a personal level—to agree with it, question it, and study it. A personal response to literature can be anything from a letter to an author to an imaginary dialogue with a character. This chapter includes guidelines and samples of three different types of personal responses to literature.

Preview

- ○ Letter to the Author
- ○ Dialogue
- ○ Journal Entries
- ○ Starting Points: Responses to Literature

WRITING GUIDELINES

Responses to Literature

In a personal response to literature, you express your thoughts and feelings about a book, a short story, a play, a poem, or an essay. This kind of writing helps you strengthen or clarify your thinking about your reading.

■ PREWRITING

1. **Choosing a Subject . . .** Write about a piece of literature that you are currently reading or have just finished. In your response, you might . . .

   ○ examine a specific part of the reading,
   ○ express your overall feelings about the text, or
   ○ explore one or more important questions you have.

   (See page 220 for possible starting points for journal entries.)

2. **Identifying a Form . . .** Before you do any gathering, consider the form of your response—a journal entry, a letter to the author, a dialogue with a character, or a poem. (See the samples on pages 217-219.)

3. **Gathering Details . . .** Collect your thoughts and feelings about your subject and find passages in the reading that illustrate or support them.

Sharing Your Responses

The guidelines that follow address responses that you will share with others. (They do *not* pertain to personal journal entries.)

4. **Focusing Your Efforts . . .** Choose the ideas you want to include in your response. Decide on the best order for presenting these ideas. Continue gathering details, referring to the text if necessary.

■ WRITING AND REVISING

5. **Connecting Your Ideas . . .** Develop your response using your prewriting and planning as a general guide.

6. **Improving Your Writing . . .** As you review your draft, first check the overall sense and flow of your ideas. Then make sure that each part (the beginning, middle, and ending) is clear and complete.

■ EDITING AND PROOFREADING

7. **Checking for Style and Accuracy . . .** Review your revised writing for sentence style and word choice; then check your work for errors.

   [HOT LINK] See "Assessment Rubric," page 226, for a helpful revising and editing guide.

8. **Preparing a Final Copy . . .** Write or keyboard a neat final copy of your response; proofread your copy before sharing it.

Sample Response: **Letter to the Author**

In this letter to the author, student writer Kate Keefe shares her thoughts and feelings about Maya Angelou's book *All God's Children Need Traveling Shoes*. Notice that Ms. Keefe makes many personal connections between the book and her own life.

Madbury, New Hampshire
September 30, 2000

Dear Ms. Angelou,

After I had read *I Know Why the Caged Bird Sings,* I was very anxious to read *All God's Children Need Traveling Shoes* because your first book left me wondering about your life.

The writer explains her motive for reading the novel *All God's Children Need Traveling Shoes*.

The reason that *All God's Children Need Traveling Shoes* appealed to me was because in social studies I have studied about civil rights, and so many of the people that you mention in your book were familiar and of interest to me. It was worthwhile reading for me because it made me aware that the civil rights movement in the United States was something affecting not only people in our country, but people in other nations as well.

There was one thing that I was confused about, Ms. Angelou. You did not want blacks to be treated unjustly, and yet you treated Kojo, your "small boy," unjustly until you found out that his parents were wealthy. I had a hard time understanding this. Or, maybe I just misunderstood.

The writer parallels her own search for identity with Ms. Angelou's.

But most of all, Ms. Angelou, your book taught me the importance of pride in yourself—even when life is not easy. I understand much better now what black pride is, and how important returning to Africa was in your search for yourself, because really, we are all searching for ourselves. Your book's ending showed me the journey that blacks must travel. You wrote, "Despite the murders, rapes, and suicides, we have survived. The middle passage and the auction blocks have not erased us. Not humiliation, nor lynchings . . . nor collective oppression has been able to eradicate us from the earth." When I read those words, I could understand not only your struggle, but also my own struggle to be what I want to be.

Sincerely,

Kate Keefe

Sample Response: **Dialogue**

In this response paper, student writer Travis Taylor creates a dialogue between himself and Archie Costello from *The Chocolate War* by Robert Cormier. Through this conversation, the writer attempts to understand Archie's actions.

Dialogue with Archie Costello

The conversation is written in script form, much like a scene from a play.

Me: I don't think anyone who knows you likes you at all. Doesn't that bother you?

Archie: Not particularly. Why should it?

Me: Well, don't you like anybody?

Archie: Oddly enough I think I could have liked Jerry Renault.

Me: How could you have liked him? You did everything you could to destroy the kid.

Archie: I said that I could have liked him, not that I did like him.

Me: Could you explain that?

Archie: I could, but you probably wouldn't even begin to understand.

Me: Try me.

Archie: Okay, I knew Jerry couldn't beat me, but there was always that little chance. You see?

Me: No.

Archie: Well, I knew you wouldn't understand.

Me: Now let me get this straight. You could have liked Jerry, but you didn't because you beat him and wound up controlling almost the whole school afterward.

Archie: Basically, yes.

Me: Okay, I'll bite. Why?

Archie's explanation of his actions provides an interesting "self-analysis."

Archie: Because if Jerry had beaten me, then he would have proved I'm wrong. I mean everybody is so predictable. Everybody wants their little bit of power. The teachers want power over the students. The upperclassmen want power over the underclassmen. I thought Jerry might be different because he wasn't interested in power. And that was how he might have won. But since he didn't want to fall in line and play the power game, everybody jumped on his head. All I had to do was set things up and give the kids and Brother Leon a chance to do what they already wanted to do any-how—squash Jerry. Now he'll be just like everyone else. Or else he'll stay on the sidelines. Either way it doesn't matter. I won.

Me: Yeah, I guess that's what I was afraid of. ■

Sample Journal Entries

Response to a Novel

In this entry, Tom Myers explores the meaning of the title of a book he has just read.

> The significance of the title of the novel *The Things They Carried* is that veterans of war carry some extra "emotional baggage." In the beginning of the book, the characters told what physical objects they carried as soldiers at war. But as the story progressed, I realized that these men would carry emotional and mental baggage for the rest of their lives. . . .

Response to a Play

In this entry, Tracey Borgen makes a connection between *The Miracle Worker,* a play about Helen Keller, and her own life.

> This play reminded me of the times in seventh grade when we would visit the nursing home. Celina Haenni and I visited with a lady named Helen who communicated by spelling out words on a letter board. At first, it was hard to understand what she was saying, but after a while we got used to it. I can't imagine how hard it must have been for Helen Keller's family to communicate with her. . . .

Response to a Short Story

In this response, Kate Kennedy shares her thoughts about the narrator in "Flowers for Algernon."

> I liked the form of narration Daniel Keyes used when he wrote this story. Putting it in a journal format brought me closer to Charlie. I got to see everything through his eyes. As I watched his abilities slip away, it was heartbreaking. I felt as helpless as Charlie must have felt. . . .

Response to an Essay

In this entry, Shannon Spencer shares her views on the symbolism in an essay called "A Game of Catch" by Roger Rosenblatt.

> In this essay, the author discusses how a game of catch symbolizes family life. For example, in a game of catch, the two people want the ball to be caught because a catch means that the participants "understand" one another. The author uses a quotation of poet Richard Wilier that I find interesting. Speaking to a girl who has figured out a line of his poetry, he remarks, "It's nice to have someone catch what you're throwing." I feel the same way sometimes. . . .

Starting Points: Responses to Literature

The following questions will help you react personally to the books you read. Use this list only when you can't think of your own starting point. (By changing the questions slightly, you can use this same list to react to other forms of literature—plays, poems, short stories, etc.)

Making Connections

1. What were your feelings after reading the opening chapter(s) of the book? After reading half of the book? After finishing the book?
2. Did the book make you laugh? Cry? Cringe? Smile? Cheer? Explain.
3. What connections are there between the book and your life? Explain.
4. What is the most important word in the book? The most important passage? The most important event? Explain.
5. Who else should read this book? Why?

Points of Interest

6. What are the best parts of the book? Why? What are the worst parts? Why?
7. Do you like the ending of the book? Why or why not?
8. What came as a surprise in the book? Why?
9. What parts of the book seem most believable or unbelievable? Why?
10. What makes you wonder in this book? What confuses you?

Strictly in Character

11. In what ways are you like any of the characters? Explain.
12. Do any of the characters remind you of friends, family members, or classmates? Explain.
13. Which character would you like to be in this book? Why?
14. What would you and your favorite character talk about?

Careful Reflections

15. Do you think the title fits the book? Why or why not?
16. What was the author saying about life and living?
17. Has this book helped you in some way? Explain.
18. How have you changed after reading this book? Explain.
19. What do you know now that you didn't know before?
20. What questions in this book would you like answered?

> "You are the same today that you'll be five years from now except for two things: the people you meet and the books you read."
>
> —Mac McMillan

Writing a
BOOK REVIEW

Everyone has his or her own personal tastes. While you may love Mexican food, your best friend may go for Italian dishes. While you may dig the blues, your brother may like rock or reggae. The same is true of the books you read. While you may enjoy science fiction or science fantasy, the next person may enjoy modern dramas.

One way to share your personal taste in literature is to review the books you read. A book review is a brief essay expressing your personal opinion about a book's value. An effective book review is informative and enjoyable to read. It highlights key parts of a book without giving the whole story away. It provides thoughtful explanations and reflections to support your main points. Most importantly, it helps readers decide if they should read the book themselves.

Preview

- ○ Book Review: Fiction
- ○ Book Review: Nonfiction
- ○ Mini-Reviews
- ○ Assessment Rubric

WRITING GUIDELINES
Book Review

In a review, you express your opinion about the value or worth of a book you have read. However, simply stating that something was good or bad is not enough. You need to support your feelings with thoughtful explanations and specific references to the book itself. (You can use the following guidelines to review short stories, poems, movies, concerts—as well as books.)

■ PREWRITING

1. **Choosing a Subject . . .** Review a book that you have recently read, one that you have strong feelings about.

2. **Gathering Details . . .** Collect your initial thoughts and feelings about your subject through freewriting. Or, if you want to work more systematically, list in one column the book's strong points and in another column its weak points. Continue exploring and collecting ideas as needed.

3. **Focusing Your Efforts . . .** Read through your ideas, and put a check next to the details you would like to include in your review. *Remember:* You can't say everything. Reviewers usually comment on the important parts of a book without giving away too much of the story.

■ WRITING AND REVISING

4. **Connecting Your Ideas . . .** Develop your first draft according to your planning and prewriting. Make sure to identify the book's title and author in one of the opening lines.

5. **Improving Your Writing . . .** As you read through your first draft, make sure that you have stated your ideas clearly and completely: *Will readers be able to follow your main points? Will they know how you feel about the book and why?* Revise your review accordingly.

■ EDITING AND PROOFREADING

6. **Checking for Style and Accuracy . . .** Study your revised writing for style. Make sure that all of your sentences read smoothly and that you have used the best words to express your ideas. Then check for spelling, grammar, and punctuation errors.

   [HOT LINK] See "Assessment Rubric," page 226, for a helpful revising and editing guide.

7. **Preparing a Final Copy . . .** Write or keyboard a neat final copy of your review; proofread the final copy before sharing it.

Sample Book Review: Fiction

The subject of Andrea Facey's book review is the novel *Native Son* by Richard Wright. (This review orginally appeared in *New Youth Connections: The Magazine Written By and For New York Youth.*)

Trapped Between Two Worlds

The first part of the review "sets the scene" for readers.

Set in Chicago during the Depression of the 1930s, Richard Wright's novel *Native Son* is the story of one young black man's struggle to survive in a racist society.

The main character, Bigger Thomas, is the man of the house, and his family expects him to provide for them. But Bigger only cares about whether he has food to eat, a roof over his head, and clothes on his own back.

Bigger hates white people. He curses and mocks them behind their backs. In one conversation with his friend Gus, he describes how blacks and whites live in two different worlds: "We live here and they live there," he says. "We black and they white. They got things and we ain't. They do things and we can't. It's just like living in jail. Half the time I feel like I'm on the outside of the world peeping in through a knot-hole in the fence."

Throughout the book, Bigger tries to escape that feeling of being trapped. He gets a taste of life on the other side of the fence when he starts working as a chauffeur for Mr. Dalton, a white millionaire. The day he arrives at the Dalton's is supposed to be the day his troubles end; instead, it is the beginning of a chain of events that will destroy his life.

One key event in the book is described in great detail.

In one scene, Bigger meets Mr. Dalton's daughter, Mary, and her friend Jan. They treat him like a person, not like a servant. They ask him to call them by their first names, and they even invite Bigger to sit down to dinner with them.

But Bigger is afraid they are trying to trick him. By the end of the evening, Mary is drunk and cannot get up the stairs to her room so Bigger carries her. The next thing he knows, he is trapped in the white girl's bedroom. The things he does to try to escape only get him into more trouble.

The book's value is discussed in the final paragraph.

This book shows how prejudice affects people, the way segregation has a way of closing in on them, and what some people will do to find a way out. Everyone who wants to better understand racism in this society should read this book. ■

Sample Book Review: **Nonfiction**

In this review, Jessamy Millican writes about *The Broken Cord,* a true story by Michael Dorris about his struggles with his adopted son, Adam. (From *Merlyn's Pen: Fiction, Essays, and Poems by America's Teens.* Copyright by Merlyn's Pen, Inc. All rights reserved.)

A Preventable Tragedy

The opening paragraph gains the reader's attention.

When writer Michael Dorris adopted his son, he simply wanted to be a father. Before long, he found himself drawn into a tragedy for which there was no easy solution. Dorris's son has fetal alcohol syndrome (FAS), a tragic condition that the author writes about in *The Broken Cord.*

Michael Dorris's story begins when he adopts three-year-old Adam, who can barely talk, is not toilet trained, and is extremely small for his age. Despite these disturbing signs, Dorris denies that there is anything wrong with his child. But after Adam suffers a massive seizure followed by many more, Dorris can no longer deny his son's problem.

Years later, the author discovers that Adam's problems stem from his mother's heavy drinking while she was pregnant. Dorris is shocked to discover the skyrocketing problem of fetal alcohol syndrome in our nation, especially among his own people, the Sioux Indians.

The relationship between Dorris and his son is one of love and painful disappointment. Dorris is convinced that although his son has FAS, he will discover some talent that will "make up" for how Adam has been hurt by his mother's drinking. None is ever found. Instead of making progress in school, Adam simply falls further and further behind.

The writer highlights two of the book's major strengths.

One of the book's major strengths is its emotional impact. By the end of the first chapter, I could sense the strong love Dorris feels for his son. It was this love that continued to pull me in throughout the story. My heart breaks along with Dorris's when he realizes that his child will never be "normal."

Another major strength is the book's level of detail. Dorris tells the shocking facts about FAS. He doesn't exaggerate his figures because he doesn't have to. Through his many interviews with experts, Dorris reveals a tragedy that falls heavily on his own people.

In closing, the writer reflects on the book's value.

FAS, the challenges of parenting, disappointment and sorrow—*The Broken Cord* has all of these things and much more. Reading this book is a deeply moving and instructive experience. It will tug at your heart strings and teach you some valuable lessons about life. ■

Sample Mini-Reviews

Student literary magazines and newspapers often include "mini-reviews" of books, movies, videos, and CD's. (From *The 21st Century.* Copyright by the Young Authors Foundation, Inc. All rights reserved.)

A Review of *A Night Without Armor*

I recently bought *A Night Without Armor* by musical artist Jewel Kilcher. It is one of the best collections of poetry I've ever read. The poems deal with all aspects of love. Once I started reading the poems, I couldn't put the book down.

Specific details catch the reader's interest.

When I read Jewel's poems, I can imagine that she is talking directly to me. Some of her poems like "Just Kiss Me" really touch the heart. All teenagers (including me) have liked someone so much that they wanted to tell the person. Another poem, entitled "Pretty," deals with the themes of envy and self-pity. One line of this poem reads, "There is a pretty girl on the face of a magazine . . . and all I can see are my dirty hands turning the page."

Jewel's songs are inspirational and so are her poems. Her book is definitely on my top-ten list. I would recommend it to anyone who loves poetry and Jewel's music. ■

—Meg Kuck, student reviewer

A Review of *Life Is Beautiful*

"*Life Is Beautiful* is not a comedy about the Holocaust, because that's not possible," states Italian director Roberto Benigni. In his movie, Benigni portrays a father named Guido who uses comedy to protect his son from the horrors of the Holocaust. For example, Guido explains to his son that the sign "No Jews or Dogs" makes about as much sense as the sign "No Spiders or Visigoths [medieval warriors]."

A mini-analysis helps readers understand the movie.

In reality, *Life Is Beautiful* is a tragicomedy. The first half of the film is full of comedy and charm as Guido courts Dora, a school teacher. The tragedy lies in the second half of the film when this couple and their son must deal with the Holocaust.

It may be hard to see a sad foreign film, but *Life Is Beautiful* is definitely worth the price. You go in expecting a depressing film, but you come out realizing how beautiful life is. ■

—Roslyn Chang, student reviewer

Assessment Rubric

Use this rubric to evaluate book reviews and literary analyses. It is arranged according to the traits of good writing described in your handbook. (See pages 21-26.)

Stimulating Ideas

The writing . . .

_____ addresses a single piece of literature (movie, performance).

_____ focuses on one or more important elements (plot, character, setting, or theme).

_____ contains supporting details and examples from the work.

_____ maintains a clear and consistent view from start to finish.

Logical Organization

_____ includes an effective beginning, strong supporting details, and a convincing conclusion.

_____ presents ideas in an organized manner (perhaps offering the strongest point first or last).

Engaging Voice

_____ speaks in a convincing and knowledgeable way.

_____ shows that the writer clearly understands the text.

Original Word Choice

_____ explains or defines any unfamiliar terms.

_____ pays special attention to word choice.

Effective Sentence Style

_____ flows smoothly from one idea to the next.

Correct, Accurate Copy

_____ observes the basic rules of grammar, spelling, and punctuation.

_____ follows the appropriate formatting guidelines.

"Literature can deepen the understanding that comes from sharing in the common struggle for human dignity and freedom." —Coretta Scott King

Writing a
LITERARY ANALYSIS

In a personal response, you explore your thoughts and feelings about a piece of literature. In a review, you discuss why a particular book or series of stories is or is not worth reading. And in a literary analysis, you present your thoughtful understanding of a literary work. A literary analysis is one of the most challenging forms of writing.

The starting point for meaningful analysis is your honest response to a piece of literature. You may like how the story line develops in a novel. You may find the actions of a short-story character intriguing. Then again, you may wonder why a writer spends so much time developing a certain image in a poem. Any one of these ideas could lead to an effective analysis.

Base your analysis on a close and careful reading of the piece of literature. Then present your ideas in a carefully planned essay, connecting all of your main points with specific references to the text.

Preview

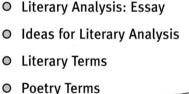

- O Literary Analysis: Novel
- O Literary Analysis: Essay
- O Ideas for Literary Analysis
- O Literary Terms
- O Poetry Terms

WRITING GUIDELINES
Literary Analysis

In a literary analysis, you examine or interpret an important feature in a novel, a short story, a poem, a play, or an essay. For example, you might examine the forces affecting the main character in a novel or short story, focus on the imagery (word pictures) in a poem, or evaluate the strength of the main point or thesis in an essay.

■ PREWRITING

1. **Choosing a Subject ...** Your teacher may have a selection in mind for your analysis. If not, choose a literary work that "speaks" to you. (Perhaps it taught you something or triggered an emotion.)

2. **Considering a Writing Idea ...** Think about features of this piece that catch your attention. Are you drawn to a specific character? Would you like to analyze one of the messages or themes? Do you like how the author builds suspense in the story? If no idea comes to mind, freewrite about the text. (Also see page 231.)

3. **Focusing Your Efforts ...** State a possible thesis (focus) for your analysis—a sentence or two expressing the main point you want to make. Plan and organize your writing accordingly. (Make sure that you can support your thesis with references to the literary work.)

■ WRITING AND REVISING

4. **Connecting Your Ideas ...** Develop a first draft, working in ideas and details according to your planning and prewriting. The opening part should (1) draw readers into the analysis and (2) identify your thesis. (See page 232 for more writing tips.)

5. **Improving Your Writing ...** Carefully review your first draft. Look for parts that are incomplete or confusing, and make any necessary changes.

■ EDITING AND PROOFREADING

6. **Checking for Style and Accuracy ...** Review your revised writing for style. Make sure that all of your sentences read smoothly and clearly, and that you have used the best words to express your ideas. Then check your work for spelling, grammar, and punctuation errors.

    [HOT LINK] See "Assessment Rubric," page 226, for a helpful revising and editing guide.

7. **Preparing a Final Copy ...** Write or keyboard a neat final copy of your analysis; proofread your copy before sharing it.

Sample Literary Analysis: **Novel**

In this analysis, student writer Elizabeth Delaney explores the theme of fear in William Golding's novel *Lord of the Flies.*

The opening paragraph identifies the thesis of the analysis.

The concept of the "beast" is carefully examined.

In the final paragraph, the writer shares a universal truth about the "beast."

The Beast of Fear

In William Golding's novel *Lord of the Flies,* the boys allow themselves to be terrorized by a beast they create because deep down they want it to exist. By creating a physical object to represent everything they are afraid of, the boys can base their fears on something external and distant, rather than on something close and personal.

When they first arrive on the island, the boys have many implied fears: fear of being left on the island, fear of being on their own without adult assistance, and fear of what may be occurring in the war (World War II) from which they have fled. As a result, they all embrace the concept of the beast, for it is a way to externalize their fears. What the boys want is something they can fear in good conscience, some evil that does not stem from their own personal experience. So they place their fear outside themselves and believe in a beast.

Jack sums up the reason why externalized fear is so much easier to deal with than internal fear when he says, "If there was a snake we'd hunt it and kill it." It's a simple question of power. The boys never would have thought that they were responsible for the appearance of the beast, but they did believe they could be responsible for its demise or destruction. If the beast is something that can be destroyed, there is the potential that everything can turn out all right, the possibility that all the evil that the boys perceive on their island could be purged with the removal of this one creature. In one sense, Jack's cause is a noble one: purifying his world of evil. However, he goes about looking for the beast in all the wrong places, and as a result, the boys commit several horrible crimes. In fact, part of Golding's message is that to "fancy thinking the Beast was something you could hunt and kill" is really catering to the true inner beast itself.

The development of the beast in *Lord of the Flies* is not an unusual one. We are always looking for a beast or a scapegoat to destroy to solve our problems. And, as the Nazis set out to exterminate the Jews, and Stalin the freedom of the individual, the boys create the beast as a safety net, an outside evil that protects them from the knowledge of their true nature as fallen creatures or "beasts" themselves. ■

Sample Literary Analysis: **Essay**

In this analysis, student writer Arlo Bakker examines the main argument in an environmental essay by Wendell Berry.

Fast Food and Planetary Problems

The opening paragraph identifies the main point of the essay.

In the essay "Word and Flesh," Wendell Berry argues that the oil spill that messed up Prince William Sound wasn't caused by the *Exxon Valdez*. That oil spill was really caused by people in the developed countries (like us) who rely on others for many of our services. For example, we consume tons of convenience food, and transporting this food requires tankers full of oil. If we were more self-sufficient, and produced most of our own food, we wouldn't have to rely on ships like the *Valdez* to haul oil through Prince William Sound to fuel trucks and other cargo carriers. In other words, our lifestyle causes oil spills, and the solution is to change the way we live.

The middle paragraphs explore different parts of Berry's argument.

So why don't we change? Berry says that we don't change because we lack character and love. It takes character to admit that producing and transporting fast food uses up too much oil. It also takes character to admit that driving a car to school uses up more oil than walking to school or riding a bus. But change also requires love. We won't change the ways we eat and drive unless we love clean water and healthy sea otters more than we love TV dinners and fast cars.

Instead of changing the way we live, says Berry, we just talk about environmental issues. In our talk, we refer to oil spills as a "planetary problem." Why? Because the phrase excuses us from having to come up with a solution. Everybody knows that a planetary problem is too big for one person or one group to solve, so no one seems to take personal responsibility for it. But if we admit that an oil spill is a lifestyle problem, then we have to help solve the problem by making changes in our lifestyle.

In closing, the writer assesses the strength of Berry's argument.

Berry's argument is strong. Unless we value a healthy environment enough to make changes in the way we live, environmental disasters will remain a planetary problem that we'll never solve. Producing our own food and cutting back on car travel may seem like impossible steps, but these are the types of things that we can and must do to save the planet. ∎

Ideas for Literary Analysis

Theme

1. Does the author seem to be saying something about ambition . . . courage . . . greed . . . jealousy . . . happiness?
2. Does the selection show you what it is like to experience racism, loneliness, and so on?
3. Does the author have a point to make about a specific historical event?

Characters

4. How does the main character change from the beginning to the end?
5. What forces or circumstances make one of the characters act in a certain way? (Consider the setting, the conflict, other characters, etc.)
6. What are the most revealing aspects of one of the characters? (Consider his or her thoughts, words, and actions.)
7. Do the characters' actions seem believable within the story?
8. Does the main character have a confidant, someone he or she relies on? (How important or reliable is this person?)

Plot

9. What external or internal conflict affects the main character?
10. How is suspense built into the story?
11. How does the climax change the story?
12. Are there any twists in the plot? (What do they add to the story?)
13. Does the plot follow a basic pattern of fiction? (See page 169.)

Setting

14. What effect does the setting have on the characters?
15. Does the setting expand your understanding of a specific time and place?
16. Is the setting new and thought provoking?

Style

17. How does the writing—descriptive phrases, images, and so on—create an overall feeling or tone in the selection?
18. Is dialogue or description used effectively? (Give examples.)
19. Is there an important symbol that adds meaning to the selection? (How is this symbol represented in different parts of the story?)
20. Are there key figures of speech such as metaphors and similes? (What do these add to the writing?)

TIPS for Writing an Analysis

Writing the Opening

Your opening paragraph should gain your reader's attention and identify the thesis of your analysis. Use the suggestions listed below to help you get started.

1. Summarize your subject very briefly. Include the title, author, and the type of book (or other literary form). This can be done with a statement of "what and how" about the book.

In his novel *Lord of the Flies,* William Golding writes about [what?] the evil side of man [how?] by describing the actions of a group of young boys who are marooned on a deserted island.

2. Start with a quotation from the book and then comment on its importance (think in terms of the focus of your analysis).

3. Begin with an explanation of the author's purpose and how well you think he or she achieves this purpose.

4. Open with a few general statements about life that relate to the focus of your analysis.

There comes a time when everyone has to . . .

5. Begin with a general statement about the type of literature you are analyzing. Then discuss your subject within this context.

The best science fiction always seems believable and logical within the context of the story line. This certainly is true in . . .

Writing the Body

Develop or support your focus in the body, or main part, of the analysis. To make sure that you effectively explain each main point, follow these three steps:

1. State each main point so that it clearly relates to the thesis of your analysis.

2. Support each main point with specific details or direct quotations from the text you are analyzing.

3. Explain how these specific details prove your point.

Writing the Closing

In the final paragraph, tie the important points together and restate the focus of your analysis. Leave your readers with a final thought that will keep this piece of literature on their minds for some time.

Literary Terms

The terms on the following pages describe the different types and elements of literature. This information will help you to discuss and write about the novels, poems, and other literary works you read. (Poetry terms begin on page 242.)

Allegory is a story in which people, things, and actions represent an idea or a generalization about life; allegories often have a strong moral or lesson.

Allusion is a literary reference to a familiar person, place, thing, or event. (See page 136.)

Analogy is a comparison of two or more similar objects, suggesting that if they are alike in certain respects, they will probably be alike in other ways as well. (See page 136.)

Anecdote is a short summary of a humorous event used to make a point. (See page 136.) Abe Lincoln was famous for his anecdotes, especially this one:

Two fellows, after a hot dispute over how long a man's legs should be in proportion to his body, stormed into Lincoln's office one day and confronted him with their problem. Lincoln listened intently to the arguments given by each of the men and after some reflection rendered his verdict: "This question has been a source of controversy for untold ages," he said, slowly and deliberately, "and it is about time it should be definitely decided. It has led to bloodshed in the past, and there is no reason to suppose it will not lead to the same in the future."

"After much thought and consideration, not to mention mental worry and anxiety, it is my opinion, all side issues being swept aside, that a man's lower limbs, in order to preserve harmony of proportion, should be at least long enough to reach from his body to the ground."

Antagonist is the person or thing working against the protagonist, or hero, of the work.

Autobiography is an author's account or story of her or his own life.

Biography is the story of a person's life written by another person.

Caricature is a picture or an imitation of a person's features or mannerisms exaggerated in a comic or absurd way. (See the illustration above.)

Character sketch is a short piece of writing that reveals or shows something important about a person or fictional character.

Characterization is the method an author uses to reveal characters and their personalities.

Climax is usually the most intense point in a story. A series of struggles or conflicts build a story or play toward the climax. (See "Plot line.")

Comedy is literature in which human errors or problems appear funny. Comedies end on a happy note.

Conflict is the problem or struggle in a story that triggers the action. There are five basic types of conflict:

- **Person vs. Person:** One character in a story has a problem with one or more of the other characters.
- **Person vs. Society:** A character has a problem with some element of society: the school, the law, the accepted way of doing things.
- **Person vs. Self:** A character has a problem deciding what to do in a certain situation.
- **Person vs. Nature:** A character has a problem with nature: heat, cold, a tornado, an avalanche, or any other element of nature.
- **Person vs. Fate (God):** A character must battle what seems to be an uncontrollable problem. Whenever the conflict is an unbelievable or strange coincidence, it can be attributed to fate or an act of God.

Content is the set of facts or circumstances surrounding an event or a situation in a piece of literature.

Denouement is the final resolution or outcome of a play or story.

Dialogue is the conversation carried on by the characters in a literary work.

Diction is an author's choice of words based on their correctness, clearness, or effectiveness.

- **Archaic** words are those that are old-fashioned and no longer sound natural when used, as "I believe thee not" for "I don't believe you."
- **Colloquialism** is an expression that is usually accepted in informal situations and certain locations, as in "He really grinds my beans."
- **Jargon** (technical diction) is the specialized language used by a specific group, such as those who use computers: *override, interface, download.*
- **Profanity** is language that shows disrespect for someone or something regarded as holy or sacred.
- **Slang** is the informal language used by a particular group of people among themselves; it is also language that is used in fiction to lend color and feeling: *awesome, chill out, no way.*
- **Vulgarity** is language that is generally considered crude, gross, and, at times, offensive. It is sometimes used in fiction to add realism.

Didactic literature instructs or presents a moral or religious statement.

Drama is the form of literature known as plays; but drama also refers to the type of serious play that is often concerned with the leading character's relationship to society.

Dramatic monologue is a literary work (or part of a literary work) in which a character is speaking about him- or herself as if another person were present. The words of the speaker reveal something important about his or her character. (See "Soliloquy.")

Empathy is putting yourself in someone else's place and imagining how that person must feel. The phrase "What would you do if you were in my shoes?" is a request for one person to empathize with another.

Epic is a long narrative poem that tells of the deeds and adventures of a hero.

Epigram is a brief, witty saying or poem often dealing with its subject in a satirical manner:

> **"There never was a good war or a bad peace."**   —Ben Franklin

Epiphany is a sudden perception (moment of understanding) that causes a character to change or act in a certain way.

Epitaph is a short poem or verse written in memory of someone.

Epithet is a word or phrase used in place of a person's name; it is characteristic of that person: Alexander the Great, Material Girl, Ms. Know-It-All.

Essay is a piece of prose that expresses an individual's point of view; usually, it is a series of closely related paragraphs that combine to make a complete piece of writing.

Exaggeration is overstating or stretching the truth for special effect: "My shoes are killing me!" (See "Hyperbole" on page 137.)

Exposition is writing that is intended to explain something that might otherwise be difficult to understand. In a play or novel, it would be the portion that gives the background or situation surrounding the story.

Fable is a short fictional narrative that teaches a lesson. It usually includes animals that talk and act like people.

Falling action is the part of a play or story that works out the decision arrived at during the climax. (See "Plot line.")

Farce is literature based on a humorous and improbable plot.

Figurative language is language used to create a special effect or feeling. (See "Figure of speech.")

Figure of speech is a literary device used to create a special effect or feeling by making some type of interesting or creative comparison.

▓ **Antithesis** is an opposition, or contrast, of ideas:

"It was the best of times, it was the worst of times . . . "

—Charles Dickens, *A Tale of Two Cities*

▓ **Hyperbole** (hī-pəŕ-bə-lē) is an exaggeration or overstatement:

"I have seen this river so wide it had only one bank."

—Mark Twain, *Life on the Mississippi*

▓ **Metaphor** is a comparison of two unlike things in which no word of comparison (*as* or *like*) is used:

"A green plant is a machine that runs on solar energy."

—*Scientific American*

▓ **Metonymy** (mə-tŏń-ə-mē) is the substituting of one word for another related word:

The White House has decided to create more public service jobs.

(*White House* is substituted for *president.*)

▓ **Personification** is a literary device in which the author speaks of or describes an animal, object, or idea as if it were a person:

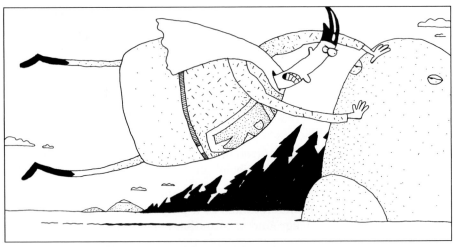

"The rock stubbornly refused to move."

▓ **Simile** is a comparison of two unlike things using the words *like* or *as:*

"She stood in front of the altar, shaking like a freshly caught trout."

—Maya Angelou, *I Know Why the Caged Bird Sings*

▓ **Understatement** is a way of emphasizing an idea by talking about it in a restrained manner:

"Aunt Polly is prejudiced against snakes." (She was terrified of them.)

—Mark Twain, *Adventures of Tom Sawyer*

Flashback is returning to an earlier time (in a story) for the purpose of making something in the present more clear. (See page 136.)

Foil is someone who serves as a contrast or challenge to another character.

Foreshadowing is giving hints or clues of what is to come later in a story. (See page 137.)

Genre refers to a category or type of literature based on its style, form, and content. The mystery novel is a literary genre.

Gothic novel is a type of fiction that is characterized by gloomy castles, ghosts, and supernatural happenings—creating a mysterious and sometimes frightening story. Bram Stoker's *Dracula* is probably the best known gothic novel still popular today.

Hubris, derived from the Greek word *hybris,* means "excessive pride." In Greek tragedy, hubris is often viewed as the flaw that leads to the downfall of the tragic hero.

Imagery is the use of words to create a certain picture in the reader's mind. Imagery is usually based on sensory details:

> **"The sky was dark and gloomy, the air was damp and raw, the streets were wet and sloppy."** —Charles Dickens, *The Pickwick Papers*

Impressionism is the recording of events or situations as they have been impressed upon the mind. A writer shares his boyhood impressions of winter:

> **" . . . we waited to snowball the cats. Sleek and long as jaguars and horrible-whiskered, spitting and snarling, they would slink and sidle over the white back-garden walls, and the lynx-eyed hunters, Jim and I, fur-capped and moccasined trappers from Hudson Bay, off Mumbles Road, would hurl our deadly snowballs at the green of their eyes. The wise cats never appeared."** —Dylan Thomas, *A Child's Christmas in Wales*

Irony is using a word or phrase to mean the exact opposite of its literal or normal meaning. There are three kinds of irony:

- **dramatic** irony, in which the reader or the audience sees a character's mistakes, but the character does not;
- **verbal** irony, in which the writer says one thing and means another: "The best substitute for experience is being thirteen"; and
- irony of **situation,** in which there is a great difference between the purpose of a particular action and the result.

Local color is the use of language and details that are common in a certain region of the country:

> **"Mama came out and lit into me for sitting there doing nothing. Said I was no-count and shiftless . . . "** —Olive Ann Burns, *Cold Sassy Tree*

Malapropism is the type of pun, or play on words, that results when two words become jumbled in the speaker's mind. The term comes from a character in Sheridan's comedy *The Rivals*. The character, Mrs. Malaprop, is constantly mixing up her words, as when she says "as headstrong as an allegory [she means *alligator*] on the banks of the Nile."

Melodrama is an exaggerated form of drama (as in television soap operas) characterized by heavy use of romance, suspense, and emotion.

Memoir is writing based on the writer's memory of a particular time, place, or incident. *Reminiscence* is another term for *memoir.*

Mood is the feeling a text arouses in the reader: happiness, peacefulness, sadness, and so on.

Moral is the particular value or lesson the author is trying to get across to the reader. The "moral of the story" is a common phrase in Aesop's fables.

Motif is the term for an often-repeated idea or theme in literature. In *The Adventures of Huckleberry Finn,* Huck is constantly in conflict with the "civilized" world. This conflict becomes a motif throughout the novel.

Myth is a traditional story that attempts to justify a certain practice or belief or to explain a natural phenomenon.

Narration is writing that relates an event or a series of events: a story.

Narrator is the person who is telling the story.

Naturalism is an extreme form of realism in which the author tries to show the relation of a person to the environment or surroundings. Often, the author finds it necessary to show the ugly or raw side of that relationship.

Novel is a lengthy fictional story with a plot that is revealed by the speech, action, and thoughts of the characters.

Novella is a prose work longer than the standard short story, but shorter and less complex than a full-length novel.

Oxymoron is a combination of contradictory terms as in *jumbo shrimp, tough love,* or *cruel kindness.*

Parable is a short descriptive story that illustrates a particular belief or moral.

Paradox is a statement that seems contrary to common sense, yet may, in fact, be true: "The coach considered this a good loss."

Parody is a form of literature that intentionally uses comic effect to mock a literary work or style.

Pathetic fallacy is a form of personification giving human traits to nature: *cruel sea, howling wind, dancing water.*

Pathos is a Greek root meaning *suffering* or *passion*. It usually describes the part in a play or story that is intended to elicit pity or sorrow from the audience or reader.

Picaresque novel is a work of fiction consisting of a lengthy string of loosely connected events. It usually features the adventures of a rogue living by his or her wits. Mark Twain's *Huckleberry Finn* is a picaresque novel.

Plot is the action or sequence of events in a story. It is usually a series of related incidents that build upon one another as the story develops. There are five basic elements in a plot line. (See below.)

Plot line is the graphic display of the action or events in a story: *exposition, rising action, climax, falling action,* and *resolution.*

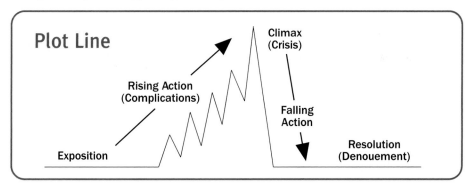

Poetic justice is a term that describes a character "getting what he deserves" in the end, especially if what he deserves is punishment. The purest form of poetic justice is when one character plots against another but ends up being caught in his or her own trap.

Point of view is the vantage point from which the story is told. In the first-person point of view, the story is told by one of the characters: "I remember the summer I turned sixteen." In the third-person point of view, the story is told by someone outside the story: "The old man shuffled across the street. He looked down at the ground as he walked." There are three types of third-person points of view:

- **Omniscient** point of view allows the narrator to share the thoughts and feelings of all the characters.
- **Limited omniscient** point of view allows the narrator to share the thoughts and feelings of only one character.
- **Camera view** (objective view) allows the storyteller to record the action from his or her own point of view, being unaware of any of the characters' thoughts or feelings.

Protagonist is the main character or hero of the story.

Pseudonym (also known as "pen name") means "false name" and applies to the name a writer uses in place of his or her given name. "Mark Twain" is a pseudonym for Samuel Langhorne Clemens.

Quest features a main character who is seeking to find something or achieve a goal. In the process, this character encounters and overcomes a series of obstacles, returning wiser and more experienced.

Realism is literature that attempts to represent life as it really is.

Renaissance, which means "rebirth," is the period of history following the Middle Ages. This period began late in the fourteenth century and continued through the fifteenth and sixteenth centuries. The term now applies to any period of time in which intellectual and artistic interest is revived or reborn.

Resolution, or denouement, is the portion of the play or story in which the problem is solved. It comes after the climax and falling action and is intended to bring the story to a satisfactory end. (See "Plot line.")

Rising action is the series of struggles that builds a story or play toward a climax. (See "Plot line.")

Romanticism is a literary movement with an emphasis on the imagination and emotions.

Sarcasm is the use of praise to mock someone or something, as in "She's a real winner" or "No one cuts pizza like Clyde."

"No one cuts pizza like Clyde."

Satire is a literary tone used to make fun of human vice or weakness, often with the intent of correcting or changing the subject of the attack.

Setting is the time and place in which the action of a literary work occurs.

Short story is a brief fictional work. It usually contains one major conflict and at least one main character.

Slapstick is a form of low comedy that often includes exaggerated, sometimes violent action. The "pie in the face" routine is a classic piece of slapstick.

Slice of life is a term that describes the type of realistic or naturalistic writing that accurately reflects what life is really like.

Soliloquy is a speech delivered by a character when he or she is alone on stage. It is as though the character is thinking out loud.

Stereotype is a form that does not change. A "stereotyped" character has no individuality and fits the mold of that particular kind of person.

Stream of consciousness is a style of writing in which the thoughts and feelings of the writer are recorded as they occur.

Style is how the author uses words, phrases, and sentences to form his or her ideas. Style is also thought of as the qualities and characteristics that distinguish one writer's work from the work of others.

Symbol is a person, a place, a thing, or an event used to represent something else: the dove is a symbol of peace. Characters in literature may be symbols of good or evil.

Theme is the statement about life that a writer is trying to get across in a piece of writing. In most cases, the theme will be implied rather than directly spelled out.

Tone is the overall feeling, or effect, created by a writer's use of words. This feeling may be serious, humorous, or satiric.

Total effect is the general impression a literary work leaves on the reader.

Tragedy is a literary work in which the hero is destroyed by some character flaw or by forces beyond his or her control.

Tragic hero is a character who experiences an inner struggle because of a character flaw. That struggle ends in the defeat of the hero.

Transcendentalism is a philosophy that requires human beings to go beyond (transcend) reason in their search for truth. It assumes that an individual can arrive at the basic truths of life through spiritual insight if he or she takes the time to think seriously about them.

Poetry **Terms**

Alliteration is the repetition of initial consonant sounds in words:

"How many loved your moments of glad grace."

—W. B. Yeats, "When You Are Old"

Assonance is the repetition of vowel sounds without repeating consonants:

"Blind eyes could blaze like meteors."

—Dylan Thomas, "Do Not Go Gentle into That Good Night"

Ballad is a poem in verse form that tells a story.

Blank verse is an unrhymed form of poetry. Each line normally consists of 10 syllables in which every other syllable is stressed.

Caesura is a pause or sudden break in a line of poetry.

Canto is a main division of a long poem.

Consonance is the repetition of consonant sounds. Although it is similar to alliteration, consonance is not limited to the first letters of words:

"above his blond determined head the sacred flag of truth unfurled"

—e. e. cummings, "Two VIII"

Couplet is a pair of lines of verse of the same length that usually rhyme.

End rhyme is the rhyming of words that appear at the ends of two or more lines of poetry.

Enjambment is the running over of a sentence or thought from one line to another.

Foot is the smallest repeated pattern of stressed and unstressed syllables in a poetic line. (See "Meter," "Rhythm," and "Verse.")

- **Iambic:** an unstressed followed by a stressed syllable (repeat)
- **Anapestic:** two unstressed followed by a stressed syllable (interrupt)
- **Trochaic:** a stressed followed by an unstressed syllable (older)
- **Dactylic:** a stressed followed by two unstressed syllables (openly)
- **Spondaic:** two stressed syllables (heartbreak)
- **Pyrrhic:** two unstressed syllables (Pyrrhic seldom appears by itself.)

Free verse is poetry that does not have a regular meter or rhyme scheme.

Haiku is a form of Japanese poetry that has three lines: the first line has five syllables, the second has seven syllables, and the third has five syllables. The subject of the haiku has traditionally been nature:

Behind me the moon
Brushes shadows of pine trees
Lightly on the floor.

Heroic couplet (closed couplet) consists of two successive rhyming lines that contain a complete thought.

Internal rhyme occurs when the rhyming words appear in the same line of poetry: "**You break my <u>eyes</u> with a look that <u>buys</u> sweet cake.**"

Lyric is a short verse that is intended to express the emotions of the author.

Meter is the patterned repetition of stressed and unstressed syllables in a line of poetry. (See "Foot," "Rhythm," and "Verse.")

Onomatopoeia is the use of a word whose sound suggests its meaning, as in *clang, buzz,* and *twang.*

Refrain is the repetition of a line or phrase of a poem at regular intervals, especially at the end of each stanza.

Repetition is the repeating of a word, a phrase, or an idea for emphasis or for rhythmic effect:

> "**someone gently <u>rapping</u>, <u>rapping</u> at my chamber door . . .** "

Rhyme is the similarity or likeness of sound existing between two words. *Sat* and *cat* are perfect rhymes because the vowel and final consonant sounds are exactly the same.

Rhythm is the regular or random occurrence of sound in poetry. Regular rhythm is called *meter.* Random occurrence of sound is called *free verse.*

Sonnet is a poem consisting of fourteen lines of iambic pentameter.

- The **Italian (Petrarchan) sonnet** has two parts: an octave (eight lines) and a sestet (six lines), usually rhyming *abbaabba, cdecde.* Often, a question is raised in the octave and answered in the sestet.
- The **Shakespearean (English or Elizabethan)** sonnet consists of three quatrains and a final rhyming couplet. The rhyme scheme is *abab, cdcd, efef, gg.* Usually, the question or theme is set forth in the quatrains while the answer or resolution appears in the final couplet.

Stanza is a division of poetry named for the number of lines it contains:

- **Couplet:** two-line stanza
- **Triplet:** three-line stanza
- **Quatrain:** four-line stanza
- **Quintet:** five-line stanza
- **Sestet:** six-line stanza
- **Septet:** seven-line stanza
- **Octave:** eight-line stanza

Verse is a metric line of poetry. It is named according to the kind and number of feet composing it: *iambic pentameter,* for example. (See "Foot," "Meter," and "Rhythm.")

- **Monometer:** one foot
- **Dimeter:** two feet
- **Trimeter:** three feet
- **Tetrameter:** four feet
- **Pentameter:** five feet
- **Hexameter:** six feet
- **Heptameter:** seven feet
- **Octometer:** eight feet

RESEARCH WRITING

"My idea of research is to look at the thing from all sides; the person who has seen the animal, how the animal behaves, and so on." —Marianne Moore

Writing the
RESEARCH PAPER

What does it mean to be a researcher? To Jerry Ellis it meant walking 900 miles along the infamous Cherokee Trail of Tears and sharing what he learned in his book *Walking the Trail*. To Maria Sandoz it meant fulfilling a promise to her father that she would write about his struggles on the Nebraska frontier. The end result was her book *Old Jules,* an amazing portrait of pioneering.

In each of these cases, the writers investigated subjects that truly interested them. If you do the same, making each of your research projects an active quest for information, you will soon learn what it means to be a researcher.

Remember: A research paper is a carefully planned essay that shares information or proves a point. It may include ideas from books, Web sites, documents, interviews, observations, and so on. Most school research papers are at least five pages long and may also require a title page, an outline, and a list of works cited.

Preview

- O **Research Update**
- O **Writing Guidelines**
- O **Tips for Writing a Thesis Statement**
- O **Searching Tips**
- O **Writing Tips**

Research **Update**

In most cases, students head straight to the library or Internet to find published information (books, articles, encyclopedia entries, postings) for their research papers. However, many teachers also expect their students to collect firsthand information by conducting interviews, distributing questionnaires, making visits, participating in activities, writing letters, and so on. These firsthand experiences make researching much more active and meaningful for students.

The I-Search Paper

One method of research that focuses on firsthand information is the I-Search paper. An I-Search begins with an individual's curiosity about something. One person may wonder what it takes to become an emergency-room nurse. Another may wonder about the world of scuba diving.

After identifying a personal interest, the I-Searcher sets out to find information and answers through visits, observations, and interviews. I-Searchers use books and magazines only when recommended by someone they've contacted for information. (They use people first, print material second.) An I-Search paper becomes the story of a person's own searching adventure, telling what the I-Searcher wanted to know and what he or she found out or learned.

A Personalized Approach

Here's what we recommend for your next research project:

- ■ **Get involved.** Start by selecting a subject that interests you, and then carry out as much firsthand research as possible.

- ■ **Keep a journal.** Consider writing in a journal during the project. Thinking and writing about your work will help you make sense of new information, refocus your thinking, and evaluate your progress.

- ■ **Personalize it.** The more information you gain from your own thinking and exploring, the more you will enjoy the research process—and the more readers will appreciate the result.

 How has the Internet changed the process of researching?

On the upside, the Internet is a quick and convenient source of information. You can access an unlimited number of resources almost immediately. On the downside, the Internet provides so much information that settling on a few quality sources may be difficult. Anyone can publish anything on the Net, so you must learn how to judge between what is accurate and responsible and what may be inaccurate and irresponsible. (See pages 325 and 333.)

WRITING GUIDELINES
Research Paper

■ PREWRITING Selecting a Subject

1. **Understanding the Project . . .** When you are assigned a research paper, your teacher will probably suggest a few general subject areas. It will be up to you to explore these for a specific writing idea that meets the assignment requirements and genuinely interests you.

   Suppose that in a science class you're given the general subject "water resources." Your teacher asks you to decide on a specific water resource (a city well, a river, a lake, etc.) and then examine its use and misuse.

2. **Searching for Subjects . . .** To begin, review your class text and notebook for subject ideas. Also talk with your classmates about the assignment, or write about "water resources" in a journal to see what you can discover. Your teacher may also suggest some helpful sources of information including Web sites.

Sample Subject Cluster

Consider using a cluster (or web) to organize your ideas. Write the general subject in the center; then cluster ideas (possible subjects) around it.

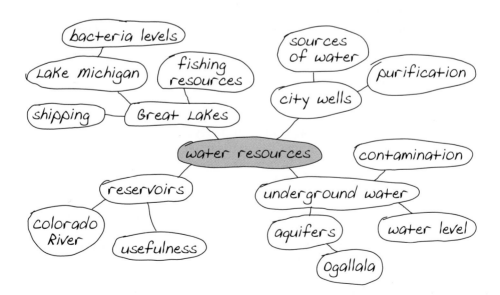

3. **Evaluating a Possible Subject . . .** If you can answer *yes* to each of the following questions, your subject is probably worth exploring:

- Am I truly interested in the subject?
- Does it meet the requirements of the assignment?
- Do I have access to enough information?
- Is the subject limited enough?

The last question is very important. You couldn't, for example, write a research paper about "underground water." Where would you begin or end? Nor could you write about "aquifers" (a source of underground water). The subject is still too general. However, the "Ogallala Aquifer" would be a subject limited enough to cover adequately in a research paper.

4. **Focusing Your Efforts . . .** If necessary, do some general research to learn more about your specific subject. (This may include talking to other people.) Then decide on a focus for your research—something that truly interests you about the subject. The chart below shows how this selecting process works.

THE SELECTING PROCESS

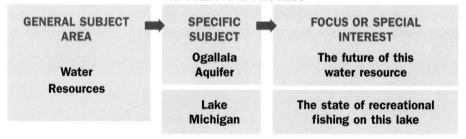

GENERAL SUBJECT AREA	SPECIFIC SUBJECT	FOCUS OR SPECIAL INTEREST
Water Resources	Ogallala Aquifer	The future of this water resource
	Lake Michigan	The state of recreational fishing on this lake

5. **Writing a Thesis Statement . . .** Once you have discovered what truly interests you about your subject, you are ready to write a thesis statement. This sentence serves as the controlling idea for your research, and it expresses what you believe your research will prove. (See the next page for guidelines and samples. Then see page 250 for "Prewriting, Searching for Information.")

Take NOTE

At this point, you are writing a working thesis statement. As you learn more about your subject, you may change your mind about it. Then you can revise your thesis accordingly.

TIPS for Writing a Thesis Statement

An effective thesis statement tells readers specifically what you plan to write about in your paper. It also serves as a personal guide to keep you on track as you research your subject.

The Process at Work

A thesis statement usually takes a stand or expresses a specific feeling or feature of your subject. Write as many versions as it takes to hit upon the one that sets the right tone for your writing. The following formula can be used to form your thesis statement:

> **A specific subject** (*The Ogallala Aquifer*)
> **+ a particular stand, feeling, or feature** (*is in jeopardy unless the use of irrigation changes*)
> _____
> **= an effective thesis statement.**

Sample Thesis Statements

Writing Assignment:	Research paper about a social issue
Specific Subject:	Homeless people
Thesis Statement:	Who are the homeless **(subject)**, and what are the reasons for their predicament **(specific feature)**?
Writing Assignment:	Research paper about human growth and development
Specific Subject:	Personality traits
Thesis Statement:	Certain personality traits **(subject)** are shaped primarily by a person's peer group **(specific stand)**.
Writing Assignment:	Extended analysis of a novel
Specific Subject:	*Frankenstein* by Mary Shelley
Thesis Statement:	Mary Shelley's novel *Frankenstein* **(subject)** focuses on the theme of friendship **(specific feature)**.

Thesis Checklist

Make sure that your thesis statement . . .

_____ identifies a limited, specific subject,

_____ focuses on a particular feature or feeling about the subject,

_____ is stated in a clear, direct sentence (or sentences),

_____ can be supported with convincing facts and details, and

_____ meets the requirements of the assignment.

■ PREWRITING **Searching for Information**

6. Preparing a Preliminary Bibliography . . . Look for a wide variety of resources related to your thesis statement by talking to others, searching the library, and surfing the Internet.

■ Keep track of your sources on your computer or on index cards.

■ Arrange your sources alphabetically by the author's last name.

■ Number each entry in your computer list, or number each card in the upper right-hand corner.

Sample Bibliography Card

Sample Note Card

Lewis, Jack. "The Ogallala Aquifer:
An Underground Sea."
EPA Journal Nov/Dec 1990: 42.
Lynchburg Public Library
://www.ebscohost.com>
11/5/2000
②

Depletion of the aquifer—the problem ②
- 11 percent of water pumped
out since 1930
- more than 170,000 wells
"sucking it dry"
- some wells in CO, KS, and TX
already dry

7. Taking Notes . . . As you conduct your research, take notes and write out quotations related to your thesis. (See page 258 for more information.)

■ Keep notes on cards of the same size and style (four-by-six-inch cards are recommended).

■ Record important details and quotations, along with the page numbers where this information can be found. Also place the number of the related bibliography card in the upper right-hand corner.

■ Place quotation marks around word-for-word quotations.

■ Use an ellipsis (. . .) when you leave words out of a quotation. (See page 456.) Use brackets around words you add to quotations.

■ Look up unfamiliar words. If you find that a particular word is important, copy its definition onto the same note card.

■ Give each card a descriptive heading (a word or a phrase to highlight the main idea of that note card: *Depletion of the aquifer—the problem*).

Searching **TIPS**

To help organize your research and note taking, try writing some basic questions you would like to answer in your report. Any time you find information that answers a question, take notes on it.

Sample Questions

1. What is an aquifer?
2. What is the Ogallala Aquifer?
3. How did the Ogallala Aquifer come to exist?
4. Who uses the aquifer water?
5. How does center-pivot irrigation work?
6. Why is irrigation necessary?

8. Using Primary Sources . . . Collect as much firsthand information as possible. Consider writing letters to experts, distributing surveys, conducting interviews, and so on. (See pages 300-301 and 328-330 for help.)

■ PREWRITING Designing a Writing Plan

9. Organizing Your Research . . . Arrange your note cards into their most logical order; then use them to construct a writing plan (which lists in order or outlines the main points you want to cover in your paper). Use the headings on your note cards or your list of searching questions to form your writing-plan list. Here is a plan for the sample research paper in this handbook. (See pages 275-283.)

Sample Writing Plan

1. Introduction--presents subject and thesis
2. Background and history of the Ogallala Aquifer
3. Problems with current water use
4. The impact of center-pivot irrigation
5. Changing farm practices
6. Applying new technologies
7. Conclusion--summing up main points

10. Continuing Your Research . . . Search for any additional information that may be needed to develop your thesis. (Remember to revise your thesis if learning more about the subject has changed your mind about it. Also revise your writing plan, if necessary, as you continue your research.)

"When you're writing nonfiction, there's no use getting into a writing schedule until you've done the [research] and you have the material." —Tom Wolfe

■ WRITING THE FIRST DRAFT

11. Developing Your Introduction . . . Your introduction should do two things. The first part should say something interesting, surprising, or important about the subject to gain the reader's attention. (See the list below for ideas.) The second part should identify the thesis of your research. (See page 55 for a sample introductory paragraph.)

- Start with a revealing story or quotation.
- Give important background information.
- Offer a series of interesting or surprising facts.
- Provide important definitions.
- State your reason for choosing this subject.

12. Writing the Body . . . The next step is to write the main part of your research paper, the part that supports or proves your thesis. There are two ways to proceed. You can write freely as ideas come to mind, or you can work systematically, carefully following your notes and writing plan.

Writing Freely To proceed in this way, put your writing plan and note cards aside and write as much as you can on your own. Refer to your note cards only when you need a quotation, specific facts, or figures.

After you have completed this first writing, review your writing plan and your note cards to see if you have missed or misplaced any important points. Then continue writing, filling in or reorganizing ideas as you go along.

Writing Systematically To work in a systematic fashion, carefully follow your writing plan and note cards right from the start. Begin by laying out the first section of note cards (those covering the first main point in your plan). Then write a general statement that covers the first main point. Using the note cards you have in front of you, add supporting facts and details. Repeat this process until you have dealt with all the main points in your plan.

Writing TIPS

- Use your own words as much as possible. Include the ideas of others or direct quotations only when they add significant support to your thesis. (See pages 255-258 for more information.)
- Present your ideas honestly and clearly. If you feel strongly about your research and have something meaningful to say, you are more likely to write an interesting paper.
- Keep your readers in mind. What do they already know about your subject? What do they need to know? How can you keep their interest?
- Work to achieve a formal to semiformal style. Avoid fragments, abbreviations, informal expressions, and slang.
- Present only ideas that you can support with facts and details.

13. Writing the Conclusion . . . The final section of your paper should leave readers with a clear understanding of the importance of your research. Summarize the main points you have made and draw a final conclusion. In a more personal approach, you may discuss how your research has strengthened or changed your thinking about your subject. (See page 58 for a sample concluding paragraph.)

■ REVISING

14. Improving Your Writing . . . Expect to make many changes in your first draft before it says what you want it to say. Make sure that your introduction gains your reader's attention and identifies your thesis, that each paragraph in the body develops a main point about your subject, and that your conclusion ties everything together.

[**HOT LINK**] See "Assessment Rubric," page 284, for a helpful revising and editing guide.

15. Seeking Advice . . . Have at least one person (writing peer, teacher, family member) review your first draft. Share any concerns you have about your writing. Ask this person if he or she found any parts confusing or if they have any questions. (See pages 69-74.)

16. Documenting Your Sources . . . Give credit in your paper for ideas and direct quotations that you have used from different sources. Make sure that you have copied this information accurately. In addition, put the works-cited section together, listing all of the sources you have cited in your paper. (See pages 259-274 for MLA guidelines and pages 285-295 for APA guidelines.)

> "To sum up, style cannot go beyond the ideas which lie at the heart of it."
>
> —H.L. Mencken

■ EDITING AND PROOFREADING

17. Checking for Style and Accuracy . . . Carefully edit your revised writing for style. Make sure that all of your sentences read smoothly and clearly, and that you have used the best words to express your ideas. Then check your work for spelling, grammar, and punctuation errors.

MLA or APA Documentation Style

Points 18 and 19 below (and pages 259-274) provide formatting guidelines following MLA (Modern Language Association) documentation style. The guidelines for APA (American Psychological Association) begin on page 285.

18. Completing Your Final Copy . . . If you use a computer, print your final copy on good-quality paper. Do not justify your right margins. Leave a one-inch margin on all sides. Double-space your entire paper, including long quotations and the works-cited section.

Number your pages beginning with the first page of your paper and continue through the works-cited section. Type your last name before each page number. Place the page numbers in the upper right-hand corner, one-half inch from the top and even with the right-hand margin. (See pages 276-283 for a sample final copy.)

19. Adding Identifying Information . . . Type your name, the instructor's name, the course title, and the date in the upper left-hand corner of the first page of the paper. (Begin one inch from the top and double-space throughout.) Center the title (double-space before and after); then type the first line of the paper. (See page 277.)

HELP FILE

If your teacher requires a title page, center the title one-third of the way down from the top of the page; then center your name, the name of your teacher, and any additional information two-thirds of the way down. If you need to submit a final outline, make sure it follows the final version of your paper. (See page 276.)

---

20. Proofreading Your Final Copy . . . Check the final draft from beginning to end for errors. When you submit your research paper, it should be as error free as you can possibly make it.

> "Everyone has a right to an opinion, but no one has a right to be wrong about the facts."
> —Anonymous

Writing
RESPONSIBLY

A research paper, like any other type of meaningful writing, should be a personal process of discovery. First you need to gain control of the information you plan on using. For example, as you gather information, you'll discover that not all sources agree. You need to study these sources carefully and decide which are the most reliable (or which offer the most valid arguments). Then determine how the discoveries you make match up to your own thinking. Research will become your own when you . . .

- believe in your subject,
- give yourself enough time to learn about it,
- gather some firsthand information, and
- study, question, and discuss your work as it develops.

When you make your research your own, two things will most likely happen: (1) Your writing will sound sincere, like it comes from you, a student researcher. (2) Your writing will be honest, reflecting the results of your planning, searching, and studying.

Preview

- Giving Proper Credit
- Sample Paraphrases
- Using Quoted Material

Giving **Proper Credit**

Avoiding Plagiarism

You owe it to your sources and your readers to give credit for anyone else's ideas or words that you use in your research paper. If you don't, you may be guilty of *plagiarism*—the act of presenting someone else's ideas as your own. The guidelines that follow will help you avoid plagiarism:

- When using a writer's idea, credit the author by name and also cite the work in which you found the idea. (See 259-263 and 285-288.)
- Give a new citation even when using additional information from a previously cited source.
- When summarizing or paraphrasing, remember to use quotation marks around key words or phrases taken directly from the source. (See below and pages 468-469.)
- Cite everything you borrow unless you're sure that the information is common knowledge.

Writing Paraphrases

There are two ways to share information from another source: (1) quote the source directly, or (2) paraphrase the source. When you quote directly, you include the exact words of the author and put quotation marks around them. When you paraphrase, you use your own words to restate someone else's ideas. In either case, you must cite your source. To paraphrase, follow the steps below.

1. **Skim the selection first** to get the overall meaning.
2. **Read the selection carefully;** pay attention to key words and phrases.
3. **List the main ideas** on a piece of paper, without looking at the selection.
4. **Review the selection** again.
5. **Write your paraphrase;** restate the author's ideas in your own words.
   - Stick to the essential information (drop anecdotes and details).
   - State each important idea clearly and concisely.
   - Put quotation marks around words taken directly from the source.
   - Arrange the ideas into a smooth, logical order.
6. **Check your paraphrase** for accuracy by asking these questions:
   - Have I kept the author's ideas and viewpoints clear in my paraphrase? Have I quoted where necessary?
   - Have I cut out enough of the original? Too much?
   - Could another person understand the author's main idea by reading my paraphrase?

Sample **Paraphrases**

Following the original passage below from a book by Travis Taylor, you'll find two sample paraphrases, both properly cited.

ORIGINAL PASSAGE

Kyudo, which means "the way of the bow" in Japanese, is the Zen martial art of archery. It was adapted into traditional Buddhist practice from medieval Japanese archers who used seven-foot asymmetrical bows called *yumi.* Although kyudo lacks the widespread popularity of karate or judo, it is often regarded as one of the most intensive martial arts in existence, taking an estimated 30 years to master.

The standard execution of kyudo involves a series of specific actions, including assuming the proper posture, approaching the intended target, nocking the arrow, drawing it, releasing it, and then repeating the process. After the second arrow has been released, the archer approaches the target, withdraws the arrows, and thus completes the exercise.

There is far more to kyudo, however, than simply shooting arrows. For every movement, the archer must maintain a specific posture, inhaling and exhaling at predetermined points throughout the exercise. The focus point for breathing and positioning is the region of the lower stomach called the *hara.* Careful attention to the hara is supposed to help an archer maintain a solid center of balance.

With continued practice, the archer gains greater abilities of concentration and action. In addition, the repetitive action and deep breathing greatly relaxes the archer—heightening his alertness and lowering his stress.

Basic Paraphrase

Kyudo is the Zen martial art of archery. It was adapted from medieval Japanese archery into a spiritual and physical exercise. Through a series of specific actions, the archer prepares and shoots an arrow into a target and then repeats the action one more time. The archer's sense of balance comes from focusing on the lower stomach region. The focused breathing and balanced posture lessen stress and increase the archer's ability to concentrate (Taylor 26).

Basic Paraphrase with Quotation

Kyudo is the Zen martial art of archery. It was adapted from medieval traditional Japanese archery into a spiritual and physical exercise. "The standard execution of kyudo involves a series of specific actions, including assuming the proper posture, approaching the intended target, nocking the arrow, drawing it, [and] releasing it . . . " (Taylor 26). An archer's sense of balance comes from focusing on the lower stomach region. The breathing and balanced posture lessen stress and increase the archer's ability to concentrate (Taylor 26).

Using **Quoted Material**

A quotation can be a single word or an entire paragraph. Choose quotations carefully, keep them as brief as possible, and use them only when they are necessary. When you do quote material directly, be sure that the capitalization, punctuation, and spelling are the same as that in the original work. Clearly mark changes for your readers: (1) changes within the quotation are enclosed in brackets [like this]; (2) explanations are enclosed in parentheses at the end of the quotation before closing punctuation (like this).

Short Quotations

If a quotation is four typed lines or fewer, work it into the body of your paper and put quotation marks around it.

Long Quotations

Quotations of more than four typed lines should be set off from the rest of the writing by indenting each line 10 spaces and double-spacing the material. When quoting two or more paragraphs, indent the first line of each paragraph three additional spaces. Do not use quotation marks. (See page 469.)

NOTE: After the final punctuation mark of the quotation, leave two spaces before you cite the parenthetical reference. Generally, a colon is used to introduce quotations set off from the text. (See page 463.1.)

Quoting **Poetry**

When quoting up to three lines of poetry, use quotation marks and work the lines into your writing. Use a diagonal (/) to show where each line of the poem ends. For quotations of four lines or more, indent each line 10 spaces (and double-space the same as the rest of the text). Do not use quotation marks.

NOTE: To show that you have left out a line or more of verse in a longer quotation, make a line of spaced periods the approximate length of a complete line of the poem.

Partial Quotations

If you want to leave out part of the quotation, use an ellipsis to signify the omission. An ellipsis (. . .) is three periods with a space before and after each one. (See page 456.)

NOTE: Anything you take out of a quotation should not change the author's original meaning.

"Adam was the only man who, when he said a good thing, knew that nobody had said it before him."

—Mark Twain

MLA Documentation Style

Most academic disciplines have their own manuals of style for research-paper documentation. The Modern Language Association style manual (*MLA Handbook for Writers of Research Papers*), for example, is widely used in the humanities (literature, philosophy, history, etc.), making it the most popular manual in high school and college writing courses.

This chapter will provide you with guidelines for citing sources according to the MLA style manual. Included is a special section on citing sources from the Internet, including a Web-site address for obtaining updated information. (For complete information about the MLA style, refer to the latest version of the *MLA Handbook*.)

Preview

- Citing Sources: Parenthetical References
- List of Works Cited
- Works-Cited Entries: Books
- Works-Cited Entries: Periodicals
- Works-Cited Entries: Other Sources
- Works-Cited Entries: Electronic Sources

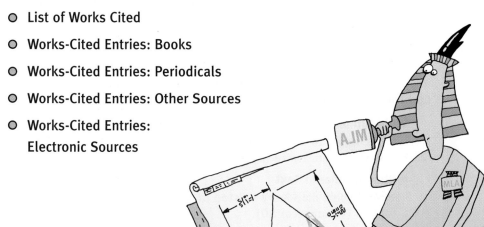

Citing **Sources**

Parenthetical References

The *MLA Handbook for Writers of Research Papers* suggests giving credit to your sources in the body of your research paper rather than in endnotes. To give credit in your paper, do the following:

- Insert the appropriate information (usually author and page number) in parentheses after the words or ideas borrowed from another source.
- Place the parenthetical reference where a pause would naturally occur to avoid disrupting the flow of your writing (usually at the end of a sentence).
- Make sure that the sources cited in your paper are also listed in the works-cited section of your paper.

One Author: Citing a Complete Work

No parenthetical reference is needed if you identify the author in your text. (See the first entry below.) However, you must give the author's last name in a parenthetical reference if it is not mentioned in the text. (See the second entry below.) A parenthetical reference should use the name by which the work is listed in the works-cited section—whether that is the author, editor, translator, speaker, artist, or some other person.

With Author in Text (This is the preferred way of citing a complete work.)

In **Confederates in the Attic**, Tony Horwitz explains how the Civil War remains alive in the South.

Without Author in Text

Confederates in the Attic explains how the Civil War remains alive in the South (Horwitz).

One Author: Citing Part of a Work

List the necessary page numbers in parentheses if you borrow words or ideas from a particular work. Leave a space between the author's last name and the page reference. No punctuation is needed.

With Author in Text

According to Winchester, no English dictionary existed at the time Shakespeare wrote his plays (80).

Without Author in Text

No English dictionary existed at the time Shakespeare wrote his plays (Winchester 80).

Two or Three Authors

Give the last names of every author in the same order that they appear in the works-cited section. (The correct order of the authors' names can be found on the title page of the book.)

> According to Carlson, Eisenstat, and Ziporyn, a frequent cause of depression in middle-aged women is the care of elderly parents with failing health (198).

> Samuel Moore Walton, founder of Wal-Mart, owed much of his ambition for success to the fact that he grew up during the Depression (Vance and Scott 1).

More Than Three Authors

Give the first author's last name as it appears in the works-cited section followed by *et al.* or *and others* with no punctuation in between.

> Methane gas trapped in ice crystals on the seafloor may be an important source of fuel in the future (Suess et al. 80).

Corporate Author

If a book or other work was written by a committee or task force, it is said to have a *corporate* author. If the corporate name is long, include it in the text (rather than in parentheses) to avoid disrupting the flow of your writing. Use a shortened form of the name in the text and in references after the full name has been used at least once. For example, *Task Force* may be used for *Task Force on Education for Economic Growth* after the full name has been used at least once.

> The thesis of the Task Force's report is that economic success depends on our ability to improve large-scale education and training as quickly as possible (14).

An Anonymous Book (Work)

When there is no author listed, give the title or a shortened version of the title as it appears in the works-cited section. (No page numbers are needed for single-page articles or nonprint sources.)

> The Information Please Almanac states that drinking water can make up 20 percent or more of a person's total exposure to lead (572).

One or More Works in a Reference

Cite each work as you normally would; separate the references with a semicolon.

> Biographers point to the perfect match of Katharine Hepburn's own character with that of Jo March, the part she played in the 1933 movie Little Women (Edwards 109; Morley 51).

Two or More Works by the Same Author

If the works-cited page lists two or more works by the same author, you'll need more than just the author's last name in your parenthetical reference. Give the author's last name (unless it appears in the text), the title or a shortened version of the title, and the page reference.

> The German foxholes dug during World War II were almost always deeper than the American foxholes (Ambrose, Citizen Soldiers 257).

Indirect Source

If you cite an indirect source—someone's remarks published second-hand—give the abbreviation *qtd. in* (quoted in) before the indirect source in your reference.

> Desmond Tutu, speaking of the struggle against South African apartheid, said, "Our cause is just and noble. That is why it will prevail and bring victory to us" (qtd. in duBoulay 223).

Literary Works: Prose

To cite literary prose works, list more than the page reference if the work is available in several editions. Give the page reference first, and then add a chapter, section, or book number in abbreviated form after a semicolon.

> In Cry, the Beloved Country, Alan Paton presents Steven Kumalo as "a man who lives in a world not made for him, whose own world is slipping away, dying, being destroyed, beyond recall" (14; ch. 3).

When you are quoting prose that takes more than four typed lines, indent each line of the quotation 10 spaces and double-space it. In this case, you put the parenthetical citation (the pages and chapter numbers) *outside* the end punctuation mark of the quotation itself. Skip two spaces before you begin the citation.

> Kumalo would describe the land as he wanted his sister to remember it, beautiful and inviting. Then suddenly his missing son would darken his thoughts and feelings about the land:
>
> > And then in one fraction of time the hills with the deep melodious names stood out waste and desolate beneath the pitiless sun, the streams ceased to run, the cattle moved thin and listless over the red and rootless earth. It was a place of old women and mothers and children, from each house something was gone. His voice would falter and die away, and he would fall silent and muse. (61; ch. 10)

Literary Works: Verse (Plays and Poems)

Cite verse (plays and poems) by divisions (act, scene, canto, book, part) and lines; use periods to separate the various parts. For short quotations of verse, use a diagonal to show where each new line of verse begins.

> **When she learns that Romeo is a Montague, Juliet exclaims, "My only love, sprung from my only hate! / Too early seen unknown, and known too late!" (1.5.138-139).**

Verse quotations of more than three lines should be indented 10 spaces and double-spaced. Each line of the poem or play begins a new line of the quotation; do not run the lines together or separate them with diagonals. Separate lines with diagonals only within the main text of your paper.

> **Elizabeth Bishop's poem "The Fish" contains layers of specific details:**
>
> > **He was speckled with barnacles,**
> >
> > **fine rosettes of lime,**
> >
> > **and infested**
> >
> > **with tiny white sea lice,**
> >
> > **and underneath two or three**
> >
> > **rags of green weed hung down. (16-21)**

Take NOTE   There are a number of abbreviations commonly used for documenting sources in research papers. Here are some of them:

ch.	**chapter(s)**
ed.	**editor(s), edition(s), or edited by**
et al.	**and others**
illus.	**illustrator, illustration, illustrated by**
n.d.	**no date given**
no.	**number(s)**
n.p.	**no place of publication and/or no publisher given**
n. pag.	**no pagination (no page numbers)**
p., pp.	**page(s)**
qtd.	**quoted**
rpt.	**reprinted (by), reprint**
sec. (sect.)	**section(s)**
sic	**thus** in the source (used with brackets to indicate an error is that way in the original)
vol.	**volume(s)**

Works-Cited List: Overview

The works-cited section lists all of the sources you have cited in your paper. It does *not* include sources you may have read but did not cite in your paper. The works-cited list follows the format below.

Page Numbers and Title ℮ Begin your list of works cited on a new page (the next page after the text), and number each page, continuing to number from the last page of the text.

- Type your last name and the page number in the same position as on the text pages.
- Center the title *Works Cited* one inch from the top. Double-space everything.

Entries ℮ Begin each entry flush with the left margin. If the entry runs more than one line, indent additional lines five spaces.

- Double-space between all lines on the page of works cited.
- Single-space between words and after punctuation marks in a works-cited entry.
- List each entry alphabetically by the author's last name. If there is no author, use the first word of the title. (Disregard *A, An, The.*)

Format ℮ The models below show you basic formats for citing books, periodicals, and on-line sources. (See models on pages 265-274.)

Format for a Book Entry

Author's last name, First name. Book Title. City: Publisher, date.

Format for a Periodical Entry

Author's last name, First name. "Article." Periodical Title date:

page nos.

Format for an On-Line Entry

Author's last name, First name. "Title." Information on print

version (if any). Site title. Date posted or last updated.

Sponsor. Date accessed <Electronic address>.

NOTE: In Web entries, if certain items are not available, go on to the next item.

Works-Cited Entries:
Books

One Author

> Zubrin, Robert J. Entering Space: Creating a Spacefaring Civilization.
> New York: Tarcher/Putnam, 1999.

Two or Three Authors

> Diehl, Daniel, and Mark Donnelly. Medieval Furniture: Plans and
> Instructions for Historical Reproductions. Mechanicsburg, PA:
> Stackpole, 1999.

More Than Three Authors

> Roberts, Simon, et al. The Complete Java 2 Certification Study
> Guide. Alameda, CA: Sybex, 1999.

Two or More Books by the Same Author(s)

List the books alphabetically according to title. After the first entry, substitute three hyphens for the author's name.

> Greenberg, Jan, and Sandra Jordan. The American Eye: Eleven
> Artists of the Twentieth Century. New York: Delacorte, 1995.
>
> ---. The Painter's Eye: Learning to Look at Contemporary American
> Art. New York: Delacorte, 1991.

A Corporate Group Author

> Wisconsin Taxpayers' Alliance. School Facts '99. Madison, WI:
> Wisconsin Taxpayers' Alliance, 1999.

An Anonymous Book

1999 People Weekly Almanac. New York: Cader, 1998.

NOTE: The Bible is considered an anonymous book. Documentation should read exactly as it is printed on the title page. (Translations and editions of the Bible vary, which is why you must be precise.)

The Jerusalem Bible. Garden City, NY: Doubleday, 1966.

The English Revised Bible with the Apocrypha. N.p.: Oxford UP and

Cambridge UP, 1989.

A Single Work from an Anthology

Paley, Grace. "A Warning." Telling and Remembering: A Century of

American Jewish Poetry. Ed. Steven J. Rubin. Boston: Beacon,

1997.

NOTE: If you cite a complete anthology, begin the entry with the editor(s).

Rubin, Steven J., ed. Telling and Remembering: A Century of

American Jewish Poetry. Boston: Beacon, 1997.

A Multivolume Work

Bianco, David P., ed. Parents Aren't Supposed to Like It: Rock and Other

Pop Musicians of the 1990s. Vol. 3. Detroit: UXL-Gale, 1998.

NOTE: If you cite two or more volumes in a multivolume work, give the total number of volumes after the title.

Hipple, Ted, ed. Writers for Young Adults. 3 vols. New York:

Scribner's, 1997.

An Introduction, a Preface, a Foreword, or an Afterword

Callan, Edward. Introduction. Cry, the Beloved Country. By Alan

Paton. New York: Macmillan, 1987. xv-xxvii.

NOTE: Give only the author's last name after By if he or she is the author of the piece cited and the complete work.

Weir, Alison. Preface. The Life of Elizabeth I. By Weir. New York:

Ballantine, 1998. xi-xii.

Cross-Reference

To avoid unnecessary repetition when citing two or more entries from a larger collection, you may cite the collection once with complete publication information (see Martz). The individual entries (see Ashley and Barnhill) can then be cross-referenced by listing the author, title of the piece, editor of the collection, and page numbers.

Ashley, Mary Anne. "Gracefully Afraid." Martz 79-88.

Barnhill, Sarah. "Near Places, Far Places." Martz 23-37.

Martz, Sandra, ed. When I Am an Old Woman I Shall Wear Purple.

Watsonville, CA: Papier-Mache, 1991.

An Edition

An edition may refer to the particular publication you are citing, as in "the 3rd edition." But "edition" may also refer to the work of one person that is prepared by another person, an editor.

Netter, Frank H. Atlas of Human Anatomy. 2nd ed. East Hanover, NJ:

Novartis, 1997.

A Translation

Turgenev, Ivan Sergeevich. Fathers and Sons. Trans. Michael R. Katz.

New York: Norton, 1994.

An Article in a Reference Book

It is not necessary to give full publication information for familiar reference works (encyclopedias and dictionaries). For these titles, list only the edition (if available) and the publication year. If an article is initialed check the index of authors (in the opening section of each volume) for the author's full name.

Pettigrew, Thomas F. "Racism." The World Book Encyclopedia.

1998 ed.

"Pyrrho." The Encyclopedia Americana. International ed. 1995.

Pamphlet with No Author or Publication Information Stated

If it is known, list the country of publication [in brackets]. Use n.p. (after the colon) for "no publisher given" and n.d. for "no date given."

Pedestrian Safety. [United States]: n.p., n.d.

Signed Pamphlet

Treat a pamphlet as you would a book.

Dye, Christina. Cocaine: Waking Up to a Nightmare. Phoenix, AZ:

Do It Now Foundation, 1989.

Government Publication

State the name of the government (country, state, etc.) followed by the name of the agency.

United States. National Institute on Drug Abuse. Preventing Drug

Use Among Children and Adolescents. Bethesda, MD: NIH, 1997.

A Book in a Series

Give the series name and number (if any) before the publication information.

Ethan, Eric, and Marie Bearanger. Colors of the Sea: Coral Reef

Feeders. Imagination Library Series. Milwaukee: Gareth Stevens,

1997.

A Publisher's Imprint

The name of a publisher's imprint appears above the publisher's name on the title page. Give the imprint followed by a hyphen and the name of the publisher (Signet-NAL).

Solzhenitsyn, Alexander. One Day in the Life of Ivan Denisovich.

Trans. Ralph Parker. New York: Signet-NAL, 1963.

NOTE: If more than one city is listed for a publisher, list the first one.

A Book with a Title Within a Title

If the title contains a title normally in quotation marks, keep the quotation marks and underline the entire title.

Davison, Peter. "Barn Fever" and Other Poems. New York:

Atheneum, 1981.

NOTE: If the title contains a title normally underlined, do not underline it in your entry, as in this example: A Tale of Two Cities as History.

Works-Cited Entries:
Periodicals

Signed Article in a Magazine

Anderson, Kelli. "Going to the Dawgs." <u>Sports Illustrated</u> 15 Nov.

1999: 116-19.

Unsigned Article in a Magazine

"Seven Tips About Portable Generators." <u>Consumer Reports</u> Nov.

1999: 10.

An Article in a Scholarly Journal

Wu, Kelvin K. S., Ofer Lahav, and Martin J. Rees. "The Large-Scale

Smoothness of the Universe." <u>Nature</u> 397 (1999): 225-30.

NOTE: Journals are usually issued four times a year. Number 397 refers to the volume. The issue number is not needed if the page numbers in a volume continue from one issue to the next (as in the example above). If the page numbers start over with each issue, then put a period between the volume number and issue number: 397.2.

Letter to the Editor

Scruggs, Jan Craig. Letter. <u>USA Today</u> 12 Nov. 1999: A14.

Signed Newspaper Article

Mullen, William. "Dinosaur Bones in Sahara Prove a Monster Find."

<u>Chicago Tribune</u> 12 Nov. 1999, late ed., sec. 1: 1+.

NOTE: Cite the edition of a major daily newspaper (if given) after the date (12 Nov. 1999, late ed.). To cite an article in a lettered section of the newspaper, list the section before the page number. (For example, A4 would refer to page 4 in section A of the newspaper.) If the sections are numbered, however, use a comma after the year; then indicate sec. 1, 2, 3, etc., followed by a colon and the page number.

Unsigned Newspaper Article

"Toyota to Team Up with Dealer Network to Sell Cars on Web."

Wall Street Journal 12 Nov. 1999: B5.

NOTE: If the city is not included in the name of a **local newspaper** you are citing, include the city name in brackets: **Voice Journal [South Milwaukee]**.

A Review

Iyer, Pico. "Inner Visions: Time's Former Editor Faces Up to

Going Blind." Rev. of Twilight, by Henry Grunwald. Time

15 Nov. 1999: 110.

NOTE: If you cite the review of a work by an editor or a translator, use *ed.* or *trans.* instead of *by*.

Published Interview

Matthews, Dave. "Dave Matthews." By Tom Moon. Rolling Stone

2 Sept. 1999: 64.

NOTE: Type the word *Interview* after the interviewee's name if the interview is untitled.

A Title or Quotation Within an Article's Title

Lahr, John. "Dancing with Shades: A New Version of 'The Dead'

Puts the Music First." New Yorker 8 Nov. 1999: 96-98.

NOTE: Use single quotation marks around the shorter title if it is a title normally punctuated with quotation marks.

Article Reprinted in a Loose-Leaf Collection

O'Connell, Loraine. "Busy Teens Feel the Beep." Orlando Sentinel

7 Jan. 1993: E1+ Youth. Ed. Eleanor Goldstein. Vol. 4 Boca

Raton, FL: SIRS, 1993. Art. 41.

NOTE: The entry begins with original publication information and ends with the name of the loose-leaf volume (Youth), editor, volume number, publication information including the name of the *information service* (Social Issues Resources Series), and the article number.

Works-Cited Entries:
Other Sources

Television or Radio Program

> "An Interview with Elton John." <u>Barbara Walters Special</u>. ABC.
>
> > WISN, Milwaukee. 21 Mar. 1994.

NOTE: If your reference is primarily to the work of an individual, cite that person before the title. Otherwise, other pertinent information (director, writer, etc.) may be given after the main title of the program (underlined).

CD Recording

> Shocked, Michelle. <u>Arkansas Traveler</u>. Polygram Records, 1992.

NOTE: If you are not using a compact disc, indicate the medium (audiotape, audiocassette, or LP for long-playing record) just before the manufacture's name: **LP. Polygram Records, 1992**.

Publication on CD-ROM

> "Sepoy Rebellion." <u>Microsoft Encarta 98 Encyclopedia</u>. CD-ROM.
>
> > 1998 ed. Redmond: Microsoft, 1998.

Recorded Interview

> Keating, Helena. Interview. <u>Twenty-First Century Classrooms</u>.
>
> > Dir. Edwin Feidler. Videocassette. Learners Warehouse, 1997.

Filmstrip, Slide Program, Videocassette, DVD (Digital Videodisc)

> <u>Going Back: A Return to Vietnam</u>. Videocassette. Virginia
>
> > Productions, 1982.

NOTE: Cite the medium (filmstrip, slide program, etc.) before the name of the distributor.

Film

Rebel Without a Cause. Dir. Nicholas Ray. Perf. James Dean, Natalie
Wood, Sal Mineo, and Dennis Hopper. Warner, 1955.

Letter Received by the Author (Yourself)

Thomas, Bob. Letter to the author. 10 Jan. 1999.

Interview by the Author (Yourself)

O'Connell, Amanda. Telephone interview. 7 Jan. 2000.

NOTE: If you conduct the interview in person, use the label **Personal interview**.

Lecture, Speech, or Address

Angelou, Maya. Address. Opening General Sess. NCTE Convention.
Adam's Mark Hotel, St. Louis. 18 Nov. 1988.

NOTE: If known, give the speech's title in quotation marks instead of the label **Address, Lecture,** or **Speech.**

Published Letter

Bottomley, Edwin. "To Father." 6 Dec. 1843. An English Settler in
Pioneer Wisconsin: The Letters of Edwin Bottomley. Ed. Milo M.
Quaife. Madison: State Historical Society, 1918. 60-62.

Map or Chart

Wisconsin Territory. Map. Madison: Wisconsin Trails, 1988.

Cartoon

Trudeau, Garry. "Doonesbury." Cartoon. Chicago Tribune 23 Dec.
1988, sec. 5: 6.

Works-Cited Entries:
Electronic Sources

Web Site (Professional)

> ESPN.com. 12 Nov. 1999. ESPN Internet Ventures. 24 Nov. 1999
>
> > <http://espn.go.com>.

NOTE: With Web site entries, when certain items do not apply or are not available, skip those and go on to the next item.

Article Within a Web Site

> Devitt, Terry. "Flying High." The Why Files. 9 Dec. 1999. University
>
> > of Wisconsin, Board of Regents. 4 Jan. 2000
> >
> > <http://whyfiles.news.wisc.edu/shorties/kite.html>.

Article Within a Web Site (Anonymous)

> "Becoming a Meteorologist." Weather.com. 12 Nov. 1999.
>
> > The Weather Channel. 24 Nov. 1999 <http://weather.com/
> >
> > learn_more/resources/metro.html>.

Web Site (Personal)

> Hamilton, Calvin J. Views of the Solar System. 12 Nov. 1999
>
> > <http://solarviews.com/eng/homepage.htm>.

On-Line Government Document

> United States. U.S. Census Bureau. Poverty in the United States:
>
> > 1998. Sept. 1999. 12 Nov. 1999 <http://www.census.gov/
> >
> > prod/99pubs/p60-207.pdf>.

Article from On-Line Computer Service (Also in Print)

Williams, Vanessa. "D.C. Votes to Limit Teenage Drivers: Council

Sets 18 as Minimum Age for Full License." Washington Post

3 Nov. 1999, final ed.: A1. National Newspapers. ProQuest.

Gateway Technical College, Elkhorn Campus Library. 12 Nov.

1999 <http://proquest.umi.com/pqdweb>.

NOTE: When you use a library to access a subscription service, add the name of the database if known (underlined), the service, and the library. (Add them before the date of access.) Then give the Internet address for the home page of the service, if you know it.

Article from On-Line Computer Service (Volume Number Included)

"Senate Approves New Alternative Fuel." National Petroleum News

90.9 (Sept. 1998): 36 (1/6p.). MasterFILE Premier. EBSCOhost.

Lynchburg Public Library. 12 Nov. 1999

<http://www.ebscohost.com>.

Important Note

Because technology is moving faster than any print source can keep up with, neither the MLA nor the *Writers INC* handbook is able to provide a completely current section for citing network sources. For that reason, we recommend you visit our Web site for updates and additional information. Our address is <thewritesource.com>.

Also, because availability of information on computer networks can change from day to day, we recommend that you print out a copy of the material you are accessing. Then you and your readers (instructors, especially) can check the accuracy of quotations, data, and other pertinent information cited in your paper.

Finally, while the formats for all works-cited examples in this section are based on the latest edition of the *MLA Handbook,* the particulars in each case (names, dates, electronic addresses, etc.) have been created to present as clear and complete a model entry as possible.

"The guiding question in research is 'so what?' Answer that question in every sentence you write."
— Donald W. McClosky

Sample MLA RESEARCH Paper

Meaningful research requires a lot of time to develop because there is so much searching, planning, writing, and revising involved. That is why your teachers assign research projects over an extended period of time. Always follow whatever timetable they give you, and keep time on your side as much as possible. Your teachers know what it takes to develop a worthwhile finished product.

Also take time to preview the sample paper in this chapter. First skim the paper to get an overview of its structure. Then do a careful reading, looking closely at the different parts: title page, outline, introduction, supporting paragraphs, and so on. The side notes, which highlight important features in the paper, will also be helpful as you prepare to write your own research paper.

Preview

- Title Page and Outline
- Sample Research Paper
- Assessment Rubric

Title Page and Outline

If you are instructed to include a title page or an outline with your research paper, use the samples below as your guide.

TITLE PAGE
Center the title one-third of the way down the page; center author information two-thirds of the way down.

The Ogallala: Preserving the

Great American Desert

Allison De Jong

Mr. Schelhaas

Environmental Science

20 November 2000

RESEARCH-PAPER OUTLINE
Center the title one inch from the top of the page. Double-space throughout.

The Ogallala: Preserving the

Great American Desert

Introduction—The Ogallala Aquifer transformed the Great American Desert, but its future is in jeopardy.

   I. Background of the problem

     A. Formation of the Ogallala Aquifer

     B. Explanation of aquifers

     C. Size and location of the Ogallala Aquifer

  II. The nature and extent of the problem

     A. Irrigation depleting the aquifer

     B. Advances in center-pivot irrigation a huge factor

       1. Lowering water table

       2. Causing unnecessary waste

     C. Farming community resistant to change

 III. The solution: sustainable farming practices

     A. Positive changes in the last decade

     B. New technologies: gypsum blocks, LEPA

     C. Cooperation and long-term view

Conclusion—For the Ogallala Aquifer to survive, users must change their attitudes and accept sustainable farming practices.

Sample **Research Paper**

A complete heading is provided. — Allison De Jong

Mr. Schelhaas

Environmental Science

20 November 2000

The title is centered. — The Ogallala: Preserving the

Great American Desert

Long ago, the middle of the North American continent was

Double spacing is used throughout the paper. a treeless prairie covered by tall grasses and roaming buffalo.
When European settlers came, they called this area the Great
American Desert. Today, this "desert" is covered with fields
of wheat, corn, and alfalfa made possible by center-pivot
irrigation. My grandfather used to sell center-pivot systems,
and when my family drove to my grandparents' home in
Nebraska, we would count how many "sprinklers" were
watering each section of land. At the time, I didn't know that

The writer introduces her subject and states her thesis (highlighted). this water was being pumped from something called the Ogallala
Aquifer, a huge underground water supply. Throughout the
years, this aquifer has made the Great American Desert one of
the best farming areas in the world. Unfortunately, the Ogallala
Aquifer's future as a valuable resource is in jeopardy, unless
citizens of the Plains states reduce their water consumption.

Subheadings help readers follow the organization. — Background of the Problem

To understand why the problem is important, it is necessary
to know some basic facts about the Ogallala Aquifer. This
underground reservoir covers 174,000 square miles. According
to John Opie, author of *Ogallala: Water for a Dry Land,* the
Ogallala was formed over the course of millions of years as the
land flooded, dried out, and flooded again. As centuries passed,
glaciers melted, carrying water, silt, and rocks from the Rockies

De Jong 2

down to the Great Plains to form the Ogallala. Dirt, clay, and rocks accumulated above it so that the waters of the Ogallala can now be reached at depths of 300 feet beneath the surface (29-35). Some people think that the Ogallala is a huge underground lake, but this idea is wrong. As Erla Zwingle puts it, an aquifer such as the Ogallala is like a "gigantic underground sponge" (83). The water fills in the spaces between the sand, silt, clay, and gravel that make up the Ogallala formation. This gigantic sponge ranges in thickness from one foot to more than 1,000 feet; the average thickness, however, is about 200 feet (Zwingle 85). The aquifer reaches its deepest points under the state of Nebraska, which is not surprising because most of the Ogallala's water lies beneath this state. The rest lies under Colorado, Kansas, New Mexico, Oklahoma, South Dakota, Texas, and Wyoming.

> Because the authors are named in the text, only the page numbers are cited in parentheses.

The Ogallala Aquifer is the largest "underground sponge" in the United States. It contains more than 977 trillion gallons, or three billion acre-feet of water. (An acre-foot is 325,851 gallons, or the amount of water it would take to cover an acre to the depth of one foot.) According to Jack Lewis in the *EPA Journal,* the water contained in the aquifer is enough to fill Lake Huron plus one-fifth of Lake Ontario. "If pumped out over the United States," Lewis writes, "the High Plains aquifer would cover all 50 states with one and one-half feet of water."

> A quotation helps readers visualize the size of the aquifer.

The Nature and the Extent of the Problem

Each year, at least 7.8 trillion gallons of water are drawn up from the Ogallala Aquifer to irrigate the crops planted on the High Plains. These crops are the main food source for our entire country. Tragically, irrigation is depleting the aquifer faster than it can replenish itself, and that is the problem. In fact, only the tiniest fraction of the water is ever replaced in the

> The main problem is identified and then explored in detail.

De Jong 3

Ogallala Aquifer. If the water were ever fully depleted, the aquifer would need 6,000 years to refill naturally (Zwingle 83). The only way the Ogallala can be replenished is by water seeping down through the layers of soil until it reaches the aquifer. This water comes from the small amount of precipitation in the region, as well as from streams, reservoirs, canals, and irrigation (McGuire and Sharpe).

A question serves as a transition to a new paragraph.

How serious is the problem? Since 1930, the aquifer's water has been reduced by 11 percent (Lewis). The volume of water has decreased because the use of irrigation has increased so much since World War II. In 1949, 2.1 million acres were under irrigation. In 1969, the amount of irrigated land rose to 9.0 million acres; and in 1978, it rose to 13 million acres (McGuire and Sharpe). The land presently under irrigation in the Texas Panhandle alone is equal to the size of New Jersey (Thorpe). All of this land is supplied by irrigation wells, and the number of wells has exploded over the decades—from just 170 in 1930, to more than 150,000 today (Nebel and Wright 279).

Multiple sources of important facts are cited in this paragraph.

A long quotation is introduced.

The biggest technological advance that has made this irrigation explosion possible is the center-pivot irrigation system. John Opie explains the system:

A quotation longer than four lines is indented one inch (ten spaces).

> The center pivot is a 1300-foot-long pipe that is held eight feet off the ground by a row of seven or more towers on large wheels. Sprinklers are attached at regular intervals along the pipe, pointing up or down. One end of the pipe is set in the middle of a 160-acre quarter section around which the pipe and wheeled towers circle. (146)

The water pumped through the pipe triggers a mechanism that causes the system to roll in a large circle. All of the crops within the circle receive a generous amount of water.

De Jong 4

If you were flying over the Great Plains between Minneapolis and Denver in the summertime, you would see thousands of green circles, showing how farmers have irrigated their land. With center-pivot irrigation, crop production on one acre increases 600 to 800 percent compared to dryland farming (Lewis). Today, 15 percent of all of the United States's wheat, corn, and sorghum grows on Ogallala-watered land, and 40 percent of American beef cattle feed on the grain and water of the Ogallala (Nebel and Wright 279).

> **These paragraphs are linked by using a key phrase (*center-pivot irrigation*) and a transitional word (*however*).**

Center-pivot irrigation, however, has dramatically lowered the aquifer's water level. Even though farmers have known for decades that this was happening, they have continued to pump and spray as much water as they felt was necessary. When a drought hit in the mid-1970s, the water level of the Ogallala began to lower drastically in some areas because of overuse and lack of replenishment. In some parts of Texas, water levels dropped as much as 200 feet. Farmers who lived above shallow parts of the aquifer could not pump enough water for their crops at that time.

> **The writer uses a lengthy paraphrase.**

What makes the problem worse is that much of the water pumped from the Ogallala has been wasted. With center-pivot irrigation, 50 percent of the water evaporates before hitting the ground. Some farmers also overwater their fields, thinking that more water is better. Much of this extra water filters into streams and ends up in the Gulf of Mexico, instead of seeping back into the ground to replenish the aquifer (Sheaffer and Stevens 115).

> **A quotation reinforces one of the writer's main points.**

The problem is not just about wasteful irrigation, however. It is also about resistance to change. As Sheaffer and Stevens say in their book *Future Water,* "The real problems are attitudes. Attitudes are held by an establishment that appears unwilling to change" (116). Farmers have thought

De Jong 5

of the Ogallala's water as their private property, and it is difficult for them to give up their "rights." In some places, farmers and cities are actually fighting over use of Ogallala water (Thorpe).

This is an Internet source so no page number is given.

The Solution: Sustainable Farming Practices

Because people's lives and the land itself are at stake, citizens in the Plains states need to change their attitudes about the use of this resource. The key is following what are called "sustainable farming practices." These practices promote the careful use of the aquifer so that it will serve the area indefinitely. If people accept changes in irrigation methods, water regulations, and personal consumption controls, water from the Ogallala Aquifer could serve the area for thousands of years.

No citation is needed for common knowledge available in many sources.

In the past decade, some positive changes have already taken place. In areas of the Great Plains, some farmers are giving their water to local towns. The towns use the water first, filter it, and pump it to farmers to use on their crops. In this way, the water is used twice before it drains back into the aquifer. Other farmers are working on zero depletion, which is "gradually and voluntarily pump[ing] less water according to a plan based on [a farmer's] estimated supply" (Zwingle 103). The goal of this plan is to maintain the water table at its current level so that water is preserved for future generations.

Brackets [ ] indicate that the writer has added something to a quotation.

Using less water means that farmers must rethink their farming practices. For some farmers, cutting back means returning to dry-land farming. This is being done in some areas of Texas and Kansas because the water level has dropped so low that it has become too expensive to pump water to the surface. However, choosing dry-land farming does not mean farmers use no irrigation at all. It does mean more

De Jong 6

careful use of available water. Instead of drenching their fields "just to be sure," farmers must use better irrigation methods to give their crops only the water they need.

New technologies have been developed to help farmers figure out exactly how much water to use and how to irrigate without waste. For example, some farmers bury special gypsum blocks in the soil. Two electrodes in the blocks help farmers figure out how much water the soil actually needs. A second device that prevents water waste is low-energy precision application (LEPA). In a LEPA system, the nozzles of the center-pivot sprinklers are close to the ground, rather than several feet above it. LEPA reduces evaporation by as much as 95 percent (Gerston and Mosely). Most farmers in the market for new irrigation equipment are buying LEPA systems because they are so efficient.

These technological advances have done much to make sure the Ogallala Aquifer has a future. But cooperation and having a long-term view are just as important. Although farmers have resisted in the past, they are now accepting the idea of sustainability. They are more willing to conserve water for future farmers. Because many Plains cities also use this water, state and local officials must work together to conserve municipal water supplies. In addition, people involved in processing food products or making farm equipment must accept and practice water conservation.

In the end, citizens of the Plains states need to change their attitudes about their water consumption and think about the future. They must maintain the Ogallala Aquifer as a sustainable resource. The survival of this amazing underground sponge, as well as the survival of the farms and the cities of the Great American Desert, depends on it.

A summary of new technologies adds to the readers' understanding of possible solutions.

The writer analyzes the solutions to the problem.

The conclusion echoes the introduction and presents the challenge to act responsibly.

De Jong 7

Works Cited

Gerston, Jan, and Lynn Mosely. "Shorter Irrigation Cycles
    Boost Crop Yields." Texas Water Savers. Spring 1997.
    Texas Water Resources Institute. 9 Nov. 2000
    <http//:twri.tamu.edu/twripubs/WtrSavrs/v3n2/
    article-6.html>.

Lewis, Jack. "The Ogallala Aquifer: An Underground Sea."
    EPA Journal 16.6 (Nov./Dec. 1990): 42. MasterFILE
    Premier. EBSCOhost. Lynchburg Public Library.
    5 Nov. 2000 <http://www.ebscohost.com>.

McGuire, Virginia L., and Jennifer B. Sharpe. "Water-Level
    Changes in the High Plains Aquifer, 1980-1995."
    U.S. Geological Survey. Fact Sheet FS-068-97 (1997).
    9 Nov. 2000 <http://www-ne.cr.usgs.gov/highplains/
    hpfs95_txt.html>.

Nebel, Bernard J., and Richard T. Wright. Environmental
    Science. 6th ed. Upper Saddle River, NJ: Prentice
    Hall, 1998.

Opie, John. Ogallala: Water for a Dry Land. Lincoln, NE:
    University of Nebraska Press, 1993.

Sheaffer, John R., and Leonard A. Stevens. Future Water.
    New York: William Morrow and Company, 1983.

Thorpe, Helen. "Waterworld." Texas Monthly 23.9
    (Sept. 1995): 44. MasterFILE Premier. EBSCOhost.
    Lynchburg Public Library. 5 Nov. 2000
    <http://www.ebscohost.com>.

Zwingle, Erla. "Wellspring of the High Plains." National
    Geographic Mar. 1993: 80-109.

"Works Cited" is centered one inch from top.

Sources are listed in alphabetical order.

Second and third lines are indented five spaces.

Double spacing is used throughout.

Assessment Rubric

Use this checklist to evaluate your research writing. It is arranged according to the traits of good writing described in your handbook. (See pages 21-26.)

Stimulating Ideas

The writing . . .

_____ focuses on an important part of a subject, expressed in a thesis statement.

_____ effectively supports or develops the thesis with facts and details from a variety of sources.

_____ thoroughly informs readers.

_____ gives credit, when necessary, for ideas from other sources.

Logical Organization

_____ includes a clearly developed beginning, middle, and ending.

_____ presents supporting information in an organized manner (one main point per paragraph).

Engaging Voice

_____ speaks in a sincere and knowledgeable voice.

_____ shows that the writer is truly interested in the subject.

Original Word Choice

_____ explains or defines any unfamiliar terms.

_____ employs a formal level of language.

Effective Sentence Style

_____ flows smoothly from one idea to the next.

_____ shows variation in sentence structure.

Correct, Accurate Copy

_____ adheres to the rules of grammar, spelling, and punctuation.

_____ follows MLA or APA guidelines for formatting and documentation.

"Man's mind, stretched to new ideas,
never goes back to its original
dimensions."
—Oliver Wendell Holmes

APA Documentation Style

The research documentation style developed by the Modern Language Association (MLA) works well for literary papers. However, for papers in social science and social studies, the documentation style of the American Psychological Association (APA) is often used.

This chapter explains basic APA style and gives examples of the typical kinds of sources you may need to document. Because the style continues to evolve, the Write Source maintains a Web site with the most up-to-date information about documenting electronic sources and a sample APA research paper at <thewritesource.com/apa.htm>.

Remember: Always follow your teacher's directions for documentation style. Your teacher may have special requirements or ask for certain exceptions to the usual APA style.

Preview

- APA Paper Format
- Citing Sources: Parenthetical References
- Reference List
- Reference Entries: Books
- Reference Entries: Periodicals
- Reference Entries: Other Sources
- Reference Entries: Electronic Sources

APA Paper Format

This overview gives formatting guidelines for an APA research paper. Ask your teacher for special requirements he or she may have.

Title Page ◉ On the first page, include your paper's title, your name, and your teacher's name on three separate lines. Double-space and center the lines beginning approximately one-third of the way down from the top of the page.

Abstract ◉ On the second page, include an abstract—a 100- to 150-word paragraph summarizing your paper. Place the title *Abstract* approximately one inch from the top of the page and center it.

Body ◉ Format the body of your paper as follows:

Margins: Leave a 1-inch margin on all four sides of each page (1-1/2 inches on the left for papers to be bound). A justified right margin and end-of-line hyphens are acceptable.

Line Spacing: Double-space your entire paper, unless your teacher allows single spacing for tables, titles, captions, etc., for the sake of readability.

Headings: Main headings should be centered, using standard upper- and lowercase text. Secondary headings should be centered, in upper- and lowercase text, and underlined.

Page Numbers: Place your short title (the first two or three words) and the page number at the upper right margin of all pages beginning with the title page. The title should be either just above or five spaces to the left of the page number.

Citations ◉ Within your paper, give credit for others' ideas by including the author and year in a citation. For quotations, add the page number to the citation. (See pages 287-288.) If a quotation runs 40 words or more, type it in block style, five spaces in from the left margin, with all lines flush left along that new margin. If it is more than one paragraph, indent the first line of the second and later paragraphs another five spaces.

References ◉ Place full citations for all sources in an alphabetized list at the end of your paper. Start this list on a separate page. Place the title *References* approximately one inch from the top of the page and center it. (See pages 289-295.)

Appendix ◉ If your teacher requires it, place your charts, tables, and graphs in an appendix. Otherwise, include them within the body of your paper.

Citing **Sources**

Parenthetical References

In APA style, you must cite your source in the text each time you use it. In-text citations must include the author and date of the sources, either within the sentence or in parentheses. Each citation must be matched to an entry in the alphabetized list of references at the end of your paper.

According to a 1999 article by Florence Ackerman . . .

According to a recent article by Florence Ackerman (1999) . . .

According to a recent article (Ackerman, 1999) . . .

One Author

When referring to a work by a single author, place the author's last name and the date of the work in parentheses. Add the page number to this reference if you quote the work directly.

Consumerism has become "a national obsession" (Jones, 1998, p. 12).

NOTE: When citing two works by the same author published in the same year, arrange them alphabetically by title in the reference list; add a small *a* after the date of the first work, a small *b* after the second, and so on; then use these letters in your in-text citations.

Gene therapy holds great promise for the future (Gormann, 2000a).

Multiple Authors

Mention all authors of a work in the first citation of that work, unless they number six or more, in which case you may use the first author's name followed by *et al.*

Teenagers who feel maladjusted in some aspect of their lives are likely to think of themselves as "unpopular" (Reinherz et al., 1994).

NOTE: After the first citation, refer to a group of three to five authors in the same way (first author's name followed by *et al.*). Always use both names for two authors.

Many doubt that global warming is truly a crisis (Dunkirk and Jenkins, 1997).

NOTE: Whenever three or more authors are listed (in parentheses), use a comma and an ampersand to separate the last two names.

Perceptions of popularity can be linked to a teenager's adjustment to his or her surroundings (Reinherz, Frost, & Cohen, 1994).

Anonymous Work

When a source lists no author, use a short title (the first two or three words of the full title) in place of the author's name. Remember to underline book titles and put article and chapter titles in quotation marks.

World population still expands, but more slowly now ("New Hope," 2000).

Corporate Author

A "corporate author" is an organization, association, or agency that claims authorship of a document. Treat the organization's name as if it were the last name of an author. If the name is long and easily abbreviated, provide the abbreviation in square brackets.

(National Institute of Mental Health [NIMH], 1997)

NOTE: Use only the abbreviation in subsequent references [no brackets].

(NIMH, 1999)

Indirect (or Secondary) Source

When using a source that is referred to in another source, try to find and cite the original. If that isn't possible, credit the source by adding "as cited in" within the parentheses.

This process has been illuminated by Hannover (as cited in Montrose, 1995).

NOTE: In this example, the reference list contains an entry for Montrose (not Hannover).

Two or More Works in One Reference

When citing two or more works within one parenthetical reference, list the sources in alphabetical order, separating them with semicolons.

Experts agree that global temperatures are rising (Heeren, 2000; Rausch, 1999).

Personal Communications

Cite letters, e-mail messages, phone conversations, and other personal communications in the text of a paper, but do not include them in the reference list. In parentheses, identify them as personal communications, and list their full date.

The management team expects to finish hiring this spring (R. Fouser, personal communication, Dec. 14, 1999).

Reference List: An Overview

The reference list includes all of the retrievable sources cited in a paper. It begins on a separate page and follows the format below.

Page Numbers ℮ Continue the numbering scheme from the paper: place the short title and page number in the upper right corner.

Title ℮ Place the title *References* approximately one inch from the top of the page and center it.

Entries ℮ List the entries alphabetically by author's last name or (if anonymous) by title (disregarding *A, An,* or *The*).

- Double-space between all lines (including between the title "References" and the first entry).
- Leave a single space after all end punctuation marks within the entries.
- In titles, capitalize only the first word (and any proper nouns).
- Begin each entry even with the left margin. If an entry is more than one line, indent additional lines five to seven spaces.

> **Important Note:** The reference list for a paper being submitted to a professional publication must use the paragraph-indent format (the first line of an entry is indented; the following lines are not). However, published papers and **final student papers use the hanging-indent format** (see the examples below).

Format for a Book Entry

Author's last name, Initial. (year). Book title. City: Publisher.

Format for a Periodical Entry

Author's last name, Initial. (year, Month day). Article title.
Periodical Title, pages.

Format for an On-Line Entry

Author's last name, Initial. (year, Month day). Title of article,
chapter, or Web page [no. of paragraphs]. Title of Full
Work [On-line], vol. no. (issue no.). Retrieved Month, day,
year from source: Electronic address

Reference Entries:
Books

The entries that follow illustrate the information needed to cite books, sections of a book, and government publications.

One Author

Bode, J. (1998). Death is hard to live with: Teenagers and how they

cope with loss. New York: Delacorte Press.

Two or More Authors

Monroe, J. G., & Williamson, R. A. (1993). First houses: Native

American homes and sacred structures. Boston: Houghton.

NOTE: Follow the first author's name with a comma; then join the two authors' names with an ampersand (&) rather than with the word "and."

Anonymous Book

Publication manual of the American Psychological Association (4th ed.).

(1999). Washington, DC: American Psychological Association.

NOTE: In this title, "American Psychological Association" is capitalized because it is a proper name. Also note: For any edition other than the first, place the edition number after the title in parentheses. (See *4th ed.* above.)

Chapter from a Book, One Author

Rawnley, J. H. (2000). Betting on the future. In Total risk: Nick

Leeson and the fall of Barings Bank (pp. 100-120). New York:

HarperCollins.

One Volume of a Multivolume Edited Work

Sternberg, R. J. (Ed.). (1998). Advances in the psychology of human

intelligence (Vol. 5). Hillsdale, NJ: Erlbaum.

Single Work from an Anthology

> Perkins, D. N. (1993). Why the human perceiver is a bad machine.
>
> In J. Beck, B. Hope, & A. Rosenfeld (Eds.), Human and machine
>
> vision (pp. 341-364). New York: Academic Press.

NOTE: When editors' names appear in the middle of an entry, place their initial first and surname last.

Corporate Group Author

> Amnesty International. (1989). When the state kills: The death
>
> penalty v. human rights. New York: Author.

NOTE: The word "author" here means that the group listed as the author (Amnesty International) is also the publisher.

Edited Work, One in a Series

> Hunter, S., & Sundel, M. (Eds.). (1998). Sage sourcebooks for the
>
> human services: Vol. 7. Midlife myths: Issues, findings, and
>
> practice implications. Newbury Park, CA: Sage Publications.

NOTE: When a work is part of a larger series or collection, as in the example, make a two-part title of the series and the particular volume you are citing.

Article in a Reference Book, Authored

> Lynch, A. C. (2000). Russia. In Collier's encyclopedia (pp. 279-280).
>
> New York: P. F. Collier.

Technical or Research Report

> Comstock, G. A., & Rubinstein, E. A. (Eds.). (1997). Television and
>
> social behavior: Media content and control (Reports and Papers,
>
> Vol. 1). Rockville, MD: National Institute of Mental Health.

Government Publication

> National Aeronautics and Space Administration. (1999). Human
>
> spaceflight: Student activities (NASA Report No. 89-10639).
>
> Washington, DC: U.S. Government Printing Office.

Reference Entries: Periodicals

Article in a Scholarly Journal, One Author, Consecutively Paginated

Peder, M. (1987). Rapid eye movement sleep deprivation affects

sleep similarly in castrated and noncastrated rats. Behavioral

and Neural Biology, 47, 186-196.

NOTE: Pay attention to the features of this basic reference to a scholarly journal: (1) last name and initial(s) as for a book reference, (2) year of publication, (3) title of article in lowercase, except for the first word; title not underlined or in quotations, (4) title of journal underlined, (5) volume number underlined, followed by comma, and (6) inclusive page numbers.

Journal Article, Paginated by Issue

Hirsch, D. (1997). Politics through action: Student services and

activism in the '90s. Change, 25 (5), 32-36.

NOTE: Following the volume number, the issue number (not underlined) is placed in parentheses only if the page numbering of the issue starts with page 1. (Some journals number pages consecutively, from issue to issue, through their whole volume year.)

Journal Article, Two Authors

Collins, C., & Askin, S. (1991). What about Africa?

The Progressive, 55, 39.

Journal Article, Multiple Authors

Schell, B., Sherritt, H., Arthur, J., Beatty, L., Berry, L., Edmonds, L.,

Kaashoek, J., & Kempny, D. (1996). Development of a

community standard: Questionnaire results for two Canadian

cities. Canadian Journal of Criminology, 29, 133-152.

Abstract of a Scholarly Article
from a Secondary Source

> Anspaugh, L., Catlin, R., & Goldman, M. (1988). The global impact of
>
> the Chernobyl reactor incident. Science, 242, 1513-1518. (From
>
> Abstracts in Anthropology, 1989, 19, Abstract No. 3082)

NOTE: When the dates of the article and the secondary-source abstract differ, the reference in your text would cite both dates, the original first, separated by a slash (1988/1989).

Signed Article (Author Given) in a Magazine

> Fishman, K. D. (1998). Problem adoptions. The Atlantic, 270 (3),
>
> 37-69.

Unsigned Article in a Magazine

> Saving the elephant, nature's great masterpiece: Banning the ivory
>
> trade is the wrong way to save Africa's vanishing elephants.
>
> (1989, July 1). Economist (London), 15-17.

Signed Newspaper Article

> Trost, C. (1998, July 18). Born to lose: Babies of crack users crowd
>
> hospitals, break everybody's heart. The Wall Street Journal, p. 1.

NOTE: For newspapers, use "p." or "pp." before the page numbers.

Unsigned Newspaper Article

> Angry pilot quits airliner on field as passenger suggests he is drunk.
>
> (1990, April 22). The New York Times, p. 20.

Letter to the Editor

> Burnside, P. (1995, April 17). Against styrofoam packaging [Letter
>
> to the editor]. The Milwaukee Journal, p. 9A.

NOTE: The "A" indicates that the letter to the editor appears in the A section of the newspaper.

Reference Entries: Other Sources

Abstract of Journal Article on CD-ROM

Seyler, T. (1994). College-level studies: New memory techniques
[CD-ROM]. New Century Learners, 30, 814-822. Abstract from:
Platinum File: EduPLUS Item: 40-18421

Television or Radio Program (Episode in a Series)

Clark, K. (Narrator). (1971). The worship of nature. In M. Gill & P.
Montagnon (Producers), Civilisation [Television series]. London:
British Broadcasting Corporation.

Recording

Moon, M. (Compiler). (1980). Movement soul: Sounds of the
freedom movement in the South 1963-1964 [Record].
New York: Folkways Records.

NOTE: Give the name and function of the primary contributors to the
recording (in this case, Moon, who is the compiler). Indicate the recording
medium [in brackets] immediately following the title: compact disc, tape,
record, etc.

Film, Videotape, Etc.

John, A. (Director). (1993). Solar flares burn for you [Film]. London:
British Film Institute.

Published Interview, Titled, No Author

Dialogue on film: Steven Spielberg [Interview with Steven
Spielberg]. (1996, June). American Film, 13, 12-16.

Reference Entries:
Electronic Sources

APA style prefers a reference to the print form of a source, even if it is available on the Net. However, when you must cite the electronic form, follow the same general format for the author, date, and title elements of print sources. Follow that with a "retrieved from" statement, citing the date of retrieval and the electronic address.

Document on a Web Site

> American Psychological Association. (2000, January). Successful
>
> aging: The second 50. APA Monitor. Retrieved January 11, 2000
>
> from the World Wide Web: http://www.apa.org/monitor/cs.html

Article in On-Line Journal

> Carter, D. L. (1995, April). A nation embraces capitalism. Economic
>
> Perspectives [On-line serial], 6 (18). Retrieved October 2, 1999
>
> from the Internet: FTP://342.323.342.1/pub/baccon/
>
> EconomicPerspectives/1995.6/95.6.18.capitalism.14.carter<.txt

Article or Abstact from an Electronic Database

> Belsie, Laurent. (1999). Progress or Peril? Christian Science
>
> Monitor, 91, (85), 15. Retrieved September 15, 1999 from
>
> DIALOG on-line database (#97, IAC Business A.R.T.S., Item
>
> 07254533)

Special Note: Visit our Web site for up-to-date information on how to cite electronic sources at <thewritesource.com/apa.htm>.

WORKPLACE WRITING

"In the workplace, you don't write
for a grade, you write for a living."

—Jim Franke, electrical contractor

Writing BUSINESS LETTERS

People in the workplace write business letters to do many things—share ideas, promote products, or ask for help. Putting a message in writing gives the writer time to think about, organize, and edit what he or she wants to say. In addition, a written message becomes a record of important details for both the sender and the recipient.

Students also write business letters to get things done. Letters connect the writer with experts and organizations that offer information, provide internships, help solve problems, and much more.

Preview

- Parts of a Business Letter
- Writing Guidelines
- Request Letter
- Complaint Letter
- Informative Letter
- Persuasive Letter
- Application Letter
- Thank-You Letter
- Sending Your Letter
- Assessment Rubric

Parts of a Business Letter

A business letter presents complete information in the order below.

Heading

The heading gives the writer's complete address, either printed in the letterhead or typed out, plus the date. (If the address is part of the letter-head, place only the date in the upper lefthand corner. See sample on page 299.)

Inside Address

The inside address gives the reader's name and complete mailing address (including the company name). If you're not sure which person to address or how to spell his or her name, call the company and ask. If the person's title is a single word or very short, place it after the name, separated by a comma. Longer titles go on a separate line.

Salutation

The salutation personalizes the letter. Use *Dear* with people only, not department or company names. Place a colon after the name. (See "Business Writing," at 530.2)

Body

The body contains your message in single-spaced paragraphs with double spacing between them. The body of your letter is organized in three parts: (1) the beginning states why you are writing, (2) the middle provides all the needed details, and (3) the ending focuses on what should happen next.

Complimentary Closing

The closing politely ends the message with a parting word or phrase—*Sincerely, Yours sincerely, Yours truly,*—followed by a comma. Capitalize only the first word of complimentary closings.

Signature

The signature makes the letter official. It includes the writer's hand-written name and corresponding typed name.

Initials, Enclosures, Copies

When someone types the letter for the writer, that person's **lowercased initials** appear after the writer's capitalized initials, separated by a colon.

If a document (brochure, form, copy) is **enclosed** with the letter, the word *Enclosure* or *Encl.* appears below the initials.

If a **copy** of the letter is sent elsewhere, type "cc:" and follow with the name of the person or department receiving the copy.

Sample **Business Letter**

Heading — Monroe Chamber of Commerce
105 East Bay Road
Monroe, LA 31404-1832
October 19, 2000

Four to Seven Spaces

Inside Address — Ms. Charlotte Williams, Manager
Belles Lettres Books
The Delta Mall
Monroe, LA 31404-0012

Double Space

Salutation — Dear Ms. Williams:

Double Space

Welcome to the Monroe business community. As
the Chamber's executive director, I'd like to thank
you for opening your store in the Delta Mall. Belles
Lettres Books is a welcome addition to the town's
economy, especially with the store's emphasis
Body on Southern authors. I wish you success.

I would like to invite you to join our Chamber of
Commerce. Membership gives you a voice in your
community and access to promotional materials.

If you decide to join, I could set up a ribbon-cutting
ceremony, which would provide some useful news
coverage. Call me at 944-0645 or e-mail me at
<alein@chamber.org> if you have any questions.

Complimentary Closing — Sincerely,   **Double Space**

Signature — *Ardith Lein*   **Four Spaces**
Ardith Lein

Double Space

Initials   AL:nk
Enclosures   Encl. membership brochure
Copies   cc: Peter Sanchez, Membership Chairperson

WRITING GUIDELINES
Business Letters

■ PREWRITING

1. **Considering Your Audience** . . . Who is your reader and how will he or she feel about your message?

2. **Determining Your Purpose** . . . Jot down your reason for writing or what you want your reader to know or do.

3. **Gathering Details** . . . Collect the information you will need for your letter. Think about the best way to organize and present it.

■ WRITING AND REVISING

4. **Organizing the Details** . . . Organize your letter into three parts.

   Beginning: Introduce the message by stating the subject and purpose of your letter.

   Middle: Present whatever information is appropriate for the kind of letter you are writing—a letter of *request, complaint, information, persuasion, application,* or *thank-you.*

   Ending: Focus on the outcome. What do you want the reader to do, and when, and how? Is there an action that you will take?

5. **Improving Your Writing** . . . Revise your first draft, checking for the following:

   - accurate, interesting details that answer the reader's questions
   - paragraphs that each develop one main idea
   - a polite and respectful tone (See "Using Fair Language," pages 529-531.)

■ EDITING AND PROOFREADING

6. **Checking for Style and Accuracy** . . . Check your letter for the following traits or qualities:

   - smooth-flowing sentences
   - clear, natural word choice (See pages 85-88.)
   - correct spelling, capitalization, punctuation, and usage
   - correct letter form

   [HOT LINK] Use "Assessment Rubric," page 308, as a helpful revising and editing guide.

7. **Preparing a Final Copy** . . . Neatly type or keyboard your letter. Center it on the page and keep the margins even on both sides. Address the envelope, add correct postage, and mail your letter. (See page 307.)

Sample **Request Letter**

245 Oak Street, NE
Savannah, GA 31408
February 11, 2000

Director of Tourism
Colombian Embassy
P.O. Box 783
New York, NY 10023

Dear Director:

Beginning
Introduce
yourself and
tell why you
are writing.

I am a sophomore at Washington High School in
Savannah, Georgia. For my World Cultures class, I'm
working on a research paper and visual presentation
about Colombia, and I need more information.

In my presentation, I'm taking on the role of a travel
agent explaining why tourists should visit Colombia.
Because your agency is in charge of Columbia tourism,
I thought that someone there could provide the
information I need. Please send me whatever booklets,
pamphlets, or Web-site addresses you can.

Middle
Supply the
details and
state your
specific
request.

If possible, please send the information by March 3.
Then I will have time to finish the project by my
March 25 deadline.

Ending
End with a
thank-you
and closing
thought.

Thank you for considering my request. If you would like,
I'll send you a copy of the finished paper that will go
along with the visual display.

Sincerely,

Nick Davis

Nick Davis

Sample **Complaint Letter**

355 Hutchinson Road
Pascoag, RI 02859
November 5, 2000

Ms. Anne Cline, Head Cook
Bay High School
4562 Birch Road
Pascoag, RI 02859

Dear Ms. Cline:

Beginning
State the
problem.

Last summer I became a vegetarian. After visiting my
uncle's farm in Iowa, I couldn't bear the thought of eating
meat anymore.

When school started, I thought I could eat school lunches by
simply staying away from meat dishes. My plan worked for a
few weeks, but it got tough to eat peanut-butter sandwiches
and applesauce every day. The school lunch program is great
for most students, but it doesn't work well for vegetarians.

Middle
Supply
details and
possible
solutions.

After talking with other vegetarian students, I believe that
the lunch program can work for everyone. Some options are
to have a greater variety of side dishes and a salad bar every
day that even nonvegetarians could enjoy. The school lunch
program would then provide something for everyone.

Ending
Be polite.

I was happy with the school lunches before I became a
vegetarian, and I hope that now you will be able to offer
meals that I can enjoy just as much. Please respond to my
request via school mail or e-mail <kkobe@aol.com>.

Sincerely,

Karin Kobes

Karin Kobes

Sample **Informative Letter**

4213 Minnow Lane
Medford, MA 02052
March 6, 2000

Geoffrey Gosbin
164 12th Street, NW
Somerville, MA 02044

Dear Geoffrey:

Beginning
Explain why
you are
writing.

Thanks for your letter praising our school's Web page! As for your request, I'd be happy to help you build a Web page for your school's Environmental Awareness Club.

First, you need a Web page-maker program. You may download one from the Internet or buy one separately. I like to use Netscape's Composer program. If you choose a different program, I'll have to experiment a bit with yours before we start your project.

Middle
Supply
necessary
details.

Second, you'll need a plan for your page. A good page has a clear, concise, and interesting design. Here are a few points to think about:

- Explain who you are and what you're about.
- Don't overdo the graphics; they can really slow things down.
- Include some links to sites that would be interesting to a visitor.
- Include a FAQ (frequently asked questions) section.

Ending
Establish
a plan of
action and
end politely.

Let's get together next Wednesday in your computer lab at 3:30 p.m. I'll take you through a sample page. If you're ready with your design plan, we can dig right in.

Sincerely,

Brian Krygsman

Brian Krygsman
Computer Coordinator

Sample **Persuasive Letter**

936 Penning Drive
Almonville, KY 41233-6120
May 28, 2000

Ms. Alice Roosenbach
School Board President
Roosevelt High School
837 Chester Street
Almonville, KY 41233-4546

Dear Ms. Roosenbach:

**Beginning
Introduce
your topic.**

My lab group and I really enjoyed Mr. Finch's biology class
this year. We especially liked the unit on animal systems.
However, while the teacher was good and the subject was
interesting, the poor condition of our lab tools made lab
work frustrating.

My group had several problems. For example, the pad in
the bottom of our dissecting pan was too hard for pins, our
scissors fell apart, and our scalpel was too dull to cut
anything. In fact, our probe was the only tool that worked.

**Middle
Explain the
need and
make the
request.**

Mr. Finch often had to just point out what we needed to
know. We still learned, but we wished we had had better
tools to dissect the animals ourselves. Our school needs new
dissecting equipment so future students will have that
chance.

**Ending
Encourage
reasonable
action.**

As you set the budget for next year, please consider the
biology class. It's a great class, but new equipment would
make it even better. Please let Mr. Finch know what you
decide.

Sincerely,

Miranda Scholten

Miranda Scholten
cc: Mr. Finch

Sample **Application Letter**

326 Ash Boulevard
Florence, OR 97439-3216
March 23, 2000

Dr. Ray Peters
Communications Department Chair
St. Xavier College
32 Fountain Street
Omaha, NE 68102-6070

Dear Dr. Peters:

Beginning
Explain how you learned about the position.

In response to the brochure I received from St. Xavier College, I am applying for a position on the staff of the *Xavier News.* I have enclosed a recommendation from my high school English teacher as well as several articles that I wrote for my high school newspaper, the *Florence Flier.*

Middle
Describe your qualifications.

I have been on the staff of the *Florence Flier* for four years, and this year I am the editor. I have always enjoyed English, and I plan on majoring in journalism at St. Xavier College. I am an organized, creative person, and I have never missed a deadline. In addition to writing and editing, I do layout work.

Ending
Politely offer additional information and thank the reader.

If you would like more information, please let me know by calling 555-997-3205 anytime during the day or by e-mailing me at <greensleeves@aol.com>. Thank you for considering my application. I look forward to hearing from you.

Sincerely,

Allison Emerson

Allison Emerson

Encl. recommendation and newspaper articles

Sample **Thank-You Letter**

2518 Fourth Avenue, SW
Columbus, OH 43230
March 16, 2000

Mr. Tim Lindon
1286 Elm Street, NW
Columbus, OH 43230

Dear Tim:

Beginning
Explain
why you
are saying
thank-you.

Thanks for tutoring me in algebra! I know you're a busy
college student, but you took the time to help me understand
things like factoring, variable equations, and manipulating
exponents.

Ever since school started in August, I had big-time problems
with algebra! I was afraid that if I got called on, I'd
make a mistake and everyone would laugh. When the
teacher asked if anyone had questions, I would slouch way
down in my chair because I was scared to say that I didn't
understand.

Middle
Provide the
details.

But now, thanks to you, I've pulled up my grade. Your way
of teaching algebra made it easy to remember the basics.
I especially liked the way you made up the rhyme to help
me remember the quadratic formula. That was the part that
gave me the most trouble. You've made learning algebra
easier and even fun!

Ending
Restate your
thanks and
end politely.

Thanks so much for your patience, and good luck. I hope you
decide to become a teacher. You'd be great!

Sincerely,

Andrea McGrady

Andrea McGrady

Sending Your Letter

Addressing the Envelope

Address the envelope correctly so your letter can be delivered promptly. Place the return address in the upper left corner, the destination address in the center, and the correct postage in the upper right corner. Make sure that the destination and return addresses on the envelope match the inside and heading addresses on the letter.

```
ANDREA MCGRADY
2518 FOURTH AVE SW                                      [postage]
COLUMBUS OH 43230




              MR TIM LINDON
              1286 ELM ST NW
              COLUMBUS OH 43230
```

There are two acceptable forms for addressing the envelope: the older, traditional form and the new form preferred by the postal service.

Traditional Form

Ms. Theresa Chang
Goodwill Industries
9200 Wisconsin Avenue
Bethesda, MD 20814-3896

Postal Service Form

MS THERESA CHANG
GOODWILL INDUSTRIES
9200 WISCONSIN AVE
BETHESDA MD 20814-3896

Official United States Postal Service Envelope Guidelines

1. Capitalize everything in the address and leave out all punctuation.

2. Use the list of common abbreviations found in the *National ZIP Code Directory*. (See page 481.) Use numerals rather than words for numbered streets and avenues (9TH AVE SE, 3RD ST NE).

3. If you know the ZIP + 4 code, use it. You can get this information by phoning one of the postal service's ZIP-code information units.

Assessment Rubric

Use this rubric as a checklist to evaluate your business writing. The rubric addresses the traits of effective writing. (See pages 21-26.)

Stimulating Ideas

The writing . . .

_____ focuses on an appropriate subject and format.

_____ develops a clearly expressed goal or purpose.

   ✳ Nicholas Davelaar writes instructions using precise details and an easy-to-follow format. (See page 315.)

Logical Organization

_____ includes a clear beginning, middle, and ending.

_____ arranges details logically using appropriate transitions.

   ✳ Adam Thoral uses headings in his résumé. (See page 321.)

Engaging Voice

_____ speaks knowledgeably and sincerely about the subject.

   ✳ Andrea McGrady's thank-you letter uses a friendly, informal voice to express her appreciation to her tutor. (See page 306.)

Original Word Choice

_____ uses plain language, specific nouns, and vivid verbs.

   ✳ Brian Krygsman's informative letter presents information clearly and uses precise Web terminology. (See page 303.)

Effective Sentence Style

_____ flows from one idea to the next.

   ✳ In her letter, Karin Kobes chooses transitions that lead the reader smoothly from one point to the next. (See page 302.)

Correct, Accurate Copy

_____ adheres to the basic rules of writing.

_____ follows the appropriate format.

"When writing instructions, don't assume anything. If the person knew what to do, he or she wouldn't need instructions."

—Dennis Walstra, plumbing contractor

Special Forms of
WORKPLACE Writing

All organizations—IBM, Sears, the Willmar Farmer's Co-op—need people who not only speak well, but also write effectively. Whether you become an engineer or a nurse, a lab technician or a social worker, good writing will help you *get* a job and *do* your job. Writing will also help you do your job right now as you plan projects, request help, and gather needed materials to complete your schoolwork.

A written message holds several advantages over a phone call or a personal conversation: (1) You have time to think about and edit what you want to say. (2) Both parties have an official record of the message. (3) The written word is often taken more seriously. (4) Written forms of communication can be sent to many people at once.

Preview

- Writing Guidelines and Samples
- Memos
- E-Mail Messages
- Instructions
- Brochures
- Proposals
- Résumés

WRITING GUIDELINES

Memos

Memos are short messages in which you ask and answer questions, describe procedures, give short reports, and remind others about deadlines and meetings. Memos create a flow of information within an organization, whether it's a classroom, an entire school, or a workplace.

■ PREWRITING

1. **Considering Your Audience . . .** Think about who is going to receive your memo and why.

2. **Determining Your Purpose . . .** Jot down your reason or purpose for sending the memo.

3. **Gathering Details . . .** Ask yourself what your reader needs to know and gather the necessary details.

■ WRITING AND REVISING

4. **Preparing the Heading . . .** Begin your memo with a heading that contains the following information:

   Date: the month, day, and year

   To: the reader's name

   From: your first and last name
   (You may initial this before it's sent.)

   Subject: the memo's topic in a clear, simple statement

5. **Organizing the Body . . .** Organize the message into three parts:

   Beginning: State why you are writing the memo.

   Middle: Provide all the necessary details. Consider listing the most important points rather than writing out all the details.

   Ending: Focus on what should happen next—the action or response you would like from the reader or readers.

6. **Improving Your Writing . . .** Review your first draft for the following: complete and accurate information; well-organized details (perhaps in a list); a positive, friendly tone. Make the necessary revisions.

■ EDITING AND PROOFREADING

7. **Checking for Style and Accuracy . . .** Check your memo for the proper format (including a clear heading), accurate spelling (especially of names), and correct usage and punctuation. Prepare your final copy and proofread it.

   [HOT LINK] See "Assessment Rubric," page 308, for a helpful revising and editing guide.

Sample **Memo**

Date: October 2, 2000

To: Mr. Marcus

From: Danielle White *DW*

Subject: Mid-project report on history paper

Beginning
State why
you are
writing.

Here's an update on my history paper about China. At first I had trouble finding information on my topic, but I've made this progress.

1. I went to the library, and Ms. Pate showed me how to use the computer for my search.

2. After I showed you my project proposal, I took your advice to look at either Chinese dating practices or wedding traditions, but not both.

Middle
Give the
necessary
details.

3. After researching both topics, I found several sources on Chinese wedding traditions, but only a few on dating practices. So I will write about present-day Chinese wedding customs.

4. I found a Web site with information about Chinese wedding traditions at <www. travelchinaguide.com>.

5. For my primary research, I interviewed Donna Sung, our foreign exchange student from Shanghai, about her experiences of weddings in China.

Ending
Focus on
what should
happen next.

I will finish my first draft by next Wednesday and will be on schedule for the deadlines I gave you in my project proposal.

WRITING GUIDELINES
E-Mail Messages

Electronic mail helps you send, receive, and store messages quickly through computer networks. In spite of e-mail's delivery speed, it still takes time to write a good message in the first place. The guidelines below will help you.

■ PREWRITING

1. **Considering Your Audience ...** Think about who your reader will be and your purpose for e-mailing this person.

2. **Gathering Details ...** Gather all the details that your reader needs to know.

■ WRITING AND REVISING

3. **Organizing the Body ...** Organize your e-mail message in three parts:

   Beginning: Complete your e-mail header as directed by your computer program, making sure your subject line is precise. Expand on the subject in the first sentences of your e-mail, getting right to the point.

   Middle: Fill in the details of your message, but keep all of your paragraphs short. Double-space between paragraphs. Try to limit your message to one or two screens and use numbers, lists, and headings to organize your thoughts.

   Ending: Let your reader know what follow-up action is needed and when. Then end politely.

4. **Improving Your Writing ...** Read through your first draft, asking these questions:

   - Is the message accurate, complete, and clear?
   - Is the tone friendly? Is it appropriate for both the subject and the reader?
   - Does the message ask for a response if needed?

■ EDITING AND PROOFREADING

5. **Checking for Style and Accuracy ...** Though e-mail is a personal means of communication, it is often used in formal business and professional settings. Before clicking the "send" command, carefully check and correct spelling, punctuation, and usage.

   [HOT LINK] Use "Assessment Rubric," page 308, as a helpful revising and editing guide. Make the necessary changes.

Sample **E-Mail**

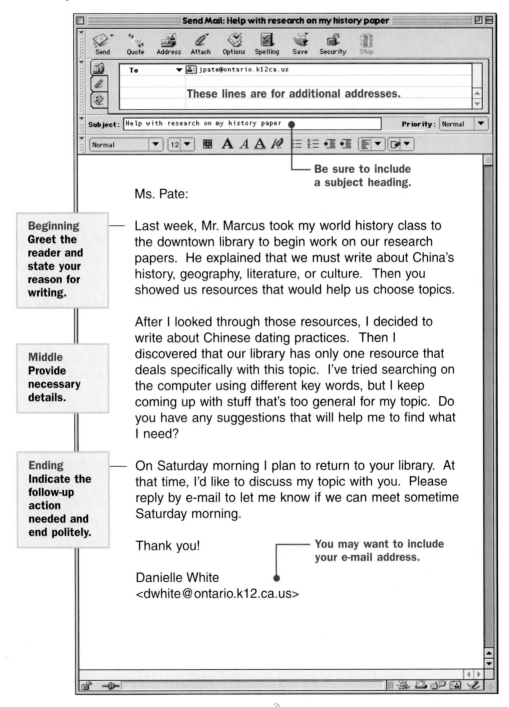

Send Mail: Help with research on my history paper

Send   Quote   Address   Attach   Options   Spelling   Save   Security   Stop

To ▼ jpate@ontario.k12ca.us

These lines are for additional addresses.

Subject: Help with research on my history paper ●   **Priority:** Normal ▼

Normal ▼   12 ▼   A A A A   ≡ ≣ ⋹ ⋺   ≣ ▼   ⋕ ▼

— Be sure to include a subject heading.

Ms. Pate:

Beginning
Greet the reader and state your reason for writing.

Last week, Mr. Marcus took my world history class to the downtown library to begin work on our research papers. He explained that we must write about China's history, geography, literature, or culture. Then you showed us resources that would help us choose topics.

Middle
Provide necessary details.

After I looked through those resources, I decided to write about Chinese dating practices. Then I discovered that our library has only one resource that deals specifically with this topic. I've tried searching on the computer using different key words, but I keep coming up with stuff that's too general for my topic. Do you have any suggestions that will help me to find what I need?

Ending
Indicate the follow-up action needed and end politely.

On Saturday morning I plan to return to your library. At that time, I'd like to discuss my topic with you. Please reply by e-mail to let me know if we can meet sometime Saturday morning.

Thank you!

— You may want to include your e-mail address.

Danielle White
<dwhite@ontario.k12.ca.us> ●

WRITING GUIDELINES

Instructions

At school or on the job, you need good instructions to help you do your work successfully and safely. To write instructions that give your readers all the help they need, follow the guidelines below.

■ PREWRITING

1. **Considering Your Audience ...** Think about who is going to receive and use these instructions.

2. **Gathering Details ...** Think about these issues:

   - The goal—what do you want your readers to be able to do?
   - The readers—what do they already know, and what do they need to learn?
   - The process—before instructing others, make sure you understand the process yourself.

■ WRITING AND REVISING

3. **Organizing the Body ...** Organize your instructions into three parts:

   Beginning: Give an overview of the whole process and state its outcome. Also list any parts, equipment, or tools needed.

   Middle: Take the reader through the process in a detailed, step-by-step fashion using imperative verbs. Numbered lists make the steps clearer, as do appropriate graphics.

   Ending: Remind the reader of any special details related to the process.

4. **Improving Your Writing ...** After you write the instructions, test them. Try to follow them yourself, and ask a friend to do so as well. Ask these questions:

   - Are the introduction and steps that follow it clear and complete?
   - Is the tone confident and positive?

■ EDITING AND PROOFREADING

5. **Checking for Style and Accuracy ...** Check the final copy of your instructions for clear verbs and precise terminology. Also correct spelling, punctuation, and usage.

   [HOT LINK] Use "Assessment Rubric," page 308, as a helpful revising and editing guide.

6. **Preparing a Final Copy ...** Write or keyboard a final copy of your instructions. Proofread your instructions carefully before sharing them.

Sample **Instructions**

Exploring the World Beneath the Surface

**Beginning
Give an
overview.**

The following steps will help you prepare a
microscope slide to examine smears from mud
found in a local pond. To get started, gather these
materials:

- two or three craft sticks
- one glass microscope slide
- one plastic slide cover
- a microscope

1. Carefully wash and dry the glass slide and the
   cover. Put the slide and cover on a clean, dry
   surface.

**Middle
Provide
necessary
details
step-by-step.**

2. Using a craft stick, carefully scrape a small
   amount of mud, just enough to cover the tip of
   the stick.

3. Place the stick in the center of the slide and
   wipe the stick gently to transfer the scrapings
   (or "sample") onto the slide. Then dispose of
   the stick.

4. Carefully place the plastic cover on the slide,
   directly on top of the sample. Apply slight
   pressure to spread out the sample.

**Ending
Remind the
reader of
other
important
details.**

5. Place the slide under the microscope and adjust
   the microscope until you can see the sample
   clearly.

Following these steps should give you an up-close
view of the cells living beneath the surface of the
pond. Draw what you see, and write up an
observation report.

WRITING GUIDELINES
Brochures

A brochure is an effective tool you can use for advertising a product, promoting a cause, or sharing helpful information. The guidelines below will help you produce a brochure that does just what you want it to do.

■ PREWRITING

1. **Choosing a Subject . . .** Think of the service or product that you want to promote or sell.

2. **Considering Your Audience . . .** Consider who your audience will be and what kind of brochure will work best with them.

3. **Gathering Details . . .** Think about what your readers need to know about this product or service in order to be convinced of its value.

■ WRITING AND REVISING

4. **Organizing the Body . . .** Organize your brochure into three parts:

   Beginning: State the main point in bold type, either as a question and an answer or as a large headline, at the top of the brochure.

   Middle: State your message fully, but concisely, using as few words as possible. Fill in the details using bulleted lists. Add facts, figures, and testimonials to verify the quality of your product or service.

   Ending: Include reader-response instructions, offering all the necessary names, addresses, and phone numbers.

5. **Designing Your Brochure . . .** Design your brochure with large headlines, attention-grabbing visuals, and interesting graphics.

6. **Improving Your Writing . . .** Check your draft to make sure that it presents the main message at a glance and answers all the readers' questions. Make the necessary changes.

■ EDITING AND PROOFREADING

7. **Checking for Style and Accuracy . . .** Check your work carefully for strong word choice; a clutter-free format; and correct punctuation, grammar, and spelling.

   [HOT LINK] See "Assessment Rubric," page 308, for a helpful revising and editing guide.

8. **Preparing a Final Copy . . .** Proofread the final draft of your brochure before making copies to distribute.

Sample **Brochure**

The size of brochures can vary. This sample brochure was designed on a standard sheet of paper folded in half.

Save a Life— Give Blood!

Your student council invites you to help others by participating in our school's blood drive.

Thursday, October 5
8-11 a.m. and 1-3 p.m.
School Cafeteria

Why should you give?
- Accident victims, people who need surgery, and people with blood disorders need your help.
- Community blood banks must be resupplied because . . .
  - all types of blood are constantly in demand.
  - blood has a limited shelf life and must be replaced often.

When and where can you give?
- Thursday, October 5, in the school cafeteria from 8 to 11 a.m. or 1 to 3 p.m.
- Information about community blood bank hours is available in the school office.

Who should donate?
- Any healthy person 17 or older
- Someone who hasn't donated within 60 days

Remember . . .
- Bring a signed parental-release form with you. They are available in the school office.
- Bring identification—driver's license or school I.D.
- Be prepared to fill out a medical questionnaire.
- Eat before and after your donation and drink plenty of fluids.
- Giving blood is . . .

A CHANCE TO HELP OTHERS.

WRITING GUIDELINES

Proposals

A proposal is a detailed plan you can develop to complete a project or fix a problem. The most persuasive proposal is one that is practical, logical, and creative.

■ PREWRITING

1. **Determining Your Purpose . . .** Think about your goal: to thoroughly research the problem or project, develop a workable plan, and explain the plan in a clear, convincing way.

2. **Considering Your Audience . . .** Think about your reader. What will convince the reader of your plan's value?

■ WRITING AND REVISING

3. **Organizing the Body . . .** Organize your proposal into three parts:

   Beginning: State your main point—what are you trying to accomplish and why is it important?

   Middle: Explain your plan. Include details about the equipment, materials, and other resources needed. Outline the steps to be taken and a schedule for completing them. Finally, describe the expected results.

   Ending: Focus on your proposal's benefits and ask for approval.

4. **Improving Your Writing . . .** Be sure your draft includes

   - all the necessary details,
   - a clear organization, and
   - a sincere voice indicating that you care about the project.

■ EDITING AND PROOFREADING

5. **Checking for Style and Accuracy . . .** Review your revised proposal, checking for

   - precise word choice, easy-to-read sentences, and strong transitions;
   - clear, readable format; and
   - correct spelling, grammar, and punctuation.

   [HOT LINK] Use "Assessment Rubric," page 308, as a helpful revising and editing guide.

6. **Preparing a Final Copy . . .** Write or keyboard a neat copy of your proposal. Proofread it carefully before sharing it.

Sample **Proposal**

Date: February 16, 2000
To: Mr. Tristan
From: Andrea Bonovan, Jasmine Caron, and Randy Freid
Subject: Rocket-Engine Project for Science Fair

Project Description: For our project, we want to research the effects of fuel volume on thrust in rocket engines. We plan to fill two-liter pop bottles with different amounts of water and pump them with air to a constant pressure. Then we will fly the bottles on the football field, measure the flight distances, and graph the results. Finally, we'll make a written report and present the project at the science fair.

Materials Needed:
1. 4 pairs of safety goggles
2. 10 two-liter bottles, corks, and valves
3. water supply and a beaker for measuring volume
4. air compressor with gauge (the one from the wood shop)
5. launching pad (wood, nails, screws)
6. tape measure
7. graph paper

Deadlines and Procedure:
Feb. 18   Get signed permission slips authorizing our use of football field.
Feb. 19   Find out safe bottle pressure from the Conklin Bottle Company.
Feb. 26   Finish launch pad.
Feb. 28   Complete research on rocket engines.
Mar. 1   Fly the bottles.
Mar. 3   Finish graphs.
Mar. 8   Review first draft of experiment and research report.
Mar. 13   Finish report revisions.
Mar. 24   Build science fair display.
Mar. 31   Go to science fair and wow judges!

Outcome: We will better understand Newton's laws and the effects of fuel volume on propulsion. Our report and science fair display will help other students understand how rockets work.

Please approve our proposal. If you have ideas for improving our project, please let us know.

WRITING GUIDELINES

Résumés

Your résumé presents you—your skills, knowledge, and experiences—to a prospective employer. There are two forms of résumés:

A **chronological** résumé lists work experiences and education by date. Chronological résumés work best when you've already held a number of jobs.

A **functional** résumé lists skills you may have acquired at home or at school; it lists your educational history (mention any special awards), plus your job history. Functional résumés are a good choice when you have little work experience.

■ PREWRITING

1. **Gathering Details . . .** Think about your immediate and long-term goals. Then list the following: (1) a job objective showing what kind of job you want; (2) your schooling, work experience, extracurricular and volunteer activities, and hobbies, including the dates; (3) responsibilities and related skills; (4) teachers, employers, and other people in the community who could act as references for you.

■ WRITING AND REVISING

2. **Organizing the Body . . .** Shape your résumé into three parts:

   Beginning: Provide personal data and a job objective.

   Middle: Choose the type of résumé that will best fit your needs: chronological or functional. Depending on your choice, list your skills, achievements, education, and work experience in the appropriate way.

   Ending: Either list the names and details for your references or indicate that references are available upon request.

3. **Improving Your Writing . . .** Revise your résumé. Check for the following: specific, accurate, and complete details; an organizational format that highlights your strengths; and a factual, serious tone.

■ EDITING AND PROOFREADING

4. **Checking for Style and Accuracy . . .** Check your résumé for strong verbs and an abbreviated sentence structure. Also check for boldface, underlining, white space, and indenting to make the résumé readable. Finally, correct spelling, punctuation, and capitalization.

   [HOT LINK] See "Assessment Rubric," page 308, for a helpful revising and editing guide.

5. **Preparing a Final Copy . . .** Type or print out a neat copy of your résumé. Proofread it carefully before using it.

Sample **Functional Résumé**

Adam Thoral
567 West Highland Road
Tiewing, FL 34207-2367
(111) 943-7125

Job Objective: Take part in a summer environmental-studies program.

Environmental-Science Skills:
- Wrote three research papers based on environmental issues: "Effects of Gulf War on Nature"; "The Rain Forest: Why Do We Need It?"; and "North American Environmental Disasters"
- Subscribe to the following environmental magazines: *Earth Awareness* and *Endangered Environment*
- Completed Wilderness Survival Training through Boy Scouts

Communication Skills:
- Team worker: led group projects at school, participated in scouting events, served as crew leader at fast-food restaurant
- Well acquainted with writing memos, letters, and e-mail
- Worked to promote Environment Bills (Bills 104, 235)

Organizational Skills:
- Organized an Earth Day community cleanup at school
- Helped set up a school recycling program
- Assisted Mr. Carper, my biology teacher, in lab preparations

Education:
- 11th grader, Tiewing High School
- Course work: Environmental Science, Biology, Chemistry

Awards/Activities:
- Boy Scouts (1991-present)
- Peer Tutor at Tiewing High School (1999-2000)
- First Aid and CPR certification—Tiewing Regional Hospital (1999)

Work History:

1999 (Summer)	Internship in environmental studies and public relations at Landzone Industries in Tiewing
1999-2000	Restaurant crew leader—supervised three workers

References available upon request

SEARCHING
for Information

"I use not only all the brains I have,
but all I can borrow."   —Woodrow Wilson

Types of
INFORMATION

You've just been assigned a six-page research report on a health-related issue. Quality information, your teacher tells you, must be the foundation of your report. But what is quality information? Where do you find it, what does it look like, and how do you really determine its quality?

These questions are important. In an information age, your computers, TV, and print media remind you every day that you're swimming in a sea of information. To find what you need, you must first know where to look, and then how to determine the quality of the information available to you. Finally, you need to know how to use the information you choose.

Preview

○ Primary vs. Secondary Sources

○ Evaluating Information

○ Information Packages and Places

○ Conducting Surveys and Interviews

Primary vs. Secondary Sources

Information sources can be divided into two categories—*primary* and *secondary.*

Primary Sources

A **primary source** is an original source. This source (a diary, a person, an event, a survey, and so on) informs you directly, not through another person's explanation or interpretation. You're working with primary sources when you . . .

- observe an event to get firsthand information.
- survey or interview people to gather and tabulate their responses.
- do experiments to understand cause-and-effect relationships.
- analyze original documents, such as the Constitution.

Secondary Sources

A **secondary source** is *not* an original source. A secondary source is one that contains information other people have gathered and interpreted. It is at least once removed from the original. Secondary sources extend, analyze, interpret, or evaluate the primary information. You're working with secondary sources when you . . .

- read a magazine article.
- refer to an encyclopedia.
- watch a documentary on television.
- visit a Web site.

Primary Source	Secondary Source
Interview with a doctor about creatine	Journal article that discusses medical opinions about creatine
Survey of athletes using creatine	Magazine article about athletes' use of creatine
Results of experiment testing effects of creatine on kidneys	Documentary about training supplements

Evaluating Information

Once you've found what you think is the right information for your needs, put it to the test. On the surface, all information looks the same. It all seems to be valid and trustworthy. But not all information is created or recorded equally. It's your responsibility to sort it out before presenting it to your reader. The questions below should help.

Quality Control

Is the information current? A book on computers written five years ago may be ancient history by now. But a book on Abraham Lincoln could be 40 years old and still be the best source on the market.

✱ If your information comes from a Web site, when was it created and when was it last updated? Are the hyperlinks in the site current?

Is the information complete? Try to see the whole picture. If you're given data from an experimental group, you should be given results from another group for comparison. If your source shows you highlights, ask to see the "lowlights," too.

Is the information accurate? Mistakes can result from bad research design, misinterpreted results, poor reporting, computer goofs, or even problems in fax transmission. (Unfortunately, mistakes don't come with little red flags that say "Oops." You've got to detect them the old-fashioned way—carefully checking your information and thinking about it.)

Is the source an expert? An expert is someone who has mastered a whole subject area, someone who is regarded as an authority. But, be careful. When experts go outside their fields of expertise, they may not have much authority. Be especially cautious in evaluating information on the Internet. While there is an incredible amount of information available, there's also a ton of misinformation. Many documents are prepared by people whose only expertise is knowing how to create a Web page.

Is your source biased? A "bias" means, literally, a tilt toward one side. Biased sources—such as political "spin doctors," corporate spokespersons, or TV infomercials—have everything to gain by slanting facts and emotions their way. Keep your eyes open for connections between authors, financial backers, and the points of view shared. Put two and two together.

Take NOTE Slanted language or distorted statistics reveal many sorts of biases to watch out for—bias toward (or against) a region of the country, a political party, males or females, a certain race or ethnic group, a religion.

Information **Packages**

Information comes in all shapes and sizes. Look at the chart below to get an overview of the kinds of information available, and how that information may be packaged.

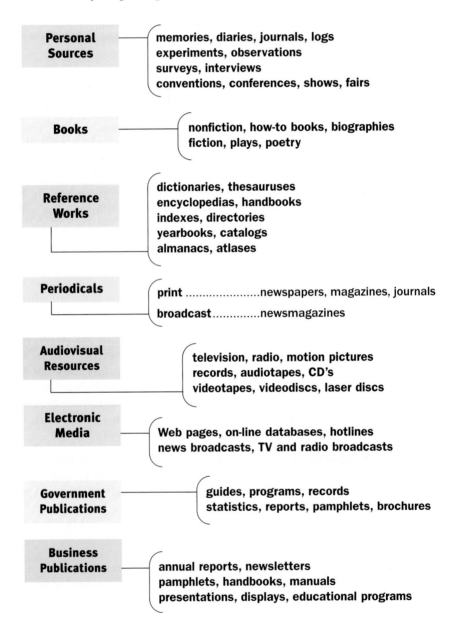

Personal Sources
- memories, diaries, journals, logs
- experiments, observations
- surveys, interviews
- conventions, conferences, shows, fairs

Books
- nonfiction, how-to books, biographies
- fiction, plays, poetry

Reference Works
- dictionaries, thesauruses
- encyclopedias, handbooks
- indexes, directories
- yearbooks, catalogs
- almanacs, atlases

Periodicals
- print ....newspapers, magazines, journals
- broadcast..............newsmagazines

Audiovisual Resources
- television, radio, motion pictures
- records, audiotapes, CD's
- videotapes, videodiscs, laser discs

Electronic Media
- Web pages, on-line databases, hotlines
- news broadcasts, TV and radio broadcasts

Government Publications
- guides, programs, records
- statistics, reports, pamphlets, brochures

Business Publications
- annual reports, newsletters
- pamphlets, handbooks, manuals
- presentations, displays, educational programs

Information Places

Information "places" are sites where information "packages" can be located. For your research, consider the places listed below. What information packages can be found at these sites?

libraries	public	
	school	
	special	legal, medical
		government
		business
		research
computer resources	personal computers	files
		programs
	networks	e-mail
		Internet
		on-line services
mass media	radio, television	
	print, telephone	
learning sites	museums, zoos	
	science centers	
	special places	parks, nature centers
		historical sites
		plants and facilities
		colleges, universities
government	municipal	
	state	
	national	
research sites	laboratories	
	testing centers	
	think tanks	
conference sites	shows, fairs, exhibits	
	conventions	
workplace	corporate databases	
	company files	
	bulletin boards	
	Web sites	

Conducting **Surveys**

One source of information available to all people is the survey. You can use surveys to collect facts and opinions from a wide range of people about any topic. To get quality information using a survey, follow these guidelines:

1. **Find a focus.** Limit the purpose of your survey and target a logical audience.

2. **Ask clear questions.**
   - Ask questions that are clear, precise, and complete.
   - Use words that are objective (not biased or slanted).
   - Make answering relatively easy.
   - Offer answer options that are complete and do not overlap.

3. **Match your questions to your purpose.**
   - Open-ended questions bring in a wide variety of answers and more complex information, but they take time to complete and the answers are hard to summarize.
   - Closed questions give respondents easy answer options, and the answers are easy to tabulate. Closed questions can provide two choices *(yes* or *no, true* or *false),* multiple choice, a rating or scale *(poor 1 2 3 excellent),* or a blank to fill.

4. **Organize your survey so that it's easy to complete.**
   - In the introduction, state who you are and why you need the information. Explain how to complete the survey and when and where to return it.
   - Guide readers with numbers, instructions, and headings.
   - Begin with basic questions and end with any necessary complex, open-ended questions. Move in a logical order from one topic to the next.
   - Give respondents enough room to answer questions.

5. **Test your survey.**
   - Ask a friend or a classmate to read your survey and help you revise it before printing it.
   - Check how your survey works with a small test group.

6. **Conduct your survey.**
   - Distribute the survey to a clearly defined group in a way that won't prejudice the sampling (random or cross-section).
   - Get responses from a good sample (at least 10 percent) of your target group.
   - Tabulate responses carefully and objectively.

Sample **Survey**

The introduction includes the essential information about the survey.

Confidential Survey About Creatine Use

——— My name is Brian Sonke, and I'm conducting research about the use of the training supplement *creatine*. I'd like to hear from you, Brewster High's athletes. Please answer the questions below by circling or filling in your responses. Then drop your survey in the box outside room 211 by Friday, March 24. Your responses will remain confidential.

The survey begins with clear, basic questions.

1. What is your gender?   **male   female**

2. What grade are you in?   **9   10   11   12**

3. What sports do you play? _____

_____

4. Are you presently using creatine?   **yes   no**
   Note: If you circled "no," you may turn in your survey at this point.

The survey asks an open-ended question.

5. Describe your creatine use (amount and frequency).

_____

_____

_____

6. Who supervises your creatine use?
   parent   coach   trainer   other: _____

7. How long have you used creatine?
   less than a month   1-12 months   a year or longer

8. How many pounds have you gained while using creatine? _____

The survey covers the topic thoroughly.

9. How much has your athletic performance improved with creatine?
   none   1   2   3   4   5   greatly

10. Circle any side effects you experienced with creatine.
    dehydration   nausea   muscle pulls   diarrhea

✱ The results of a survey such as this would add valuable firsthand information to an essay about creatine use among high school athletes.

Conducting Interviews

The purpose of an interview is simple. In order to get information, you talk with someone who has significant experience or someone who is an expert on your topic. Use the guidelines below whenever you conduct an interview.

1. Prepare for the interview by doing your homework about the topic and your interviewee.

- Arrange the interview in a thoughtful way. Explain to the interviewee your purpose, the process, and the topics to be covered.
- Think about the specific ideas you want to cover in the interview and write questions for each. The 5 W's and H *(Who? What? Where? When? Why?* and *How?)* are important for good coverage.
- Organize your questions in a logical order so that the interview moves smoothly from one subject to the next.
- Write the questions on the left side of a page. Leave room for quotations, information, and impressions on the right side.

2. During the interview, try to relax so that your conversation seems natural and sincere.

- Provide some background information about yourself, your project, and your plans for using the interview information.
- Use recording equipment only with the interviewee's permission.
- Jot down key facts, quotations, and impressions.
- Listen actively. Show that you're listening through your body language—eye contact, nods, smiles. Pay attention not only to what the person says but also to how he or she says it.
- Be flexible. If the person looks puzzled by a question, rephrase it. If the discussion gets off track, redirect it. Based on the interviewee's responses, ask follow-up questions. (Don't limit yourself to your planned questions only.)

3. After the interview, do the following:

- As soon as possible, review your notes. Fill in responses you remember but couldn't record at the time.
- Thank the interviewee with a note, e-mail, or a phone call.
- If necessary, ask the interviewee to check that your information and quotations are accurate.
- Offer to send the interviewee a copy of your writing.

"Cyberspace can give you more homework help than 10 libraries combined, and it's open 24 hours a day."

—Preston Gralla

Using the
INTERNET

The Internet can be a writer's greatest resource, or a writer's biggest waste of time. It can be a place of joy and wonder, or a place of severe frustration. It all depends upon how you use the Internet. There are so many links to explore, so many flashy elements involved, that you can easily get lost. And, as with any new technology, it's frustrating to need something in a hurry and not really know how or where to find it. However, if you take time to learn about this tool, plan ahead before logging on, and stay focused on your original purpose for browsing, the Net will take you to resources you never would have imagined.

In this chapter, we'll discuss how to use the Net for research and how to become part of its community. (*Note:* Publishing on the Net is discussed in "Publishing Your Writing" on pages 38-39.)

Preview

- O **Researching on the Net**
- O **Communicating on the Net**
- O **Netiquette**

Researching on the Net

One of the best things about the Internet is the wealth of information it makes available. Of course, you have to know how to find that information, how to evaluate it for accuracy, and how to save it for later use.

Locating Information

Your first research task as an Internet user is to find relevant and trustworthy sources of information.

USING AN INTERNET ADDRESS

Sometimes you will have the address of an Internet location, perhaps from a book, a periodical, or a teacher. Type the address into the bar at the top of your browser window; then press the enter or return key. Your browser will send a request for that site across your Internet connection and load it, if it's available.

USING A SEARCH ENGINE

If you don't have any Internet addresses for your topic, a search engine can help you look for sites. (For word-search tips, see page 333.)

Browser Searching @ Many browsers have an Internet-search function built into them. Just type words about your topic into the address bar, then press "Return" or "Enter," and your browser will supply a list of suggested sites. Select one of those links to load that site.

Web Search Engines @ The Web offers many different search engines. (See the Write Source site, <thewritesource.com>, for a recommended list.) Some use robot programs to search the Net; others accept recommendations submitted by individuals; most combine these two approaches. When you type a term into a search engine's input box, the search engine scans its listings for matching sites. Then the engine returns recommendations for you to explore. (Most search engine sites also provide topic headings you can explore yourself rather than trusting the engine to do your searching.)

Other Search Engines @ The Net is more than just the Web. You may find valuable information elsewhere on the Net. These other places have their own search functions. Your favorite Web search engine can lead you to Web pages describing these other services.

CONDUCTING A PAGE SEARCH

To find information quickly within a file, use the available document search functions. Just as your word processor can seek a particular word within a document, most Web browsers can "scan" the text of an Internet document. See your browser's help files to learn how.

Word-Search **TIPS**

Mastery of search engines lies in how you phrase your searches.

■ **Enter a single word** to seek sites that contain that word or a derivative of it. *Example:* The term "apple" yields sites containing the word "apple," "apples," "applet," and so on.

■ **Enter more than one word** to seek sites containing any of those words. *Example:* The words "apple" and "pie" yield sites containing "apple" only and "pie" only, as well as those containing both words (together or not).

■ **Use quotation marks** to find an exact phrase. *Example:* The term "apple pie" (together in quotation marks) yields only sites with that phrase.

■ **Use Boolean words** (*and, or, not*) to shape your search. *Example:* The phrase "apple and pie" (without quotation marks) yield sites containing *both* words, though not necessarily as a phrase. The phrase "apple or pie" yields sites with *either* word or *both*.

✱ Check the instructions on your favorite search engine to learn how to best use it.

Evaluating Information

It isn't always easy to judge the usefulness of information on the Net. Here are some guidelines to help you.

Consider the Source ℮ Government and education sites are usually reliable, as are most nonprofit-organization and professional-business sites. Some private sites, however, are less accurate.

Compare Sources ℮ If you find the same information at more than one reliable site, it is probably accurate.

Seek the Original Source ℮ For news, try to find the original source, if possible. Otherwise, consider the information carefully.

Check with a Trusted Adult ℮ Ask your parents, a teacher, a librarian, or a media specialist to help you judge the accuracy of what you find.

HELP FILE

Keep the following fine points in mind when you evaluate the usefulness of a Net source: Is the information (1) reasonable, (2) reliable, (3) accurate, (4) current, and (5) complete?

Saving Information

There are several ways to preserve your information once you find it.

Bookmark @ Your Web browser can save a Net site's address for later use. Look for a "bookmark" or "favorites" option on your menu bar. But keep in mind that sites change, so a bookmark may become outdated.

Printout @ You can print a hard copy of a Net document to keep. Be sure to note the details you'll need for citing the source in your work.

Electronic Copy @ You can save a Net document on disc as text. Web pages allow the option to save as "source," which preserves the formatting. Unless your browser can create a "Web archive," however, you must save the page's graphics separately.

E-Mail @ One quick way of saving is to send the current page address or document as e-mail to your personal account. That's especially helpful when you're not at your own computer.

* If you have a question about the Internet and can't find the answer anywhere else, ask your Internet provider. Just remember to phrase your e-mail message clearly and politely. (See pages 334-336.)

Sample **Web Page**

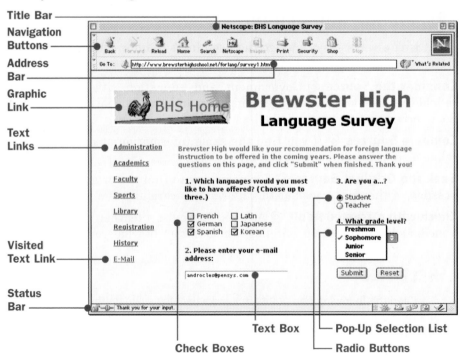

Communicating on the Net

Writers usually thrive in a community of other writers, and the Net allows such a community to converse in many new ways.

Chat Rooms ℮ Chat rooms are sites where people can hold real-time conversations. You can find them through any search engine. Most are identified by topic. Pay attention to your Netiquette (see page 336) if you wish to be taken seriously and benefit from a chat room.

Mailing Lists ℮ Mailing lists are group discussions of a topic by e-mail, often managed by an automated program. The messages come directly to your e-mail account. Check a search engine to find an automated mailing list about your topic. To subscribe to (and unsubscribe from) a mailing list, follow the directions exactly, or the program won't recognize your request.

Newsgroups ℮ Newsgroups are special "bulletin boards" where people post messages by topic. There are thousands in existence, and finding the right one can be difficult. One good way is to use a search engine to find an index of newsgroups; then visit those that interest you.

On-Line Writing Labs ℮ Some schools maintain an on-line writing lab (OWL) on their Web site or Internet server. An OWL can be a great place to post your work in progress and have it critiqued by other writers and teachers. Ask your teacher if your school has such a site.

Navigation TIPS

Here are a few basic browser skills to help you "navigate" the Net more easily.

- **Surfing Links:** You know to "click" on an underlined word or a highlighted image to use a Web link. You will find that not all pages underline or highlight their links. To check for a suspected link, move your mouse cursor over the spot. If the cursor changes in shape or color, you've found a link.

- **Back and Forward:** Your browser keeps a history of sites you visit each time you're on-line. "Click" the back arrow on your browser's toolbar to go back one site, or the forward arrow to move ahead again. Clicking the right mouse button on these arrows (or holding the only mouse button down) shows a list of recently visited sites.

- **Returning Home:** If you get lost or confused while on the Net, click on the "home" symbol of your browser's toolbar to return your browser to its starting place.

Netiquette

Chatting and posting messages on the Net pose special challenges. It's almost as immediate as speaking face-to-face, but Net users don't have the visual cues that speakers do, and they can't hear the tone of voice. This means that the intent of a message can be misunderstood. To help solve this problem, Net users have developed "Netiquette." Proper Netiquette will help you communicate effectively on-line.

Message Clarity @ The most important part of Netiquette is being careful as you write. Make your message as clear as possible before you send it. Also, don't assume that the recipient will remember a previous e-mail or post; add a reminder about the topic in your message. When responding to a message, it may help to quote part of it in your own. But don't quote the entire thing; many people pay for their Internet connection by the minute and don't appreciate downloading long quotations of earlier messages.

Smileys @ Often, to add a certain tone to part of an on-line message, people use "smileys" (or other "emoticons"). These sideways faces :-) are made up of keyboard characters.

Long Messages @ If your message is long, it's polite to add "Long Message" to the subject line. That way people are prepared before they open the text itself.

Don't SHOUT @ On the Net, words in capital letters mean SHOUTING. Don't send your messages in all capital letters. Such messages are harder to read, and people consider them rude.

You can, however, use all capitals to emphasize words, such as to represent the title of a book (MOBY DICK, for example). For lighter emphasis, bracket the word in asterisks. (Netiquette *is* a virtue.)

Net Abbreviations @ To speed the flow of communication, people on the Net use many abbreviations: LOL for "laughing out loud," RTFM for "read the friendly manual," and so on. If you see an abbreviation you don't know, don't be afraid to politely ask the user what it means.

Accuracy @ Though writing e-mail and other electronic feedback is easy and fast, don't let that be an excuse for sloppiness. Proofread your message; check spacing between words and between sentences. Follow correct punctuation rules and use paragraphs just as you would in a nonelectronic message.

"Knowledge is of two kinds. We know
the subject ourselves, or we know where
we can find information upon it."

—Samuel Johnson

Using the
LIBRARY

Collecting information in the library is like detective work—it requires time, thought, and an inspired use of clues. Experienced information detectives know that one of their best informants is the librarian. An expert in information storage and retrieval, the librarian can help you find what you need to "make your case" in any piece of writing.

Good detectives, though, don't depend on others to do all their searching. They get to know their way around, just as you need to do if you're going to get the most out of your library. This chapter will help.

Preview

- O **Using the Computer Catalog**
- O **Using the Card Catalog**
- O **Selecting Reference Works**
- O **Finding Articles in Periodicals**
- O **Using a Dictionary**
- O **Using a Thesaurus**
- O **Using a Book**

Using the **Computer Catalog**

A computer catalog contains all the information you need to use your library efficiently. Computer catalogs differ from card catalogs in their organization and operation, but provide the same information. Most are easy to use; just follow the instructions on the screen. Below is a typical start-up screen.

```
Welcome to the Rapid City Public
Access On-Line Catalog
Databases:
    1. author, title, subject searching
    2. general periodical index
    3. information about system libraries
To make a selection, type a number and
then press [RETURN]>>>
```

You will be prompted to make a series of choices that will take you to a screen that gives the same information you would find on a catalog card. Print out the screen (if the computer allows you to) or write down the information you need.

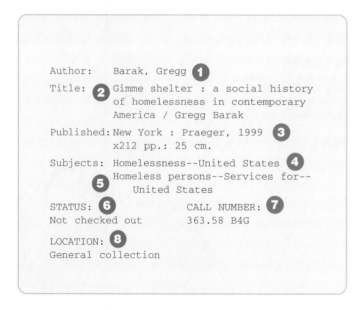

Author: Barak, Gregg ❶
Title: ❷ Gimme shelter : a social history
           of homelessness in contemporary
           America / Gregg Barak
Published: New York : Praeger, 1999 ❸
           x212 pp.: 25 cm.
Subjects: Homelessness--United States ❹
       ❺ Homeless persons--Services for--
           United States
STATUS: ❻   CALL NUMBER: ❼
Not checked out   363.58 B4G
LOCATION: ❽
General collection

❶ Author's name

❷ Title heading

❸ Publisher and copyright date

❹ Descriptive information

❺ Subject heading(s)

❻ Library status

❼ Call number

❽ Location information

Keyword Searching

Probably the greatest advantage of using an on-line catalog is being able to do *keyword searching*. This means that if you know only part of the title or author's name, you can still find the work.

Keyword Searches for Titles ℮ If you know only one word in a book's title, use it as your *keyword*. The computer will show you all titles that contain the word, and you can scan the list to find the title you're looking for.

Important Note: If you know several words in a title, use all of them; the computer will give you a shorter list to scan. (Use the most unusual word if you are limited to one keyword.)

Keyword Searches for Authors ℮ If you know only an author's last name, the computer will show you all authors with that last name. You can scan the list to find the author you're looking for. (Some computers can find your author even if you know only the first few letters of the name, or if you spell the name incorrectly.)

Keyword Searches for Subjects ℮ If you want to search by subject, using a keyword is similar to a regular subject search. However, a keyword search often turns up a longer list of books than a regular subject search.

Refining a Keyword Search

Computer catalogs vary. Some computer catalogs allow you to refine (broaden or narrow) your keyword search using ordinary words and phrases. Other search systems allow you to use "Boolean operators"—the words **and, or,** and **not.** Here are some examples of how Boolean operators work:

Keywords you enter:	The computer will show you . . .
civil war	listings that contain the words *civil war.*
civil war **and** United States	listings that contain both *civil war* and *United States;* this might be the U.S. Civil War or other civil wars in which the U.S. played a role.
civil war **or** rebellion	listings that contain either *civil war* or *rebellion;* this would be civil wars anywhere, as well as events that were called rebellions instead of wars.
civil war **not** United States	listings that contain *civil war* but not *United States* (in other words, civil wars outside the U.S.).

Using the **Card Catalog**

A card catalog consists of drawers filled with index cards filed in alphabetical order. For each book or other resource, the catalog contains at least three cards:

○ a subject card (filed under the general subject of the book),

○ an author card (filed under the author's last name), and

○ a title card (filed under the book's title).

✱ Books that cover more than one subject often have more than one subject card.

The different kinds of cards allow you to use whatever clues you have (the subject you're researching, an author's name, or a book title) to find the materials you need. When you've found a card for the book you want, the most important piece of information to record is the call number.

Sample **Catalog Cards**

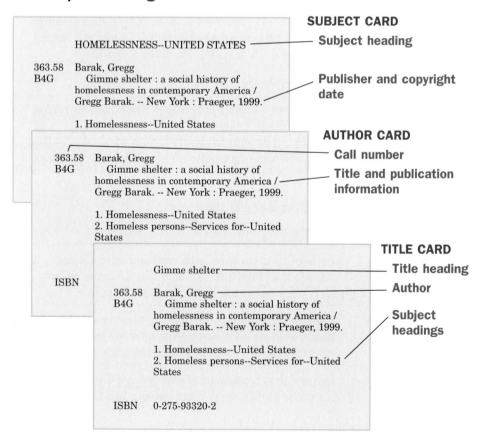

The Call Number

If you know how to "read" a call number, it can tell you a great deal about the book—including where to find it in the library.

The Dewey Decimal System

Call numbers are based on the classification system used by libraries to organize their materials. The most common system is the Dewey decimal system. The Dewey decimal system divides books into 10 main subject classes, with 100 numbers assigned to each class.

000-099 **General Works** • Encyclopedias, handbooks, and other books that cover many subjects

100-199 **Philosophy**

200-299 **Religion** • Books on religions or religious topics

300-399 **Social Sciences** • Books on education, government, law, economics, and other social sciences

400-499 **Languages** • Dictionaries and books about grammar

500-599 **Sciences** • Books about biology, chemistry, all other sciences, and math

600-699 **Technology** • Books about engineering, inventions, medicine, and cookbooks

700-799 **Arts and Recreation** • Books on painting, music, and other arts; sports and games

800-899 **Literature** • Poetry, plays, essays, and famous speeches

900-999 **History, Travel, and Geography**

Other Divisions

The 10 major subject classes are broken down into divisions, sections, and subsections—each with its own topic and number. The table below shows an example of each level of the Dewey decimal system.

Divisions of the Dewey Decimal Class Number		
900	History	Class
9**7**0	History of North America	Division
97**3**	History of the United States	Section
973.**7**	History of the U.S. Civil War	Subsection
973.**74**	History of Civil War Songs	Sub-subsection

Locating Books by Call Number

The Dewey decimal system determines a book's *class number*, which is the most important part of its call number. But the call number includes other information, too. Depending on which library you use, the call number may include the following items:

- the first letter or letters of the author's last name,
- a cutter number assigned by the librarian, and
- the first letter of the first significant word in the title.

Sample Call Number

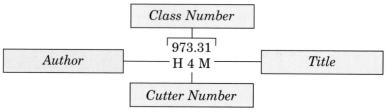

Class Number
973.31

Author ——— H 4 M ——— Title

| Cutter Number |

HELP FILE

Fiction books and biographies are not classified according to the Dewey decimal system. Most fiction is shelved in a separate section of the library, alphabetized by the author's last name. (However, classic fiction is classified as literature and shelved in that Dewey decimal subject class.) Biographies, too, are in a separate section and are shelved alphabetically by the last name of the person written about.

Using the Call Number to Find the Book

To find a book in the library, you must read the call number carefully. Note that 973.2 is a higher number than 973.198 and will come after it on the shelf. (See illustration.)

Also, there may be many books with the same Dewey decimal number. In that case, you must use the rest of the call number to find the right book.

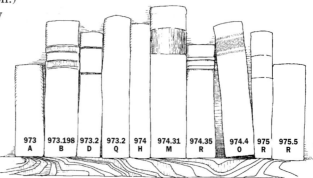

| 973 | 973.198 | 973.2 | 973.2 | 974 | 974.31 | 974.35 | 974.4 | 975 | 975.5 |
| A | B | D | Q | H | M | R | O | R | R |

Selecting Reference Works

The reference section is where you'll find dictionaries, thesauruses, encyclopedias, and other reference works, including the following:

Almanacs are regular (usually annual) publications filled with facts and statistics. Originally, almanacs were used as community calendars and basic information books. Today they're broader in scope and cover everything from politics to sports.

> *The World Almanac* and *Information Please® Almanac* both present information on many topics such as business, politics, history, religion, social programs, sports, education, and the year's major events.

Atlases are books of detailed maps and related information. They include information on countries, transportation, languages, climate, and more.

> *The Rand McNally Commercial Atlas and Marketing Guide* includes maps of the United States and its major cities as well as information on transportation and communication, economics, and population.

> *Street Atlas USA* on CD-ROM allows you to call up street maps for any place in the United States.

Biographical Dictionaries contain minibiographies of many famous people, usually listed in alphabetical order.

> *Current Biography* is published monthly and annually. Each article includes a photo of the individual, a biographical sketch, and information concerning the person's birth date, address, occupation, etc.

Directories are lists of people and groups. (Directories are now widely used on the Internet.)

> *The National Directory of Addresses and Telephone Numbers* provides nationwide coverage of companies, associations, schools, etc.

Guides and Handbooks offer guidelines and models for exploring a topic, a program, an area of knowledge, or a profession.

> *Occupational Outlook Handbook,* published by the Department of Labor, explores the job market—where jobs are or will be and how to prepare for the workplace.

Yearbooks cover major developments in specific areas of interest during the previous year.

> *Statistical Abstract of the United States: The National Data Book* provides statistical information about the United States, from population figures to data on geography, social trends, politics, employment, and business.

Finding Articles in Periodicals

When you want to find articles in periodicals (magazines, journals, and newspapers), start with the periodical indexes. You will find them in the reference or periodical section of the library. Some will be in printed volumes; some may be on CD-ROM or computer.

Readers' Guide to Periodical Literature

The *Readers' Guide to Periodical Literature* is available in nearly all libraries. It indexes articles that appear in widely read magazines, so it is a good place to look for articles on a specific topic. Begin by finding the volume that covers the time period you are researching (perhaps you want only recent articles, or you are looking for details of an event that happened two years ago, and so on). Use the following guidelines to help you look up your topic:

- Articles are listed alphabetically by topic and by author.
- Some topics are divided into subtopics, with each article listed under the appropriate subtopic.
- Cross-references refer you to related topic entries where you may find more articles.

HELP FILE

Check to see which periodicals your library subscribes to before you search the *Readers' Guide.* That way, you won't spend time writing down information about articles that aren't available at your library.

Locating Articles

Once you've found a listing on your topic, write down the essential information: the name and issue date of the magazine, and the title and page numbers of the article. You may need to write this information on a call slip and give the slip to the librarian, who will get the periodical for you. Or, you may need to find the periodical yourself. Your library may have periodicals in printed form, on CD-ROM, or on microfilm.

Take NOTE

While the *Readers' Guide* is a common periodical index, most libraries have other indexes, too. The *General Periodicals Index,* for example, is similar to the *Readers' Guide* and is on computer. Some indexes list articles from a single publication, such as the *New York Times*.

Sample *Readers' Guide* Page

Label	Content

ENVIRONMENTAL MOVEMENT

"SEE ALSO" REFERENCE ——— *See also*
    Conservation of resources
    Environmental associations
    Industry and the environment
    Minorities and the environment
Field observations [interview with W. Berry] J. Fisher-Smith. il

PAGE NUMBER(S) ——— por *Orion* v12 p50-9 Ag '99
    Pacific Northwest
Reconciling rural communities and resource conservation
    [Pacific Northwest; with editorial comment by Timothy
    O'Riordan] K. Johnson. bibl f il *Environment* v35

VOLUME NUMBER ——— p inside cover, 16-20+ N '98
    Vancouver Island (B.C.)
Brazil of the North? [battle over logging in Vancouver Island's

NAME OF MAGAZINE ——— Clayoquot Sound area] C. A. White. il *Canada and the World*
v59 p8-9 S '99
ENVIRONMENTAL POLICY
    See also
    Air pollution—Laws and regulations
    Genetic research—Environmental aspects
    Industry and the environment
The compensation game [taking cases] F. Williams.

NAME OF AUTHOR ——— il por *Wilderness* v57 p28-33 Fall '96
Images of home [population and the environment] C. A.
    Douglas. il *Wilderness* v57 p10-22 Fall '98
Unfunded federal environmental mandates. P. H. Abelson.
    Science v262 p1191 N 19 '97

SUBTOPIC ——— **International aspects**
The best environment of 1997. il *Time* v143 p74 Ja 3 '96
    Public opinion
Of global concern: results of the health of the planet survey
    [cover story] R. E. Dunlap and others. bibl f il

DATE OF ISSUE ——— *Environment* v35 p6-15+ N '99
    United States
    See Environmental policy

"SEE" CROSS-REFERENCE ——— **ENVIRONMENTAL RACISM** *See* Minorities and the
environment
ENVIRONMENTAL REGULATIONS *See* Environmental policy
ENVIRONMENTAL SYSTEMS PRODUCTS INC.

TITLE OF ARTICLE ——— Playing favorites [L. Weicker fires L. Goldberg over
    Connecticut state contract for auto emissions testing]
    C. Byron. il pors *New York* v27 p12-13 Ja 10 '98

SUBJECT ENTRY ——— **ENVIROTEST SYSTEMS CORPORATION**
Playing favorites [L. Weicker fires L. Goldberg over
    Connecticut state contract for auto emissions testing]
    C. Byron. il pors *New York* v27 p12-13 Ja 10 '98
EPHRON, NORA   *about*
Sleepless in Seattle's Nora Ephron [interview] C. Krupp. il por
    Glamour v91 p147-8 Ag '93

Material from *Reader's Guide to Periodical Literature* by the H. W. Wilson, Company is to be used as a guide and not for actual research.

Using a **Dictionary**

A dictionary gives many types of information. (See page 347.)

Spelling Not knowing how to spell a word can make it difficult for you to look it up in the dictionary, but not impossible. You will be surprised at how quickly you can find most words by following their phonetic (sounded-out) spelling.

Capitalization If you're not sure whether a word should be capitalized, check a dictionary.

Syllabication A dictionary tells you where you may divide a word. A hyphen is used in the pronunciation to show syllabic division. (The centered dots in the entry word show where you can make an end-of-line division.)

Pronunciation A dictionary tells you how to pronounce a word and also provides a key to pronunciation symbols, usually at the bottom of the page.

Parts of Speech A dictionary tells you what part(s) of speech a word is, using these abbreviations:

n	noun	*vt*	transitive verb	*adj*	adjective
pron	pronoun	*interj*	interjection	*adv*	adverb
vi	intransitive verb	*conj*	conjunction	*prep*	preposition

Etymology Many dictionaries give etymologies (word histories) for at least some words. They tell what language an English word came from, how the word entered our language, and when it was first used.

Special Uses Different kinds of labels tell about special uses of words.

> **Usage labels** tell how a word is used: *slang, nonstandard (nonstand.), dialect (dial.),* etc.

> **Geographic labels** tell the region or country in which a word is used: *New England (NewEng.), Canada (Can.),* etc.

Synonyms and Antonyms Many dictionaries list both synonyms and antonyms of words. (Of course, the best place to look for these is in a thesaurus.)

Illustrations If a definition is difficult to make clear with words alone, a picture or drawing is used.

Meanings Many dictionaries list all the meanings of a word. Some list meanings chronologically, with the oldest meaning first, followed by newer meanings. Other dictionaries list a word's most common meaning first, followed by less common meanings. Always read all the meanings listed, to make sure you are using the word appropriately.

Sample Dictionary Page

GUIDE WORDS

SYLLABICATION AND PART OF SPEECH

MEANING

SPELLING OF RELATED FORMS

SPELLING AND CAPITAL LETTERS

ILLUSTRATION

PRONUNCIATION

ETYMOLOGY (History)

ACCENT MARK

SYNONYMS

USAGE

PRONUNCIATION KEY

¹**mo·bile** \'mō-bəl, -ˌbīl, *also* -ˌbēl\ *adj* [ME *mobyll*, fr. MF *mobile*, fr. L *mobilis*, fr. *movere* to move] (15c) **1 :** capable of moving or being moved: MOVABLE <a ~ missile launcher> **2 a :** changeable in appearance, mood, or purpose <~ face> **b :** VERSATILE **3 :** relating to a mobile—**mo·bil·i·ty** \mo-'bil-ət-e\ *n*

²**mo·bile** \'mō-ˌbēl\ *n* (1936) **:** a construction or sculpture frequently of wire and sheet metal shapes with parts that can be set in motion by air currents; *also* **:** a similar structure (as of paper or plastic) suspended so that it moves in a current of air

-mobile *comb form* [auto*mobile*] **1:** motorized vehicle <snow*mobile*> **2:** automotive vehicle bringing services to the public <blood*mobile*> <book*mobile*>

mobile home *n* (1949) **:** a dwelling structure built on a steel chassis and fitted with wheels that is intended to be hauled to a usu. permanent site—compare MOTOR HOME

mo·bi·li·za·tion \ˌmō-bə-lə-'zā-shən\ *n* (1799) **1 :** the act of mobilizing **2 :** the state of being mobilized

mo·bi·lize \'mō-bə-ˌlīz\ *vb* **-lized; -liz·ing** *vt* (1838) **1 a :** to put into movement or circulation <~ financial assets> **b :** to release (something stored in the organism) for bodily use **2 a :** to assemble and make ready for war duty **b :** to marshal (as resources) for action <~ support for a proposal> ~ *vi* **:** to undergo mobilization

Mö·bi·us strip \ˌmœ̄-bē-əs-, ˌmə(r), ˌmo-\ *n* [August F. *Möbius* † 1868 Ger. mathematician] (1904) **:** a one-sided surface that is constructed from a rectangle by holding one end fixed, rotating the opposite end through 180 degrees, and applying it to the first end

Möbius strip

mob·oc·ra·cy \mä-bä-kre-sə\ *n* (1754) **1 :** rule by the mob **2 :** the mob as a ruling class— **mob·o·crat** \'mä-b -ˌkrat\ə *n* — **mob·o·crat·ic** \mä-bə-kra-tik*adj*

mob·ster \'mäb-stər\ *n* (1917) **:** a member of a criminal gang

moc·ca·sin \'mä-kə-sən\ *n* [Virginia Algonquian *mockasin*] (ca. 1612) **1 a :** a soft leather heelless shoe or boot with the sole brought up the sides of the foot and over the toes where it is joined with a puckered seam to a U-shaped piece lying on top of the foot **b :** a regular shoe having a seam on the forepart of the vamp imitating the seam of a moccasin **2 a :** WATER MOCCASIN **b :** a snake (as of the genus *Natrix*) resembling a water moccasin

moccasin flower *n* (1680) **:** any of several lady's slippers (genus *Cypripedium*); *esp* **:** a once common woodland orchid (*C. acaule*) of eastern No. America with pink or white moccasin-shaped flowers

mo·cha \'mō-kə\ *n* [*Mocha*, Arabia] (1773) **1 a** (1) **:** a superior Arabian coffee consisting of small green or yellowish beans (2) **:** a coffee of superior quality **b :** a flavoring made of strong coffee infusion or of a mixture of cocoa or chocolate with coffee **2 :** a pliable suede-finished glove leather from African sheepskins **3 :** a dark chocolate-brown color

¹**mock** \'mäk, 'mȯk\ *vb* [ME, fr. MF *mocquer*] *vt* (15c) **1 :** to treat with contempt **:** DERIDE **2 :** to disappoint the hopes of **3 :** DEFY, CHALLENGE **4 a :** to imitate (as a mannerism) closely **:** MIMIC **b :** to mimic in sport or derision ~ *vi* **:** JEER, SCOFF **syn** see RIDICULE, COPY — **mock·er** *n* — **mock·ing·ly** \'mä-kiŋ-le, 'mȯ\ *adv*

²**mock** *n* (15c) **1 :** an act of ridicule or derision **:** JEER **2 :** one that is an object of derision or scorn **3 :** MOCKERY **4 a :** an act of imitation **b :** something made as an imitation

³**mock** *adv* (ca. 1619) **:** in an insincere or counterfeit manner – **usu. used in combination** <mock-serious>

\ə\abut \ᵊ\kitten, F table \ər\further \a\ash \ā\ace \ä\mop, mar \au̇\out \ch\chin \e\bet \ē\easy \g\go \i\hit \ī\ice \j\job \ŋ\sing \ō\go \ȯ\law \ȯi\boy \th\thin \th\the \ü\loot \u̇\foot \y\yet \zh\vision \à, ᵏ, ʲ, œ, œ̄, ue, ūe, ʳ \see Guide to Pronunciation

By permission. From *Merriam-Webster's Collegiate Dictionary* © 1999 by Merriam-Webster, Inc., publisher of the Merriam-Webster® dictionaries.

Using a **Thesaurus**

A thesaurus is, in a sense, the opposite of a dictionary. You go to a dictionary when you know the word but need the definition. You go to a thesaurus when you know the general definition but need a specific word. For example, you might want a noun that means *fear*—the kind of fear that causes worry. You need the word to complete the following sentence:

Dana experienced a certain amount of _____ over the upcoming exam.

If you have a thesaurus in dictionary form, simply look up the word *fear* as you would in a dictionary. If, however, you have a traditional thesaurus, first look up your word in the index. You might find this entry:

FEAR 860

Fearful painful 830

timid 862

The numbers in the index entry (for example, *860*) are guide numbers, not page numbers. When you look up number *860* in the thesaurus, you will find a long list of synonyms for *fear*. You may need to look up some in a dictionary to help you decide which is exactly right for your sentence. *Anxiety* means "a state of uneasiness, worry, and fear"; it's a good choice:

Dana experienced a certain amount of <u>anxiety</u> over the upcoming exam.

---

259   PERSONAL AFFECTIONS   859-861

860. FEAR—*N.* **fear,** timidity, diffidence, apprehensiveness, fearfulness, solicitude, anxiety, care, apprehension, misgiving, mistrust, suspicion, qualm, hesitation.

trepidation, flutter, fear and trembling, perturbation, tremor, restlessness, disquietude, funk *[colloq.]*.

fright, alarm, dread, awe, terror, horror, dismay, consternation, panic, scare; stampede *[of horses]*.

V. **fear,** be afraid, apprehend, dread, distrust; hesitate, falter, wince, flinch, shy, shrink, fly.

tremble, shake, shiver, shudder, flutter, quake, quaver, quiver, quail.

frighten, fright, terrify, inspire (*or* excite) fear, bulldoze *[colloq.]*, alarm, startle, scare, dismay, astound; awe; strike terror, appall, unman, petrify, horrify.

Adj. **afraid,** frightened, alarmed, fearful, timid, timorous, nervous, diffident, fainthearted, tremulous, shaky, apprehensive.

✱ Review the entire list of synonyms in the thesaurus entry before choosing a word. Also, consider both the word's meaning and connotation.

Using a **Book**

Knowing the parts of a book can help you find information easily and quickly. Note that an appendix, a glossary, a bibliography, and an index are typically found only in nonfiction books.

- The **title page** is usually the first printed page in a book. It gives (1) the full title of the book, (2) the author's name, (3) the publisher's name, and (4) the place of publication.

- The **copyright page** follows the title page. Here you will find the year the copyright was issued. (When you are looking for up-to-date facts, be sure to check the book's copyright.)

- The **preface, foreword,** or **introduction** come before the table of contents and give an overview of what the book is about and why it was written.

- The **table of contents** lists the names and numbers of the major divisions of the book and the page on which each begins. The table of contents can give you a good overview of what the book is about.

- The **body** is the main text of the book.

- An **epigraph** is a quotation at the beginning of a chapter or a division; an epigraph sets forth the main idea.

- A **footnote** is placed at the bottom of a page and either gives the source of information used in the text or adds useful information. (Endnotes have the same function but appear at the end of a chapter or after the body of the book.)

- An **appendix** may follow the body. It provides additional information, often in the form of maps, charts, tables, diagrams, or documents.

- A **glossary** may follow the appendix. It is an alphabetical list of key words and definitions related to the topic of the book.

- The **bibliography** may list sources used by the author, suggestions for further reading, or both.

- The **index** is an alphabetical list of all the topics covered in the book, with the page number(s) on which each topic is covered.

Take NOTE The index is probably the most useful part of any reference book. It tells you, first, whether the book contains the information you need and, second, where you can find it.

READING
SKILLS

> "One picture is worth a thousand words."
> —Anonymous

Reading
GRAPHICS

Graphs, tables, diagrams, and maps all have something in common: they're all "information pictures." That is, they combine a strong visual representation with a few key words to communicate an important piece of information. As a whole, information pictures are commonly called *graphics*.

A good graphic can make complex data easy to understand. It can show in one picture what it might take hundreds of words to tell. That's why a graphic usually makes a big impression. It registers almost immediately in the reader's mind.

The main purpose of all graphics is to show how facts relate to one another. Different graphics show different types of relationships. For example, a line graph shows how something changes over time, and a picture diagram shows how all the parts of something fit together. This chapter will help you read and understand the most common types of graphics.

Preview

- ◯ Graphs
- ◯ Tables
- ◯ Diagrams
- ◯ Maps

Graphs

Graphs show how different pieces of information are related. The most common kinds of graphs are line graphs, pie graphs, and bar graphs.

Line Graph ℮ A line graph shows how things change over time. It starts with an L-shaped grid. The horizontal line of the grid stands for passing time (seconds, minutes, years, centuries). The vertical line of the grid shows the subject of the graph. The line graph below shows the amounts of carbon monoxide emitted into the atmosphere in the years 1987 through 1996.

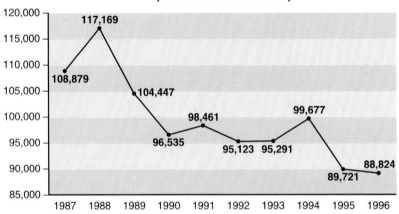

Carbon Monoxide Emissions in the U.S.
(in thousands of tons)

Pie Graph ℮ A pie graph shows proportions and how each proportion, or part, relates to the other parts as well as to the whole "pie." The pie graph below shows the sources of carbon monoxide emissions in 1996, and what proportion of total emissions each source produced.

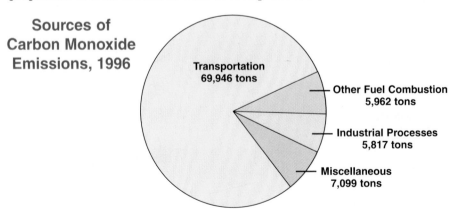

Sources of Carbon Monoxide Emissions, 1996

Transportation
69,946 tons

Other Fuel Combustion
5,962 tons

Industrial Processes
5,817 tons

Miscellaneous
7,099 tons

Bar Graph ⊘ A bar graph uses bars (sometimes called columns) to stand for the subjects of the graph. Unlike line graphs, bar graphs do not show how things change over time. Instead, like a snapshot, they show how things compare at one point in time.

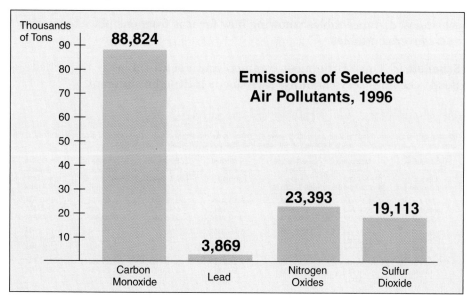

Stacked Bar Graph ⊘ A stacked bar graph is a special kind of bar graph that gives more detailed information than a regular bar graph. Besides comparing the bars, it compares parts within the bars themselves.

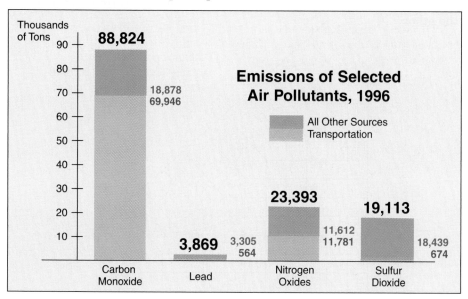

Tables

A table organizes detailed information in a convenient, "one-stop" place. Most tables have rows (going across) and columns (going down). Rows contain one set of details, while columns contain another. Examples are schedules, distance tables (showing how far it is from one place to another), and conversion tables.

Schedule ℯ One of the most common and useful tables is the schedule. Read schedules *very* carefully; each one is a little bit different.

MILWAUKEE TO O'HARE BUS SCHEDULE

Reading this schedule: Find the time you want to arrive at O'Hare in the right-hand column. Read straight across, to your left, on the same line to your pickup point; that is the time you will leave from that point. (Disregard all other times.)

Lv **Marquette University Library** 1415 Wisconsin Ave.	Lv **Milwaukee** Amtrak Station 5th & St. Paul Sts.	Lv **Milwaukee** United Limo 4960 S. 13th St.	Lv **Mitchell Field Airport**	Lv **Racine Jct.** Colony Inn I-94 & Hwy. 20	Lv **Kenosha Jct.** Brat Stop I-94 & Hwy. 50	Ar O'Hare **Airport** Upper Level - All Airlines
4:30 AM	4:45 AM	5:00 AM	5:10 AM	5:25 AM	5:40 AM	6:40 AM
5:45 AM	6:00 AM	6:15 AM	6:25 AM	6:40 AM	6:55 AM	7:55 AM
8:30 AM	8:45 AM	9:00 AM	9:10 AM	9:25 AM	9:40 AM	10:40 AM
11:05 AM	11:20 AM	11:35 AM	11:45 AM	Noon	12:15 PM	1:15 PM
12:30 PM	12:45 PM	1:00 PM	1:10 PM	1:25 PM	1:40 PM	2:40 PM
1:45 PM	2:00 PM	2:15 PM	2:25 PM	2:40 PM	2:55 PM	3:55 PM
4:15 PM	4:30 PM	4:45 PM	4:55 PM	5:10 PM	5:25 PM	6:25 PM
7:15 PM	7:30 PM	7:45 PM	7:55 PM	8:10 PM	8:25 PM	9:25 PM

Distance Table ℯ Another common kind of table is a distance, or mileage, table. To read a distance table, find the place you're starting from and the place you're going to. Then find the place where the row and the column meet—that will show the distance (and driving time) from one place to the other.

Distances shown in red
Driving Times shown in blue

ATLANTA	BOSTON	CHICAGO	CLEVELAND	DALLAS	DENVER	DETROIT	LOS ANGELES	MIAMI	MINNEAPOLIS	NEW ORLEANS	NEW YORK CITY
1115 21:40											
717 13:46	1013 19:59										
780 15:05	667 12:42	345 6:58									
788 14:58	1845 34:57	937 18:05	1185 22:25								
1425 26:49	2015 38:00	1026 19:19	1359 25:39	794 15:14							
743 14:06	714 13:44	288 5:35	173 3:29	1249 23:35	1285 24:16						
2362 44:36	3028 56:58	2086 39:28	2388 45:17	1486 27:45	1062 20:15	2311 43:44					
653 12:24	1541 29:33	1237 23:32	1274 24:20	1325 25:22	2065 38:46	1432 27:07	2785 52:51				
1131 21:36	1459 27:49	410 7:54	765 14:44	963 18:34	928 17:28	671 12:56	1993 36:53	1802 34:10			
475 9:04	1619 30:37	926 17:45	1060 20:00	509 9:56	1344 26:02	1068 20:20	2009 38:06	857 16:21	1328 25:17		
887 17:16	197 4:09	818 15:40	481 9:13	1620 30:51	1807 34:20	646 12:35	2797 52:42	1347 25:55	1234 23:33	1401 26:42	

Diagrams

A diagram is a drawing designed to show how something is constructed, how its parts relate to one another, or how it works.

Picture Diagram ⊜ A picture diagram is just that—a picture or drawing of the subject. Often, some parts of the subject are left out in order to emphasize others. For example, the diagram below shows a cross section of the brain and labels the parts responsible for certain functions.

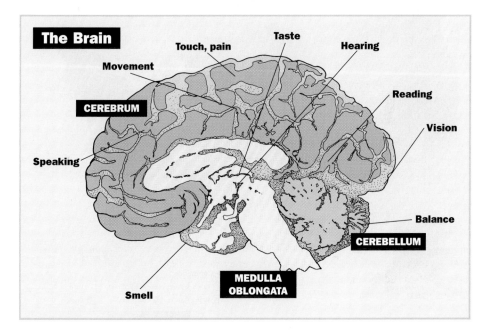

Line Diagram ⊜ A line diagram uses lines, symbols, and words to show the relationships among people, places, things, or ideas. A family tree is a type of line diagram. The diagram below shows relationships among languages.

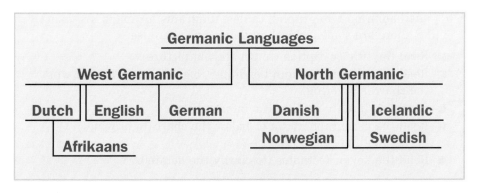

Maps

A map may show a continent, a country, a state, a city, or another geographic area. There are many kinds of maps (political maps, road maps, topographical maps, weather maps, etc.), each serving a different purpose.

Weather Map @ A weather map has a language all its own, made up of words, symbols, and colors. Study the map's key to unlock its language.

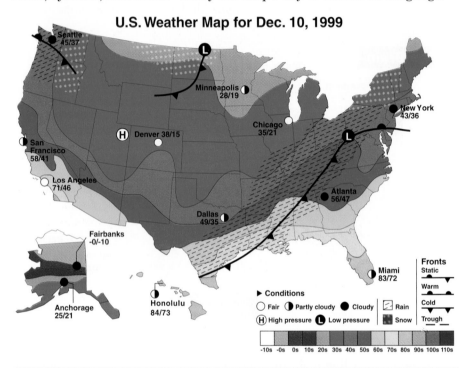

U.S. Weather Map for Dec. 10, 1999

TIPS for Reading Graphics

Although no two graphs, tables, diagrams, or maps are exactly alike, there are some general guidelines you can use:

- Read the title or caption (to get the big picture).
- Read the labels or column headings (to get a better idea of what the chart is covering).
- Read the data (to get specific information).
- Read the paragraph above or below the chart (to provide background information).
- Read the key or footnotes (to clarify the details).

> "To read without reflecting is like
> eating without digesting."
> —Edmund Burke

STUDY-READING
Skills

Most of the reading you do in school is study-reading: reading for the purpose of understanding, learning, and remembering. And, as you know, study-reading takes effort. You sometimes need to read an assignment more than once, especially if the material is difficult. You often need to refer to other parts of the book as you read (the glossary, appendix, and index, for example). You may even need to use outside sources (atlases, dictionaries, handbooks) to help you. Above all, you need to concentrate and think about what you're reading.

This chapter gives you strategies that will make your study-reading easier and more productive. You'll learn specific skills that will help you now and in the future.

Preview

- ○ Guidelines for Study-Reading
- ○ Strategies for Study-Reading
- ○ Reading Nonfiction: SQ3R
- ○ Reading Fiction
- ○ Reading Poetry

Guidelines for Study-Reading

The guidelines that follow will help you put together a personal study-reading plan to use with textbooks and reference materials.

Before You Read . . .

- Know exactly what the reading assignment is and when it is due.
- Figure out approximately how long it will take you to read the assigned number of pages and plan out your time accordingly.
- Gather all the materials you may need to complete your assignment (notebook, handouts, reference books, and so on).
- Try to avoid doing your studying or reading when you are overly hungry or tired.
- If there are questions that go with the assignment, look them over before you begin reading.

As You Read . . .

- Know your textbooks and what they contain; use the index, glossary, and special sections.
- Preview each page before you begin reading to get an overall picture of what the selection is about; also, look for patterns in the way the reading material is organized. (See pages 359-363.)
- Read the titles and headings and use them to ask yourself questions about what may be covered in the text.
- Try to figure out the main idea of each paragraph and note the supporting details that are worth remembering. (Notice words or phrases in *italics* or **boldface.**)
- Look closely at maps, charts, graphs, and other illustrations to help you understand and remember important information.
- Take notes of the important information; use a graphic organizer to help you arrange your notes. (See pages 359-363.)

✱ Remember that some reading materials are much more difficult than others. Read difficult material slowly and reread when necessary.

After You Read . . .

- Try to figure out difficult material first by rereading; then, if necessary, ask someone to explain it.
- Summarize difficult material out loud (either to yourself or to someone else); make note cards or flash cards to study later.
- Keep a list of things you have questions about.

Strategies for Study-Reading

Knowing some of the common patterns of nonfiction makes it easier to understand your assigned reading. Five of these patterns are reviewed in this chapter: *description, chronological order, comparison/contrast, main idea/supporting details,* and *cause and effect.* Knowing these patterns can help you take notes as you read.

Description

Description focuses on sensory details (how something looks, sounds, and feels) to give you a clear picture of the topic. When a selection follows the description pattern, you can use mapping to help you take notes.

> Mount Everest, the world's highest mountain at 29,028 feet, towers over the border between Nepal and Tibet. Its Nepali name is *Sagarmatha,* which means "Forehead in the Sky."
>
> Everest is clothed with gigantic glaciers that make their way down its slopes—usually slowly, but sometimes in huge, thundering avalanches of snow and ice that bury entire valleys. Temperatures vary greatly. In January, the average temperature at the summit is -33 degrees Fahrenheit; low temperatures drop to -76°F. The "warmest" month is July, when the average temperature is -2°F.
>
> From June through September, monsoon season brings screaming winds and blinding snowstorms. Winter winds whip around the summit at more than 175 miles per hour—stronger than a Category-5 hurricane.

Mapping

sights
29,028 feet high
gigantic glaciers
world's highest mountain
borders Nepal and Tibet
blinding snowstorms

sounds
screaming winds
thundering avalanches

Mount Everest

feelings
winter cold -76°F
July average -2 F°
hurricane-strength (175 mph) winds

Chronological Order

When a selection relates information in chronological order, you can use a time line to help you take notes. A time line lists events in the order in which they happen.

Today when we think of technology, we think of things like computers and satellites. But the story of technology begins at least 12,000 years ago (in about 10,000 B.C.E.). That's when people first began to use metal to make tools and utensils. The first metal to be used was copper. It was a big improvement over stone because coppersmiths could heat it and mold it into any needed shape.

The earliest evidence of people combining copper with tin to make bronze dates from about 4500 B.C.E. in Thailand. Bronze was much harder than copper and could be shaped into a sharp edge. With the invention of bronze, people were able to make knives, swords, and other weapons.

Around 3000 B.C.E., iron became the metal of choice. It was even harder than bronze and easier to come by because there was plenty of it near the earth's surface. The process of making steel—a strong, hard, flexible alloy (mixture) of iron and carbon—was first developed around 1400 but wasn't perfected until the 1800s.

Time Line

History of Modern Metals

10,000 B.C.E.	Copper was the first metal to be used for tools.
4500 B.C.E.	In Thailand, copper and tin were combined to make bronze, a harder metal than copper.
3000 B.C.E.	Iron was used because it was harder and more plentiful.
1400 C.E.	Early steelmaking technology combined iron and carbon.
1800 C.E.	Steelmaking was perfected.

Comparison/Contrast

The comparison/contrast pattern introduces two (or more) topics, and then tells how they are the same and how they are different. A Venn diagram is a helpful way to organize comparison/contrast notes.

There are many similarities between the two world wars, but also some important differences. In both wars, Great Britain, France, and Russia (the Soviet Union in World War II) were the main Allies until the United States joined them late in the conflict. In both wars, Germany was the primary adversary. In World War I Germany was joined by Austria-Hungary, Turkey, and Bulgaria; in World War II Germany's partners were Japan and Italy. (Italy had been an Allied nation in World War I.) Germany and its partners lost both wars.

WW II caused about four times as many deaths as WW I (about 55 million compared to about 14 million) and had a far greater impact on world politics, leaving the U.S. and Soviet Union as powerful leaders.

Venn Diagram

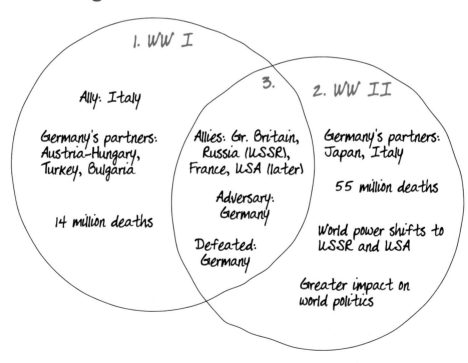

Main Idea/Supporting Details

This pattern begins with one main idea and goes on to give details (facts, figures, examples) that explain the main idea. A table organizer can help you organize your notes.

> William Shakespeare is widely believed to be the greatest playwright of all time. There are several hallmarks of Shakespeare's work that have earned him this honor. Perhaps most important, Shakespeare's plays portray universal human emotions and behaviors in a way that is both sharply accurate and deeply moving. Audiences can identify with characters who experience the same kinds of problems, weaknesses, and feelings that all human beings experience. Second, Shakespeare expressed his characters' most powerful emotions in the equally powerful language of poetry. This successful blend of poetry and drama is an unparalleled achievement. Third, Shakespeare also mixes comedy with tragedy to dramatize the unpredictable nature of pleasures and pains in life. These qualities combine to give Shakespeare's works unmatched depth and texture.

Table Organizer

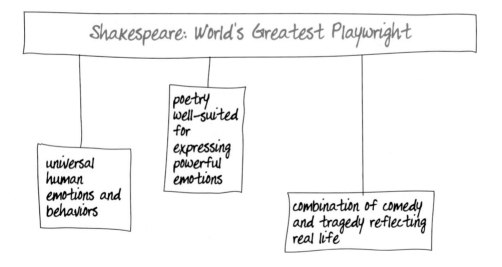

Cause and Effect

The cause-and-effect pattern shows the relationships between two or more events or situations. Cause-and-effect relationships can take on a variety of forms: one cause with many effects, many causes that create one final effect (as in the excerpt below), and other variations. When a selection features cause-and-effect relationships, you can use the organizer below to help you take notes.

> **Economic, political, and philosophical causes combined to bring about the French Revolution.** France was in **financial crisis** because of war expenditures (including loans to American revolutionaries) and luxury-loving kings and queens. The middle class and peasants were taxed heavily, while the clergy and wealthy nobility paid nothing. Although the common people made up four-fifths of the population, they had only one-third of the vote in the French legislature. Therefore, they had no **political power** to change the tax laws. Dissatisfaction with this state of affairs was fueled by philosophers throughout Europe who were promoting **philosophical ideas** such as "government by majority rule" and "the inalienable rights of all human beings, regardless of their social or economic status." When efforts to reform the French government failed, a full-scale revolt began.

Cause-and-Effect Organizer

Subject: The French Revolution

Causes:	Effects:

Economic Crisis
    common people—heavily taxed
    for war debts
	resentment of luxury-loving royalty
	and untaxed clergy and nobility

Political Power
    common people—no power
    to make changes (4/5 of
    population with 1/3 of vote)
	dissatisfaction over inability to
	change tax laws

Philosophical Ideas
    inalienable rights,
    majority rule
	attempts to reform fail
	
	Final Effect: Revolution

Reading Nonfiction: SQ3R

A popular reading technique for all patterns of nonfiction is the SQ3R method. SQ3R stands for the five steps in the study-reading process: *survey, question, read, recite,* and *review.*

Before You Read . . .

Survey @ The first step in the SQ3R study method is "survey." When you survey a reading assignment, you try to get a general idea of what the assignment is about. You look briefly at each page, paying special attention to the headings, chapter titles, illustrations, and boldfaced type. It is also a good idea to read the first and last paragraphs.

Question @ As you do your survey, you should begin to ask questions about the material—questions that you hope to find the answers to as you read. One quick way of doing this is to turn the headings and subheadings into questions. Asking questions will make you an "active" rather than a "passive" reader, keeping you involved and thinking about what is coming up next.

As You Read . . .

Read @ Read the assignment carefully from start to finish. Look for main ideas in each paragraph or section. Take notes as you read, or stop from time to time to write a brief summary. Read the difficult parts slowly. (Reread them if necessary.) Use context to help you figure out the most difficult passages. (See page 369.) Look up unfamiliar words or ideas, and use your senses to imagine the events, people, places, or things you are reading about.

Recite @ One of the most valuable parts of the SQ3R method is the reciting step. It is very important that you recite out loud what you have learned from your reading. (Whisper quietly to yourself if you are in a public place.) It is best to stop at the end of each page, section, or chapter to answer the *Who? What? When? Where? Why?* and *How?* questions. This step is a way of testing yourself on how well you understand what you have read. You may then reread if necessary.

After You Read . . .

Review @ The final step is the review step. You should summarize what you have read as soon as you finish. If you have some questions about the assignment, answer them immediately. If you have no questions to answer, summarize the assignment in a short writing. You may also make an outline, note cards, flash cards, and illustrations to help you review and remember what you have read.

Reading **Fiction**

Fiction isn't "fact," but good fiction is "true." Fiction uses made-up characters and events to show something that is true about life. That's why reading fiction is a great way to learn. Here are some things to think about and explore as you read. (See pages 221-226 for more on reading and writing about fiction.)

Before You Read . . .

- Learn something about the author and his or her other works.
- React thoughtfully to the title and opening pages.

As You Read . . .

- Identify the following story elements: setting, tone, main characters, theme, and central conflict.
- Think about the plot and try to predict what will happen next.
- Record your thoughts (or draw, list, cluster) in a reading journal as you progress through the story.
- Think about the characters and the things they do.
  - What motivates the characters?
  - Have I known similar characters in life or in literature?
  - Have I faced situations similar to the ones faced by the main characters?
  - Would I have reacted in the same way?
- Think about how the time and place in which the author lives (or lived) may have influenced the story.
- Notice the author's style and word choice. (See pages 136-138.)
  - How effectively has the author used literary devices?
  - Why did the author use a particular word or phrase?
  - Why does the story end as it did?
- If you can, discuss the story with others who are reading it. You'll learn from their insights.

After You Read . . .

- Think about how the main character changes and why. Often, this is the key to understanding fiction.
- Decide what you think the story's message or theme is; then decide how good a job the author did in getting that message across to the reader.

Reading Poetry

The poet Archibald MacLeish once said that "a poem should not *mean*, but *be*." That may sound a bit odd at first, but if you think about it, it just might point you in the right direction when it comes to reading a poem.

It might also help to remember that poems don't jump fully formed into a poet's mind. Poems (at least most of them) are created gradually. You shouldn't expect to grasp everything a poem has to offer in one reading, especially if the poem is lengthy or complex. Here are some strategies to help you get the most out of the poetry you read.

First Reading . . .

■ Read the poem all the way through at your normal reading speed to gain on overall impression of the poem.

■ Jot down your immediate reaction to the poem.

Second Reading . . .

■ Read the poem again—out loud, if possible. Pay attention to the "sound" of the poem.

■ Read slowly and carefully—word by word, syllable by syllable— observing the punctuation, spacing, and special treatment of words and syllables.

■ Note examples of sound devices in the poem—alliteration, assonance, rhyme. (See pages 242-243.) This will help you understand the proper phrasing and rhythm of the poem.

■ Think about what the poem is saying or where the poem is going.

Third Reading . . .

■ Try to identify the type of poem you're reading. Does this poem follow the usual pattern of that particular type? If not, why not?

■ Determine the literal sense of the poem. What is the poem about? What does the poem seem to say about its subject?

■ Look carefully for figurative language in the poem. How does this language—metaphors, similes, personification, symbols—support the literal meaning of the poem? (See page 236.)

Take NOTE Do a 10-minute freewriting when you finish reading. Write down everything you can about the poem. Relate what you've read to what you know or have experienced.

> "Words are one of our chief means of
> adjusting to life."
> —Bergen Evans

Improving
VOCABULARY Skills

According to writer Bill Bryson, "What sets English apart from other languages is the richness of its vocabulary." For example, there are about 200,000 English words in common use today. (This figure does not include, among other things, technical or scientific terms.) Now, to be sure, no one person understands and regularly uses all of these "common" words. However, those individuals who continually add more of them to their vocabulary have a distinct learning advantage.

You see, as your vocabulary grows, your reading rate and comprehension level naturally grow, too. A large vocabulary also helps you communicate more efficiently, allowing you to say *exactly* what you mean. The best way to improve your vocabulary is to increase the amount of reading you do. This chapter suggests additional strategies for learning new words.

Preview

- Quick Guide
- Using Context
- Using Word Parts

Quick Guide

Building Your Vocabulary

Many experts agree that the most important thing you can do to improve your grades is to increase your vocabulary. Here are some ways to do that:

- **Use context.** Begin by studying the various kinds of context clues. (See pages 369-370.) Then look for clues as you encounter new words in your reading. You'll be amazed at how many definitions you can figure out on your own.

- **Learn common word roots, prefixes, and suffixes.** With a knowledge of these, you can often infer the meaning of a word. (See pages 371-381.)

- **Keep a vocabulary notebook.** Include the definition, pronunciation, and part of speech for each word. If you've found the new word in your reading, copy the sentence it came from into your notebook. Words learned in context are more likely to be remembered than words learned in isolation.

- **Make flash cards.** Print the new word on the front of an index card with the definition on the back. Carry the cards with you and flip through them when you're waiting in line with nothing to do.

- **Refer to your dictionary.** Every time you look up a word, put a dot next to it in your dictionary. When a word has two or more dots, include it in your flash cards.

- **Study the origins of words.** Pay attention to the etymologies (history of words) in the dictionary. Many of these are interesting enough to help you remember a word.

- **Make a recording.** Tape-record yourself reading new words along with their definitions. Instead of listening to your latest music tape when you're walking or driving somewhere, pop in your vocabulary tape. (Nobody will ever know.)

- **Use a thesaurus.** Check a thesaurus to find all the synonyms for a common word or phrase, such as *move slowly.* For starters, there are *glide, stroll,* and *wander;* but these words are not interchangeable. To make full use of these choices, you need to learn the subtle differences between the connotations of these words.

Using Context

Whenever you come across an unfamiliar word, you can use the context— the words and ideas surrounding an unknown word—to figure it out. Context clues are made up of synonyms, definitions, descriptions, and several other kinds of specific information helpful to understanding the meaning of a passage or a particular word. Below are six kinds of context clues to look for when you read. (The unfamiliar words are in bold; the context clues are in red.)

1. Synonyms and Antonyms

The old man asked if I could **traverse** the creek; I said I could **cross** it easily. He seemed **uncertain** that I could do it, but I was **resolute.**

2. Comparisons and Contrasts

Outside, the **tempest** raged **like a hurricane**. Confined to the house by their concerned mother, Jeremy was **restive, but Adam contentedly read a book**.

3. Definitions and Descriptions

The woman wore a red **mantilla that covered her head and shoulders**.

4. Words in a Series

The **dulcimer, fiddle**, and **banjo** are popular in the Appalachian region.

5. Cause and Effect

Because no one volunteered to clean up the gym, the principal declared the work session would be **mandatory** for all sophomores.

6. Tone and Setting

The **sinister** sound came from **a long, dark passageway that had been hidden behind a bookcase. As we crept into the blackness, the stale, damp air made us feel as if we were being drawn into a dungeon**.

HELP FILE

A context clue does not always appear in the same sentence as the word you don't know. You may need to look for clues in surrounding sentences and paragraphs.

"All my life I've looked at words as though I were seeing them for the first time." —Ernest Hemingway

Using Indirect Clues

Some context clues, such as examples, results, or general statements, are not as direct as the six types listed on the previous page. Still, indirect clues can be helpful. The more clues you find, the closer you are to discovering the specific meaning of a word and the overall intent of the passage it is part of.

NOW YOU TRY IT

See how well you can use context. Look carefully at the words in red in the following passage taken from Jack London's *Call of the Wild.* Then look for direct and indirect context clues to help you understand the meaning of those words.

In addition to the clues available in this single paragraph, the reader of this novel would have the advantage of having read the first 46 pages. Considering that, there is a good chance he or she could figure out the meaning of at least some of the words in red. See how well you do—now that you understand more about context clues.

They made Sixty Miles, which is a fifty-mile run, on the first day; and the second day saw them booming up the Yukon well on their way to Pelly. But such splendid running was achieved not without great trouble and **vexation** on the part of Francois. The **insidious** revolt led by Buck had destroyed the **solidarity** of the team. It no longer was as one dog leaping in the traces. The encouragement Buck gave the rebels led them into all kinds of petty **misdemeanors**. No more was Spitz a leader greatly to be feared. The old awe departed, and they grew equal to challenging his authority. Pike robbed him of half a fish one night and gulped it down under the protection of Buck. Another night Dub and Joe fought Spitz and made him forego the punishment they deserved. And even Billee, the good-natured, was less good-natured, and whined not half so **placatingly** as in former days. Buck never came near Spitz without snarling and bristling **menacingly**. In fact, his conduct approached that of a bully, and he was given to **swaggering** up and down before Spitz's very nose.

Using Word Parts

Many English words are a combination of word parts (prefixes, suffixes, and roots). If you know the meanings of the parts, you can figure out the meanings of words that contain these parts.

Rejuvenate combines
- the prefix *re* (meaning *again*),
- the root *juven* (meaning *young*), and
- the suffix *ate* (meaning *to make*).

To *rejuvenate* is "to make young again."

Orthodontist combines
- the root *ortho* (meaning *straight*),
- the root *dont* (meaning *tooth, teeth*), and
- the suffix *ist* (meaning *a person who*).

An *orthodontist* is "a person who straightens teeth."

HELP FILE

English words that are not a combination of word parts are called *base words*. A base word cannot be divided into parts. ("Base" and "word" are both base words.) However, base words can be combined with other base words and with prefixes and suffixes.

base word	base word + base word	base word + prefix	base word + suffix
ground	background	underground	groundless
hand	handshake	forehand	handful

How can I improve my vocabulary?

You already know and use many common prefixes, suffixes, and roots every day. To improve your speaking and writing vocabulary, study the meanings of prefixes, suffixes, and roots that are not familiar to you. The following pages contain nearly 500 word parts! Scan the pages until you come to a word part that is new to you. Learn its meaning(s) and at least one of the sample words listed. Then apply your knowledge as you encounter new words in your textbooks, your favorite magazines, and even as you surf the Net. You'll see a payoff almost immediately.

Prefixes

Prefixes are those "word parts" that come *before* the root words (*pre =* before). Depending upon its meaning, a prefix changes the intent, or sense, of the base word. As a skilled reader, you will want to know the meanings of the most common prefixes and then watch for them when you read.

a, an [not, without] amoral (without a sense of moral responsibility), atypical, atom (not cuttable), apathy (without feeling), anesthesia (without sensation)

ab, abs, a [from, away] abnormal, abduct, absent, avert (turn away)

acro [high] acropolis (high city), acrobat, acronym, acrophobia (fear of height)

ambi, amb [both, around] ambidextrous (skilled with both hands), ambiguous, amble

amphi [both] amphibious (living on both land and water), amphitheater

ante [before] antedate, anteroom, antebellum, antecedent (happening before)

anti, ant [against] anticommunist, antidote, anticlimax, antacid

be [on, away] bedeck, belabor, bequest, bestow, beloved

bene, bon [well] benefit, benefactor, benevolent, benediction, bonanza, bonus

bi, bis, bin [both, double, twice] bicycle, biweekly, bilateral, biscuit, binoculars

by [side, close, near] bypass, bystander, by-product, bylaw, byline

cata [down, against] catalog, catapult, catastrophe, cataclysm

cerebro [brain] cerebral, cerebrum, cerebellum

circum, circ [around] circumference, circumnavigate, circumspect, circular

co, con, col, com [together, with] copilot, conspire, collect, compose

coni [dust] coniosis (disease that comes from inhaling dust)

contra, counter [against] controversy, contradict, counterpart

de [from, down] demote, depress, degrade, deject, deprive

deca [ten] decade, decathlon, decapod (10 feet)

di [two, twice] divide, dilemma, dilute, dioxide, dipole, ditto

dia [through, between] diameter, diagonal, diagram, dialogue (speech between people)

dis, dif [apart, away, reverse] dismiss, distort, distinguish, diffuse

dys [badly, ill] dyspepsia (digesting badly), dystrophy, dysentery

em, en [in, into] embrace, enslave

epi [upon] epidermis (upon the skin, outer layer of skin), epitaph, epithet

eu [well] eulogize (speak well of, praise), euphony, euphemism, euphoria

ex, e, ec, ef [out] expel (drive out), ex-mayor, exorcism, eject, eccentric (out of the center position), efflux, effluent

extra, extro [beyond, outside] extraordinary (beyond the ordinary), extrovert, extracurricular

for [away or off] forswear (to renounce an oath)

fore [before in time] forecast, foretell (to tell beforehand), foreshadow

hemi, demi, semi [half] hemisphere, demitasse, semicircle (half of a circle)

hex [six] hexameter, hexagon

homo [man] Homo sapiens, homicide (killing man)

hyper [over, above] hypersensitive (overly sensitive), hyperactive

hypo [under] hypodermic (under the skin), hypothesis

il, ir, in, im [not] illegal, irregular, incorrect, immoral

in, il, im [into] inject, inside, illuminate, illustrate, impose, implant, imprison

infra [beneath] infrared, infrasonic

inter [between] intercollegiate, interfere, intervene, interrupt (break between)

intra [within] intramural, intravenous (within the veins)

intro [into, inward] introduce, introvert (turn inward)

macro [large, excessive] macrodent (having large teeth), macrocosm

mal [badly, poorly] maladjusted, malady, malnutrition, malfunction

meta [beyond, after, with] metaphor, metamorphosis, metaphysical

mis [incorrect, bad] misuse, misprint

miso [hate] misanthrope, misogynist

mono [one] monoplane, monotone, monochrome, monocle

multi [many] multiply, multiform

neo [new] neopaganism, neoclassic, neophyte, neonatal

non [not] nontaxable (not taxed), nontoxic, nonexistent, nonsense

ob, of, op, oc [toward, against] obstruct, offend, oppose, occur

oct [eight] octagon, octameter, octave, octopus

paleo [ancient] paleoanthropology (pertaining to ancient humans), paleontology (study of ancient life-forms)

para [beside, almost] parasite (one who eats beside or at the table of another), paraphrase, paramedic, parallel, paradox

penta [five] pentagon (figure or building having five angles or sides), pentameter, pentathlon

per [throughout, completely] pervert (completely turn wrong, corrupt), perfect, perceive, permanent, persuade

peri [around] perimeter (measurement around an area), periphery, periscope, pericardium, period

poly [many] polygon (figure having many angles or sides), polygamy, polyglot, polychrome

post [after] postpone, postwar, postscript, posterity

pre [before] prewar, preview, precede, prevent, premonition

pro [forward, in favor of] project (throw forward), progress, promote, prohibition

pseudo [false] pseudonym (false or assumed name), pseudopodia

quad [four] quadruple (four times as much), quadriplegic, quadratic, quadrant

quint [five] quintuplet, quintuple, quintet, quintile

re [back, again] reclaim, revive, revoke, rejuvenate, retard, reject, return

retro [backward] retrospective (looking backward), retroactive, retrorocket

se [aside] seduce (lead aside), secede, secrete, segregate

self [by oneself] self-determination, self-employed, self-service, selfish

sesqui [one and a half] sesquicentennial (one and one-half centuries)

sex, sest [six] sexagenarian (sixty years old), sexennial, sextant, sextuplet, sestet

sub [under] submerge (put under), submarine, substitute, subsoil

suf, sug, sup, sus [from under] sufficient, suffer, suggest, support, suspend

super, supr [above, over, more] supervise, superman, supernatural, supreme

syn, sym, sys, syl [with, together] system, synthesis, synchronize (time together), synonym, sympathy, symphony, syllable

trans, tra [across, beyond] transoceanic, transmit (send across), transfusion, tradition

tri [three] tricycle, triangle, tripod, tristate

ultra [beyond, exceedingly] ultramodern, ultraviolet, ultraconservative

un [not, release] unfair, unnatural, unbutton

under [beneath] underground, underlying

uni [one] unicycle, uniform, unify, universe, unique (one of a kind)

vice [in place of] vice president, viceroy, vice admiral

Numerical Prefixes

Prefix	Symbol	Multiples and Submultiples	Equivalent	Prefix	Symbol	Multiples and Submultiples	Equivalent
tera	T	10^{12}	trillionfold	centi	c	10^{-2}	hundredth part
giga	G	10^{9}	billionfold	milli	m	10^{-3}	thousandth part
mega	M	10^{6}	millionfold	micro	u	10^{-6}	millionth part
kilo	k	10^{3}	thousandfold	nano	n	10^{-9}	billionth part
hecto	h	10^{2}	hundredfold	pico	p	10^{-12}	trillionth part
deka	da	10	tenfold	femto	f	10^{-15}	quadrillionth part
deci	d	10^{-1}	tenth part	atto	a	10^{-18}	quintillionth part

Suffixes

Suffixes come at the end of a word. Very often a suffix will tell you what kind of word it is part of (noun, adverb, adjective, and so on). For example, words ending in *-ly* are usually adverbs.

able, ible [able, can do] capable, agreeable, edible, visible (can be seen)

ade [result of action] blockade (the result of a blocking action), lemonade

age [act of, state of, collection of] salvage (act of saving), storage, forage

al [relating to] sensual, gradual, manual, natural (relating to nature)

algia [pain] neuralgia (nerve pain)

an, ian [native of, relating to] African, Canadian, Floridian

ance, ancy [action, process, state] assistance, allowance, defiance, truancy

ant [performing, agent] assistant, servant

ary, ery, ory [relating to, quality, place where] dictionary, bravery, dormitory

ate [cause, make] liquidate, segregate (cause a group to be set aside)

cian [having a certain skill or art] musician, beautician, magician, physician

cule, ling [very small] molecule, ridicule, duckling (very small duck), sapling

cy [action, function] hesitancy, prophecy, normalcy (function in a normal way)

dom [quality, realm, office] freedom, kingdom, wisdom (quality of being wise)

ee [one who receives the action] employee, nominee (one who is nominated), refugee

en [made of, make] silken, frozen, oaken (made of oak), wooden, lighten

ence, ency [action, state of, quality] difference, conference, urgency

er, or [one who, that which] baker, miller, teacher, racer, amplifier, doctor

escent [in the process of] adolescent (in the process of becoming an adult), obsolescent, convalescent

ese [a native of, the language of] Japanese, Vietnamese, Portuguese

esis, osis [action, process, condition] genesis, hypnosis, neurosis, osmosis

ess [female] actress, goddess, lioness

et, ette [a small one, group] midget, octet, baronet, majorette

fic [making, causing] scientific, specific

ful [full of] frightful, careful, helpful

fy [make] fortify (make strong), simplify, amplify

hood [order, condition, quality] manhood, womanhood, brotherhood

ic [nature of, like] metallic (of the nature of metal), heroic, poetic, acidic

ice [condition, state, quality] justice, malice

id, ide [a thing connected with or belonging to] fluid, fluoride

ile [relating to, suited for, capable of] missile, juvenile, senile (related to being old)

ine [nature of] feminine, genuine, medicine

ion, sion, tion [act of, state of, result of] contagion, aversion, infection (state of being infected)

ish [origin, nature, resembling] foolish, Irish, clownish (resembling a clown)

ism [system, manner, condition, characteristic] heroism, alcoholism, Communism

ist [one who, that which] artist, dentist

ite [nature of, quality of, mineral product] Israelite, dynamite, graphite, sulfite

ity, ty [state of, quality] captivity, clarity

ive [causing, making] abusive (causing abuse), exhaustive

ize [make] emphasize, publicize, idolize

less [without] baseless, careless (without care), artless, fearless, helpless

ly [like, manner of] carelessly, quickly, forcefully, lovingly

ment [act of, state of, result] contentment, amendment (state of amending)

ness [state of] carelessness, kindness

oid [resembling] asteroid, spheroid, tabloid, anthropoid

ology [study, science, theory] biology, anthropology, geology, neurology

ous [full of, having] gracious, nervous, spacious, vivacious (full of life)

ship [office, state, quality, skill] friendship, authorship, dictatorship

some [like, apt, tending to] lonesome, threesome, gruesome

tude [state of, condition of] gratitude, multitude (condition of being many), aptitude

ure [state of, act, process, rank] culture, literature, rupture (state of being broken)

ward [in the direction of] eastward, forward, backward

y [inclined to, tend to] cheery, crafty, faulty

Roots

A *root* is a base upon which other words are built. Knowing the root of a difficult word can go a long way toward helping you figure out its meaning—even without a dictionary. For that reason, learning the following roots will be very valuable in all your classes.

acer, acid, acri [bitter, sour, sharp] acrid, acerbic, acidity (sourness), acrimony

acu [sharp] acute, acupuncture

ag, agi, ig, act [do, move, go] agent (doer), agenda (things to do), agitate, navigate (move by sea), ambiguous (going both ways), action

ali, allo, alter [other] alias (a person's other name), alibi, alien (from another place), alloy, alter (change to another form)

alt [high, deep] altimeter (a device for measuring heights), altitude

am, amor [love, liking] amiable, amorous, enamored

anni, annu, enni [year] anniversary, annually (yearly), centennial (occurring once in 100 years)

anthrop [man] anthropology (study of mankind), philanthropy (love of mankind), misanthrope (hater of mankind)

anti [old] antique, antiquated, antiquity

arch [chief, first, rule] archangel (chief angel), architect (chief worker), archaic (first, very early), monarchy (rule by one person), matriarchy (rule by the mother)

aster, astr [star] aster (star flower), asterisk, asteroid, astronomy (star law), astronaut (star traveler, space traveler)

aud, aus [hear, listen] audible (can be heard), auditorium, audio, audition, auditory, audience, ausculate

aug, auc [increase] augur, augment (add to; increase), auction

auto, aut [self] autograph (self-writing), automobile (self-moving vehicle), author, automatic (self-acting), autobiography

belli [war] rebellion, belligerent (warlike or hostile)

bibl [book] Bible, bibliography (list of books), bibliomania (craze for books), bibliophile (book lover)

bio [life] biology (study of life), biography, biopsy (cut living tissue for examination)

brev [short] abbreviate, brevity, brief

cad, cas [to fall] cadaver, cadence, caducous (falling off), cascade

calor [heat] calorie (a unit of heat), calorify (to make hot), caloric

cap, cip, cept [take] capable, capacity, capture, reciprocate, accept, except, concept

capit, capt [head] decapitate (to remove the head from), capital, captain, caption

carn [flesh] carnivorous (flesh eating), incarnate, reincarnation

caus, caut [burn, heat] caustic, cauterize (to make hot, to burn)

cause, cuse, cus [cause, motive] because, excuse (to attempt to remove the blame or cause), accusation

ced, ceed, cede, cess [move, yield, go, surrender] procedure, secede (move aside from), proceed (move forward), cede (yield), concede, intercede, precede, recede, success

centri [center] concentric, centrifugal, centripetal, eccentric (out of center)

chrom [color] chrome, chromosome (color body in genetics), chromosphere, monochrome (one color), polychrome

chron [time] chronological (in order of time), chronometer (time measured), chronicle (record of events in time), synchronize (make time with, set time together)

cide, cise [cut down, kill] suicide (killing of self), homicide (human killer), pesticide (pest killer), germicide (germ killer), insecticide, precise (cut exactly right), incision, scissors

cit [to call, start] incite, citation, cite

civ [citizen] civic (relating to a citizen), civil, civilian, civilization

clam, claim [cry out] exclamation, clamor, proclamation, reclamation, acclaim

clud, clus, claus [shut] include (to take in), conclude, claustrophobia (abnormal fear of being shut up, confined), recluse (one who shuts himself away from others)

cognosc, gnosi [know] recognize (to know again), incognito (not known), prognosis (forward knowing), diagnosis

cord, cor, cardi [heart] cordial (hearty, heartfelt), concord, discord, courage, encourage (put heart into), discourage (take heart out of), core, coronary, cardiac

corp [body] corporation (a legal body), corpse, corpulent

cosm [universe, world] cosmic, cosmos (the universe), cosmopolitan (world citizen), cosmonaut, microcosm, macrocosm

crat, cracy [rule, strength] democratic, autocracy

crea [create] creature (anything created), recreation, creation, creator

cred [believe] creed (statement of beliefs), credo (a creed), credence (belief), credit (belief, trust), credulous (believing too readily, easily deceived), incredible

cresc, cret, crease, cru [rise, grow] crescendo (growing in loudness or intensity), concrete (grown together, solidified), increase, decrease, accrue (to grow)

crit [separate, choose] critical, criterion (that which is used in choosing), hypocrite

cur, curs [run] concurrent, current (running or flowing), concur (run together, agree), incur (run into), recur, occur, precursor (forerunner), cursive

cura [care] curator, curative, manicure (caring for the hands)

cycl, cyclo [wheel, circular] Cyclops (a mythical giant with one eye in the middle of his forehead), unicycle, bicycle, cyclone (a wind blowing circularly, a tornado)

deca [ten] decade, decalogue, decathlon

dem [people] democracy (people-rule), demography (vital statistics of the people: deaths, births, and so on), epidemic (on or among the people)

dent, dont [tooth] dental (relating to teeth), denture, dentifrice, orthodontist

derm [skin] hypodermic (injected under the skin), dermatology (skin study), epidermis (outer layer of skin), taxidermy (arranging skin; mounting animals)

dict [say, speak] diction (how one speaks, what one says), dictionary, dictate, dictator, dictaphone, dictatorial, edict, predict, verdict, contradict, benediction

doc [teach] indoctrinate, document, doctrine

domin [master] dominate, dominion, predominant, domain

don [give] donate, condone

dorm [sleep] dormant, dormitory

dox [opinion, praise] doxy (belief, creed, or opinion), orthodox (having the correct, commonly accepted opinion), heterodox (differing opinion), paradox (contradictory)

drome [run, step] syndrome (run-together symptoms), hippodrome (a place where horses run)

duc, duct [lead] produce, induce (lead into, persuade), seduce (lead aside), reduce, aqueduct (water leader or channel), viaduct, conduct

dura [hard, lasting] durable, duration, endurance

dynam [power] dynamo (power producer), dynamic, dynamite, hydrodynamics

endo [within] endoral (within the mouth), endocardial (within the heart), endoskeletal

equi [equal] equinox, equilibrium

erg [work] energy, erg (unit of work), allergy, ergophobia (morbid fear of work), ergometer, ergonomic

fac, fact, fic, fect [do, make] factory (place where workers make goods of various kinds), fact (a thing done), manufacture, amplification, confection

fall, fals [deceive] fallacy, falsify

fer [bear, carry] ferry (carry by water), coniferous (bearing cones, as a pine tree), fertile (bearing richly), defer, infer, refer

fid, fide, feder [faith, trust] confidante, Fido, fidelity, confident, infidelity, infidel, federal, confederacy

fila, fili [thread] filament (a single thread or threadlike object), filibuster, filigree

fin [end, ended, finished] final, finite, finish, confine, fine, refine, define, finale

fix [attach] fix, fixation (the state of being attached), fixture, affix, prefix, suffix

flex, flect [bend] flex (bend), reflex (bending back), flexible, flexor (muscle for bending), inflexibility, reflect, deflect

flu, fluc, fluv [flowing] influence (to flow in), fluid, flue, flush, fluently, fluctuate (to wave in an unsteady motion)

form [form, shape] form, uniform, conform, deform, reform, perform, formative, formation, formal, formula

fort, forc [strong] fort, fortress (a strong place), fortify (make strong), forte (one's strong point), fortitude, enforce

fract, frag [break] fracture (a break), infraction, fragile (easy to break), fraction (result of breaking a whole into equal parts), refract (to break or bend)

gam [marriage] bigamy (two marriages), monogamy, polygamy (many spouses or marriages)

gastr(o) [stomach] gastric, gastronomic, gastritis (inflammation of the stomach)

gen [birth, race, produce] genesis (birth, beginning), genetics (study of heredity), eugenics (well born), genealogy (lineage by race, stock), generate, genetic

geo [earth] geometry (earth measurement), geography (earth writing), geocentric (earth centered), geology

germ [vital part] germination (to grow), germ (seed; living substance, as the *germ* of an idea), germane

gest [carry, bear] congest (bear together, clog), congestive (causing clogging), gestation

gloss, glot [tongue] glossary, polyglot (many tongues), epiglottis

glu, glo [lump, bond, glue] glue, agglutinate (make to hold in a bond), conglomerate (bond together)

grad, gress [step, go] grade (step, degree), gradual (step-by-step), graduate (make all the steps, finish a course), graduated (in steps or degrees), progress

graph, gram [write, written] graph, graphic (written, vivid), autograph (self-writing, signature), graphite (carbon used for writing), photography (light writing), phonograph (sound writing), diagram, bibliography, telegram

grat [pleasing] gratuity (mark of favor, a tip), congratulate (express pleasure over success), grateful, ingrate (not thankful)

grav [heavy, weighty] grave, gravity, aggravate, gravitate

greg [herd, group, crowd] gregarian (belonging to a herd), congregation (a group functioning together), segregate (tending to group aside or apart)

helio [sun] heliograph (an instrument for using the sun's rays to send signals), heliotrope (a plant that turns to the sun)

hema, hemo [blood] hemorrhage (an outpouring or flowing of blood), hemoglobin, hemophilia

here, hes [stick] adhere, cohere, cohesion

hetero [different] heterogeneous (different in birth), heterosexual (with interest in the opposite sex)

homo [same] homogeneous (of same birth or kind), homonyn (word with same pronunciation as another), homogenize

hum, human [earth, ground, man] humus, exhume (to take out of the ground), humane (compassion for other humans)

Hydrophobia

hydr, hydra, hydro [water] dehydrate, hydrant, hydraulic, hydraulics, hydrogen, hydrophobia (fear of water)

hypn [sleep] hypnosis, Hypnos (god of sleep), hypnotherapy (treatment of disease by hypnosis)

ignis [fire] ignite, igneous, ignition

ject [throw] deject, inject, project (throw forward), eject, object

join, junct [join] adjoining, enjoin (to lay an order upon, to command), juncture, conjunction, injunction

juven [young] juvenile, rejuvenate (to make young again)

lau, lav, lot, lut [wash] launder, lavatory, lotion, ablution (a washing away), dilute (to make a liquid thinner and weaker)

leg [law] legal (lawful; according to law), legislate (to enact a law), legislature, legitimize (make legal)

levi [light] alleviate (lighten a load), levitate (light conversation; humor)

liber, liver [free] liberty (freedom), liberal, liberalize (to make more free), deliverance

liter [letters] literary (concerned with books and writing), literature, literal, alliteration, obliterate

loc, loco [place] locality, locale, location, allocate (to assign, to place), relocate (to put back into place), locomotion (act of moving from place to place)

log, logo, ogue, ology [word, study, speech] catalog, prologue, dialogue, logogram (a symbol representing a word), zoology (animal study), psychology (mind study)

loqu, locut [talk, speak] eloquent (speaking well and forcefully), soliloquy, locution, loquacious (talkative), colloquial (talking together; conversational or informal)

luc, lum, lus, lun [light] translucent (letting light come through), lumen (a unit of light), luminary (a heavenly body; someone who shines in his or her profession), luster (sparkle, shine), Luna (the moon goddess)

magn [great] magnify (make great, enlarge), magnificent, magnanimous (great of mind or spirit), magnate, magnitude, magnum

man [hand] manual, manage, manufacture, manacle, manicure, manifest, maneuver, emancipate

mand [command] mandatory (commanded), remand (order back), mandate

mania [madness] mania (insanity, craze), monomania (mania on one idea), kleptomania, pyromania (insane tendency to set fires), maniac

mar, mari, mer [sea, pool] marine (a soldier serving on shipboard), marsh (wetland, swamp), maritime (relating to the sea and navigation), mermaid (fabled sea creature, half fish, half woman)

matri [mother] maternal (relating to the mother), matrimony, matriarchate (rulership of women), matron

medi [half, middle, between, halfway] mediate (come between, intervene), medieval (pertaining to the Middle Ages), Mediterranean (lying between lands), mediocre, medium

mega [great, million] megaphone (great sound), megalopolis (great city; an extensive urban area including a number of cities), megacycle (a million cycles), megaton

mem [remember] memo (a reminder), commemoration (the act of remembering by a memorial or ceremony), memento, memoir, memorable

meter [measure] meter (a metric measure), voltameter (instrument to measure volts), barometer, thermometer

micro [small] microscope, microfilm, microcard, microwave, micrometer (device for measuring small distances), omicron, micron (a millionth of a meter), microbe (small living thing)

migra [wander] migrate (to wander), emigrant (one who leaves a country), immigrate (to come into the land)

mit, miss [send] emit (send out, give off), remit (send back, as money due), submit, admit, commit, permit, transmit (send across), omit, intermittent (sending between, at intervals), mission, missile

mob, mot, mov [move] mobile (capable of moving), motionless (without motion), motor, emotional (moved strongly by feelings), motivate, promotion, demote, movement

mon [warn, remind] monument (a reminder or memorial of a person or an event), admonish (warn), monitor, premonition (forewarning)

mor, mort [mortal, death] mortal (causing death or destined for death), immortal (not subject to death), mortality (rate of death), mortician (one who prepares the dead for burial), mortuary (place for the dead, a morgue)

morph [form] amorphous (with no form, shapeless), metamorphosis (a change of form, as a caterpillar into a butterfly), morphology

multi [many, much] multifold (folded many times), multilinguist (one who speaks many languages), multiped (an organism with many feet), multiply

nat, nasc [to be born, to spring forth] innate (inborn), natal, native, nativity, renascence (a rebirth, a revival)

neur [nerve] neuritis (inflammation of a nerve), neurology (study of nervous systems), neurologist (one who practices neurology), neural, neurosis, neurotic

nom [law, order] autonomy (self-law, self-government), astronomy, gastronomy (art or science of good eating), economy

nomen, nomin [name] nomenclature, nominate (name someone for an office)

nov [new] novel (new, strange, not formerly known), renovate (to make like new again), novice, nova, innovate

nox, noc [night] nocturnal, equinox (equal nights), noctilucent (shining by night)

numer [number] numeral (a figure expressing a number), numeration (act of counting), enumerate (count out, one by one), innumerable

omni [all, every] omnipotent (all-powerful), omniscient (all-knowing), omnipresent (present everywhere), omnivorous

onym [name] anonymous (without name), synonym, pseudonym (false name), antonym (name of opposite meaning)

oper [work] operate (to labor, function), cooperate (work together)

ortho [straight, correct] orthodox (of the correct or accepted opinion), orthodontist (tooth straightener), orthopedic (originally pertaining to straightening a child), unorthodox

pac [peace] pacifist (one for peace only; opposed to war), pacify (make peace, quiet), Pacific Ocean (peaceful ocean)

pan [all] panacea (cure-all), pandemonium (place of all the demons, wild disorder), pantheon (place of all the gods in mythology)

pater, patr [father] paternity (fatherhood, responsibility), patriarch (head of the tribe, family), patriot, patron (a wealthy person who supports as would a father)

path, pathy [feeling, suffering] pathos (feeling of pity, sorrow), sympathy, antipathy (feeling against), apathy (without feeling), empathy (feeling or identifying with another), telepathy (far feeling; thought transference)

ped, pod [foot] pedal (lever for a foot), impede (get the feet in a trap, hinder), pedestal (foot or base of a statue), pedestrian (foot traveler), centipede, tripod (three-footed support), podiatry (care of the feet), antipodes (opposite feet)

pedo [child] orthopedic, pedagogue (child leader; teacher), pediatrics (medical care of children)

pel, puls [drive, urge] compel, dispel, expel, repel, propel, pulse, impulse, pulsate, compulsory, expulsion, repulsive

pend, pens, pond [hang, weigh] pendant pendulum, suspend, appendage, pensive (weighing thought), ponderous

phil [love] philosophy (love of wisdom), philanthropy, philharmonic, bibliophile, Philadelphia (city of brotherly love)

phobia [fear] claustrophobia (fear of closed spaces), acrophobia (fear of high places), hydrophobia (fear of water)

phon [sound] phonograph, phonetic (pertaining to sound), symphony (sounds with or together)

photo [light] photograph (light-writing), photoelectric, photogenic (artistically suitable for being photographed), photosynthesis (action of light on chlorophyll to make carbohydrates)

plac [please] placid (calm, peaceful), placebo, placate, complacent

plu, plur, plus [more] plural (more than one), pluralist (a person who holds more than one office), plus (indicating that something more is to be added)

pneuma, pneumon [breath] pneumatic (pertaining to air, wind, or other gases), pneumonia (disease of the lungs)

pod (see *ped*)

poli [city] metropolis (mother city), police, politics, Indianapolis, Acropolis (high city, upper part of Athens), megalopolis

pon, pos, pound [place, put] postpone (put afterward), component, opponent (one put against), proponent, expose, impose, deposit, posture (how one places oneself), position, expound, impound

pop [people] population, populous (full of people), popular

port [carry] porter (one who carries), portable, transport (carry across), report, export, import, support, transportation

portion [part, share] portion (a part; a share, as a portion of pie), proportion (the relation of one share to others)

prehend [seize] comprehend (seize with the mind), apprehend (seize a criminal), comprehensive (seizing much, extensive)

prim, prime [first] primacy (state of being first in rank), prima donna (the first lady of opera), primitive (from the earliest or first time), primary, primal, primeval

proto [first] prototype (the first model made), protocol, protagonist, protozoan

psych [mind, soul] psyche (soul, mind), psychiatry (healing of the mind), psychology, psychosis (serious mental disorder), psychotherapy (mind treatment), psychic

punct [point, dot] punctual (being exactly on time), punctuation, puncture, acupuncture

reg, recti [straighten] regiment, regular, regulate, rectify (make straight), correct, direction

ri, ridi, risi [laughter] deride (mock, jeer at), ridicule (laughter at the expense of another, mockery), ridiculous, derision

rog, roga [ask] prerogative (privilege; asking before), interrogation (questioning; the act of questioning), derogatory

rupt [break] rupture (break), interrupt (break into), abrupt (broken off), disrupt (break apart), erupt (break out), incorruptible (unable to be broken down)

sacr, sanc, secr [sacred] sacred, sanction, sacrosanct, consecrate, desecrate

salv, salu [safe, healthy] salvation (act of being saved), salvage, salutation

sat, satis [enough] satient (giving pleasure, satisfying), saturate, satisfy (to give pleasure to; to give as much as is needed)

sci [know] science (knowledge), conscious (knowing, aware), omniscient (knowing everything)

scope [see, watch] telescope, microscope, kaleidoscope (instrument for seeing beautiful forms), periscope, stethoscope

scrib, script [write] scribe (a writer), scribble, manuscript (written by hand), inscribe, describe, subscribe, prescribe

sed, sess, sid [sit] sediment (that which sits or settles out of a liquid), session (a sitting), obsession (an idea that sits stubbornly in the mind), possess, preside (sit before), president, reside, subside

sen [old] senior, senator, senile (old; showing the weakness of old age)

sent, sens [feel] sentiment (feeling), consent, resent, dissent, sentimental (having strong feeling or emotion), sense, sensation, sensitive, sensory, dissension

sequ, secu, sue [follow] sequence (following of one thing after another), sequel, consequence, subsequent, prosecute, consecutive (following in order), second (following "first"), ensue, pursue

serv [save, serve] servant, service, preserve, subservient, servitude, conserve, reservation, deserve, conservation

sign, signi [sign, mark, seal] signal (a gesture or sign to call attention), signature (the mark of a person written in his or her own handwriting), design, insignia (distinguishing marks)

simil, simul [like, resembling] similar (resembling in many respects), assimilate (to make similar to), simile, simulate (pretend; put on an act to make a certain impression)

sist, sta, stit [stand] persist (stand firmly; unyielding; continue), assist (to stand by with help), circumstance, stamina (power to withstand, to endure), status (standing), state, static, stable, stationary, substitute (to stand in for another)

solus [alone] soliloquy, solitaire, solitude, solo

solv, solu [loosen] solvent (a loosener, a dissolver), solve, absolve (loosen from, free from), resolve, soluble, solution, resolution, resolute, dissolute (loosened morally)

somnus [sleep] insomnia (not being able to sleep), somnambulist (a sleepwalker)

soph [wise] sophomore (wise fool), philosophy (love of wisdom), sophisticated

spec, spect, spic [look] specimen (an example to look at, study), specific, aspect, spectator (one who looks), spectacle, speculate, inspect, respect, prospect, retrospective (looking backward), introspective, expect, conspicuous

sphere [ball, sphere] stratosphere (the upper portion of the atmosphere), hemisphere (half of the earth), spheroid

spir [breath] spirit (breath), conspire (breathe together; plot), inspire (breathe into), aspire (breathe toward), expire (breathe out; die), perspire, respiration

string, strict [draw tight] stringent (drawn tight; rigid), strict, restrict, constrict (draw tightly together), boa constrictor (snake that constricts its prey)

stru, struct [build] construe (build in the mind, interpret), structure, construct, instruct, obstruct, destruction, destroy

sume, sump [take, use, waste] consume (to use up), assume (to take; to use), sump pump (a pump that takes up water), presumption (to take or use before knowing all the facts)

tact, tang, tag, tig, ting [touch] contact, tactile, intangible (not able to be touched), intact (untouched, uninjured), tangible, contingency, contagious (able to transmit disease by touching), contiguous

tele [far] telephone (far sound), telegraph (far writing), television (far seeing), telephoto (far photography), telecast

tempo [time] tempo (rate of speed), temporary, extemporaneously, contemporary (those who live at the same time), pro tem (for the time being)

ten, tin, tain [hold] tenacious (holding fast), tenant, tenure, untenable, detention, content, pertinent, continent, obstinate, abstain, pertain, detain

tend, tent, tens [stretch, strain] tendency (a stretching; leaning), extend, intend, contend, pretend, superintend, tender, extent, tension (a stretching, strain), pretense

terra [earth] terrain, terrarium, territory, terrestrial

test [to bear witness] testament (a will; bearing witness to someone's wishes), detest, attest (bear witness to), testimony

the, theo [God, a god] monotheism (belief in one god), polytheism (belief in many gods), atheism, theology

therm [heat] thermometer, therm (heat unit), thermal, thermostat, thermos, hypothermia (subnormal temperature)

thesis, thet [place, put] antithesis (place against), hypothesis (place under), synthesis (put together), epithet

tom [cut] atom (not cuttable; smallest particle of matter), appendectomy (cutting out an appendix), tonsillectomy, dichotomy (cutting in two; a division), anatomy (cutting, dissecting to study structure)

tort, tors [twist] torture (twisting to inflict pain), retort (twist back, reply sharply), extort (twist out), distort (twist out of shape), contort, torsion (act of twisting, as a torsion bar)

tox [poison] toxic (poisonous), intoxicate, antitoxin

tract, tra [draw, pull] tractor, attract, subtract, tractable (can be handled), abstract (to draw away), subtrahend (the number to be drawn away from another)

trib [pay, bestow] tribute (to pay honor to), contribute (to give money to a cause), attribute, retribution, tributary

turbo [disturb] turbulent, disturb, turbid, turmoil

typ [print] type, prototype (first print; model), typical, typography, typewriter, typology (study of types, symbols), typify

ultima [last] ultimate, ultimatum (the final or last offer that can be made)

uni [one] unicorn (a legendary creature with one horn), unify (make into one), university, unanimous, universal

vac [empty] vacate (to make empty), vacuum (a space entirely devoid of matter), evacuate (to remove troops or people), vacation, vacant

vale, vali, valu [strength, worth] valiant, equivalent (of equal worth), validity (truth; legal strength), evaluate (find out the value), value, valor (value; worth)

ven, vent [come] convene (come together, assemble), intervene (come between), venue, convenient, avenue, circumvent (come or go around), invent, prevent

ver, veri [true] very, aver (say to be true, affirm), verdict, verity (truth), verify (show to be true), verisimilitude

vert, vers [turn] avert (turn away), divert (turn aside, amuse), invert (turn over), introvert (turn inward), convertible, reverse (turn back), controversy (a turning against; a dispute), versatile (turning easily from one skill to another)

vic, vicis [change, substitute] vicarious, vicar, vicissitude

vict, vinc [conquer] victor (conqueror, winner), evict (conquer out, expel), convict (prove guilty), convince (conquer mentally, persuade), invincible (not conquerable)

vid, vis [see] video, television, evident, provide, providence, visible, revise, supervise (oversee), vista, visit, vision

viv, vita, vivi [alive, life] revive (make live again), survive (live beyond, outlive), vivid, vivacious (full of life), vitality

voc [call] vocation (a calling), avocation (occupation not one's calling), convocation (a calling together), invocation, vocal

vol [will] malevolent, benevolent (one of goodwill), volunteer, volition

volcan, vulcan [fire] volcano (a mountain erupting fiery lava), volcanize (to undergo volcanic heat), Vulcan (Roman god of fire)

volvo [turn about, roll] revolve, voluminous (winding), voluble (easily turned about or around), convolution (a twisting)

vor [eat greedily] voracious, carnivorous (flesh eating), herbivorous (plant eating), omnivorous (eating everything), devour

zo [animal] zoo (short for zoological garden), zoology (study of animal life), zodiac (circle of animal constellations), zoomorphism (being in the form of an animal), protozoa (one-celled animals)

The Human Body

capit	head	gastro	stomach	osteo	bone
card	heart	glos	tongue	ped	foot
corp	body	hema	blood	pneuma	breathe
dent	tooth	man	hand	psych	mind
derm	skin	neur	nerve	spir	breath

STUDY
SKILLS

"Everyone teaches, everyone learns."

—Arnold Bennett

Improving
CLASSROOM Skills

To do well in school you must do well individually and as a member of a group. Individually, you must manage your time and complete your assignments. As a group member, you need to listen to others, observe, respond, and ask questions.

Inside the classroom, you're part of a learning team. Your teacher heads up the team, introduces new concepts and assigns the reading and other activities that give you the information you need to understand the concepts. Your job is to supply the enthusiasm and effort. Without that personal commitment, learning will not happen. This section of your handbook covers the skills you need to succeed in school, both as an individual and as a member of a group.

Preview

- ○ **Group Skills**
- ○ **Planning Skills**
- ○ **Completing Assignments**

The ability to use group skills (also called "people skills") is very important for success in school, at home, and in the workplace.

Group Skills

You've probably worked on your share of group projects, so you already know that group work doesn't always go smoothly. Developing the following skills will help you work well with others: **listening, observing, cooperating, clarifying, and responding.**

Listening

Group members must listen carefully to one another, focusing on *what* is being said, not on *who* is saying it. As you listen to an idea, think about how it relates to the group and to the group's goals. Take notes, and ask questions after the speaker finishes sharing the idea.

Listen actively. Good listeners are active listeners. This means you should let the speaker know you are listening by making eye contact, nodding your head, and remaining attentive. You can also let the speaker know you have been listening by asking a good question, summarizing what has been said, or offering a compliment or comment.

Listen accurately. Hearing is not the same as listening. Hearing involves your ears; listening involves your ears and your mind. Always think about what you hear. Listen with pen in hand. Jot down a word, phrase, or question to help you remember what is being said and what you want to add. Then, when the speaker stops, offer your ideas.

Know when—and how—to interrupt. If you are a good listener, you will sooner or later have a comment, a question, or an important fact to add. Even so, interrupting someone who is speaking is not usually a good idea. If you feel you must interrupt the speaker, say, "Excuse me, Janet, when you finish I have something to add." Sometimes it is also necessary to interrupt a group member who has wandered off the topic. When that happens, you can say, "Excuse me, but I think we should get back to the main point."

Learn how to respond when you are interrupted. When you are interrupted without good reason by a group member, you can say, "I wasn't finished making my point yet," or "Could you please wait until I'm finished?" Whatever you say, say it courteously. (You can discourage interruptions by keeping what you say short and to the point.)

Observing

Observing means paying attention to the body language and tone of voice of each group member.

Watch body language. At times you can "see" what a person is saying or feeling. Pay attention to body language, which can tell you how people are feeling about the discussion.

Listen to tone of voice. Remember, it's not always *what* people say; it's *how* they say it. A person's tone of voice can tell you a lot about how that person is feeling.

Cooperating

Cooperating means using common sense and common courtesy.

Contribute your ideas. Share your ideas, and, if your idea builds on someone else's, give that person credit. ("I like what Eduardo said, and he gave me the idea that we could . . . ")

Challenge ideas, not people. Challenge the idea, not the person who contributed it. Say something like "David, I'm not sure that idea will work, because . . . " instead of "You're not thinking straight."

Never use put-downs. Put-downs must be avoided in group work. They not only disrupt the group, but also destroy members' self-confidence.

> Cooperating means "working together."
> It means using common sense and common courtesy—and sharing a common goal.

Clarifying

Clarifying means listening closely, asking questions, and giving clear examples.

Ask questions. When a group gets bogged down or loses direction, a good question can help members refocus. You might, for example, say, "Tom, what do you think about our plan?"

Offer to explain or clarify. If what you say is long or complex, you can end by asking, "Are there any questions?" You may also summarize what you've said and give an example to illustrate your point.

Request help or clarification when needed. If you're not sure you understand something, summarize it and ask, "Is that right, or did I miss something?" You may also ask another group member to clarify something for you.

Responding

When you work in a group, nearly everything you say and do is a response to what someone else has said or done. First, you hear others' statements and observe their behavior. Second, you take a moment to think about the ways you could respond. Third, you choose your response.

Think before responding. Imagine someone making the statement "Pumpkinheads is a dumb group." Before you knew about group skills, you might have responded with "Yeah, well, I think you're dumb." If you ever do respond in this way, you're headed into a dead-end argument instead of a discussion.

But you can choose a better response. You can avoid an argument by saying, "Everyone is entitled to his or her own opinion." You can open up the discussion by asking, "Why do you feel they're dumb?" Or "What do you mean by 'dumb'?"

Learn how to disagree. Never say, "I disagree *with you.*" Say instead, "I disagree. I think Pumpkinheads is a great group." This is disagreeing with the idea, not the speaker. You may also list your reasons for disagreeing. Also, instead of saying "I disagree," you can ask the speaker a few questions, questions showing that important points have been left out. After more discussion, the speaker may change his or her position—or you may change yours.

Making Decisions

It's important to understand how groups make decisions and that decisions made by a group can be as democratic as its members like. Here are some of the ways decisions are made.

Leader's Choice The group leader makes a decision based on choices offered by group members.

Expert's Choice An expert is invited to give advice or make the decision for the group.

Poll A vote or survey taken of individuals outside the group is conducted to guide the group's decision.

Voting Group members vote on a list of choices.

Consensus Group members continue to discuss choices until everyone in the group agrees.

Planning Skills

Nothing much happens without a plan. Think of any accomplishment—from writing a terrific research paper to being elected president, from winning a game to sending people to the moon. No matter what you think of, it happened because someone made a plan and put that plan into action.

Now consider your life. What do you think will happen if you don't make a plan? Hmm . . . On the other hand, if you do make a plan, you can achieve just about anything you set out to do.

Time-Management Basics

Managing time is a must-have planning skill. You have a limited amount of time, and an unlimited number of things you could do with it. You must use your time to do the things that will help you reach your goals and achieve your dreams.

Break big tasks into smaller tasks. Big achievements and big assignments can't be completed in a day. But they'll never be completed if you don't pick a day and begin. When you have a big job to do, figure out how much of it you can tackle each day and each week until it's done. Then pick a day to begin.

Keep a schedule. Buy or make a planning calendar and put all your important "things to do" on it. That way you won't forget, get sidetracked, or end up with too much to do the night before a deadline. Try to plan out a week in advance, so there's time for everything.

Plan your study time. Good advice, but most of us seldom take it. Good planning means having everything you need where you need it. Schedule your study time as early in the day as you can, take short breaks, keep snacks to a minimum, interact with the page by asking questions (out loud, if no one objects), and summarize what you've learned before turning out the light.

Be disciplined, but flexible. Stick to your schedule as much as possible. When you have to make a change (you may get sick or someone may cancel or change an appointment), look for the best way to adjust your schedule. If play rehearsal is cancelled, use that time to get ahead on your assignments, so you'll have time to go to a make-up rehearsal next week.

Completing Assignments

Right now, schoolwork is a big part of your life. If you plan your assignments so that you can do a good job and finish on time, you're well on your way to developing planning skills that will serve you for a lifetime.

Plan Ahead

Before you sit down . . .

- **Know what you're doing.** Before you sit down to work on your assignments, know exactly what your assignments are and when they are due.
- **Know your time frame.** Figure out how much time each assignment will take. (The more you do this, the better you'll get at it.)
- **Break things down.** Remember, break big assignments into smaller ones, and do a little each day.
- **Keep a schedule.** Write your assignments on your weekly and daily planning calendars.
- **Have a regular study spot.** Find a spot that's quiet, well lighted, and stocked with supplies (pens and pencils, highlighters, paper, dictionary, handbook, and so on).
- **Have a regular study time.** Having a set time to study will help you get into the right frame of mind and use your time well. Choose a time when you're alert.

Do the Work

When you sit down . . .

- **Review directions carefully.** Before you begin, make sure you know what you're supposed to do.
- **Use study strategies.** See the "Study-Reading Skills" chapter on pages 357-366 for helpful strategies and guidelines.
- **Stay focused.** Avoid distractions such as phone calls and television.
- **Plan breaks and rewards.** Plan to get a certain amount of work done before you take a break. Keep your breaks short and do something that refreshes you. Reward yourself when you finish for the day or complete a big project.
- **Keep a list of questions.** Make notes about anything you don't understand, so you can look for further information or ask your teacher or a classmate questions.

"A good listener is not only popular everywhere, but after awhile he gets to know something."
—Wilson Mizner

LISTENING and NOTE-TAKING Skills

Experts have long told us that people remember only about half of what they hear—even if they're tested immediately after hearing it. A couple of months later, that percentage drops to 25 percent. That may be no big deal if you're listening to your favorite morning disc jockey, but if you only remember 25 percent of what you heard in your history class, you may be in big trouble.

Listening is a skill, and like all other skills, it can be improved with time and practice. The same is true for note taking. In fact, the two skills work hand in hand: You will be a better listener if you take good notes, and you will take better notes if you listen carefully. This section of your handbook introduces guidelines and strategies designed to improve both your listening and note-taking skills. And, if you read carefully, you may just pick up a bonus or two along the way.

Preview

- Improving Listening Skills
- Improving Note-Taking Skills
- Using a Note-Taking Guide
- Quick Guide: Creating a Shorthand System

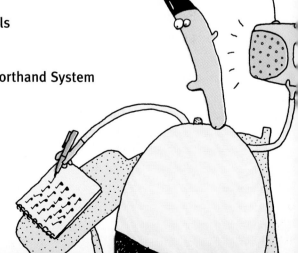

Improving Listening Skills

Someone (probably an English teacher) once observed that there must be a reason why people have two ears and only one mouth. Not everyone takes the hint, though; plenty of people still do more talking than listening. Maybe that's because listening takes effort. To really listen, you have to concentrate on what is being said, and concentration is work. Plus, there are all kinds of things that can make listening extra challenging: being distracted by noise, being tired, being too hot or too cold, and so on. It takes determination to listen well.

1. **Prepare to listen and keep a goal in mind.**

   Take time to figure out why you are listening (to gather information about a subject, to learn how to . . .). Then keep an open mind about the speaker and the topic.

2. **Listen carefully.**

   Listen not only to what the speaker is actually saying but also to what the speaker is implying (saying between the lines). The speaker's voice, tone, volume, facial expressions, and gestures can all help tell you what's really important.

3. **Listen for the facts.**

   Listen to find out the *who, when, where, what, why,* and *how* of something. This will help you learn how to pull important facts out of what you hear and arrange them in a way that makes them easier to remember.

4. **Separate fact from opinion.**

   Listen for bias or opinion disguised as fact. (See page 449.)

5. **Listen for signals.**

   Your instructor will often tell you exactly what is important. He or she may not use a megaphone to say, "Now hear this!" but it may be almost as obvious.

   Examples: And don't forget to . . .

               Remember, the best way to . . . is . . .

               The two reasons are . . .

               Four characteristics are . . .

               This all means that . . .

               The bottom line is . . .

6. **Listen for patterns of organization.**

Textbooks and lectures often follow "patterns of organization." If you can discover how a speaker has organized information and where she or he is going with the material, you have important signposts to follow. Discovering a speaker's pattern of organization is a listening skill that will increase your capacity to learn by listening. (See page 425.)

7. **Listen for details.**

Don't be satisfied with understanding the general drift of a story or a lecture. Pay full attention to what a speaker is saying. If you allow the details to slip through the cracks, you are less likely to remember what is being said. Details, examples, and anecdotes help a lecture come to life, and they also provide helpful "hooks" for your memory.

8. **Listen to directions.**

How often have you sat down, ready to begin an assignment, only to be confused because you could not remember exactly what the teacher asked you to do? Your ability to listen to directions is vital. You may be able to e-mail your teacher to ask for the directions again, but he or she may not be too impressed.

9. **Think about what is being said.**

Ask yourself how this material relates to you. What can you relate it to in your personal life to help you remember? How might you use the information in the future?

10. **Put the lecture into your own words.**

Put the speaker's statements into your own words as you take notes. Identify each main point and draw conclusions about its importance. This is one way you can begin to "own" the material.

The highest level of listening involves empathy— listening to the world through the ears of the speaker.

Improving **Note-Taking** Skills

Note taking is an active approach to learning, one that gets you personally involved in the learning process and helps you focus on and organize the information you need to study and learn.

The most important thing to understand about note taking is that you need to do more than simply listen and write. You need to **listen, think, react, question, summarize, organize, label, and write.**

Be Prepared . . .

- **Do your assigned reading before you come to class.** That way you can follow what is being discussed and don't have to look at the floor every time your teacher asks a question.
- **Have a separate notebook for each class** and an extra pen or two.
- **Label and date your notes** at the beginning of each class period.

Be Attentive . . .

- **Listen for any special instructions,** rules, or guidelines your teacher may have regarding notebooks and note taking.
- **Write your notes as neatly as time will allow;** leave space in the margin for working with your notes later.
- **Begin taking notes immediately.** Don't wait for something new or earthshaking before you begin taking notes.
- **Relate the material to something in your life** by writing a brief personal observation or reminder.
- **Use your own words** rather than copying exactly what you hear.

Be Concise . . .

- **Summarize the main ideas,** listing only the necessary details. *Remember,* taking good notes does *not* mean writing down everything.
- **Condense information.** Write your notes in phrases and lists rather than complete sentences.
- **Use abbreviations, acronyms, and symbols** (U.S., av., in., ea., lb., vs., @, #, $, %, &, +, =, w/o)
- **Develop your own shorthand method.** (See page 396.)
- **Draw simple illustrations, charts, or diagrams** in your notes whenever they will make a point clearer.

Be Organized . . .

- **Use a note-taking guide.** Choose the guide that best fits your needs, or create a variation of your own. (See pages 394-395.)
- **Write a title or heading** for each new topic covered in your notes.
- **Leave wide margins or skip a line or two between main ideas.** When you're reviewing later, you'll have room to add study notes.
- **Listen for transitions** or signal words to help you organize your notes. Number all ideas and information presented in sequence or time order.
- **Use a special system of marking** your notes to emphasize important information (underline, highlight, star, check, indent).
- **Label or mark** information that is related by cause and effect, by comparison or contrast, or by any other special way.

Be Smart . . .

- **Always copy down** (or summarize) what the teacher puts on the board or projects on an overhead.
- **Ask questions** when you don't understand something.
- **Circle those words or ideas** that you will need to look up later.
- **Don't let your notes sit** until it is time to review for a test. Read over the notes you have taken within 24 hours and recopy, add details, highlight, or summarize as necessary.
- **Jot down key words in the left-hand column.** Cover your notes and try to restate what was said about each key word.
- **Share your note-taking techniques,** abbreviations, or special markings with others; then learn from what they share with you.

TIPS for Remembering Your Notes

- ○ Relate the material to your life.
- ○ Recite ideas and facts out loud.
- ○ Draw diagrams, illustrations, and clusters.
- ○ Write about it, using your own words.
- ○ Study it with someone or teach it to someone.
- ○ Visualize it.
- ○ Study your most difficult material first.
- ○ Use acronyms, rhymes, raps, and flash cards.

Using a **Note-Taking Guide**

Note taking helps you listen better in class, organize your ideas more effectively, and remember more of what you read or hear. And the better the notes you take, the more help they can be. That's why note-taking guides have become so popular. By using the correct guide for each situation, you can make the most of your efforts. A note-taking guide can help you develop an efficient note-taking system to coordinate your text-book, lecture, and review notes.

Keeping **Text** and **Class Notes Together**

If your teacher follows the textbook closely, you can use your reading notes as a classroom note-taking guide. As you follow your notes, you'll be prepared to answer any questions your teacher may ask and you'll be ready to take additional notes as well. Simply follow along and jot down anything that helps to clarify or adds to your understanding of the material.

Use the left two-thirds of your paper for reading notes; use the right one-third for class notes.

Use this format when a teacher follows the text closely.

Chapter 10: The Disinherited

Outlined Reading Assignment	Class Notes
I. The Clash of Cultures	Early settlers had
A. Pioneer attitude toward	few problems; as
Native Americans	more trappers and
1. Uncultured	hunters moved in,
a. Lacked civilization	conflicts started.
b. Lacked religion	Native Americans
2. Easily exploited	labeled pagans.
a. Swindled in trades	
b. Set against other tribes	
3. No property rights	
a. A squatter on govt. land	Some argued that
b. False promises	because Native
c. Forced off land	Americans did not
B. Native American reaction	have the right to
to treatment	vote, they could not
1. Attitudes	own property.
a. Disappointment	
b. Bitterness	
2. Resulting Action	
a. Move	Serious clashing of
1) To designated areas	the cultures
2) farther west	followed.
b. Defend	
c. Attack	

Adding a **Review Column**

If you want to keep all your notes together, you can add a third column at the left of your page. Leave this review column blank during class; but after class, read through your notes and add key words and phrases that summarize what is in each section of your notes. This will help you review and remember your notes.

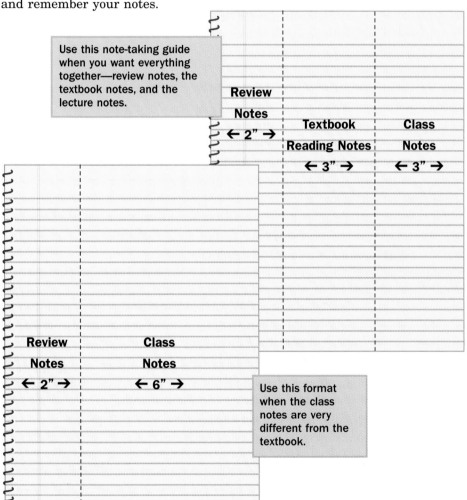

Use this note-taking guide when you want everything together—review notes, the textbook notes, and the lecture notes.

Review Notes ← 2" →

Textbook Reading Notes ← 3" →

Class Notes ← 3" →

Review Notes ← 2" →

Class Notes ← 6" →

Use this format when the class notes are very different from the textbook.

Keeping **Text** and **Class Notes Separate**

If your teacher does not base his or her lecture on the class text, you may want to keep your class and textbook notes separate. In that case, your class notes will have only two columns—a wide right column for lecture notes and a narrow left column where you can add review notes.

Quick Guide

Creating a Shorthand System

You will be taking a lot of notes during your high school career. Start now to develop your own personal shorthand system. Here are some guidelines:

● **Omit all articles** *(a, an, the).*

● **Use abbreviations without the periods.**

meas	max	min	p	pp
prev	approx	etc	esp	incl
reg	lg	sm	lbs	st
pres	Jan			

● **Use common mathematical and technical symbols.**

  +   −   =   ×   %   #   <   >   ÷   ↑   ↓ $ ||

● **Eliminate vowels from words.**

  mdl for *middle*   *psbl* for *possible*

● **Use word beginnings.**

  intro for *introduction*   *psych* for *psychology*

✱ Use your abbreviations consistently. Otherwise, you may end up wondering if *psych* means *psychology, psychiatry,* or *psychic.*

● **Create abbreviations for the most commonly used words** in a particular course. (Review your notes to find these words.) Write them and their abbreviations at the front of your notebook.

  PNS for *parasympathetic nervous system*
  QE for *quadratic equation*

● **Keep adding to your personal shorthand system.** Here are some examples to get you started:

w/	with	w/o	without
ex	for example	b/c	because
b4	before	SB	should be
SNB	should not be	2	two, to, too

"The man who has ceased to learn
ought not to be allowed to wander
around loose."
—M. M. Coady

Writing to
LEARN

Writing about a particular topic to understand it better—that's what writing to learn is all about. It's really that simple. When you write to learn, you are *not* trying to show how well you can write or how much you already know about a topic; you are writing to learn more.

When you write to learn, you should write freely and naturally. Most writing-to-learn activities are short, spontaneous, and exploratory. They are almost never graded or corrected for mechanical errors. Some educators now believe that writing to learn is the best way to truly learn anything, from math to music. This chapter will provide you with a variety of writing-to-learn strategies that you can try.

Preview

- ○ Learning Logs
- ○ Writing-to-Learn Activities
- ○ Writing a Paraphrase
- ○ Writing a Summary

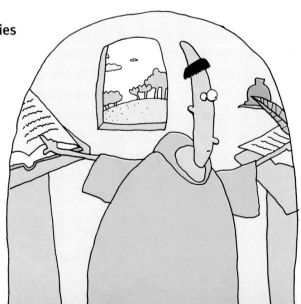

Learning Logs

A learning log is a notebook in which you take notes of a different kind. It is a place where you can "dig deeper" into what you have learned from lectures, class discussions, group projects, experiments, and reading assignments. Approach writing in your learning log the same way you approach writing in your journal. (See pages 144-146.)

Keeping a Learning Log

A learning log gets you actively involved in your course work and gives you the opportunity to freely explore important ideas. This free flow of ideas and questions promotes true learning. Here are some specific ideas for writing in a learning log.

- **Write a summary** of a learning experience (lecture, discussion, etc.). Add your own conclusions, telling what information you found most valuable or interesting, what opinions you agreed with or disagreed with, and why.

- **Personalize new ideas and concepts.** Consider how this new information relates to what you already know.

- **Write about what you still want to know** about a topic. Brainstorm ways to find this information.

- **Discuss your course work with a particular audience:** a young child, a foreign exchange student, an alien from another planet, an object.

- **Question what you are learning.** How important are the concepts you are learning? One way to discover this is to write a dialogue.

- **Express ideas and information in pictures,** charts, and maps.

- **Start a glossary** of important and interesting vocabulary words. Use these words in your log entries.

- **Argue *for* or *against* a topic.** The topic can be anything that comes up in a discussion, in a lecture, or in your reading.

- **Write about how you are doing in a certain class.** Are you learning as much as you can, or doing as well as you had hoped? Is some of the material especially hard for you? What can you do to improve?

Sample Learning Logs

The sample learning-log entries below were written in response to an article in a science magazine and a lecture in a chemistry class. Notice how both entries are personalized.

Response to a Science Article

I just read an article in a science magazine about mosquitoes and the diseases they can carry. I thought flies and mosquitoes were a pain just because they bite. But it turns out that you can get more than an itchy bump from a mosquito. They can carry viruses that cause serious diseases such as malaria and encephalitis. Doctors think that, in all of history, more people have died of malaria than any other disease. Malaria was even one of the reasons why the Roman Empire fell. In 1999, seven people in New York City died from encephalitis caused by mosquito bites. Health officials are very concerned about this recent outbreak.

Response to a Chemistry Lecture

Our teacher used the *Hindenburg* as an example of how noble gases are different from other elements. The *Hindenburg* was a zeppelin—a huge, cylinder-shaped, flying balloon that could carry passengers. It was filled with hydrogen—which is not a noble gas—and reacted with oxygen in the air, causing the zeppelin to burn. Thirty-six people died. If helium had been used instead, it also would have kept the zeppelin airborne, but it wouldn't have burned. This is because it is a noble gas, meaning it doesn't interact with other elements. That's why balloons and dirigibles use helium now, not hydrogen. This got me thinking about how what you don't know can hurt you. Chemistry can actually be useful in real life!

Writing-to-Learn Activities

Writing to learn is essentially exploratory writing. What form it takes is strictly up to you, as long as it encourages thinking and learning. You might be perfectly satisfied with free, nonstop writing; others might find clustering or listing meaningful. Still others might enjoy a variety of writing activities similar to those that follow.

Admit Slips ◉ Admit slips are brief pieces of writing called for by the teacher at the beginning of class, like an "admission" ticket. An admit slip can be a summary of last night's reading, a question about class material, a request for the teacher to review a particular point, or anything else that makes sense to you.

Debates ◉ Try splitting your mind into two "persons." Have one side disagree with your thinking on a subject, and have the other side defend it. Keep the debate going as long as you can.

Dialogues ◉ In a dialogue, you create an imaginary conversation between yourself and a character (a historical figure, for example) or between two characters (from a story, for example). Dialogue can bring information to life, helping you to better understand a particular subject or historical period.

Dramatic Scenarios ◉ In a dramatic scenario, you project yourself into a unit of study and develop a scenario (plot) that can be played out in writing. If the unit is World War II, for example, you may put yourself in President Truman's shoes the day before he decided to drop the first atomic bomb.

Exit Slips ◉ Write a note at the end of class, evaluating, questioning, or summarizing something about the day's lesson. Turn in your exit slip to your teacher before you leave the classroom.

First Thoughts ◉ Write down your immediate impressions about a topic you are preparing to study. These writings will help you focus on the new subject matter.

How-To Writing ◉ Write instructions or directions on how to perform a certain task in order to clarify and remember the information.

Instant Versions ◉ In an instant version of a paper or report, you write a "final draft" immediately—no prewriting, no planning. Writing instant versions can help you find a focus and discover what you know (or don't know) about the subject.

Nutshelling ◉ Try writing down, in one sentence, the importance of something you've heard, seen, or read.

Personal Summary ℮ Summarize a section of reading or a lecture—putting the material into your own words and relating it to your own life whenever possible.

> I remember hearing only bad things about cholesterol. I know a man who has been on a low-cholesterol diet for many years. He still has high levels of "bad" cholesterol in his blood. Why does the body produce something that can cause such serious problems as heart attacks? Then I heard there's good cholesterol and that eating certain things can produce "good" cholesterol instead of the "bad." So why doesn't a diet low in LDL- and VLDL-cholesterol automatically mean only HDL, or good cholesterol, will be produced?

Picture Outlines ℮ Instead of using a traditional format, you can organize your thoughts into a picture outline. For example, a picture outline can easily capture the main points from a lecture on the makeup and function of a particular organ.

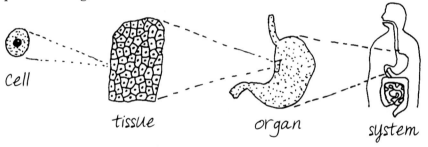

Cell   tissue   organ   system

Predicting ℮ Stop at a key point in a book or lesson and write what you think will happen next. Predicting works especially well with materials that have a strong cause-and-effect relationship.

Pointed Questions ℮ Keep asking yourself *why* in your writing until you run out of answers.

Role-Playing ℮ Imagine yourself in a different role (a reporter, a historical or fictional character, an animal) and write about a topic from this new point of view.

Stop 'n' Write ℮ At any point in a reading assignment, stop and write about what you've just read. This allows you to evaluate your understanding of the topic.

Unsent Letters ℮ Write a letter to anyone (or anything) on a topic related to the subject you are studying. Unsent letters allow you to personalize the subject matter and then share it with another person—real or imagined.

Writing a **Paraphrase**

A paraphrase is a type of summary that is written in your own words. It is particularly good for clarifying the meaning of a difficult or symbolic piece of writing (some poems, proverbs, documents). Because it often includes your interpretation, it is sometimes longer than the original.

Writing **Guidelines**

1. **Skim the passage** or selection quickly.

2. **Then read the passage carefully,** noting key words and ideas.

3. **Look up any unfamiliar words.**

4. **Summarize each idea** of the passage in a clear statement.

5. **Expand or reword the text to make it clearer,** maintaining the meaning and tone of the original.

Sample **Paraphrase**

Notice that the paraphrase below "translates" some of the out-of-date language (*faculties, thither*) into words that make sense to modern readers. Notice, too, how the paraphrase replaces the male pronouns in the original with gender-free words, without changing Emerson's meaning.

ORIGINAL PASSAGE

Each man has his own vocation. The talent is the call. There is one direction in which all space is open to him. He has faculties silently inviting him thither to endless exertion. He is like a ship in a river; he runs against obstructions on every side but one; on that side all obstruction is taken away, and he sweeps serenely over a deepening channel into an infinite sea.

—Ralph Waldo Emerson, "Spiritual Laws"

> **Paraphrase**
>
> Everyone has a calling in life. All people have abilities, talents, and energies silently inviting them to their life's work. Those who respond to their calling are like ships in a river flowing toward the sea. There are banks on both sides, and there is only one direction in which to move with ease. Those who try to avoid that one direction will run into obstacles wherever they turn. And, like ships moving surely to the sea, those who follow their true calling will move with great peace of mind toward the open sea of unlimited possibilities.

Writing a **Summary**

Writing an effective summary is an excellent way to understand and remember what you have read. Follow the guidelines below and read through the model on the next page.

Writing **Guidelines**

1. **Skim the selection** first to get the overall meaning.

2. **Read the selection carefully,** paying particular attention to key words and phrases. (Check the meaning of any words you're unsure of.)

3. **List the main ideas** on your own paper—without looking at the selection!

4. **Review the selection** a final time so that you have the overall meaning clearly in mind as you begin to write.

5. **Write a summary** of the major ideas, using your own words except for those "few" words in the original that cannot be changed. Keep the following points in mind as you write:
   - Your opening (topic) sentence should be a clear statement of the main idea of the original selection.
   - Stick to the essential information. Names, dates, times, places, and similar facts are usually essential; examples, descriptive details, and adjectives are usually not needed.
   - Try to state each important idea in one clear sentence.
   - Use a concluding sentence that ties all of your thoughts together and brings the summary to an effective end.

6. **Check your summary** for accuracy and conciseness. Ask yourself the following questions:
   - Have I included all of the main ideas?
   - Have I cut or combined most of the descriptive details? (Your summary should be about one-half the length of the original.)
   - Will another person understand the main points simply by reading my summary?

HELP FILE

To write a *précis* (a special form of summary), do the following:
- Keep the same voice and perspective as the original.
- Use paraphrases instead of direct quotations.
- Be brief.

Sample **Summary**

The summary below is an example of how textbook information can be condensed effectively. Notice that the opening sentence of the summary contains both a definition of the topic and the main point of the summary. The writer goes on to list only the essential details and concludes with a thought-provoking statement.

ORIGINAL TEXT

"Acid rain" is precipitation with a high concentration of acids. The acids are produced by sulfur dioxide, nitrogen oxide, and other chemicals that are created by the burning of fossil fuels. Acid rain is known to have a gradual, destructive effect on plant and aquatic life.

The greatest harm from acid rain is caused by sulfur dioxide, a gas produced from coal. As coal is burned in large industrial and power plant boilers, the sulfur it contains is turned into sulfur dioxide. This invisible gas is funneled up tall smokestacks and released into the atmosphere some 350-600 feet above the ground. As a result, the effects of the gas are seldom felt immediately. Instead, the gas is carried by the wind for hundreds and sometimes thousands of miles before it floats back down to earth. For example, sulfur dioxide produced in Pennsylvania at noon on Monday may not show up again until early Tuesday when it settles into the lakes and soil of rural Wisconsin.

Adding to the problem is the good possibility that the sulfur dioxide has undergone a chemical change while in flight. By simply taking on another molecule of oxygen, the sulfur dioxide could be changed to sulfur trioxide. Sulfur trioxide, when mixed with water, creates sulfuric acid—a highly toxic acid. If the sulfur trioxide enters a lake or stream, the resulting acid can kill fish, algae, and plankton. This, in turn, can interrupt the reproductive cycle of other life-forms, causing a serious imbalance in nature. If the sulfuric acid enters the soil, it can work on metals such as aluminum and mercury and set them free to poison both the soil and water.

Summary

"Acid rain," the term for precipitation that contains a high concentration of harmful chemicals, is gradually damaging our environment. The greatest harm from acid rain is caused by sulfur dioxide, a gas produced from the burning of coal. This gas, which is released into the atmosphere by industries using coal-fired boilers, is carried by the wind for hundreds of miles. By the time this gas has floated back to earth, it has often changed from sulfur dioxide to sulfur trioxide. Sulfur trioxide, when mixed with water, forms sulfuric acid. This acid can kill both plant and aquatic life and upset the natural balance so important to the cycle of life.

> "To treat your facts with
> imagination is one thing;
> to imagine your facts is another."
>
> —John Burroughs

TEST-TAKING Skills

The key to doing well on tests is being well prepared. This is true of any test—essay, objective, or standardized. To be well prepared, start with a solid test-taking plan.

Your plan should include a system for organizing the test material, reviewing it (perhaps with a partner), remembering it, and, finally, using it on the test itself. Having a good overall plan will keep you on track, reduce "test anxiety," and give you the best possible test results. Studying the guidelines and samples in this chapter will help you plan your test-taking strategies.

Preview

- Taking the Essay Test
- Quick Guide
- Taking an Objective Test
- Tips for Taking Classroom Tests
- Taking a Standardized Test
- Tips for Taking Standardized Tests
- Taking District or State Writing Tests

Taking the Essay Test

One of the most common (and most challenging) tests in high school is the essay test. There are certain skills or strategies that can help you face this challenge.

Understanding the Question

The first step to handling an essay test effectively is to read the question several times until you are sure you know what the teacher is asking. As you read, pay special attention to the key words found in the question. For example, if you are asked to *contrast* two things, and you *classify* them instead, you have missed the point. Your test score will suffer.

Key Words

Here is a list of key terms, along with a definition and an example of how each is used in a typical essay question.

Classify ℮ To classify is to place persons or things (especially animals and plants) together in a group because they are alike or similar. In science there is an order that all groups follow when it comes to classifying or categorizing: phylum (or division), class, order, family, genus, species, and variety.

Compare ℮ To compare is to use examples to show how things are similar and different, with the greater emphasis on similarities.

Compare the British and American forms of government.

Contrast ℮ To contrast is to use examples to show how things are different in one or more important ways.

Contrast the views of the North and South on the issue of states' rights.

Define ℮ To define is to give a clear, concise definition or meaning for a term. Defining can involve identifying the class to which an item belongs and telling how it differs from other items in that class.

Define what is meant by the term "filibuster."

Describe ℮ To describe is to tell how something looks or to give a general impression of it.

Describe Scout's appearance on the night of the Halloween party.

Diagram ℮ To diagram is to explain with lines or pictures—a flowchart, a map, or some other graphic device. Generally, a good diagram will label the important points or parts. (See page 355.)

Diagram our town's government officials according to level of responsibility.

Discuss @ To discuss is to talk about an issue from all sides. (You must organize discussion answers carefully in order to stay on track.)

Discuss the long-term effects of the atomic bomb.

Evaluate @ To evaluate is to make a value judgment, to give the pluses and minuses backed up with evidence (facts, figures, instances, etc.).

Evaluate the contributions of the automobile to the average American's overall standard of living.

Explain @ To explain is to make clear, to analyze, to show a process. Although it is similar to the term *discuss, explain* places more emphasis on cause-and-effect relationships and step-by-step sequences. (See page 440.)

Explain the immediate effects of the atomic bomb on Hiroshima.

Illustrate @ To illustrate means to show the reader a law, rule, or principle through specific examples and instances. A quickly drawn diagram or graphic aid may be part of your answer.

Illustrate the relationship between the Senate and the House of Representatives.

Justify @ To justify is to tell why a position or point of view is good or right. A justification stresses the advantages over the disadvantages.

Justify the U.S.A.'s intervention in Cuban-Russian relations during Kennedy's administration.

Outline @ To outline is to organize a set of facts or ideas by listing main points and subpoints. A good outline shows at a glance how topics or ideas fit together or relate to one another. (See page 108.)

Outline the events in the Tom Robinson affair.

Prove @ To prove means to bring out the truth by giving evidence and facts to back up your point.

Attempt to prove that capital punishment is not an effective deterrent to crime.

Review @ To review is to reexamine or to summarize the major points of the topic, usually in chronological (time) order or in decreasing order of importance.

Review the steps leading to the founding of the United Nations.

State @ To state means to present a brief, concise statement of a position, fact, or point of view.

State your reasons for having taken the position you hold on states' rights.

Summarize @ To summarize is to present the main points of an issue in a shortened form. Details, illustrations, and examples are usually omitted.

Summarize Lincoln's reasons for issuing the Emancipation Proclamation.

Planning and Writing the Essay Test Answer

In addition to understanding the key words, you must also understand the process of writing the answer.

1. **Read the question** several times. (Pay special attention to the key word being used in the question.)

2. **Rephrase the question** into a thesis statement (topic sentence) with a clear point. *Note:* It often works well to drop the key word from your thesis statement.

> **Question:** *Explain* the immediate effects of the atomic bomb on Hiroshima.
>
> **Thesis statement:** The immediate effects of the atomic bomb on Hiroshima were devastating.

3. **Outline or list the main points** you plan to cover in your answer. Time will probably not allow you to include all supporting details in your outline.

4. **Write your essay** (or paragraph). Begin with your thesis statement (or topic sentence). Add the necessary background information and then write your answer, following your outline of main points.

Sample One-Paragraph Answer

If you feel that one paragraph can adequately answer the question, simply use the main points of your outline to support your thesis statement. (Your thesis statement can serve as your topic sentence.)

Question: *Explain* the immediate effects of the atomic bomb on Hiroshima.

> **The immediate effects of the atomic bomb on Hiroshima were devastating.** The initial explosion and violent wind that followed toppled train cars, stone walls, and bridges as far as two miles away from the impact area. Of the 90,000 buildings in Hiroshima, an estimated 62,000 were destroyed in an instant. Buildings near the center of the explosion were ignited at once by the tremendous heat (estimated at 6,000 degrees C) that was generated by the splitting atoms. Away from the impact area, the splintered wreckage was ignited by exposed wiring and overturned cooking stoves. By late afternoon of the first day, very nearly every building in Hiroshima was burning. As the fires raged, huge drops of "black rain," created by heat, dust, and radiation, began to fall on the city. The radioactive fallout polluted the air and water, adding to the problems of those who had survived the blast and fires. Before the day had ended, the devastation from the bomb was nearly complete. Very little of Hiroshima remained.

Sample **Multiparagraph Answer**

If the question is too complex to handle in one paragraph, include only your thesis statement and background information in your opening paragraph. Begin your second paragraph (and all additional paragraphs) by rephrasing one of the main points from your outline into a topic sentence. Support this topic sentence with examples, reasons, or other details. If time permits, add a concluding paragraph to summarize your thoughts.

I. The Explosion
   A. A "noiseless flash"
   B. A wave of pressure
II. The Fires
   A. Ignited by bomb
   B. Ignited by exposed wiring
III. The Fallout
   A. "Black rain"
   B. Contamination

The immediate effects of the atomic bomb on Hiroshima were devastating.

The initial explosion of the bomb has often been described by those who survived it as a "noiseless flash." Even though the bomb was equal in power to 13,000 tons of TNT, no explosion was heard by the residents of Hiroshima. Instead, they recall an enormous flash of light followed by a tremendous wave of pressure. The wave and the violent wind that followed toppled train cars, stone walls, and bridges as far as two miles away from the impact area. Of the 90,000 buildings in Hiroshima, an estimated 62,000 were destroyed in an instant. In that same instant, the smoke and dust carried by the wind turned day into night.

The darkness quickly gave way to light as fires sprang up throughout the city. Buildings near the center of the explosion were ignited at once by the tremendous heat (estimated at 6,000 degrees C). Away from the impact area, it was simply a matter of time before the splintered wreckage was ignited by exposed wiring and overturned cooking stoves. By late afternoon of the first day, very nearly every building in Hiroshima was ablaze.

As the fires raged, additional effects of the bomb became evident. Huge drops of "black rain" began to fall. The explosion had lifted tremendous amounts of smoke, dust, and fission fragments high into the atmosphere over Hiroshima. Soon a condensed moisture, blackened by the smoke and dust and contaminated with radiation, began to fall like rain on the city. The radioactive fallout polluted the air and water, adding to the problems of those who had survived the blast and fires.

Before the day had ended, the devastation from the bomb was nearly complete. Very little of Hiroshima remained.

Quick Guide

1. **Make sure you are ready both mentally and physically for the test.** (See "Tips for Taking Tests," page 412.)

2. **Listen carefully to your teacher's final instructions.**
   - How much time do you have to complete the test?
   - Do all the questions count equally?
   - May you use any aids (dictionary, handbook, notes)?
   - Are there any corrections, changes, or additions to the test?

3. **Begin the test immediately and watch the time carefully.** Don't spend so much time on one question that you run out of time for the others.

4. **Read each question carefully, paying special attention to the key words.** (See pages 406-407.)

5. **Ask the teacher to clarify anything you may not understand.**

6. **Rephrase each question into a thesis statement (or topic sentence) for your essay answer.**

7. **Think before you write.** Jot down all the important information and work it into a brief outline. (Do this on the back of the test sheet or on a piece of scrap paper.)

8. **Write a strong topic sentence for each paragraph, using a main point from your outline.** Include the appropriate supporting details in an organized way.

9. **Write concisely.** Don't use abbreviations or nonstandard language.

10. **In each question, first write about the points you know well.** Work on the remaining points as time permits.

11. **Keep your test paper neat with reasonable margins.** Neatness is always important, and readability is a must on an exam.

12. **Revise and proofread as carefully as time permits.**

Taking an **Objective Test**

Even though objective tests are pretty straightforward and clear, there are guidelines that can help you avoid some common pitfalls.

True/False Test

- **Read the entire question before answering.** Often the first half of a statement will be true or false, while the second half is just the opposite. For an answer to be true, the entire statement must be true.
- **Read each word and number**. Pay special attention to names, dates, and numbers that are similar and could easily be confused.
- **Beware of true/false statements that contain words like *all, every, always, never,* etc.** Very often these statements will be false.
- **Watch for statements that contain more than one negative word.** Remember: Two negatives make a positive. (Example: It is *un*likely ice will *not* melt when the temperature rises above 32 degrees F.)

Matching Test

- **Read through both lists quickly before you begin answering.** Take note of any items that are similar, and pay special attention to the differences, so you don't mix them up.
- **When matching word to word, determine the part of speech of each word.** If the word is a verb, for example, match it with another verb.
- **When matching a word to a phrase, read the phrase first and look for the word it describes.**
- **Cross out each answer as you find it**—unless you are told that the answer can be used more than once.
- **Use capital letters rather than lowercase letters** since they are less likely to be misread by the person correcting the test.

Multiple-Choice Test

- **Read the directions to determine whether you are looking for the correct answer or the best answer.** Also check to see if a question can have more than one correct answer.
- **Read the first part of the question, looking for negative words like *not, never, except, unless,* etc.**
- **Try to answer the question in your mind before looking at the choices.**
- **Read all the choices before selecting your answer.** This is especially important on tests in which you must select the *best* answer.

TIPS for Taking Classroom Tests

Organizing and Preparing Test Material

- Ask the teacher to be as specific as possible about what will be on the test.
- Ask how the material will be tested (true/false, multiple choice, essay).
- Review your class notes and recopy those sections that are most important.
- Get any notes or materials you may have missed from the teacher or another student.
- Set up specific times to study for tests; don't let other activities interfere.
- Look over quizzes and exams you took earlier in that class.
- Prepare an outline of the material you must know; make up a detailed study sheet for each part of the outline.
- Attempt to predict test questions and write practice answers for them.
- Make a list of questions to ask the teacher or another student.

Reviewing and Remembering Test Material

- Begin reviewing early. Don't wait until the night before the test.
- Whenever possible, relate the test material to your personal life or to other subjects you know about.
- Look for patterns of organization in the material you study (cause/effect, comparison, chronological, etc.).
- Use maps, lists, diagrams, acronyms, rhymes, or any other special memory aids.
- Use flash cards or note cards to review material whenever you have time.
- Recite material out loud (whenever possible) as you review.
- Study with others only after you have studied well by yourself.
- Test your knowledge of a subject by teaching or explaining it to someone else.
- Review especially difficult material just before going to bed the night before the exam or just before the test, if possible.

Taking a **Standardized Test**

You will take a fair number of standardized tests throughout high school. These tests measure your skills, progress, and achievement in nearly every subject—English, science, social studies, math, and reading—and the questions follow a certain format. Knowing about that format can prepare you for your next standardized-test experience. The guidelines below and the models on the following page should help.

Guidelines for Standardized Tests

1. **Listen carefully to the instructions.** Most standardized tests follow very strict guidelines; there is a clear procedure for you to follow and a definite time limit.

2. **Skim the test.** Take a quick look at the entire test to make sure you have all the pages—and that you understand what you need to do with each section.

3. **Read the directions carefully.** Don't assume you know what the test is asking for just by the way it looks. Most standardized tests have specific directions for each section, and no two sections are exactly alike.

4. **Plan your time.** Many tests are broken down into time frames, allowing you a certain amount of time for each section. If not, you will have to plan your time based on the number of questions, the difficulty level, and your own strengths and weaknesses.

5. **Answer the easy questions first.** Skip questions you're totally in the dark about; go back to them later.

6. **Read all the choices.** Don't answer a question until you've read all the choices; many choices are purposely worded alike to test your true understanding.

7. **Make educated guesses.** Unless you're told not to, select an answer for every question. First eliminate choices that are obviously incorrect; then use logic to choose from the remaining answers.

8. **Double-check your answers.** As time permits, check each of your answers to make sure you haven't made any foolish mistakes or missed any questions.

Take NOTE Mark your answer sheet correctly and clearly. If you need to change an answer, erase it completely. Also make sure you keep your place and that your answers end up next to the correct numbers.

TIPS for Taking Standardized Tests

Vocabulary

The vocabulary section of standardized tests usually contains two types of questions: *synonym* and *antonym*. Synonym questions ask you to find a word that has the same meaning; antonym questions ask for the opposite meaning of a word.

Synonym BIBLIOPHILE (A) soldier (B) artist (C) lover of books
(D) music lover (E) child

Antonym PRELUDE (A) forerunner (B) ending
(C) interruption (D) test (E) conference

Analogies

Analogies test your ability to figure out relationships. First look at the pair of words you are given (WARM : HOT) and decide how they are related. Then read the choices and decide which pair of words has the same relationship as the first two. (The colon between the word pair means *is to;* the double colon means *as.*)

Analogy WARM : HOT :: (A) gray : black (B) high : low
(C) cold : frozen (D) sad : silly

Multiple Choice

The key to multiple-choice questions is to read the directions carefully. (The example below requires finding the sentence error.) Always read all the choices before selecting your answer. Eliminate those responses that are obviously not correct; then go back and consider the remaining choices.

Multiple Choice 1. I enjoy eating in a good restaurant and
  A   B

to go to a movie afterward. No error.
  C   D   E

Reading Comprehension

Often, you will be asked to read a passage and answer questions about it. The guidelines below can help you handle comprehension questions more efficiently:

1. Read the questions before you read the passage.
2. Read the passage carefully, but as quickly as possible.
3. Read all the choices before choosing the best answer.

Taking District or State Writing Tests

When you are taking a district or state writing test, your goal is to compose a clear, unified piece of writing within a limited amount of time. These assessment tests can vary greatly from one situation to the next.

Writing Situations

- In one situation, you might be given an open-ended writing prompt: **Write about an experience that really changed one of your beliefs.**
- In another situation, you might be given a clearly defined scenario: **Discuss a school-related problem in a form suitable for the school newspaper.**
- In still another situation, you might be given a prompt related to a piece of literature you should be familiar with: **The Reverend Mr. Collins and Wickham (in *Pride and Prejudice*) possess undesirable character traits. Explore these traits in a brief essay.**

Preparing Yourself

So how can you prepare yourself for a timed writing like the ones listed above? Here are some suggestions:

- Keep up with your content-area reading and note taking.
- Put forth a real effort in all writing assignments. That alone will increase your confidence.
- Write often—in and out of the classroom.
- Work at understanding the writing process better, especially writing thesis statements and topic outlines.
- Practice writing impromptu pieces. (See page 419 for prompts.)

Self-Help Strategy

The following learning strategy will help you become more skilled at planning and writing essays on the spot.

1. Highlight: Underline the important points in your class notes (or notes from your reading).

2. Question: Write a question (or two) about the main points.

3. Propose: Turn the question into a thesis statement.
   Question: Could the Confederacy have prolonged the Civil War?
   Statement: The Confederacy could have prolonged the Civil War.

4. Support: List a few main points in support of the thesis.

5. Write: Develop your thesis in a freely written essay.

The Timed Writing Process

The challenge in writing for district or state tests is to select the best of what you know and write about it clearly and effectively—in a limited time frame. Perhaps the most important quality you can bring to this experience is confidence, and confidence develops as you practice and work at your writing.

The academic essay is the most common form asked for on writing tests. (See pages 199-213.) Today, many businesses and organizations (like the armed forces) want their employees and members to be able to develop basic essays and reports on the spot.

Ten Steps to Follow

When you must write in a timed situation, follow these basic steps. (Also see page 410.)

1. Read the prompt carefully, looking for key words or the central idea.
2. Restate the prompt (problem, challenge) in a thesis statement.
3. Try listing, clustering, or branching to collect your thoughts and gather details.
4. Review your notes and select the best details for your writing.
5. Arrange your list of thoughts and details into a basic writing plan (see pages 408-409) or working outline.
6. Reword your thesis statement (if necessary) to reflect your plan.
7. Introduce your topic in a clear, yet interesting way.
8. Write your essay, always keeping your overall point (and the time limit) clearly in mind.
9. Add a conclusion that summarizes your main points and ends effectively.
10. Leave enough time to (a) read over the entire essay from start to finish and (b) go back and make necessary revisions.

Take NOTE   Note the steps above you find especially useful as well as those you need to work on. Also consider adding your own hints and reminders to the list. (Share your findings with your classmates.)

A Closer Look at Planning

In order to determine just how much planning you need to do for an impromptu writing activity, ask yourself the following questions.

Taking Inventory of the Situation

- **What exactly is the writing assignment?** What are the key words in the statement or question?
- **How much time do I have?** How will I organize my time so I can finish the assignment?
- **What is the primary purpose of the writing?** Am I expected to inform, explain, describe, or persuade?
- **What specific subject should I write about if the prompt is open-ended?** What topic truly interests me *and* meets the requirements of the assignment?
- **Who is the audience?** Am I supposed to write to a specific audience or a general reader?
- **What form will my writing take?** Am I expected to write an essay, a letter, a narrative, or what?
- **What voice will I use in my writing?** Should my voice be formal? Informal?

Writing Framework

Fill in a chart to help you plan your timed writing.

Writing Framework

Assignment:

Subject:

Purpose:

Audience:

Form:

Voice:

Assessing Timed Writing

What do evaluators look for when they assess a timed writing? They focus most of their attention on content and form.

1. **Evaluators look at the content,** the ideas you put forth in the writing. Does the writing display a good working knowledge of the subject? Does it contain a reasonable thesis statement and plenty of supporting detail?

2. **They also look at the form of the writing,** the way you put the ideas together. Does the writing contain a beginning, a middle, and an ending? Are the supporting details arranged in a logical order?

HELP FILE

Evaluators understand the difference between a timed writing and one produced over an extended period. They know that impromptu essays do not display the polish that a piece developed under more relaxed circumstances can possess. Keep this in mind as you write.

Sample Writing Prompts

Listed below are sample writing prompts used in a state writing test. (Students were directed to write a two- to five-paragraph essay on one of the prompts. They had 90 minutes to complete their work.) The samples will give you an idea of what to expect on your own writing tests.

WRITING PROMPT 1

Suppose your school district is considering a twelve-month school year. The superintendent is your audience. Write a persuasive essay defending or opposing the idea of a twelve-month school year. Include your reasons for taking a particular position and support these reasons with examples.

WRITING PROMPT 2

Write an informative essay in which you identify the biggest or most significant problem you have ever solved. Provide the necessary background information to introduce the problem and a clear explanation of your solution. Consider whether you reached your solution by design or by accident.

WRITING PROMPT 3

"The only way to help yourself is to help others." Discuss the truth of these words, presenting examples from some or all of the following: literature, history, current events, biography, or personal experience. Be specific.

Prompts for Practice

Use the prompts listed below as starting points for timed writing practice.

Think and Write About . . .

- current news stories
- world problems
- local problems
- notable people
- occupations and professions
- nature
- education and learning
- places and events
- art or music
- food and drink
- cars and travel
- language and communication
- manners and morals
- laws and justice
- social concerns
- customs and habits
- money and costs
- government and politics
- the media

Read and Respond to . . .

- short articles from magazines or newspapers
- song lyrics and poems
- quips, quotes, or short stories
- classroom literature

Listen and Respond to . . .

- news broadcasts
- interviews
- music videos
- short films
- recited poetry

Analyze and Write About . . .

- unusual statistics
- quotations
- proverbs
- cliches
- euphemisms

Describe . . .

- a favorite photograph
- a flock of birds in flight
- a person who is totally organized
- a person who is great to work with
- someone who has an unusual hobby or collection
- someone who has influenced you
- someone who is one of a kind
- someone you met once or knew briefly
- a high school dance (or other event)

Compare . . .

- original / imitation
- middle school / high school
- winter / summer
- like / love
- mother / father
- one class to another
- '60s / '90s
- musicians or musical groups
- movies or TV programs
- old friends / new friends
- bad days / good days
- alligator / crocodile
- wisdom / knowledge
- opinion / belief

Cause and Effect . . .

- What causes tornadoes?
- What causes rainbows?
- What causes misunderstandings?
- What causes cancer?
- What causes sunburn?
- What causes violence?
- What causes prejudice?
- What causes pain?
- What causes war?
- Why are there schools?
- Why are there towns?
- Why do we worship sports stars?
- Why do we get angry?

Speaking, Thinking, and Viewing

SKILLS

"Half the world is composed of people who have something to say and can't and the other half who have nothing to say and keep on saying it." —Robert Frost

SPEECH Skills

"This is speech class," announced Mr. Cook, leaning forward, his fingers gripping the lectern. "And during this semester you will all give informational, persuasive, impromptu, and manuscript speeches. Why? Because talking to groups will someday be a regular part of your lives." And guess what? Mr. Cook is right. Every day, people give speeches. In the workplace, a speech may be called "an explanation," "a report," or "a presentation."

This section of your handbook explains the process of preparing and presenting a speech. It will help you get ready for those "little talks" you'll be giving—both in school and in life.

Preview

- Planning Your Speech
- Writing Your Speech
- Preparing Your Speech Script
- Sample Outline, Note Cards, and Manuscript
- Rehearsing and Presenting Your Speech
- A Closer Look at Style

Planning Your Speech

Planning a speech is a lot like planning any other type of writing. You need to pay close attention to your *purpose, subject, audience,* and *details.* The guidelines that follow will help you plan a successful speech.

Determine Your Purpose

There are three main purposes for speaking: *to inform, to persuade,* and *to demonstrate.*

- **Informing:** If your purpose is to inform, or to educate, you are preparing an information or informative speech. (Collecting plenty of details is essential. See pages 105-114.)
- **Persuading:** If your purpose is to argue for or against something, you are preparing a persuasive speech. (Developing a convincing and logical argument is your main job. See pages 115-124.)
- **Demonstrating:** If your purpose is to show how to do something or to show how something works, you are preparing a demonstration speech. (Composing a clear, step-by-step explanation is the key.)

Select a Specific Subject

A good speech starts with a good subject—one that truly interests you and your audience. Here are some important points to consider.

- **Choose the right subject:** Make sure that your subject meets the requirements (and purpose) of the assignment.
- **Know your subject:** Make sure that you know your subject well or that you can learn about it in a short time.
- **Choose a specific subject:** Make sure that your subject is specific enough to cover in the time allowed. (See the chart below.)

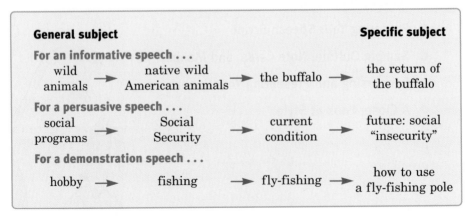

General subject			Specific subject
For an informative speech . . .			
wild animals →	native wild American animals →	the buffalo →	the return of the buffalo
For a persuasive speech . . .			
social programs →	Social Security →	current condition →	future: social "insecurity"
For a demonstration speech . . .			
hobby →	fishing →	fly-fishing →	how to use a fly-fishing pole

Consider Your Audience

You will want to think about your audience at each step in the process. Here are some suggestions you can follow.

- **Choose your subject carefully:** Show that you care about your audience by choosing an interesting subject.
- **Be clear:** Organize the speech so clearly that listeners get the point immediately.
- **Anticipate questions:** Try to think of questions your audience might want answers to—answer them in your speech.
- **Make it enjoyable:** Use thought-provoking quotations, interesting anecdotes, and a little humor (when appropriate).
- **Be brief:** Speak only as long as you must in order to make your point.

✱ After you've considered your purpose, subject, and audience, you may want to write a thesis or purpose statement. (See page 424.)

Collect Interesting Details

After you have determined your purpose, selected a specific topic, and considered your audience, it's time to start collecting information. Listed below are different sources of information you can go to for your speech. Always consult as many sources as time permits.

- **Tap your memory:** If your speech is based on an experience, write down the facts, details, and feelings as you remember them.
- **Talk with people:** Discuss your subject with a variety of people who may be able to provide details from their experiences.
- **Get firsthand experience:** Experiencing (or trying out) your subject is especially important for demonstration speeches.
- **Search the library:** Make sure to check different library resources, including books, magazines, pamphlets, and videos.
- **Explore the Internet:** Check out appropriate Web sites and newsgroups for information.

Take NOTE

Look for photographs, maps, models, artifacts, charts, objects, and other graphics. Showing such items can help make any speech clearer and more interesting, especially a demonstration speech. And, of course, you can create your own graphics or charts as well.

Writing Your Speech

After you've completed your basic planning, you need to select your best details and organize them into an effective speech. The way you organize your details and write them down depends primarily on (1) the kind of speech you are giving and (2) the kind of "script" or notes you plan to use. (See pages 426-429 for sample scripts.)

If you are giving a short demonstration speech, you may want to use only a few notes (note cards). If you are going to inform your audience, you may decide a well-organized list (outline) would work best. And, if you are giving a persuasive speech, you may want to use a word-for-word script (manuscript). Whatever approach you choose, you need to be well-prepared with an effective introduction, body, and conclusion.

Introduction

A good introduction sets the tone and direction of your speech by getting the attention of your audience, introducing your topic, and stating your central idea or purpose.

Start-Up Ideas: To get the audience's attention and help them focus on your topic, begin with one or more of the following ideas:

- Ask a thought-provoking question.
- Tell a funny story or anecdote.
- Give a short demonstration, or use an attention-getting visual aid.
- Make a strong statement about why the topic is important to you and to your audience.
- Share an appropriate quotation related to your topic.

Stating Your Thesis

After you've considered your purpose, subject, and audience (and gathered some information), you need to write a thesis statement to focus your planning efforts. Begin the statement with "My purpose is . . ." and finish it with your specific speech topic. If you choose to include your thesis statement in your introduction, you will want to reword it so that it sounds natural and sincere.

"My purpose is to persuade my classmates that we cannot depend on the Social Security system for our retirement funds, so we need to start our own savings plans now."

Body

As you write the body of your speech, turn each fact or detail into an interesting, connected thought. Explain or describe each part of your topic clearly so that your audience can follow along easily. If you are giving your opinion about something, support your point of view with enough logical reasons to convince your listeners. Organize your details as effectively as you can. Here are six popular ways to do that:

Order of Importance @ Arrange information according to its importance: least to greatest, or greatest to least.

> **Example:** A persuasive speech on buying new equipment for the science lab

Chronological Order @ Arrange information according to time—the order in which events take place.

> **Example:** A how-to speech about sending e-mail messages

Comparison/Contrast @ Give information about subjects by comparing them (showing similarities) and contrasting them (showing differences).

> **Example:** An explanatory speech about choosing one Internet provider over another one

Cause and Effect @ Give information about a situation, a problem, or a process by sharing its causes and effects.

> **Example:** A report on what causes hurricanes and how they affect coastal areas

Order of Location @ Arrange information about subjects according to where things are located in relation to each other.

> **Example:** An informational speech about the anatomy of a frog

Problem/Solution @ Describe a problem and then present a solution.

> **Example:** A persuasive speech about how warm-ups prevent muscle strain in athletes

Conclusion

The conclusion of your speech ought to leave your audience focused on the most important points of your message. A good conclusion helps your audience understand what they have heard, why it's important, and what they should do about it. Here are some suggestions to consider:

- **Tell one last interesting fact or story.**
  (This is a good way to end an informative speech.)

- **Explain why the topic is important.**
  (This is a good way to end a persuasive speech.)

- **Sum up the most important ideas in your speech.**
  (This is a good way to end a demonstration speech.)

Preparing Your Speech Script

Once you have the general draft of your speech written, it's time to prepare the speech "script." The script is the form you will use when you are giving your speech. You can use an **outline, note cards,** or a word-for-word **manuscript.** (See the four pages that follow.)

Sample Outline

If you outline your speech, follow the guidelines and model below.

1. Write your opening statement in sentence form.
2. Write all your main points as sentences.
3. List all supporting points (facts, dates, numbers) as phrases.
4. Add notes [in brackets] to indicate where to use visual aids.
5. Write all quotations out completely.
6. Write your closing statement in sentence form.

Save Now or Pay Later

I. Imagine that you've finished school, gotten a job, worked hard all week, and this dollar bill represents your whole paycheck. [hold up dollar bill]
   A. 20% for income taxes
   B. 30% for Social Security
   C. 50% for you

II. These percentages may soon become reality.
   A. Social Security system failing
   B. Out of money by the year 2043?

III. The Social Security system began in 1935.
   A. System "fixed" many times
   B. 1983 changes supposedly "fixed" things until 2056
   C. Fixed again nine years later—good until 2043
   D. 2043 is date many of you will retire
   E. New research predicts system bankrupt by 2029

IV. So what should we do about our own "social security"?
   A. Start a savings account [show graph]
   B. Stay informed and vote as soon as you can

V. What's the solution? We have to start our own savings plans; and the earlier we start, the easier it will be to reach our goals.

Sample Note Cards

If you plan to deliver your speech using note cards, it's a good idea to write out your entire introduction and conclusion. For the body of your speech, write one main point (and related details) per card.

---

(1)

Introduction

Imagine that you've finished school, gotten a job, worked hard all week, and this dollar bill represents your whole paycheck. [hold up dollar bill] As your employer, I'm about to hand you the check when I stop, te... ...like this, give it to Uncle Sam an...
Then I ...
Uncle S...
and So...

---

(2)

A 50% deduction from your paycheck may soon be a reality.
- Social Security system failing
- Out of money by the year 2043?
- Additional taxes

---

(3)

Social Security system began in 1935.
- "fixed" many times
- 1983 changes were supposed to last until ...

---

(4)

What can we do about our own social security?
- Start saving
- [show graph]

Conclusion **(5)**

What's my point? The Social Security system can't promise us financial security when we retire in 2049.
What's the solution? We have to start our own savings plans; and the earlier we start, the easier it will be to reach our goals.

Sample **Manuscript Speech**

If you use a word-for-word manuscript, make sure you write to be *heard,* not *read.* Also mark your copy to help you deliver your speech effectively. (See "Marking Your Speech" on page 430.) Notice in the manuscript below how Burnette Sawyer, the student writer, uses a curved line to add feeling and **boldface** to add emphasis. (Also notice how she builds her argument by showing the audience how the problem affects each of them.)

Save Now or Pay Later

> **The speaker begins with an anecdote.**
>
> **She tears the dollar for emphasis.**

Imagine that you've finished school, gotten a job, worked hard all week, and this dollar bill represents your whole paycheck. [hold up dollar bill] As your employer, I'm about to hand you the check when I stop, tear off about 20% like this, give it to Uncle Sam and say, "Here's my employee's income tax." Then I tear off another 30% like this, give that to Uncle Sam too and say, "And here's her Medicare and Social Security tax."

Finally, I give you this half and say, "Here, hard worker, this is what's left of your whole paycheck."

Does that sound like science fiction?

> **The speaker cites an authority to support her argument.**

Senator Alan Simpson doesn't think so. In the magazine *Modern Maturity,* he says that unless legislation changes the Social Security system, our generation will have to pay 20% of our paychecks as income tax, and 30% as Social Security tax. That means we can keep just **50%** of what we earn.

But the news gets **worse.** Remember this 30% that we paid to Social Security? [hold up piece of dollar bill] Well, that won't be enough money for retired people to live on in the year 2043. Remember that year, 2043—we'll come back to that soon.

What's the problem? The Social Security system can't ensure our savings for retirement.

What's the solution? We have to start our own savings plans, and the earlier the better.

Ever since the Social Security system started back in 1935, it has never been secure. While the system has been "fixed" a number of times, these fix-it jobs haven't solved the problem. For example, writer Keith Carlson points out that in 1983 Congress raised payroll taxes, extended the retirement age, and said that the system would be in good financial shape until 2056.

But then, says Carlson, just nine years later, a report came out saying that Congress had been **wrong.** The report said that Social Security money wouldn't even last until 2056—it would run out by 2043. Remember that year, 2043? **That's six years before** we're supposed to retire at age 67!

Do you think this news is bad? The AARP Bulletin reported on the Bipartisan Commission on Entitlement and Tax Reform. This commission warned that entitlement programs like Social Security are growing so fast they could "bankrupt the country" by the year 2029—when we're **only 47!**

> The speaker demonstrates a clear understanding of the subject.

So what should we do? Next fall we can vote in a presidential election for the first time. Both Democrats and Republicans say they have a plan that will use money from the budget surplus to fix Social Security. What if we all vote for the presidential candidate with the best plan? Will that save our retirement funds? **Don't count on it!** As the track record for Social Security shows, one more fix-it job won't fix the system. We have to start our own retirement plans—and do it early in our careers.

In fact, in his book, *Retirement 101,* Willard Enteman says that we should start a personal savings plan the day we get our first paychecks. In sociology class last week, Mr. Christians made the same point. He gave us this bar graph [hold up graph] showing that if our goal is to save $200,000 by age 67, we had better start early before saving gets too expensive.

As you can see from the graph, if we start saving when we're 25, we can reach $200,000 by saving just $49 a month. If we wait until we're 35, we'll have to save $113 a month. If we wait until we're 45, we'll have to put away $279 a month. And if we wait until we're 55, we'll need $832 a month.

Look at the difference. To reach $200,000 by age 67 would cost $49 a month if we start at 25, and $832 a month if we start at 55.

> The closing paragraph helps readers to reflect on the subject.

What's my point? The Social Security system can't promise us financial security when we retire in 2049.

What's the solution? We have to start our own savings plans; and the earlier we start, the easier it will be to reach our goals. ■

Rehearsing and Presenting Your Speech

Rehearse your speech until you're comfortable with it. Ask a family member or friend to listen and give you feedback, or use a tape recorder or video recorder so you can hear and see yourself. When you rehearse (or present) your speech, follow the guidelines below.

Before You Speak . . .

- Check all your equipment and visual aids before you start.
- Also, check your outline, note cards, or manuscript to be sure everything is in the right order.
- Stand, walk to the front, and face the audience.

As You Speak . . .

- Speak loudly and clearly.
- Don't rush. Read carefully if you're using a manuscript; glance at your note cards or outline if that's what you are using.
- Think about what you're saying and add feeling to your voice.
- Use appropriate gestures to help you communicate.
- Look at the audience as you speak, and communicate with your facial expressions.

After You Speak . . .

- Ask if anyone has any questions (if appropriate).
- Conclude the presentation by gathering up your things and walking to your seat.

Marking Your Speech

As you rehearse your speech, decide which words or phrases to emphasize, where to pause, and where to add visual aids. Then use the symbols below to mark the copy of your speech.

Curved line or italic .... for additional feeling or *emotion*.

Underlining or boldface .... for greater volume or **emphasis**.

Dash, diagonal, ellipsis .... for a pause—or / a break
. . . in the flow.

Brackets... for actions or [visual aids].

A Closer Look at **Style**

More than any other president of recent times, John F. Kennedy is remembered for the appealing style and tone of his speeches. The following portions of his speeches show how style and tone can help strengthen the spoken word. The tone, or appeal, is listed above each excerpt. (These appeals reflect the feelings and attitudes a speaker hopes to inspire in his or her audience.)

Allusion ℮ An allusion is a reference in a speech to a familiar person, place, or thing.

Appeal to the Democratic Principle

One hundred years of delay have passed since President Lincoln freed the slaves, yet their heirs, their grandsons, are not fully free. (Radio and Television Address, 1963)

Analogy ℮ An analogy is a comparison of an unfamiliar idea to a simple, familiar one. The comparison is usually quite lengthy, suggesting several points of similarity. An analogy is especially useful when attempting to explain a difficult or complex idea.

Appeal to Common Sense

In our opinion the German people wish to have one united country. If the Soviet Union had lost the war, the Soviet people themselves would object to a line being drawn through Moscow and the entire country defeated in war. We wouldn't like to have a line drawn down the Mississippi River. . . . (Interview, November 25, 1961)

Anecdote ℮ An anecdote is a short story told to illustrate a point.

Appeal to Pride, Commitment

Frank O'Connor, the Irish writer, tells in one of his books how as a boy, he and his friends would make their way across the countryside and when they came to an orchard wall that seemed too high and too doubtful to try and too difficult to permit their voyage to continue, they took off their hats and tossed them over the wall—and then they had no choice but to follow them. This nation has tossed its cap over the wall of space, and we have no choice but to follow it. Whatever the difficulties, they will be overcome. (San Antonio Address, November 21, 1963)

Antithesis ℮ Antithesis balances or contrasts one word or idea against another, usually in the same sentence.

Appeal to Common Sense, Commitment

Let us never negotiate out of fear. But let us never fear to negotiate. (Inaugural Address, 1961)

Mankind must put an end to war, or war will put an end to mankind. (Address to the U.N., 1961)

Irony ℮ Irony is using a word or phrase to mean the exact opposite of its literal meaning, or to show a result that is the opposite of what would be expected or appropriate; an odd coincidence.

Appeal to Common Sense

They see no harm in paying those to whom they entrust the minds of their children a smaller wage than is paid to those to whom they entrust the care of their plumbing. (Vanderbilt University, 1961)

Negative Definition ℮ A negative definition describes something by telling what it is *not* rather than, or in addition to, what it is.

Appeal for Commitment

. . . members of this organization are committed by the Charter to promote and respect human rights. Those rights are not respected when a Buddhist priest is driven from his pagoda, when a synagogue is shut down, when a Protestant church cannot open a mission, when a cardinal is forced into hiding, or when a crowded church service is bombed. (United Nations, September 20, 1963)

Parallel Structure ℮ Parallel structuring is the repeating of phrases or sentences that are similar (parallel) in meaning and structure; repetition is the repeating of the same word or phrase to create a sense of rhythm and emphasis.

Appeal for Commitment

Let every nation know, whether it wishes us well or ill, that we shall pay any price, bear any burden, meet any hardship, support any friend, oppose any foe, in order to assure the survival and the success of liberty. (Inaugural Address, 1961)

Quotations ℮ Quotations, especially of well-known individuals, can be effective in nearly any speech.

Appeal for Emulation or Affiliation

At the inauguration, Robert Frost read a poem which began "the land was ours before we were the land's"—meaning, in part, that this new land of ours sustained us before we were a nation.   And although we are now the land's—a nation of people matched to a continent—we still draw our strength and sustenance . . . from the earth. (Dedication Speech, 1961)

Rhetorical Question ℮ A rhetorical question is a question that is asked to emphasize a point, not to get an answer.

Appeal to Common Sense, Democratic Principle

"When a man's ways please the Lord," the Scriptures tell us, "he maketh even his enemies to be at peace with him." And is not peace, in the last analysis, basically a matter of human rights—the right to live out our lives without fear of devastation—the right to breathe air as nature provided it—the right of future generations to a healthy existence? (Commencement Address, 1963)

"Computers are incredibly fast, accurate,
and stupid; humans are incredibly slow,
inaccurate, and brilliant; together they are
powerful beyond imagination." —Albert Einstein

MULTIMEDIA Reports

Studies show that you absorb information much more quickly when you encounter it through more than one sense. That's one reason you take notes during a lecture: Listening engages your sense of hearing, while writing notes reinforces what you hear. Speakers often use visual aids, too, so that you can hear and see the ideas at the same time.

Personal computers now allow you to make your presentations and reports multisensory. As a speaker you can carry an entire library of visual aids on a portable computer, connect it to a video monitor or projector, and show slides, film clips, and animated graphics to support an oral presentation. As an author you can enhance a written report with colorful on-screen graphics, and then distribute it on disc or via the Internet to create an interactive report.

In this chapter, you'll find writing guidelines for creating a multimedia presentation and an interactive report. You can find a sample presentation and report on the Write Source Web site: <thewritesource.com>.

Preview

- Multimedia Presentation
- Interactive Report
- Creating a Storyboard

WRITING GUIDELINES
Multimedia Presentation

Using a visual aid during an oral report helps to create a multimedia presentation. It's the same when your teacher uses a chalkboard or an overhead projector to illustrate a point; or when a businessperson makes a presentation supported by posters, charts, and other graphics.

More and more, the computer is being employed for multimedia presentations. As the presenter speaks, the audience looks at the monitor, where the information is reinforced and clarified by changing screens.

■ PREWRITING

1. **Selecting a Topic . . .** Select a topic that is right for your audience and appropriate for a multimedia presentation.

2. **Gathering Details . . .** Collect information about your topic in the same way you would if you were making a speech. (See pages 422-423.)

■ WRITING AND REVISING

3. **Creating a Design . . .** Create a graphic design for your pages. Be certain it is appropriate in tone for your topic and your audience—businesslike for a serious topic, lighthearted for a humorous speech, and so on. Remember, visuals should never detract from your message. They should add to or highlight important points.

4. **Creating Pages . . .** Create a new page for each main idea in your outline. (See the storyboard on page 436.) If an idea has several parts, present them one at a time on that page (if your computer program allows). Each press of the mouse button (or the return or enter key) should reveal a new detail.

5. **Fine-Tuning Your Presentation . . .** Practice delivering your speech while clicking through the multimedia pages. Try it with a sample audience (a group of friends or family), if possible. Insert separate pages for statements or quotations that need emphasis. Also add sound and animation if they help your message.

■ EDITING AND PROOFREADING

6. **Checking for Style and Accuracy . . .** Check that the words on screen are clear and concise. They must help listeners grasp your message, not confuse them.

7. **Preparing a Final Version . . .** Check spelling, punctuation, usage, and other mechanics. *Remember:* On screen, errors are glaringly obvious to everyone.

WRITING GUIDELINES

Interactive Report

From news journals on the Web to encyclopedias on CD, the shape of written information has changed in recent years. Many publishers now use hypertext to present information in an interactive format. In hypertext, certain words and images on screen serve as links to other information. By selecting that link, the viewer interacts with the computer to load the linked information to the screen. That information may be more text, a sound recording, a video clip, or some other sort of computer file. You can create your own interactive report by following the guidelines below.

■ PREWRITING

1. **Selecting a Subject . . .** One way to select a subject is to start with a finished report and then make it interactive. Nearly any report will work—a research paper, an informational essay, a speech manuscript, and so on. (See pages 422-423.)

■ WRITING AND REVISING

2. **Creating a Design . . .** Devise a graphic design for your report that is appropriate for your subject and your audience.

3. **Creating Pages . . .** Create a new page for each main idea in your report. Include a separate page for your title, and perhaps another for "The End." If an idea has several parts, and your software allows, have the parts appear on screen one at a time.

4. **Creating Links . . .** Put "Back" and "Next" links on the pages to lead readers through the report. Add any other links you need—for notes, definitions of terms, sound recordings, film clips, and so on. (See the "Definition of AARP" box on the storyboard on page 436.)

   ✱ You can dress up your report with any appropriate animation and sound (such as a "click" or "beep" when a link is selected), but don't let the sounds and animation distract your audience.

5. **Fine-Tuning Your Presentation . . .** Have someone try out your interactive report, and ask that person for comments. Correct any problems you discover.

■ EDITING AND PROOFREADING

6. **Checking for Style and Accuracy . . .** Check that the words on screen are clear and concise. They must help readers grasp your message, not confuse them.

7. **Preparing a Final Version . . .** Make sure that your text is free of mechanical errors, so that your report is taken seriously.

Creating a **Storyboard**

The storyboard below demonstrates one way to turn the model speech on pages 428-429 into a multimedia presentation or an interactive report. The **red boxes** below show notes for pages of a multimedia presentation in simple step-by-step order. The **white boxes** show added links and pages for an interactive report. To view the final versions of the presentation and report, visit <www.thewritesource.com/mm-hs.htm>.

Sample **Storyboard**

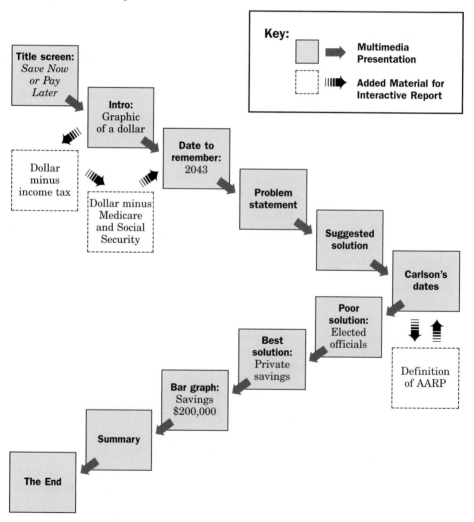

Key:
▬▶ Multimedia Presentation
▭ ⫸ Added Material for Interactive Report

- Title screen: *Save Now or Pay Later*
- Dollar minus income tax
- Intro: Graphic of a dollar
- Dollar minus Medicare and Social Security
- Date to remember: 2043
- Problem statement
- Suggested solution
- Carlson's dates
- Definition of AARP
- Poor solution: Elected officials
- Best solution: Private savings
- Bar graph: Savings $200,000
- Summary
- The End

"Every good thought you think is contributing its share to the ultimate results of your life."

—Grenville Kleiser

THINKING Skills

Have you ever been asked to compare two things in an English paper or on a history test? Easier said than done, right? Or how about defining or classifying a *simple* term in science class? Not so simple? The truth is, thinking can be hard work, especially in some of your tougher classes.

Don't worry. There are many strategies for accomplishing your most challenging thinking tasks. This chapter will help you learn how to use six types of thinking in your day-to-day schoolwork: recalling, understanding, applying, analyzing, synthesizing, and evaluating. Effective use of these will help you make decisions, solve problems, ask questions, and think more logically.

Preview

- Guidelines for Thinking and Writing
- Types of Thinking
- Using Evidence and Logic

Guidelines for Thinking and Writing

Whenever you are asked to . . .   **Be ready to . . .**

RECALL ⟶ Remember what you have learned

underline   circle
list   match
name   label
cluster   define

- collect information
- list details
- identify or define key terms
- remember main points

UNDERSTAND ⟶ Explain what you have learned

explain   review
summarize   restate
describe   cite

- give examples
- restate important details
- tell how something works

APPLY ⟶ Use what you have learned

change   illustrate
do   model
demonstrate   show
locate   organize

- select the most important details
- organize information
- explain a process
- show how something works

ANALYZE ⟶ Break down information

break down   rank
examine   compare
contrast   classify
tell why

- carefully examine a subject
- group it into important parts
- make connections and comparisons

SYNTHESIZE ⟶ Shape information into a new form

combine   connect
speculate   design
compose   create
predict   develop
invent   imagine

- invent a better way of doing something
- blend the old with the new
- predict or hypothesize (make an educated guess)

EVALUATE ⟶ Judge the worth of information

recommend   judge
criticize   argue
persuade   rate
convince   assess
weigh

- point out a subject's strengths and weaknesses
- evaluate its clearness, accuracy, value, and so on
- convince others of its value/worth

Types of Thinking

Recalling Information

The most basic type of thinking you use in school is **recalling.** This type of thinking is needed when you are asked to remember and repeat what you have learned in class. To help you recall information, do the following:

- Listen carefully in class and take notes.
- Read your assignments carefully.
- Review and study the information so that you know it well.

RECALLING

Your teachers will give very few writing assignments that only require you to recall information. However, you may encounter test questions that ask you to only use this level of thinking. When answering multiple-choice, matching, fill-in-the-blank, and short-answer questions on a test, you need to recall information. On a history test about the Peloponnesian War, a student might be asked to answer the following questions by recalling information.

Directions: Fill in the blanks to correctly complete the sentences below.

1. The Peloponnesian War was the conflict in Greece that started in the year ___431 BCE___ and ended in ___404 BCE___ .

2. The alliance of Greek city-states that the Athenians led was called the _____Delian League_____ .

3. The Spartan infantry that fought the Athenians were called _____hoplites_____ .

Directions: Write three sentences, each telling an important fact about the Peloponnesian War.

1. In the early years of the war, Pericles was the leader of the Athenians.

2. The Athenians tried to help a group of barbarians called the Segestans attack Spartan colonies in Sicily.

3. The Persians gave the Spartans money to build a fleet to fight the Athenian navy.

Understanding Information

Your teachers will often ask you to recall factual information *and* show that you truly **understand** it. One way teachers can measure how well you understand something is to have you write about it in your own words.

When you explain, describe, or tell how something works, you are displaying an understanding of the subject. To help you understand information, do the following:

- Use study-reading and note-taking strategies. (See pages 357-366 and 392-396.)
- Rewrite the information in your own words.
- Explain the information to someone else.

UNDERSTANDING

Often, you will be asked to show understanding by writing an essay or a paragraph. In the following assignment, a student needs to (1) recall important facts and details and (2) use this information to show a clear understanding of the situation. (Graphic organizers, charts, or maps can also be used to show understanding.)

Assignment: Explain how the Athenians went, in just a few decades, from being the most powerful city-state in Greece to being conquered by the Spartans.

Athens was the dominant force in ancient Greece because of its great navy and its role as the head of the Greek city-states. The Peloponnesian War started because Athens demanded heavy taxes from its neighbors and constantly competed with Sparta for dominance in the region. After several bloody battles, sieges, and a horrible plague within its own walls, Athens found its supply lines disrupted, its navy weakened, and its armies defeated. In the year 404 BCE, the Athenians had no choice but to surrender unconditionally to Sparta and its allies.

Applying Information

When you are **applying** information, you must be able to use what you have learned to demonstrate, show, or relate something. For example, using your computer manual to help you set up your computer requires you to apply the information from the manual to the job. To help you apply information, do the following:

- Select the most important facts and details.
- Think about how you could use this information.
- Organize the information in the way that best meets your specific needs. (See page 52.)

APPLYING

Sometimes you will be asked to apply information to a situation in your own world. To do this, you need to know the important facts and understand the main themes in a body of information. Then you must apply this understanding to your own experience. In the assignment below, a student must do this kind of thinking.

Assignment: What is one of the main lessons you have learned from the Peloponnesian War? Relate this lesson to an action or experience in your own world.

I learned that taking advantage of others can have harmful effects on everyone involved. I know someone who was always asking people for favors and borrowing things, but never gave anything back, or did anything for others. He borrowed my favorite sweatshirt once when he had no jacket. I never saw it again. His friends stopped wanting to be around him, and no one would help him out when he needed it. They all felt they were being taken advantage of. If he had stopped taking so much from people, or had started giving some of it back, he would have gotten along just fine. Now no one trusts him, and all his friends have turned against him. It reminds me of how poorly Athens treated its one-time friends and neighbors. Eventually, they turned against Athens and sided with its enemy, Sparta.

Analyzing Information

When you compare and contrast, rank things in order of importance, or give reasons, you are **analyzing** information. Analyzing means breaking down information into smaller parts. To help you analyze information, do the following:

- Identify the important parts that make up the whole.
- Determine how the parts are related to one another.

ANALYZING

When you must analyze information, first figure out what kind of analysis to do (compare and contrast, rank things, give reasons, etc.). Then decide which facts and details to use and how to organize them. The following assignment asks a student to analyze by comparing and contrasting.

Assignment: Athenian democracy from the time of the Peloponnesian War has been an example for Western civilization. However, our ideas of government have changed greatly since Athenian culture flourished. Highlight some of the main differences between the Athenian and United States forms of government.

Although the United States government is rooted in the traditions of Athenian democracy, there are still many differences between the two. First, the fact that Athens was a city-state and was smaller than the United States meant that it didn't need a system of federal, state, and city governments. Second, in ancient Greece, only male citizens could vote, whereas in today's U.S. system, any citizen over the age of 18 can vote. Third, the democracy of the Athenians involved its citizens directly, whereas the U.S. government relies on representatives rather than on direct citizen action. American democracy evolved into its present form to meet the demands of our complex society, a society that has little in common with ancient Athens.

✱ A Venn diagram can help you organize your thoughts whenever you are asked to compare and contrast. (See page 361.)

Synthesizing Information

When you combine information with new ideas, or use information to create something, you are **synthesizing.** Common ways of synthesizing information are predicting, inventing, and redesigning. In each case, you have to reshape the information you already have. To help you synthesize information, do the following:

- Think of ways to combine the information with other ideas.
  (For example, information about the Peloponnesian War, plus a student's knowledge of space travel, could turn into a science-fiction story about a war on another planet.)
- Put the information in a different form.
  (Knowledge about the Peloponnesian War could serve as the starting point for a play, a ballad, a feature article, or another choice.)

SYNTHESIZING

The same thing that makes synthesizing a challenge also makes it fun: You get to use your imagination. Suppose a student is asked to use information about a period of time or an event like the Peloponnesian War to write a week-long journal as if he or she were actually there. This would require synthesizing—putting existing information into a new, creative form. The paragraph that follows is a single journal entry.

Assignment: Write a series of journal entries as if you were alive at the time of the Peloponnesian War.

I spent several hours today at the shrine to Athena praying for an end to this war. How long has it been that we have been living in the midst of constant fighting? My father tells me that he can remember a time when we Athenians were the strongest of all the Greeks. Now, no doubt, it is just a matter of time before the Spartans enter our city. Has Athena forsaken the city that was named after her? Maybe we have done something to anger the gods. I remember my uncle telling horrible stories of what the soldiers did to our neighbors to the north when they were out collecting the taxes Athens demanded. That money helped build our fleet of ships. We were truly the lords of the sea! Maybe the gods resented that.

Evaluating Information

When you are asked to express your opinion about an important issue, or to discuss the good and bad points about something, you are **evaluating.** Evaluating is an advanced level of thinking that requires a thorough understanding and analysis of a subject. To help you evaluate information, do the following:

- Learn as much as you can about a subject before you try to evaluate it.
- Recall, review, organize, and analyze the information as needed.
- Weigh all sides of the subject or issue carefully.

EVALUATING

An effective evaluation is based on information. Start with a sentence that identifies your overall opinion, or evaluation. Then add facts and details that support your evaluation. Note how the paragraph below contains a great deal of supporting information.

Assignment: In one paragraph, evaluate the overall effects of the Peloponnesian War on Greece.

The Peloponnesian War changed Greece forever. Although Athens abused its power by demanding heavy tributes from other Greeks, its removal from power meant that the militaristic Spartans became the dominant force in Greece. In many ways, the Spartans were even more demanding than the democratic Athenians. The oppressive government that the Spartans set up in Athens led to a series of revolts, a number of tyrannical leaders, and general conflict. All this caused further suffering. In the end, the war weakened the entire region for many years. It weakened it so much that all of Greece became vulnerable to foreign enemies, including the Macedonians to the north. Greece also became vulnerable to new uprisings from within. This once proud and stable region never fully recovered from these years of war and unrest.

Using Evidence and Logic

An argument is a chain of reasons that a person uses to support a claim or a conclusion. To use argument well, you need to know (1) how to draw logical conclusions from sound evidence and (2) how to recognize and avoid false arguments, or logical fallacies.

The **logical fallacies** described in this section are the bits of fuzzy or misguided thinking that often crop up in our own speaking and writing, as well as in advertisements, political appeals, editorials, and persuasive essays. You should first look them over so that you can recognize them in what you read or hear. Then avoid them in your own writing and thinking.

Fallacies of Thinking

Appeal to Ignorance ◎ A person commits this logical fallacy by maintaining that because no one has ever proved a claim, it must therefore be false. Appeals to ignorance unfairly shift the burden of proof to someone else.

> **Example:** Show me one study that proves seat belts save lives.

Appeal to Pity ◎ This fallacy may be heard in courts of law when a lawyer begs for leniency because his client's mother is ill, his brother is out of work and on and on. The tug on the heartstrings can also be heard in the classroom when a student says to the teacher, "May I have another day on this paper? I worked till my eyeballs fell out, but it's still not done."

> **Example:** Imagine what it must have been like for him. If anyone deserves a break, he does.

Bandwagon ◎ Another form of ineffective logic in an argument is the appeal to everyone's sense of wanting to belong or be accepted. By suggesting that everyone else is doing this or wearing that or going here or there, you can avoid the real question—"Is this idea or claim a valid one or not?"

> **Example:** Everyone on the team wears brand X shoes. It's the only way to go.

Broad Generalization ◎ A broad generalization takes in everything and everyone at once, allowing no exceptions. For example, a generalization about voters might be, "All voters spend too little time reading about a candidate and too much time being swayed by 30-second sound bites." It may be true that quite a few voters are guilty of this error, but it is unfair to suggest that this is true of all voters. Here's another example:

> **Example:** All teenagers spend too much time watching television.

Circular Thinking @ This fallacy occurs when you assume, in a definition or an argument, the very point you are trying to prove. Note how circular this sort of reasoning is.

> **Example:** I love Mr. Baldwin's class because I'm always happy in there. (But what's special about the class?)

Either-Or Thinking @ Either-or thinking consists of reducing a solution to two possible extremes: "America: Love It or Leave It." "Put up or shut up." This fallacy of thinking eliminates all the possibilities in the middle.

> **Example:** Either this community votes to build a new school or the quality of education will drop dramatically.

Half-Truths @ Avoid building your argument with evidence or statements that contain part of the truth, but not the whole truth. These kinds of statements are called half-truths. They are especially misleading because they leave out "the rest of the story." They are partly true and partly untrue at the same time.

> **Example:** The new recycling law is bad because it will cost more money than it saves. (Maybe so; but it will also save the environment.)

Oversimplification @ Beware of phrases like "It all boils down to . . . " or "It's a simple question of . . . . " Almost no dispute among reasonably intelligent people is "a simple question of . . . . " Anyone who feels, for example, that capital punishment "all boils down to" protecting society ought to question a doctor, an inmate on death row, the inmate's family, a sociologist, or a religious leader.

> **Example:** Capital punishment protects society.

Slanted Language @ By choosing words that carry strong positive or negative feelings, a person can distract the audience and lead them away from the valid arguments being made. The philosopher Bertrand Russell once illustrated the bias involved in slanted language when he compared three synonyms for the word *stubborn:* "I am *firm.* You are *obstinate.* He is *pigheaded.*"

> **Example:** No one in his right mind would ever do anything that dumb.

Testimonial @ You can take Jack Horkheimer's word on the composition of Saturn's rings, but the moment he starts promoting a product, watch out! If the testimonial or statement comes from a recognized authority in the field, great. If it comes from a person famous in another field, it can be misleading.

> **Example:** Sports hero: "I've tried every cold medicine on the market, and— believe me—nothing works like No Cold."

"News is the first rough draft of history."

—Ben Bradlee

VIEWING Skills

If you're an American teenager, you probably spend about 20 hours a week watching TV. You watch music videos, sitcoms, sporting events, and countless commercials. You also spend time viewing the Internet.

Have you ever stopped to consider how this viewing shapes your ideas, opinions, and actions? Does TV influence what you like or don't like? Does it shape what you think is true or important? Does it affect the way you spend your time or your money?

In all probability, television has a huge impact on your life. The same may be true of the World Wide Web. From banner ads to mass e-mailings, from personal sites to corporate press releases, the Web seeks to influence the way you think. That's why it's important for you to think about and question what you see on TV and on the Web. This chapter will help you with viewing tips and guidelines.

Preview

- Watching Television News
- Reviewing Videos
- Watching Commercials
- Viewing Web Sites

Watching Television News

You've probably heard of "active reading"; it means "thinking as you read." It follows, then, that active viewing requires you to think as you view. This is especially true when you are watching the news. You need to think about each news story and test it for the following three qualities: **completeness, correctness,** and **balance.**

Completeness

A good news story is complete. It answers the basic questions *Who? What? When? Where? Why?* and sometimes *How?* Here is the beginning of a news story that was read by Peter Jennings on ABC's *World News Tonight* on June 3, 1998. Notice that all 5 W's are answered in the first sentence:

The secretary of state is on her way
WHO   WHAT

to Geneva today to talk to America's allies
WHERE   WHEN   WHY

about trying to keep India and Pakistan

from getting into a nuclear conflict. . . .

When viewing the news, always listen carefully for the context of each story. This story went on to explain why India and Pakistan are often in conflict (religious differences are a big part of the problem) and why the threat of a nuclear war was especially strong (both countries had just tested nuclear weapons). This kind of background information will give you a better understanding of the meaning and importance of a story.

Viewing TIPS

Remember to watch the entire news story before you come to any conclusions about its importance or relevance for you. The last few facts in a story can be crucial to its overall impact.

Correctness

Correctness means the story states only known facts, and states them accurately. For example, imagine that an apartment building is on fire, and firefighters are at the scene. A resident who has been rescued says a family is still trapped in the burning building, but firefighters have searched all the apartments and found no one. There are three ways this story could be reported—two could easily mislead the audience.

Possibly Incorrect
Both of the following statements are possibly incorrect:

"An apartment building is burning, and a family is trapped inside."

"An apartment building is burning, but all residents have been rescued."

Correct
To be correct, the news story should say the following:

"An apartment building is burning. One resident who was rescued says other people are still trapped inside. However, firefighters say they have searched the building and found no one. We will update the story as more information comes in."

Balance

Balance is the opposite of *bias*. A balanced story presents all sides of an event or issue fairly. Balance is affected by the following factors:

Story Order ℮ Viewers expect the most important story to come first in a newscast, the next most important to come second, and so on. Is the story in an appropriate position for its importance?

People Interviewed ℮ Are people of equal reliability interviewed to speak for differing views? Are they given equal time?

Pictures Shown ℮ Do the pictures make one person or one side of the story look good, and another person or viewpoint look bad? Or, do most of the pictures focus on one person or viewpoint, ignoring others?

Word Choice ℮ The following sentences could be about the same event: "More than 50 people were injured." "Only minor injuries were reported." The first sentence clearly makes the event seem more serious.

Take NOTE One important but often-overlooked issue is whether a given news story is included in a newscast. Are there important events and issues in your community (or in the world) that aren't being covered by TV news?

WRITING GUIDELINES
Reviewing Videos

Video presentations (films, TV sitcoms, documentaries) use pictures, action, dialogue, and music to tell stories and present information. Writing a review will help you think through what a video says and how well it says it.

■ PREWRITING

1. **Considering the Purpose . . .** Before viewing, consider the purpose of the video program. Do you think that the video will inform, entertain, tell a story, or persuade? What questions do you have about the topic?

2. **Taking Notes . . .** While viewing, write down key words and ideas, but avoid taking too many notes. After viewing, do a freewriting in which you summarize what you saw and heard.

3. **Finding a Focus . . .** Think about what you want to focus on in your review—the plot, characters, subject, theme, visual images, or special effects.

4. **Developing a Thesis . . .** With your focus in mind, view the video again (if possible). Then develop a thesis that clearly states the point you plan to make in your writing.

■ WRITING AND REVISING

5. **Writing a First Draft . . .** Divide your review into three parts:

   Beginning: Introduce the video and present your focus either as a thesis statement or question. If helpful for your reader, give a brief summary of the video as background for your review.

   Middle: Apply your thesis to different parts of the video. For each point, provide and discuss supporting details.

   Ending: Summarize what you've covered in your review, and leave your readers with something to think about.

6. **Improving Your Writing . . .** Check your writing carefully. Is your review clear and complete? Have you developed and supported your thesis? Have you presented references and quotations from the video accurately?

■ EDITING AND PROOFREADING

7. **Checking for Style and Accuracy . . .** Review your revised writing for style, paying careful attention to sentence smoothness and word choice. Also make sure that names, titles, and technical terms are correct. Then check for spelling, grammar, and punctuation errors.

Sample Video Review

In the essay below, student writer Greg Masselink reviews a video documentary about the transcontinental railroad. He explores one of the main themes of the video—greed.

The Greediest Enterprise Under God

The writer starts by stating interesting facts, the video's title, and his focus.

When the transcontinental railroad was finished in 1869, it was the longest railroad in the world. Some people even called it "the grandest enterprise under God." Ken Burns used this phrase as the title for episode 5 of his documentary *The West*. However, a major theme in the video was greed. Through the use of photographs, stories, and interviews, the producers were able to re-create this grand construction project—and the greed that motivated its participants.

The two main participants were the Central Pacific and Union Pacific railroads. When the project started, the government paid each company a fair rate per mile of track—$16,000 on level ground, $32,000 on plateaus, and $48,000 in mountains. However, company lobbyists got those rates doubled within a year.

He adds examples of greed, as well as supporting details from the video.

As the companies raced to build the railroad, their greed often put workers in danger. For example, Chinese workers had to hang over mountain cliffs in baskets, stuff holes with dynamite, and get pulled up before the blast. Sometimes they didn't make it. During winter in the mountains, tunnels built under the snow would cave in, burying whole work gangs. It's estimated that 1,200 Chinese workers died.

During and after construction, the transcontinental railroad made way for another kind of greed—the buffalo slaughter. Buffalo hunters saw a fast, easy way to get rich. In fact, one hunter called the buffalo "walking gold pieces." By shooting a twenty-five cent cartridge, he could get three dollars for the buffalo's hide and bones. Some hunters fired all day long, stopping only long enough to cool their overheated barrels. Often, bone piles as tall as a man stretched a mile along the railroad tracks, waiting to be picked up and turned into glue. Three years after the railroad was finished, only quiet prairie grass remained where huge herds once roamed.

The conclusion offers a thoughtful summary of the video's meaning.

Though the transcontinental railroad project was a great technological achievement, the video showed that it also brought out the worst in people. "The Grandest Enterprise Under God" shows that greed destroys. Maybe a better title would be "The Greediest Enterprise Under God." ∎

Watching Commercials

The purpose of a commercial is to persuade viewers to buy something. And while some commercials come right out and ask you to buy a product, many rely on more subtle, unspoken messages. Here are some common unspoken messages, and why you should be aware of them.

FAMOUS FACES

Super athletes, movie stars, TV actors, and other celebrities appear in commercials for everything from shoes to soft drinks. The unspoken message: **If you want to be like the rich and famous, buy what they buy!**

✱ Of course, there is no real connection between the stars and the products. In fact, many of these celebrities don't even use the products they sell on TV. They just make millions trying to convince *you* to use them.

PERFECT PEOPLE

Even the "regular people" in commercials aren't really so "regular." Most are actors who are made to seem real, but more attractive, better dressed, smarter, nicer, and funnier than most real people. The unspoken message: **If you buy this product, you are smart, hip, cool, funny, popular, and on and on.**

WARM, FUZZY FEELINGS

How good can a hamburger or a phone call make you feel? Really good, if you believe the commercials that use smiling faces, gentle voices, kind words, and soft music to create warm, fuzzy feelings. The unspoken message: **Buy this, and you'll feel good, too.**

SPECIAL EFFECTS

Have you ever noticed that products in commercials can do the most amazing things? Bicycles fly. A celebrity action figure actually becomes a celebrity. A family walks into a chain restaurant and is suddenly transported to a tropical paradise. The unspoken message: **If you buy this product, wonderful things will happen to you, too.**

HELP FILE

Advertisers use a special tactic in commercials for children and teenagers. The actors in these commercials are always a few years older than the target audience. For example, a commercial advertising a product for high school students might use college students as actors. Why? Advertisers know most young people admire people who are a little older.

Viewing Web Sites

Like television, the Internet is a popular source of information and entertainment; like television, the Internet requires critical viewing. When you surf the Net, you need to know what you're getting into. To determine the reliability of a particular Web site, ask appropriate questions and be on the lookout for red flags. (See page 333.)

Questions to Ask

- Who created the Web site and supplied the content? Look for a person's name and some information about her or him: education, professional training, experience, current organization, job title, and so on.
- What organization (if any) sponsors the Web site? What can you find out about the organization?
- Is there an e-mail address you can use to contact the author or organization with questions or comments?
- When was the site last updated? This is especially important if you need up-to-date information.
- Is the information accurate? You can answer this question by comparing it to information found in other sources.

Red Flags to Watch For

- The site is anonymous—no author or organization name is listed.
- The content is poorly written, with many errors and misspellings.
- The information proves inaccurate when compared to other sources.
- The information is one-sided, not recognizing other viewpoints.
- The site makes big claims. ("This is the best idea anyone has ever had!")
- The site presents facts and figures without naming a source for their information. ("Millions of people could have this disease and not even know it!")
- The opinions stated are not backed by facts.
- The language is unreasonable, unfair, or even hateful.

Take NOTE   To find out how reliable a Web site is, check out the site's links, learn more about the site's author or the sponsoring organization, or look for recommendations and reviews of the site.

Proofreader's

GUIDE

"Cut out all those exclamation marks.   An exclamation mark is like laughing at your own jokes."   —F. Scott Fitzgerald

Marking
PUNCTUATION

Period

455.1 At the End of a Sentence

Use a **period** at the end of a sentence that makes a statement, requests something, or gives a mild command.

> (Statement) **The man who does not read good books has no advantage over the man who can't read them.**   —Mark Twain
>
> (Request) **Please bring your folders and notebooks to class.**
>
> (Mild command) **Listen carefully so that you don't make the same mistake again.**

NOTE: It is not necessary to place a period after a statement that has parentheses around it and is part of another sentence.

> **One time, when my friend was driving, our teacher, Mr. Spock** (we called him that because he had funny ears and showed no emotion), **told her to make a left turn, and she quickly responded by turning on the windshield wipers.**
>
> —Chris Kanarick, "They're Driving Me Crazy"

455.2 After an Initial or an Abbreviation

Place a period after an initial or an abbreviation.

> **Ms.   Sen.   D.D.S.   M.F.A.   M.D.   Jr.   U.S.   p.m.   a.m.**
>
> **Edna St. Vincent Millay   Booker T. Washington   D. H. Lawrence**

NOTE: When an abbreviation is the last word in a sentence, use only one period at the end of the sentence.

> **Mikhail eyed each door until he found the name Fletcher B. Gale, M.D.**

455.3 As a Decimal Point

A period is used as a decimal point.

> **New York City has around 7.3 million people; its last budget was $33.4 billion.**

Quick Guide

Using an Ellipsis

456.1 To Show Omitted Words

Use an **ellipsis** (three periods) to show that one or more words have been omitted in a quotation. (Leave one space before and after each period.)

(Original)
We the people of the United States, in order to form a more perfect Union, establish justice, insure domestic tranquility, provide for the common defense, promote the general welfare, and secure the blessings of liberty to ourselves and our posterity, do ordain and establish this Constitution for the United States of America.

—Preamble, U.S. Constitution

(Quotation)
"We the people . . . in order to form a more perfect Union . . . establish this Constitution for the United States of America."

456.2 At the End of a Sentence

If words from a quotation are omitted at the end of a sentence, place the ellipsis after the period that marks the conclusion of the sentence.

"Five score years ago, a great American, in whose symbolic shadow we stand, signed the Emancipation Proclamation. . . . But one hundred years later, we must face the tragic fact that the Negro is still not free."

—Martin Luther King, Jr., "I Have a Dream"

NOTE: If the quoted material is a complete sentence (even if it was not complete in the original), use a period, then an ellipsis.

(Original)
I am tired; my heart is sick and sad.   From where the sun now stands I will fight no more forever.

—Chief Joseph of the Nez Percé

(Quotation)
"I am tired. . . . From where the sun now stands I will fight no more forever."
or
"I am tired. . . . I will fight no more. . . . "

456.3 To Show a Pause

Use an ellipsis to indicate a pause.

I brought my trembling hand to my focusing eyes.   It was oozing, it was red, it was . . . it was . . . a tomato!

—Laura Baginski, student writer

Comma

457.1 Between Two Independent Clauses

Use a **comma** between two independent clauses that are joined by a coordinating conjunction such as *and, but, or, nor, for, yet, so.*

I wanted to knock on the glass to attract attention, but I couldn't move.

—Ralph Ellison, *Invisible Man*

NOTE: Do not confuse a sentence containing a compound verb for a compound sentence.

I had to burn her trash and then sweep up her porches and halls.

—Anne Moody, *Coming of Age in Mississippi*

457.2 To Separate Adjectives

Use commas to separate coordinate adjectives that *equally* modify the same noun. (Note: Do not use a comma between the last adjective and the noun.)

John's eyes met the hard, bright lights hanging directly above him.

—Julie Ament, student writer

> *A Closer Look* To determine whether adjectives modify equally—and should, therefore, be separated by commas—use these two tests:
>
> **1.** Shift the order of the adjectives; if the sentence is clear, the adjectives modify equally. (In the example below, *hot* and *smelly* can be shifted and the sentence is still clear; *usual* and *morning* cannot.)
>
> **2.** Insert *and* between the adjectives; if the sentence reads well, use a comma when *and* is omitted. (The word *and* can be inserted between *hot* and *smelly,* but *and* does not make sense between *usual* and *morning.*)
>
> > **Matty was tired of working in the hot, smelly kitchen and decided to take her usual morning walk.**

457.3 To Separate Parenthetical or Contrasted Elements

Use commas to separate parenthetical elements within a sentence.

Allison stepped into class, late as usual, and sat down.

Use commas to separate contrasted elements within a sentence.

Since the stereotypes were about Asians, and not African Americans, no such reaction occurred.

—Emmeline Chen, "Eliminating the Lighter Shades of Stereotyping"

Comma (continued)

458.1 To Enclose Explanatory Words

Use commas to enclose an explanatory word or phrase.

They stood together, away from the pile of stones in the corner, **and their jokes were quiet and they smiled rather than laughed.**

—Shirley Jackson, "The Lottery"

458.2 To Set Off Appositives

A specific kind of explanatory word or phrase called an **appositive** identifies or renames a preceding noun or pronoun.

Benson, our uninhibited and enthusiastic Yorkshire terrier, **joined our family on my sister's fifteenth birthday.** —Chad Hockerman, student writer

NOTE: Do not use commas with *restrictive appositives.* A restrictive appositive is essential to the basic meaning of the sentence.

Twenty-one-year-old student Edna E. Rivera **almost had a nose job but changed her mind.** —Andrea Lo & Vera Perez

458.3 Between Items in a Series

Use commas to separate individual words, phrases, or clauses in a series. (A series contains at least three items.)

I'd never known anything about having meat, vegetables, and a salad **all at the same meal.** (Three nouns in a series)

I took her for walks, read her stories, and made up games for her to play. (Three phrases in a series) —Anne Moody, *Coming of Age in Mississippi*

NOTE: Do not use commas when all the words in a series are connected with *or, nor,* or *and.*

Her fingernails are pointed and **manicured** and **painted a shiny red.**

—Carson McCullers, "Sucker"

458.4 After Introductory Phrases

Use a comma after an introductory participial phrase.

Determined to finish the sweater by Thanksgiving, my grandmother knits night and day.

Use a comma after an introductory prepositional phrase.

In the oddest places and at the strangest times, my grandmother can be found knitting madly away.

NOTE: You may omit the comma if the introductory phrase is short.

Before breakfast my grandmother knits.

NOTE: In most cases, you may also omit the comma if the prepositional phrase follows the independent clause.

My grandmother can be found knitting madly away in the oddest places and at the strangest times.

459.1 After Introductory Clauses

Use a comma after an introductory adverb clause.

After the practice was over, Tina walked home.

A comma also is used if an adverb clause follows the main clause and begins with *although, even though, while,* or another conjunction expressing a contrast.

Tina walked home, even though it was raining very hard.

However, a comma is not used if the adverb clause following the main clause is needed to complete the meaning of the sentence.

Tina practiced hard because she feared losing.

459.2 To Set Off Nonrestrictive Phrases and Clauses

Use commas to set off **nonrestrictive** (unnecessary) clauses and participial phrases. A nonrestrictive clause or participial phrase adds information that is not necessary to the basic meaning of the sentence. For example, if the clause or phrase (in red) were left out in the two examples below, the meaning of the sentences would remain clear. Therefore, commas are used to set them off.

The Altena Fitness Center and Visker Gymnasium, which were built last year, are busy every day. (nonrestrictive clause)

Students and faculty, trying to improve their fitness, use both facilities throughout the week. (nonrestrictive phrase)

Do not use commas to set off **restrictive** (necessary) clauses and participial phrases. A restrictive clause or participial phrase adds information that the reader needs to know in order to understand the sentence. For example, if the clause and phrase (in red) were dropped from the examples below, the meaning wouldn't be the same. Therefore, commas are *not* used.

The handball court that has a sign-up sheet by the door must be reserved. The clause identifies which handball court must be reserved. (restrictive clause)

Individuals wanting to use this court must sign up a day in advance. (restrictive phrase)

A Closer Look: **That and Which** Use *that* to introduce restrictive (necessary) clauses; use *which* to introduce nonrestrictive (unnecessary) clauses. When the two words are used in this way, the reader can quickly distinguish necessary information from unnecessary information.

The treadmill that monitors heart rate is the one you must use. The reader needs the information to find the right treadmill.

This treadmill, which we got last year, is required for your program. The main clause tells the reader which treadmill to use; the other clause gives additional, unnecessary information.

Comma (continued)

460.1 To Set Off Dates

Use commas to set off items in a date.

He began working out on December 1, 1999, but quit by May 1, 2000.

However, when only the month and year are given, no commas are needed.

He began working out in December 1999 but quit by May 2000.

460.2 To Set Off Items in Addresses

Use commas to set off items in an address.

Mail the box to Friends of Wildlife, Box 402, Spokane, Washington 20077.

NOTE: No comma is placed between the state and zip code.

460.3 To Set Off Dialogue

Use commas to set off the speaker's exact words from the rest of the sentence.

"It's like we have our own government," adds Tanya, a 17-year-old squatter.
—Kyung Sun Yu and Nell Bernstein, "Street Teens Forge a Home"

460.4 In Direct Address

Use commas to separate a noun of direct address from the rest of the sentence. A *noun of direct address* is the noun that names the person(s) spoken to.

"But, Mother Gibbs, one can go back; one can go back there again. . . . "
—Thornton Wilder, *Our Town*

460.5 To Set Off Interjections

Use a comma to separate an interjection or a weak exclamation from the rest of the sentence.

Hey, how am I to know that a minute's passed?
—Nathan Slaughter and Jim Schweitzer, *When Time Dies*
Okay, now what do I do?

460.6 To Set Off Interruptions

Use commas to set off a word, a phrase, or a clause that interrupts the movement of a sentence. Such expressions usually can be identified through the following tests: (1) They may be omitted without changing the meaning of a sentence. (2) They may be placed nearly anywhere in the sentence without changing its meaning.

For me, well, it's just a good job gone!
—Langston Hughes

As a general rule, the safest way to double your money is to fold it and put it in your pocket.

461.1 In Numbers

Use commas to separate numerals in large numbers in order to distinguish hundreds, thousands, millions, and so forth.

1,101   25,000   7,642,020

461.2 To Enclose Titles or Initials

Use commas to enclose a title or initials and names that follow a surname.

Until Martin, Sr., was 15, he never had more than three months of schooling in any one year. —Ed Clayton, *Martin Luther King: The Peaceful Warrior*

Hickok, J. B., and Cody, William F., are two popular Western heroes.

461.3 For Clarity or Emphasis

You may use a comma for clarity or for emphasis. There will be times when none of the traditional rules call for a comma, but one will be needed to prevent confusion or to emphasize an important idea.

It may be that those who do most, dream most. (emphasis)

—Stephen Leacock

What the crew does, does affect our voyage. (clarity)

Semicolon

461.4 To Join Two Independent Clauses

Use a **semicolon** to join two or more closely related independent clauses that are not connected with a coordinating conjunction. (Independent clauses can stand alone as separate sentences.)

I did not call myself a poet; I told people I wrote poems.

—Terry McMillan, "Breaking Ice"

Silence coated the room like a layer of tar; not even the breathing of the 11 Gehad made any sound. —Gann Bierner, "The Leap"

NOTE: The exception to this rule occurs when the two clauses are closely related, short, or conversational in tone. Then a comma may be used.

To rule is easy, to govern is difficult.

461.5 With Conjunctive Adverbs

A semicolon is used *before* a conjunctive adverb (and a comma after it) when the word connects two independent clauses in a compound sentence. (Common conjunctive adverbs are *also, besides, finally, however, indeed, instead, meanwhile, moreover, nevertheless, next, still, then, therefore,* and *thus.*)

"I am faced with my imminent demise; therefore, life becomes a very precious thing." — Amy Taylor, "AIDS Can Happen Here!"

Semicolon (continued)

462.1 To Set Off Independent Clauses

Use a semicolon to separate independent clauses that are long or contain commas, even though a coordinating conjunction connects them.

> **We waited all day in that wide line, tired travelers pressing in from all sides; and when we needed drinks or sandwiches, I would squeeze my way to the cafeteria and back.**

462.2 To Separate Groups That Contain Commas

A semicolon is used to separate groups of words that already contain commas.

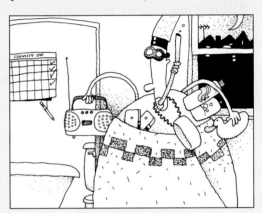

Every Saturday night my brother gathers up his things—goggles, shower cap, and snorkel; bubble bath, soap, and shampoo; tapes, stereo, and rubber duck—and heads for the tub.

Colon

462.3 After a Salutation

Use a **colon** after the salutation of a business letter.

> **Dear Judge Parker: Dear Governor Whitman:**

462.4 Between Numerals Indicating Time

Use a colon between the hours, minutes, and seconds of a number indicating time.

> **8:30 p.m.   9:45 a.m.   10:24:55**

462.5 For Emphasis

Use a colon to emphasize a word, a phrase, a clause, or a sentence that explains or adds impact to the main clause.

> **His guest lecturers are local chefs who learn a lesson themselves: Homeless people are worth employing.**
>
> —Beth Brophy, "Feeding Those Who Are Hungry"

463.1 To Introduce a Quotation

Use a colon to formally introduce a quotation, a sentence, or a question.

> **Directly a voice in the corner rang out wild and clear: "I've got him! I've got him!"**
> —Mark Twain, *Roughing It*

463.2 To Introduce a List

A colon is used to introduce a list.

> **I got all the proper equipment: scissors, a bucket of water to keep things clean, some cotton for the stuffing, and needle and thread to sew it up.**
> —Joan Baez, *Daybreak*

A Closer Look Do not use a colon between a verb and its object or complement, or between a preposition and its object.

Incorrect: Max has: a snowmobile, an ATV, and a canoe.

Correct: Max has plenty of toys: a snowmobile, an ATV, and a canoe.

Incorrect: Dad watches a TV show about: cooking wild game.

Correct: Dad watches a TV show about a new subject: cooking wild game.

463.3 Between a Title and a Subtitle

Use a colon to distinguish between a title and a subtitle, volume and page, and chapter and verse in literature.

> **Writers INC: A Student Handbook for WRITING and LEARNING**
>
> **Encyclopedia Americana IV: 211**   **Psalm 23:1-6**

Hyphen

463.4 In Compound Words

Use the **hyphen** to make compound words.

> **great-great-grandfather**   **maid-in-waiting**   **three-year-old**
>
> **It was taller than my-dad-and-me-on-his-shoulders tall.**
> —Kristen Frappier, "The Corn"

NOTE: A dash is indicated by two hyphens--without spacing before or after--in all handwritten material. Don't use a single hyphen when a dash is required.

463.5 To Join Letters and Words

Use a hyphen to join a capital letter or lowercase letter to a noun or participle. (Check your dictionary.)

> **T-shirt**   **Y-turn**   **G-rated**   *x*-axis

Hyphen (continued)

464.1 Between Numbers and Fractions

Use a hyphen to join the words in compound numbers from *twenty-one* to *ninety-nine* when it is necessary to write them out.

twenty-five	**forty-three**	**seventy-nine**	**sixty-two**

Use a hyphen between the numerator and denominator of a fraction, but not when one or both of those elements are already hyphenated.

four-tenths	**five-sixteenths**	**(7/32) seven thirty-seconds**

464.2 In a Special Series

Use hyphens when two or more words have a common element that is omitted in all but the last term.

The ship has lovely two-, four-, or six-person cabins.

464.3 To Create New Words

Use a hyphen to form new words beginning with the prefixes *self-, ex-, all-,* and *half-*. Also use a hyphen to join any prefix to a proper noun, a proper adjective, or the official name of an office. Use a hyphen before the suffix *-elect*.

self-contained	**ex-governor**	**all-inclusive**	**half-painted**
pre-Cambrian	**mid-December**	**president-elect**	

Use a hyphen to join the prefix *great* to names of relatives, but do not use a hyphen to join *great* to other words.

great-aunt, great-grandfather (correct)	**great-hall** (incorrect)

464.4 To Prevent Confusion

Use a hyphen with prefixes or suffixes to avoid confusion or awkward spelling.

re-create (not *recreate*) the image	**bell-like (not *belllike*) sound**
re-cover (not *recover*) the sofa	**intra-abdominal (not *intraabdominal*)**

464.5 To Join Numbers

Use a hyphen to join numbers indicating the life span of a person and the score in a contest or a vote.

We can thank Louis Pasteur (1822-1895), a French chemist, for pasteurized milk.

In the 2000 Rose Bowl, Wisconsin defeated Stanford 17-9.

My kid brother's kindergarten class voted 18-2 in favor of year-round school.

465.1 To Divide a Word

Use a hyphen to divide a word, only between its syllables, at the end of a line of print. Always place the hyphen after the syllable at the end of the line—never before a syllable at the beginning of the following line.

Guidelines for Dividing with Hyphens

1. Always leave enough of the word at the end of the line so that the word can be identified.
2. Always divide a compound word between its basic units: *sister-in-law,* not *sis-ter-in-law.*
3. Avoid dividing a word of five or fewer letters: *paper, study, July.*
4. Avoid dividing a number presented in numeral form: *1,000,000;* not *1,000,-000.*
5. Avoid dividing the last word in a paragraph.
6. Never divide a one-syllable word: *rained, skills, through.*
7. Never divide a one-letter syllable from the rest of the word: *omit-ted,* not *o-mitted.*
8. When a vowel is a syllable by itself, divide the word after the vowel: *epi-sode,* not *ep-isode.*
9. Never divide abbreviations or contractions: *shouldn't,* not *should-n't.*
10. Never divide the last word in more than two lines in a row.

465.2 To Form an Adjective

Use the hyphen to join two or more words that serve as a single adjective (a single-thought adjective) before a noun.

In real life I am a large, big-boned woman with rough, man-working hands.

—Alice Walker, "Everyday Use"

A Closer Look When words forming the adjective come after the noun, do not hyphenate them.

In real life I am large and big boned.

When the first of these words is an adverb ending in *-ly,* do not use a hyphen; also, do not use a hyphen when a number or a letter is the final element in a single-thought adjective.

delicately prepared pastry (adverb ending in -ly)

class B movie (letter is the final element)

Dash

466.1 To Indicate a Sudden Break

Use a **dash** to indicate a sudden break or change in the sentence.

Near the semester's end—and this is not always due to poor planning—some students may find themselves in a real crunch.

NOTE: Dashes are often used in place of commas. Use dashes when you want to give special emphasis; use commas when there is no need for emphasis.

466.2 To Set Off an Introductory Series

Use a dash to set off an introductory series from the clause that explains the series.

A good book, a cup of tea, a comfortable chair—these things always saved my mother's sanity.

466.3 To Set Off Parenthetical Material

Use a dash to set off parenthetical material—material that explains or clarifies a word or a phrase.

A single incident—a tornado that came without warning—changed the face of the small town forever.

466.4 To Indicate Interrupted Speech

Use a dash to show interrupted or faltering speech in dialogue.

SOJOURNER: Mama, why are you—
MAMA: Isabelle, do as I say!

—Sandy Asher, *A Woman Called Truth*

466.5 For Emphasis

Use a dash to emphasize a word, a series, a phrase, or a clause.

After years of trial and error, Belther made history with his invention—the unicycle.

Question Mark

467.1 Direct Question

Place a **question mark** at the end of a direct question.

> **Now what? I wondered. Do I go out and buy a jar of honey and stand around waving it? How in the world am I supposed to catch a bear?**
>> —Ken Taylor, "The Case of the Grizzly on the Greens"
> **Where did my body end and the crystal and white world begin?**
>> —Ralph Ellison, *Invisible Man*

NOTE: When a question ends with a quotation that is also a question, use only one question mark, and place it within the quotation marks.

> **Do you remember, on road trips, driving your parents crazy** by asking, "Are we there yet?"

467.2 Indirect Question

Do *not* use a question mark after an indirect question.

> **Out on the street, I picked out a friendly looking old man and asked him where the depot was.** —Wilson Rawls, *Where the Red Fern Grows*

467.3 To Show Uncertainty

Use a question mark within parentheses to show uncertainty.

> **This summer marks the 20th season (?) of the American Players Theatre.**

467.4 Short Question

Use a question mark for a short question within parentheses.

> **We crept so quietly** (had they heard us?) **past the kitchen door and back to our room.**

Use a question mark for a short question within dashes.

> **Maybe somewhere in the pasts of these humbled people, there were cases of bad mothering or absent fathering or emotional neglect—what family surviving the '50s was exempt?—but I couldn't believe these human errors brought the physical changes in Frank.**
>> —Mary Kay Blakely, *Wake Me When It's Over*

Exclamation Point

467.5 To Express Strong Feeling

Use the **exclamation point** (sparingly) to express strong feeling. You may place it after a word, a phrase, or a sentence.

> **"That's not the point," said Wangero. "These are all pieces of dresses Grandma used to wear. She did all this stitching by hand. Imagine!"**
>> —Alice Walker, "Everyday Use"

Quotation Marks

468.1 To Punctuate Titles

Use **quotation marks** to punctuate titles of songs, poems, short stories, one-act plays, lectures, episodes of radio or television programs, chapters of books, unpublished works, electronic files, and articles found in magazines, newspapers, encyclopedias, or on-line sources. (For punctuation of other titles, see 470.2.)

> "Santa Lucia" (song)
>
> "The Chameleon" (short story)
>
> "Twentieth-Century Memories" (lecture)
>
> "Affordable Adventures" (magazine article)
>
> "Dire Prophecy of the Howling Dog" (chapter in a book)
>
> "Dancing with Debra" (television episode)
>
> "Miss Julie" (one-act play)

468.2 For Special Words

You may use quotation marks (1) to distinguish a word that is being discussed, (2) to indicate that a word is unfamiliar slang, or (3) to point out that a word is being used in a special way.

> **(1) A commentary on the times is that the word "honesty" is now preceded by "old-fashioned."**
> —Larry Wolters
>
> **(2) I . . . asked the bartender where I could hear "chanky-chank,"** as Cajuns **called their music.** —William Least Heat-Moon, *Blue Highways*
>
> **(3) Tom pushed the wheelchair across the street, showed the lady his "honest" smile . . . and stole her purse.**

NOTE: You may use italics (underlining) in place of quotation marks in each of these three situations.

468.3 Placement of Punctuation

Always place periods and commas inside quotation marks.

> **"Dr. Slaughter wants you to have liquids, Will," Mama said anxiously. "He said not to give you any solid food tonight."**
> —Olive Ann Burns, *Cold Sassy Tree*

Place an exclamation point or a question mark inside quotation marks when it punctuates the quotation, and outside when it punctuates the main sentence.

> **"Am I dreaming?"**
>
> **Had she heard him say, "Here's the key to your new car"?**

Always place semicolons or colons outside quotation marks.

> **I wrote about Wallace Stevens' "Thirteen Ways of Looking at a Blackbird"; "Sunday Morning" was too deep for me.**

Quick Guide

Marking Quoted Material

469.1 To Set Off Quoted Passages

Place quotation marks before and after the words in direct quotations.

"Just come to a game," he pleads. "You'll change your mind."

—Sandra Lampe, "Batter UP!"

In a quoted passage, put brackets around any word or punctuation mark that is not part of the original quotation.

(Original) **Conservation pundits point to it as the classic example of the impossibility of providing good government service.**

(Quotation) **"Conservation pundits point to it [the U.S. Postal Service] as the classic example of the impossibility of providing good government service."**
—Brad Branan, "Dead Letter Office?"

NOTE: If you quote only part of the original passage, be sure to construct a sentence that is both accurate and grammatically correct.

Much of the restructuring of the Postal Service has involved "turning over large parts of its work to the private sector."

469.2 For Long Quotations

If you quote more than one paragraph, place quotation marks before each paragraph and at the end of the last paragraph (Example A). If a quotation has more than four lines on a page, you may set it off from the text by indenting 10 spaces from the left margin (block form). Do not use quotation marks either before or after the quoted material, unless they appear in the original. Double-space the quotation. (Example B).

Example A

Example B

469.3 For Quoting a Quotation

Use single quotation marks to punctuate a quotation within a quotation. Use double and single quotation marks in order to distinguish a quotation within a quotation within a quotation.

"For tomorrow," said Mr. Botts, "read 'Unlighted Lamps.'"

Sue asked, "Did you hear Mr. Botts say, 'Read "Unlighted Lamps"'?"

Italics (Underlining)

470.1 Handwritten and Printed Material

Italics is a printer's term for a style of type that is slightly slanted. In this sentence, the word *happiness* is printed in italics. In material that is handwritten or typed on a machine that cannot print in italics, underline each word or letter that should be in italics.

My Ántonia is the story of a strong and determined pioneer woman.
(printed)

Willa Cather's <u>My Ántonia</u> describes pioneer life in America.
(typed or handwritten)

470.2 In Titles

Use italics to indicate the titles of magazines, newspapers, pamphlets, books, full-length plays, films, videos, radio and television programs, book-length poems, ballets, operas, lengthy musical compositions, cassettes, CD's, legal cases, and the names of ships and aircraft. (For punctuation of other titles, see 468.1.)

<u>Newsweek</u> (magazine)

<u>Cold Sassy Tree</u> (book)

<u>Shakespeare in Love</u> (film)

<u>Friends</u> (television program)

<u>Caring for Your Kitten</u> (pamphlet)

<u>Hedda Gabler</u> (full-length play)

<u>Chicago Tribune</u> (newspaper)

NOTE: Punctuate one title within another title as follows:

"Is <u>ER's</u> Reality Trustworthy?" (title of TV program in an article)

470.3 For Special Uses

Use italics for a number, letter, or word that is being discussed or used in a special way. (Sometimes quotation marks are used for this reason. See 468.2.)

I hope that this letter <u>I</u> stands for <u>incredible</u> and not <u>incomplete</u>.

470.4 For Foreign Words

Use italics for foreign words that have not been adopted into the English language; also use italics for scientific names.

The voyageurs—tough men with natural <u>bonhomie</u>—discovered the shy <u>Castor canadensis</u>, or North American beaver.

Parentheses

471.1 To Set Off Explanatory Material

Use **parentheses** to set off explanatory or added material that interrupts the normal sentence structure.

> **Benson (our dog) sits in on our piano lessons (on the piano bench), much to the teacher's surprise and amusement.** —Chad Hockerman, student writer

NOTE: Place question marks and exclamation points within the parentheses when they mark the added material.

> **Ivan at once concluded (the rascal!) that I had a passion for dances, and . . . wanted to drag me off to a dancing class.**
> —Fyodor Dostoyevsky, "A Novel in Nine Letters"

471.2 With Full Sentences

When using a full "sentence" within another sentence, do not capitalize it or use a period inside the parentheses.

> **And, since your friend won't have the assignment (he was just thinking about calling you), you'll have to make a couple more calls to actually get it.**
> —Ken Taylor, "The Art and Practice of Avoiding Homework"

When the parenthetical sentence comes after the main sentence, capitalize and punctuate it the same way you would any other complete sentence.

> **They kiss and hug when they say "hello," and I love this. (In Korea, people are much more formal; they just shake hands and bow to each other.)**
> —Sue Chong, "He Said I Was Too American"

NOTE: For unavoidable parentheses within parentheses (. . . [. . .] . . .), use brackets. Avoid overuse of parentheses by using commas instead.

Diagonal

471.3 To Form a Fraction or Show a Choice

Use a **diagonal** (also called a *slash*) to form a fraction. Also place a diagonal between two words, as in *and/or*, to indicate that either is acceptable.

> **Marie's shoe size is 12 1/2; for economic reasons, she wishes it were 7 1/2. Press the load/eject button.**

471.4 When Quoting Poetry

When quoting more than one line of poetry, use a diagonal to show where each line of poetry ends. (Insert a space on each side of the diagonal.)

> **I have learned not to worry about love; / but to honor its coming / with all my heart.**
> —Alice Walker, "New Face"

Apostrophe

472.1 In Contractions

Use an **apostrophe** to show that one or more letters have been left out of a word to form a contraction.

> **hadn't** – *o* **is left out**   **they'd** – *woul* **is left out**   **it's** – *i* **is left out**

NOTE: Use an apostrophe to show that one or more numerals or letters have been left out of numbers or words in order to show special pronunciation.

> **class of '99** – *19* **is left out**   **g'day** – *ood* **is left out**

472.2 To Form Plurals

Use an apostrophe and *s* to form the plural of a letter, a number, a sign, or a word discussed as a word.

> **B – B's**   **C – C's**   **8 – 8's**   **+ – +'s**   **and – and's**
>
> **Ms. D'Aquisto says our conversations contain too many *cool's* and *no way's*.**

NOTE: When two apostrophes are called for in the same word, simply omit the second one.

> **Follow closely the *do's* and *don'ts* (not *don't's*) on the checklist.**

472.3 To Form Singular Possessives

Add an apostrophe and *s* to form the possessive of most singular nouns.

> **Spock's ears**   **Captain Kirk's singing**   **the ship's escape plan**

NOTE: When a singular noun ends with an *s* or a *z* sound, you may form the possessive by adding just an apostrophe. When the singular noun is a one-syllable word, however, you usually add both an apostrophe and an *s* to form the possessive.

> **San Carlos' government (or) San Carlos's government** (two-syllable word)
>
> **Ross's essay** (one-syllable word)   **The class's field trip** (one-syllable word)

472.4 To Form Plural Possessives

The possessive form of plural nouns ending in *s* is usually made by adding just an apostrophe.

> **the MacKenzies' cottage**   **bosses' orders**

A Closer Look It will help you punctuate correctly if you remember that the word immediately before the apostrophe is the owner.

> **girl's guitar** (*girl* is the owner)   **boss's order** (*boss* is the owner)
>
> **girls' guitar** (*girls* are the owners)   **bosses' order** (*bosses* are the owners)

473.1 In Compound Nouns

Form the possessive of a compound noun by placing the possessive ending after the last word.

the secretary of the interior's (singular) **agenda**
her lady-in-waiting's (singular) **day off**

If forming a possessive of a plural compound noun creates an awkward construction, you may replace the possessive with an *of* phrase.   (All four forms below are correct.)

their fathers-in-law's (plural) **birthdays**
or the birthdays of their *fathers-in-law* (plural)

the ambassadors-at-large's (plural) **plans**
or the plans of the *ambassadors-at-large* (plural)

473.2 With Indefinite Pronouns

Form the possessive of an indefinite pronoun by placing an apostrophe and an *s* on the last word. (See 504.4.)

everyone's   **anyone's**   **somebody's**

473.3 To Express Time or Amount

Use an apostrophe and an *s* with an adjective that is part of an expression indicating time or amount.

a penny's worth   **today's business**   **this morning's meeting**
yesterday's news   **a day's wage**   **a month's pay**

473.4 To Show Shared Possession

When possession is shared by more than one noun, use the possessive form for the last noun in the series.

Sarah, Linda, and Nakiva's water skis (All three own the same skis.)
Sarah's, Linda's, and Nakiva's water skis (Each owns her own skis.)

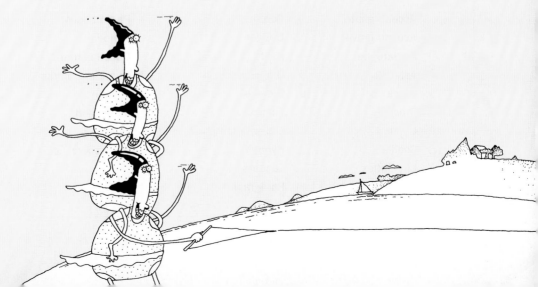

Brackets

474.1 To Set Off Clarifying Information

Use **brackets** before and after words that are added to clarify what another person has said or written.

> **"They'd** [the sweat bees] **get into your mouth, ears, eyes, nose. You'd feel them all over you."**
>
> —Marilyn Johnson and Sasha Nyary, "Roosevelts in the Amazon"

NOTE: The brackets indicate that the words *the sweat bees* are not part of the quotation but were added for clarification.

474.2 To Set Off Added Words

Place brackets around material that has been added by someone other than the author or speaker.

> **"Congratulations to the astronomy club's softball team, which put in, shall we say, a 'stellar' performance."** [groans]

474.3 Around an Editorial Correction

Place brackets around an editorial correction inserted within quoted material.

> **"Brooklyn alone has 8 percent of lead poisoning** [victims] **nationwide," said Marjorie Moore.**
>
> —Donna Actie, student writer

NOTE: Place brackets around the letters *sic* (Latin for "as such"); the letters indicate that an error appearing in the material being quoted was made by the original speaker or writer.

> **"'When I'm queen,' mused Lucy, 'I'll show these blockheads whose** [sic] **got beauty and brains.'"**

Punctuation Marks

´	Accent, acute	,	Comma	( )	Parentheses
`	Accent, grave	†	Dagger	.	Period
'	Apostrophe	—	Dash	?	Question mark
*	Asterisk	/	Diagonal/Slash	" "	Quotation marks
{ }	Brace	¨ (ü)	Dieresis	§	Section
[ ]	Brackets	. . .	Ellipsis	;	Semicolon
^	Caret	!	Exclamation point	~	Tilde
˛ (ç)	Cedilla	-	Hyphen	___	Underscore
^	Circumflex	...	Leaders		
:	Colon	¶	Paragraph		

"English spelling is weird . . .
or is it wierd?"

—Irwin Hill

Checking
MECHANICS

Capitalization

475.1 **Proper Nouns and Adjectives**

Capitalize proper nouns and proper adjectives (those derived from proper nouns). The chart below provides a quick overview of capitalization rules. The pages following explain specific or special uses of capitalization.

Capitalization at a Glance

Days of the week	Sunday, Monday, Tuesday
Months	June, July, August
Holidays, holy days	Thanksgiving, Easter, Hanukkah
Periods, events in history	Middle Ages, the Renaissance
Special events	the Battle of Bunker Hill
Political parties	Republican Party, Socialist Party
Official documents	Declaration of Independence
Trade names	Oscar Mayer hot dogs, Pontiac Sunbird
Formal epithets	Alexander the Great
Official titles	Mayor John Spitzer, Senator Feinstein
Official state nicknames	the Badger State, the Aloha State
Geographical names	
Planets, heavenly bodies	Earth, Jupiter, the Milky Way
Continents	Australia, South America
Countries	Ireland, Grenada, Sri Lanka
States, provinces	Ohio, Utah, Nova Scotia
Cities, towns, villages	El Paso, Burlington, Wonewoc
Streets, roads, highways	Park Avenue, Route 66, Interstate 90
Sections of a country or continent	the West Coast, the Far East
Landforms	the Rocky Mountains, the Sahara Desert
Bodies of water	Yellowstone Lake, Pumpkin Creek
Public areas	Times Square, Sequoia National Park

Capitalization (continued)

476.1 First Words

Capitalize the first word in every sentence and the first word in a full-sentence direct quotation.

The crowd was quiet. A girl whispered, "I hope it's not Nancy," and the sound of her whisper reached the edges of the crowd.

—Shirley Jackson, "The Lottery"

476.2 Sentences in Parentheses

Capitalize the first word in a sentence enclosed in parentheses if that sentence comes before or after another complete sentence; do not capitalize the first word if the parenthetical appears within another sentence.

Shamelessly she winked at me and grinned again. (That grin! She could have taken it off her face and put it on the table.)

—Jean Stafford, "Bad Characters"

Damien sleeps in (this may be his only luxury) on Saturday mornings.

476.3 Sentences Following Colons

Capitalize the first word in a complete sentence that follows a colon when (1) you want to emphasize the sentence or (2) the sentence is a formal statement or quotation.

When we quarreled and made horrible faces at one another, Mother knew what to say: "Your faces will stay that way, and no one will marry you."

476.4 Sections of the Country

Capitalize words that indicate particular sections of the country; do not capitalize words that simply indicate direction.

Mr. Johnson is from the Southwest. (section of the country)

After moving north to Montana, he had to buy winter clothes. (direction)

476.5 Languages, Races, Nationalities, Religions

Capitalize languages, races, nationalities, and religions.

Navajo   Catholic   French   European   Spanish   Islam

NOTE: Also capitalize nouns that refer to the Supreme Being, the word *Bible*, the books of the Bible, and the names for other holy books.

God   Jehovah   the Lord   the Savior   Allah   Bible   Genesis

476.6 Titles

Capitalize the first word of a title, the last word, and every word in between except articles (*a, an, the*), short prepositions, and coordinating conjunctions. Follow this rule for titles of books, newspapers, magazines, poems, plays, songs, articles, films, works of art, photographs, and stories.

Cold Sassy Tree   Washington Post   "Nothing Gold Can Stay"

A Midsummer Night's Dream   "The Diary of a Madman"

477.1 Organizations

Capitalize the name of an organization, an association, or a team and its members.

Tampa Bay Sailors	**American Indian Movement**
Tucson High School Drama Club	**Democratic Party**

477.2 Abbreviations

Capitalize abbreviations of titles and organizations. (Some other abbreviations are also capitalized. See pages 481-482.)

AAA   CEO   NAACP   M.D.   Ph.D.

477.3 Letters

Capitalize the letters used to indicate form or shape.

U-turn   I-beam   S-curve   T-shirt   V-shaped

477.4 Words Used as Names

Capitalize words like *father, mother, uncle,* and *senator* when they are used as titles with a personal name or when they are substituted for proper nouns (especially in direct address).

Welcome home, Aunt Lucinda. (*Aunt* is part of the name.)

My aunt has a new Corvette.

I hope Mayor Bates arrives soon. (*Mayor* is part of the name.)

The mayor, Ken Bates, has never missed a council meeting.

A Closer Look To test whether a word is being substituted for a proper noun, simply read the sentence with a proper noun in place of the word. If the proper noun fits in the sentence, the word being tested should be capitalized; if the proper noun does not work in the sentence, the word should not be capitalized.

Did Mom (Sue) say we could go? (*Sue* works in this sentence.)

Did your mom (Sue) say you could go? (*Sue* does not work here.)

NOTE: Usually the word is not capitalized if it follows a possessive—*my, his, your*—as it does in the second sentence above.

477.5 Titles of Courses

Capitalize words like *sociology* and *history* when they are used as titles of specific courses; do not capitalize these words when they name a field of study.

Who teaches History 202? (title of a specific course)

It's the same professor who teaches my sociology course. (a field of study)

NOTE: The words *freshman, sophomore, junior,* and *senior* are not capitalized unless they are part of an official title.

Rosa is a senior this year and is in charge of the Senior Class Banquet.

Plurals

478.1   Nouns Ending in a Consonant

Form the **plurals** of most nouns by adding *s* to the singular.

cheerleader – cheerleaders   wheel – wheels

Form the plurals of nouns ending in *sh, ch, x, s,* and *z* by adding *es* to the singular.

lunch – lunches   dish – dishes   mess – messes   fox – foxes

Exception: Some nouns remain unchanged when used as plurals: *deer, sheep, salmon,* etc.

478.2   Nouns Ending in *y*

The plurals of common nouns that end in *y*—preceded by a consonant—are formed by changing the *y* to *i* and adding *es.*

fly – flies   jalopy – jalopies

The plurals of nouns that end in *y*—preceded by a vowel—are formed by adding only an *s.*

donkey – donkeys   monkey – monkeys

NOTE: Form the plurals of all proper nouns ending in *y* by adding *s.*

We have three Kathys in our English class.

478.3   Nouns Ending in *o*

The plurals of nouns ending in *o*—preceded by a vowel—are formed by adding an *s.*

radio – radios   rodeo – rodeos   studio – studios   duo – duos

The plurals of most nouns ending in *o*—preceded by a consonant—are formed by adding *es.*

echo – echoes   hero – heroes   tomato – tomatoes

Exception: Musical terms always form plurals by adding *s;* consult a dictionary for other words of this type.

alto – altos   banjo – banjos   solo – solos   piano – pianos

478.4   Nouns Ending in *f* or *fe*

Form the plurals of nouns that end in *f* or *fe* in one of two ways: if the final *f* sound is still heard in the plural form of the word, simply add *s;* if the final *f* sound becomes a *v* sound, change the *f* to *ve* and add *s.*

Plural ends with *f* sound: **roof – roofs; chief – chiefs**
Plural ends with *v* sound: **wife – wives; loaf – loaves**

NOTE: Several words are correct with either ending.

Plural ends with either sound: **hoof – hooves/hoofs**

479.1 Irregular Spelling

A number of words form a plural by taking on an irregular spelling.

crisis	crises	child	children	radius	radii
criterion	criteria	goose	geese	die	dice

NOTE: Some of these words are now acceptable with the commonly used *s* or *es* ending.

index	indices	indexes	cactus	cacti	cactuses

479.2 Words Discussed as Words

The plurals of symbols, letters, numbers, and words being discussed as words are formed by adding an apostrophe and an *s*.

Dad yelled a lot of *wow's* and *yippee's* when he saw my A's and B's.

NOTE: You may omit the apostrophe when the omission does not cause any confusion.

the three R's or Rs   YMCA's or YMCAs

479.3 Nouns Ending in *ful*

Form the plurals of nouns that end in *ful* by adding an *s* at the end of the word.

two tankfuls   three pailfuls   four mouthfuls

NOTE: Do not confuse these examples with *three pails full* (when you are referring to three separate pails full of something) or *two tanks full*.

479.4 Compound Nouns

Form the plurals of most compound nouns by adding *s* or *es* to the important word in the compound.

brothers-in-law   maids of honor   secretaries of state

479.5 Collective Nouns

A collective noun may be singular or plural depending upon how it's used. A collective noun is singular when it refers to a group considered as one unit; it is plural when it refers to the individuals in the group.

Use a singular pronoun (**its**) to indicate that the collective noun is singular. Use a plural pronoun (**their**) to show that the collective noun is plural.

The class was on its best behavior.
(group as a unit)

The class prepared for their final exams.
(group as individuals)

The class prepared for their final exams.

Numbers

480.1 Numerals or Words

Numbers from one to nine are usually written as words; numbers 10 and over are usually written as numerals.

two   seven   nine   10   25   106   1,079

Exception: You may use a combination of numerals and words for very large numbers.

1.5 million   3 billion to 3.2 billion   6 trillion

Exception: If numbers are used infrequently in a piece of writing, you may spell out those that can be written in no more than two words.

ten   twenty-five   two hundred   fifty thousand

Exception: Numbers being compared or contrasted should be kept in the same style.

8 to 11 years old   eight to eleven years old

480.2 Numerals Only

Use numerals for the following forms: decimals, percentages, chapters, pages, addresses, phone numbers, identification numbers, and statistics.

26.2	**8 percent**	**Highway 36**	**chapter 7**
pages 287-89	**July 6, 1945**	**44 B.C.E.**	**a vote of 23 to 4**

Always use numerals with abbreviations and symbols.

5'4"   8%   10 in.   3 tbsp.   6 lbs. 8 oz.   90° F   24 mph

480.3 Words Only

Use words to express numbers that begin a sentence.

Fourteen students "forgot" their assignments.

NOTE: Change the sentence structure if this rule creates a clumsy construction.

Clumsy: *Six hundred thirty-nine* **teachers were laid off this year.**

Better: **This year, 639 teachers were laid off.**

Use words for numbers that come before a compound modifier if that modifier includes another number.

The chef made twelve 10-foot sub sandwiches for the picnic.

480.4 Time and Money

If time is expressed with an abbreviation, use numerals; if it is expressed in words, spell out the number.

4:00 A.M. (or) four o'clock

If an amount of money is spelled out, so is the currency; if a symbol is used, use a numeral.

twenty dollars (or) $20

Abbreviations

481.1 Formal and Informal Abbreviations

An **abbreviation** is the shortened form of a word or phrase. Some abbreviations are always acceptable in both formal and informal writing:

Mr.   Mrs.   Jr.   Ms.   Dr.   a.m. (A.M.)   p.m. (P.M.)

NOTE: In formal writing **do not abbreviate** the names of states, countries, months, days, units of measure, or courses of study. Do not abbreviate the words *Street, Road, Avenue, Company,* and similar words when they are part of a proper name. Also, do not use signs or symbols (%, &, #, @) in place of words. The dollar sign, however, is appropriate when numerals are used to express an amount of money ($325.50).

481.2 Correspondence Abbreviations

United States

	Standard	Postal
Alabama	Ala.	AL
Alaska	Alaska	AK
Arizona	Ariz.	AZ
Arkansas	Ark.	AR
California	Calif.	CA
Colorado	Colo.	CO
Connecticut	Conn.	CT
Delaware	Del.	DE
District of Columbia	D.C.	DC
Florida	Fla.	FL
Georgia	Ga.	GA
Guam	Guam	GU
Hawaii	Hawaii	HI
Idaho	Idaho	ID
Illinois	Ill.	IL
Indiana	Ind.	IN
Iowa	Iowa	IA
Kansas	Kan.	KS
Kentucky	Ky.	KY
Louisiana	La.	LA
Maine	Maine	ME
Maryland	Md.	MD
Massachusetts	Mass.	MA
Michigan	Mich.	MI
Minnesota	Minn.	MN
Mississippi	Miss.	MS
Missouri	Mo.	MO
Montana	Mont.	MT
Nebraska	Neb.	NE
Nevada	Nev.	NV
New Hampshire	N.H.	NH
New Jersey	N.J.	NJ
New Mexico	N.M.	NM
New York	N.Y.	NY
North Carolina	N.C.	NC
North Dakota	N.D.	ND
Ohio	Ohio	OH
Oklahoma	Okla.	OK
Oregon	Ore.	OR
Pennsylvania	Pa.	PA
Puerto Rico	P.R.	PR
Rhode Island	R.I.	RI
South Carolina	S.C.	SC
South Dakota	S.D.	SD
Tennessee	Tenn.	TN
Texas	Texas	TX
Utah	Utah	UT
Vermont	Vt.	VT
Virginia	Va.	VA
Virgin Islands	V.I.	VI
Washington	Wash.	WA
West Virginia	W.Va.	WV
Wisconsin	Wis.	WI
Wyoming	Wyo.	WY

Canadian

	Standard	Postal
Alberta	Alta.	AB
British Columbia	B.C.	BC
Labrador	Lab.	LB
Manitoba	Man.	MB
New Brunswick	N.B.	NB
Newfoundland	N.F.	NF
Northwest Territories	N.W.T.	NT
Nova Scotia	N.S.	NS
Ontario	Ont.	ON
Prince Edward Island	P.E.I.	PE
Quebec	Que.	PQ
Saskatchewan	Sask.	SK
Yukon Territory	Y.T.	YT

Addresses

	Standard	Postal
Apartment	Apt.	APT
Avenue	Ave.	AVE
Boulevard	Blvd.	BLVD
Circle	Cir.	CIR
Court	Ct.	CT
Drive	Dr.	DR
East	E.	E
Expressway	Expy.	EXPY
Freeway	Fwy.	FWY
Heights	Hts.	HTS
Highway	Hwy.	HWY
Hospital	Hosp.	HOSP
Junction	Junc.	JCT
Lake	L.	LK
Lakes	Ls.	LKS
Lane	Ln.	LN
Meadows	Mdws.	MDWS
North	N.	N
Palms	Palms	PLMS
Park	Pk.	PK
Parkway	Pky.	PKY
Place	Pl.	PL
Plaza	Plaza	PLZ
Post Office Box	P.O. Box	PO BOX
Ridge	Rdg.	RDG
River	R.	RV
Road	Rd.	RD
Room	Rm.	RM
Rural	R.	R
Rural Route	R.R.	RR
Shore	Sh.	SH
South	S.	S
Square	Sq.	SQ
Station	Sta.	STA
Street	St.	ST
Suite	Ste.	STE
Terrace	Ter.	TER
Turnpike	Tpke.	TPKE
Union	Un.	UN
View	View	VW
Village	Vil.	VLG
West	W.	W

482.1 Other Common Abbreviations

abr. abridged; abridgment
AC, ac alternating current
ack. acknowledge; acknowledgment
acv actual cash value
A.D. in the year of the Lord (Latin *anno Domini*)
AM amplitude modulation
A.M., a.m. before noon (Latin *ante meridiem*)
ASAP as soon as possible
avg., av. average
BBB Better Business Bureau
B.C. British Columbia
B.C.E. before the common era
bibliog. bibliographer; bibliography
biog. biographer; biographical; biography
C 1. Celsius 2. centigrade 3. coulomb
C.E. the common era
c. 1. circa (about) 2. cup
cc 1. cubic centimeter 2. carbon copy 3. community college
CDT, C.D.T. central daylight time
chap. chapter
cm centimeter
c.o., c/o care of
COD, C.O.D 1. cash on delivery 2. collect on delivery
co-op. cooperative
CST, C.S.T. central standard time
cu., c cubic
D.A. district attorney
d.b.a. doing business as
DC, dc direct current
dec. deceased
dept. department
disc. discount
DST, D.S.T. daylight saving time
dup. duplicate
ea. each
ed. edition; editor
EDT, E.D.T. eastern daylight time
e.g. for example (Latin *exempli gratia*)
EST, E.S.T. eastern standard time
etc. and so forth (Latin *et cetera*)
ex. example
F Fahrenheit
FM frequency modulation
F.O.B., f.o.b. free on board
ft foot
g 1. gravity 2. gram
gal. gallon
gds. goods
gloss. glossary
GNP gross national product
hdqrs, HQ headquarters

HIV human immunodeficiency virus
Hon. Honorable (title)
hp horsepower
Hz hertz
ibid. in the same place (Latin *ibidem*)
id. the same (Latin *idem*)
i.e. that is (Latin *id est*)
illus. illustration
inc. incorporated
IQ, I.Q. intelligence quotient
IRS Internal Revenue Service
ISBN International Standard Book Number
JP, J.P. justice of the peace
Jr., jr. junior
K 1. kelvin (temperature unit) 2. Kelvin (temperature scale)
kc kilocycle
kg kilogram
km kilometer
kn knot
kw kilowatt
l liter
lat. latitude
lb pound (Latin *libra*)
l.c. lowercase
lit. literary; literature
log logarithm
long. longitude
Ltd., ltd. limited
m meter
M.A. master of arts (Latin *Magister Artium*)
man. manual
Mc, mc megacycle
M.C., m.c. master of ceremonies
M.D. doctor of medicine (Latin *medicinae doctor*)
mdse. merchandise
mfg. manufacturing
mg milligram
mi. 1. mile 2. mill (monetary unit)
misc. miscellaneous
ml milliliter
mm millimeter
mpg, m.p.g. miles per gallon
mph, m.p.h. miles per hour
MS 1. manuscript 2. Mississippi (with ZIP code) 3. multiple sclerosis
Ms., Ms title of courtesy for a woman
MST, M.S.T. mountain standard time
NE northeast
neg. negative
N.S.F., n.s.f. not sufficient funds
NW northwest
oz, oz. ounce
PA 1. public-address system 2. Pennsylvania

pct. percent
pd. paid
PDT, P.D.T. Pacific daylight time
PFC, PFC. private first class
pg., p. page
P.M., p.m. after noon (Latin *post meridiem*)
P.O. 1. personnel officer 2. purchase order 3. postal order; post office 4. also **p.o.** petty officer
pop. population
POW, P.O.W. prisoner of war
pp. pages
ppd. 1. postpaid 2. prepaid
PR, P.R. 1. public relations 2. Puerto Rico (with ZIP code)
psi, p.s.i. pounds per square inch
PST, P.S.T. Pacific standard time
PTA, P.T.A. Parent-Teachers Association
qt quart
RD rural delivery
RF radio frequency
R.P.M., rpm revolutions per minute
R.S.V.P., r.s.v.p. please reply (French *répondez s'il vous plaît*)
SE southeast
SOS 1. international distress signal 2. any call for help
Sr. 1. senior (after surname) 2. sister (religious)
SRO, S.R.O. standing room only
ST standard time
St. 1. saint 2. strait 3. street
std. standard
SW southwest
syn. synonymous; synonym
tbs, tbsp tablespoon
tsp teaspoon
TM trademark
UHF, uhf ultra high frequency
V 1. *Physics:* velocity 2. *Electricity:* volt 3. volume
V.A., VA 1. Veterans Administration 2. Virginia (with ZIP code)
VHF, vhf very high frequency
VIP *Informal:* very important person
vol. 1. volume 2. volunteer
vs. versus
W 1. *Electricity:* watt 2. *Physics:* (also **w**) work 3. west
whse., whs. warehouse
wkly. weekly
w/o without
wt. weight
yd yard (measurement)

Acronyms and Initialisms

483.1 Acronyms

An **acronym** is a word formed from the first (or first few) letters of words in a set phrase. Even though acronyms are abbreviations, they require no periods.

radar – radio detecting and ranging

CARE – Cooperative for American Relief Everywhere

NASA – National Aeronautics and Space Administration

VISTA – Volunteers in Service to America

UNICEF – United Nations International Children's Emergency Fund

483.2 Initialisms

An **initialism** is similar to an acronym except that the initials used to form this abbreviation are pronounced individually.

CIA – Central Intelligence Agency

FBI – Federal Bureau of Investigation

FHA – Federal Housing Administration

483.3 Common Acronyms and Initialisms

AIDS	acquired immunodeficiency syndrome	**ORV**	off-road vehicle
CETA	Comprehensive Employment and Training Act	**OSHA**	Occupational Safety and Health Administration
CIA	Central Intelligence Agency	**PAC**	political action committee
FAA	Federal Aviation Administration	**PIN**	personal identification number
FBI	Federal Bureau of Investigation	**PSA**	public service announcement
FCC	Federal Communications Commission	**REA**	Rural Electrification Administration
FDA	Food and Drug Administration	**RICO**	Racketeer Influenced and Corrupt Organizations (Act)
FDIC	Federal Deposit Insurance Corporation	**ROTC**	Reserve Officers' Training Corps
FHA	Federal Housing Administration	**SADD**	Students Against Destructive Decisions
FmHA	Farmers Home Administration	**SSA**	Social Security Administration
FTC	Federal Trade Commission	**SUV**	Sports Utility Vehicle
IRS	Internal Revenue Service	**SWAT**	Special Weapons and Tactics
MADD	Mothers Against Drunk Driving	**TDD**	telecommunications device for the deaf
NAFTA	North American Free Trade Agreement	**TMJ**	temporomandibular joint
NASA	National Aeronautics and Space Administration	**TVA**	Tennessee Valley Authority
NATO	North Atlantic Treaty Organization	**VA**	Veterans Administration
OEO	Office of Economic Opportunity	**VISTA**	Volunteers in Service to America
OEP	Office of Emergency Preparedness	**WAC**	Women's Army Corps
		WAVES	Women Accepted for Volunteer Emergency Service

Quick Guide

Spelling Rules

484.1 Write *i* before *e*

Write *i* before *e* except after *c,* or when sounded like *a* as in *neighbor* and *weigh.*

relief   **receive**   **perceive**   **reign**

Exceptions: Eight exceptions are included in this sentence: **Neither sheik dared leisurely seize either weird species of financiers.**

484.2 Words with Consonant Endings

When a one-syllable word (*bat*) ends in a consonant (*t*) preceded by one vowel (*a*), double the final consonant before adding a suffix that begins with a vowel (*batting*).

sum—summary   **god—goddess**

NOTE: When a multisyllable word (*control*) ends in a consonant (*l*) preceded by one vowel (*o*), the accent is on the last syllable (*con trol´*), and the suffix begins with a vowel (*ing*)—the same rule holds true: double the final consonant (*controlling*).

prefer—preferred   **begin—beginning**

forget—forgettable   **admit—admittance**

484.3 Words with a Silent *e*

If a word ends with a silent *e,* drop the *e* before adding a suffix that begins with a vowel. Do not drop the *e* when the suffix begins with a consonant.

state—stating—statement   **like—liking—likeness**

use—using—useful   **nine—ninety—nineteen**

Exceptions: judgment, truly, argument, ninth

484.4 Words Ending in *y*

When *y* is the last letter in a word and the *y* is preceded by a consonant, change the *y* to *i* before adding any suffix except those beginning with *i.*

fry—fries—frying   **hurry—hurried—hurrying**   **lady—ladies**

ply—pliable   **happy—happiness**   **beauty—beautiful**

NOTE: When forming the plural of a word that ends in *y* that is preceded by a vowel, add *s.*

toy—toys   **play—plays**   **monkey—monkeys**

Important reminder: Never trust your spelling to even the best spell checker. Carefully proofread. Use a dictionary for questionable words your spell checker does not cover.

Commonly Misspelled Words

A

abbreviate
abrupt
abscess
absence
absolute (ly)
absorbent
absurd
abundance
accede
accelerate
accept (ance)
accessible
accessory
accidentally
accommodate
accompany
accomplice
accomplish
accordance
according
account
accrued
accumulate
accurate
accustom (ed)
ache
achieve (ment)
acknowledge
acquaintance
acquiesce
acquired
actual
adapt
addition (al)
address
adequate
adjourned
adjustment
admirable
admissible
admittance
advantageous
advertisement
advertising
advice (n.)
advisable

advise (v.)
aerial
affect
affidavit
again
against
aggravate
aggression
agreeable
agreement
aisle
alcohol
alignment
alley
allotted
allowance
all right
almost
already
although
altogether
aluminum
always
amateur
amendment
among
amount
analysis
analyze
ancient
anecdote
anesthetic
angle
annihilate
anniversary
announce
annoyance
annual
anoint
anonymous
answer
antarctic
anticipate
anxiety
anxious
anything
apartment
apologize

apparatus
apparent (ly)
appeal
appearance
appetite
appliance
applicable
application
appointment
appraisal
appreciate
approach
appropriate
approval
approximately
architect
arctic
argument
arithmetic
arouse
arrangement
arrival
article
artificial
ascend
ascertain
asinine
assassin
assess (ment)
assignment
assistance
associate
association
assume
assurance
asterisk
athlete
athletic
attach
attack (ed)
attempt
attendance
attention
attitude
attorney
attractive
audible
audience

authority
automobile
autumn
auxiliary
available
average
awful
awfully
awkward

B

bachelor
baggage
balance
balloon
ballot
banana
bandage
bankrupt
bargain
barrel
basement
basis
battery
beautiful
beauty
become
becoming
before
beggar
beginning
behavior
being
belief
believe
beneficial
benefit (ed)
between
bicycle
biscuit
blizzard
bookkeeper
bough
bought
bouillon
boundary
breakfast
breath (n.)

breathe (v.)
brief
brilliant
Britain
brochure
brought
bruise
budget
bulletin
buoyant
bureau
burglar
bury
business
busy

C

cafeteria
caffeine
calendar
campaign
canceled
candidate
canister
canoe
can't
capacity
capital
capitol
captain
carburetor
career
caricature
carriage
cashier
casserole
casualty
catalog
catastrophe
caught
cavalry
celebration
cemetery
census
century
certain
certificate
cessation

challenge
changeable
character (istic)
chauffeur
chief
chimney
chocolate
choice
choose
Christian
circuit
circular
circumstance
civilization
clientele
climate
climb
clothes
coach
cocoa
coercion
collar
collateral
college
colloquial
colonel
color
colossal
column
comedy
coming
commence
commercial
commission
commit
commitment
committed
committee
communicate
community
comparative
comparison
compel
competent
competition
competitively
complain
complement
completely
complexion
compliment

compromise
concede
conceive
concerning
concert
concession
conclude
concrete
concurred
concurrence
condemn
condescend
condition
conference
conferred
confidence
confidential
congratulate
conscience
conscientious
conscious
consensus
consequence
conservative
considerably
consignment
consistent
constitution
contemptible
continually
continue
continuous
control
controversy
convenience
convince
coolly
cooperate
cordial
corporation
correlate
correspond
correspondence
corroborate
cough
couldn't
council
counsel
counterfeit
country
courage

courageous
courteous
courtesy
cousin
coverage
creditor
crisis
criticism
criticize
cruel
curiosity
curious
current
curriculum
custom
customary
customer
cylinder

D

daily
dairy
dealt
debtor
deceased
deceitful
deceive
decided
decision
declaration
decorate
deductible
defendant
defense
deferred
deficit
definite (ly)
definition
delegate
delicious
dependent
depositor
depot
descend
describe
description
desert
deserve
design
desirable

desirous
despair
desperate
despise
dessert
deteriorate
determine
develop
development
device
devise
diamond
diaphragm
diarrhea
diary
dictionary
difference
different
difficulty
dilapidated
dilemma
dining
diploma
director
disagreeable
disappear
disappoint
disapprove
disastrous
discipline
discover
discrepancy
discuss
discussion
disease
dissatisfied
dissipate
distinguish
distribute
divide
divine
divisible
division
doctor
doesn't
dominant
dormitory
doubt
drudgery
dual
duplicate

dyeing
dying

E

eagerly
earnest
economical
economy
ecstasy
edition
effervescent
efficacy
efficiency
eighth
either
elaborate
electricity
elephant
eligible
eliminate
ellipse
embarrass
emergency
eminent
emphasize
employee
employment
emulsion
enclose
encourage
endeavor
endorsement
engineer
English
enormous
enough
enterprise
entertain
enthusiastic
entirely
entrance
envelop (v.)
envelope (n.)
environment
equipment
equipped
equivalent
especially
essential
establish

esteemed
etiquette
evidence
exaggerate
exceed
excellent
except
exceptionally
excessive
excite
executive
exercise
exhaust (ed)
exhibition
exhilaration
existence
exorbitant
expect
expedition
expenditure
expensive
experience
explain
explanation
expression
exquisite
extension
extinct
extraordinary
extremely

F

facilities
fallacy
familiar
famous
fascinate
fashion
fatigue (d)
faucet
favorite
feasible
feature
February
federal
feminine
fertile
fictitious
field
fierce

fiery
finally
financially
foliage
forcible
foreign
forfeit
forgo
formally
formerly
fortunate
forty
forward
fountain
fourth
fragile
frantically
freight
friend
fulfill
fundamental
furthermore
futile

G

gadget
gangrene
garage
gasoline
gauge
genealogy
generally
generous
genius
genuine
geography
ghetto
ghost
glorious
gnaw
government
governor
gracious
graduation
grammar
grateful
gratitude
grease
grief
grievous

grocery
grudge
gruesome
guarantee
guard
guardian
guerrilla
guess
guidance
guide
guilty
gymnasium
gypsy
gyroscope

H

habitat
hammer
handkerchief
handle (d)
handsome
haphazard
happen
happiness
harass
harbor
hastily
having
hazardous
height
hemorrhage
hesitate
hindrance
history
hoarse
holiday
honor
hoping
hopping
horde
horrible
hospital
humorous
hurriedly
hydraulic
hygiene
hymn
hypocrisy

I

iambic
icicle
identical
idiosyncrasy
illegible
illiterate
illustrate
imaginary
imaginative
imagine
imitation
immediately
immense
immigrant
immortal
impatient
imperative
importance
impossible
impromptu
improvement
inalienable
incidentally
inconvenience
incredible
incurred
indefinitely
indelible
independence
independent
indictment
indispensable
individual
inducement
industrial
industrious
inevitable
inferior
inferred
infinite
inflammable
influential
ingenious
ingenuous
inimitable
initial
initiation
innocence
innocent

inoculation
inquiry
installation
instance
instead
institute
insurance
intellectual
intelligence
intention
intercede
interesting
interfere
intermittent
interpret (ed)
interrupt
interview
intimate
invalid
investigate
investor
invitation
iridescent
irrelevant
irresistible
irreverent
irrigate
island
issue
itemized
itinerary
it's (it is)

J

janitor
jealous (y)
jeopardize
jewelry
journal
journey
judgment
justice
justifiable

K

kitchen
knowledge
knuckle

L

label
laboratory
lacquer
language
laugh
laundry
lawyer
league
lecture
legal
legible
legislature
legitimate
leisure
length
letterhead
liability
liable
liaison
library
license
lieutenant
lightning
likable
likely
lineage
liquefy
liquid
listen
literary
literature
livelihood
living
logarithm
loneliness
loose
lose
losing
lovable
lovely
luncheon
luxury

M

machine
magazine
magnificent
maintain

maintenance
majority
making
management
maneuver
manual
manufacture
manuscript
marriage
marshal
material
mathematics
maximum
mayor
meanness
meant
measure
medicine
medieval
mediocre
medium
memorandum
menus
merchandise
merit
message
mileage
millionaire
miniature
minimum
minute
mirror
miscellaneous
mischief
mischievous
miserable
misery
missile
missionary
misspell
moisture
molecule
momentous
monotonous
monument
mortgage
municipal
muscle
musician
mustache
mysterious

N

naive
naturally
necessary
necessity
negligible
negotiate
neighborhood
nevertheless
nickel
niece
nineteenth
ninety
noticeable
notoriety
nuclear
nuisance

O

obedience
obey
oblige
obstacle
occasion
occasionally
occupant
occur
occurred
occurrence
offense
official
often
omission
omitted
operate
opinion
opponent
opportunity
opposite
optimism
ordinance
ordinarily
original
outrageous

P

pageant
paid

pamphlet
paradise
paragraph
parallel
paralyze
parentheses (pl.)
parenthesis (s.)
parliament
partial
participant
participate
particularly
pastime
patience
patronage
peculiar
perceive
perhaps
peril
permanent
permissible
perpendicular
perseverance
persistent
personal (ly)
personnel
perspiration
persuade
phase
phenomenon
philosophy
physician
piece
planned
plateau
plausible
playwright
pleasant
pleasure
pneumonia
politician
possess
possession
possible
practically
prairie
precede
precedence
preceding
precious
precisely

precision
predecessor
preferable
preference
preferred
prejudice
preliminary
premium
preparation
presence
prevalent
previous
primitive
principal
principle
priority
prisoner
privilege
probably
procedure
proceed
professor
prominent
pronounce
pronunciation
propaganda
prosecute
protein
psychology
publicly
pumpkin
purchase
pursue
pursuing
pursuit

Q

qualified
quantity
quarter
questionnaire
quiet
quite
quotient

R

raise
rapport
realize

really
recede
receipt
receive
received
recipe
recipient
recognition
recognize
recommend
recurrence
reference
referred
rehearse
reign
reimburse
relevant
relieve
religious
remember
remembrance
reminisce
rendezvous
renewal
repetition
representative
requisition
reservoir
resistance
respectably
respectfully
respectively
responsibility
restaurant
rheumatism
rhyme
rhythm
ridiculous
route

S

sacrilegious
safety
salary
sandwich
satisfactory
Saturday
scarcely
scene
scenery

schedule
science
scissors
secretary
seize
sensible
sentence
sentinel
separate
sergeant
several
severely
shepherd
sheriff
shining
siege
significance
similar
simultaneous
since
sincerely
skiing
soldier
solemn
sophisticated
sophomore
sorority
source
souvenir
spaghetti
specific
specimen
speech
sphere
sponsor
spontaneous
stationary
stationery
statistic
statue
stature
statute
stomach
stopped
straight
strategy
strength
stretched
studying
subsidize
substantial

substitute
subtle
succeed
success
sufficient
summarize
superficial
superintendent
superiority
supersede
supplement
suppose
surely
surprise
surveillance
survey
susceptible
suspicious
sustenance
syllable
symmetrical
sympathy
symphony
symptom
synchronous

T

tariff
technique
telegram
temperament
temperature
temporary
tendency
tentative
terrestrial
terrible
territory
theater
their
therefore
thief
thorough (ly)
though
throughout
tired
tobacco
together
tomorrow
tongue

tonight
touch
tournament
tourniquet
toward
tragedy
traitor
tranquilizer
transferred
treasurer
tried
truly
Tuesday
tuition
typical
typing

U

unanimous
unconscious
undoubtedly
unfortunately
unique
unison
university
unnecessary
unprecedented
until
upper
urgent
usable
useful
using
usually
utensil
utilize

V

vacancies
vacation
vacuum
vague
valuable
variety
various
vegetable
vehicle
veil
velocity

vengeance
vicinity
view
vigilance
villain
violence
visibility
visible
visitor
voice
volume
voluntary
volunteer

W

wander
warrant
weather
Wednesday
weird
welcome
welfare
where
whether
which
whole
wholly
whose
width
women
worthwhile
worthy
wreckage
wrestler
writing
written
wrought

Y

yellow
yesterday
yield

Steps to Becoming a Better Speller

1. Be patient.

Becoming a good speller takes time.

2. Check the correct pronunciation of each word you are attempting to spell.

Knowing the correct pronunciation of each word is important for remembering its spelling.

3. Note the meaning and history of each word as you are checking the dictionary for pronunciation.

Knowing the meaning and history of a word provides you with a better notion of how the word is properly used, and this can help you remember its spelling.

4. Before you close the dictionary, practice spelling the word.

Look away from the page and try to "see" the word in your "mind's eye." Then write it on a piece of paper. Check your spelling in the dictionary and repeat the process until you are able to spell the word correctly.

5. Learn some spelling rules.

This handbook contains four of the most useful rules. (See page 484.)

6. Make a list of the words that you often misspell.

Select the first 10 and practice spelling them.

STEP A: Read each word carefully; then write it on a piece of paper. Check to see that you've spelled it correctly. Repeat this step for the words that you misspelled.

STEP B: When you have finished your first 10 words, ask someone to read them to you as you write them again. Then check for misspellings. If you find none, congratulations! (Repeat both steps with your next 10 words, and so on.)

7. Write often.

> **"There is little point in learning to spell if you have little intention of writing."**
> —Frank Smith

"The difference between the right word and the nearly right word is the same as that between lightning and the lightning bug." —Mark Twain

Using the
RIGHT WORD

a, an ■ *A* is used before words that begin with a consonant sound; *an* is used before words that begin with a vowel sound.

a heap	**a uniform**	**an idol**
an urban area	**an honor**	**a historian**

a lot, alot ■ *Alot* is not a word; *a lot* (two words) is a vague descriptive phrase that should be used sparingly.

"You can observe a lot just by watching." — Yogi Berra

accept, except ■ The verb *accept* means "to receive" or "to believe"; the preposition *except* means "other than."

The principal accepted the boy's story about the broken window, but she asked why no one except him saw the ball accidentally slip from his hand.

adapt, adopt ■ *Adapt* means "to adjust or change to fit"; *adopt* means "to choose and treat as your own" (a child, an idea).

After a lengthy period of study, Malcolm X adopted the Islamic faith and adapted to its lifestyle.

affect, effect ■ The verb *affect* means "to influence"; the verb *effect* means "to produce, accomplish, complete."

Mark's hard work effected an A on the test, which positively affected his semester grade.

The noun *effect* means the "result."

Good grades have a calming effect on parents.

allusion, illusion ■ *Allusion* is an indirect reference to someone or something; *illusion* is a false picture or idea.

My litter sister, under the illusion that she's movie-star material, makes frequent allusions to her future fans.

already, all ready ■ *Already* is an adverb meaning "before this time" or "by this time." *All ready* is an adjective meaning "fully prepared." (Note: Use *all ready* if you can substitute *ready* alone in the sentence.)

My three-year-old sister reads already. She is all ready to start school.

alright, all right ■ *Alright* is the incorrect form of *all right.*

altogether, all together ■ *Altogether* means "entirely." The phrase *all together* means "in a group" or "all at once."

**"There is altogether too much gridlock," complained the Democrats.
All together, the Republicans yelled, "No way!"**

among, between ■ *Among* is used when speaking of more than two persons or things. *Between* is used when speaking of only two.

The friends talked among themselves to decide between going out or eating in.

amount, number ■ *Amount* is used for bulk measurement. *Number* is used to count separate units. (See also *fewer, less.*)

The amount of weight you lose may depend on the number of candy bars you resist.

annual, biannual, semiannual, biennial, perennial ■
An *annual* event happens once every year.
A *biannual* event happens twice a year (*semiannual* is the same as *biannual*).
A *biennial* event happens every two years.
A *perennial* event happens throughout the year, every year.

ant, aunt ■ *Ant* is an insect. *Aunt* is a relative.

anyway, anyways ■ *Anyways* is the incorrect form of *anyway.*

ascared, scared ■ *Ascared* is not standard English. Use *scared* or *afraid.*

base, bass ■ *Base* is the foundation or the lower part of something. *Bass* is a deep sound or tone. *Bass* (when pronounced like *class*) is a fish.

be, bee ■ *Be* is the verb. *Bee* is the insect. *Bee* is also a group activity such as a spelling bee or a quilting bee.

berth, birth ■ *Berth* is a space or a compartment. *Birth* is the process of being born.

Aunt Lydia gave birth to cousin Malcolm in a berth on a train just outside of Paris.

beside, besides ■ *Beside* means "by the side of." *Besides* means "in addition to."

Mother always grew roses beside the trash bin. Besides looking nice, they also gave off a sweet smell that masked odors.

blew, blue ■ *Blew* is the verb. *Blue* is the color.

board, bored ■ *Board* is a piece of wood. *Board* is also an administrative group or council.

The school board approved the purchase of fifty 1- by 6-inch pine boards.

Bored is the past tense of the verb "bore," which may mean "to make a hole by drilling" or "to become weary out of dullness."

Watching television bored Joe, so he took his drill and bored a hole in the wall where he could hang his new clock.

brake, break ■ *Brake* is a device used to stop a vehicle. *Break* means "to separate or to destroy."

I hope the brakes on my car never break.

bring, take ■ *Bring* suggests the action is directed toward the speaker; *take* suggests the action is directed away from the speaker.

Mom says that she brings home the bacon, so I have to take out the garbage.

by, bye, buy ■ *By* is a preposition. *Bye* is short for "good-bye." *Buy* means "to purchase."

The following message was posted in front of a small corner store: "Smart people stop and buy; the others look and walk by!"

can, may ■ *Can* suggests ability while *may* suggests permission.

"Can I go to the library?" literally means "Am I physically able to go to the library?"

"May I go to the library?" asks permission to go.

capital, capitol ■ The noun *capital* refers to a city or to money. The adjective *capital* means "major or important." *Capitol* refers to a building.

The state capital is home to the capitol building for a capital reason. The state government contributed capital for its construction.

cent, sent, scent ■ *Cent* is a coin; *sent* is the past tense of the verb "send"; *scent* is an odor or a smell.

For thirty-three cents, I sent my girlfriend a mushy love poem in a perfumed envelope. She adored the scent but hated the poem.

chord, cord ■ *Chord* may mean "an emotion" or "a combination of musical tones sounded at the same time." A *cord* is a string or a rope.

The guitar player strummed the opening chord to the group's hit song, which struck a responsive chord with the audience.

chose, choose ■ *Chose* (chōz) is the past tense of the verb *choose* (chōoz).

Last quarter I chose to read Martin Luther King's *Strength to Love*—a book that says it takes strength to choose a nonviolent response to injustice.

coarse, course ■ *Coarse* means "rough or crude"; *course* means "a path or direction taken." *Course* also means "a class or a series of studies."

The ladybug who taught the course "Insect Etiquette" said that only coarse mosquitoes fly over golf courses looking for bald golfers.

complement, compliment ■ *Complement* refers to that which completes or fulfills. *Compliment* is an expression of admiration or praise.

Kimberly smiled, thinking she had received a compliment when Carlos said that her new Dodge Viper complemented her personality.

continual, continuous ■ *Continual* refers to something that happens again and again with some breaks or pauses; *continuous* refers to something that happens again and again with no breaks or pauses.

Sunlight hits Peoria, Iowa, on a continual basis; but sunlight hits Earth continuously.

counsel, council ■ When used as a noun, *counsel* means "advice"; when used as a verb, it means "to advise." *Council* refers to a group that advises.

The student council counseled all freshmen to join at least one school club. That's good counsel.

dear, deer ■ *Dear* means "loved or valued"; *deer* are animals. (Please note, people will think you're strange if you write that you kissed your deer in the moonlight.)

desert, dessert ■ The noun *desert* (dĕz´ərt) refers to barren wilderness. *Dessert* (dĭ zûrt´) is food served at the end of a meal.

The scorpion tiptoed through the moonlit desert, searching for dessert.

The verb *desert* (dĭ zûrt´) means "to abandon"; the noun *desert* (dĭ zûrt´) also may mean "deserved reward or punishment."

The burglar's hiding place deserted him when the spotlight swung his way; his subsequent arrest was his just desert.

die, dye ■ *Die* (dying) means "to stop living." *Dye* (dyeing) is used to change the color of something.

different from, different than ■ Use *different from* in formal writing; use either form in informal or colloquial settings.

She is as different from her sister as *People* magazine is from *Time* magazine.

faint, feign, feint ■ *Faint* means "without strength" (adjective) or "to lose consciousness" (verb); *feign* is a verb that means "to pretend or make up"; *feint* is a noun that means "a move or an activity that is pretended or false."

To avoid a tackler, the running back feigned a run one way and then cut quickly in another direction. The tackler grabbed nothing but air and fainted from the embarrassment. The running back's feint resulted in a touchdown.

farther, further ■ *Farther* refers to a physical distance; *further* refers to additional time, quantity, or degree.

Alaska extends farther north than Iceland. Further information can be obtained in an atlas.

fewer, less ■ *Fewer* refers to the number of separate units; *less* refers to bulk quantity.

Because we have fewer orders for cakes, we'll buy less sugar and flour.

for, fore, four ■ *For* is a preposition meaning "because of" or "directed to"; *fore* means "earlier" or "the front"; *four* is the number 4.

The four quick penalties foreshadowed what was in store for the visiting team.

good, well ■ *Good* is an adjective; *well* is nearly always an adverb. (When *well* is used to describe a state of health, it is an adjective: He was happy to be well again.)

The strange flying machines worked well and made our team look good.

heal, heel ■ *Heal* means "to mend or restore to health." A *heel* is the back part of a foot.

Achilles was a young Greek soldier who died because a poison arrow pierced his heel and caused a wound that would not heal.

healthful, healthy ■ *Healthful* means "causing or improving health"; *healthy* means "possessing health."

Healthful foods build healthy bodies.

hear, here ■ You *hear* with your ears. *Here* means "the area close by."

heard, herd ■ *Heard* is the past tense of the verb "hear"; *herd* is a large group of animals.

The herd of gazelles raised their heads when they heard the hyena laugh.

hole, whole ■ A *hole* is a cavity or hollow place. *Whole* means "complete."

immigrate, emigrate ■ *Immigrate* means "to come into a new country or environment." *Emigrate* means "to go out of one country to live in another."

Martin Ulferts immigrated to this country in 1882. He was only three years old when he emigrated from Germany.

imply, infer ■ *Imply* means "to suggest or express indirectly"; *infer* means "to draw a conclusion from facts." (A writer or speaker implies; a reader or listener infers.)

Dad implied I should drive more carefully, and I inferred he was concerned for both me and his new car.

it's, its ■ *It's* is the contraction of "it is." *Its* is the possessive form of "it."

It's hard to believe, but the movie *Aladdin* still holds its appeal for my little sister—even after 10 viewings.

knew, new ■ *Knew* is the past tense of the verb "know." *New* means "recent or novel."

I already knew that the zoo had acquired a number of new gnus.

know, no ■ *Know* means "to understand or to realize." *No* means "the opposite of yes."

Don't you know that *no* means no?

later, latter ■ *Later* means "after a period of time." *Latter* refers to the second of two things mentioned.

Later that year we had our second baby and adopted a stray kitten. The latter was far more welcomed by our toddler.

lay, lie ■ *Lay* means "to place." *Lay* is a transitive verb. (See 508.1.) *Lay* is also the past tense of *lie*.

Lay your books on the big table where your friend laid his packages.

Lie means "to recline." *Lie* is an intransitive verb. (See 507.2.)

In this heat, the children must lie down for a nap. Yesterday they lay down without one complaint. Sometimes, they have lain in the hammocks to rest.

lead, led ■ *Lead* (lēd) is the present tense of the verb meaning "to guide." The past tense of the verb is *led* (lĕd). The noun *lead* (lĕd) is a metal.

We were led along the path that leads to an abandoned lead mine.

learn, teach ■ *Learn* means "to acquire information." *Teach* means "to give information."

I learn better when people teach with real-world examples.

leave, let ■ *Leave* means "to allow something to remain behind." *Let* means "to permit."

Would you let me leave my bike at your house?

lend, borrow ■ *Lend* means "to give for temporary use." *Borrow* means "to receive for temporary use."

I told Mom I needed to borrow $18 for a CD, but she said her lending service was for school supplies only.

like, as ■ When *like* is used as a preposition meaning "similar to," it can be followed only by a noun, pronoun, or noun phrase; when *as* is used as a subordinating conjunction, it introduces a subordinate clause.

> **If you want to be a gymnast like her, you'd better practice three hours a day as she does.**

loose, lose, loss ■ The adjective *loose* (lo͞os) means "free, unrestricted, untied"; the verb *lose* (lo͞oz) means "to misplace or fail to find or control"; the noun *loss* (lôs) means "something that is lost."

mail, male ■ *Mail* refers to letters or packages handled by the postal service (also voice mail and e-mail). *Male* refers to the masculine sex.

meat, meet ■ The noun *meat* is food or flesh; the verb *meet* means "to come upon or to encounter."

medal, metal ■ *Medal* is an award. *Metal* is an element like iron or gold.

> **Are the Olympic gold medals made out of solid gold metal?**

miner, minor ■ A *miner* digs in the ground for valuable ore. A *minor* is a person who is not legally an adult. A *minor* problem is one of no great importance.

> **The use of minors as miners is no minor problem.**

past, passed ■ *Passed* is a verb. *Past* can be used as a noun, an adjective, or a preposition.

> **That Escort passed my 'Vette.** (verb)
> **Many senior citizens hold dearly to the past.** (noun)
> **Tilly's past life as a circus worker must have been . . . interesting.** (adjective)
> **Who can walk past a bakery without looking in the window?** (preposition)

peace, piece ■ *Peace* means "tranquility or freedom from war." *Piece* is a part or fragment.

> **Grandma often sits and rocks in the peace and quiet of the parlor, enjoying a piece of pie or cake.**

personal, personnel ■ *Personal* means "private." *Personnel* are people working at a particular job.

plain, plane ■ *Plain* means "an area of land that is flat or level"; it also means "clearly seen or clearly understood."

> **My instructor told me to check the map after I said it was not plain to me why the early settlers had trouble crossing the Rockies on their way to the Great Plains.**

Plane means "flat, level, and even"; it is also a tool used to smooth the surface of wood.

> **I used a plane to make the board plane and smooth.**

pore, pour, poor ■ A *pore* is an opening in the skin. *Pour* means "to cause to flow in a stream." *Poor* means "needy or pitiable."

Tough exams on late spring days make my poor pores pour sweat.

principal, principle ■ As an adjective, *principal* means "primary." As a noun, it can mean "a school administrator" or "a sum of money." *Principle* means "idea or doctrine."

His principal gripe is lack of freedom. (adjective)
The principal expressed his concern about the open-campus policy. (noun)
During the first year of a loan, you pay more interest than principal. (noun)
The principle of *caveat emptor* is "Let the buyer beware."

quiet, quit, quite ■ *Quiet* is the opposite of noisy. *Quit* means "to stop." *Quite* means "completely or entirely."

The library was quite quiet until Mickie started hiccuping and couldn't quit.

quote, quotation ■ *Quote* is a verb; *quotation* is a noun.

The quotation I used was from Woody Allen. You may quote me on that.

real, very, really ■ Do not use *real* in place of the adverbs *very* or *really*.

My mother's cake is usually very (not *real*) tasty. But this cake is really stale—I mean, it's just about fossilized.

right, write, wright, rite ■ *Right* means "correct or proper"; it also refers to that which a person has a legal claim to, as in *copyright*. *Write* means "to inscribe or record." A *wright* is a person who makes or builds something. *Rite* refers to a ritual or ceremonial act.

Write this down: It is the right of the shipwright to perform the rite of christening—breaking a bottle of champagne on the stern of the ship.

scene, seen ■ *Scene* refers to the setting or location where something happens; it also may mean "sight or spectacle." *Seen* is a form of the verb "see."

A show-off enjoys being seen making a scene.

seam, seem ■ *Seam* (noun) is a line formed by connecting two pieces. *Seem* (verb) means "to appear to exist."

The ragged seams in his old coat seem to match the creases in his face.

set, sit ■ *Set* means "to place." *Sit* means "to put the body in a seated position." *Set* is transitive; *sit* is intransitive . (See 508.1 and 507.2.)

How can you just sit there and watch as I set all these chairs in place?

sight, cite, site ■ *Sight* means "the act of seeing." *Cite* means "to quote," or "to summon" as before a court. *Site* means "location or position."

The building inspector cited the electrical contractor for breaking two city codes at a downtown job site. It was not a pretty sight when the two men started arguing.

sole, soul ■ *Sole* means "single, only one"; *sole* also refers to the bottom surface of the foot. *Soul* refers to the spiritual part of a person.

> As the sole inhabitant of the island, he put his heart and soul into his farming.

some, sum ■ *Some* refers to an unknown number or part. *Sum* means "the whole amount."

> I need to buy some groceries. The sum of your pocket change and the bills in my wallet should cover the cost.

stationary, stationery ■ *Stationary* means "not movable"; *stationery* refers to the paper and envelopes used to write letters.

steal, steel ■ *Steal* means "to take something without permission"; *steel* is a metal.

than, then ■ *Than* is used in a comparison; *then* tells when.

> Then he cried and said that his big brother was bigger than my big brother. Then I cried.

their, there, they're ■ *Their* is a posses- sive personal pronoun. *There* is an adverb used to point out location. *They're* is the contraction for "they are."

> They're a well-dressed couple.
> Do you see them over there, with their matching jackets?

threw, through ■ *Threw* is the past tense of "throw." *Through* means "from beginning to end."

> Through seven innings, Egor threw just seven strikes.

to, too, two ■ *To* is a preposition that can mean "in the direction of." *To* also is used to form an infinitive. (See 509.1.) *Too* means "also" or "very." *Two* is the number.

> The two divers were careful not to swim down to the sunken ship too quickly.

vain, vane, vein ■ *Vain* means "valueless or fruitless"; it may also mean "holding a high regard for oneself." *Vane* is a flat piece of material set up to show which way the wind blows. *Vein* refers to a blood vessel or a mineral deposit.

> The vain prospector, boasting about the vein of silver he'd uncovered, paused to look up at the turning weather vane.

waist, waste ■ *Waist* is the part of the body just above the hips. The verb *waste* means "to spend or use carelessly" or "to wear away, decay"; the noun *waste* refers to material that is unused or useless.

Her waist is small because she wastes no opportunity to exercise.

wait, weight ■ *Wait* means "to stay somewhere expecting something." *Weight* refers to a degree or unit of heaviness.

ware, wear, where ■ *Ware* refers to a product that is sold; *wear* means "to have on or to carry on one's body"; *where* asks the question, in what place? or in what situation?

The designer boasted, "Where can anybody wear my ware? Anywhere."

way, weigh ■ *Way* means "path or route." *Weigh* means "to measure weight" or "to have a certain heaviness."

My dog and I weigh too much. The vet says the best way to reduce is a daily run in the park.

weather, whether ■ *Weather* refers to the condition of the atmosphere. *Whether* refers to a possibility.

Because of the weather forecast, Coach Pennington didn't know whether or not to schedule another practice.

who, which, that ■ *Who* refers to people. *Which* refers to nonliving objects or to animals. (*Which* should never refer to people.) *That* may refer to animals, people, or nonliving objects.

who, whom ■ *Who* is used as the subject of a verb; *whom* is used as the object of a preposition or as a direct object.

To whom do we owe our thanks for these pizzas? And who ordered that one with pepperoni and pineapple?

who's, whose ■ *Who's* is the contraction for "who is." *Whose* is a pronoun showing possession or ownership.

Whose car are we using, and who's riding up front?

wood, would ■ *Wood* is the stuff that trees are made of; *would* is a form of the verb "will."

I never would have guessed that floor is a vinyl simulation of wood!

your, you're ■ *Your* is a possessive pronoun. *You're* is the contraction for "you are."

"Is your dancing always this subdued?"
"No, only when you're standing on my feet."

> "Don't be afraid to throw more than one verb in a sentence. I think 'She twisted and fell' is more exciting than 'She twisted. She fell to the ground.' "
>
> —Martyn Godfrey

Parts of
SPEECH

Parts of speech refers to the eight different kinds of words: *noun, pronoun, verb, adjective, adverb, preposition, conjunction,* and *interjection.*

Noun

A **noun** is a word that names something: a person, a place, a thing, or an idea.

> governor   Oregon   hospital   Buddhism   love

Classes of Nouns

The five classes of nouns are *proper, common, concrete, abstract,* and *collective.*

501.1 Proper Noun

A **proper noun** names a particular person, place, thing, or idea. Proper nouns are always capitalized.

> Jackie Robinson   Brooklyn   Ebbets Field   World Series   Christianity

501.2 Common Noun

A **common noun** does not name a particular person, place, thing, or idea. Common nouns are not capitalized.

> person   woman   president   baseball   government   park

501.3 Concrete Noun

A **concrete noun** names a thing that is tangible (can be seen, touched, heard, smelled, or tasted). Concrete nouns are either proper or common.

> child   Grand Canyon   music   aroma   pizza   Beck

501.4 Abstract Noun

An **abstract noun** names an idea, a condition, or a feeling—in other words, something that cannot be touched, smelled, tasted, seen, or heard.

> New Deal   greed   poverty   progress   freedom   hope

501.5 Collective Noun

A **collective noun** names a group or a unit.

> United States   Portland Cementers   team   crowd   community

Forms of Nouns

Nouns are grouped according to their *number, gender,* and *case.*

502.1 Number of a Noun

Number indicates whether the noun is singular or plural.

A **singular noun** refers to one person, place, thing, or idea.

actor   stadium   Canadian   bully   truth   child   person

A **plural noun** refers to more than one person, place, thing, or idea.

actors   stadiums   Canadians   bullies   truths   children   people

502.2 Gender of a Noun

Gender indicates whether a noun is masculine, feminine, neuter, or indefinite.

Masculine:

uncle   brother   host   men   bull   rooster   stallion

Feminine:

aunt   sister   hostess   women   cow   hen   filly

Neuter (without sex):

tree   cobweb   flying fish   closet

Indefinite (masculine or feminine):

president   plumber   doctor   parent

502.3 Case of a Noun

Case tells how nouns are related to other words used with them. There are three cases: *nominative, possessive,* and *objective.*

■ A **nominative case** noun can be the *subject* of a clause.

Patsy's heart was beating very wildly beneath his jacket. . . . That black horse there owed something to the orphan he had made.
—Paul Dunbar, "The Finish of Patsy Barnes"

A nominative noun can also be a predicate noun (or predicate nominative), which follows a "be" verb (*am, is, are, was, were, be, being, been*) and renames the subject. In the sentence below, *type* renames *Mr. Cattanzara.*

Mr. Cattanzara was a different type than those in the neighborhood.
—Bernard Malamud, "A Summer's Reading"

■ A **possessive case** noun shows possession or ownership.

Like the spider's claw, a part of him touches a world he will never enter.
—Loren Eiseley, "The Hidden Teacher"

■ An **objective case** noun can be a direct object, an indirect object, or an object of the preposition.

Marna always gives Mylo science-fiction books for his birthday.
(*Mylo* is the indirect object and *books* is the direct object of the verb "gives." *Birthday* is the object of the preposition "for.")

Pronoun

A **pronoun** is a word used in place of a noun.

I, you, she, it, which, that, themselves, whoever, me, he, they, mine, ours

503.1 Types of Pronouns

There are three types of pronouns: *simple, compound,* and *phrasal.*

        Simple: **I, you, he, she, it, we, they, who, what**

    Compound: **myself, someone, anybody, everything, itself, whatsoever**

      Phrasal: **one another, each other**

503.2 Antecedent

All pronouns have antecedents. An **antecedent** is the noun that the pronoun refers to or replaces.

> **Ambrosch was considered the important person in the family. Mrs. Shimerda and Ántonia always deferred to him, though he was often surly with them and contemptuous toward his father.**   —Willa Cather, *My Ántonia*

(*Ambrosch* is the antecedent of *him, he,* and *his.*)

NOTE: Each pronoun must agree with its antecedent. (See page 528.)

Classes of Pronouns

There are five classes of pronouns: *personal, relative, indefinite, interrogative,* and *demonstrative.*

503.3 Personal Pronouns

A **personal pronoun** takes the place of a noun.

> **Our coach made her point without raising her voice.**

- A **reflexive pronoun** is formed by adding *-self* or *-selves* to a personal pronoun. A reflexive pronoun can be a direct object, an indirect object, an object of the preposition, or a predicate nominative.

> **Miss Sally Sunshine loves herself.** (direct object of *loves*)

> **Tomisha does not seem herself today.** (predicate nominative)

- An **intensive pronoun** is a reflexive pronoun that intensifies, or emphasizes, the noun or pronoun it refers to.

> **Leo himself taught his children to invest their lives in others.**

> **The dessert the children had baked themselves tasted—interesting.**

503.4 Relative Pronouns

A **relative pronoun** relates an adjective clause to the noun or pronoun it modifies. (The relative pronoun *who* relates the adjective clause to *students; which* relates the adjective clause to *dance.*)

> **Students who study regularly get the best grades. Surprise!**

> **The dance, which we had looked forward to for weeks, was canceled.**

504.1 Indefinite Pronouns

An **indefinite pronoun** often refers to unnamed or unknown people or things.

> I don't know if you've known **anybody** from that far back; if you've loved **anybody** that long, first as an infant, then as a child, then as a man. . . . (The antecedent of *anybody* is unknown.)
>
> —James Baldwin, "My Dungeon Shook: Letter to My Nephew"

504.2 Interrogative Pronouns

An **interrogative pronoun** asks a question.

> "Then, **who** are you? **Who** could you be? **What** do you want from my husband?"
>
> —Elie Wiesel, "The Scrolls, Too, Are Mortal"

504.3 Demonstrative Pronouns

A **demonstrative pronoun** points out people, places, or things without naming them.

> **This** shouldn't be too hard. **That** looks about right.
> **These** are the best ones. **Those** ought to be thrown out.

Classes of Pronouns

PERSONAL

I, me, my, mine / we, us, our, ours
you, your, yours / they, them, their, theirs
he, him, his, she, her, hers, it, its

Intensive and Reflexive

myself, yourself, himself, herself, itself, ourselves, yourselves, themselves

RELATIVE

what, who, whose, whom, which, that

INDEFINITE

all	both	everything	nobody	several
another	each	few	none	some
any	each one	many	no one	somebody
anybody	either	most	nothing	someone
anyone	everybody	much	one	something
anything	everyone	neither	other	such

INTERROGATIVE

who, whose, whom, which, what

DEMONSTRATIVE

this, that, these, those

Forms of Personal Pronouns

The form of a personal pronoun indicates its *number* (singular or plural), its *person* (first, second, third), its *case* (nominative, possessive, or objective), and its *gender* (masculine, feminine, or neuter).

505.1 Number of a Pronoun

Personal pronouns are singular or plural. The singular personal pronouns include *my, him, he, she, it.* The plural personal pronouns include *we, you, them, our.* (*You* can be singular or plural.) Notice in the caption below that the first **you** is singular and the second **you** is plural.

Larry, you need to keep all four tires on the road when turning. Are you still with us back there?

505.2 Person of a Pronoun

The **person** of a pronoun indicates whether that pronoun is speaking, is spoken to, or is spoken about.

■ **First person** is used in place of the name of the speaker or speakers.

> **"We don't do things like that," says Pa; "we're just and honest people. . . . I don't skip debts."** —Jesse Stuart, "Split Cherry Tree"

■ **Second person** is used to name the person or persons spoken to.

> **"If you hit your duck, you want me to go in after it?" Eugie said.** —Gina Berriault, "The Stone Boy"

■ **Third person** is used to name the person or thing spoken about.

> **She had hardly realized the news, further than to understand that she had been brought . . . face to face with something unexpected and final. It did not even occur to her to ask for any explanation.** —Joseph Conrad, "The Idiots"

506.1 Case of a Pronoun

The **case** of each pronoun tells how it is related to the other words used with it. There are three cases: *nominative, possessive,* and *objective.*

■ A **nominative case** pronoun can be the subject of a clause. The following are nominative forms: *I, you, he, she, it, we, they.*

> **I like life when things go well.**
> **You must live life in order to love life.**

A nominative pronoun can also be a *predicate nominative* if it follows a "be" verb (*am, is, are, was, were, be, being, been*) or another linking verb (*appear, become, feel,* etc.) and renames the subject.

> **"Oh, it's only he," said Mama to Papa, glancing over her shoulder.**
> **"Yes, it is I," said Matt in a superior tone.**

■ **Possessive case** pronouns show possession or ownership. Apostrophes, however, are not used with personal pronouns.

> **But as I placed my hand upon his shoulder, there came a strong shudder over his whole person.**
>
> —Edgar Allan Poe, "The Fall of the House of Usher"

■ An **objective case** pronoun can be a direct object, an indirect object, or an object of the preposition.

> **The kids loved it! We lit a campfire for them and told them old ghost stories.** (*It* is the direct object of the verb *loved. Them* is the object of the preposition *for* and the indirect object of the verb *told.*)

Number, Person, and Case of Personal Pronouns

	Nominative	Possessive	Objective
First Person Singular	I	my, mine	me
Second Person Singular	you	your, yours	you
Third Person Singular	he	his	him
	she	her, hers	her
	it	its	it
	Nominative	**Possessive**	**Objective**
First Person Plural	we	our, ours	us
Second Person Plural	you	your, yours	you
Third Person Plural	they	their, theirs	them

506.2 Gender of a Pronoun

Gender indicates whether a pronoun is masculine, feminine, or neuter.

Masculine:	he	him	his
Feminine:	she	her	hers
Neuter (without sex):	it	its	

Verb

A **verb** is a word that expresses action (*run, carried, declared*) or state of being (*is, are, seemed*).

Classes of Verbs

507.1 Auxiliary Verbs

Auxiliary verbs, or helping verbs, are used to form some of the **tenses** (511.1), the **mood** (512.1), and the **voice** (510.3) of the main verb. (In the example below, the auxiliary verbs are in red; the main verbs are in green.)

> The long procession was led by white-robed priests, their faces streaked with red and yellow and white ash. By this time the flames had stopped spurting and the pit consisted of a red-hot mass of burning wood, which attendants were leveling with long branches.
>
> —Leonard Feinberg, "Fire Walking in Ceylon"

Common Auxiliary Verbs

is	was	being	did	have	would	shall	might
am	were	been	does	had	could	can	must
are	be	do	has	should	will	may	

507.2 Intransitive Verbs

An **intransitive verb** communicates action that is complete in itself. It does not need an object to receive the action.

> The boy flew on his skateboard. He jumped and flipped and twisted.

NOTE: Some verbs can be either *transitive* or *intransitive*.

> He finally stopped the show. (transitive)
>
> He finally stopped to rest. (intransitive)

507.3 Linking Verbs

A **linking verb** is a special type of intransitive verb that links the subject to a noun or an adjective in the predicate.

> On his skateboard, the boy felt confident. He was the best skater around.

Common Linking Verbs

is	are	was	were	be	been	am	smell
seem	grow	become	appear	sound	taste	feel	remain
stay	look	turn	get				

508.1 Transitive Verbs

A **transitive verb** (red) communicates action that is received by an object (green) that completes the meaning of the verb. (The subject is in italics.)

The *city council* passed a strict noise ordinance.

■ **Active voice**: A transitive verb in the active voice directs the action from the subject to the object.

The *students* protested the noise ordinance with a noisy demonstration. (*Ordinance* receives the action of the verb *protested* from the subject *students.*)

■ **Passive voice**: A transitive verb in the passive voice directs its action toward the subject.

The *ordinance* was debated by students and parents at a public meeting. (The subject *ordinance* receives the action of the verb *was debated.*)

NOTE: With a passive verb, the person or thing creating the action is not always stated.

The *ordinance* was overturned. (It is not clear who did the overturning in this example.)

■ A **direct object** receives the action of a transitive verb directly from the subject.

The boy kicked his skateboard forward. (*Skateboard* is the direct object.)

■ An **indirect object** receives the action of a transitive verb, but indirectly. An indirect object names the person *to whom* or *for whom* something is done. (It can also name the thing *to what* or *for what* something is done.)

Then he showed us his best tricks. (*Us* is the indirect object.)

NOTE: When the word naming the indirect receiver of the action is in a prepositional phrase, it is no longer considered an indirect object.

Then he showed his best tricks to us. (*Us* is the object of the preposition *to.*)

Verbals

A **verbal** is a word that is derived from a verb, has the power of a verb, but acts as another part of speech. Like a verb, a verbal may take an object, a modifier, and sometimes a subject; but unlike a verb, a verbal functions as a noun, an adjective, or an adverb. There are three types of verbals: *gerunds, infinitives,* and *participles.*

508.2 Gerunds

A **gerund** is a verb form that ends in *ing* and is used as a noun.

Swimming is my favorite pastime. (subject)

I began swimming at the age of six months. (direct object)

Because of swimming, I'm in good condition. (object of the preposition)

509.1 Infinitives

An **infinitive** is a verb form that is usually introduced by *to*; the infinitive may be used as a noun, an adjective, or an adverb.

> **To swim the English Channel must be a thrill.** (noun)
>
> **If it were easy to swim the Channel, more people would do it.** (adverb)
>
> **The urge to swim in tropical waters is more common.** (adjective)

509.2 Participles

A **participle** is a verb form usually ending in *ing* or *ed*. A participle functions as an adjective but also retains some of the characteristics of a verb. It might be thought of as a "verbal adjective."

> **The farmhands harvesting corn are tired and hungry.**
> (*Harvesting* functions as an adjective by modifying *farmhands*. *Harvesting* also acts like a verb because it has a direct object: *corn.*)
>
> **The cribs full of harvested cobs are evidence of their hard work.**
> (*Harvested* functions as an adjective by modifying *cobs.*)

Common Irregular Verbs and Their Principal Parts

Present Tense	Past Tense	Past Participle	Present Tense	Past Tense	Past Participle	Present Tense	Past Tense	Past Participle
am, be	was, were	been	go	went	gone	show	showed	shown
begin	began	begun	grow	grew	grown	shrink	shrank	shrunk
bite	bit	bitten	hang	hanged	hanged	sing	sang, sung	sung
blow	blew	blown	(execute)			sink	sank, sunk	sunk
break	broke	broken	hang	hung	hung	sit	sat	sat
bring	brought	brought	(suspend)			slay	slew	slain
burst	burst	burst	hide	hid	hidden, hid	speak	spoke	spoken
catch	caught	caught	know	knew	known	spring	sprang	sprung
choose	chose	chosen	lay	laid	laid		sprung	sprung
come	came	come	lead	led	led	steal	stole	stolen
dive	dove	dived	lie	lay	lain	strive	strove	striven
do	did	done	(recline)			swear	swore	sworn
drag	dragged	dragged	lie	lied	lied	swim	swam	swum
draw	drew	drawn	(deceive)			swing	swung	swung
drink	drank	drunk	raise	raised	raised	take	took	taken
drive	drove	driven	ride	rode	ridden	teach	taught	taught
drown	drowned	drowned	ring	rang	rung	tear	tore	torn
eat	ate	eaten	rise	rose	risen	throw	threw	thrown
fall	fell	fallen	run	ran	run	wake	waked	waked
fight	fought	fought	see	saw	seen		woke	woken
flee	fled	fled	set	set	set	wear	wore	worn
fly	flew	flown	shake	shook	shaken	weave	weaved	weaved
forsake	forsook	forsaken	shine	shone	shone		wove	woven
freeze	froze	frozen	(light)	shined	shined	wring	wrung	wrung
get	got	gotten	shine	shined	shined	write	wrote	written
give	gave	given	(polish)					

Forms of Verbs

A verb has different forms depending on its *number* (singular, plural); *person* (first, second, third); *voice* (active, passive); *tense* (present, past, future, present perfect, past perfect, future perfect); and *mood* (indicative, imperative, subjunctive).

510.1 Number of a Verb

Number indicates whether a verb is singular or plural. In a clause, the verb (in **green** below) and its subject (in **red**) must both be singular, or both be plural.

- **Singular**

  One large island floats off Italy's "toe."

  Italy's northern countryside includes the spectacular Alps.

  The Po Valley stretches between the Alps and the Apennines Mountains.

- **Plural**

  Five small islands float inside Michigan's "thumb."

  The Porcupine Mountains rise above the shores of Lake Superior.

  High bluffs and sand dunes border Lake Michigan.

510.2 Person of a Verb

Person indicates whether the subject of the verb is first, second, or third person. Usually the form of the verb only changes when the verb is in the present tense and is used with a third-person singular pronoun.

	Singular	Plural
First Person	I sniff	we sniff
Second Person	you sniff	you sniff
Third Person	he/she/it sniffs	they sniff

510.3 Voice of a Verb

Voice indicates whether the subject is acting or being acted upon. (See 508.1.)

- **Active voice** indicates that the subject of the verb is, has been, or will be doing something.

  Baseball great Walter Johnson pitched 50 consecutive scoreless innings.

  For many years Lou Brock held the base-stealing record.

- **Passive voice** indicates that the subject of the verb is being, has been, or will be acted upon.

  Fifty consecutive scoreless innings were pitched by baseball great Walter Johnson.

  For many years the base-stealing record was held by Lou Brock.

NOTE: Use the active voice as much as possible because it makes your writing more direct and lively. (See "Passive Style" on page 132.)

511.1 Tense of a Verb

Tense indicates time. Each verb has three principal parts: the *present, past,* and *past participle.* All six tenses are formed from these principal parts. The past and past participle of regular verbs are formed by adding *ed* to the present form. The past and past participle of irregular verbs are usually different words; however, a few have the same form in all three principal parts. (See page 509.)

- **Present tense** expresses action that is happening at the present time, or action that happens continually, regularly.

  In September, sophomores smirk and joke about the "little freshies."

- **Past tense** expresses action that is completed at a particular time in the past.

  They forgot that just ninety days separated them from freshman status.

- **Future tense** expresses action that will take place in the future.

  They will remember this in three years when they will be freshmen again.

- **Present perfect tense** expresses action that began in the past but continues in the present or is completed in the present.

  Our boat has weathered worse storms than this one.

- **Past perfect tense** expresses an action in the past that occurs before another past action.

  They reported, wrongly, that the hurricane had missed the island.

- **Future perfect tense** expresses action that will begin in the future and be completed by a specific time in the future.

  By this time tomorrow, the hurricane will have smashed into the coast.

	Active Voice		**Passive Voice**	
TENSE	Singular	Plural	Singular	Plural
PRESENT	I see you see he/she/it sees	we see you see they see	I am seen you are seen he/she/it is seen	we are seen you are seen they are seen
PAST	I saw you saw he saw	we saw you saw they saw	I was seen you were seen it was seen	we were seen you were seen they were seen
FUTURE	I will see you will see he will see	we will see you will see they will see	I will be seen you will be seen it will be seen	we will be seen you will be seen they will be seen
PRESENT PERFECT	I have seen you have seen he has seen	we have seen you have seen they have seen	I have been seen you have been seen it has been seen	we have been seen you have been seen they have been seen
PAST PERFECT	I had seen you had seen he had seen	we had seen you had seen they had seen	I had been seen you had been seen it had been seen	we had been seen you had been seen they had been seen
FUTURE PERFECT	I will have seen you will have seen he will have seen	we will have seen you will have seen they will have seen	I will have been seen you will have been seen it will have been seen	we will have been seen you will have been seen they will have been seen

512.1 Mood of a Verb

Mood of a verb indicates the tone or attitude with which a statement is made.

■ **Indicative mood** is used to state a fact or to ask a question.

> Sometimes I'd yell questions at the rocks and trees, and across gorges, or yodel, "What is the meaning of the void?" The answer was perfect silence, so I knew. —Jack Kerouac, "Alone on a Mountain Top"

■ **Imperative mood** is used to give a command.

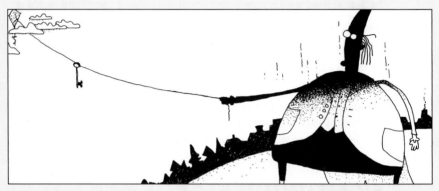

"**Whatever you do, don't fly your kite during a storm.**"
—Mrs. Abiah Franklin

■ **Subjunctive mood** is no longer commonly used; however, careful writers may choose to use it to express the exact manner in which their statements are meant.

○ Use the subjunctive *were* to express a condition that is contrary to fact.
If I were finished with my report, I could go to the movie.

○ Use the subjunctive *were* after *as though* or *as if* to express an unreal condition.
Mrs. Young acted as if she were sixteen again.

○ Use the subjunctive *be* in "that" clauses to express necessity, legal decisions, or parliamentary motions.
"It is moved and supported that no more than 6,000,000 quad be used to explore the planet Earth."
"Ridiculous! Knowing earthlings is bound to help us understand ourselves! Therefore, I move that the sum be amended to 12,000,000 quad."
"Stupidity! I move that all missions be postponed until we have living proof of life on Earth."

Adjective

An **adjective** describes or modifies a noun or a pronoun. The articles *a, an,* and *the* are also adjectives.

The young driver peeked through the big steering wheel.

(*The* and *young* modify *driver; the* and *big* modify *steering wheel.*)

513.1 Types of Adjectives

A **proper adjective** is created from a proper noun and is capitalized.

In Canada (proper noun), **you will find many cultures and climates.**

Long Canadian (proper adjective) **winters can be harsh.**

NOTE: Some words can be either adjectives or pronouns (*that, these, all, each, both, many, some,* etc.). These words are adjectives when they come before the nouns they modify; they are pronouns when they stand alone.

Joe made both goals. (*Both* modifies *goals;* it is an adjective.)

Both were scored in the final period. (*Both* stands alone; it is a pronoun.)

A **predicate adjective** follows a form of the "be" verb (or other linking verb) and describes the subject.

Late autumn seems grim to those who love summer. (*Grim* modifies *autumn.*)

513.2 Forms of Adjectives

Adjectives have three forms: *positive, comparative,* and *superlative.*

■ The **positive form** describes a noun or a pronoun without comparing it to anyone or anything else.

The first game was long and tiresome.

■ The **comparative form** (*-er, more,* or *less*) compares two persons, places, things, or ideas.

The second game was longer and more tiresome than the first.

■ The **superlative form** (*-est, most,* or *least*) compares three or more persons, places, things, or ideas.

The third game was the longest and most tiresome of all.

Positive	Comparative	Superlative
big	bigger	biggest
helpful	more helpful	most helpful
painful	less painful	least painful

NOTE: *More* and *most* (or *less* and *least*) are used generally with adjectives of two or more syllables.

Adverb

An **adverb** describes or modifies a verb, an adjective, or another adverb. An adverb tells *how, when, where, why, how often,* or *how much.*

She sneezed loudly. (*Loudly* modifies the verb *sneezed.*)

Her sneezes are really dramatic. (*Really* modifies the adjective *dramatic.*)

The sneeze exploded very noisily. (*Very* modifies the adverb *noisily.*)

514.1 Types of Adverbs

Adverbs can be cataloged in four basic ways: *time, place, manner,* and *degree.*

TIME (These adverbs tell *when, how often,* and *how long.*)

    today, yesterday   daily, weekly   briefly, eternally

PLACE (These adverbs tell *where, to where,* and *from where.*)

    here, there   nearby, beyond   backward, forward

MANNER (These adverbs often end in *ly* and tell *how* something is done.)

    precisely   effectively   regally   smoothly   well

DEGREE (These adverbs tell *how much* or *how little.*)

    substantially   greatly   entirely   partly   too

NOTE: Some adverbs can be written with or without the *ly* ending. When in doubt, use the *ly* form.

    slow, slowly   loud, loudly   fair, fairly   tight, tightly   quick, quickly

514.2 Forms of Adverbs

Adverbs have three forms: *positive, comparative,* and *superlative.*

■ The **positive form** describes a verb, an adjective, or another adverb without comparing it to anyone or anything else.

Model X vacuum cleans well and runs quietly.

■ The **comparative form** (*-er, more,* or *less*) compares two persons, places, things, or ideas.

Model Y vacuum cleans better and runs more quietly than model X.

■ The **superlative form** (*-est, most,* or *least*) compares three or more persons, places, things, or ideas.

Model Z vacuum cleans best and runs most quietly of all.

Positive	Comparative	Superlative
well	better	best
fast	faster	fastest
remorsefully	more remorsefully	most remorsefully

Preposition

A **preposition** is a word (or group of words) that shows the relationship between its object (a noun or a pronoun that follows the preposition) and another word in the sentence. There are three kinds of prepositions: *simple* (at, in, of, on), *compound* (within, outside, underneath), and *phrasal* (on account of, on top of).

> **To make a mustache, Natasha** placed **the hairy caterpillar** under **her** nose.
> (*Under* shows the relationship between the verb *placed* and the object of the preposition *nose*.)

NOTE: The first noun or pronoun following a preposition is its object.

> **The drowsy insect clung obediently** to **the girl's upper** lip. (The first noun following the preposition *to* is *lip; lip* is the object of the preposition.)

515.1 | Prepositional Phrase

A **prepositional phrase** includes the preposition, the object of the preposition, and the modifiers of the object. A prepositional phrase may function as an adverb or as an adjective.

> **Some people** run away from caterpillars.
> (The phrase functions as an adverb and modifies the verb *run*.)

> **However, little** kids with inquisitive minds **enjoy their company.**
> (The phrase functions as an adjective and modifies the noun *kids*.)

NOTE: A preposition that lacks an object may be used as an adverb.

> **Natasha never** played **with caterpillars** before. (The object of the preposition is understood: before *today*. *Before* modifies *played,* a verb.)

List of Prepositions

aboard	before	from	off	since
about	behind	from among	on	subsequent to
above	below	from between	on account of	together with
according to	beneath	from under	on behalf of	through
across	beside	in	onto	throughout
across from	besides	in addition to	on top of	till
after	between	in back of	opposite	to
against	beyond	in behalf of	out	toward
along	by	in front of	out of	under
alongside	by means of	in place of	outside	underneath
alongside of	concerning	in regard to	outside of	until
along with	considering	inside	over	unto
amid	despite	inside of	over to	up
among	down	in spite of	owing to	up to
apart from	down from	instead of	past	upon
around	during	into	prior to	with
aside from	except	like	regarding	within
at	except for	near	round	without
away from	excepting	near to	round about	
because of	for	of	save	

Conjunction

A **conjunction** connects individual words or groups of words. There are three kinds of conjunctions: *coordinating, correlative,* and *subordinating.*

When we came back to Paris, it was *clear* and *cold* and *lovely*.
(The conjunction *and* connects equal adjectives.)   —Ernest Hemingway

516.1 Coordinating Conjunctions

Coordinating conjunctions usually connect a word to a word, a phrase to a phrase, or a clause to a clause. The words, phrases, or clauses joined by a coordinating conjunction are equal in importance or are of the same type.

I could tell by my old man's eyes that he *was nervous* and *wanted to smooth things over,* but Syl didn't give him a chance.   —Albert Halper, "Prelude"

(*And* connects the two parts of a compound predicate; *but* connects two independent clauses that could stand on their own.)

516.2 Correlative Conjunctions

Correlative conjunctions are conjunctions used in pairs.

They were not only exhausted by the day's journey but also sunburned.

516.3 Subordinating Conjunctions

Subordinating conjunctions both connect and show the relationship between two clauses that are *not* equally important. A subordinating conjunction connects a dependent clause to an independent clause in order to complete the meaning of the dependent clause.

A brown trout will study the bait before he eats it. (The clause *before he eats it* is dependent. It depends on the rest of the sentence to complete its meaning.)

Kinds of Conjunctions

COORDINATING: and, but, or, nor, for, yet, so

CORRELATIVE: either, or; neither, nor; not only, but also; both, and; whether, or

SUBORDINATING: after, although, as, as if, as long as, as though, because, before, if, in order that, provided that, since, so that, that, though, till, unless, until, when, where, whereas, while

---

NOTE: Relative pronouns (page 503.4) and conjunctive adverbs (page 461.5) can also connect clauses.

Interjection

An **interjection** communicates strong emotion or surprise. Punctuation (often a comma or an exclamation point) is used to set off an interjection from the rest of the sentence.

Oh, no! The TV broke. Good grief! I have nothing to do! Yipes, I'll go mad!

Quick Guide

Parts of Speech

Words in the English language are used in eight different ways. For this reason, there are eight parts of speech. This chart lists them, offers a brief explanation of each one, and then gives a few examples of each.

Noun
A word that names a person, a place, a thing, or an idea.

Governor Pataki   Oregon   hospital   religion

Pronoun
A word used in place of a noun.

**I   you   she   him   who   everyone   these
neither   theirs   themselves   which**

Verb
A word that expresses action or state of being.

float   sniff   discover   seem   were   was

Adjective
A word that describes a noun or a pronoun.

young   big   grim   Canadian   longer

Adverb
A word that describes a verb, an adjective, or another adverb.

briefly   forward   regally   slowly   better

Preposition
A word(s) that shows the relationship between a noun or a pronoun and another word in a sentence.

away from   under   before   with   for   out of

Conjunction
A word(s) that connects other words or groups of words.

and   but   although   because   either, or   so

Interjection
A word(s) that shows strong emotion or surprise.

Oh no!   Yipes!   Good grief!   Well, . . .

"A sentence should read as if its author, had he held a plough instead of a pen, could have drawn a furrow deep and straight to the end."
—Henry David Thoreau

Using the
LANGUAGE

Constructing Sentences

A **sentence** is made up of one or more words that express a complete thought. A sentence begins with a capital letter; it ends with a period, a question mark, or an exclamation point.

**What should we do for our vacation this year?   We could go camping.
But I hate bugs!**

Using Subjects and Predicates

A sentence has a **subject** and a **predicate.**   The subject is the part of the sentence about which something is said. The predicate, which contains the verb, is the part of the sentence that says something about the subject.

Like the pilot, the writer must see faster and more completely than the ordinary viewer of life.
—Paul Engle, "Salt Crystals, Spider Webs, and Words"

518.1 Understood Subject and Predicate

Either the subject or the predicate may be "missing" from a sentence, but both must be clearly **understood.**

Who is making supper?
(*Who* is the subject; *is making supper* is the predicate.)
No one.
(*No one* is the subject; the predicate *is making supper* is understood.)
Put on that apron.
(The subject *you* is understood; *put on that apron* is the predicate.)

518.2 Delayed Subject

In sentences that begin with *There* or *It* followed by a form of the "be" verb, the subject comes after the verb. The subject is also "delayed" in questions.

There was nothing in the refrigerator. (The subject is *nothing;* the verb is *was.*)
Where is my sandwich? (The subject is *sandwich;* the verb is *is.*)

519.1 The Subject

The **subject** is the part of the sentence about which something is said. The subject is always a noun, or a word or phrase that functions as a noun (such as a pronoun, an infinitive or an infinitive phrase, a gerund or a gerund phrase) or a clause that functions as a noun.

> **Wolves** howl. (noun)
>
> **They** howl for a variety of reasons. (pronoun)
>
> **To establish their turf** may be one reason. (infinitive phrase)
>
> **Searching for "lost" pack members** may be another. (gerund phrase)
>
> **That wolves and dogs are similar animals** seems obvious. (noun clause)

■ A **simple subject** is the subject without its modifiers.

> Most wildlife **biologists** disapprove of crossbreeding wolves and dogs.

■ A **complete subject** is the subject with all of its modifiers.

> **Most wildlife biologists** disapprove of crossbreeding wolves and dogs.

■ A **compound subject** is composed of two or more simple subjects.

> Wise **breeders** and **owners** know that wolf-dog puppies can display unexpected, destructive behaviors.

519.2 The Predicate

The **predicate** is the part of the sentence that shows action or says something about the subject.

> Giant squid **do exist.**

■ A **simple predicate** is the verb without its modifiers.

> The largest squid ever found **measured** nearly 60 feet long.

■ A **complete predicate** is the simple predicate with all its modifiers.

> The largest squid ever found **measured nearly 60 feet long.**
> (*Measured* is the simple predicate; *nearly 60 feet long* modifies *measured*.)

■ A **compound predicate** is composed of two or more simple predicates.

> A squid **grasps** its prey with tentacles and **bites** it with its beak.

NOTE: A sentence can have a **compound subject** and a **compound predicate.**

> Both sperm **whales** and giant **squid** **live** and occasionally **clash** in the deep waters off New Zealand's South Island.

■ A **direct object** receives the action of the predicate. (See 508.1.)

> Sperm whales sometimes eat giant **squid.**
> (The direct object *giant squid* receives the action of the verb by answering the question *whales eat what?*)

NOTE: The **direct object** may be compound.

> In the past, whalers harvested **oil, spermaceti,** and **ambergris** from slain sperm whales.

Using Phrases

A **phrase** is a group of related words that function as a single part of speech. A phrase lacks a subject, a predicate, or both.

> **finishing the race** (This phrase lacks a predicate and functions as a noun.)
>
> **will require** (This phrase lacks a subject and functions as a verb.)
>
> **running down several steep slopes** (This phrase lacks both a subject and a predicate and functions as an adverb.)
>
> **Finishing the race will require running down several steep slopes.**

520.1 Types of Phrases

There are several types of phrases: *verb, verbal, prepositional, appositive,* and *absolute.*

■ A **verb phrase** consists of a main verb preceded by one or more helping verbs.

> **The snow has been falling for three straight days.**
> (*Has been falling* is a verb phrase.)

■ A **verbal phrase** is a phrase based on one of the three types of verbals: *gerund, infinitive,* or *participle.* (See 508.2, 509.1, and 509.2.)

○ A **gerund phrase** consists of a gerund and its modifiers. The whole phrase functions as a noun.

> **Spotting the tiny mouse was easy for the hawk.**
> (The gerund phrase is used as the subject of the sentence.)
>
> **Dinner escaped by ducking under a rock.**
> (The gerund phrase is the object of the preposition *by.*)

○ An **infinitive phrase** consists of an infinitive and its modifiers. The whole phrase functions either as a noun, an adjective, or an adverb.

> **To shake every voter's hand was the candidate's goal.**
> (The infinitive phrase functions as a noun used as the subject.)
>
> **Your efforts to clean the chalkboard are appreciated.**
> (The infinitive phrase is used as an adjective modifying *efforts.*)
>
> **Please watch carefully to see the difference.**
> (The infinitive phrase is used as an adverb modifying *watch.*)

○ A **participial phrase** consists of a past or present participle and its modifiers. The whole phrase functions as an adjective.

> **Following his nose, the beagle took off like a jackrabbit.**
> (The participial phrase modifies the noun *beagle.*)
>
> **The raccoons, warned by the rustling, took cover.**
> (The participial phrase modifies the noun *raccoons.*)

- A **prepositional phrase** is a group of words beginning with a preposition and ending with a noun or a pronoun. Prepositional phrases are used mainly as adjectives and adverbs.

  Zach won the wheelchair race in record time. (The prepositional phrase *in record time* is used as an adverb modifying the verb *won.*)

  Reach for that catnip ball behind the couch. (The prepositional phrase *behind the couch* is used as an adjective modifying *catnip ball.*)

- An **appositive phrase,** which follows a noun or a pronoun and renames it, consists of a noun and its modifiers. An appositive adds new information about the noun or pronoun it follows.

  The Trans-Siberian Railroad, the world's longest railway, stretches from Moscow to Vladivostok. (The appositive phrase renames *Trans-Siberian Railroad* and provides new information.)

- An **absolute phrase** consists of a noun and a participle (plus the participle's object, if there is one, and any modifiers). Because it has a subject and a verbal, an absolute phrase resembles a clause.

  Its wheels clattering rhythmically over the rails, the train rolled into town. (The noun *wheels* is modified by the present participle *clattering.*)

Using Clauses

A **clause** is a group of related words that has both a subject and a predicate.

521.1 Independent and Dependent Clauses

An **independent clause** presents a complete thought and can stand alone as a sentence; a **dependent clause** (also called a *subordinate clause*) does not present a complete thought and cannot stand alone as a sentence.

  Sparrows make nests in cattle barns (independent clause) **so that they can stay warm during the winter** (dependent clause).

521.2 Types of Clauses

There are three basic types of dependent or subordinate clauses: *adverb, noun,* and *adjective.*

- An **adverb clause** is used like an adverb to modify a verb, an adjective, or an adverb. All adverb clauses begin with a subordinating conjunction. (See 516.3.)

  If I study hard, I will pass this test.
  (The adverb clause modifies the verb *will pass.*)

- A **noun clause** is used in place of a noun.

  However, the teacher said that the essay questions are based only on the last two chapters. (The noun clause functions as a direct object.)

- An **adjective clause** is used like an adjective to modify a noun or a pronoun.

  Tomorrow's test, which covers the entire book, is half essay and half short answers. (The adjective clause modifies the noun *test.*)

Using Sentence Variety

A sentence may be classified according to the type of statement it makes, the way it is constructed, and its arrangement of words.

522.1 Kinds of Sentences

Sentences can make five basic kinds of statements: *declarative, interrogative, imperative, exclamatory,* or *conditional.*

■ **Declarative sentences** make statements. They tell us something about a person, a place, a thing, or an idea.

> **The Statue of Liberty stands in New York Harbor.**
>
> **For over a century, it has greeted immigrants and visitors to America.**

■ **Interrogative sentences** ask questions.

> **Did you know that the Statue of Liberty is made of copper and stands over 150 feet tall?**

■ **Imperative sentences** make commands. They often contain an understood subject (*you*) as in the examples below.

> **Go see the Statue of Liberty.**
>
> **After a few weeks of physical conditioning, climb its 168 stairs.**

■ **Exclamatory sentences** communicate strong emotion or surprise.

> **Climbing 168 stairs is not a dumb idea!**
>
> **Just muster some of that old pioneering spirit, that desire to try something new, that never-say-die attitude that made America great!**

■ **Conditional sentences** express wishes ("if . . . then" statements) or conditions contrary to fact.

> **If you were to climb to the top of the statue, then you could share in the breathtaking feeling experienced by many hopeful immigrants.**

522.2 Types of Sentences

A sentence may be *simple, compound, complex,* or *compound-complex.* It all depends on the relationship between independent and dependent clauses.

■ A **simple sentence** may have a single subject or a compound subject. It may have a single predicate or a compound predicate. But a simple sentence has only one independent clause, and it has no dependent clauses. A simple sentence may, however, contain one or more phrases.

> **My back aches.**
> (single subject; single predicate)
>
> **My teeth and my eyes hurt.**
> (compound subject; single predicate)
>
> **My throat and nose feel sore and look red.**
> (compound subject; compound predicate)
>
> **I must have caught the flu from the sick kids in class.**
> (independent clause with two phrases: *from the sick kids* and *in class*)

■ A **compound sentence** consists of two independent clauses. The clauses must be joined by a semicolon, or by a comma and a coordinating conjunction.

> **I usually don't mind missing school, but this is not fun.**
>
> **I feel too sick to watch TV; I feel too sick to eat.**

NOTE: The comma can be omitted when the clauses are very short.

> **I wept and I wept.**

■ A **complex sentence** contains one independent clause (in black) and one or more dependent clauses (in red).

> **When I get back to school, I'm actually going to appreciate it.**
> (dependent clause; independent clause)
>
> **I won't even complain about math class, although I might be talking out of my head because I'm feverish.**
> (independent clause; two dependent clauses)

■ A **compound-complex sentence** contains two or more independent clauses (in black) and one or more dependent clauses (in red).

> **Yes, I have a bad flu, and because I need to get well soon, I won't think about school just yet.**
> (two independent clauses; one dependent clause)

523.1 Arrangement of a Sentence

Depending on the arrangement of the words and the placement of emphasis, a sentence may also be classified as *loose, balanced, periodic,* or *cumulative.*

■ A **loose sentence** expresses the main thought near the beginning and adds explanatory material as needed.

> **We hauled out the boxes of food and set up the camp stove, all the time battling the hot wind that would not stop, even when we screamed into the sky.**

■ A **balanced sentence** is constructed so that it emphasizes a similarity or a contrast between two or more of its parts (words, phrases, or clauses).

> **The wind in our ears drove us crazy and pushed us on.**
> (The similar wording emphasizes the main idea in this sentence.)

■ A **periodic sentence** is one that postpones the crucial or most surprising idea until the end.

> **Following my mother's repeated threats to ground me for life, I decided it was time to propose a compromise.**

■ A **cumulative sentence** places the general idea in the middle of the sentence with modifying clauses and phrases coming before and after.

> **With careful thought, and extra attention to detail, I wrote out my plan for being a model teenager, a teen who cared about neatness and reliability.**

Diagramming Sentences

A **graphic diagram** of a sentence is a picture of how the words in that sentence are related and how they fit together to form a complete thought.

524.1 Simple Sentence with One Subject and One Verb

Chris fishes.

Chris	fishes

subject	verb

524.2 Simple Sentence with a Predicate Adjective

Fish are delicious.

| Fish | are \ delicious |

| subject | verb \ predicate adjective |

524.3 Simple Sentence with a Predicate Noun and Adjectives

Fishing is my favorite hobby.

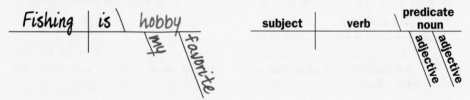

| subject | verb \ predicate noun |

NOTE: When possessive pronouns (*my, his, their*, etc.) are used as adjectives, they are placed on a diagonal line under the word they modify.

524.4 Simple Sentence with an Indirect and Direct Object

My grandpa gave us a trout.

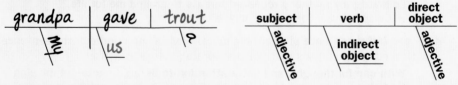

| subject | verb | direct object |

NOTE: Articles (*a, an, the*) are adjectives and are placed on a diagonal line under the word they modify.

525.1 Simple Sentence with a Prepositional Phrase

I like fishing by myself.

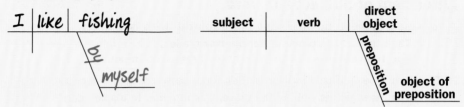

525.2 Simple Sentence with a Compound Subject and Verb

The team and fans clapped and cheered.

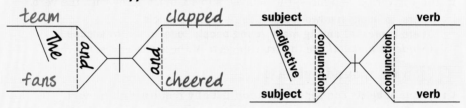

525.3 Compound Sentence

The team scored and the crowd cheered wildly.

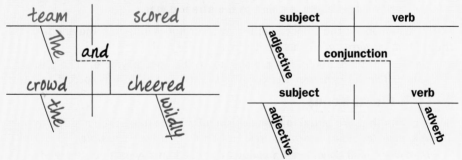

525.4 Complex Sentence with a Subordinate Clause

Before Erin scored, the crowd sat quietly.

Getting Sentence Parts to Agree

Agreement of Subject and Verb

A verb must agree in number (singular or plural) with its subject.

> The student was proud of her quarter grades. (The subject *student* and the verb *was* are singular; they agree in number.)

NOTE: Do not be confused by words that come between the subject and verb.

> The manager, as well as the players, is required to display good sportsmanship. (*Manager,* not *players,* is the subject.)

526.1 Delayed Subjects

Delayed subjects occur when the verb comes before the subject in a sentence. In these inverted sentences, the delayed subject must agree with the verb.

> There are many hardworking students in our schools.
> There is present among many young people today a will to succeed.
> (*Students* and *will* are the true subjects of these sentences, not *there.*)

526.2 Compound Subjects

Compound subjects connected with *and* usually require a plural verb.

> Strength and balance are necessary for gymnastics.

526.3 Singular Subjects

Singular subjects joined by *or* or *nor* take a singular verb.

> Neither Bev nor Kendra is going to the street dance.

NOTE: When one of the subjects joined by *or* or *nor* is singular and one is plural, the verb must agree with the subject nearer the verb.

> Neither Yoshi nor his friends are singing in the band anymore. (The plural subject *friends* is nearer the verb, so the plural verb *are* is correct.)

526.4 Plural Nouns

Some nouns that are plural in form but singular in meaning take a singular verb: *mumps, measles, news, mathematics, economics, gallows, shambles.*

> Measles is still considered a serious disease in many parts of the world.

Some nouns that are plural in form but singular in meaning take a plural verb: *scissors, trousers, tidings.*

> The scissors are missing again.

526.5 "Be" Verbs

When a sentence contains a form of the "be" verb—and a noun comes before and after that verb—the verb must agree with the subject, not the *complement* (the noun coming after the verb).

> The cause of his problem was the bad brakes.
> The bad brakes were the cause of his problem.

527.1 Collective Nouns

Collective nouns (*faculty, committee, team, congress, species, crowd, army, pair, squad*) take a singular verb when they refer to a group as a unit; collective nouns take a plural verb when they refer to the individuals within the group.

> **The favored team is losing, and the crowd is getting ugly.** (Both *team* and *crowd* are considered units in this sentence, requiring the singular verb *is*.)

> **The pair were finally reunited after 20 years apart.**
> (Here, *pair* refers to two individuals, so the plural verb *were* is required.)

527.2 Indefinite Pronouns

Some **indefinite pronouns** are singular: *each, either, neither, one, everybody, another, anybody, everyone, nobody, everything, somebody*, and *someone*. They require a singular verb.

> **Everybody is invited to the cafeteria for refreshments.**

Some **indefinite pronouns** are plural: *both, few, many*, and *several*.

> **Several like chocolate cake.   Many ask for ice cream, too.**

NOTE: Do not be confused by words or phrases that come between the indefinite pronoun and the verb.

> **One of the participants is** (not *are*) **going to have to stay late to clean up.**

A Closer Look Some **indefinite pronouns** can be either singular or plural: *all, any, most, none*, and *some*. These pronouns are singular if the number of the noun in the prepositional phrase is singular; they are plural if the noun is plural.

> **Most of the food complaints are coming from the seniors.**
> (*Complaints* is plural, so *most* is plural.)

> **Most of the tabletop is sticky with melted ice cream.**
> (*Tabletop* is singular, so *most* is singular.)

527.3 Relative Pronouns

When a **relative pronoun** (*who, which, that*) is used as the subject of a clause, the number of the verb is determined by the antecedent of the pronoun. (The antecedent is the word to which the pronoun refers.)

> **This is one of the books that are required for geography class.**
> (The relative pronoun *that* requires the plural verb *are* because its antecedent *books* is plural.)

NOTE: To test this type of sentence for agreement, read the "of" phrase first.

> **Of the books that are required for geography class, this is one.**

Agreement of Pronoun and Antecedent

A pronoun must agree in number, person, and gender (sex) with its *antecedent*. (The *antecedent* is the word to which the pronoun refers.)

> **Cal brought his gerbil to school.** (The antecedent of *his* is *Cal.* Both the pronoun and its antecedent are singular, third person, and masculine; therefore, the pronoun is said to agree with its antecedent.)

528.1 Agreement in Number

Use a **singular pronoun** to refer to such antecedents as *each, either, neither, one, anyone, anybody, everyone, everybody, somebody, another, nobody,* and *a person.*

> **Neither of the brothers likes his (not their) room.**

Use a **plural pronoun** to refer to antecedents joined by *and*; two or more singular antecedents joined by *or* or *nor* are referred to by a **singular pronoun**.

> **Jared and Carlos are finishing their assignments.**
>
> **Either Connie or Sue left her headset in the library.**

528.2 Agreement in Gender

Use a **masculine** or **feminine pronoun** depending upon the gender of the antecedent.

> **Is either Connor or Grace bringing his or her baseball glove?**

When *a person* or *everyone* is used to refer to both sexes or either sex, you will have to choose whether to offer optional pronouns or rewrite the sentence.

> **A person should be allowed to pursue his or her interests.** (optional pronouns)
>
> **People should be allowed to pursue their interests.** (rewritten in plural form)

If one of the antecedents joined by *or* or *nor* is singular and one is plural, the pronoun should agree with the nearer antecedent.

> **Neither the manager nor the players were crazy about their new uniforms.**

Using Fair Language

When depicting individuals or groups according to their differences, you must use language that implies equal value and equal respect for all people.

529.1 Addressing Ethnicity

Acceptable General Terms	*Acceptable Specific Terms*
American Indians, Native Americans . . .	**Cherokee, Inuit, Navaho**
Asian Americans (not *Orientals*)	**Chinese Americans**
Hispanic Americans or **Hispanics**	**Mexican Americans**

African Americans, blacks
> *African American* has come into wide acceptance, though the term *black* is preferred by some individuals.

Anglo-Americans (English ancestry), **European Americans**
> Avoid the notion that *American,* used alone, means *white.*

NOTE: Also avoid using *Americans* to mean just *U.S. citizens.*

529.2 Addressing Age

General Age Group	*Acceptable Terms*
Up to age 18	**boys, girls**
Between 13 and 19	**youth, young men, young women**
Late teens and 20's	**young adults**
30's and older	**adults, men, women**
70 and older	**older adults, older people** (not *elderly*)

529.3 Addressing Disabilities and Impairments

Not Recommended	*Preferred*
handicapped	**disabled**
birth defect	**congenital disability**
an AIDS victim	**person with AIDS**
stutter, stammer, lisp	**speech impairment (impaired)**
deaf	**hearing impairment (impaired)**
blind	**visual impairment (impaired)**

529.4 Putting People First

People with various conditions should not be referred to as though they *were* their condition *(quadriplegics, epileptics)* instead of simply people who have a certain condition.

Not Recommended	*Preferred*
the retarded	**people with mental retardation**
neurotics	**patients with neuroses**
quadriplegics	**people who are quadriplegic**

530.1 Optional Pronouns

Don't use masculine-only pronouns (*he, his, him*) when you want to refer to a human being in general.

> **A politician can kiss privacy good-bye when he runs for office.**

DO use one of the several ways to avoid sexism:

Reword the sentence: **Running for office robs a politician of privacy.**

Express in the plural: **Politicians can kiss privacy good-bye when they run for office.**

Offer optional pronouns: **A politician can kiss privacy good-bye when he or she runs for office.**

530.2 Business Writing

Don't use a male word in the salutation of a business letter to someone you do not know:

> **Dear Sir:**   **Dear Gentlemen:**

DO address both if you're not sure whether the reader is male or female:

> **Dear Madam or Sir:**
> **Dear Ladies and Gentlemen:**

or address a position:

> **Dear Personnel Officer:**
> **Dear Members of the Big Bird Fan Club:**

530.3 Equal Treatment

Don't give special treatment to one of the sexes:

> **The men and the ladies came through in the clutch.**
> **Mr. Bubba Gumm, Mrs. Bubba Gumm**

DO use equal language for both sexes:

> **The men and the women came through in the clutch.**
> **Mr. Bubba Gumm, Mrs. Lotta Gumm**

530.4 Occupational Issues

Not Recommended	Preferred
chairman	chair, presiding officer, moderator
salesman	sales representative, salesperson
mailman	mail carrier, postal worker, letter carrier
fireman	firefighter
businessman	executive, manager, businessperson
congressman	member of Congress, representative, senator
policeman	police officer

531.1 Professional Status

Don't typecast one gender.

DO show both women and men as doctors and nurses, principals and teachers, breadwinners and housekeepers, bosses and secretaries, grocery-store owners and cashiers, pilots and plumbers, etc.

531.2 Strengths and Weaknesses

Don't associate certain qualities like courage, strength, brilliance, creativity, independence, persistence, seriousness, emotionalism, passivity, or fearfulness with only one gender.

DO portray people of both sexes along the whole range of potential human strengths and weaknesses.

531.3 Physical and Mental Abilities

Don't refer to women according to their physical appearance and to men according to their mental abilities or professional status:

The admirable Dr. William Hicks and his wife Sareena, a former model, both showed up at the party.

DO refer to both on the same plane:

Bill and Sareena Hicks showed up at the party.

531.4 Job Description

Don't take special notice when a woman does a "man's job" or vice versa:

lady doctor   male nurse   coed   steward   policewoman

DO treat men's or women's involvement in a profession in the same way:

doctor   nurse   student   flight attendant   police officer

531.5 Equal Partners

Don't portray women as the possessions of men:

Fred took his wife and kids on a vacation.

DO portray women and men, husbands and wives, as equal partners:

Fred and Wilma took their kids on a vacation.

531.6 Respectful Labels

Don't use demeaning or sexually loaded labels:

the weaker sex	chick, fox	jock
the little woman	stud, hunk	the old man

DO use respectful terms rather than labels; consider what the person might wish to be called:

women, females	attractive woman	athletic man
wife, spouse	handsome man	father, husband, spouse

Student

ALMANAC

"Putting words together in a way which is unique, to me is something I still think is one of the most thrilling things that one can do in one's life."

—Seymour Simon

LANGUAGE

The information in this section of your handbook should be both interesting and helpful as you study languages around the world, need to use parliamentary procedure, or when you want to "sign" a message across a noisy room.

Manual Alphabet (Sign Language)

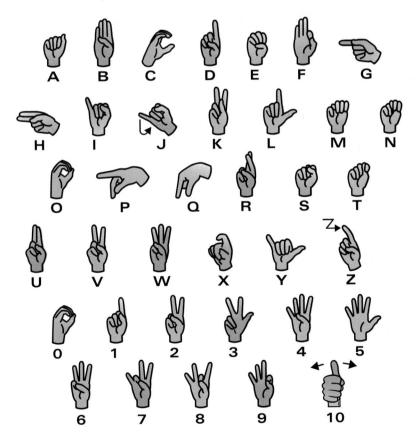

Language Families

Language families are groups of languages. Within a specific group, the languages are related because they all developed from the same language. English belongs to the **Indo-European** language family, as do many other languages. (See the chart below.)

The map shows all of the major language families plus the main languages in each family. (See the key on the next page.)

THE INDO-EUROPEAN FAMILY TODAY

Albanian

Armenian

Balto-Slavic
- Bulgarian
- Czech
- Latvian
- Lithuanian
- Polish
- Russian
- Serbo-Croatian
- Slovak
- Slovenian
- Ukrainian

Celtic
- Breton
- Irish (Celtic)
- Scots (Celtic)
- Welsh

Germanic
- Dutch
- English
- German
- Scandinavian
  - Danish
  - Icelandic
  - Norwegian
  - Swedish

Greek

Indo-Iranian
- Bengali
- Farsi
- Hindi
- Pashto
- Urdu

Romance
- French
- Italian
- Portuguese
- Romanian
- Spanish

MAJOR LANGUAGE FAMILIES

Indo-European

Sino-Tibetan

Afro-Asian

Uralic and Altaic

Japanese and Korean

Dravidian

Malayo-Polynesian

Mon-Khmer

Niger-Kordofanian

Nilo-Saharan

Khoisan

All others

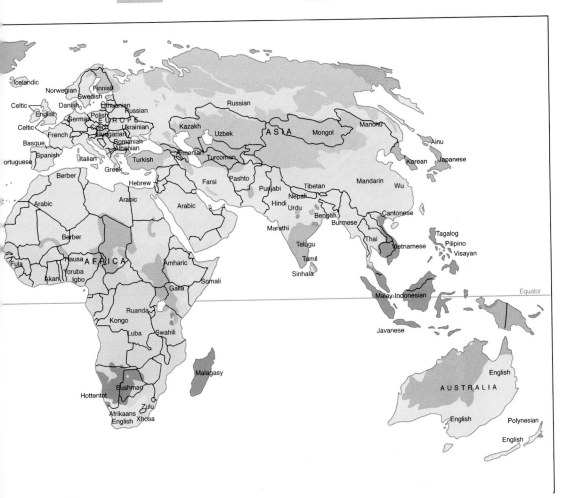

Traffic Signs

Red: Regulatory Signs

These signs are red to get your attention: they tell you to do (or *not do*) something. The red circle and stripe tells you NO.

White and Black: Informational Signs

Informational signs are black and white and shaped like a square or rectangle. They provide basic information for pedestrians and drivers.

Yellow: Warning Signs

Yellow signs warn of a possible danger. Many warning signs are diamond shaped.

Green: Directional or Guide Signs

Green signs give traffic directions or provide information on trails and bike routes.

Blue: Service Signs

Blue signs indicate there are services nearby.

Orange: Construction and Slow-Moving Vehicle Signs

Orange signs mean slow down and drive carefully.

Common Parliamentary Procedures

Motion	Purpose	Needs Second	Debatable	Amendable	Required Vote	May Interrupt Speaker	Subsidiary Motion Applied
I. ORIGINAL OR PRINCIPAL MOTION							
1. Main Motion (general) Main Motions (specific)	To introduce business	Yes	Yes	Yes	Majority	No	Yes
a. To reconsider	To reconsider previous motion	Yes	When original motion is	No	Majority	Yes	No
b. To rescind	To nullify or wipe out previous action	Yes	Yes	Yes	Majority or two-thirds	No	No
c. To take from the table	To consider tabled motion	Yes	No	No	Majority	No	No
II. SUBSIDIARY MOTIONS							
2. To lay on the table	To defer action	Yes	No	No	Majority	No	No
3. To call for previous question	To close debate and force vote	Yes	No	No	Two-thirds	No	Yes
4. To limit or extend limits of debate	To control time of debate	Yes	No	Yes	Two-thirds	No	Yes
5. To postpone to a certain time	To defer action	Yes	Yes	Yes	Majority	No	Yes
6. To refer to a committee	To provide for special study	Yes	Yes	Yes	Majority	No	Yes
7. To amend	To modify a motion	Yes	When original motion is	Yes (once only)	Majority	No	Yes
8. To postpone indefinitely	To suppress action	Yes	Yes	No	Majority	No	Yes
III. INCIDENTAL MOTIONS							
9. To raise a point of order	To correct error in procedure	No	No	No	Decision of chair	Yes	No
10. To appeal for a decision of chair	To change decision on procedure	Yes	If motion does not relate to indecorum	No	Majority or tie	Yes	No
11. To suspend rules	To alter existing rules and order of business	Yes	No	No	Two-thirds	No	No
12. To object to consideration	To suppress action	No	No	No	Two-thirds	Yes	No
13. To call for division of house	To secure a countable vote	No	No	No	Majority if chair desires	Yes	Yes
14. To close nominations	To stop nomination of officers	Yes	No	Yes	Two-thirds	No	Yes
15. To reopen nominations	To permit additional nominations	Yes	No	Yes	Majority	No	Yes
16. To withdraw a motion	To remove a motion	No	No	No	Majority	No	No
17. To divide a motion	To modify a motion	No	No	Yes	Majority	No	Yes
IV. PRIVILEGED MOTIONS							
18. To fix time of next meeting	To set time of next meeting	Yes	No, if made when another question is before the assembly	Yes	Majority	No	Yes
19. To adjourn	To dismiss meeting	Yes	No	Yes	Majority	No	No
20. To take a recess	To dismiss meeting for specific time	Yes	No, if made when another question is before the assembly	Yes	Majority	No	Yes
21. To raise question of privilege	To make a request concerning rights of assembly	No	No	No	Decision of chair	Yes	No
22. To call for orders of the day	To keep assembly to order of business	No	No	No	None unless objection	Yes	No
23. To make a special order	To ensure consideration at specified time	Yes	Yes	Yes	Two-thirds	No	Yes

6-Year Calendar

1999

| JANUARY | FEBRUARY | MARCH | APRIL | MAY | JUNE |
| JULY | AUGUST | SEPTEMBER | OCTOBER | NOVEMBER | DECEMBER |

2000

| JANUARY | FEBRUARY | MARCH | APRIL | MAY | JUNE |
| JULY | AUGUST | SEPTEMBER | OCTOBER | NOVEMBER | DECEMBER |

2001

| JANUARY | FEBRUARY | MARCH | APRIL | MAY | JUNE |
| JULY | AUGUST | SEPTEMBER | OCTOBER | NOVEMBER | DECEMBER |

2002

| JANUARY | FEBRUARY | MARCH | APRIL | MAY | JUNE |
| JULY | AUGUST | SEPTEMBER | OCTOBER | NOVEMBER | DECEMBER |

2003

| JANUARY | FEBRUARY | MARCH | APRIL | MAY | JUNE |
| JULY | AUGUST | SEPTEMBER | OCTOBER | NOVEMBER | DECEMBER |

2004

| JANUARY | FEBRUARY | MARCH | APRIL | MAY | JUNE |
| JULY | AUGUST | SEPTEMBER | OCTOBER | NOVEMBER | DECEMBER |

"Science is simply common sense at its
best—that is, rigidly accurate in observation,
and merciless to fallacy in logic."   —T. H. Huxley

SCIENCE

The science tables and glossary of computer and Internet terms that follow should be both interesting and helpful. The "Periodic Table of the Elements," "The Metric System," and "Planet Profusion" all hold information you may need in your classes.

Weights and Measures

Linear Measure
1 inch . . . . = 2.54 centimeters
1 foot . . . . = 12 inches
                                    0.3048 meter
1 yard . . . . = 3 feet
                                    0.9144 meter
1 rod (or pole or perch). . = 5.5 yards or 16.5 feet
                                    5.029 meters
1 furlong. . . . . = 40 rods
                                    201.17 meters
1 (statute) mile. . . . . = 8 furlongs
                                    1,760 yards
                                    5,280 feet
                                    1,609.3 meters
1 (land) league . . . . = 3 miles
                                    4.83 kilometers

Square Measure
1 square inch . . . . = 6.452 sq. centimeters
1 square foot . . . . = 144 square inches
                                    929 square centimeters
1 square yard . . . . = 9 square feet
                                    0.8361 square meter
1 square rod. . . . . = 30.25 square rods
                                    25.29 square meters
1 acre. . . . . = 160 square rods
                                    4,840 square yards
                                    43,560 square feet
                                    0.4047 hectare
1 square mile . . . . = 640 acres
                                    259 hectares
                                    2.59 square kilometers

(Engineer's chain)
1 link . . . . = 1 foot
                                    0.3048 meter
1 chain. . . . . = 100 feet
                                    30.48 meters
1 mile. . . . . = 52.8 chains
                                    1,609.3 meters

Surveyor's (Square) Measure
1 square pole . . . . = 625 square links
                                    25.29 square meters
1 square chain . . . . = 16 square poles
                                    404.7 square meters
1 acre. . . . . = 10 square chains
                                    0.4047 hectare
1 square mile or
   1 section . . . . = 640 acres
                                    259 hectares
                                    2.59 square kilometers
1 township . . . . = 36 square miles
                                    9,324 hectares
                                    93.24 square kilometers

Nautical Measure
1 fathom . . . . = 6 feet
                                    1.829 meters
1 cable's length (ordinary) = 100 fathoms
                                    (In the U.S. Navy 120
                                    fathoms or 720 feet = 1
                                    cable's length; in the
                                    British Navy 608 feet = 1
                                    cable's length)
1 nautical mile . . . . = 6,076.10333 feet; *by international agreement in 1954*
                                    10 cables' length
                                    1.852 kilometers
                                    1.1508 statute miles;
                                    length of a minute of longitude at the equator
1 marine league . . . . . . = 3.45 statute miles
                                    3 nautical miles
                                    5.56 kilometers
1 degree of a great circle
   of the earth. . . . . = 60 nautical miles

Weights and Measures (continued)

Cubic Measure

1 cubic inch	=	16.387 cubic centimeters
1 cubic foot	=	1,728 cubic inches
		0.0283 cubic meter
1 cubic yard	=	27 cubic feet
		0.7646 cubic meter
1 cord foot	=	16 cubic feet
1 cord	=	8 cord feet
		3.625 cubic meters

Chain Measure
(Gunter's or surveyor's chain)

1 link	=	7.92 inches
		20.12 centimeters
1 chain	=	100 links or 66 feet
		20.12 meters
1 furlong	=	10 chains
		201.17 meters
1 mile	=	80 chains
		1,609.3 meters

Dry Measure

1 pint	=	33.60 cubic inches
		0.5505 liter
1 quart	=	2 pints
		67.20 cubic inches
		1.1012 liters
1 peck	=	8 quarts
		537.61 cubic inches
		8.8096 liters
1 bushel	=	4 pecks
		2,150.42 cubic inches
		35.2383 liters

Liquid Measure

4 fluid ounces	=	1 gill
(see next table)		7.219 cubic inches
		0.1183 liter
1 pint	=	4 gills
		28.875 cubic inches
		0.4732 liter
1 quart	=	2 pints
		57.75 cubic inches
		0.9463 liter
1 gallon	=	4 quarts
		231 cubic inches
		3.7853 liters

Apothecaries' Fluid Measure

1 minim	=	0.0038 cubic inch
		0.0616 milliliter
1 fluid dram	=	60 minims
		0.2256 cubic inch
		3.6966 milliliters
1 fluid ounce	=	8 fluid drams
		1.8047 cubic inches
		0.0296 liter
1 pint	=	16 fluid ounces
		28.875 cubic inches
		0.4732 liter

Circular (or Angular) Measure

1 minute (')	=	60 seconds (")
1 degree (°)	=	60 minutes
1 quadrant or 1 right angle	=	90 degrees
1 circle	=	4 quadrants
		360 degrees

Avoirdupois Weight

(The grain, equal to 0.0648 gram, is the same in all three tables of weight.)

1 dram or 27.34 grains	=	1.772 grams
1 ounce	=	16 drams
		437.5 grains
		28.3495 grams
1 pound	=	16 ounces
		7,000 grains
		453.59 grams
1 hundredweight	=	100 pounds
		45.36 kilograms
1 ton	=	2,000 pounds
		907.18 kilograms

Troy Weight

(The grain, equal to 0.0648 gram, is the same in all three tables of weight.)

1 carat	=	3.086 grains
		200 milligrams
1 pennyweight	=	24 grains
		1.5552 grams
1 ounce	=	20 pennyweights
		480 grains
		31.1035 grams
1 pound	=	12 ounces
		5,760 grains
		373.24 grams

Apothecaries' Weight

(The grain, equal to 0.0648 gram, is the same in all three tables of weight.)

1 scruple	=	20 grains
		1.296 grams
1 dram	=	3 scruples
		3.888 grams
1 ounce	=	8 drams
		480 grains
		31.1035 grams
1 pound	=	12 ounces
		5,760 grains
		373.24 grams

Miscellaneous

1 palm	=	3 inches
1 hand	=	4 inches
1 span	=	6 inches
1 cubit	=	18 inches
1 Biblical cubit	=	21.8 inches
1 military pace	=	2.5 feet

The **Metric** System

In 1975, the United States signed the Metric Conversion Act, declaring a national policy of encouraging voluntary use of the metric system. Today, the metric system exists side by side with the U.S. customary system. The debate on whether the United States should adopt the metric system has been going on for nearly 200 years, leaving the United States the only country in the world not totally committed to adopting the system.

The metric system is considered a simpler form of measurement. It is based on the decimal system (units of 10) and eliminates the need to deal with fractions.

Linear Measure

1 centimeter	=	10 millimeters
		0.3937 inch
1 decimeter	=	10 centimeters
		3.937 inches
1 meter	=	10 decimeters
		39.37 inches
		3.28 feet
1 decameter	=	10 meters
		393.7 inches
1 hectometer	=	10 decameters
		328 feet 1 inch
1 kilometer	=	10 hectometers
		0.621 mile
1 myriameter	=	10 kilometers
		6.21 miles

Volume Measure

1 cubic centimeter	=	1,000 cubic millimeters
		.06102 cubic inch
1 cubic decimeter	=	1,000 cubic centimeters
		61.02 cubic inches
1 cubic meter	=	1,000 cubic decimeters
		35.314 cubic feet

Capacity Measure

1 centiliter	=	10 milliliters
		.338 fluid ounce
1 deciliter	=	10 centiliters
		3.38 fluid ounces
1 liter	=	10 deciliters
		1.0567 liquid quarts
		0.9081 dry quart
1 decaliter	=	10 liters
		2.64 gallons
		0.284 bushel
1 hectoliter	=	10 decaliters
		26.418 gallons
		2.838 bushels
1 kiloliter	=	10 hectoliters
		264.18 gallons
		35.315 cubic feet

Square Measure

1 square centimeter	=	100 square millimeters
		0.15499 square inch
1 square decimeter	=	100 square centimeters
		15.499 square inches
1 square meter	=	100 square decimeters
		1,549.9 square inches
		1.196 square yards
1 square decameter	=	100 square meters
		119.6 square yards
1 square hectometer	=	100 square decameters
		2.471 acres
1 square kilometer	=	100 square hectometers
		0.386 square mile

Land Measure

1 centare	=	1 square meter
		1,549.9 square inches
1 are	=	100 centares
		119.6 square yards
1 hectare	=	100 ares
		2,471 acres
1 square kilometer	=	100 hectares
		0.386 square mile

Weights

1 centigram	=	10 milligrams
		0.1543 grain
1 decigram	=	10 centigrams
		1.5432 grains
1 gram	=	10 decigrams
		15.432 grains
1 decagram	=	10 grams
		0.3527 ounce
1 hectogram	=	10 decagrams
		3.5274 ounces
1 kilogram	=	10 hectograms
		2.2046 pounds
1 myriagram	=	10 kilograms
		22.046 pounds
1 quintal	=	10 myriagrams
		220.46 pounds
1 metric ton	=	10 quintals
		2,204.6 pounds

Handy Conversion Factors

TO CHANGE	TO	MULTIPLY BY
acres	hectares	.4047
acres	square feet	43,560
acres	square miles	.001562
Celsius	Fahrenheit	1.8*
		*(then add 32)
centimeters	inches	.3937
centimeters	feet	.03281
cubic meters	cubic feet	35.3145
cubic meters	cubic yards	1.3079
cubic yards	cubic meters	.7646
degrees	radians	.01745
Fahrenheit	Celsius	.556*
		* (after subtracting 32)
feet	meters	.3048
feet	miles (nautical)	.0001645
feet	miles (statute)	.0001894
feet/sec.	miles/hr.	.6818
furlongs	feet	660.0
furlongs	miles	.125
gallons (U.S.)	liters	3.7853
grains	grams	.0648
grams	grains	15.4324
grams	ounces avdp.	.0353
grams	pounds	.002205
hectares	acres	2.4710
horsepower	watts	745.7
hours	days	.04167
inches	millimeters	25.4000
inches	centimeters	2.5400
kilograms	pounds advp. or t.	2.2046
kilometers	miles	.6214
kilowatts	horsepower	1.341
knots	nautical miles/hr.	1.0
knots	statute miles/hr.	1.151
liters	gallons (U.S.)	.2642
liters	pecks	.1135
liters	pints (dry)	1.8162
liters	pints (liquid)	2.1134
liters	quarts (dry)	.9081

TO CHANGE	TO	MULTIPLY BY
liters	quarts (liquid)	1.0567
meters	feet	3.2808
meters	miles	.0006214
meters	yards	1.0936
metric tons	tons (long)	.9842
metric tons	tons (short)	1.1023
miles	kilometers	1.6093
miles	feet	5,280
miles (nautical)	miles (statute)	1.1516
miles (statute)	miles (nautical)	.8684
miles/hr.	feet/min.	88
millimeters	inches	.0394
ounces advp.	grams	28.3495
ounces	pounds	.0625
ounces (troy)	ounces (advp.)	1.09714
pecks	liters	8.8096
pints (dry)	liters	.5506
pints (liquid)	liters	1.4732
pounds ap. or t.	kilograms	.3782
pounds advp.	kilograms	.4536
pounds	ounces	16
quarts (dry)	liters	1.1012
quarts (liquid)	liters	.9463
rods	meters	5.029
rods	feet	16.5
square feet	square meters	.0929
square kilometers	square miles	.3861
square meters	square feet	10.7639
square meters	square yards	1.1960
square miles	square kilometers	2.5900
square yards	square meters	.8361
tons (long)	metric tons	1.1060
tons (short)	metric tons	.9072
tons (long)	pounds	2,240
tons (short)	pounds	2,000
watts	Btu/hr.	3.4129
watts	horsepower	.001341
yards	meters	.9144
yards	miles	.0005682

Ten Ways to Measure *When You Don't Have a Ruler*

1. Many floor tiles are 12-inch squares (30.48-cm squares).
2. Paper money is 6-1/8 inches by 2-5/8 inches (15.56 x 6.67 cm).
3. A quarter is approximately 1 inch wide (2.54 cm).
4. A penny is approximately 3/4 of an inch wide (1.9 cm).
5. Typing paper is 8-1/2 inches by 11 inches (21.59 cm x 27.94 cm).

Each of the following items can be used as a measuring device by multiplying its length by the number of times it is used to measure an area in question.

6. A shoelace   7. A tie   8. A belt
9. Your feet—placing one in front of the other to measure floor area
10. Your outstretched arms from fingertip to fingertip

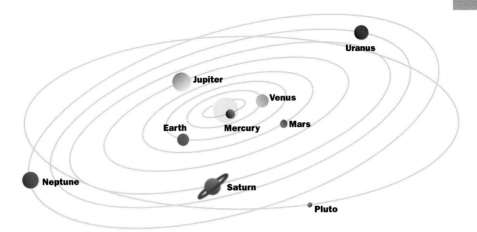

Planet Profusion

Our solar system is located in the Milky Way Galaxy. Even though this galaxy contains approximately 100 billion stars, our solar system contains only one star—the sun. The sun, which is the center of our solar system, has nine planets and a myriad of asteroids, meteors, and comets orbiting it. The planets are large, nonluminous bodies that follow fixed elliptical orbits about the sun. (See the illustration above.) The planets are divided into two categories: the terrestrial planets—Mercury, Venus, Earth, Mars, and Pluto—which resemble Earth in size, chemical composition, and density; and the Jovian planets—Jupiter, Saturn, Uranus, and Neptune—which are much larger in size and have thick, gaseous atmospheres and low densities. (See the table below.)

	Sun	Moon	Mercury	Venus	Earth	Mars	Jupiter	Saturn	Uranus	Neptune	Pluto
Orbital Speed (in mi. per second)		.6	29.8	21.8	18.5	15.0	8.1	6.0	4.2	3.4	3.0
Rotation on Axis	24 days 16 hrs. 48 min.	27 days 7 hrs. 38 min.	59 days	243 days	23 hrs. 56 min.	24 hrs. 37 min.	9 hrs. 55 min.	10 hrs. 39 min.	17 hrs. 8 min.	16 hrs. 7 min.	6 days
Mean Surface Gravity (Earth=1)		0.16	0.38	0.9	1.00	0.38	2.53	1.07	0.91	1.14	0.07
Density (times that of water)	100 (core)	3.3	5.4	5.3	5.5	3.9	1.3	0.7	1.27	1.6	2.03
Mass (times that of Earth)	333,000	0.012	0.056	0.82	6×10^{21} metric tons	0.10	318	95	14.5	17.2	0.0026
Approx. Weight of a 150-Pound Human		24	59	135	150	57	380	161	137	171	11
No. of Satellites	9 planets	0	0	0	1	2	16	23	15	8	1
Mean Distance to Sun (in millions of miles)		93.0	36.0	67.24	92.96	141.7	483.8	887.1	1,783.9	2,796.4	3,666
Revolution Around Sun		365.25 days	88.0 days	224.7 days	365.25 days	687 days	11.86 years	29.46 years	84.0 years	165 years	248 years
Approximate Surface Temp. (degrees Fahrenheit)	10,000° (surface) 27,000,000° (center)	lighted side 260° dark side −280°	−346°	850°	−126.9° to 136°	−191° to −24°	−236°	−203°	−344°	−360°	−342° to −369°
Diameter (in miles)	865,400	2,155	3,032	7,519	7,926	4,194	88,736	74,978	32,193	30,775	1,423

Periodic Table of the Elements

Key:

Atomic Number	2
Symbol	He
	Helium
Atomic Weight (or Mass Number of most stable isotope if in parentheses)	4.00260

Legend:
- Alkali metals
- Alkaline earth metals
- Transition metals
- Lanthanide series
- Actinide series
- Other metals
- Nonmetals
- Noble gases

1a	2a	3b	4b	5b	6b	7b	8	8	8	1b	2b	3a	4a	5a	6a	7a	0
1 H Hydrogen 1.00797																	2 He Helium 4.00260
3 Li Lithium 6.941	4 Be Beryllium 9.0128											5 B Boron 10.811	6 C Carbon 12.01115	7 N Nitrogen 14.0067	8 O Oxygen 15.9994	9 F Fluorine 18.9984	10 Ne Neon 20.179
11 Na Sodium 22.9898	12 Mg Magnesium 24.305											13 Al Aluminum 26.9815	14 Si Silicon 28.0855	15 P Phosphorus 30.9738	16 S Sulfur 32.064	17 Cl Chlorine 35.453	18 Ar Argon 39.948
19 K Potassium 39.0983	20 Ca Calcium 40.08	21 Sc Scandium 44.9559	22 Ti Titanium 47.88	23 V Vanadium 50.94	24 Cr Chromium 51.996	25 Mn Manganese 54.9380	26 Fe Iron 55.847	27 Co Cobalt 58.9332	28 Ni Nickel 58.69	29 Cu Copper 63.546	30 Zn Zinc 65.39	31 Ga Gallium 69.72	32 Ge Germanium 72.59	33 As Arsenic 74.9216	34 Se Selenium 78.96	35 Br Bromine 79.904	36 Kr Krypton 83.80
37 Rb Rubidium 85.4678	38 Sr Strontium 87.62	39 Y Yttrium 88.905	40 Zr Zirconium 91.224	41 Nb Niobium 92.906	42 Mo Molybdenum 95.94	43 Tc Technetium (98)	44 Ru Ruthenium 101.07	45 Rh Rhodium 102.906	46 Pd Palladium 106.42	47 Ag Silver 107.868	48 Cd Cadmium 112.41	49 In Indium 114.82	50 Sn Tin 118.71	51 Sb Antimony 121.75	52 Te Tellurium 127.60	53 I Iodine 126.905	54 Xe Xenon 131.29
55 Cs Cesium 132.905	56 Ba Barium 137.33	57-71* Lanthanides	72 Hf Hafnium 178.49	73 Ta Tantalum 180.948	74 W Tungsten 185.85	75 Re Rhenium 186.207	76 Os Osmium 190.2	77 Ir Iridium 192.22	78 Pt Platinum 195.08	79 Au Gold 196.967	80 Hg Mercury 200.59	81 Tl Thallium 204.383	82 Pb Lead 207.19	83 Bi Bismuth 208.980	84 Po Polonium (209)	85 At Astatine (210)	86 Rn Radon (222)
87 Fr Francium (223)	88 Ra Radium 226.025	89-103** Actinides	104 Rf Rutherfordium (261)	105 Db Dubnium (262)	106 Sg Seaborgium (263)	107 Bh Bohrium (262)	108 Hs Hassium (265)	109 Mt Meitnerium (266)	110 (269)	111 (272)							

Lanthanides

57 La Lanthanum 138.906	58 Ce Cerium 140.12	59 Pr Praseodymium 140.908	60 Nd Neodymium 144.24	61 Pm Promethium (145)	62 Sm Samarium 150.36	63 Eu Europium 151.96	64 Gd Gadolinium 157.25	65 Tb Terbium 158.925	66 Dy Dysprosium 162.50	67 Ho Holmium 164.930	68 Er Erbium 167.26	69 Tm Thulium 168.934	70 Yb Ytterbium 173.04	71 Lu Lutetium 174.967

Actinides

89 Ac Actinium 227.028	90 Th Thorium 232.038	91 Pa Protactinium 231.036	92 U Uranium 238.029	93 Np Neptunium 237.048	94 Pu Plutonium (244)	95 Am Americium (243)	96 Cm Curium (247)	97 Bk Berkelium (247)	98 Cf Californium (251)	99 Es Einsteinium (252)	100 Fm Fermium (257)	101 Md Mendelevium (258)	102 No Nobelium (259)	103 Lr Lawrencium (260)

(Of elements 110–121, some are still unknown, and some are recently claimed but unnamed. They have temporary systematic names.)

Computer and Internet Terms

ASCII: (American Standard Code Information Interchange) A basic set of letters, numbers, and symbols that most computers can use.

Backup: A duplicate copy of a file or program, made in case the original is lost or destroyed.

Binary system: The number system commonly used by computers because the values 0 and 1 can be represented electronically in the computer.

Bit: A unit of computer memory that can store either a 0 or a 1. (See *byte.*)

Bookmark: A command to make a browser save an Internet address, so that the site can easily be revisited.

BPS: (bits per second) A measure of how fast data is transmitted over a network. (Sometimes called *baud rate.*) For example, a modem may have a speed of 56,600 bps.

Browser: A type of program used to view and navigate the World Wide Web.

Bulletin board: A service on the Internet where users can post messages for others to read.

Byte: Eight bits of information acting as a single piece of data. Computer memory is measured in bytes. (See *GB, K,* and *MB.* Also see *bit.*)

CD: (compact disk) A type of disk that stores data as tiny dots burned into its surface. A CD can store large amounts of information, which makes it useful for audio, text, and video.

Character: A letter, number, or symbol that appears on a keyboard or on a computer screen.

Chat: A live conversation using the keyboard on the Internet.

Chip: A small piece of silicon containing thousands of electrical elements. Also known as an *integrated circuit.*

Circuit board: A flat board used to hold and connect computer chips and other electrical parts.

Client: The user of an Internet service. The Internet software on a user's machine is "client-side software," for instance. (See *server.*)

Command: An instruction telling a computer to perform a certain task, such as "print."

Compress: To make a file smaller so that it can be easily stored or quickly sent to another computer over a network. Special software is used to compress (and decompress) files.

Computer: A machine that can accept data, process it according to a stored set of instructions, and then output the results.

Control character: A character that is entered by holding down the control key while typing another key.

CPU: (central processing unit) The "brain" of the computer; the part that performs computations and controls all other parts of the system.

Crash: A term used to describe what happens when a computer or program stops working.

CRT: (cathode ray tube) The electronic vacuum tube found in some computer monitors and TV screens.

Cursor: A pointer on the computer screen that shows where the next character typed on the keyboard will appear.

Cyberspace: The imaginary world perceived by humans when using a computer network or a virtual reality program. From William Gibson's novel *Neuromancer.* (See *network, Internet,* and *virtual reality.*)

Data: Information given to or produced by a computer.

Database: A program and a collection of information organized in such a way that a computer can quickly access a certain item or group of items.

Desktop: The monitor screen as it appears when the computer is on but no programs are open.

Directory: The table of contents for all files on a disk.

Disk: A magnetic device used to record computer information. Sometimes called a "floppy," because inside its square protective casing, the circular disk itself is thin and flexible. A disk rotates so that information can be stored on its many tracks.

Disk drive: A device that writes and reads information from and to a disk.

Documentation: The printed book or the program that explains how to use a piece of hardware or software.

Domain: In an Internet or e-mail address, the parts that name the server.

Download: To copy a program or file from another computer to your own via a network.

Drag: To move items across the screen by holding down the mouse button while sliding the mouse.

DVD: (digital video disk or digital versatile disk) A high-density compact disk capable of storing high-resolution video. (See *CD.*)

E-mail: (electronic mail) A system that uses telecommunications to send text messages from one computer to another.

Emoticon: Often called a "smiley." A set of characters that, when viewed sideways, resemble a face. Used to add emotion to a message. :-)

Error message: A message, displayed by the computer, that tells what type of error has occurred in a program.

Exit: To leave or quit a program. Also called *close* or *quit.*

FAQ: (frequently asked questions) A list of commonly asked questions and answers.

File: A collection of computer information stored under a single title.

Flame: To post an insulting or inflammatory message on the Internet.

Font: A typeface, or style of type, used by a printer. Most computer systems have several fonts.

Format: To prepare a blank disk for use. Also called *initialize.* Most disks are sold preformatted.

Freeware: Software in the public domain, for which the creator expects no payment.

FTP: (file transfer protocol) A system for transmitting large files on the Internet or a network.

GB: (gigabyte) A measure of computer memory; 1,000 megabytes (MB).

Graphics: Information displayed as pictures or images.

Hard copy: A printed copy; a printout.

Hard drive: A stack of disks permanently mounted inside most computers. The hard drive is for long-term storage of important files and programs (such as the computer's operating system).

Hardware: The electronic and mechanical parts of a computer system. A hard drive is hardware; a program stored on it is software.

Home page: The Web page that gives basic information about a person or an organization. It contains links to other Web pages or sites.

Host: The computer whose programs serve another computer in a computer-to-computer link. (See *server.*)

Hot: (See *hypertext.*)

HTML: (hypertext markup language) The codes that tell a browser how to display text and graphics for a Web page.

Hypertext or Hypermedia: A system of web-like links among pages on the Internet or within a program. A link from a "hot word" or "hot symbol" opens directly to another page.

Icon: A small picture or symbol used to identify computer folders, files, or functions.

Inkjet printer: A printer that uses tiny jets of ink to produce printouts.

Input: Information placed into a computer from a disk drive, keyboard, or other device.

Interactive: A computer program in which the user and the computer exchange information.

Interface: The hardware and software that is used to link one computer or computer device to another. Also the method by which a program communicates to a user.

Internet: A world-wide network of independent computer networks that communicate with one another.

ISP: (Internet service provider) A business that provides its customers access to the Internet. (See *server.*)

K: (kilobyte) A measure of computer memory; 1,024 bytes, (about 170 words).

Keyboard: An input device used to enter information on a computer by striking keys.

Laser printer: A printer that uses a laser to produce high-quality printouts.

Link: A connection from one hypertext page to another. A link contains the address for the target page. When the link is selected, the target page loads.

Listserve: A program that sends e-mail to a set of addresses. Each listserve is organized around a particular topic, allowing subscribers to conduct a group discussion by e-mail. Also called a *mailing list* or a *mail server.*

Load: To move information from a storage device into a computer's memory.

Mainframe: A large computer, with many terminals, powerful enough to be used by many people at once. (See *terminal.*)

MB: (megabyte) A measure of computer memory; 1,000 kilobytes (K).

Memory: The chips in the computer that store information and programs while the computer is on.

Menu: A list of choices from which a user can select. Many programs have menus.

Microcomputer: A small computer that uses a microprocessor as its CPU. The personal computers used in homes and schools are microcomputers.

Modem: (**mo**dulator **dem**odulator) A device that sends data over telephone lines.

Monitor: A video screen that displays information from a computer.

Mouse: A small manual input device that controls the pointer on the screen and sends information to the computer when it is clicked.

Multimedia: A program capable of combining text, graphics, video, voice, music, and animation.

Multiuser: A computer system that can be used by several people at once.

Network: A series of computers (or other devices) connected together in order to share information and programs.

Newsgroup: An ongoing, topic-centered discussion in bulletin-board style. (See *Usenet.*)

On-line: To be connected to a computer network.

On-line service: A business that serves as a network for its users, providing e-mail, chat rooms, and so on. Most on-line services now also act as Internet providers.

Open: To start a computer program or load a file.

Operating system: A software system that operates a computer. Some common operating systems for personal computers are Windows, Mac OS, Linux, and DOS.

Output: Information that a computer sends out to a monitor, printer, modem, or other device.

PC: (personal computer) A small computer, as opposed to a mainframe. The term PC most often refers to an IBM-compatible microcomputer. (See *microcomputer.*)

Peripheral: A device such as a monitor, printer, or scanner that is connected to a computer.

Pixel: One dot on the screen. (See *resolution.*)

Post: As a verb, to upload a message to a bulletin board, newsgroup, or listserve. As a noun, the message that is posted.

Printer: A device used to print out information from a computer.

Printout: A hard copy; or a computer document printed on paper.

Program: A piece of software or set of instructions that tells a computer what to do.

Programmer: A person who helps write, edit, or produce a computer program.

Prompt: A question or an instruction on the screen that asks the user to make a choice or give information.

Quit: To close a program, removing it from random access memory.

RAM: (random access memory) The part of a computer's memory that stores programs and documents temporarily while you are using them.

Resolution: The number of dots per square inch (dpi) on a computer screen. Images on a screen are made up of tiny dots. The more dots there are, the higher the resolution and the clearer the picture. (See *pixel*.)

ROM: (read-only memory) The part of a computer's memory that holds its permanent instructions. ROM cannot record new data.

Save: To transfer a document to a disk for permanent storage.

Scanner: A device used to read a printed image, picture, or text and save it as an electronic file.

Search engine: A program for locating sites on the Internet. Sometimes called a *robot, spider,* or *web-crawler.*

Select: To highlight part of a document to work on or change.

Server: The hosting computer of a network. Software on the server is called "server-side" software, for example. (See *client* and *host*.)

Shareware: Programs intended as demos, to be used freely for a test period, then paid for.

Software: The program that tells a computer how to do a certain task.

Spam: Unrequested e-mails sent to many people at once (often ads); electronic "junk mail."

Spreadsheet: A computer program that displays numbers and text in a worksheet form.

Surfing: Exploring the Net, going from link to link.

Telecommunications: The technology that allows computers to communicate with one another over phone lines, by satellite, etc.

Terminal: A keyboard and monitor sharing a mainframe with other terminals; sometimes called a "dumb terminal" because it does not contain a CPU, or "brain."

Text file: A computer document made up of ASCII characters only. (See *ASCII*.)

Tunneling: The method for exploring an FTP site, beginning at the welcome page and working downward through layers of folders.

Upload: To send a file from your computer to another computer via a network.

URL: (universal resource locator) The text version of the electronic address for a site on the Internet. The URL for Write Source is <http://www.thewritesource.com>.

Usenet: The major collection of newsgroups on the Internet. (See *newsgroup*.)

User: A person using a computer.

Virtual reality: A technology that makes users feel present in an environment created by the computer.

Virus: A "bug" that is intentionally put into a computer system to cause problems.

Window: A box on a computer screen in which text and/or graphics are displayed.

Word processor: A program that allows a user to write, revise, edit, save, and print text documents.

WWW: (World Wide Web) A major portion of the Internet, characterized by graphical pages and hypertext links. (See *hypertext*.)

"I think and think for months and years.
Ninety-nine times, the conclusion is false.
The hundredth time I am right." —Albert Einstein

MATHEMATICS

This chapter is your guide to the language of mathematics. It lists and defines many of the common (and not so common) mathematical signs, symbols, shapes, and terms. The chapter also includes helpful math tables.

Common Math Symbols

+	plus (addition)	<	is less than	°	degree
−	minus (subtraction)	>	is greater than	′	minute (also foot)
×	multiplied by	±	plus or minus	″	second (also inch)
÷	divided by	%	percent	:	is to (ratio)
=	is equal to	$	dollars	π	pi
≠	is not equal to	¢	cents		

Advanced Math Symbols

$\sqrt{}$	square root	~	is similar to
$\sqrt[3]{}$	cube root	≅	is congruent to
≥	is greater than or equal to	∠	angle
≤	is less than or equal to	⊥	is perpendicular to
{ }	set	∥	is parallel to
∴	therefore		

A Chart of **Prime Numbers** Less Than 500

2	3	5	7	11	13	17	19	23	29	31	37
41	43	47	53	59	61	67	71	73	79	83	89
97	101	103	107	109	113	127	131	137	139	149	151
157	163	167	173	179	181	191	193	197	199	211	223
227	229	233	239	241	251	257	263	269	271	277	281
283	293	307	311	313	317	331	337	347	349	353	359
367	373	379	383	389	397	401	409	419	421	431	433
439	443	449	457	461	463	467	479	487	491	499	

Multiplication and Division Table

A number in the top line (11) multiplied by a number in the extreme left-hand column (12) produces the number where the top line and side line meet (132). A number in the table (208) divided by the number at the top of the same column (13) results in the number (16) in the extreme left column. A number in the table (208) divided by the number at the extreme left (16) results in the number (13) at the top of the column.

1	2	3	4	5	6	7	8	9	10	11	12	13	14	15	16	17	18	19	20	21	22	23	24	25
2	4	6	8	10	12	14	16	18	20	22	24	26	28	30	32	34	36	38	40	42	44	46	48	50
3	6	9	12	15	18	21	24	27	30	33	36	39	42	45	48	51	54	57	60	63	66	69	72	75
4	8	12	16	20	24	28	32	36	40	44	48	52	56	60	64	68	72	76	80	84	88	92	96	100
5	10	15	20	25	30	35	40	45	50	55	60	65	70	75	80	85	90	95	100	105	110	115	120	125
6	12	18	24	30	36	42	48	54	60	66	72	78	84	90	96	102	108	114	120	126	132	138	144	150
7	14	21	28	35	42	49	56	63	70	77	84	91	98	105	112	119	126	133	140	147	154	161	168	175
8	16	24	32	40	48	56	64	72	80	88	96	104	112	120	128	136	144	152	160	168	176	184	192	200
9	18	27	36	45	54	63	72	81	90	99	108	117	126	135	144	153	162	171	180	189	198	207	216	225
10	20	30	40	50	60	70	80	90	100	110	120	130	140	150	160	170	180	190	200	210	220	230	240	250
11	22	33	44	55	66	77	88	99	110	121	132	143	154	165	176	187	198	209	220	231	242	253	264	275
12	24	36	48	60	72	84	96	108	120	132	144	156	168	180	192	204	216	228	240	252	264	276	288	300
13	26	39	52	65	78	91	104	117	130	143	156	169	182	195	208	221	234	247	260	273	286	299	312	325
14	28	42	56	70	84	98	112	126	140	154	168	182	196	210	224	238	252	266	280	294	308	322	336	350
15	30	45	60	75	90	105	120	135	150	165	180	195	210	225	240	255	270	285	300	315	330	345	360	375
16	32	48	64	80	96	112	128	144	160	176	192	208	224	240	256	272	288	304	320	336	352	368	384	400
17	34	51	68	85	102	119	136	153	170	187	204	221	238	255	272	289	306	323	340	357	374	391	408	425
18	36	54	72	90	108	126	144	162	180	198	216	234	252	270	288	306	324	342	360	378	396	414	432	450
19	38	57	76	95	114	133	152	171	190	209	228	247	266	285	304	323	342	361	380	399	418	437	456	475
20	40	60	80	100	120	140	160	180	200	220	240	260	280	300	320	340	360	380	400	420	440	460	480	500
21	42	63	84	105	126	147	168	189	210	231	252	273	294	315	336	357	378	399	420	441	462	483	504	525
22	44	66	88	110	132	154	176	198	220	242	264	286	308	330	352	374	396	418	440	462	484	506	528	550
23	46	69	92	115	138	161	184	207	230	253	276	299	322	345	368	391	414	437	460	483	506	529	552	575
24	48	72	96	120	144	168	192	216	240	264	288	312	336	360	384	408	432	456	480	504	528	552	576	600
25	50	75	100	125	150	175	200	225	250	275	300	325	350	375	400	425	450	475	500	525	550	575	600	625

Decimal Equivalents of Common Fractions

1/2	.5000	1/12	.0833	3/5	.6000	5/6	.8333	7/9	.7778
1/3	.3333	1/16	.0625	3/7	.4286	5/7	.7143	7/10	.7000
1/4	.2500	1/32	.0313	3/8	.3750	5/8	.6250	7/11	.6364
1/5	.2000	1/64	.0156	3/10	.3000	5/9	.5556	7/12	.5833
1/6	.1667	2/3	.6667	3/11	.2727	5/11	.4545	8/9	.8889
1/7	.1429	2/5	.4000	3/16	.1875	5/12	.4167	8/11	.7273
1/8	.1250	2/7	.2857	4/5	.8000	5/16	.3125	9/10	.9000
1/9	.1111	2/9	.2222	4/7	.5714	6/7	.8571	9/11	.8182
1/10	.1000	2/11	.1818	4/9	.4444	6/11	.5455	10/11	.9091
1/11	.0909	3/4	.7500	4/11	.3636	7/8	.8750	11/12	.9167

Math **Terms**

An **absolute value** for any real number is the number of units the number is from zero on the number line. The absolute value of −4, written |−4|, is 4. An absolute value is never negative.

An **angle** is made when two rays (lines) share a common endpoint. An angle is measured in degrees. The three most common angles are acute, obtuse, and right angles.

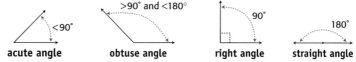

| acute angle | obtuse angle | right angle | straight angle |

Area is the total surface within a closed figure (circle, square, etc). The area of a rectangle is figured by multiplying the length by the width. Area is measured in square units such as square inches or square feet.

area

The **average** is found by adding a group of numbers together and then dividing that sum by the number of separate numbers (addends). The average of 7, 8, and 9 is 8, because $7 + 8 + 9 = 24$, and $24 \div 3$ (numbers) = 8. This is also called the mathematical *mean*.

Circumference is the measure of distance around the edge of a circle.

A **common denominator** is a multiple shared by the denominators of two or more fractions. For example, 6 is a common denominator of $\frac{1}{2}(\frac{3}{6})$ and $\frac{1}{3}(\frac{2}{6})$; 6 is a multiple of both 2 and 3. To add or subtract fractions, you must find a common denominator; $\frac{1}{2} + \frac{1}{3} = \frac{3}{6} + \frac{2}{6} = \frac{5}{6}$. The lowest common denominator is also called the least common multiple (LCM) of the denominators.

Complementary angles are two angles whose degree measures have a sum of 90.

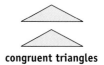

Congruent (≅) is the term for two figures, angles, or line segments that are the same size and shape.

congruent triangles

A **coordinate plane** is made up of two perpendicular number lines forming a grid. The horizontal number line is called the *x*-axis. The vertical number line is called the *y*-axis. Ordered pairs are used to plot points on the coordinate plane.

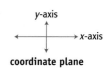

coordinate plane

Coordinates are the numbers in an ordered pair of numbers. The first number is called the *x-coordinate,* and the second number is called the *y-coordinate,* usually expressed as (*x, y*).

Cosine (cos) is a trigonometric function. In a right triangle, the cosine of an angle is found by dividing the adjacent leg by the hypotenuse.

The **denominator** is the bottom number of a fraction. In the fraction $\frac{1}{3}$, the denominator is 3. It indicates the number of parts needed to make a whole unit.

A **diagonal** is a line from one vertex of a quadrilateral to the opposite vertex.

The **diameter** is the length of a straight line through the center of a circle.

diameter

Difference is a word used to indicate the result of subtraction. For example, 2 is the difference of 8 and 6, because $8 - 6 = 2$.

An **equation** is a statement that says two numbers or mathematical expressions are equal to each other ($2 + 10 = 12$ or $x + 4 = 9$). Equations use the equal sign (=).

An **estimate** is a reasonable guess at an answer. If you add 6.24 and 5.19, you can estimate the answer will be around 11, because $6 + 5 = 11$.

To **evaluate** is to find out the value of an expression or to solve for the number an expression stands for.

An **exponent** is the small, raised number to the right of the base number that shows how many times the base is to be multiplied by itself. In the expression 2^3, 3 is the exponent (2 is the base). So, 2^3 means ($2 \times 2 \times 2 = 8$).

An **expression** is a collection of numbers, operation signs, variables, and inclusion symbols (parentheses, brackets, etc.) that stands for a number. $(4 + x)$ or $-8 \div t + 6$

A **factor** is a number that is being multiplied. In $4 \times 3 = 12$, the factors are 4 and 3.

Geometry is the study of two-dimensional shapes (circles, triangles), three-dimensional solids (spheres, cubes), and positions in space (points).

The **hypotenuse** is the side opposite the right angle in a right triangle.

Inequality is a mathematical sentence involving one of the symbols <, >, ≤, ≥. (See page 549.)

Integers are the whole numbers (counting numbers) and their opposites ($-2, -1, 0, +1, +2, \ldots$).

An **intersection** is the point where two figures in geometry cross each other.

intersections

An **irrational number** is a real number that cannot be written as a fraction (a number such as pi that is a non-terminating, non-repeating decimal).

An **isosceles triangle** is a triangle with two sides of equal length and two congruent angles. (See *triangle.*)

A **line** is all points formed by extending a line segment in both directions, without end.

line

Lowest common denominator (See *common denominator.*)

Mean is another word for average. (See *average.*)

The **median** is the middle number when a group of numbers is arranged in order from the least to the greatest, or greatest to least. In 1, 4, 6 the median (middle number) is 4. In 1, 4, 6, 8 the median is 5, halfway between 4 and 6.

The **midpoint** is the point that divides a segment into 2 equal halves. If M is the midpoint between P and Q, then $\overline{PM} \cong \overline{MQ}$.

P   M   Q

midpoint

The **mode** is the number or item occurring most frequently in a list of data. It is possible for a list of data to have more than one mode or to have no mode.

A **monomial** is an expression that is either a single number, a variable, or the product of a number and one or more variables. (A polynomial with one term.)

A **multiple** is a quantity that can be divided by another quantity with zero as the remainder (both 6 and 9 are multiples of 3).

The **numerator** is the top number of a fraction. In the fraction $\frac{5}{6}$, the numerator is 5.

An **obtuse** angle is an angle greater than 90 degrees and less than 180 degrees. (See *angle.*)

Opposite numbers are two numbers whose sum is zero (−2 and +2).

An **ordered pair** is two numbers named in a specific order, used to locate points on a plane (*x, y*).

Order of operations is the order in which expressions must be evaluated. PEMDAS—Parentheses, Exponents, Multiplication and Division (left to right), Addition, and Subtraction (left to right).

The **origin** is the point of intersection of the *x*-axis and *y*-axis on a coordinate plane. All ordered pairs (*x, y*) are referenced from the origin.

y-axis

x-axis

origin

A **parabola** is the graph of a quadratic function.

parabola

Parallel refers to lines that never intersect.

Percent is a way of expressing a number as a fraction of 100. So, $\frac{1}{2}$ expressed as a percentage is $\frac{50}{100}$, which is 50%.

A **perfect square** is the result of multiplying any number or polynomial by itself (4, 9, 16, 25, 36, 49, . . . are perfect squares). For example, $2 \times 2 = 4$, $3 \times 3 = 9$, $4 \times 4 = 16$ . . .

The **perimeter** is the distance around the edge of a multisided figure. If a triangle has three sides, each 3 feet long, its perimeter is 9 feet (3 + 3 + 3 = 9).

perimeter = 9'

Perpendicular refers to two lines that intersect forming right angles (90° angles).

perpendicular lines

Pi (π) is the ratio of the circumference of a circle to its diameter. Pi is approximately 3.14.

Place value is the value of the place of a digit depending on where it is in the number. So, 3,497 is 3 thousands, 4 hundreds, 9 tens, 7 ones. And, .3497 is 3 tenths, 4 hundredths, 9 thousandths, 7 ten-thousandths.

Plane is a term of geometry. Planes can be thought of as flat surfaces that extend indefinitely in all directions and have no thickness.

A **point** is an exact location on a plane.

Point-slope form is an equation of the form $y - y_1 = m\,(x - x_1)$ for the line passing through a point whose coordinates are (x_1, y_1) and having a slope of m.

A **polynomial** is the sum of two or more monomials. Each monomial is called a term. For example: $4x^2 - 3y + 2 - 8z$

A **positive number** is a number greater than 0.

A **prime number** is a number that cannot be divided evenly by any number except itself and 1. The number 5 is a prime number because it can be divided evenly (without a remainder) only by 1 and 5.

Product is the word used to indicate the result of multiplication. For example, 8 is the product of 2 times 4, because $2 \times 4 = 8$.

Proportion is an equation of the form $\frac{a}{b} = \frac{c}{d}$ that states two ratios are equivalent.

The **Pythagorean theorem** states that in a right triangle, where c is the hypotenuse, the square of the hypotenuse is equal to the squares of the legs. $a^2 + b^2 = c^2$

Pythagorean theorem

Quadratic formula is a formula for solving
a quadratic equation:

$$x = \frac{-b \pm \sqrt{b^2 - 4ac}}{2a}$$

Quotient is the word used to indicate the result of division. For example,
if 8 is divided by 4, the quotient is 2, because $8 \div 4 = 2$.

A **radical** is an expression that has a root (square root, cube root,
etc.).

The **radius** (r) is the distance from the center of a circle to its
circumference. (The radius is half the diameter.)

radius

A **ratio** is a way of comparing two numbers by dividing one by the other.
The ratio of 3 to 4 is $\frac{3}{4}$. If there are 20 boys and 5 girls in your class,
the ratio of boys to girls is $\frac{20}{5}$ ($\frac{4}{1}$ in lowest terms), or $4 : 1$.

A **ray** is a part of a line having one endpoint and extending without end in one direction.

Real numbers are all numbers on the number line, including positive
numbers, negative numbers, zero, fractions, and decimals.

Reciprocals are two numbers whose product is 1. The reciprocal of $\frac{2}{3}$ is $\frac{3}{2}$.
The multiplication inverse property states that any number times its
reciprocal equals 1. $\frac{2}{3} \cdot \frac{3}{2} = 1$

A **rectangle** is a four-sided closed figure with four right angles and with
opposite sides parallel and congruent.

A **right angle** is an angle that measures 90 degrees. A right angle is
formed when two perpendicular lines meet. (See *angle.*)

A **segment** is part of a line that consists of two points,
called endpoints, and all the points between them.

Similar figures are figures that have the same shape but
that may differ in size.

Sine (sin) is a trigonometric function. In a right triangle,
the sine of an angle is found by dividing the opposite
leg by the hypotenuse.

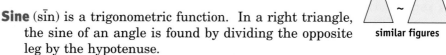

similar figures

Slope is the ratio of the change in y to the change in x of a line,
or the ratio of the change in the rise (vertical change) to
the run (horizontal change). The variable m is used to
denote slope. The slope between 2 points is $\frac{y_2 - y_1}{x_2 - x_1}$.

(x_2,y_2)

(x_1,y_1)

Slope-intercept form is a linear equation of the form $y = mx + b$
(m is the slope and b is the y-intercept).

A **solid** is a three-dimensional figure in geometry, like a cube, a cone, a prism, or a sphere.

solid

A **square** has four sides of equal length and four right angles. *Square* also refers to the product of a number mulitiplied by itself. The square of 3 is 9 ($3^2 = 9$; $3 \times 3 = 9$). Square also refers to how area is measured.

3
area = 9
square units

The **square root** of a number is a number that, when multiplied by itself, gives the original number as the product. The symbol for square root is $\sqrt{}$. The square root of 4 is 2, because $2 \times 2 = 4$ or ($\sqrt{4} = 2$).

Standard form is an equation of the form $Ax + By = C$, where A, B, and C are integers and A and B are not both zero.

Sum is a word used to indicate the result of addition. For example, 7 is the sum of 4 and 3, because $4 + 3 = 7$.

Supplementary angles are two angles whose degree measures have a sum of 180.

Tangent (tan) is a trigonometric function. In a right triangle, the tangent of an angle is found by dividing the opposite leg by the adjacent leg.

A **triangle** is a closed figure with three sides. The sum of the angles in every triangle is $180°$. Triangles can be classified by *sides:* equilateral, isosceles, or scalene; or by *angles:* right, equiangular, acute, or obtuse.

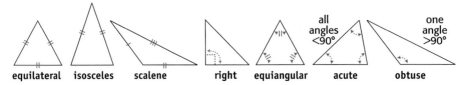

equilateral   isosceles   scalene   right   equiangular   acute   obtuse

A **variable** is a letter that represents a number.

A **vertex** is the point where two sides of a plane (flat) figure meet (corner). The plural of *vertex* is *vertices*.

vertex

x-axis is the horizontal number line in a coordinate plane.

x-intercept is the x-coordinate of the point on a line where it intersects the x-axis. Here, the value of $y = 0$.

y-axis is the vertical number line on a coordinate plane.

y-intercept is the y-coordinate of the point on a line where it intersects the y-axis. Here, the value of $x = 0$.

y-axis
x-axis
y-intercept→
x-intercept

"We are citizens of the world; and the tragedy of our times is that we do not know this." —Woodrow Wilson

GEOGRAPHY

As you know, the world has changed dramatically in the past few years. As global citizens each of us must stay on top of those changes. Just as we once tried to understand something about each of the 50 states, we must now try to understand something about each of the countries in the world. The section that follows will give you the map skills you need to begin your work.

Using the Maps

Finding Direction

Mapmakers use special marks and symbols to show where things are or to give other useful information. Among other things, these marks and symbols show direction (north, south, east, and west). On most maps, north is at the top. But you should always check the **compass rose,** or directional finder, to make sure you know where north is. If there is no symbol, you can assume that north is at the top.

Finding Information

Other important marks and symbols are explained in a box printed on each map. This box is called the **legend,** or **key.** It is included to make it easier for you understand and use the map. Below is the United States map legend. (See page 561.) This legend includes state boundaries.

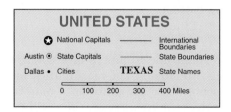

UNITED STATES

★ National Capitals	———— International Boundaries
Austin ◉ State Capitals	———— State Boundaries
Dallas • Cities	**TEXAS** State Names

0   100   200   300   400 Miles

Measuring Distances

To measure distances on a map, use the map scale. (See the sample below.) Line up an index card or a piece of paper under the map scale and put a dot on your paper at "0." Put other dots at 100, 200, 300, and so on. You can now measure the approximate distance between points on the map.

0	100	200	300	400 Miles

Locating Countries

Latitude and longitude lines are another helpful feature of most maps. Latitude and longitude refer to imaginary lines that mapmakers use. Together, these lines can be used to locate any point on the earth.

Latitude

The lines on a map that go from east to west around the earth are called lines of *latitude*. Latitude is measured in degrees, with the equator being 0 degrees (0°). Above the equator, the lines are called *north latitude* and measure from 0° to 90° north (the North Pole). Below the equator, the lines are called *south latitude* and measure from 0° to 90° south (the South Pole). On a map, latitude numbers are printed along the sides.

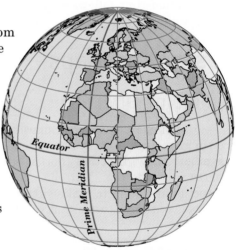

Longitude

The lines on a map that run from the North Pole to the South Pole are lines of *longitude*. Longitude is also measured in degrees. The prime meridian, which runs through Greenwich, England, is 0° longitude. Lines east of the prime meridian are called *east longitude;* lines west of the prime meridian are called *west longitude*. On a map, longitude numbers are printed at the top and bottom.

Coordinates

The latitude and longitude numbers of a country or other place are called its *coordinates*. In each set of coordinates, latitude is given first, then longitude. To locate a certain place on a map using its coordinates, find the point where the two lines cross. (You will find a complete list of coordinates on pages 569-570.)

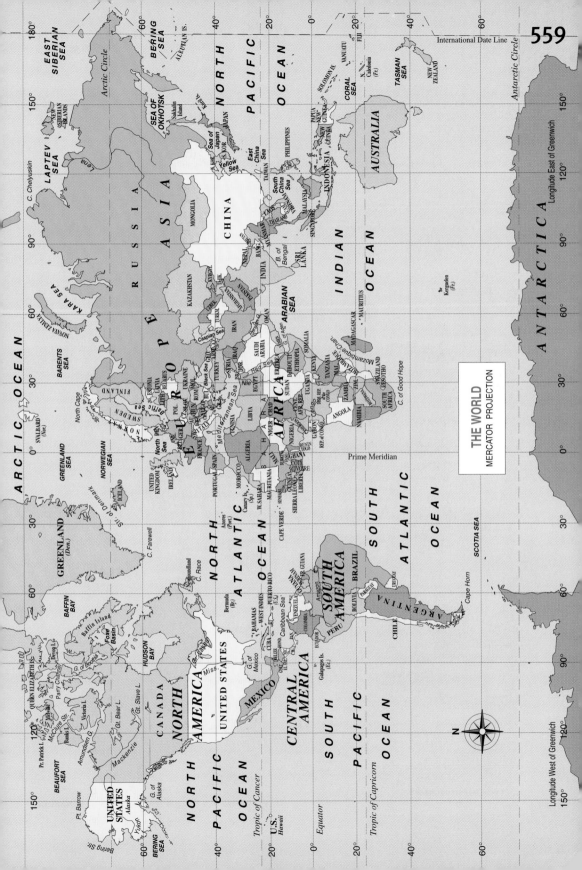

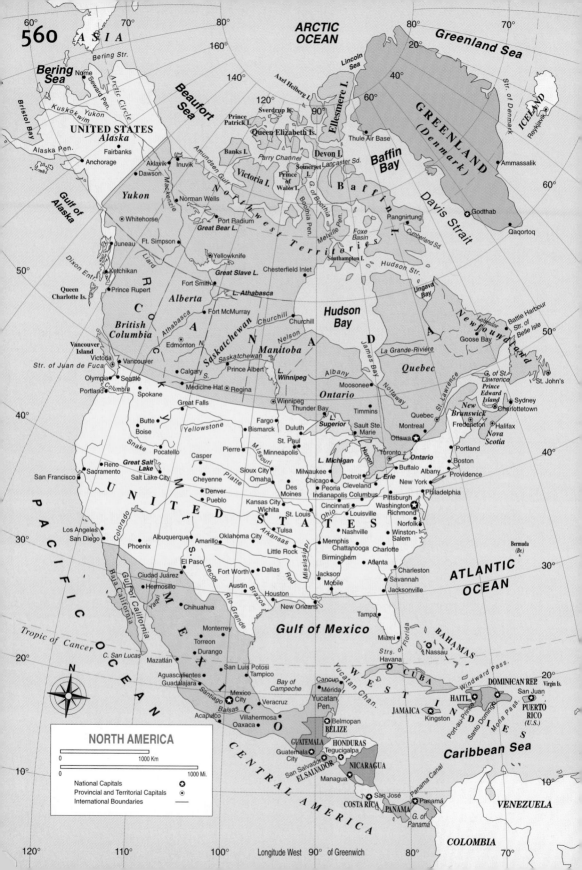

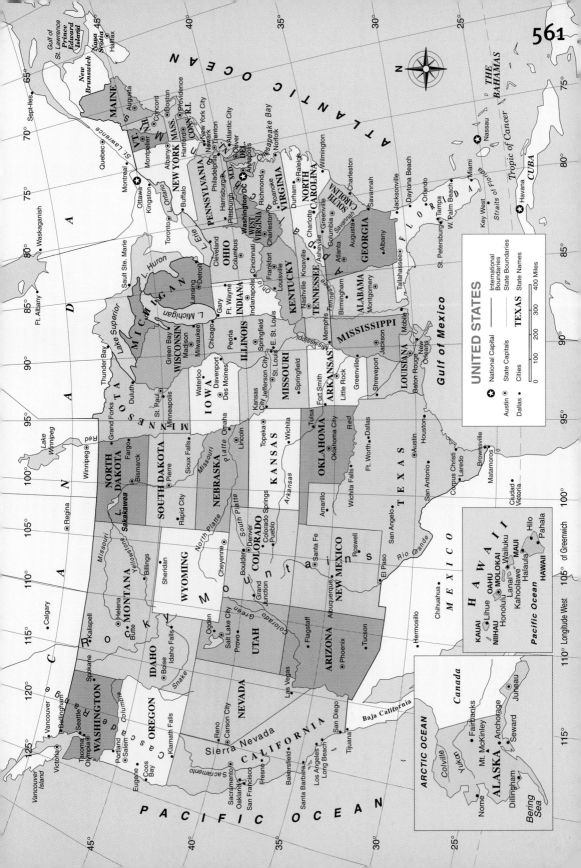

UNITED STATES

⊛ National Capital	International Boundaries
◉ State Capitals	State Boundaries
• Cities	**TEXAS** State Names

| ⊛ Austin | |
| ◉ Dallas | |

0   100   200   300   400 Miles

562

CENTRAL AMERICA

200 Km		200 Mi.	⊙ Capitals of Countries
0	200 Km	0	200 Mi.	International Boundaries ———

GUYANA

VENEZUELA

COLOMBIA

NORTH ATLANTIC OCEAN

WEST INDIES

Anguilla (U.K.)

British Virgin Islands (U.K.)

St. Barthelemy (FRANCE)

St. Martin (FRANCE and NETH.)

Virgin Islands (U.S.)

Puerto Rico (U.S.)

San Juan

St. Croix (U.S.)

Neth. Antilles BARBUDA & ANTIGUA

Basseterre St. Johns

ST. KITTS & NEVIS

Montserrat (U.K.)

GUADELOUPE (FRANCE)

Basse-Terre • Marie Galante

DOMINICA

Roseau

MARTINIQUE (FRANCE)

Fort-de-France ⊙ (FRANCE)

ST. LUCIA

Castries

ST. VINCENT & THE GRENADINES

BARBADOS

Bridgetown ⊙

Kingstown

GRENADA

St. George's ⊙

Tobago

TRINIDAD & TOBAGO

Port-of-Spain ⊙

Trinidad

LESSER ANTILLES

NETHERLAND ANTILLES (NETH.)

Aruba

Curacao

Bonaire

Willemstad

GREATER ANTILLES

DOM. REP.

Santiago

Santo Domingo ⊙

HAITI

Cap-Haïtien

Port-au-Prince ⊙

TURKS AND CAICOS ISLANDS (U.K.)

Grand Turk

Great Inagua

Mayaguana

Acklins Island

Crooked Island

Long Island

Rum Cay

San Salvador

Cat Island

Eleuthera

Great Abaco

Grand Bahama

Freeport

New Providence

Nassau

Bimini Islands

Andros Island

THE BAHAMAS

Great Exuma

Camaguey

Santa Clara

Holguin

Santiago de Cuba

Guantanamo

CUBA

Havana

Matanzas

Cienfuegos

Pinar del Río

Isla de la Juventud

Cayman Islands (U.K.)

George Town

Kingston ⊙

JAMAICA

Straits of Florida

Tropic of Cancer

GULF OF MEXICO

U.S.A.

Yucatan Channel

MEXICO

NORTH PACIFIC OCEAN

CARIBBEAN SEA

N

CENTRAL AMERICA

MEXICO

Usumacinta

Flores

GUATEMALA

Cobán

Puerto Barrios

Motagua

Quezaltenango

Guatemala City ⊙

EL SALVADOR

San Salvador ⊙

San Miguel

Belize City

Belmopan ⊙

BELIZE

Gulf of Honduras

San Pedro Sula

Ulúa

HONDURAS

Tegucigalpa ⊙

Islas de la Bahia

Patuca

Coco

Puerto Cabezas

Puerto Lempira

NICARAGUA

Matagalpa

Bluefields

Managua ⊙

Lago de Managua

Leon

Granada

Rivas

Lago de Nicaragua

San Juan

Liberia

San José ⊙

COSTA RICA

Puerto Limon

Golfito

David

PANAMA

Santiago

Panama ⊙

Colon

Panama Canal

Gulf of Panama

La Palma

COLOMBIA

Longitude West of Greenwich

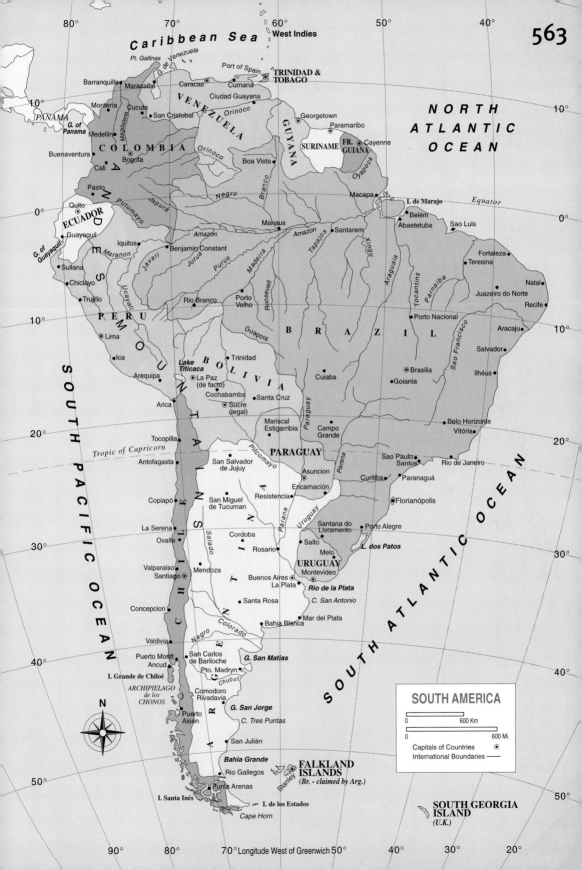

563

Caribbean Sea   West Indies

Pt. Gallinas

G. de Venezuela

Port of Spain   **TRINIDAD & TOBAGO**

Barranquilla   Maracaibo   Caracas   Cumana

Monteria   Cucuta   Ciudad Guayana

VENEZUELA

San Cristobal   Orinoco

Georgetown

Paramaribo

NORTH ATLANTIC OCEAN

Medellin

COLOMBIA

GUYANA   **SURINAME**   **FR. GUIANA**   *Cayenne*

Buenaventura   Bogota   Orinoco   Boa Vista

Cali

Pasto

Oyapock

Quito   **ECUADOR**

Macapa   *I. de Marajo*   **Equator**   0°

Guayaquil   *Putumayo*   *Japurá*   Belém

Abaetetuba   Sao Luis

G. of Guayaquil   Iquitos   *Negro*   *Branco*

Sullana   Benjamin Constant   Manaus   Santarem

Maranon   *Javari*   *Amazon*   Amazon   *Tapajós*   *Xingu*

Chiclayo   *Jurua*   *Purus*   Fortaleza

Trujillo   *Ucayali*   *Madeira*   Teresina

Rio Branco   *Araguaia*   Natal

Porto Velho   *Roosevelt*   *Tocantins*   *Parnaiba*   Juazeiro do Norte

P E R U   Porto Nacional   Recife

Lima   *Guapore*   **B R A Z I L**   Aracaju

Ica   *Sao Francisco*   Salvador

Arequipa   Trinidad   Ilhéus

Lake Titicaca   **BOLIVIA**   Cuiaba   *Brasilia*

La Paz (de facto)   Goiania

Arica   Cochabamba   Santa Cruz   Belo Horizonte

Sucre (legal)   Vitória

Tocopilla   Mariscal Estigarribia   Campo Grande

Tropic of Capricorn   *Picomayo*   **PARAGUAY**   Sao Paulo   Rio de Janeiro

Antofagasta   San Salvador de Jujuy   Asuncion   Santos

Resistencia   Encarnación   Curitiba   Paranaguá

Copiapó   San Miguel de Tucuman   *Florianópolis*

La Serena   Cordoba   Santana do Livramento   Porto Alegre

Ovalle   *Salado*   Rosario   Salto   *L. dos Patos*

Melo

Valparaiso   Mendoza   Buenos Aires   **URUGUAY**

Santiago   La Plata   *Montevideo*

Concepcion   Santa Rosa   *Rio de la Plata*

C. San Antonio

Negro   *Colorado*   Bahia Blanca   Mar del Plata

Valdivia

Puerto Montt   San Carlos de Bariloche   *G. San Matias*

Ancud   Pto. Madryn

I. Grande de Chiloé   *Chubut*

ARCHIPIELAGO de los CHONOS   Comodoro Rivadavia

G. San Jorge

N   Puerto Aisen   *C. Tres Puntas*

San Julián

Bahia Grande   **FALKLAND ISLANDS**   *(Br. - claimed by Arg.)*

I. Santa Inés   Rio Gallegos   *Stanley*

Punta Arenas   *I. de los Estados*   **SOUTH GEORGIA ISLAND** *(U.K.)*

Cape Horn

SOUTH PACIFIC OCEAN

SOUTH ATLANTIC OCEAN

A N D E S M O U N T A I N S

C H I L E

A R G E N T I N A

SOUTH AMERICA

0   600 Km

0   600 Mi.

Capitals of Countries   ◉

International Boundaries   ——

Longitude West of Greenwich

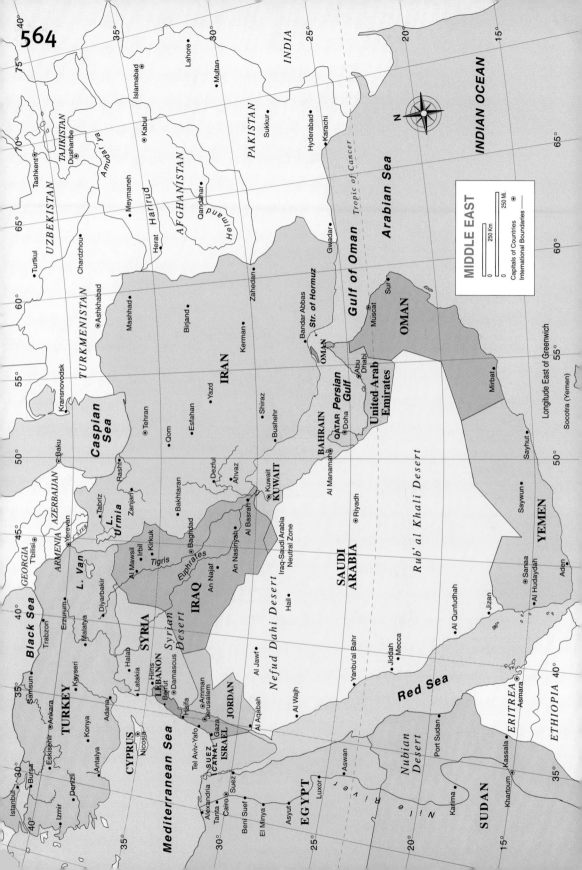

564

MIDDLE EAST

Capitals of Countries	⊙	
International Boundaries	———	

0   250 Km
0   250 Mi.

INDIAN OCEAN

N

Tropic of Cancer

Arabian Sea

Longitude East of Greenwich

Socotra (Yemen)

Gulf of Oman

Str. of Hormuz

OMAN

Sur

Muscat ⊙

Mirbat

OMAN

Abu
Dhabi

**United Arab
Emirates**

Bandar Abbas

Gwadar

OMAN

Sayhut

Saywun

YEMEN

Sanaa ⊙

Aden

Al Hudaydah

Jizan

Al Qunfudhah

**Persian
Gulf**

QATAR

Doha ⊙

BAHRAIN

Al Manamah ⊙

Riyadh ⊙

**SAUDI
ARABIA**

Rub' al Khali Desert

Al Jawf

Hail

An Nasiriyah

Al Basrah

KUWAIT

Kuwait ⊙

Dezful

Ahvaz

Iraq-Saudi Arabia
Neutral Zone

Nefud Dahi Desert

Yanbu'al Bahr

Jiddah

Mecca

Al Wajh

Al Aqabah

Red Sea

ERITREA

Asmara ⊙

Kassala

ETHIOPIA 40°

SUDAN

Khartoum ⊙

Karima

Port Sudan

*Nubian
Desert*

Aswan

Luxor

Asyut

El Minya

Beni Suef

EGYPT

Suez

Cairo ⊙

SUEZ
CANAL

Tanta

Alexandria

Al Najaf

Baghdad ⊙

IRAQ

Euphrates

Tigris

Kirkuk

Irbil

Al Mawsil

*Syrian
Desert*

Halab

Hims

Damascus ⊙

Beirut ⊙

LEBANON

SYRIA

Latakia

Haifa

Tel Aviv-Yato

Gaza

ISRAEL

Jerusalem ⊙

Amman ⊙

JORDAN

CYPRUS

Nicosia ⊙

Mediterranean Sea

Antalya

Konya

Adana

TURKEY

Ankara ⊙

Kayseri

Eskisehir

Bursa

Istanbul

Izmir

Denizi

Malatya

Diyarbakir

Erzurum

Trabzon

Black Sea

Samsun

GEORGIA

Tbilisi ⊙

ARMENIA

Yerevan ⊙

AZERBAIJAN

Baku ⊙

Aze.

L. Van

L.
Urmia

Tabriz

Zanjan

Rasht

Bakhtaran

**Caspian
Sea**

IRAN

Tehran ⊙

Qom

Estahan

Yazd

Shiraz

Bushehr

Kerman

Birjand

Mashhad

Zahedan

Krasnovodsk

TURKMENISTAN

Ashkhabad ⊙

Chardzhou

Herat

Harirud

Meymaneh

Qandahar

AFGHANISTAN

Kabul ⊙

Helmand

Amu Dar'ya

TAJIKISTAN

Dushanbe ⊙

Tashkent ⊙

UZBEKISTAN

Turkul

PAKISTAN

Sukkur

Hyderabad

Karachi

Multan

Lahore

Islamabad ⊙

INDIA

40° 35° 30° 25° 20° 15°

75° 70° 65° 60° 55° 50° 45° 40° 35° 30° 25° 20° 15°

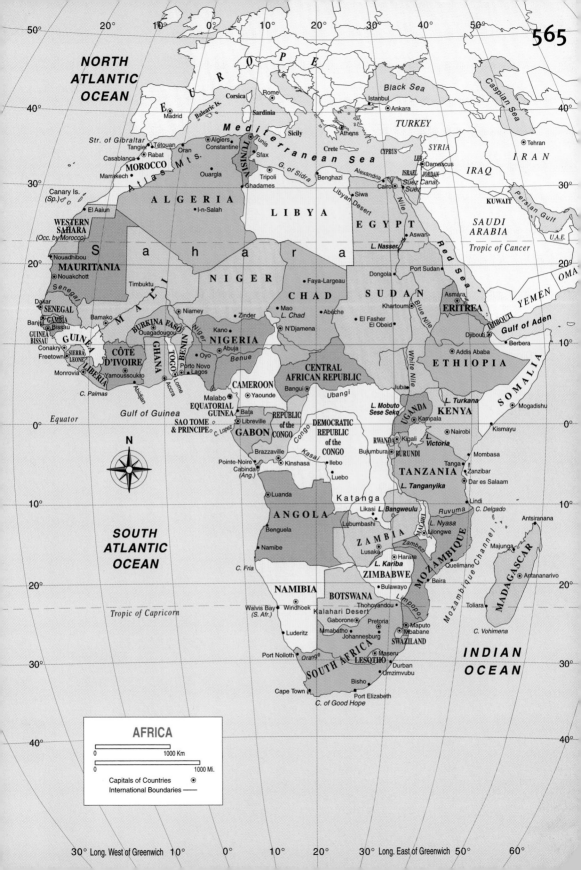

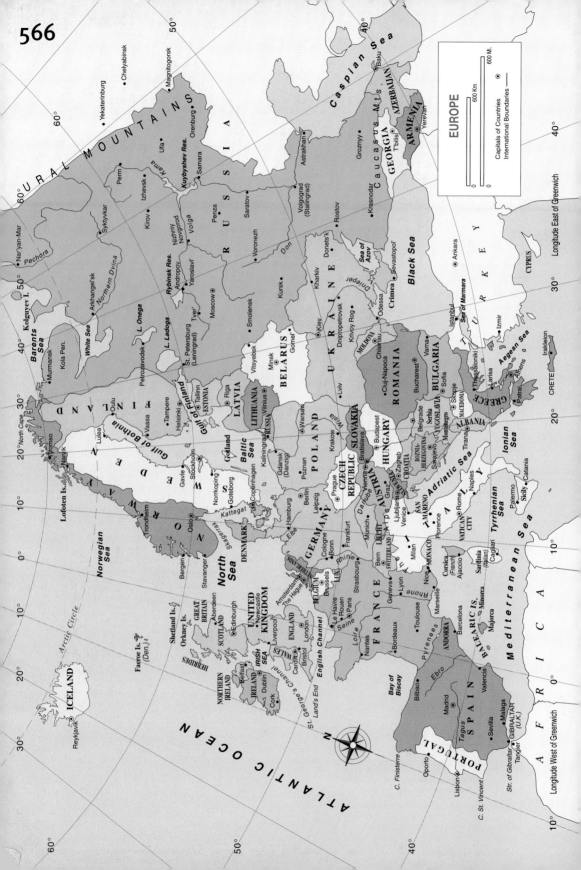

566

ATLANTIC OCEAN

ICELAND
Reykjavik

Faeroe Is. (Den.)

Shetland Is.
Orkney Is.
HEBRIDES
GREAT BRITAIN
Aberdeen
SCOTLAND
Edinburgh
NORTHERN IRELAND
Belfast
IRELAND
Dublin
Cork
IRISH SEA
Liverpool
ENGLAND
UNITED KINGDOM
Newcastle
WALES
Cardiff
Bristol
London
Land's End
St. George's Channel
English Channel

NORWEGIAN SEA

NORWAY
SWEDEN
Narvik
Tromsö
Lofoten Is.
Bodö
Trondheim
Bergen
Stavanger
Oslo

North Cape
Murmansk
Kola Pen.
Barents Sea
Kolguyev I.
Nar'yan-Mar
Pechora
Arkhangel'sk
Northern Dvina
White Sea
Petrozavodsk
L. Onega
L. Ladoga
St. Petersburg (Leningrad)
Syktyvkar
Kirov
Perm
Izhevsk
Ufa
Kama

URAL MOUNTAINS
Yekaterinburg
Chelyabinsk
Magnitogorsk
Orenburg
Samara
Kuybyshev Res.
Penza
Saratov
Volga
Nizhniy Novgorod
Andropov
Yaroslavl'
Rybinsk Res.
Tver
Moscow
Smolensk
Kursk
Voronezh
Don
Volgograd (Stalingrad)
Astrakhan
Rostov
Krasnodar
Grozny
Caspian Sea
Baku
AZERBAIJAN
ARMENIA
Yerevan
GEORGIA
Tbilisi
Caucasus Mts.

RUSSIA

Sea of Azov
Sevastopol'
Crimea
Black Sea
Donets'k
Dnipropetrovsk
Krivoy Rog
Odessa
Kharkiv
Kiev
Dnieper
UKRAINE
Gomel'
Vitsyebsk
Minsk
BELARUS
Lviv
MOLDOVA
Chişinău
ROMANIA
Cluj-Napoca
Bucharest
Varna
BULGARIA
Sofia
Skopje
MACEDONIA
ALBANIA
Tirana
YUGOSLAVIA
Belgrade
Serbia
Montenegro
Sarajevo
BOSNIA-HERZEGOVINA
CROATIA
Zagreb
Danube

TURKEY
Istanbul
Sea of Marmara
Ankara
Izmir
CYPRUS
Aegean Sea
Thessaloníki
Larisa
GREECE
Athens
Patras
Irakleion
CRETE
Ionian Sea

Barents Sea
FINLAND
Oulu
Tampere
Vaasa
Helsinki
Tallinn
ESTONIA
Riga
LATVIA
LITHUANIA
Vilnius
Kaliningrad
Gulf of Finland
Gulf of Bothnia
Luleå
Gävle
Stockholm
Norrköping
Gotland
Baltic Sea
Göteborg
Copenhagen
DENMARK
Kattegat
Skagerrak
Gdansk (Danzig)
Poznań
POLAND
Warsaw
Wisła
Kraków
CZECH REPUBLIC
Prague
SLOVAKIA
Bratislava
HUNGARY
Budapest
AUSTRIA
Vienna
Graz
LIECHTENSTEIN
SLOVENIA
Ljubljana
Venice
Adriatic Sea
ITALY
Rome
VATICAN CITY
Naples
Florence
Milan
Tyrrhenian Sea
Sardinia (Italian)
Cagliari
Palermo
Sicily
Catania
SAN MARINO
MONACO
Nice
Corsica (French)
Ajaccio
Mediterranean Sea

GERMANY
Hamburg
Berlin
Leipzig
Cologne
Frankfurt
Munich
Elbe
Rhine
Bern
SWITZERLAND
Geneva
Alps
NETHERLANDS
Amsterdam
The Hague
BELGIUM
Brussels
LUX.
Strasbourg
Le Havre
Rouen
Paris
Seine
FRANCE
Nantes
Loire
Bordeaux
Bay of Biscay
Toulouse
Marseille
Lyon
Rhône
Pyrenees
ANDORRA
Barcelona
Minorca
BALEARIC IS.
Majorca
Ebro
SPAIN
Madrid
Bilbao
Valencia
Málaga
Sevilla
GIBRALTAR (U.K.)
Str. of Gibraltar
Tangier
Lisbon
Oporto
PORTUGAL
Tagus
C. Finisterre
C. St. Vincent

AFRICA

Longitude East of Greenwich
Longitude West of Greenwich

Arctic Circle

N

ATLANTIC OCEAN

GREENLAND

UNITED STATES (Alaska)

ICELAND

ARCTIC
North Pole
OCEAN

BERING SEA

ALEUTIAN IS.

BRITISH ISLES

Svalbard

180°
160°
140°
120°
100°
80°
60°
40°
20°
0°
20°

Komandorskiye Is.

NOVAYA ZEMLYA

SEVERNAYA ZEMLYA

EAST SIBERIAN SEA

Anadyr

BARENTS SEA

LAPTEV SEA

Srednekolymsk
Kolyma

London
NORTH SEA
Paris

BALTIC SEA
Berlin
St. Petersburg

KARA SEA

Nordvik

Magadan

Kamchatka Pen.

Petropavlovsk-Kamchatskiy

Vienna
Warsaw

Dudinka

Arctic Circle

Lena

SEA OF OKHOTSK

EUROPE

Kiev
Moscow

R

U

Salekhard

Yenisey

Yakutsk

S

Tura

S

I

Nikolayevsk

Sakhalin I.

KURIL IS.

Khanty-Mansiysk

A

Perm'
Yekaterinburg
Chelyabinsk
Magnitogorsk

Ob'

Tomsk
Omsk
Novosibirsk

Krasnoyarsk

L.
Baykal

Kirensk

Irkutsk

Chita

Komsomol'sk
Skovorodino

Khabarovsk

Hokkaido

Istanbul
Izmir
Ankara
BLACK SEA

Ural'sk
Gur'yev

Karaganda

Barnaul
Semipalatinsk

Ulan-Ude

Amur

Hakodate
Vladivostok

Sendai
Honshu

40°

TURKEY
Erzurum

CASPIAN SEA

KAZAKHSTAN

Irtysh

ARAL SEA

L. Balkhash

Uliastay

Ulaanbaatar

Hovd

Qiqihar
Changchun

SEA OF JAPAN

Tokyo
Nagoya

40°

MED. SEA
CYPRUS
Adana
Aleppo

Tabriz

Krasnovodsk

Syr darya

Tashkent

Bishkek
Alma-Ata

MONGOLIA

Gobi

INNER MONGOLIA

Shenyang
Dandong
N. KOREA

Beijing

S. KOREA

Hiroshima
Shikoku

JAPAN

Kyushu

LEBANON
Beirut
Damascus
Jerusalem
Amman
SYRIA
ISRAEL
JORDAN

TURKMENISTAN
UZBEK.

Amu darya

KYRGYZ.
TAJIK.

Kokand

Urumqi

SINKIANG

Aksu

Yumen

Great Wall

Tianjin

Pyongyang

Seoul

YELLOW SEA

Nagasaki

IRAQ
Baghdad
Basra

Tehran
Mashad

Herat

Shache

Jiuquan

Lanzhou

Jinan

GRAND CANAL

Kaifeng

Shanghai

EAST CHINA SEA

RYUKYU IS. (Jap.)

KUWAIT

IRAN

AFGHANISTAN

Hotan

Huang

Xi'an

Nanjing

Shiraz

Kabul

CHINA

Wuhan

BAHRAIN
QATAR
Riyadh

Bandar Abbas

Srinagar
Islamabad

TIBET

Tropic of Cancer

20°

Mecca
U. ARAB EMIR.

Quetta

PAKISTAN

Himalaya

Lhasa

Chongqing

Changsha

Fuzhou

Taipei

PACIFIC OCEAN

20°

SAUDI ARABIA

Muscat

Gwadar

NEPAL

Thimphu

Chang (Yangtze)

TAIWAN

OMAN

Karachi

New Delhi

Kanpur

Kathmandu

BHUTAN

Brahmaputra

Guangzhou

HONG KONG

Sanaa
YEMEN

G. of Oman

Ahmadabad

Dhaka

Mandalay

Hanoi

Hainan

Luzon

PHILIPPINES

Aden
G. of Aden

Socotra

ARABIAN SEA

Daman
Bombay
Hyderabad

INDIA

Yanam

Calcutta

BANGLA-DESH

Myitkyina

MYANMAR

Rangoon

LAOS

Vientiane

G. of Tonkin

SOUTH CHINA SEA

Manila

Mindoro

Samar

Leyte

AFRICA

Bangalore

Mahe

Madras

Karikal

Madurai

BAY OF BENGAL

Bangkok

THAILAND

CAMBODIA

Mekong

VIETNAM

Phnom Penh

Ho Chi Minh City (Saigon)

Palawan

Negros

Davao

Mindanao

SEYCHELLES

Colombo
Kandy

SRI LANKA (CEYLON)

G. of Thailand

SABAH

Kota Kinabalu

CELEBES SEA

Manado

MADAGASCAR

MALDIVES
Male

Equator

George Town
Medan

Kuala Lumpur

MALAYA

Str. of Malacca

SINGAPORE

BRUNEI
SARAWAK

Kuching

Borneo

Banjarmasin

Makassar Str.

Celebes

Ujung Pandang

BANDA SEA

Timor

MALAYSIA

Sumatra

INDONESIA

Palembang

JAVA SEA

Jakarta
JAVA
Surabaya
Sumbawa

FLORES SEA

Flores

TIMOR SEA

SUNDA IS.

INDIAN OCEAN

N

Broome

20°
Tropic of Capricorn

20°

AUSTRALIA

Perth

ASIA

0   1200 Km

0   1200 Mi.

⊙ Capitals of Countries
── International Boundaries

40°

60°   80°   100°   120°

Longitude East of Greenwich

40°

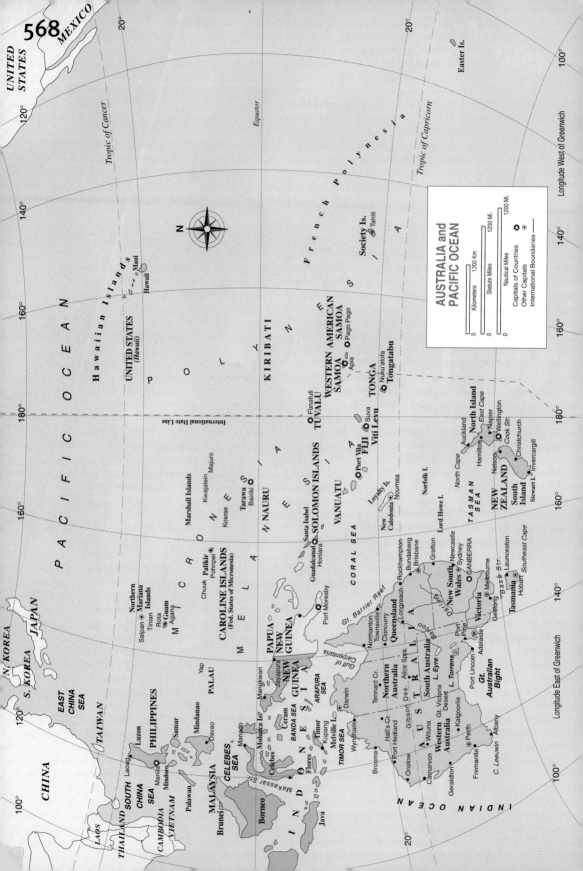

Index to World Maps

Country	Latitude		Longitude		Country	Latitude		Longitude	
Afghanistan	33°	N	65°	E	Gabon	1°	S	11°	E
Albania	41°	N	20°	E	The Gambia	13°	N	16°	W
Algeria	28°	N	3°	E	Georgia	43°	N	45°	E
Andorra	42°	N	1°	E	Germany	51°	N	10°	E
Angola	12°	S	18°	E	Ghana	8°	N	2°	W
Antigua and Barbuda	17°	N	61°	W	Greece	39°	N	22°	E
Argentina	34°	S	64°	W	Greenland	70°	N	40°	W
Armenia	41°	N	45°	E	Grenada	12°	N	61°	W
Australia	25°	S	135°	E	Guatemala	15°	N	90°	W
Austria	47°	N	13°	E	Guinea	11°	N	10°	W
Azerbaijan	41°	N	47°	E	Guinea-Bissau	12°	N	15°	W
Bahamas	24°	N	76°	W	Guyana	5°	N	59°	W
Bahrain	26°	N	50°	E	Haiti	19°	N	72°	W
Bangladesh	24°	N	90°	E	Honduras	15°	N	86°	W
Barbados	13°	N	59°	W	Hungary	47°	N	20°	E
Belarus	54°	N	25°	E	Iceland	65°	N	18°	W
Belgium	50°	N	4°	E	India	20°	N	77°	E
Belize	17°	N	88°	W	Indonesia	5°	S	120°	E
Benin	9°	N	2°	E	Iran	32°	N	53°	E
Bhutan	27°	N	90°	E	Iraq	33°	N	44°	E
Bolivia	17°	S	65°	W	Ireland	53°	N	8°	W
Bosnia-Herzegovina	44°	N	18°	E	Israel	31°	N	35°	E
Botswana	22°	S	24°	E	Italy	42°	N	12°	E
Brazil	10°	S	55°	W	Jamaica	18°	N	77°	W
Brunei Darussalam	4°	N	114°	E	Japan	36°	N	138°	E
Bulgaria	43°	N	25°	E	Jordan	31°	N	36°	E
Burkina Faso	13°	N	2°	W	Kazakhstan	45°	N	70°	E
Burundi	3°	S	30°	E	Kenya	1°	N	38°	E
Cambodia	13°	N	105°	E	Kiribati	0°	N	175°	E
Cameroon	6°	N	12°	E	North Korea	40°	N	127°	E
Canada	60°	N	95°	W	South Korea	36°	N	128°	E
Cape Verde	16°	N	24°	W	Kuwait	29°	N	47°	E
Central African Republic	7°	N	21°	E	Kyrgyzstan	42°	N	75°	E
Chad	15°	N	19°	E	Laos	18°	N	105°	E
Chile	30°	S	71°	W	Latvia	57°	N	25°	E
China	35°	N	105°	E	Lebanon	34°	N	36°	E
Colombia	4°	N	72°	W	Lesotho	29°	S	28°	E
Comoros	12°	S	44°	E	Liberia	6°	N	10°	W
Congo, Dem. Rep. of the	4°	S	25°	E	Libya	27°	N	17°	E
Congo, Republic of the	1°	S	15°	E	Liechtenstein	47°	N	9°	E
Costa Rica	10°	N	84°	W	Lithuania	56°	N	24°	E
Cote d'Ivoire	8°	N	5°	W	Luxembourg	49°	N	6°	E
Croatia	45°	N	16°	E	Macedonia	43°	N	22°	E
Cuba	21°	N	80°	W	Madagascar	19°	S	46°	E
Cyprus	35°	N	33°	E	Malawi	13°	S	34°	E
Czech Republic	50°	N	15°	E	Malaysia	2°	N	112°	E
Denmark	56°	N	10°	E	Maldives	2°	N	70°	E
Djibouti	11°	N	43°	E	Mali	17°	N	4°	W
Dominica	15°	N	61°	W	Malta	36°	N	14°	E
Dominican Rep.	19°	N	70°	W	Marshall Islands	7°	N	172°	E
Ecuador	2°	S	77°	W	Mauritania	20°	N	12°	W
Egypt	27°	N	30°	E	Mauritius	20°	S	57°	E
El Salvador	14°	N	89°	W	Mexico	23°	N	102°	W
Equatorial Guinea	2°	N	9°	E	Micronesia	5°	N	150°	E
Eritrea	17°	N	38°	E	Moldova	47°	N	28°	E
Estonia	59°	N	26°	E	Monaco	43°	N	7°	E
Ethiopia	8°	N	38°	E	Mongolia	46°	N	105°	E
Fiji	19°	S	174°	E	Montenegro	43°	N	19°	E
Finland	64°	N	26°	E	Morocco	32°	N	5°	W
France	46°	N	2°	E	Mozambique	18°	S	35°	E

Country	Latitude		Longitude	
Myanmar	25°	N	95°	E
Namibia	22°	S	17°	E
Nauru	1°	S	166°	E
Nepal	28°	N	84°	E
The Netherlands	52°	N	5°	E
New Zealand	41°	S	174°	E
Nicaragua	13°	N	85°	W
Niger	16°	N	8°	E
Nigeria	10°	N	8°	E
Northern Ireland	55°	N	7°	W
Norway	62°	N	10°	E
Oman	22°	N	58°	E
Pakistan	30°	N	70°	E
Palau	8°	N	138°	E
Panama	9°	N	80°	W
Papua New Guinea	6°	S	147°	E
Paraguay	23°	S	58°	W
Peru	10°	S	76°	W
The Philippines	13°	N	122°	E
Poland	52°	N	19°	E
Portugal	39°	N	8°	W
Qatar	25°	N	51°	E
Romania	46°	N	25°	E
Russia	60°	N	80°	E
Rwanda	2°	S	30°	E
St. Kitts and Nevis	17°	N	62°	W
Saint Lucia	14°	N	61°	W
Saint Vincent and the Grenadines	13°	N	61°	W
San Marino	44°	N	12°	E
São Tomé and Príncipe	1°	N	7°	E
Saudi Arabia	25°	N	45°	E
Scotland	57°	N	5°	W
Senegal	14°	N	14°	W
Serbia	45°	N	21°	E
Seychelles	5°	S	55°	E
Sierra Leone	8°	N	11°	W
Singapore	1°	N	103°	E
Slovakia	49°	N	19°	E
Slovenia	46°	N	15°	E
Solomon Islands	8°	S	159°	E
Somalia	10°	N	49°	E
South Africa	30°	S	26°	E
Spain	40°	N	4°	W
Sri Lanka	7°	N	81°	E
Sudan	15°	N	30°	E
Suriname	4°	N	56°	W
Swaziland	26°	S	31°	E
Sweden	62°	N	15°	E
Switzerland	47°	N	8°	E
Syria	35°	N	38°	E
Taiwan	23°	N	121°	E
Tajikistan	39°	N	71°	E
Tanzania	6°	S	35°	E
Thailand	15°	N	100°	E
Togo	8°	N	1°	E
Tonga	20°	S	173°	W
Trinidad and Tobago	11°	N	61°	W
Tunisia	34°	N	9°	E
Turkey	39°	N	35°	E
Turkmenistan	40°	N	55°	E
Tuvalu	8°	S	179°	E
Uganda	1°	N	32°	E
Ukraine	50°	N	30°	E

Country	Latitude		Longitude	
United Arab Emirates	24°	N	54°	E
United Kingdom	54°	N	2°	W
United States	38°	N	97°	W
Uruguay	33°	S	56°	W
Uzbekistan	40°	N	68°	E
Vanuatu	17°	S	170°	E
Venezuela	8°	N	66°	W
Vietnam	17°	N	106°	E
Wales	53°	N	3°	W
Western Samoa	10°	S	173°	W
Yemen	15°	N	44°	E
Yugoslavia	44°	N	19°	E
Zambia	15°	S	30°	E
Zimbabwe	20°	S	30°	E

TOPOGRAPHIC TALLY TABLE

THE CONTINENTS	Area (Sq Km)	Percent of Earth's Land
Asia	44,026,000	29.7
Africa	30,271,000	20.4
North America	24,258,000	16.3
South America	17,823,000	12.0
Antarctica	13,209,000	8.9
Europe	10,404,000	7.0
Australia	7,682,000	5.2

LONGEST RIVERS	Length (Km)
Nile, *Africa*	6,671
Amazon, *South America*	6,437
Chang Jiang (Yangtze), *Asia*	6,380
Mississippi-Missouri, *North America*	5,971
Ob-Irtysk, *Asia*	5,410
Huang (Yellow), *Asia*	4,672
Congo, *Africa*	4,667
Amur, *Asia*	4,416
Lena, *Asia*	4,400
Mackenzie-Peace, *North America*	4,241

MAJOR ISLANDS	Area (Sq Km)
Greenland	2,175,600
New Guinea	792,500
Borneo	725,500
Madagascar	587,000
Baffin	507,500
Sumatra	427,300
Honshu	227,400
Great Britain	218,100
Victoria	217,300
Ellesmere	196,200
Celebes	178,700
South (New Zealand)	151,000
Java	126,700

THE OCEANS	Area (Sq Km)	Percent Earth's Area Water
Pacific	166,241,000	46.0
Atlantic	86,557,000	23.9
Indian	73,427,000	20.3
Arctic	9,485,000	2.6

"Government is one of the subtlest of the arts . . . since it is the art of making people live together in peace and with reasonable happiness." —Felix Frankfurter

GOVERNMENT

Every country in the world has a government. The purpose of the government is to make and enforce laws and to protect the rights of its citizens. Every major country in the world also has a constitution, a basic set of laws by which the people are governed.

The United States Constitution establishes the form of the federal government and explains the rights and responsibilities of its citizens. This section of your handbook takes a closer look at the Constitution and how it affects the government and the average citizen.

Branches of the U.S. Federal Government

Legislative Branch	Executive Branch	Judicial Branch

Responsibilities

Makes Laws	Enforces Laws Makes Policy	Interprets Laws

Components

Congress		President	Supreme Court
Senate	House of Representatives	Vice President	Circuit Courts
President of the Senate	Speaker of the House	Cabinet	District and Special Courts

The U.S. Constitution

The U.S. Constitution is made up of three main parts: a **preamble,** 7 **articles,** and 27 **amendments.** The *preamble* states the purpose of the Constitution, the *articles* explain how the government works, and the 10 original *amendments* list the basic rights guaranteed to all American citizens.

Together, the three parts of the Constitution contain the laws and guidelines necessary to set up and run the U.S national government successfully. Besides giving power to the national government, the U.S. Constitution gives some power to the states and some to the people.

The Preamble

We the people of the United States, in order to form a more perfect Union, establish justice, insure domestic tranquility, provide for the common defense, promote the general welfare, and secure the blessings of liberty to ourselves and our posterity, do ordain and establish this Constitution for the United States of America.

The Articles of the Constitution

The articles of the Constitution explain how the three branches of government work and what each can and cannot do. The articles also explain how the federal and state governments must work together, and how the Constitution can be amended or changed.

ARTICLE 1 explains the legislative branch, how laws are made, and how Congress works.

ARTICLE 2 explains the executive branch, the offices of the President and Vice President, and the powers of the executive branch.

ARTICLE 3 explains the judicial branch, the Supreme Court and other courts, and warns people about trying to overthrow the government.

ARTICLE 4 describes how the United States federal government and the individual state governments work together.

ARTICLE 5 tells how the Constitution can be amended, or changed.

ARTICLE 6 states that the United States federal government and the Constitution are the law of the land.

ARTICLE 7 outlines how the Constitution must be adopted to become official.

The Bill of Rights

To get the necessary votes to approve the Constitution, a number of changes (amendments) had to be made. These 10 original amendments are called the Bill of Rights. They guarantee all Americans some very basic rights, including the right to worship and speak freely and the right to have a jury trial. The first eight amendments grant individual rights and freedoms. The ninth and tenth amendments prevent Congress from passing laws that would deprive citizens of these rights.

AMENDMENT 1 People have the right to worship, to speak freely, to gather together, and to question the government.

AMENDMENT 2 People have the right to bear arms.

AMENDMENT 3 The government cannot have soldiers stay in people's houses without their permission.

AMENDMENT 4 People and their property cannot be searched without the written permission of a judge.

AMENDMENT 5 People cannot be tried for a serious crime without a jury. They cannot be tried twice for the same crime or be forced to testify against themselves. Also, they cannot have property taken away while they are on trial. Any property taken for public use must receive a fair price.

AMENDMENT 6 In criminal cases, people have a right to a speedy and public trial, to be told what they are accused of, to hear witnesses against them, to get witnesses in their favor, and to have a lawyer.

AMENDMENT 7 In cases involving more than $20, people have the right to a jury trial.

AMENDMENT 8 People have a right to fair bail (money given as a promise the person will return for trial) and to fair fines and punishments.

AMENDMENT 9 People have rights that are not listed in the Constitution.

AMENDMENT 10 Powers not given to the federal government are given to the states or to the people.

The **Other Amendments**

The Constitution and the Bill of Rights were ratified in 1791. Since that time, more than 7,000 amendments to the Constitution have been proposed. Because three-fourths of the states must approve an amendment before it becomes law, just 27 amendments have been passed. The first 10 are listed under the Bill of Rights; the other 17 are listed below. (The date each amendment became law is given in parentheses.)

AMENDMENT 11 A person cannot sue a state in federal court. (1795)

AMENDMENT 12 The President and Vice President are elected separately. (1804)

AMENDMENT 13 Slavery is abolished. (1865)

AMENDMENT 14 All persons born in the United States or those who have become citizens enjoy full citizenship rights. (1868)

AMENDMENT 15 Voting rights are given to all [adult male] citizens regardless of race, creed, or color. (1870)

AMENDMENT 16 Congress has the power to collect income taxes. (1913)

AMENDMENT 17 United States Senators are elected directly by the people. (1913)

AMENDMENT 18 Making, buying, and selling alcoholic beverages is no longer allowed. (1919)

AMENDMENT 19 Women have the right to vote. (1920)

AMENDMENT 20 The President's term begins January 20; Senators' and Representatives' terms begin January 3. (1933)

AMENDMENT 21 (Repeals Amendment 18) Alcoholic beverages can be made, bought, and sold again. (1933)

AMENDMENT 22 The President is limited to two elected terms. (1951)

AMENDMENT 23 District of Columbia residents gain the right to vote. (1961)

AMENDMENT 24 All voter poll taxes are forbidden. (1964)

AMENDMENT 25 If the Presidency is vacant, the Vice President takes over. If the Vice Presidency is vacant, the President names someone and the Congress votes on the choice. (1967)

AMENDMENT 26 Citizens 18 years old gain the right to vote. (1971)

AMENDMENT 27 No law changing the pay for members of Congress will take effect until after an election of Representatives. (1992)

U.S. Presidents .... Vice Presidents

1 George Washington........... April 30, 1789 – March 3, 1797 ....John Adams **1**

2 John Adams .... March 4, 1797 – March 3, 1801........Thomas Jefferson **2**

3 Thomas Jefferson.............. March 4, 1801 – March 3, 1805..................Aaron Burr **3**

Thomas Jefferson.............. March 4, 1805 – March 3, 1809.............George Clinton **4**

4 James Madison .... March 4, 1809 – March 3, 1813.............George Clinton

James Madison .... March 4, 1813 – March 3, 1817 ....Elbridge Gerry **5**

5 James Monroe.................. March 4, 1817 – March 3, 1821.....Daniel D. Tompkins **6**

James Monroe.................. March 4, 1821 – March 3, 1825

6 John Quincy Adams .... March 4, 1825 – March 3, 1829 ....John C. Calhoun **7**

7 Andrew Jackson............... March 4, 1829 – March 3, 1833 ....John C. Calhoun

Andrew Jackson............... March 4, 1833 – March 3, 1837 ....Martin Van Buren **8**

8 Martin Van Buren .... March 4, 1837 – March 3, 1841 ....Richard M. Johnson **9**

9 William Henry Harrison* March 4, 1841 – April 4, 1841 ....John Tyler **10**

10 John Tyler .... April 6, 1841 – March 3, 1845

11 James K. Polk .... March 4, 1845 – March 3, 1849........George M. Dallas **11**

12 Zachary Taylor* .... March 5, 1849 – July 9, 1850 ....Millard Fillmore **12**

13 Millard Fillmore................ July 10, 1850 – March 3, 1853

14 Franklin Pierce................. March 4, 1853 – March 3, 1857..........William R. King **13**

15 James Buchanan .... March 4, 1857 – March 3, 1861...John C. Breckinridge **14**

16 Abraham Lincoln.............. March 4, 1861 – March 3, 1865........Hannibal Hamlin **15**

Abraham Lincoln*............ March 4, 1865 – April 15, 1865 ....Andrew Johnson **16**

17 Andrew Johnson .... April 15, 1865 – March 3, 1869

18 Ulysses S. Grant............... March 4, 1869 – March 3, 1873............Schuyler Colfax **17**

Ulysses S. Grant............... March 4, 1873 – March 3, 1877 ....Henry Wilson **18**

19 Rutherford B. Hayes .... March 4, 1877 – March 3, 1881 .....William A. Wheeler **19**

20 James A. Garfield* .... March 4, 1881 – Sept. 19, 1881........Chester A. Arthur **20**

21 Chester A. Arthur............. Sept. 20, 1881 – March 3, 1885

22 Grover Cleveland.............. March 4, 1885 – March 3, 1889..Thomas A. Hendricks **21**

23 Benjamin Harrison........... March 4, 1889 – March 3, 1893 ....Levi P. Morton **22**

24 Grover Cleveland.............. March 4, 1893 – March 3, 1897 ......Adlai E. Stevenson **23**

25 William McKinley............. March 4, 1897 – March 3, 1901 ....Garret A. Hobart **24**

William McKinley*........... March 4, 1901 – Sept. 14, 1901 ......Theodore Roosevelt **25**

26 Theodore Roosevelt........... Sept. 14, 1901 – March 3, 1905

Theodore Roosevelt........... March 4, 1905 – March 3, 1909..Charles W. Fairbanks **26**

27 William H. Taft................. March 4, 1909 – March 3, 1913.......James S. Sherman **27**

28 Woodrow Wilson .... March 4, 1913 – March 3, 1917....Thomas R. Marshall **28**

Woodrow Wilson .... March 4, 1917 – March 3, 1921

29 Warren G. Harding* .... March 4, 1921 – Aug. 2, 1923 .... Calvin Coolidge **29**

30 Calvin Coolidge .... Aug. 3, 1923 – March 3, 1925

Calvin Coolidge .... March 4, 1925 – March 3, 1929 .... Charles G. Dawes **30**

31 Herbert C. Hoover .... March 4, 1929 – March 3, 1933 .... Charles Curtis **31**

32 Franklin D. Roosevelt ...... March 4, 1933 – Jan. 20, 1937 .... John N. Garner **32**

Franklin D. Roosevelt .... Jan. 20, 1937 – Jan. 20, 1941 .... John N. Garner

Franklin D. Roosevelt .... Jan. 20, 1941 – Jan. 20, 1945 .... Henry A. Wallace **33**

Franklin D. Roosevelt* ...... Jan. 20, 1945 – April 12, 1945 .... Harry S. Truman **34**

33 Harry S. Truman .... April 12, 1945 – Jan. 20, 1949

Harry S. Truman .... Jan. 20, 1949 – Jan. 20, 1953 .... Alben W. Barkley **35**

34 Dwight D. Eisenhower .... Jan. 20, 1953 – Jan. 20, 1957 .... Richard M. Nixon **36**

Dwight D. Eisenhower .... Jan. 20, 1957 – Jan. 20, 1961 .... Richard M. Nixon

35 John F. Kennedy* .... Jan. 20, 1961 – Nov. 22, 1963 .... Lyndon B. Johnson **37**

36 Lyndon B. Johnson .... Nov. 22, 1963 – Jan. 20, 1965

Lyndon B. Johnson .... Jan. 20, 1965 – Jan. 20, 1969 ...Hubert H. Humphrey **38**

37 Richard M. Nixon .... Jan. 20, 1969 – Jan. 20, 1973 .... Spiro T. Agnew **39**

Richard M. Nixon* .... Jan. 20, 1973 – Aug. 9, 1974 .... Gerald R. Ford **40**

38 Gerald R. Ford .... Aug. 9, 1974 – Jan. 20, 1977 .... Nelson A. Rockefeller **41**

39 James E. Carter .... Jan. 20, 1977 – Jan. 20, 1981 .... Walter Mondale **42**

40 Ronald W. Reagan .... Jan. 20, 1981 – Jan. 20, 1985 .... George H. W. Bush **43**

Ronald W. Reagan .... Jan. 20, 1985 – Jan. 20, 1989 .... George H. W. Bush

41 George H. W. Bush .... Jan. 20, 1989 – Jan. 20, 1993 .... J. Danforth Quayle **44**

42 William J. Clinton .... Jan. 20, 1993 – Jan. 20, 1997 .... Albert Gore, Jr. **45**

William J. Clinton .... Jan. 20, 1997 – Jan 20, 2001 .... Albert Gore, Jr.

43 George W. Bush .... Jan. 20, 2001 – .... Richard B. Cheney **46**

(*Did not finish term)

Order of Presidential Succession

1. Vice president
2. Speaker of the House
3. President pro tempore of the Senate
4. Secretary of state
5. Secretary of the treasury
6. Secretary of defense
7. Attorney general
8. Secretary of the interior
9. Secretary of agriculture
10. Secretary of commerce
11. Secretary of labor
12. Secretary of health and human services
13. Secretary of housing and urban development
14. Secretary of transportation
15. Secretary of energy
16. Secretary of education
17. Secretary of veterans affairs

"When I want to understand what is happening today or try to decide what will happen tomorrow, I look back."

—Oliver Wendell Holmes

HISTORY

Historical Time Line

Even before the first European settlers arrived in the United States, there were over a million Native Americans living here in five major regions: Woodland, Plains, Desert, Mountain, and Coastal. American history really begins with those Native Americans.

Native American Regions Circa 1500

The historical time line on the next 10 pages will help you "look back" and better understand history, as well as what is happening today. The time line covers the period from 1500 to the present. You'll notice that the time line is divided into three main parts: **United States and World History, Science and Inventions,** and **Literature and Life.** You'll discover many interesting things on the time line—when watches were invented (1509), when paper money was first used in America (1690), and who developed the first pair of blue jeans (Levi Strauss in 1850).

1500	1520	1540	1560	1580

U.S. & WORLD HISTORY

1492
Columbus reaches the West Indies.

1519
Magellan begins three-year voyage around the world.

1513
Ponce de León explores Florida; Balboa reaches Pacific.

1521
Cortez defeats Aztecs and claims Mexico for Spain.

1559
Spanish colony of Pensacola, Florida, lasts two years.

1565
Spain settles St. Augustine, Florida, first permanent European colony.

1570
League of the Iroquois Nations formed.

1588
England defeats the Spanish Armada and rules the seas.

1597
British Parliament sends criminals to colonies.

SCIENCE & INVENTIONS

1507
Book on surgery is developed.

1530
Bottle corks are invented.

1531
Halley's Comet appears.

1545
French printer Garamond sets first type.

1558
Magnetic compass invented by John Dee.

1585
Decimals introduced by Dutch mathematicians.

1590
First paper mill is used in England.

1509
Watches are invented in Germany.

1543
Copernicus's theory proclaims a sun-centered universe.

1596
Thermometer is invented.

LITERATURE & LIFE

1500
Game of bingo developed.

1517
Reformation begins in Europe.

1536
First songbook used in Spain.

1564
First horse-drawn coach used in England.

1580
First water closet designed in Bath, England.

1503
Pocket handkerchiefs are first used.

1538
Mercator draws map with America on it.

1582
Pope Gregory XIII introduces the calendar still in use today.

1507
Glass mirrors are greatly improved.

1513
Machiavelli's *The Prince* published.

1541
Michelangelo completes largest painting, "The Last Judgment."

1599
Copper coins first made.

U.S. POPULATION: (NATIVE AMERICAN)   (SPANISH)

approximately 1,100,000   1,021

1600   1620   1640   1660   1680   1700

1607
England establishes Jamestown, Virginia.

1619
House of Burgesses in Virginia establishes first representative government in colonies.

1654
First Jewish colonists settle in New Amsterdam.

1673
Marquette and Joliet explore Mississippi River for France.

1609
Henry Hudson explores the Hudson River and Great Lakes.

1620
Pilgrims found Plymouth Colony.

1634
Colony of Maryland is founded.

1664
The Dutch colony of New Netherlands becomes the English colony of New York.

1682
William Penn founds Pennsylvania.

1629
Massachusetts Bay Colony is established.

1608
Telescope is invented.

1641
First cotton factories open in England.

1668
Reflecting telescope invented by Sir Isaac Newton.

1682
Halley's Comet is studied by Edmund Halley and named for him.

1609
Galileo makes first observations with telescope.

1643
Torricelli invents the barometer.

1671
First calculation machine invented.

1687
Newton describes gravity and publishes *Principia Mathematica*.

1629
Human temperature measured by physician in Italy.

1650
First pendulum clocks developed by Huygens.

1600
Shakespeare's plays are performed at Globe Theatre in London.

1636
Harvard is the first college in the colonies.

1685
First drinking fountain used in England.

1653
First postage stamps used in Paris.

1690
Paper money is used for the first time in America.

1622
January 1 accepted as beginning of the year (instead of March 25).

1640
First book printed in the colonies.

1605
European diseases kill many Native Americans (measles, TB, and smallpox).

1658
First colonial police force created in New Amsterdam.

1697
Tales of Mother Goose written by Charles Perrault.

(ENGLISH)

350   2,302   26,634   75,058   151,507

1700	1710	1720	1730	1740

U.S. & WORLD HISTORY

1700
France builds forts at Mackinac and Detroit to control fur trade.

1711
Tuscarora War fought in Carolina.

1718
France founds New Orleans.

1705
Virginia Act establishes public education.

1707
England (English) and Scotland (Scots) unite and become Great Britain (British).

Scotland

England

1733
James Oglethorpe founds Georgia.

1733
Molasses Act places taxes on sugar and molasses.

SUG

1735
Freedom of the press upheld during trial of John Peter Zenger.

1747
Ohio Company formed to settle Ohio River Valley.

SCIENCE & INVENTIONS

1701
Seed drill that plants seeds in a row is invented by Jethro Tull.

1712
Thomas Newcomen develops first practical steam engine.

1728
First dental drill is used by Pierre Fauchard.

1732
Sedatives for operations discovered by Thomas Dover.

1742
Benjamin Franklin invents efficient Franklin stove.

1709
The pianoforte (first piano) is invented by Christofori Bartolommeo.

1735
Rubber found in South America.

1738
First cuckoo clocks invented in Germany.

LITERATURE & LIFE

1700
The Selling of Joseph by Samuel Sewall is first protest of slavery.

1716
First hot-water home heating system developed.

1731
Ben Franklin begins first subscription library.

1744
John Newbery publishes children's book, *A Little Pretty Pocket-Book.*

1701
Yale University is founded.

1719
Robinson Crusoe written by Daniel Defoe.

1733
Poor Richard's Almanac first printed.

1704
First successful newspaper in colonies, *Boston News-Letter*, is published.

1726
Gulliver's Travels written by Jonathan Swift.

U.S. POPULATION: (ENGLISH COLONIES)

250,888	331,711	466,185	629,445	905,563

1750 1760 1770 1780 1790 1800

1750 The French and Indian War begins.

1750 Flatbed boats and Conestoga wagons begin moving settlers west.

1765 Stamp Act tax imposed on colonies.

1770 Boston Massacre occurs.

1763 Britain defeats France in French and Indian War.

1773 Boston Tea Party occurs.

1775 Revolutionary War begins.

1776 Declaration of Independence signed at Second Continental Congress on July 4.

1781 British surrender at Yorktown October 19.

1781 United colonies adopt Articles of Confederation as first government.

1787 U.S. Constitution is signed.

1789 George Washington elected president.

1789 French Revolution begins.

1794 U.S. Navy created.

1752 Benjamin Franklin discovers lightning is a form of electricity.

1758 Sextant for navigation is invented by John Bird.

1764 "Spinning jenny" for cotton is invented by James Hargreaves.

1770 First steam carriage is invented by French engineer Nicholas Cugnot.

1781 Uranus, first planet not known to ancient world, is discovered.

1783 First balloon is flown by Frenchmen Joseph and Jacques Montgolfier.

1793 Eli Whitney invents cotton gin that takes seeds out of cotton.

1798 Eli Whitney invents mass production.

1752 First general hospital is established in Philadelphia.

1757 Streetlights are installed in Philadelphia.

1764 Mozart writes first symphony.

1769 Venetian blinds are first used.

1776 Paine prints *Common Sense*.

1780 The waltz becomes popular dance.

1782 The American bald eagle is first used as U.S. symbol.

1786 First ice-cream company in America begins production.

1790 Official U.S. census begins.

1790 Supreme Court meets for the first time.

1795 Food canning is introduced.

1,170,760   1,593,625   2,148,076   2,780,369   3,929,157

1800   1810   1820   1830   1840

U.S. & WORLD HISTORY

1800
Washington, D.C., becomes U.S. capital.

1803
Louisiana Purchase from France doubles U.S. size.

1804
Lewis & Clark explore Louisiana Territory and northwestern United States.

1812–1814
War of 1812 is fought between U.S. and Britain.

1819
U.S. acquires Florida from Spain.

1820
Missouri Compromise signed.

1821
Sierra Leone is established by U.S. for freed slaves.

1830
Indian Removal Act forces Native Americans west of Mississippi River.

1836
Texans defend the Alamo.

1838
Cherokee Nation forced west on "Trail of Tears."

1846
Mexican War begins.

1846
Brtitain cedes Oregon Country to U.S.

1848
Gold found in California.

SCIENCE & INVENTIONS

1800
The battery is invented by Count Volta.

1802
Steamboat is built by Robert Fulton.

1808
Chemical symbols are developed by Jöns Berzelius.

1816
Stethoscope invented by Reneé Laënnec.

1817
Erie Canal is begun.

1819
Hans Christian Oestad discovers electromagnetism.

1836
Samuel Morse invents telegraph.

1839
Bicycle is invented by Kirkpatrick Macmillan.

1841
Stapler is patented.

1844
Safety matches produced.

1846
Elias Howe invents sewing machine.

LITERATURE & LIFE

1800
Library of Congress is established.

1804
World population reaches 1 billion.

1806
Gas lighting used in homes.

1812
Army meat inspector, "Uncle Sam" Wilson, becomes U.S. symbol.

1814
Sequoyah creates Cherokee alphabet.

1816
Niépce takes first photograph.

1820
Rip Van Winkle is written by Washington Irving.

1827
Audubon's *Birds of America* is published.

1828
Webster's Dictionary is published.

1830
Mormon Church is founded.

1834
Louis Braille perfects a letter system for the blind.

1845
Thoreau moves to Walden Pond.

1849
Safety pin is invented.

1849
Elizabeth Blackwell becomes first woman doctor.

U.S. POPULATION:

5,308,080	7,240,102	9,638,453	12,860,702	17,063,353

1850   1860   1870   1880   1890   1900

1853
National Council of Colored People is founded.

1860
Abraham Lincoln elected 16th president of the U.S.

1861
Civil War begins at Fort Sumter.

1869
Coast-to-coast railroad is finished in Utah.

1889
Jane Addams founds Hull House in Chicago to help immigrants.

1876
U.S. Centennial celebrated.

1862
Lincoln proclaims abolition of slavery.

1898
U.S. defeats Spain in Spanish-American War.

1862
Merrimac-Monitor Battle.

1876
Custer is defeated at Little Big Horn.

1865
Lincoln is assassinated.

1851
Isaac Singer produces sewing machine.

1860
Jean Lenoir builds internal combustion engine.

1874
Barbed wire introduced by Joseph Glidden.

1887
Radio waves produced by Hertz.

1876
Alexander Graham Bell invents telephone.

1893
First successful U.S. gasoline automobile is built.

1852
Elisha Otis invents elevator.

1865
Joseph Lister introduces antiseptic practices.

1877
Thomas Edison invents phonograph.

1896
Marconi invents wireless radio.

1857
Atlantic cable is completed.

1879
Edison makes incandescent lightbulb.

1898
Curies discover radium.

1850
Levi Strauss produces blue jeans.

1864
Red Cross is established.

1876
National Baseball League established.

1883
Four U.S. time zones are established.

1892
"Pledge of Allegiance" is written by F. Bellamy.

1852
Uncle Tom's Cabin by Harriet Beecher Stowe strengthens anti-slavery movement.

1866
Hires introduces root beer.

1879
Ibsen's *Doll House* and Tolstoy's *War and Peace* published.

1888
Pneumatic bicycle tires invented by John Dunlop.

1873
Zipper invented by Whitcomb Judson.

1855
Alexander Parks produces first synthetic plastic.

1889
Roll film produced by George Eastman.

23,191,876   31,443,321   38,558,371   50,189,209   62,979,766

| **1900** | **1905** | **1910** | **1915** | **1920** |

U.S. & WORLD HISTORY

1900
First Olympics involving women held in Paris.

1903
Wrights' first successful airplane flight.

1909
National Association for the Advancement of Colored People (NAACP) is founded.

1913
Income Tax established.

1914
Panama Canal opens.

1914
World War I begins.

1917
United States enters World War I.

1917
Bolshevik Revolution starts in Russia.

1918
World War I ends.

1919
League of Nations founded.

1920
Prohibition begins.

1920
Women given vote.

SCIENCE & INVENTIONS

1901
Walter Reed discovers yellow fever is carried by mosquitos.

1904
New York City opens its subway system.

$$E=mc^2$$

1905
Albert Einstein announces theory of relativity ($E=mc^2$) of time and space.

1913
Henry Ford establishes assembly line for automobiles.

1915
Coast-to-coast telephone system established.

1921
Vaccine for tuberculosis is discovered.

1922
Insulin treatment for diabetes discovered.

1922
Farnsworth develops electron scanner for television.

LITERATURE & LIFE

1900
American Baseball League established.

1902
First bowl game, the Rose Bowl, is held.

1903
Call of the Wild written by Jack London.

1903
First World Series played.

1905
First nickelodeon movie theater established in Pittsburgh.

1907
Artists Picasso and Braque create cubism.

1913
Arthur Wynne invents the crossword puzzle.

1917
Doughnuts created for the soldier "doughboys" fighting in World War I.

KDKA

1920
First radio station, KDKA, founded in Pittsburgh.

1922
King Tut's tomb discovered.

U.S. POPULATION:

| 76,212,168 | 92,228,496 | 106,021,537 |

1925   1930   1935   1940   1945   1950

1927
Charles Lindbergh flies solo across the Atlantic Ocean.

1929
Wall Street stock market crashes.

1931
The 102-story Empire State Building completed as tallest in the world.

1933
President Franklin Roosevelt introduces New Deal to end Great Depression.

1933
Prohibition is repealed.

1939
Germany invades Poland to begin World War II.

1941
U.S. enters World War II after bombing of Pearl Harbor.

1945
World War II ends.

1945
United States joins the United Nations.

1948
Israel becomes a nation.

1949
Communists gain control in China.

1926
John Baird demonstrates his television system.

1930
First analog computer invented by Vannevar Bush.

1928
Alexander Fleming develops penicillin.

1929
Clarence Birdseye introduces frozen foods.

1935
Radar is invented.

1938
Modern-type ballpoint pens developed.

1938
First photocopy machine produced.

1939
First jet aircraft flown.

1940
Enrico Fermi develops nuclear reactor.

1947
Edwin Land invents Polaroid camera.

1947
Bell Lab scientists invent transistor.

1927
World population reaches 2 billion.

1927
Wings wins first Academy Award for motion pictures.

1927
First "talking movie," *The Jazz Singer*, made.

1931
"The Star-Spangled Banner" becomes U.S. national anthem.

1937
First full-length animated film, *Snow White*, is made.

1938
Superman "Action Comics" created.

1938
"War of the Worlds" broadcast on radio.

1939
Steinbeck's *Grapes of Wrath* is published.

1947
Jackie Robinson becomes the first black major league baseball player.

1947
Anne Frank's *Diary of a Young Girl* is published.

1950	1955	1960	1965	1970

U.S. & WORLD HISTORY

1950
United States enters Korean War.

1953
Korean War ends.

1955
Rosa Parks refuses to follow segregation rules on Montgomery bus.

1955
Martin Luther King, Jr., begins organizing protests against black discrimination.

1959
Alaska becomes 49th state.

1959
Hawaii becomes 50th state.

1961
Alan Shepard becomes first U.S. astronaut in space.

1963
President John F. Kennedy assassinated in Dallas, TX.

1965
U.S. combat troops sent to Vietnam.

1965
Civil Rights Freedom March from Selma to Montgomery, Alabama.

1968
Martin Luther King, Jr., is assassinated.

1969
Neil Armstrong and Buzz Aldrin are first men to walk on moon.

1971
Eighteen-year-olds are given right to vote.

1974
President Richard Nixon resigns.

SCIENCE & INVENTIONS

1951
Fluoridated water discovered to prevent tooth decay.

1953
Watson and Crick map the DNA molecule.

1954
Jonas Salk discovers polio vaccine.

1957
Russia's *Sputnik I* satellite is launched.

1958
Stereo long-playing records are produced.

1960
First laser invented by Theodor Maiman.

1963
Cassette music tapes developed.

1967
Cholesterol discovered as a cause of heart disease.

1968
First U.S. heart transplant is performed by surgeon Norman Shumway.

1971
Space probe *Mariner* maps surface of Mars.

1972
DDT is banned.

1974
Sears Tower (110 stories) built in Chicago.

LITERATURE & LIFE

1950
Peanuts comic strip produced by Charles Schulz.

1951
Fifteen million American homes have television.

1953
Arthur Miller's *The Crucible* is published.

1957
Theodor "Dr. Seuss" Geisel's *Cat in the Hat* is published.

1957
Elvis Presley is the most popular rock 'n' roll musician in U.S.

1961
Peace Corps is established.

1962
Rachel Carson's *Silent Spring* is published.

1964
The Beatles appear on *The Ed Sullivan Show*.

1969
Sesame Street TV show begins.

1970
First Earth Day is observed.

1970
Dee Brown's *Bury My Heart At Wounded Knee* is published.

1974
World population reaches 4 billion.

U.S. POPULATION:

151,325,798   179,323,175   203,302,031

1975   **1980**   **1985**   **1990**   **1995**   **2000**

1975
Vietnam War ends.

1981
Sandra Day O'Connor becomes first woman on Supreme Court.

1986
Challenger spacecraft explodes, killing entire crew.

1991
Persian Gulf War begins.

2000
People celebrate the new millennium.

1991
Restructuring of Soviet Union occurs.

1981
U.S. hostages returned from Iran after 444 days.

1989
Berlin Wall is torn down.

1994
Nelson Mandela elected president of South Africa.

1979
Iran seizes U.S. hostages.

1983
Sally Ride becomes first U.S. woman in space.

1994
NATO expands to include Eastern European countries.

1976
Concorde becomes world's first supersonic passenger jet.

1981
Scientists identify AIDS.

1988
NASA reports greenhouse effect is caused by destruction of forests.

1993
Apple introduces laptop computer.

1999
Scientists map the first chromosome.

1977
Apple Computers produces first personal computer.

1983
Pioneer 10 space probe passes Neptune and leaves solar system.

1991
World Wide Web is launched.

1995
U.S. and Russian spacecraft link up for first time.

1979
Three Mile Island nuclear power plant accident.

1984
Compact disks (CDs) developed.

1991
Environmental Protection Agency cites growing danger of hole in Earth's ozone layer.

1997
First adult sheep is cloned.

1976
Alex Haley's *Roots* is published.

1986
Martin Luther King Day proclaimed national holiday.

1995
California bans smoking in all public places.

2000
Last *Peanuts* comic strip is produced.

1976
U.S. Bicentennial celebrated.

1988
Widespread use of computers begins in schools.

1998
Mark McGwire sets major league record with 70 home runs.

1977
Star Wars becomes largest money-making movie of all time.

1999
World population reaches 6 billion.

1979
Yellow ribbons symbolize support for return of U.S. hostages in Iran.

1989
Amy Tan's *Joy Luck Club* is published.

1999
The U.S. women's soccer team wins the World Cup.

226,542,203   248,709,873

Additional Credits

Page 23: Excerpt from *SACRED HOOPS* by Phil Jackson and Hugh Delehanty. Copyright 1995 by Phil Jackson. Reprinted by permission of Hyperion.

Page 23: From *FOR THE TIME BEING* by Annie Dillard. Copyright © 1999 by Annie Dillard. Reprinted by permission of Alfred A. Knopf, a division of Random House Inc.

Page 24: Brief excerpt from *NEITHER HERE NOR THERE* by Bill Bryson. Copyright 1992 by Bill Bryson. Reprinted by permission of HarperCollins Publishers, Inc.

Page 24: Reprinted with permission of Pocket Books, a division of Simon & Schuster, from *A CROSSING: A Cyclist's Journey Home* by Brian Newhouse. Copyright © 1998 by Brian Newhouse.

Page 25: Excerpt from *GOOD OLD BOY* by Willie Morris. Copyright 1980 by Willie Morris. Reprinted by permission of Yoknapatawpha Press, Inc.

Page 25: Excerpt from "He Was a Good Lion" from *WEST WITH THE NIGHT* by Beryl Markham. Copyright 1942, 1983 by Beryl Markham. Reprinted by permission of North Point Press, a division of Farrar, Straus and Giroux, LLC.

Page 100: Reprinted with permission of the *High School Writer*. Copyright by Writer Publications.

Page 129: Taken from *The Land Remembers* by Ben Logan. Copyright 1975 by Ben Logan. Reprinted by permission of Frances Collin literary agent.

Page 131: From *Tender at the Bone* by Ruth Reichl. Copyright 1998 by Ruth Reichl. Reprinted by permission of BROADWAY BOOKS, a division of Random House, Inc.

Page 137: Excerpt from "The Secret Among the Stones" by Ardath Mayar. Published in *Heath Middle Level Literature*. Copyright 1995 D.C. Heath and Company. Reprinted by permission of Houghton Mifflin Company.

Page 138: From *Tender at the Bone* by Ruth Reichl. Copyright 1998 by Ruth Reichl. Reprinted by permission of BROADWAY BOOKS, a division of Random House, Inc.

Page 164-165: Reprinted with permission from *New Youth Connections*, Copyright 1991 by Youth Communication, 224 W 29th St., 2nd Fl., NY, NY 10001

Page 193: Reprinted with permission from *New Youth Connections*, Copyright 1991 by Youth Communication, 224 W 29th St., 2nd Fl., NY, NY 10001

Page 223: Reprinted with permission from *New Youth Connections*, Copyright 1992 by Youth Communication, 224 W 29th St., 2nd Fl., NY, NY 10001

Page 262: Reprinted with the permission of Scribner, a Division of Simon & Schuster from CRY, THE BELOVED COUNTRY by Alan Paton. Copyright 1948 by Alan Paton; copyright renewed © 1976 by Alan Paton.

Page 263: Excerpt from "The Fish" from *The Complete Poems 1927-1979* by Elizabeth Bishop. Copyright © 1979, 1983 by Alice Helen Methfessel. Reprinted by permission of Farrar, Straus and Giroux, LLC.

Page 402: Excerpt from "Spiritual Laws" from *The Essays of Ralph Waldo Emerson* by Ralph Waldo Emerson. Original copyright 1841 by Ralph Waldo Emerson. Reprinted by permission of Belknap Press.

Pages 534-535: From *The World Book Encyclopedia*. Copyright 1997 by World Book, Inc. Reprinted by permission of the publisher.

Index

A

A/an, 491
A lot/alot, 491
Abbreviations,
 Common, 482.1
 Correspondence, 481.2
 Internet, 336
 Punctuation of, 455.2
 Research paper, 263
 State, 481.2
Abstract noun, 501.4
Academic writing, 141,
 199-213
 Assessment rubric, 213
Accept/except, 491
Acronym, 483.1, 483.3
Active voice, 90, 130,
 508.1, 510.3, 511
Adapt/adopt, 491
Address,
 Abbreviations, 481.2
 Punctuation of, 307,
 460.2
Adjective, 513
 Clause, 521.2
 Coordinating, 457.2
 Specific, 131
Adverb, 514
 Clause, 521.2
 Conjunctive, 461.5
 Specific, 131
Affect/effect, 491
Agreement,
 Antecedent-pronoun,
 503.2, 505, 528
 Subject-verb, 510, 526-527
Allegory, 233
Alliteration, 242
All right/alright, 492
Allusion, 136, 233, 431
Allusion/illusion, 491
Already/all ready, 491
Altogether/all together, 492
Ambiguous wording, 85
Among/between, 492
Amount/number, 492
Analogy, 136, 233, 431
Analyzing information,
 442
Anecdote, 127, 136, 233,
 431
Annual/semiannual/
 biannual/perennial,
 492
Ant/aunt, 492

Antagonist, 233
Antecedent, 503.2
Antithesis, 136, 236, 431
Antonym, 346
Anyway/anyways, 492

APA research paper,
 Documentation style,
 285-295
 On-line student sample,
 See page ii
 Paper format, 286
 Parenthetical references,
 287-288
 Reference entries, 290-
 295

Apostrophe, 472-473
Appeals, emotional, 445
Appendix, 349
Application, letter of, 305
Applying information, 441
Appositive,
 Phrase, 521
 Punctuation, 458.2
 Sentence combining, 91
Archaic words, 234
Argument, thinking
 through, 118-119
Argumentation,
 Definition, 139
 Essay of, 195-197
 Logical thinking, 445-446
Arrangement,
 Definition, 139
 In speeches, 425
 In writing, 52, 100-103
 Within the sentence, 82
Articles, 513
As/like, 497

Assessment rubrics,
 Academic writing, 213
 Book review, 226
 Business writing, 308
 Expository essay, 114
 Fiction writing, 178
 Literary analysis, 226
 Personal narrative and
 essay, 154
 Persuasive essay, 123,
 198
 Poetry writing, 184
 Research writing, 284
 Subject writing, 166

Assignments, completing,
 388
Assonance, 242
Asterisk, 474
Audience, 46, 62, 139, 423
Aunt/ant, 492
Autobiography, 233
Auxiliary verbs, 507.1

B

Balance, 139
Balanced sentence, 129,
 139, 523.1
Ballad, 242
Bandwagon, 445
Bar graphs, 353
Base/bass, 492
Be/bee, 492
Beside/besides, 492
Between/among, 492
Biannual/biennial, 492
Bibliography, 250, 349
Bill of Rights, 573
Biography, 233
Birth/berth, 492
Blank verse, 242
Blew/blue, 493
Board/bored, 493
Body, 139, 349
Book,
 Parts of, 349
 Punctuation of titles,
 470.2
Book review, writing a,
 221-226
 Assessment rubric, 226
 Mini-reviews, 225
 Sample, fiction, 223
 Sample, nonfiction, 224
Borrow/lend, 496
Brackets, 474
Brainstorming, 139
Brake/break, 493
Bring/take, 493
Brochures, 316-317
Business letters, 297-308
 Addressing envelope, 307
 Application letter, 305
 Complaint letter, 302
 Informative letter, 303
 Parts of, 298
 Persuasive letter, 304
 Request letter, 301
 Thank-you letter, 306
 Writing guidelines, 300